Research Series on the Chinese Dream and China's Development Path

Drawing on a large body of empirical studies done over the last two decades, this Series provides its readers with in-depth analyses of the past and present and forecasts for the future course of China's development. It contains the latest research results made by members of the Chinese Academy of Social Sciences. This series is an invaluable companion to every researcher who is trying to gain a deeper understanding of the development model, path and experience unique to China. Thanks to the adoption of Socialism with Chinese characteristics, and the implementation of comprehensive reform and opening-up, China has made tremendous achievements in areas such as political reform, economic development, and social construction, and is making great strides towards the realization of the Chinese dream of national rejuvenation. In addition to presenting a detailed account of many of these achievements, the authors also discuss what lessons other countries can learn from China's experience.

More information about this series at http://www.springer.com/series/13571

Lin Li · Jihong Mo · Guoqiang Zhai
Editors

Constitutional Development in China, 1982–2012

SSAP

Springer

Editors
Lin Li
Institute of Law
Chinese Academy of Social Sciences
Beijing, China

Jihong Mo
Institute of Law
Chinese Academy of Social Sciences
Beijing, China

Guoqiang Zhai
Chinese Academy of Social Sciences
Beijing, China

Translated by Liyun Shi

ISSN 2363-6866 ISSN 2363-6874 (electronic)
Research Series on the Chinese Dream and China's Development Path
ISBN 978-981-32-9259-8 ISBN 978-981-32-9261-1 (eBook)
https://doi.org/10.1007/978-981-32-9261-1

Jointly published with Social Sciences Academic Press
The print edition is not for sale in China. Customers from China please order the print book from: Social Sciences Academic Press.

This Springer imprint is published by the registered company Springer Nature Singapore Pte Ltd.
The registered company address is: 152 Beach Road, #21-01/04 Gateway East, Singapore 189721, Singapore

Series Preface

Since China's reform and opening began in 1978, the country has come a long way on the path of socialism with Chinese characteristics, under the leadership of the Communist Party of China. Over 30 years of reform, efforts and sustained spectacular economic growth have turned China into the world's second largest economy and wrought many profound changes in the Chinese society. These historically significant developments have been garnering increasing attention from scholars, governments, and the general public alike around the world since the 1990s, when the newest wave of China studies began to gather steam. Some of the hottest topics have included the so-called "China miracle," "Chinese phenomenon," "Chinese experience," "Chinese path" and the "Chinese model." Homegrown researchers have soon followed suit. Already hugely productive, this vibrant field is putting out a large number of books each year, with Social Sciences Academic Press alone having published hundreds of titles on a wide range of subjects.

Because most of these books have been written and published in Chinese, however, readership has been limited outside China—even among many who study China—for whom English is still the lingua franca. This language barrier has been an impediment to efforts by academia, business communities, and policy-makers in other countries to form a thorough understanding of contemporary China, of what is distinct about China's past and present may mean not only for her future but also for the future of the world. The need to remove such an impediment is both real and urgent, and the *Research Series on the Chinese Dream and China's Development Path* is my answer to the call.

This series features some of the most notable achievements from the last 20 years by scholars in China in a variety of research topics related to reform and opening. They include both theoretical explorations and empirical studies, and cover economy, society, politics, law, culture, and ecology, the six areas in which reform and opening policies have had the deepest impact and farthest-reaching consequences for the country. Authors for the series have also tried to articulate their visions of the "Chinese Dream" and how the country can realize it in these fields and beyond.

All of the editors and authors for the *Research Series on the Chinese Dream and China's Development Path* are both longtime students of reform and opening and recognized authorities in their respective academic fields. Their credentials and expertise lend credibility to these books, each of which having been subjected to a rigorous peer review process for inclusion in the series. As part of the Reform and Development Program under the State Administration of Press, Publication, Radio, Film, and Television of the People's Republic of China, the series is published by Springer, a Germany-based academic publisher of international repute, and distributed overseas. I am confident that it will help fill a lacuna in studies of China in the era of reform and opening.

Xie Shouguang

Preface

The year 2012 marked the 30th anniversary of the promulgation of the Constitution of China. This Constitution has played an extremely important role in China's economy, politics, culture and social life. Over the past three decades, the Constitution has provided the needed legal safeguard for China's reform and opening up and socialist modernization to proceed. At the same time, the Constitution has propelled the building of socialist democracy in China and facilitated the implementation of the governance by law as the fundamental strategy. The Constitution has promoted the development of China's cause of human rights and various social undertakings. It is a socialist constitution with Chinese characteristics and suitable for China's national conditions.

I. Development History of the Constitution of China

Looking back, we can trace the history of China's socialist constitution to the Congress of Soviets system in place during the 1927–1937 Civil War between the Kuomintang and the Communist Party of China. Its very name—this Congress of Soviets—leaves little doubt that the system was modeled on the organizational form of state power adopted by the Soviet Union after the October Revolution.[1] The First National Congress of Chinese Soviet Republic was held in Yeping Village, Ruijin County of Jiangxi Province on November 7, 1931. On 11, the Presidium of the National Congress decided to set up the Committee for Revision of the Constitution consisting of Ren Bishi, Wang Jiaxiang and Mao Zedong, among others. After discussions, *the Outline of the Constitution of the Soviet Republic of China* (*the Constitution Outline* for short) was hammered out and adopted according to the

[1]The original meaning of "Soviet" was "congress of workers and peasants" in Russian. The so-called Congress of Soviets referred to the Congress of Workers, Peasants and Soldiers, meaning an organizational form of state power with workers, peasants and soldiers as the power subjects.

principles proposed by the temporary central government in a telegram. *The Constitution Outline* was the first constitutional document developed by the people under the leadership of the Communist Party of China (CPC) and opened a new chapter of China's constitutional history. *The Constitution Outline* also represented the first people's democratic constitution in China's history and had an epoch-making significance in China's history of constitutional government. According to *the Constitution Outline*, the supreme political power of the Chinese Soviet Republic was the National Congress of Soviets of Workers, Peasants and Soldiers. When the Congress was not in session, the Temporary Central Executive Committee of the National Soviets was the supreme organ of state power. The People's Council organized under the Central Executive Committee was responsible for handling daily government affairs and issuing all decrees and resolutions. The Soviet system was a useful attempt of the socialist constitutional government in early stage and was in the state of "adaptation" to national conditions as a new system. Given CPC's lack of firsthand experience in building political power, the Soviet Union's Congress of Soviets system was once dogmatically and mechanically copied. This was closely related to the fact that the revolutionary struggles back then were led by the Communist International. This blind imitation did not factor in China's unique national conditions and developmental needs.

With the all-round victory of the socialist revolution led by the CPC, the First Plenary Session of the Chinese People's Political Consultative Conference (CPPCC) was convened in September 1949. The session adopted *the Common Program of the Chinese People's Political Consultative Conference* (*Common Program* for short) and formulated *the Organic Law of the Chinese People's Political Consultative Conference, the Organic Law of Central People's Government of the People's Republic of China* and the *Resolution on the Capital, the Way of Numbering the Years, the Anthem and the National Flag*. Back then, the CPPCC exercised the functions of the National People's Congress (which had not yet been established) and confirmed the legitimacy of the new state power within a relatively short time. Many scholars agree that the convocation of this session had the nature of and significance for enacting the Constitution. Apart from the preamble, *the Common Program* included 60 articles of 7 chapters, namely general principles, organs of political power, military system, economic policies, cultural and educational policies, ethnic politics and diplomatic policies. In terms of the contents, *the Common Program* affirmed the basic rights of the people and designed the basic political system at that time. *The Common Program* had much in common with the 1954 Constitution in structure and had an important significance in the history of China's constitutional government. Chinese legal historians Zeng Xianyi and Zhang Jinfan once pointed out that the *Common Program* had the general characteristics of Constitution in both content and form. In terms of the content, *the Common Program* stipulated the basic principles and legislative principles of China's social system and state institution, and thus gave the legal basis for various state activities. When it comes to the form, *the Common Program* was like a general constitution as well, with the provisions on state nature, political regime, economic system, people's basic rights and duties and regional autonomy of ethnic minorities the similar as that of a general constitution.[2]

The Central People's Government Committee decided to set up the Committee for Draft of the Constitution of the People's Republic of China on January 13, 1953. Drawn out by the Committee, the draft constitution was published by the Central People's Government Committee on June 14, 1954, for 3-month discussions by the whole nation. The Committee for Draft of the Constitution amended the draft constitution for many times based on the opinions of all the people and all walks of life. On September 20, 1954, the First Session of the First National People's Congress (NPC) adopted *the Constitution of the People's Republic of China* by secret ballot. Liu Shaoqi said in *the Report on the Draft Constitution of the People's Republic of China* that, from 1953, China had entered the period of planned economic development toward the socialist target. He said that it is therefore absolutely necessary to go further on the basis of *the Common Program* to enact a Constitution just like what's being proposed to all deputies and use legal means to define the general task for China's transitional period. He noted in the report that it is an arduous and complicated task to realize socialist industrialization and socialist transformation in China. He observed that the task could only be completed through motivating the strength of all the people of the whole country, giving full play to the enthusiasm and creativity of the broad masses of the people and overcoming all kinds of difficulties under the correct and highly unified leadership. He concluded in the report that there was a must to further promote people's democracy, expand the scale of democratic system on the one hand and establish a highly unified leadership system of the state on the other. As he said, for that to happen, it is completely necessary to hammer out a constitution more perfect than *the Common Program*, just like the one being proposed to the session. That is the first constitution in the history of the People's Republic of China. This constitution defined people's democracy and socialist principles in the form of fundamental law. This constitution had more detailed stipulations on the assignment of state power and on the fundamental rights of citizens. This Constitution established the basic pattern and framework of China's constitutional system.

However, as Mencius said, state governance would not be effective only with decrees. During the Cultural Revolution, stipulations of the 1954 Constitution failed to be effectively implemented, were even impracticable and finally amended. The 1975 Constitution and 1978 Constitution followed fell behind the times and failed to adapt to the needs of national development. In September 1980, the Third Session of the Fifth National People's Congress decided to establish a Committee for Revision of the Constitution to completely amend the 1978 Constitution. In April 1982, the draft amendment to the Constitution proposed by the Committee for Revision of the Constitution was published by the Standing Committee of the NPC for discussions by the people of the entire nation. The Committee for Revision of the Constitution revised the draft amendment to the Constitution based on the

[2]Zeng Xianyi and Zhang Jinfan: *Brief History of the Constitution of China*, People's Publishing House, 1979 edition, page 242.

opinions raised by the entire nation. On December 4, 1982, the Fifth Session of the Fifth National People's Congress adopted *the Constitution of the People's Republic of China* which is the current constitution. This Constitution contains 138 articles which are divided into five parts, namely the preamble, Chapter one covering general principles, Chapter two on the fundamental rights and duties of citizens, Chapter three the structure of the state and Chapter four the national flag, the national emblem and the national's capital.

After being adopted, the current constitution has been amended for four times. The First Session of the Seventh National People's Congress held on April 12, 1988, amended the Constitution by adding the provisions allowing the existence and development of private economy within the limits prescribed by law, lifting the ban on land lease and permitting the transfer of land use right in accordance with the law. On March 29, 1993, the First Session of the Eighth National People's Congress revised the Constitution again. This time, the provision of Article 15 on practicing the planned economy was modified into "practicing the socialist market economy" and "strengthening economic legislation and improving macroeconomic regulation and control." On March 15, 1999, the Second Session of the Ninth National People's Congress added the provision that "the People's Republic of China implements governance by law and builds a socialist country under the rule of law" to Article 5 of the Constitution. In March 2004, the Second Session of the Tenth National People's Congress made necessary amendments to the Constitution according to the suggestions put forward by the Central Committee of the CPC. New contents were added to the Constitution, including the important thoughts of "Three Represents," harmonious development of the "Three Civilizations," respecting and guaranteeing human rights and protecting the citizens' private property from being encroached.

Since its development, China's Constitution has identified the basic values of constitutionalism, namely democracy, rule of law and human rights as the fundamental principles of the socialist constitution with Chinese characteristics. The Constitution has confirmed the achievements of Chinese people of all ethnic groups and stipulated the basic system and basic tasks of the nation and the most important principles in national life in the form of law. The Constitution has the highest authority and legal effects. The Constitution in force is the fundamental law of the state and the fundamental legal basis for maintaining national unification, ethnic unity, economic development, social progress and lasting peace and stability of the country. It is the fundamental legal rules for behaviors of all state organs, social groups and citizens. It provides fundamental guarantee for citizens' basic rights and freedom and party leadership in the country's quest to build socialism with Chinese characteristics. The constitutional system implemented by a state is determined by the national conditions and nature of the state eventually. There are no completely same political models in the world, and even in countries with the same social system, the political models are different. There is absolutely none, and there will never have a political development path that is universally applicable. The development of China's Constitution is the product of combining foreign institutional experience with China's national conditions. It is the outcome of Marxist localization in China. The socialist constitution with Chinese characteristics is the choice of history and the people. It represents the unity of the Party's propositions and the people's will. It is the recordation and affirmation of the achievements of socialist revolution, construction, and reform and opening up. It is also the fundamental confirmation and guarantee of the socialist system and people's rights.

II. Essential Characteristics of the Current Constitution of China

Constitution is the fundamental law of China and the general principle for ensuring sound administration of state affairs and national security. It is the legal basis for maintaining national unification, ethnic unity, economic development, social progress and lasting peace and stability of the country. It is also the legal system guaranteeing the CPC's governance and rejuvenation of the country and uniting all ethnic groups to build socialism with Chinese characteristics. With the Four Fundamental Principles (the path of socialism, Marxism–Leninism and Mao Zedong Thought, the people's democratic dictatorship and the leadership of the Communist Party) as the guiding ideology, the existing constitution has defined China's basic political, economic, cultural and social systems. Besides, the Constitution has played a crucial role in pushing forward the reform and opening up and provided a solid legal foundation for China's socialism construction.

(I) Adhere to the Four Fundamental Principles, and Take the Road of Socialism with Chinese Characteristics

The Four Fundamental Principles is the summary of the long-term accumulated experience of the CPC as the ruling party and has been written into the Constitution. The Four Fundamental Principles comes as the crystallization of China's revolution and construction experience. Therefore, the Four Fundamental Principles must be consistently upheld at any time and under any circumstance. According to Marxist theory, the Constitution reflects a country's economic foundation and the development of political pattern. In the semicolonial and semifeudal era, all kinds of political forces and progressive people with lofty ideals proposed their solutions for saving the country and the nation. The Revolution of 1911, led by Mr. Sun Yat-sen, abolished the feudal monarchy and founded the Republic of China. Yet, the Chinese people had not accomplished the historic mission of overthrowing imperialism and feudalism. After going through protracted, arduous and tortuous struggles, armed and otherwise, the Chinese people led by the CPC finally overthrew the rule of imperialism, feudalism and bureaucrat capitalism, won the great victory of the new-democratic revolution and founded the People's Republic of China. Therefore, at the time of making the Constitution, it is reasonable to incorporate the Four Fundamental Principles into the Constitution as a fundamental principle.

The Four Fundamental Principles is interdependent, indivisible and organically integrated with the core of staying committed to the path of socialism and the Party's leadership. Apart from the clear stipulations in the preamble of the Constitution, the Four Fundamental Principles is also reflected in articles of the Constitution. As provided in the first article of the Constitution, the People's Republic of China is a socialist state under the people's democratic dictatorship led by the working class and based on the alliance of workers and peasants. This article directly defines two of the Four Fundamental Principles, namely people's democracy and socialism. The statement of "led by the working class and based on the alliance of workers and peasants" gives expression to the principle of upholding the leadership of the Communist Party. The principles of Marxism–Leninism and Mao Zedong Thought are reflected in the system and structure of articles on the constitution, such as the principle of economic system and materialism. According to constitutional theories, Constitution is classified into formal constitution and substantive constitution. Formal constitution represents articles on the Constitution and regulations. Substantive constitution focuses on revealing the overall state of Constitution and political operations, namely the actual constitution. Therefore, we can say that the Four Fundamental Principles is the essence of China's substantive constitution. China is now in the state of social transformation, so it must develop the socialist constitution and staying committed to the Four Fundamental Principles as the time changes. Comrade Jiang Zemin pointed out that there is a must to unify the reform and opening up with the Four Fundamental Principles. He said that the vigorous vitality of socialism with Chinese characteristics lied in the implementation of the reform and opening-up policy. As he said, China's reform and opening up can develop healthily because it helps consolidate and develop the socialism.[3]

(II) The People's Congress System

China's people's congress system is the political governmental system with Chinese characteristics. It is formed by referring to the Congress of Workers, Peasants and Soldiers of the Soviet Union in line with China's actuality. The early form of the people's congress system Congress of Soviets system in the revolutionary base period. The people's congress system gradually took shape with the continuous consolidation and improvement of the political power of the CPC. Since the First National People's Congress held in 1954, the people's congress system has also gone through a development of twists and turns. Especially during the Cultural Revolution, the people's congress system only existed in name and was sabotaged seriously in various functions. That was the harsh times for China's constitutional development. With the convocation of the Third Plenary Session of the 11th Central Committee of the CPC, the Party Central Committee attached great importance to the building of the people's congress system and synchronized it with the reform and opening up and the economic development. Accordingly, the democratic rule

[3]*Selected Important Documents of All Plenary Sessions of the CPC Central Committee since the Third Plenary Session of the 11th Central Committee of the CPC*, Volume II, Central Party Literature Press, 1997, first edition, page 165–166.

of law went on the right track step by step. The people's congress system kept developing and improving and became mature in various specific systems. Consequently, the people's congress system with Chinese characteristics took shape. The people's congress system contains various specific systems in itself. These various specific systems are mutually coordinated and complemented and together make up the people's congress system.

According to constitutional principles and system inheritance, China does not implement the tripartite political system with regard to the framework of power organs. Instead, China implements the people's congress system based on the principle of people's sovereignty and democratic centralism. The main characteristics of the people's congress system are as follows.

1. When it comes to the relationship between the people and the organs of the state power, the people directly or indirectly select the deputies to the NPC to constitute people's congresses of all levels; deputies and people's congresses are elected by, responsible for and supervised by the people. In regions implementing direct elections, voters have the right to dismiss incompetent deputies directly. In regions choosing indirect elections, the original electoral units have the right to dismiss deputies selected and assigned to the upper level of people's congress by them.
2. In terms of the relationship between the ruling party and people's congress, the Party must act within the framework of the Constitution and the law. At the same time, people's congresses of all levels and their standing committees must voluntarily accept the leadership of the Party due to the ruling status of the CPC. Also, the Party assumes the overall control and coordinates all parties to support people's congresses to exercise their functions according to the law. The Party mainly exercises the political, ideological and organizational leadership. The Party asserts its leadership mainly through formulating fundamental policies, putting forward legislative suggestions, recommending important leaders and carrying out ideological publicity. The Party gives full play to the Party organization and members, and leads the nation and society by persisting in governance by law.
3. As regards the relationship between people's congresses and other state organs, people's congresses are organs of state power. Other state organs are created by, responsible for and supervised by people's congresses. According to the stipulations of the Constitution, the National People's Congress is the supreme organ of state power. The State Council, the Central Military Commission, the Supreme People's Procuratorate and the Supreme People's Court are elected by and responsible for the NPC and supervised by the NPC and the Standing Committee of the NPC. Local people's congresses of all levels are local organs of state power. Local people's governments, people's courts and people's procuratorates at all levels are elected by and responsible for the people's congresses of the same level and supervised by the people's congresses and their standing committees of the same level.

4. Regarding the relationship between the NPC and local people's congresses of all levels, the principle is to exercise initiatives at local level under the unified leadership of the Central Committee. Mao Zedong incisively pointed out in the article titled *On the Ten Major Relationships* that it is imperative to have a strong and unified central government leadership and unified planning and discipline throughout the country to build a powerful socialist country, and it is impermissible to disrupt this indispensable unity. He added in the article that it is essential to bring the initiative of the local authorities into full play and let each locality enjoy the particularity suited to its local conditions. He noted that this particularity was not the particularity for the senior posts but the one necessary for the interest of the whole and for the strengthening of national unity. These words of Mao Zedong are just the principles guiding the relationship between the NPC and local people's congresses at all levels.
5. As for the relationship between people's congresses and their standing committees, the Standing Committee of people's congress is the standing organization of the people's congress. The standing committees of people's congresses at all levels hold responsibility and report to and accept the supervision of the people's congresses of the same level. People's congresses may change or revoke the decisions of the standing committees of the same level.
6. With respect to the relationship between the central government and special administrative regions, the "one country, two systems" policy is adopted. Under the premise of fully respecting the original system of special administrative regions, the NPC enacts the basic law for special administrative regions and regulates that special administrative regions implement the political–legal system different from that of the mainland China. In the meantime, the NPC also has deputies from special administrative regions. They can represent their special administrative regions to participate in the administration and discussion of state affairs and exercise democratic powers.
7. In regard to ethnic relationship, people's congresses of areas inhabited by ethnic minorities exercise the right to national autonomy and may formulate flexible ethnic regulations and specific regulations of their respective regions. Deputies to the NPC shall include an appropriate number of deputies of minority nationalities. This kind of autonomous system fully respects the special living habit, cultural tradition, religious belief, etc., of minority areas and guarantees the right of minority areas to subsistence and development.

(III) Staying Committed to the CPC-led Multi-party Cooperation and Political Consultation System

The CPC-led multi-party cooperation and political consultation system is different from both the two-party or multi-party competition system and the single-party system implemented by other countries. The CPC-led multi-party cooperation and political consultation system is an important part of China's constitutional system. Its basic principles are: The CPC and democratic parties closely cooperate and mutually supervise but not oppose each other; the CPC governs the country by law while all democratic parties participate in government and political affairs by law rather than ruling in turn with the CPC. The political consultation system used to play a pivotal role in establishing the state power. In 1949, large-scale military actions were not yet over, national production and life were not yet on the right track, and the National People's Congress was not yet established. In this case, the First CPPCC exercised the functions of the NPC. The First CPPCC formulated *the Common Program* and government organization law and elected the central government. In September 1954, the First Session of the First National People's Congress was held and adopted *the Constitution of the People's Republic of China.* In December of the same year, the First Session of the Second National Committee of the CPPCC was held. At this session, *the Constitution of the Chinese People's Political Consultative Conference* was rolled out, signifying the completion of the establishment of the CPPCC as an organizational form of political consultation and multi-party cooperation.

The CPPCC represents an important organization carrying forward people's democracy and liaising people of all walks of life.[4] The Constitution has further specified this system: In the chronic years of revolution and construction, abroad patriotic united front that is composed of all socialist laborers and patriots standing up for socialism and national reunification, led by the CPC and participated by various democratic parties and people's organizations, has taken shape. This united front will be further solidified and developed. The CPPCC is a unified front organization with extensive representativeness and played an important historical role in the past. Going forward, the CPPCC will further play its vital role in national political life, social life and friendly foreign activities, socialist modernization and struggles safeguarding national unification and solidarity. On this basis, Article 4 of the Amendments to the Constitution stipulates that the multi-party cooperation and political consultation system led the Communist Party of China (CPC) will exist and develop for a long time.

The CPPCC is similar to the upper house of foreign parliament in some functions. Some theories state that China may refer to this bicameralism in constitutional reform, developing the people's political consultation system into the "upper house" paralleling the NPC, and realize legalization. However, China's Constitution clearly defines the identity and function of the CPPCC as a unified front organization instead of a state organ. As a matter of fact, the political consultation system has played an essential role in developing and implementing policies and laws. The political consultation system is not confirmed in the form of law, but it has formed a series of practices and institutions for conducting activities, such as the Constitution of the CPPCC. These institutions and practices have in effect certain binding power and are similar to the "constitutional conventions" of some countries without a written constitution. In practice, these institutions and practices have provided the basis for the CPPCC to implement activities. With the stipulations of the Constitution on its nature and status, the political consultation system has a flexible and broad development space with the development of the

[4] *Selected Works of Deng Xiaoping*, Volume 2, People's Publishing House, 1994, 2nd edition, page 187.

society. If we must legalize the CPPCC, such as turning it into the "upper house," it would not only increase the costs for institutional reform but also trigger political unrests. Beyond that, staying committed to the people's political consultation system does not mean the rejection of learning and drawing on the beneficial fruits of human political civilization. The CPPC, as an important political form and organizational form of China's consultative democracy, is in necessity and condition to critically study the democratic system, form, contents, procedures, etc., of the West. In particular, some foreign institutions similar to the CPPCC merit our studies and imitations.[5]

(IV) Insist on the Regional Autonomy System and the "One Country, Two Systems" Policy

With different and diversified cultural traditions and lifestyles, different countries uniformly give much autonomous space to minority areas. One practice of them is using the principle of federalism to render different autonomous authorities to different regions. As a result of political, cultural and historical traditions, China does not implement the federalist form of state but the unitary form of state and the system of regional national autonomy. This renders special authorities and preferential measures to regions inhabited by ethnic minorities to solve their special issues. The Constitution of China stipulates that China is a united multiethnic state founded jointly by the people of all ethnic groups and has 56 ethnic minorities except for the Han nationality. The population of ethnic minorities accounts for 8% of China's total population, and the areas inhabited by them make up for 60% of the total area of China. In order to safeguard the legitimate rights and interests of all ethnic groups and protect and develop the equal, united and mutually assistant relationship, China implements regional autonomy in regions inhabited by ethnic minorities in concentration. The areas implementing the autonomy system include autonomous regions, autonomous prefectures and autonomous counties. There are altogether 5 autonomous regions (Inner Mongolia Autonomous Region, Xinjiang Uygur Autonomous Region, Guangxi Zhuang Autonomous Regions, Ningxia Hui Autonomous Regions and Tibet Autonomous Regions), 30 autonomous prefectures, 116 autonomous counties and 3 autonomous banners in China. All autonomous areas are an inalienable part of the People's Republic of China. The autonomous organs of ethnic autonomous areas are people's congresses and people's governments of autonomous regions, autonomous prefectures and autonomous counties. Autonomous authorities of ethnic autonomous areas exercise autonomy by law apart from exercising the functions of local state organs and enforce national laws and policies in line with local actual conditions. People's congresses of ethnic autonomous areas have the right to formulate autonomous regulations and specific regulations according to local national political, economic and cultural characteristics. In case that any resolution, decision, order or instruction of a state organ of the upper level is unsuitable for the national autonomous area,

[5]Li Changjian: "30-Year Remarkable Development and Reform Path and Future Development of the CPPCC," *Publication of the CPPCC Theory Research Institute*, 2008, Issue 4.

the autonomous authority may report to the upper level of state organ and ask for the approval for flexible or suspended implementation. Under the guidance of state plans, autonomous authorities of ethnic autonomous areas autonomously arrange and manage local economic development undertakings. Autonomous authorities have the autonomy to manage local finance. Autonomous authorities autonomously manage local educational, scientific, cultural, health and sports undertakings. While developing resources and establishing enterprises in ethnic autonomous areas, the state should take the interests of ethnic autonomous areas into consideration. The state helps ethnic minorities speed up economic and cultural development in the aspects of finance, materials, technologies, etc. The state also helps ethnic autonomous areas cultivate cadres of all levels, talents and technicians of various professionals from local people.

In order to solve the issues related to Taiwan, Hong Kong and Macao, the Constitution stipulates the special administrative region system, which is more flexible than the federal system. For the sake of safeguarding national unity and territorial integrity and help Hong Kong and Macao maintain prosperity, development and social stability, the central government decided to implement the "one country, two systems" policy rather than the socialist system and policy in Hong Kong and Macao. Their previous capitalist system and way of life may remain unchanged for 50 years. According to the Constitution, special administrative regions enjoy a high degree of autonomy which has more extensive authorities than the autonomous units under the federal system. This kind of autonomy has fully guaranteed the special political and cultural traditions of special administrative regions. The Third Session of the Seventh National People's Congress held in April 4, 1990, determined to establish Hong Kong Special Administrative Region (Hong Kong SAR) as of July 1, 1997, and adopted *the Basic Law of the Hong Kong Special Administrative Region of the People's Republic of China* (hereinafter referred to as *the Basic Law of the Hong Kong Special Administrative Region*). The First Session of the Eighth National People's Congress held on March 31, 1993, decided the establishment of Macao Special Administrative Region (Macao SAR) since December 20, 1999, and adopted *the Basic Law of the Macao Special Administrative Region of the People's Republic of China* (hereinafter referred to as *the Basic Law of the Macao Special Administrative Region*).

Hong Kong SAR and Macao SAR are local administrative regions directly under the governance of central government, and they both implement different systems and policies with that of the mainland and enjoy a high degree of autonomy. The high degree of autonomy of special administrative regions includes the administrative power, legislative power, independent judicial power and power of final adjudication. Besides, authorized by the central people's government, special administrative regions may also autonomously handle some foreign affairs. To assure central government's leadership and governance of special administrative regions, the national defense and foreign affairs of special administrative regions are taken charge by the central people's government. The chief executive and governmental leading officials of special administrative regions are appointed by the central people's government. A few national laws on national defense, and diplomatic affairs and matters excluded from the range of autonomy of special administrative regions are issued or enforced as legislation in special administrative regions.

(V) Stay Committed to an Organic Unity of the Party's Leadership, the People's Role as Masters of the Country and Governance by Law, and Accomplish the Socialist Constitutional Government with Chinese Characteristics

Just like such terms as democracy, freedom, equality, constitution, human right and republic, constitutional government is not the patent of the bourgeoisie but the commonwealth of human political civilization and an appropriate system for socialism. In the past, a minority of people questioned and even heckled the use of concepts such as rule of law, human right, equity and justice, democracy and freedom, but they were still incapable of blocking the scientific and historical advancement. Just like the market economy is neither capital nor socialist exclusive system, constitutional government is also not exclusive to the bourgeoisie. Constitutional government is a realization form of democratic politics. Capitalism has the constitutional government, but socialism may also and should also have the constitutional government that is more superior and authentic than that of capitalism. The bourgeoisie uses constitutional government to serve the bourgeois dictatorship and capitalist society. The proletariat should give more play to the role of constitutional government in consolidating the people's democratic dictatorship and realizing socialist modernization.

During the new-democratic revolution and great practice of socialist construction and reform, Chinese communists have taken people's democracy, fairness and justice, governance by law, equity and freedom, human rights and rule of law as their objectives. Besides, Chinese communists have also put a high premium on making, amending and implementing the Constitution and advocated ruling the country by the Constitution and building a socialist constitutional government. We stand for a constitutional government with Chinese characteristics guided by localized Marxism in China and adhering to the Four Fundamental Principles as the political prerequisites. The constitutional government has the fundamental nature of an organic unity of the Party's leadership, the people's role as masters of the country and the governance by law and upholds the people's congress system as the basic political system. The constitutional government refers to the socialist democracy with the purpose of governing for the people, respecting and protecting human rights and realizing an overall liberation of the people.

Adhering to the organic unity of the Party's leadership, the people's role as masters of the country and the governance by law represents a major theoretical achievement of the Communist Party made in constant explorations of the relations among the three ever since the founding of the People's Republic of China. The Party's leadership is the fundamental guarantee for people's democracy and governance by law. Enabling the people to become masters of the country is an essential requirement of socialist democracy. Governance by law is the fundamental strategy for the ruling party to lead the people to govern the country. The Party's leadership, enabling the people to be master of the country and governance by law are the essential characteristics of the socialist political civilization and three essential elements of the constitutional government with Chinese characteristics. The three are organically united and dialectically unified and supplement each other. In ideology, the three are united in the localized Marxism in China and the philosophy of putting people first and the scientific outlook on an all-round, coordinated and sustainable development. In practical form, the three are united in the practices of socialist democratic development and the entire process of socialist modernization. In institutional form, the three are united in the Constitution with Chinese characteristics. The Party's leadership, enabling the people to be masters of the country and governance by law are defined and organically united through institutionalized and constitutionalized arrangement of the constitutional government with Chinese characteristics and in the form of fundamental law and democratic system. Thus, the constitutional system with Chinese characteristics effectively guarantees the implementation of Party's principles, policies and guidelines and the Party's political authority and status. The constitutional system with Chinese characteristics also guarantees the leading and core role of the CPC in grasping the overall situation and coordinating all parties to enable the people to become masters of the country and govern the country by law.

In terms of deepening the political system reform, the constitutional government with Chinese characteristics requires transforming the constitutional government with Chinese characteristics from the past "separating the functions of the party from those of the government" to "an organic unity of the three." It also requires building harmonious and orderly relationships between the Party and the government, between the Party and the law, between the ruling party and democratic parties, between the Party and the people, between the central government and local governments, between nationalities, etc. When it comes to the content of deepening the political system reform, the constitutional government with Chinese characteristics requires comprehensively strengthening institutional building and institutional reform and incorporating economic system, cultural system, social system, political system, legal system and other systems into the scope of institutional building and generalized political system reform. The constitutional government with Chinese characteristics requires united planning, coordinated execution and orderly advancement under the leadership of the Party. In terms of the principle of deepening the political system reform, the constitutional government with Chinese characteristics requires that political system building and political system reform must help strengthen the vigor and vitality of the Party and the state and motivate the enthusiasm, initiative and creativity of the masses. It also requires that the political system building and political system reform must help safeguard national unification, ethnic unity and social harmony and promote economic development and social progress.

III. The Universality and Particularity of China's Constitution

Constitution is the critique and summary of historical experiences and an important development form of law-based civilization of humanity. The socialist constitution with Chinese characteristics has both the characteristics of a general constitution and the particularity that is different from a general constitution.

(I) **People's Democracy**

Democracy is the outcome of the development of human political civilization and a universal demand for people all over the world. Democracy is not peculiar to bourgeoisie. It also exists in socialism. There would be no socialism and socialist modernization without democracy. The democratic principle in China's Constitution has certain universalities with that of other countries, but it also has its particularities. Deng Xiaoping once pointed out that the old China had left us more tradition of feudal autocracy than tradition of democracy and legal system. After the liberation, China also failed to consciously and systematically put in place various systems to safeguard the people's democratic rights, and its legal system was neither complete nor being valued.[6] Due to the lack of democratic political and cultural tradition, China should lay special emphasis on the constitutional value of democracy. Just like the constitutions of other countries, China's Constitution stipulates that all power rests with the people, which is the constitutional principle of people's democracy. On this basis, China's Constitution clearly defines the path and way to realize democracy. According to China's Constitution, the people elect their representatives through democratic general elections to constitute people's congresses at all levels. People's congresses at all levels are responsible for and supervised by the people. Chinese people of all ethnic groups exercise democratic election, democratic decision making, democratic management and democratic supervision in accordance with the law and enjoy the extensive democracy, freedom and rights as stipulated by the Constitution and laws. Moreover, the political consultation system is also an effective form to realize democracy, but this form is different from the bicameralism of other countries. Democratic parties and all sectors of society discuss state affairs and take part in the formulation and execution of national laws and policies through participating in political consultative meetings. In order to guarantee the democratic power of ethnic minorities, China implements regional national autonomy system in areas inhabited by ethnic groups. Preferential treatment is given to ethnic groups in the organization of people's congresses and governments to ensure their representatives to take part in political process. Another route to realize socialist democracy is the implementation of grassroots self-governance system in urban communities and rural areas. How to guarantee citizens to actively and orderly take part in grassroots political life remains to be one of the issues for realizing socialist democracy.

[6] *Selected Works of Deng Xiaoping*, Volume 2, People's Publishing House, 1994 edition, page 348.

Over the six decades after the founding of the People's Republic of China, the constitutional principle of people's democracy has gone through a tortuous yet constantly improving development. Especially after the Third Plenary Session of the 11th Central Committee of CPC, the meaning of people's democracy has been continuously developed and perfected. In 2004, the amendment to the Constitution established the important position of the "Three Represents." "Representing the fundamental interests of the overwhelming majority of the people" in the important thought of the "Three Represents" emphasizes the universality of people's democracy, further expands the main body of democracy and maximizes the understanding of the main body of people's democracy. For instance, the changes of this democratic meaning have been illustrated by the representatives of private entrepreneurs in people's congresses of all levels. Due to the ruling status of CPC, the fundamental issue in developing socialist democratic politics in China is how to organically unite the Party's leadership, people's role as masters of the country and governance by law. In China, the development of socialist democracy should be a progressive process. CPC is the ruling party and the core of China's political power. There would be no democracy of the core power without democracy within the Party. Socialist democracy and rule of law are mutually complementary and inseparable. It is the same between intra-party democracy and people's democracy. They are all indispensable and important contents of the development of socialist constitutional government and political civilization. Therefore, developing intra-party democracy and using intra-party democracy to drive people's democracy represent a feasible and easily achievable road for China to develop democratic politics. The proposition of using intra-party democracy to drive people's democracy signifies that people's democracy rather than intra-party democracy is the fundamental and ultimate goal of China's democratic politics.[7] Comrade Hu Jintao pointed out in the Report to the 17th National Congress that the fundamental target of deepening the political system reform is to widen people's democracy and ensure people's role as masters of the country. Ensuring the people to be masters of the country is the essence and core of socialist democratic politics. In this connection, developing intra-party democracy is basically the path and condition for promoting people's democracy. While staying committed to governance by law, the Party also needs to further develop intra-party democracy, practically guarantee the democratic rights of party members and keep improving intra-party democratic system and decision-making mechanism. The Party also needs to give full play to the important, exemplary and leading role of intra-party democracy in people's democracy and drive and promote people's democracy by intra-party democracy.

(II) Governance by Law

The rule of law is an important mark of civilization and one of the values countries around the world pursue in their constitutions. When scholars in the West refer to the "rule of law," they are usually talking about "governance by law" and "law-based country" in China. The American scholar Fuller put forward eight principles of

[7]Yu Keping: *Democracy is the Life of the Republic*, *People's Tribune*, 2007, Issue 22.

legality, namely generality, publicity, non-retroactivity, clarity, non-contradiction, possibility of compliance, stability and congruity.[8] The International Congress of Jurists held in India in 1959 adopted the *Declaration of Delhi*. The declaration defines the concept of rule of law into three principles. First, the function of legislative body is to create and maintain various conditions for safeguarding human dignity. Second, the principles of rule of law shall provide legal guarantee for curbing administrative power abuse and enable the government to effectively maintain the legal order and thus guarantee sufficient conditions for people's social and economic life. Third, judicial independence and lawyer freedom are also essential conditions for the implementation of principles of rule of law.

The principles of rule of law are also one of the basic principles of China's Constitution. Deng Xiaoping profoundly pointed out while summarizing the painful lessons from the Cultural Revolution that the mistakes made in the past certainly had something to do with the ideological style of some leaders, but it is more serious in the organizational system and working system. Institutional issues are even featured by fundamentality, overall influence, stability and chronicity, so they must be taken seriously by the entire Party. Deng Xiaoping also indicated that there is a must to pay high attention to the building of the socialist democratic legal system. There would be no socialism and socialist modernization without democracy. To build a socialist modernized country, there is a must to develop socialist democracy, improve the socialist legal system and institutionalize and legalize democracy. The Constitution is the fundamental law of the state and the general principle for ensuring well administration of state affairs and national security. A perfect and well-thought-out constitution is the must for implementing the legal system. In August 1980, Deng Xiaoping systematically stated issues related to the reform of the Party and state's leadership system at the enlarged meeting of the Political Bureau of CPC Central Committee. He said that CPC Central Committee was considering a major reform and the first step of the major reform was to raise suggestions to the NPC for amending the constitution. Deng Xiaoping pointed out the need to make the Constitution more perfect, well-thought-out and accurate, and practically guarantee the people to truly enjoy the power to manage national organizations at all levels and enterprises and full civic rights. He also noted the need to truly implement regional national autonomy system in ethnic minority areas and improve the people's congress system, etc. Regarding the principle of allowing no excessive concentration of power, Deng Xiaoping said that it would be reflected in the Constitution. This speech of Deng Xiaoping at the enlarged meeting actually established the important guiding thought for drafting the 1982 Constitution. The report of the Party to its Twelfth National Congress put forward that the building of socialist democracy must be closely connected with the building of the socialist legal system and the legal system must be institutionalized and legalized. The report also required that "the Party must act within the framework of the Constitution and the law." From the central level to the grassroots level, the activities of all party

[8]Shen Zongling: *Modern Western Jurisprudence*, Peking University Press, 1992 edition, page 58-62.

organizations and members should not collide with the Constitution and the law. The Party is part of the people. The Party leads the people to enact the Constitution and the law that must be strictly abided by the entire party once being adopted by organs of state power. The 1982 Constitution formulated under the guidance of the spirit of the Twelfth National Congress clearly provided that all parties must take the Constitution as the basic guidelines for activities and take responsibility for protecting and guaranteeing the dignity and implementation of the Constitution. The 1982 Constitution also required that all state organs and armed forces, political parties and social organizations, enterprises and public institutions must abide by the Constitution and the law. All acts violating the Constitution and the law must be prosecuted. No organization or individual shall have the privilege over the Constitution and the law. The Fifteenth National Congress of the Party held in 1997 made a high degree of summary of the scientific meaning and significance of governance by law and changed the "ruled by law" to "governance by law." The First Session of the Ninth NPC held in 1999 adopted an amendment to the Constitution and wrote "the People's Republic of China implements governance by law and builds a socialist country under the rule of law" into the Constitution. Specifically speaking, the socialist rule of law with Chinese characteristics has the following ten points of meaning: perfect legal system, people's sovereignty, protection of human rights, power balance, legal equality, supremacy of law, administration by law, judicial independence, proper procedure and the Party's abidance by the law.[9]

(III) **Safeguarding Human Rights**

Human right is the confirmation of the reified and legalized will, interest and dignity of people as sovereignty subject and legal subject. Human right is the formal institutional arrangement of specific individual conforming to legal norms and the delimitation and definition of the individual private domain and the government public domain. Enjoying full human rights is the long-cherished ideal of humanity. Concern for human right is what fuels constitutional movements around the world, and it is both the starting point and end result of constitutionalism. For socialist China, safeguarding human rights and continuously improving human rights situation are the fundamental purposes determined by the nature of socialist state. CPC's governance and its support and guarantee of the people's role as masters of the country are also for the purpose of enabling the people to have human rights and basic freedom. The basic target of governing the country by law is not for managing and ruling the common people but for bringing state act under rule of law and fully ensuring the realization of every individual's rights and basic freedom.

Respecting and protecting human rights are the value targets commonly pursued by constitutions of all countries, but different countries have different specific regulations and practices in their respective constitution as a result of their different historical and cultural traditions. In China's Constitution, the protection of human rights is described as "the basic rights of citizens." The rights of citizens as

[9]Li Buyun: *Milestones of Governance by Law*, April 6, 1999, the theoretic edition.

stipulated by the Constitution and laws are the crystalized and legalized dignity and interests of citizens, including political, economic and cultural interests. No matter in what way the civic rights are being encroached by state functionaries, the encroachment would trigger the dissatisfaction of the masses with the Party and government and may deteriorate the relationship between the Party and the masses and make the Party become the opposites of the people in serious cases, thereby undermining the Party's ruling foundation. The rights and obligations of citizens are unified, which is the basic principle stipulated by the Constitution for the rights of citizens. However, for the ruling party governing for the people and for the government administering for the people, they should pay more attention to guaranteeing civic rights. In so doing, they could better reflect the advancement of the working class party serving the interests of the people and governing for the people, better embody the advanced nature of the people's government serving the people and actively promote the citizens to earnestly fulfill their obligations. The Constitution was revised at the Second Session of the Tenth National People's Congress held in March 2004. This time, the provision of "the state respects and safeguards human rights" was added to the Constitution. The protection of human rights cannot be talked about without a specific legal system and social and economic conditions. Therefore, an important task for safeguarding our people's basic rights is to legalize all basic rights declared by the Constitution and comprehensively improve all legal provisions and related systems for guaranteeing human rights on the basis of our national conditions.

IV. Improvement and Development of the Socialist Constitutional System with Chinese Characteristics

(I) Putting People First and Embracing People's Democracy

The core tenet of Marxism around which it developed was the aspiration for the complete emancipation of humanity. After unveiling the historical development law of human society, the Marxist theory points out that socialism takes the full and free development of humanity as the basic principle and provides all people with healthy and beneficial jobs, plenty of material life and leisure time, and real and full freedom. The political civilization of socialism is the democratic politics in which people are masters of the country, and state authority is responsible for and elected, performed and supervised by the people. The report of the Party to its 17th National Congress especially made "putting people first" the core of the Scientific Outlook on Development. The report pointed out the must to put people first and stipulated the respect and protection of human rights in the General Program of the Party Constitution. Building the socialist constitutional government and political civilization should adhere to people first, promote people's democracy and continuously improve various constitutional systems.

First of all, China should further uphold and improve the people's congress system, which is the essential requirement of socialist democracy and the key and soul of building the socialist constitutional government and political civilization. The people's congress system is the basic political system under which people of all ethnic groups are masters of the country. The Constitution clearly stipulates that the NPC is the supreme organ of state power and enjoys the legislative power, decision-making power in major events, power of appointment and removal of personnel and right of supervision. Therefore, there is a need to establish specific systems to further guarantee the constitutional power of people's congress and implement the constitutional status of people's congress. There is also a need to establish working mechanisms to give a practical play to the role of people's congress in democratic legislation, democratic election, democratic decision making, democratic supervision, etc. At the same time, there is a need to further perfect and improve the multi-party cooperation and political consultation system under the leadership of CPC, ethnic regional national autonomy system, grassroots democratic system, citizens' democratic participation system, etc.

Second, there is a need to highly value the specific system and operational procedure construction of socialist democracy. In the past, we generally laid more emphasis on the essential feature and superiority of socialist democracy but insufficient emphasis on the construction of specific socialist democratic system and operational procedure. This has affected a further play of the superiority of the fundamental political system and basic political system of socialist democracy to a certain extent. This has also restrained the specific realization process of people's democracy. This has exerted influence on the initiative, motivation and creativity of the masses and weakened the realization degree of people's role as masters of the country. Therefore, there is a need to further improve democracy in the election process and candidate nomination procedure of people's congresses, the procedure of dismissing the leaders elected by people's congresses and the decision-making procedure for major issues. There is also a need to further perfect democracy in legislative procedure, voting procedure, monitoring procedure, etc. There is a need to establish and improve democracy in the legislative transparency system, system of auditing at people's congresses, legislation auditing system, system of citizens' orderly participation in legislation, etc.

Third, there is a need to extend citizens' orderly participation in politics in accordance with the law with the economic and cultural development. Participating in politics is the basic right of citizens and is protected by the Constitution and the law. Citizens should exercise their rights and orderly participate in democratic politics in accordance with the law. Any disorderly political expression and participation of "great democracy" violating the law are uncivilized political expressions and shall be banned or regulated in accordance with the law. The scope and area of citizens' direct election should be gradually extended under the leadership of the Party and on the track of rule of law. All systems for citizens' participation in decision making and exercise of democratic management and democratic supervision shall be further perfected and improved. Citizens' democratic rights shall be practically safeguarded, such as the right to vote and to be elected, the right to know, right of participation in the administration and discussion of state affairs, right of criticism and suggestion, right of petition, accusation and disclosure and so on and so forth.

Fourth, grassroots democracy should be further expanded. Expanding grassroots direct democracy can help motivate people's enthusiasm and creativity to manage their own affairs in accordance with the law. Expanding grassroots democracy is conducive to the improvement of the democratic quality of the entire nation. In rural areas, there is a must to keep improving villagers' self-governance and perfect the autonomous mechanism of villagers with full vitality under the leadership of village party organizations. In urban areas, there is a must to advance urban community construction across the board, clearly define the functions of community committees and the relations between government and communities and form new-type communities featuring orderly administration, civilization and harmony. In enterprises and public institutions, there is a must to keep staying committed to and improving congresses of workers and staff and other forms of democratic management systems and practically guarantee the lawful rights and interests of workers.

Fifth, the socialist democratic system should be adhered to and improved. There is a must to properly handle the relations between direct election and indirect election,[10] between representative democracy and direct democracy and between intra-party democracy and people's democracy, and promote an all-round and coordinated development of socialist democracy. There is a must to properly handle the relations between organs of state power and administrative organs, judicial organs and procuratorial organs to ensure a positive development of the fundamental political system. There is a must to properly handle the relations between political democracy, economic democracy and social democracy to realize harmonious development of the three. There is a must to properly handle the relations between the protection of civic rights and the requirement for citizens' fulfillment of legal obligations and assumption of social responsibilities, and remain committed to the unity of rights and obligations and the unity of rights and responsibilities.[11] There is a must to properly handle the relations between developing democracy and propelling the political system reform for one part and maintaining social stability for another, comprehensively develop people's democracy and actively and orderly reform the political system under the precondition of maintaining stability. Among all these relationships, the primary is to handle the relations between Party's

[10]Both direct election and indirect election are the realization forms of democracy. A higher degree of direct election does not necessarily mean more democratic. Likewise, more universal indirect election does not necessarily mean less democratic. Both direct election and indirect election are democratic approaches and both adapt to the national conditions and cultural, economic and social development level, so they should not be understood as a whole.

[11]However, government should not emphasize citizens' performance of obligations but stress how the government could provide guarantees and services to citizens and better realize the rights of citizens. For instance, in terms of citizens' fulfillment of the obligation of paying taxes, competent government departments should also assume the obligation of protecting taxpayers' rights, especially their right to know where and how their tax payments are used, and their right of supervision derived from this. In a society under the rule of law, an important aspect for citizens to fulfill obligations is that the government guarantees an effective realization of civic rights.

leadership, people's role as masters of the country and governance by law and guarantee an organic unity of the three in system, procedure and law.

(II) Implement Governance by Law as the Fundamental Strategy, and Guarantee Full-Scale Enforcement of Laws

Firstly, it is to continuously develop and modify the socialist system of law. The socialist system of law is the foundation for implementing the governance by law as the fundamental strategy and an important systematic premise for ensuring national unification, ethnic unity, social stability and people's life and work in peace and contentment. The socialist system of law is also the basic requirement for safeguarding the authority of the socialist rule of law and an indispensable guarantee for building and improving a uniformed socialist market economic system. The quality of the socialist system of law has been affected by departmental protectionism in legislative works and the inconsistency and even conflicts existing in laws and regulations. To further improve China's system of law, the existing system of law should be modified across the board according to the amendment to the Constitution to ensure the coordination and consistency of various laws, regulations, local laws and regulations, government rules, etc., for one part and the Constitution for another especially after the adoption of the amendment to the Constitution at the Second Session of the Tenth NPC. At the same time, there is a must to intensify the implementation of *the legislation law*. State organs should strictly observe corresponding legislative authority and shall neither excessively exercise and extend their powers nor derelict their duties and shirk responsibilities. Local organs shall not encroach on the exclusive legislative authority of central organs, still less develop regulative documents conflicting with the Constitution, laws and administrative regulations.

Secondly, there is a must to try to solve issues related to the uniformity of legal interpretations and further strengthen the recording review works of the Standing Committee of the NPC in legal interpretation. The current situation in China is that laws or regulations are interpreted by drafting organs, which can easily result in arbitrary and amplified interpretation of laws and regulations. In the interpretation of law enforcement of administrative organs, there are such phenomena as taking what they need, establishing their own systems, passing the buck and even "fighting by law." The phenomenon of incompliance with the current Constitution and laws also exists in judicial interpretation, such as expanding and excessively exercising their powers. The solutions to these problems are: (1) Relevant subjects shall correctly exercise the interpretation power and prevent the abuse or disuse of the interpretation power in accordance with the Constitution and the law; (2) the Standing Committee of the NPC shall reinforce legislative interpretations and effectively supervise and review judicial interpretations.

Thirdly, the mechanism for law enforcement shall be perfected. After nearly 30 years of building the rule of law, the socialist system of law with Chinese characteristics has basically taken shape and laws are generally available. Currently, the principal contradiction in building the rule of law in China is in the aspect of law enforcement, mainly demonstrated by the rather serious behaviors such as noncompliance with the law, slack law enforcement and unpunished lawbreakers.[12] To strive to improve the overall level of China's rule of law, we should further strengthen law enforcement while continuously valuing and improving legislative works, take effective law enforcement as the priority of the next step of building the rule of law and finally realize a coordinated development of law enforcement and lawmaking. To improve the effectiveness of law enforcement, we should start from leading cadres of all levels by constantly improving their concepts and level of governance by law, making decisions by law and acting by law. We should also put in place a strict law enforcement system and practically realize governance by law and law enforcement for the people. We should practically guarantee in system and law that judicial organs and procuratorial organs independently and impartially exercise their judicial powers and procuratorial powers in accordance with law. In law enforcement, we should guarantee the uniformity of law enforcement and judicature, which is the basic requirement of the principles of socialist rule of law for guaranteeing uniformed law enforcement. We should firmly curb local protectionism existing in judicature and prevent people's procuratorates and people's courts from becoming the tool of local protectionism and even from becoming "local procuratorates" and "local courts" serving local interests.

(III) Maintain the Constitutional Authority, and Reinforce Constitutional Supervision

The socialist constitution with Chinese characteristics has given expression to the Party's propositions and the people's will. The socialist constitution with Chinese characteristics represents the institutional and regulative basis for staying committed to the Party's leadership, enabling the people to become masters of the country and governing the country by law. In the process of building the socialist constitutional government, we should practically govern the country, hold the power in accordance with the Constitution, use constitutional, democratic and law-based methods to adhere to the Party's leadership, build the Party for public interests and govern for the people in order to maintain the socialist constitutional authority. On September 15, 2004, General Secretary Hu Jintao delivered a speech marking the 50th anniversary of the founding of the NPC. In the speech, he clearly pointed out the must to improve the constitution protection system in order to ensure a comprehensive implementation of the Constitution. There is a must to pay close attention to studying and modifying the constitution supervision mechanism, further clarify the constitution supervision procedures and make all behaviors

[12]The phenomenon of replacing the law by personal views of administrative leaders and powers of administrative leaders exists in some local areas. Some local areas settle for pragmatism in law enforcement, namely implementing what is beneficial to them and leaving those unbeneficial to them unimplemented. Some local areas are facing such problems as denial of justice, low efficiency and difficulty in enforcing some laws. The lacking of effectiveness of laws is sometimes the result of legislation. For example, in some local areas laws are made by "leaders," neglecting the democratic procedure of legislation and lacking law enforcement evaluation; they face high cost of law enforcement and have no conditions for enforcement, which have made it difficult to enforce some local laws and regulations.

violating the Constitution be timely corrected. As provided in China's Constitution, the NPC and the Standing Committee of the NPC supervise the implementation of the Constitution. This supervision mainly covers the following aspects. First, the NPC has the right to change or repeal inappropriate laws and decisions made by the Standing Committee of the NPC to guarantee that the laws and decisions made by the Standing Committee of the NPC do not conflict with the Constitution. Second, the Standing Committee of the NPC has the right to repeal the administrative laws, regulations, decisions and orders made by the State Council but conflicting with the Constitution and laws. Third, the NPC and the Standing Committee of the NPC have the right to supervise the works and judicial interpretations of the Supreme People's Court and the Supreme People's Procuratorate. Fourth, the Standing Committee of the NPC has the right to abolish local laws, regulations and resolutions formulated and approved by organs of provinces, autonomous regions and municipalities directly under the central government of state power but conflicting with the Constitution, laws and administrative laws and regulations. On top of that, the Constitution also stipulates that local people's congresses of all levels shall guarantee the observance and implementation of the Constitution within their respective administrative regions.

However, due to the lacking of laws and systems and incompletely adaptable quality of law enforcers, there are many issues, such as the failure to abide by the law, slack law enforcement and impunity of lawbreakers. Violations of the Constitution still exist to various degrees. Given these phenomena, some scholars pointed out that violation of the Constitution is the most serious violation of laws and that governing the country by law should be firstly governing the country in accordance with the Constitution. So, they proposed that the constitution supervision becomes the core and top priority of people's congresses. In their opinion, the function of constitution supervision has not been effectively exercised because the constitution supervision mechanism and procedures remain to be further improved.[13] The NPC in 2000 adopted *the Legislation Law of the People's Republic of China* with clear stipulation on the hierarchical system of the force of law of China. The legislation law provides that lower-level laws shall not collide with upper-level laws. The legislation law also stipulates the mutual relations between laws at the same level (including the superiority of special laws to general laws and superiority of new laws to old laws) and the circumstances of altering or repealing laws, regulations, autonomous regulations, specific regulations, rules, etc. It can be said that there are many clauses, provisions and requirements in Chinese laws for constitution supervision. Nevertheless, there is still a lack of institutions and procedures for inspecting and supervising violations of the Constitution and some relations in political system have not been straightened out, so it is difficult to launch and carry out constitution supervisions in most cases and legislative remedies and measures and supervision mechanisms usually exist in name only. In practices, some departments pass the buck by extending legislative powers and

[13]Cheng Xiangqing: *On Improving the Supervising Mechanism of People's Congresses*, *National People's Congress of China*, 2004, Issue 8.

choose departmental protectionism. Some local areas make laws for private interests and choose local protectionism. There are also some other departments or local areas that advocate the idea of "omnipotent law" (or known as "legislative principle"), make laws random and arbitrary and seem to believe that laws are the panacea for social issues. They believe that all social issues result from the insufficient supply of legislative resources, which has led to unnecessary and over-elaborate formalities of lawmaking. Some laws and regulations unnecessarily adjusted some social relations and some unnecessarily controlled some issues. The existence and spread of above-mentioned phenomena have much to do with the absence of effective constitution supervision system.

The Office for Recording and Examining Laws under the Legislative Affairs Commission of the Standing Committee of the NPC handles the conflict of administrative laws and regulations, local laws and regulations, departmental rules, etc., with the Constitution and laws. This approach certainly has a positive significance in maintaining the unity of national legal system and safeguarding the constitutional rights of citizens. But ever since its establishment, the Office for Recording and Examining Laws has not yet made any decision on compliance with or violation of the Constitution. Currently, the Chinese society has no lack of applications by citizens to the NPC for examining violations of the Constitution. We believe that the constitution supervision system should be further improved and comprehensively implemented on the basis of thorough investigations and scientific demonstrations. Constitutional decisions can be made for state acts mentioned in these applications that do not collide with the Constitution. On the one hand, these constitutional decisions can remove the doubts of all walks of life about the constitutionality of state acts. On the other hand, these constitutional decisions can help provide a legitimate basis for state acts in the Constitution and establish the authority of law-based government. Acts in violation of the constitution should be called as such without delay and corrected. The ultimate goal is to subject socialist democratic politics to the rule law and maintain the supreme authority of the Constitution.

V. Theoretical Development of the Socialist Constitution with Chinese Characteristics (Chinese p. 21)

China's existing constitution is a constitution with Chinese characteristics. Marxism–Leninism served as the ideological foundation and theoretical basis for the formulation, amendment and implementation of China's Constitution. Therefore, Marxism–Leninism had an indispensable guiding role in the development of China's socialist constitutional theory and the improvement of the constitutional system. The three generations of leadership represented by Mao Zedong, Deng Xiaoping and Jiang Zemin combined the basic principle of Marxism with China's reality to summarize the long-term and practical experiences of the Party and the Chinese people in building democracy and the rule of law and study and draw on the beneficial achievements of human constitutional civilization. The socialist constitutional theory with Chinese characteristics has taken shape gradually through pooling the collective wisdom of the Party and the whole nation.

The constitutional theory of Marxism–Leninism has revealed the basic law of formation and development of constitution by applying the principles of dialectical materialism and historical materialism. The constitutional theory of Marxism–Leninism points out that constitution is also a social–historical phenomenon, just like a state, so it has historical conditions and evolution process from emergence, development to extinction. Constitution should be based on the society. When constitution is unrealistic, it would be ostensible and vice versa. From the perspective of the relationship between constitution and economy, the constitutional theory of Marxism–Leninism correctly reveals the dialectical relationship between constitution and economic foundation. The constitutional theory of Marxism–Leninism believes that constitution as an integral part of the superstructure is determined by the economic foundation in the final analysis and is bound to change with the economic foundation and react upon the economic foundation for its formation and existence. According to the constitutional theory of Marxism–Leninism, Constitution promotes the development of productivity and boosts social progress through adjusting social relations. While acknowledging the historical progress of capitalist constitution, the constitutional theory of Marxism–Leninism profoundly unveils that the Constitution of capitalist countries is the fundamental legal system for maintaining the bourgeois political rule. The constitutional theory of Marxism–Leninism concludes that socialist constitution is the fundamental law and system established by the proletariat and the masses of working people, reflecting the people's will as a whole and protecting the fundamental interests of the people.

The constitutional theory of Marxism–Leninism thinks highly of the dominant role of man (people) in constitution and law, puts people first and safeguards people's basic rights. The constitutional theory of Marxism–Leninism further points out that the right to vote and recall and the freedom of publication and assembly are essential parts of people's rights. The constitutional theory of Marxism–Leninism also clearly states that equality is an important principle of socialist constitution, and the state respects religious freedom and stays out of all religious affairs. In terms of the relationship between right and obligation, Marxism–Leninism believes that rights come with obligations. According to Marxism–Leninism, a person has the responsibility to demand human rights and civil rights not only for himself or herself but also for everyone fulfilling his or her obligations, and there is no right without obligation or obligation without right. The constitutional theory of Marxism–Leninism thinks that democracy is the rule by most people and democracy should be realized through general, direct and equal elections. The constitutional theory of Marxism–Leninism holds that socialist political power should implement the principle of integrating parliament with administration and the principle of democratic centralism, and the structural form of socialist countries should be the unitary form of state in principle. In the aspect of building the legal system, Marxism–Leninism stands for unified socialist legal system but enforcing laws differently in line with local actuality and diversified enforcing means and rules in specific.

The first generation of leading collectives of the Party with Mao Zedong as the core formed the Mao Zedong Thought and proposed a series of socialist constitutional awareness and principles. The first generation of leading collectives creatively developed the constitutional theory of Marxism and provided the ideological basis for making the constitution and building the socialist democratic legal system of China. Mao Zedong made it loud and clear that Constitution is the general principle and fundamental law of a country, the fact of democracy is the foundation of Constitution, and Constitution is the confirmation of democracy. He pointed out that all constitutional governments in the world, including that of the UK, France, the USA or the Soviet Union, would issue and accept a fundamental law after the success of a revolution and the availability of democracy, namely the constitution. On this basis, he classified Constitution into capitalist constitution and socialist constitution. He observed that socialist constitution is more advanced although capitalist constitution is an earlier comer from the perspective of the historical development process. He concluded that China's Constitution is a socialist constitution. In the aspect of drafting and formulating the socialist constitution, he stressed the need to combine the scientific nature with principle and flexibility and combine learning foreign advanced experience in making Constitution with China's actual conditions. He emphasized to fix the socialist principle and democratic principle and enact a people-satisfied constitution. When it comes to the observation and implementation of the Constitution, he required the whole nation to study and comply with the Constitution after its adoption. He also highlighted that working staff of state organs, especially high-level leading cadres of the Party and the state, should take the lead to abide by and implement the Constitution, otherwise, it would be a violation of the Constitution, and so on and so forth.

Mao Zedong clearly proposed to take people's democracy as the fundamental way to jump out of the historical rise and fall periodic law. He emphasized that only people's supervision could make the government dare not to slack off, and only when everyone takes on the responsibility, could the people and the government avoid failures. In order to realize people's democracy, Mao Zedong raised a host of constitutional theories and thoughts. In the aspect of the nature of the state, he profoundly analyzed the status of different social classes based on China's specific practices in revolutionary constructions and demonstrated the necessity of implementing people's democratic dictatorship in the People's Republic of China. He also stressed that the leadership of the proletariat and the alliance of workers and peasants are crucial guarantees for enabling the people to become masters of the country. With regard to the organization form of state power, he scientifically threw light upon the basic principles of the people's congress system and the basic principles of democratic centralism. Regarding the political party system, he generalized the historical experiences of CPC in long-term cooperation with various democratic parties and drew lessons from the experiences and lessons of the International Communist Movement. He put forward the principle of "long-term coexistence, mutual supervision" for the cooperation of CPC with democratic parties and non-party personages, which fundamentally solved issues related to the development prospect of democratic parties and established the basic pattern of a new-type political party system featuring multi-party cooperation under the socialist conditions. As regards issues related to ethnic groups, he proposed to implement the ethnic regional national autonomy system but not federal system in areas inhabited by ethnic minorities, which laid a theoretical basis for properly handling national issues within the united multiethnic country. When it comes to the relations between central and local governments, he advocated for the expansion of local powers, more independent local authorities and more actively played local powers under the precondition of consolidating the unified leadership of the central government.

The socialist constitutional theory with Chinese characteristics is an organic part of the socialist theory with Chinese characteristics and a major theoretical result of the localization of Marxist constitutional theory in China. The socialist constitutional theory with Chinese characteristics has enriched and developed the constitutional theory of Marxism in a series of key issues and become an important thought guiding China's building of socialist democracy and rule of law.

(I) Theory of Socialist Democracy and Legal System

On the basis of summarizing the experiences and lessons of China in building socialist democracy, Deng Xiaoping concluded that there would be no socialism and socialist modernization without democracy. He made democracy the key to the success of China's socialist cause. He emphasized the need to institutionalize and subject socialist democracy to the rule of law and make this system remain unchanged amid the change of leaders and the change of leaders' opinions and attentions. He put forward the "sixteen-character guideline" in building the socialist legal system. The "sixteen-character guideline" can be explained as the establishment, the strict and punitive enforcement of the law. He underlined that all citizens are equal before laws and systems and everyone has equal rights and obligations in accordance with legal provisions.

(II) Theory of "One Country, Two Systems"

"One country, two systems" offers a pragmatic and feasible way to address issues related to Taiwan, Hong Kong and Macao and for realizing peaceful reunification of the country. Implementing the "one country, two systems" policy involves allowing Taiwan, Hong Kong and Macao to retain their capitalist system and way of life in the foreseeable future under the fundamental premise of there being only one China whose basic system is socialism. This entails "letting the people of Hong Kong govern Hong Kong" and "letting the people of Macao govern Macao" with a high degree of autonomy, and in strict accordance with the basic law of special administrative regions. The long-term aim is to promote a long-lasting prosperity and stability of Hong Kong and Macao. China stays committed to the principles of "peaceful reunification, and one country, two systems" and the eight proposals for developing the cross-strait relations and boosting peaceful reunification of the country. The Chinese government adheres steadfastly to the four points in developing cross-strait relations and the principle of peaceful development of cross-strait relations and will resolutely strive toward cross-strait relations toward peace and stability.

(III) Respect for and Protection of Human Rights

Respecting and protecting human rights come as an intrinsic requirement of developing socialist democratic politics and building socialist political civilization. Human rights issues have universal significance. Given the reality of so many countries in the world, the realization of human rights requires the efforts of all countries. Fundamentally speaking, the issue of human rights falls within the sovereignty of each country. Human rights are the product of history, and their full realization is a gradual development process associated with the economic and cultural level of each country. Collective human rights and individual rights, economic, social and cultural rights, civic and political rights are inseparable. In terms of respecting and safeguarding human rights, there is a need to respect the principle of universality of human rights and act upon the basic national conditions to practically prioritize people's subsistence right and development right. There is also a need to ensure the equal participation and development right of all social members on the basis of promoting a sound and rapid social and economic development. For China, the most important human right is the subsistence right and gradual realization of a higher level of and more extensive human rights with the development of modernization.

(IV) Put Forward Governance by Law as the Fundamental Strategy

The governance by law is the basic strategy for the Party to lead the people to rule the state and deal with politics. Governing the country by law is an objective requirement for developing the socialist market economy. It is also an important symbol of the progress of social civilization and an important guarantee for China's long-lasting peace and stability. Under this theoretical guidance, "the People's Republic of China implements governance by law and builds a socialist country under the rule of law" that has been written into the Constitution in the form of amendment and has become an important constitutional principle. The requirement is to combine the governance by law with the rule by virtue, combine building the rule of law with spiritual civilization and combine legislation with major reform and development policies so as to provide a strong law-based guarantee for the socialist modernization.

(V) Persevere in Governing the Country and Exercising Power in Accordance with the Constitution

In the process of deeply implementing the governance by law as the fundamental strategy, the CPC attaches great importance to the core position and vital role of the Constitution as the fundamental law in state politics and social life. The CPC came up with the constitutional ideas of governing the country and exercising power in accordance with the Constitution from a strategically advantageous position. The CPC commands and guides the implementation of the Constitution and laws on the basis of governing the country and exercising power in accordance with the Constitution. Hu Jintao noted that governing the country by law requires first of all governing the country in accordance with the Constitution while ruling by law requires first of all exercising power in accordance with the Constitution. The Constitution and laws are the embodiment of the Party's propositions and people's will and the scientific summary of China's great revolution, construction and reform practices. The Constitution is the fundamental law of the country and the general principle for ensuring well administration of state affairs and national security. The Constitution is the legal basis for guaranteeing national unification, ethnic unity, economic development, social progress and lasting political stability. The Constitution is the legal system guarantee for the Party to govern and rejuvenate the country and lead people of all ethnic groups to build the socialism with Chinese characteristics. All Party members, working staff of state organs and people of all ethnic groups should earnestly study, observe and safeguard the Constitution and ensure its implementation in the entire society.

(VI) **Theory About the Implementation of the Constitution**

According to the theory of constitution with Chinese characteristics, the life of Constitution lies in its implementation, so there is a must to strengthen the enforcement of the Constitution. This is an essential task for building a socialist political civilization and the groundwork for building a socialist country under the rule of law. In this connection, the implementation of the Constitution must be strengthened unswervingly for long. The implementation of the Constitution should be advanced from the following three aspects. First, there is a must to study and propagate the Constitution. There is a must to constantly improve the Party and all people's understanding of the important position and role, the basic knowledge and contents of the Constitution and the significance of the implementation of the Constitution. There is also a must to form a good atmosphere of upholding, observing and safeguarding the Constitution. Second, there is a must to improve the constitution guarantee system and carry out regular examinations and supervisions of the implementation of the Constitution. There is also a must to timely correct violations of the Constitution and practically implement various stipulations of the Constitution in right place. Third, there is a must to adhere to the Party's leadership. Party organizations and members of all levels should abide by the Constitution and act in strict accordance with the Constitution. The Constitution and laws reflect the unity of the Party's propositions and people's will. The Party leads the people to make the Constitution and laws, so it should also lead the people to obey the Constitution and laws. Party members and cadres, especially party leaders, should play an exemplary role in abiding by the Constitution and laws. All party organizations and members, especially party leaders' words and deeds, shall not conflict with the Constitution and laws.

As the think tank and brain trust of the Party Central Committee, Chinese Academy of Social Sciences (CASS) has played an important role in drafting and amending the Constitution. Hu Qiaomu, Hu Sheng, Li Tieying, Chen Kuiyuan and other leaders of CASS played their essential roles in drafting the current

Constitution. The Institute of Law of CASS has been attaching importance to studying constitutional jurisprudence ever since its establishment. The Institute of Law of CASS has also been committed to combining theoretical studies on constitutions with China's practices. In the process of drafting the 1982 Constitution, Zhang Youyu, Wang Shuwen and some other senior constitutional scholars of the Institute of Law assisted Comrade Hu Qiaomu and the Secretariat of the Committee for Revision of the Constitution to carry out a lot of theoretical studies and collect data. In all previous constitution revising processes, scholars in constitutional studies from the Institute of Law conducted abundant studies, consultations and propaganda works through various formal and informal channels and contributed to the improvement of the constitutional system and the building of the authority of the Constitution. Over the past three decades, many new phenomena and new issues occurring in China's constitutional practices merit our studies and thinking. Theorists in constitutional jurisprudence have compiled many outstanding research results by centering on the development of the existing Constitution, which have exerted positive influences on facilitating theoretical innovation, increasing the consciousness of all walks of life in maintaining and observing the Constitution and safeguarding the authority of the Constitution. In order to review the development of China's constitutional system ever since the implementation of the Constitution in force and summarize China's achievements in theoretical studies on the constitutional jurisprudence, the Institute of Law of CASS has published a series of books on 30-year development of the Constitution with the hope of contributing their part to the prosperity and development of China's study of law.

September 2012

Lin Li
Member of the Academic Divisions of the Chinese
Academy of Social Sciences (CASS Academic Divisions)

Head of the Institute of Law of CASS
Beijing, China

Contents

Review and Outlook of the "1982 Constitution" 1
Buyun Li

Constitutional Research in China: A Thirty-Year Review and Future Outlook: Marking the 30th Anniversary of the Promulgation of the 1982 Constitution and the First Anniversary of the Founding of China Constitutional Research Association 15
Dayuan Han and Honghong Hu

Continuous Growth in Reform and Opening-up: Three Decades of Development of Constitutional Law Studies in China 47
Jihong Mo and Guoqiang Zhai

The International Perspective: Thirty Years of International Outreach and Exchanges (1981–2012) 131
Jihong Mo

The Chinese Constitution as the Fundamental Law and Supreme Law of the Land: Marking the 30th Anniversary of the Adoption of the 1982 Constitution 141
Jinxue Fan

Constitutionalism and Revolution: Reflections on and Outlook for the 1982 Constitution 167
Xiaobing Li

Toward Academic Consciousness: Review of Theoretical Studies on Basic Rights Over the Past Thirty Years 189
Hailiang Yan and Xiaobiao Cui

The 1982 Constitution and Human Rights: Thirty Years of Social Change and Its Constitutional Implications 221
Zhang Zhen

State Organs: Three Decades of Structural Change and Institutional Development 235
Hongchang Jiao and Qiang Ye

The President as the Head of State: Review and Reflections 265
Ling Ma

Values in the Constitution: Fifteen Years of Exploration 283
Qian Zhao

Implementation of the Constitution: Evaluation Method and Impact Assessment 299
Jihong Mo

Legislative Application of the Constitution: Key Features and Critical Analysis 319
Jihong Mo

Study of the Applicability of the Constitution in Judicial Proceedings 363
Mo Jihong

Postscript I 389

Postscript II 393

References 395

Review and Outlook of the "1982 Constitution"

Buyun Li

[Editor's Note] Mr. Li Buyun, the author of the book, reviewed the formation process and major achievements of the 1982 Constitution with his personal experience. He believes that the current Constitution has reflected the ideological guideline of seeking truth from facts upheld by the Party and the state over the past three decades of reform and opening-up. He also believes that the constitution in force has demonstrated the major achievements and progress of the Party and the state in political, economic, cultural, and social areas. In his opinion, the current constitution has truly mirrored the present situation of China, but it has not yet reached the level of an ideal constitutional government and needs to be constantly improved with the development of China's constitutional government. The principal challenge at present is how to build the supreme authority of the Constitution and boost the development of democracy and rule of law in an comprehensive and holistic manner. For being a senior Chinese jurist and a history witness of the 1982 Constitution, Mr. Li Buyun together with Mr. Jiang Ping and Mr. Guo Daohui are called "Three Senior Figures in Rule of Law." At the time of the publication of the series of books titled *China's Constitution over the Past Three Decades (1982–2012)*, the transcript of an academic lecture titled *Review and Outlook of the "1982 Constitution"* by Li Buyun is especially chosen as the preamble of Volume I of this series of books to mark the 30th anniversary of the promulgation and implementation of the existing 1982 Constitution.

Thank you, the moderator and all friends present here. The organizer of the meeting has designated a topic to me which is *Review of the 1982 Constitution: Progress, Difficulties and Outlook*. This requires giving a speech from a macro-

---

Honorary member of the Academic Divisions and researcher of the Institute of Law of CASS.

B. Li (✉)
Chinese Academy of Social Sciences, Beijing, China
e-mail: 13263169197@163.com

L. Li et al. (eds.), *Constitutional Development in China, 1982–2012*,
Research Series on the Chinese Dream and China's Development Path,
https://doi.org/10.1007/978-981-32-9261-1_1

scopic perspective. Before talking about this specific topic, I would like to say a bit of my personal understandings of it today.

The so-called "transformation toward modernization" is a holistic concept. It requires the transition from an agricultural society to an industrial society, from the originally planned economy to a market economy, and from seclusion to opening-up to the outside world. It also covers the transformation of culture from monism to diversity including ideology. Of course, it also covers the theme we are talking about, namely the transforming constitution and constitutional government toward modernization.

I agree with the viewpoint that now China has a constitution but not constitutional government. I think I should make a supplement to it. Constitution has taken shape in China, but it is not perfect. The constitution has only basically mirrored our current situation, but it has not yet reached an ideal state required by a constitutional government. Modern constitutional government requires not only a good constitution but also its thorough implementation, great authority, and all the basic principles are carried out. I boil modern constitution down to three major basic principles, namely democracy, rule of law, and human rights. I also sum up constitutional government into four elements, namely democracy, rule of law, human rights, and supremacy of constitution. The former three elements are substantial contents. The supremacy of constitution means that constitution has the supreme authority, which is formal necessity. We have already stepped on the track of transformation toward a modernized constitutional government. We are heading toward this objective, but we still have a long way to go. It is the transformation from excessive centralization to democracy; from rule of man to rule of law; from no rights and unguaranteed rights of people to fully guaranteed rights of people; and from no authority of constitution to supreme authority of constitution. That is my understanding of the scope of this topic. This is what we need to study today. Now, let me go back to the theme.

I was a graduate student at Peking University between 1962 and 1965. I was majoring in jurisprudence under the supervision of Professor Zhang Youyu. I started to study constitution by chance. In July 1980, I was temporarily transferred to the Research Office of the Secretariat of the CPC Central Committee to take charge of legal affairs. My supervisor Professor Zhang Youyu was the Deputy Secretary General of the Secretariat of the 1982 Constitution Drafting Committee. He asked me whether I could work with the Secretariat and take part in the drafting in person. I said that it might be inappropriate as I already worked in the Secretariat of the CPC Central Committee, and most of drafts requiring the approval of the Central Committee would be reviewed by me. He said that's quite right. Later, my first task at the Research Office of the Secretariat of the CPC Central Committee was to draft the speech for Chairman Ye Jianying to be delivered at the first meeting of the 1982 Constitution Drafting Committee, which set the tone for the 1982 Constitution on behalf of the Party Central Committee. I drafted the speech together with Chen Jinyu. Since then, every draft would be modified by me and then submitted to Deng Liqun and other central government leaders for their opinions.

Back then, I was quite energetic. I worked 16 h a day and stayed overnight in my office in Zhongnanhai. In one and a half months in 1981, I published ten articles consecutively on the *People's Daily* to provide suggestions for the amendments to the Constitution, and most of them were adopted. I later also attended two expert meetings held by the central leading group for amending the Constitution. I proposed to write "governance by law" and "safeguarding human rights" into the Constitution, which was adopted.

My comment on the 1982 Constitution is that it basically reflected the achievements of our Party in governing the state and dealing with politics since the reform and opening-up. The actuality was basically mirrored in the field of political system reform, certainly including the economic system reform. The 1982 Constitution went beyond the 1954 Constitution. The 1975 Constitution was a bad one as it was formulated during the Cultural Revolution. The 1978 Constitution did not eliminate its influence completely but had a great improvement. The greatest improvement was that it deleted "under the leadership of the Central Committee of the CPC" from the statement "the National People's Congress under the leadership of the Central Committee of the CPC is the supreme organ of state power." However, there were still some deficiencies. For instance, the guiding thought of "continuous revolution under the proletarian dictatorship" and "speaking out freely, airing views fully, holding great debates and writing big-character posters" remained unchanged. I think the 1982 Constitution had improvements in the following aspects.

First, in terms of democracy, the preamble of the constitution contained a paragraph stating that all state organs, armed forces, political parties, social organizations, enterprises, and public institutions must observe the constitution as the fundamental rules for their activities and assume the responsibility of safeguarding constitutional dignity and guaranteeing constitutional implementation. Political parties herein included the Communist Party. All political parties must defend the authority of the constitution. This was consistent with one of my suggestions adopted by the Party Constitution of the Party's Twelfth National Congress—party organizations must act within the framework of the constitution and the law. This suggestion of mine was firstly put forward on *Guangming Daily* and was later written in the Party Constitution. It could be written in the Party Constitution but not in the constitution. This principle was reflected in the preceding sentence referring to all political parties in the preamble of the constitution reflected this principle.

Regarding the tenure system, I should not be attributed to the abolition of life tenure of leading posts. Yan Jiaqi firstly spoke out his disagreement to life tenure. Later on July 9, 1982, I published an article titled *A Reform with Far-reaching Significance* on *People's Daily*, which played a certain role in abolishing the life tenure system.

Second, the progress in the rule of law was mainly the restoration of the two major principles: judicial independence and equality before the law. The 1975 Constitution abrogated these two principles contained in 1954 Constitution, but they were not restored in the 1978 Constitution. For this reason, I published two articles, on in *People's Daily the other in The Red Flag* (refer to "Staying Committed to Equality of All Citizens before the Law," *People's Daily*, December 6, 1978, and "Staying Committed to Equality of All People before the Law," *The Red Flag*, 1979, Issue 23). I thought that this issue was basically resolved because the Party's official newspaper and periodical had clearly affirmed it. Therefore, I put forward my suggestion of "staying committed to two principles in amending the Constitution, one is judicial independence and the other is democratic legislation" while drafting the "speech at the first meeting of the 1982 Constitution Drafting Committee" for Ye Jianying. This suggestion was accepted. These two basic principles were written in the 1982 Constitution. Of course, some other principles were also included in the constitution.

Third, in the aspect of human rights, one of my proposals was adopted, that is to arrange the chapter of safeguarding The Fundamental Rights of Citizens in front of the chapter of The Structure of The State. This reflected that state is the means while citizens are the purpose, and state organs exist to serve the people. Therefore, the chapter on fundamental rights of citizens was placed before the chapter on the structure of the state, which was also mentioned in my articles in *People's Daily* and was adopted in the constitutional amendment.

I once wrote an article titled *What Is a Citizen* (*People's Daily*, December 18, 1981). In the past, many people held the view that the "five groups of people," namely landowners, rich peasants, counterrevolutionaries, evildoers and rightists, and people with criminal convictions, especially those deprived of political rights, were not citizens. That is a vague statement for many people and also for the Central Committee and the National People's Congress. I then proposed to write "every person who has the nationality of the People's Republic of China is a citizen of the People's Republic of China" into the new constitution, which was adopted. Since then, tens of millions of Chinese people have obtained their deserved legal personality and are no longer "second-class citizens" who are not clearly and legally guaranteed in rights. A new sentence was added about the rights of citizens: "the personal dignity of citizens is inviolable," and so on and so forth. There were also some suggestions on the usage of language. For example, I didn't agree with such figurative statements as "the People's Liberation Army (PLA) is the strong pillar of proletarian dictatorship and the own army of workers and peasants," etc.

So, in my assessment, the 1982 Constitution was a good constitution. It is good in two ways. First, it affirms the country's commitment to reform and opening-up and the emancipation of the mind. Second, it reflected the depth of our understandings back then. This depth not only went beyond that of the Cultural Revolution but also that of the period between 1954 and the Cultural Revolution and of course the period before 1954. The 1982 Constitution was a huge step forward in the reform and design of the political system. The governance by law and human rights protection were incorporated into the constitution, respectively, in 1999 and 2004, which have basically reflected, together with private property protection, the progress, and achievement in the reform and opening-up over the past three decades. Speaking from an ideal state of constitutional government, this constitution had its shortage due to certain stipulations on some regimes. For example, the Party's leadership, with or without election, I'm always the leader; Mao Zedong Thought, Deng Xiaoping Theory and Three Represents are all written into the constitution, when will be the end of this?

From the perspective of an ideal constitutional government, it is not a perfect constitution. However, it had great progress. It had progressed step by step from its establishment to the four amendments, especially when the two major principles, namely the rule of law and human rights were written into the constitution. I witnessed the process, which was by no means an easy one.

Let's take the admission of human rights to the constitution as an example. At the time, comrade Wu Bangguo chaired six panel meetings on this matter. On one occasion with the participation of five constitutional scholars, he asked one of them, a senior professor to say something first, but the senior professor declined the offer out of concern for undesirable consequences. So then I was asked to speak. I raised four points, and two and a half were adopted. My suggestion on establishing a review for constitutionality system and modifying Article 126, namely the article about judicial independence, failed to be adopted. According to Article 126, people's courts independently exercise judicial powers without the interference of administrative organs, social groups, and individuals. My suggestion was "without the interference of any organs," people's congresses and the Party could supervise but not interfere with people's courts. The suggestion was not adopted. But my suggestion on incorporating protection of human rights in the constitution was adopted. Another suggestion of mine was related to the Sun Zhigang Case and was also adopted. I asked whether we could carry out a review for constitutionality which was absent in the past 50 years and abolish the *Measures for Assisting Vagrants and Beggars* which was formulated by the State Council. Three citizens submitted petitions on the abolition, so we should accept it as it is a right suggestion. So, what should we do? How about the first-ever constitutionality review in 50 years? Premier Wen Jiabao personally announced the abolition of the ordinance later. It was changed to "assistance by civil affairs department."

Another suggestion was about the functions and powers of state president. I cited a long-existing unconstitutional example while suggesting the establishment of a constitutionality review system. According to the provisions of China's constitution in force, state president is titular head who cannot intervene in affairs of state. That said, our president has traveled around the world, had substantive talks with foreign leaders, issued communiques, signed treaties, and engaged in other activities in recent years, which are unconstitutional. An article was added to the amendments to the constitution: State president may engage in state affairs. That's how it was amended.

During the process of amending the constitution, I realized that our political system reform has been moving forward as a whole. From a holistic perspective, our constitution basically conforms to the current national conditions. Many people have certain reasons to complain that the political system reform lags behind the economic system reform and the overall social development. This is an objective reality. We should be faster in reforming the political system. But, some issues that should be addressed and addressed sooner still fail to get done as expected, such as review for constitutionality. Since 1982, I've written many articles about it and spoken of it on various occasions, but it is still not accepted. It might be because of worrying about supervisions over Party documents and over military commissions. What if a proposal on a review for constitutionality in these two areas is raised? I stand for adding a constitution commission to the current nine commissions. There is no need to revise the constitution as the NPC has the power to set up a commission. A leader asked about the missions of the review for constitutionality. I pointed out the missions in eight aspects. He asked who should be the members. I said that it should not be a problem as we could choose two or three vice chairmen from the NPC and some senior experts to be the members. One month prior to the convocation of this year's NPC, I made a speech at the work meeting on celebrating the Spring Festival held by the Legislative Affairs Commission of the Standing Committee of the NPC. I said it would be Hu Jintao's great political legacy if he could see to it that the Legislative Affairs Commission was established before the end of his term in office. I noted that it was a great opportunity and all participants at the work meeting could play a big role and contribute their part. I expressed my wish to see its establishment as soon as possible since there was only one year to go before the change of the term of office.

This kind of issue will not affect the political situation, still less the Party's leadership. It could only add marks to the Party's leadership. This is about political wisdom.

Next, I would share my general estimation of the constitution. In terms of the constitutional government, the principal problem at present is that some stipulations of the constitution in force fail to be put in place. The people's congress system is an example. According to constitutional concept, it should be a "steel seal." The supreme organ of state power should be the NPC but not the Party Central Committee. In contrast, the Party Central Committee is our supreme organ of state power. Some powers fail to be given to the NPC. That is to say the NPC is not yet the "steel seal." When I contacted with some ministerial leaders of the NPC, they said that our people's congress system is not bad in itself but not completely in place. Even a conservative vice chairman of the NPC complained about having limited powers. How and when, even the agenda of convening the meetings are all strictly examined by the Party Central Committee. The bicameralism we mentioned yesterday is good, but it is difficult to put it in place.

Speaking of the outlook, I have a few thoughts. I would like to share some of my viewpoints on democracy. I agree with what Mr. Zhou said yesterday.

First, we need to stay committed to the Party's leadership. If we turn to a multi-party system and lift party banning, China would fall into a chaos. This chaos may last 10 to 20 years before stability is fully restored. In addition, it would impede both economic growth and improvements in people's living standards. Therefore, we still need to move forward step by step within the system of Party's leadership.

Second, we need to move forward in an all-round way. Yesterday, Professor Tong Zhiwei raised an important issue: The Party provides overarching oversight and decides where breakthroughs should be made. The question is which one?

We need to ease restrictions now, but there are so many places requiring corrections. I strongly agree with what Mr. Zhou said. We need to make breakthroughs in all areas and in a comprehensive and holistic manner. We will not pass up even the slightest possibility for improving things. We need to push forward comprehensively in various specific issues related to democracy, rule of law, human rights, and the supremacy of the constitution. Of course, there are some key points, such as the rule of law. I think we need to make breakthroughs in two areas regarding the rule of law.

The first is review for constitutionality. I once participated in a panel meeting held at the Great Hall of the People. At the meeting, I said to former Vice Chairman Peng Chong that it would be a great contribution if he could take the lead with comrade Wan Li to establish a constitutionality review system. He asked whether he could play such a big role. I said yes. I said it would be difficult to require the people to strictly observe the law if the Party Central Committee doesn't respect the constitution. I told him that no one would dare to disrespect the constitution if the Party set an example.

(Chinese p. 30) In its September 2009 issue, *Southern Weekly* published an article I wrote titled "It is Time to Establish a Constitutionality Review System." In the article, I brought up the issue again and noted that if the central government leaders could establish such a system it would do a country a great deal of good and be a significant milestone. An oversight system is what allows the implementation of the constitution to have real bite.

The second point is judicial independence. At an expert meeting on constitution amendment held at the Great Hall of the People on June 13, 2003, I put forward four opinions. One of them was to revise Article 126 of the Constitution. The Supreme People's Court convened an expert meeting on this matter and I attended. I talked about the history of judicial independence in China. However, the proposal of the Supreme People's Court was not adopted. I think the reason was that it is the Party Committee who has the authority to approve proposals. The so-called coordination is in reality the Political and Legislative Affairs Committee calling the shots. While taking part in drafting Document No. 64 in 1979, I suggested abolishing the review system that lets the Party Central Committee decide cases. That was added to the document, only to have the inclusion reversed later.

Local protectionism is also an obstacle to judicial independence. Moreover, some of what goes on are simply illegal, such as various ways for politicians to exert influence on cases. Speaking of the system, the top priority is not the supervision over individual cases, which has already been addressed. I am very impressed by a book published recently by the Party School of the Central Committee of CPC. The first article in the book is written by a professor of the Party School of Sichuan Committee of CPC (PSSC), who offers a comprehensive plan for political system reform. One suggestion was to experiment with abolishing Political and Legislative Affairs Committee in some provinces. I learned that the Central Committee had in fact considered doing, on two occasions, but never did follow through. The first time was in drafting the document of the Central Committee on dividing authorities between the State Council and the Secretariat of the CPC Central Committee in early 1980s. The second time, some provinces abolished the Political and Legislative Committee but restored it later. This consideration is mainly for correctly handling the relations between the Party and judicial organs. Judicial independence is a prime concern both internationally and domestically and indeed requires discussions. Many Chinese judges take various relationships into consideration in judging cases. They don't consider whether it complies with the law. Instead, they care about whether there is an instruction from the superior. So many cases of this kind can be citied.

I once put forward 12 suggestions on the reform of the people's congress system. I observe that we are moving toward this direction, but we are moving slowly and have seen little progress.

In reforming the electoral system, it is to expand competitive election and reform how nominations are made. Candidates must meet voters and let people know what they think. These three points haven't been completely implemented under the current system. There is another suggestion about improving the quality of deputies of the people's congresses.

When giving lectures to provincial leaders, I often cite two examples. One is about a deputy to the National People's Congress who is also a world-class scientist. He used to tell his high schoolmates that he usually read books when others made speeches at NPC sessions because he believed in the Party, so he voted based on the Party's will. The other example happened in a province. One deputy who served for 5 years never spoke at People's Congress sessions except for saying "Thank You" at the closing panel just before he stepped down. We also mentioned the professionalization of members of the Standing Committee of the NPC yesterday, which could be quite effective. We have many cadres but not enough positions to place them in. They can be members of the Standing Committee of the NPC to work full-time and do nothing else. Some deputies may work part-time and reach out to voters, undertake investigations for 4 months to 6 months every year. It is feasible to improve the people's congress system by implementing rigorous standards for what members of the Standing Committee of the NPC do.

Moreover, regarding making reports by the Military Commission to the NPC, I once said in the article titled *Constitutional Government and China* that the former and present chairmen of the Military Commission would greatly promote democracy if they could deliver a work report to the NPC. These 12 suggestions also include an issue about whether it is democratic regarding the chairman of NPC and the director of a provincial people's congress because we are implementing the commission system, and act at the will of officials, and some others.

Under the current system, there are still three major areas in which there is room for further advancing reform of the people's congress system. One is the issue related to political parties. At the moment, democratic parties enroll party members on a scale of only increasing 5% each year. Could that be increased to 10%, or 20% several years later or completely unlimited some years later. I often talk to members of democratic parties and tell them not to not to write themselves off. I tell them that, if they work hard, they would have a very good foundation when there are no more bans on political parties. We must appreciate the independent character of political parties, which is the key. As Mr. Zhou said, all these systems, including the political consultative system and the ethnic autonomy system and grassroots self-governance system, are areas requiring comprehensive breakthroughs and advancement within the framework of the constitutional government.

Finally, it is my conclusion remarks. Why am I optimistic? In 1987 when I was a visiting scholar in the USA, Louis Henkin once invited me to dinner, the day after Hu Yaobang stepped down. He asked me about my outlook on democracy in China at that historic juncture. I replied without much thinking that I was optimistic. He asked why. I gave him four reasons.

First, democracy, rule of law, human rights, freedom, equality, and fraternity are the fundamental interests and strong desires of humanity, including the 1.3 billion Chinese people. The political consciousness of Chinese ordinary people has been greatly improved. Going forward, no political party or leader would dare to go against this will.

Second, after the implementation of the reform and opening-up, the market economy is bound to change the two major social relationships and five major social concepts. Firstly, it is the change "from status to contract" and from "big state, small society" to "strong state, big society." The five major concepts refer to subject consciousness, democracy consciousness, equality consciousness, freedom ideology, and concept of rights. These ideas would gradually and imperceptibly take roots and blossom in the minds of the Chinese people.

Third, opening to the outside world is an irreversible step. China is destined to be connected with the rest of the world in a comprehensive and holistic manner in economy, politics, and culture. It is impracticable to turn back either in economy or in politics as the pressure would be unbearable.

Fourth, the younger generations to come will be more knowledgeable, younger, know more about the world, and not burdened by historical legacies. At present, people with vested interests still bear historical burdens. Some others may think that things were different back in the old days during the revolution. And now capitalism is enjoying brisk growth, which can itself something of a historical burden. The younger generations to come would not have such historical burdens in mind. Generally speaking, cadres at either the central or local level would have higher education attainment, more knowledge, and less burdens.

I asked Louis Henkin about his thoughts on these four points. He said he would wait and see. I told him that Americans are pragmatists and only care about the present and who is in power. I'm not. I told him that I'm an idealist and I cared about which direction China must and was bound to go, not how many years either Deng Xiaoping or Hu Yaobang would serve in office.

Why am I optimistic? I'm a communist, so I certainly wish to see the long-lasting rule of the Communist Party. Having said that, I should add that I am not in favor of holding onto political power by force. In this connection, I stand for the so-called transformation. I'm not saying that the Communist Party must or will definitely be replaced. I'm not so pessimistic the way some are who believe relaxing restrictions on forming parties or on the freedom of expression would necessarily spell the doom for the CPC. This may not happen. The key is how our party would do. I have confidence in it.

At a meeting I attended lately in Harbin, Guo Daohui and I were not interrupted by applause. The only speech interrupted by applause was given by a vice president of the Party School of the CPC. As he said, we often say that the ruling status of our party is something the people chose for themselves. But why couldn't there be a second or third round of choosing? This was met with applauses from the audience. This is not to be taken to mean that we want to see the CPC gone as the ruling party. No one supporting the reforms wishes that. We simply wish to see that the political system and the Communist Party become culturally more sophisticated. We wish to see that people support the Communist Party because it has done well by them rather than because of some sense of entitlement by the Party or feeling of indebtedness among the people. Now do we wish to see extreme measure used by the CPC to stay in power? In fact, we all have a sense of crisis, which is tenable in theory. The core issue of anti-corruption is within the system. The constitutional government has not yet been fully established, which is a fundamental reason. Without addressing this issue, it would be very difficult to eliminate corruption, even in eight or nine more years. That's all what I want to say. Thank you!

I would like to share some of my views on what we talked about just now. First, it is the interpretation of the name of the country as Prof. Jiao Hongchang pointed out. I intended to write an article titled "New Interpretation of the Name of the Country" or "A New Understanding of the Republic." In the name of this country, the People's Republic of China, "China" refers to a collection of 56 ethnic groups while "people" has two interpretations and two meanings. Not long ago, leaders of the Legislative Affairs Commission of the Standing Committee of the NPC held a meeting. On the meeting I said I had thought the principle that "the state respects and protects human rights" would be added to the amendment to the *Criminal Procedure Law* without any questions. But the result was unexpected. I said that it is a shame to have that result. Now, the focus is only on cracking down on criminals and protecting the people. But, what's the meaning of people? It is a big step backward. In my opinion, "people" has two meanings. "People" is a legal concept in China, equivalent to "citizen," so "people" in the name of the country is synonymous with "citizen." All people with Chinese nationality are part of the People's Republic of China and thus the people. Its other meaning is a political concept which is the opposite of "enemy." The political concept is rarely used now because it is difficult to clarify who is enemy. Comrade Hu Qiaomu upholds that all criminals except those committing crimes against the state should be considered anti-social. Many such statements have yet to be clarified. Nowadays, it is not common to have people and so-called enemy pitted against each other in politics, and this sense of the terms is little used. The concept of "the people" contained in "the name of the country" must be understood in connection with the state and the law.

When the 1982 Constitution was being drafted, I said to an expert of the Secretariat that it is a fundamental mistake to say that "the people's democratic dictatorship is the nature of state and democratic centralism is the form of government." It makes little sense. Democratic centralism is not a form of government. Instead, it is an organizational principle and principle governing the conduct of state organs. Professor Wang Yicheng explained that people's democratic dictatorship is the nature of state and people's congress is the form of government. This is also incorrect in my view. So, how should we explain it? The people constitute the substance of the state as all powers of this state should belong to the people (or citizens) of the People's Republic of China. This should be the nature of state rather than people's democratic dictatorship. How could people's democratic dictatorship be the nature of state? It doesn't make sense. What's the form of government? It is republic, such as the Republic of France and the Republic of China. It requires the state to be democratically elected and the implementation of parliamentary system and people's congress system. There are also other various forms, such as the presidential system and cabinet system. People's congress is not the form of government but a specific form of republican government.

There should be a new interpretation of "republic." I have identified eight key points. On the one hand, republic means: state power is shared by the people; state affairs are decided by the people; national main resources are shared by the people; national development achievements are shared by the people. On the other hand, republic also means officials and the people have a harmonious relationship; ethnic groups coexist harmoniously; the rich and the poor work together with one heart; the country coexists peacefully with other countries. This has demonstrated not only the commonality but also some characteristics of republic. For instance, the share of national resources by the people has the characteristic of socialism in which the rich and the poor are equal. Equality between the rich and the poor is the proposition of both socialism and communism. Republic should be like this. This summary might be worthy of the name of republic. Now, the CPC Central Committee has played down the concept of people's democratic dictatorship and rarely uses it. Republic must be emphasized in the form of government. We need to emphasize more in republic.

Second, it is about the relationship between the Party and the government. I went to Guangzhou for a meeting a few days ago. They introduced an experience of integration of the Party and the government. That means the judicial bureau and the political and law committee of a city are composed of the same group of members. I made it clear at the meeting that non-separation between the party and the government is a great retrogression. The Party should be separated from the government, which is the general direction. In the past, the biggest disadvantage of our political system is non-separation between the Party and the government. I think highly of the Party School of the Central Committee of CPC. I once gave two lectures at the school open to all of the students. I told them that I had been paying close attention to them for the past 30 years. I expressed how impressed I had been of their commitment to the four principles, including seeking truth from facts, reform and opening-up, theoretical innovation, and academic tolerance. I once published an interview titled "30-year Rule of Law in China: Review and Outlook" on the school's journal Chinese Cadres Tribune (2008, Issue 10). In the last paragraph, I wrote that we should by no means mix the Party with the government.

(Chinese: p. 33) In December 1996, the NPC held a high-level seminar in Shenzhen (200 people attended the seminar, including chairmen and secretary-generals of provincial people's congresses and principals of the NPC Special Committee). Three participants were invited to deliver keynote speeches. I talked about governing the country by law; Wu Jialin talked about constitution; Li Yining talked about market economy. The day before I made the report, I was told that my presentations had been read already and was asked to say something new. That evening, I drafted 12 suggestions on reforming the people's congress system. Next day during lunch, I sat with five chairmen of people's congresses. Chairman Ye Gongqi from Shanghai Municipal People's Congress said that they agreed with my 12 suggestions, but there was one flaw. I asked what it was. He said I should not have put improving relations between the Party and people's congress at the very end, as the twelfth of twelve suggestions. I replied that he might have missed something I had said, at the very end, which was that the last suggestion was the key. He felt relieved and assured upon hearing this. Becoming a People's Congress deputy would change the way a person things, just like "where you stand depends on where you sit." This was the theory put forward by a former party secretary of Guangdong province. Future reform relies on people's congress which is a huge driver. Once you became a deputy to people's congress, you would promote democratic politics. A book published by the Institute of Law suggested that party secretary may also serve as the chairman of people's congress since we staying committed to the Party's leadership. This suggestion was adopted later. At a meeting of the NPC, I asked a minister of the NPC about this suggestion. He said that he personally proposed that those retired from the party committee and the most prestigious to serve as chairman of people's congress. He said that chairman of people's congress must be senior and prestigious. This merits more studies.

With regard to the chairman of military committee, what Professor Ma Ling said is true. But there is one problem. In Obama's party, there is no military committee. In the west, no party has its own military committee. That there is no separation between the party and the government is the biggest challenge at present. The Central Discipline Inspection Commission and the Ministry of Supervision work out of one office, but whether this is a good thing needs to be studied.

I attended a conference in Germany on modern party transformation. Head of our delegation was from the Central Compilation & Translation Bureau. Many well-known scholars in public law from Germany were at the conference. To show their respect, they asked me to speak first. I told them that the CPC was also in the middle of transformation toward modernization. But, how was the transformation being carried out? I explained in four sentences. First, all parties big or small are equal; second, state power is higher than party's power; third, national laws trump party rules; fourth, the Party complies with democratic principles in its organization and operations. The Party would be a modern party only when these four principles are fulfilled. Since the implementation of reform and opening-up policy 30 years ago, our party has made notable progress in this direction.

The Party's leadership might be the key to building a country under the rule of law. A country under the rule of law must meet ten criteria. The tenth one is that the Party must obey the law. A foreign expert commented that in the West the first nine criteria apply, but not the tenth one. I replied that the tenth one is the most important one out of the 12 suggestions, for two reasons. First, China is a single-party state with multi-party cooperation. In multi-party or two-party systems that exist in the West, if a party does something unconstitutional, they will just suffer at the polls in the next election. Everything is open and transparent. Second, it is the culture of constitutional government. The history of constitutional government goes back 200 years in the West, and by now just about everybody knows that the Constitution and the laws are to be obeyed. In China, things are different. China is a one-party state with the cooperation of different parties. The advantage of the one-party system is that the party can call all the shots. But the biggest drawback of such a system, at least right now, has to do with the Party itself.

Many people talked about bicameralism. A central government leader said that it is not good for China. As a matter of fact, there is room for discussion. Bicameralism was firstly proposed at the time of drafting the 1982 Constitution by Hu Qiaomu who suggested one professional chamber and one local chamber. But it failed to be adopted. If someone like Hu Qiaomu, who represented the orthodox within the Party, would not shy away from broaching the subject, why couldn't we look into it? It is the job of politicians to decide whether to adopt or not. But, scholars may and have the right and responsibility to make the proposal. That was an effective meeting insofar as issues like that were put on the table for serious discussions. I might talk too much. However, I would like to thank Mr. Zhou and his friends for offering us this platform to exchange views frankly. We are all old friends. I'm really happy to meet with you again to freely talk about and review the 1982 Constitution and look into its future!

Constitutional Research in China: A Thirty-Year Review and Future Outlook: Marking the 30th Anniversary of the Promulgation of the 1982 Constitution and the First Anniversary of the Founding of China Constitutional Research Association

Dayuan Han and Honghong Hu

Constitutional law study is a discipline, and its growth and development are closely linked with the community of constitutional scholars. Neither can either exist or thrive without the other. This year happens to be the 30th anniversary of the promulgation of the 1982 Constitution and the first anniversary of the founding of China Constitutional Research Association. We especially write articles describing the development course, analyzing the status quo and looking into the future of China's constitutional scholars to mark this occasion. At the same time, we wish to probe into the consensus of Chinese constitutional scholars on their academic missions and explore diversified channels to develop constitutional law. Furthermore, we could effectively integrate research resources and adapt to the requirement of social practical development. And eventually, we could have mature and in-depth studies on constitutional theories, boost the development of constitutional practices and realize the rule of law.

Honghong Hu: Thank doctoral student Yu Wenhao of the Renmin University of China Law School and postgraduates Zhang Danzhuo and Zhu Xiaomei of the Law School of Zhongnan University of Economics and Law for their data compilation and statistical works.

D. Han (✉)
China Constitutional Research Association, Renmin University of China Law School, Beijing, China
e-mail: 13263169197@163.com

H. Hu
Constitutional Research Association of China, Zhongnan University of Economics and Law, Wuhan, China

L. Li et al. (eds.), *Constitutional Development in China, 1982–2012*,
Research Series on the Chinese Dream and China's Development Path,
https://doi.org/10.1007/978-981-32-9261-1_2

1 Importance of a Community of Constitutional Scholars

By constitutional scholars, we mean those individuals engaged in the theoretical study of the constitution through teaching, legal practices and publishing. This is a sizeable group. Its very existence presupposes broad acknowledgment by the society at large of the subject matter, and the impact research findings in this field would have on society. The makeup of the community is marked by dynamic continuity.

The constitution and the legal studies of the subject have proceeded hand in hand since the very beginning. When ideas related to constitutionalism were first introduced into China, they were met with ready reception, indicating the existence of those who are prepared to study the constitution professionally. When constitutional scholars as a group become a source of influence on the society, a community of constitutional scholars can be said to have taken shape. This community is the subject and foundation of the development of constitutional theories. Constitutional studies cannot thrive except through the creativity of a large number of constitutional scholars.

The development of the community of constitutional scholars is directly proportional to the demand for the constitution in a state. In 1999, "building a socialist country under the rule of law" was formally written into the Constitution. As is known to all, the essential difference between the rule of law and the rule of man is that the authority of law is superior to the will of the individual when they are in conflicts with each other. In term of state power, the rule of law requires the acceptance of regulation and constraint, and the constitution is the utmost constraint of state power. The foremost requirement of the rule of law is the supremacy of the constitution.[1] The status of a country's constitutional scholars usually reflects the position of the constitution in the country to a certain degree. Insofar as we recognize three modes of existence for the constitution, namely the written, the conceptual and the de facto,[2] constitutional scholars leave their marks on all three through their participation in drafting, revising and annulling the written constitution, their efforts in helping to raise awareness about the constitution among the general public and their guidance on the *de facto* constitution. Research achievements and activities of the constitutional scholars can affect the construction of the rule of law fairly directly. Since constitutional revisions and amendments are mostly aimed at fine-turning the relationship between state power and civic rights, to the degree that constitutional scholars work toward elevating the status of the constitution by, this will ultimately help bring the exercise of state power under proper norms, guarantee civic rights and build the rule of law.

The community of constitutional scholars is of great significance to constitutional law, to the constitution itself and to the building of the rule of law of the country. However, for too long we have focused almost exclusively on the study of

---

[1]Zhou [1].

[2]Liu [2].

the constitution at the expense of neglecting the people who are engaged in this work. Such studies are few and hard to find. For example, in his 1998 article "Historical Review of Constitutional Law"[3] professor Dong Chengmei devoted some space to discussions about constitutional scholars, and the topic came up at the Symposium Marking the 20th Anniversary of the Convocation of the Third Plenary Session of the 11th Central Committee of the Chinese Communist Party and the 16th Anniversary of the Promulgation of the Constitution held by Constitutional Research Association of China Law Society, the Constitutional Law Association of Beijing Law Society.[4] Researcher Zhang Qingfu touched upon the subject in "A Brief Introduction to Constitutional Law Research.".[5] In 2005, the theme of the Constitutional Research Association of China Law Society annual conference was "academic community of constitutional scholars."[6] Apart from these, systematic discussions could not be found. Strengthening studies on China's community of constitutional scholars is a long-term strategy in China's undertaking of law. Only stable, high quality and active research team could ensure continuous academic sources. Only building the research team could integrate research resources and give full play to the charm of theoretical studies. This chapter especially recaps the current situation, elaborates the characteristics, summarizes the contributions and looks into the future development of the community of constitutional scholars.

2 Evolution of China's Community of Constitutional Scholars

The evolution of China's community of constitutional scholars is correlated with the development of constitutional law. In late Qing Dynasty and the early Republic of China when the course of constitutional law appeared, there had been constitutional law researchers. However, it was the emergence of the constitution of the People's Republic of China that led to qualitative changes of the constitution and of the intellectual team studying constitutional law. Since the founding of the People's Republic of China, building upon the release of the new nation's first constitution, China's constitutional scholars acquired rich experience and strong expertise in their field of study. During the Cultural Revolution, these individuals suffered serious setbacks, and things did not make a substantial turn for the better until the Third Plenary Session of the 11th Central Committee of the CPC in 1978. Constitutional studies went through an exuberant period till the promulgation of the 1982 Constitution. During this period, the community of constitutional scholars

[3]Dong [3].

[4]Zhang [4].

[5]Refer to Zhang [5].

[6]Refer to Han and Hu [6].

kept expanding in general and demonstrated a blooming and flourishing picture with minor fluctuations in between.

2.1 *Difficult Start: 1949–1978*

We can trace the start of the community of constitutional scholars to the drafting and rollout of the 1954 Constitution. In the years leading up to the release of this constitution, the academic community had been deeply involved. Afterward, the nationwide campaign to raise awareness of and cultivate reverence for the constitution and related theoretical studies were ratcheted up. More instructional manuals, textbooks and other research materials have become available, and the number of publications in the field had grown considerably. Most colleges and universities of political science and law offered four standard courses on the constitution, namely "Constitution of the Bourgeois," "Constitution of Socialist Countries," "Constitution of People's Democratic Countries" and "Chinese Constitution." Normal universities also began to introduce such courses in the political science department.[7] Thus began China's homegrown constitutional scholarship, which at the time could claim but twenty or no more than thirty practitioners.[8]

After the scale of the anti-right movement was increased in 1957, many constitutional courses were canceled, and the subject field was seriously limited in terms of what could be studied. Despite this, however, "constitutional law studies did not come to a grinding halt, and even saw progress made in a number of areas."[9] For instance, the Institute of Law of the Chinese Academy of Social Sciences (CASS) was established in October 1958. The institute's first researchers studied jurisprudence and constitutional law, making the institute the first in China specializing in constitutional law studies. During the Cultural Revolution, most teaching materials on the constitution were considered a worthless hodgepodge of feudalism, capitalism and revisionism, and research institutions were closed down, their teaching staff being sent away to undergo reform through labor. As a result, the study of the constitution was arbitrarily suspended, and the community of constitutional scholars fell apart.

We can identify a few things about constitutional scholars during this period. Firstly, there were not very many of them, but the few who stuck around had solid training in the field and were already quite influential. These individuals would later play an instrumental role in integrating constitutional law studies into the broader academic landscape. Secondly, most constitutional scholars at the time displayed limited intellectual independence and were instead primarily driven by the desire to serve the government's political objectives. For example, Mr. Zhang Youyu

---

[7]Dong [7].

[8]Dong [3].

[9]Han [8].

devoted his entire life to this field and published many books on constitutional law and constitutional theories. He was a firm believer of the principle that theories and practices must work together and that scholarship is a means to political ends[10] and swore to keep promoting Chinese constitutionalism. Thirdly, the creativity of constitutional law study was restricted. This was mainly manifested in copying other countries' constitutional studies, and study of annotations was popular. A certain scholar recorded that all other studies were centered on annotations of the 1954 Constitution, only the object of constitutional law study was a rather new topic and there had never been academic debates in a strict sense.[11] Besides, constitutional scholars were faced with personal safety in politics. Due to frequent political movements, most of them were cautious in their words and dared not to speak except for repeating Marxist–Leninist works and central documents and remarks of leaders. Naturally, academic studies lacked creativity.

2.2 Increasing in Number, Becoming Better Organized: 1978–1985

The Third Plenary Session of the 11th Central Committee of the CPC restored order emancipated people's minds and provided strong stimulus for academic studies. The comprehensive amendment to the constitution gave a strong sense of mission to Chinese constitutional researchers. From 1980 to 1982, numerous laymen and academics alike showed great interest in and concern for constitutional issues, and scholarly studies in the area reached a climax. New constitutional text was adopted at the Fifth Session of the Fifth National People's Congress on December 4, 1982. Since then, Chinese constitutional studies have entered a period of rapid development.[12]

During this period, China's constitutional scholars saw a number of developments. First, their number and academic caliber increased greatly compared to what they were in the years preceding the Cultural Revolution. In 1979, besides the restoration of departments of law that once existed but were then suspended, nearly 20 legal departments were newly established that specialized in constitutional law. Many colleges also admitted graduate students majoring in constitutional law. A large number of young constitutional workers emerged, and they later became young constitutional scholars. Second, scholars felt freshly energized and motivated, despite the many limitations they faced to what they could do. In particular, their work was mostly focused on publicizing and interpreting the new constitution. According to one characterization, "in this period a good deal of research work was concerned with doctrinal interpretations and analyses in relation to the 1982

---

[10]Zhang [9].

[11]Wen [10].

[12]Han [11].

Constitution, with the aim of offering critical reflections that would help make the constitution normatively more rigorous and practically more effective.[13] Third, there was a shift from researchers working largely by themselves toward teams of researchers working together. For instance, political science universities and law schools initiated research projects to be undertaken by the faculty, organized colloquiums and produced publications. Chinese and foreign scholars were invited to give talks at these conferences and workshops. Chinese constitutional scholars also travel outside the country to attend conferences. After the release of the 1982 Constitution, the Institute of Sociology, Chinese Academy of Social Sciences, China Law Society and local law societies organized a number of symposiums. The establishment of China Constitutional Research Association in October 1985 signaled the coming into being of a community of Chinese constitutional scholars. "Some provinces and cities established local constitutional research societies. The number of constitutional scholars reached was somewhere between 100 and 200 nationwide.[14] These societies provided constitutional scholars with the platform on which to engage in academic exchanges and cooperations.

2.3 Stabilization and Fluctuations: 1985–1993

When the Constitutional Research Association of China Law Society was just established, it was expected to contribute toward the theoretical and practical development of constitutional law by bringing together those engaged in teaching, research and practical works nationwide.[15] The Annual Meeting of China Constitutional Research Association had already developed into a system. The Annual Meeting represented not only one of the major forms of academic activities carried out by China Constitutional Research Association but also an important proof of its development. According to written records, a review of the number of participants[16] in the Annual Meeting of China Constitutional Research Association from 1985 to 1993 reflects the relative stability of the community of constitutional scholars from one side (see Fig. 1).

Constitutional scholars enjoyed steady increases in the number of platforms on which they could exchange ideas and work together. International academic exchanges also began to thrive. In addition to groups joining the International Association of Constitutional Law as institutional members, more and more Chinese scholars were being invited to attend conferences held outside the country.

---

[13]Han [11].

[14]Dong [3].

[15]*Summary of the Conference on the Establishment of Constitutional Research Association of China Law Society*, published in *China Legal Science*, 1986, Issue 1.

[16]The recorded numbers of participants in each annual meeting was all approximate numbers by using such words as "about," "nearly" and "more than," but concrete numbers are required for making the graph, so integers are used hereby.

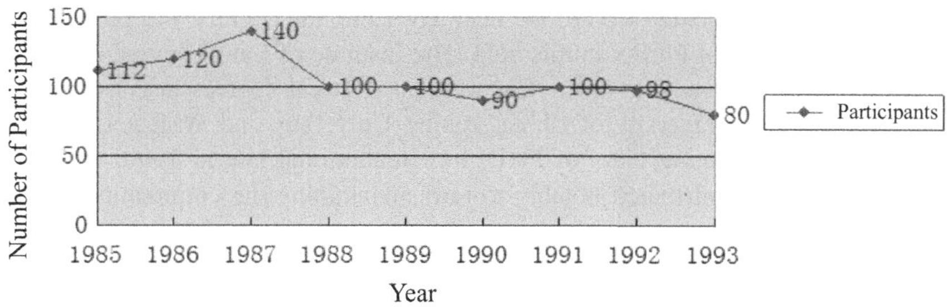

Fig. 1 Number of participants in annual meetings between 1985 and 1993

In June 1986, researcher Wang Shuwen visited Japan on an exchange program on Japan's constitutional review system. In September 1987, professor Gong Xiangrui spoke about the features and achievements of China's constitution at the meeting commemorating the 200th Anniversary of the birth of the US Constitution.

While the community of constitutional scholars in China maintained a certain measure of stability, occasional perturbations did occur. In 1998, the legality of compensated land transfers and privately owned enterprises were officially given constitutional recognition in the newly adopted amendments. The change boosted economic growth and was part of a series of profound economic transformations in the country. The academic community as a whole also felt the effects of these developments strongly, and a growing number of constitutional scholars began to explore and pursue options previously unavailable to them, including studying abroad, leaving academia, working for the government and even starting their own business. While the community of constitutional scholars suffered some loss during this period, on the whole it stayed intact.

The year of 1993 is considered a landmark moment because it saw a significant shift in the subject matter to be studied, which also helped draw more scholars to enter this field. Nine constitutional amendments, a significant number, were approved in 1993. In addition to these revisions to the main text, the preamble was amended for the first time. Both procedurally and substantively the amendments attracted the interests of a growing number of scholars. And the amendments sparked lively discussions about their backdrop and impact. So while economic transformation led to some constitutional scholars to leave the field, the [1993] constitutional amendments brought about new research opportunities.

2.4 *Continued Expansion and Field Development: 1993–2010*

During this period, the field of constitutional law studies enjoyed a large infusion of undergraduates, M.A. and even some Ph.D. students, as well as professional researchers who gravitated toward the field. By 1993, the country was producing a respectable number of Ph.D.s in this field. The Institute of Law, Chinese Academy of Social Sciences, was one of the first to grant doctoral degrees in constitutional law. The Renmin University of China, Peking University and Wuhan University had their first graduating class of Ph.D. in constitutional law in 1990, 1994 and 1994. All of this contributed notably toward maintaining the community of constitutional scholars and the deepening of theoretical studies in this field.

The gradual expansion of the community of constitutional scholars during this period was also reflected by the number of participants[17] in each of the annual meeting on the constitution from 1994 to 2010 (see Fig. 2).

During this stage, the number of articles about constitutional research also increased sharply. According to the statistics compiled by Zhang Zhen, more than 300 articles about the constitution were published in an influential law journal. Of those, two were published in *Social Sciences in China* between 1994 and 1999; 15 in *Chinese Journal of Law* between 1994 and 1999; 36 in *China Legal Science* between 1990 and 1999; 22 in *Peking University Law Journal* between 1994 and 1999; 21 in *The Jurist* between 1994 and 1999; 41 in *Law Review* between 1990 and 1999; 43 in *Modern Law Science* between 1990 and 1999; 29 in *Studies in Law and Business* between 1994 and 1999; 39 in *Science of Law* between 1990 and 1999; 20 in *Tribune of Political Science and Law* between 1990 and 1999; and 65 in *Law Science* between 1990 and 1999 and so forth. The representative works included *Fundamental Theory of Constitutional Theory* by Xu Xiuyi and Han Dayuan, *Basic Theory of Constitutional Law* and *Constitutionalism Review* by Zhang Qingfu and *Comparative Study on Constitution* by Li Buyun and so forth.[18]

Through dialogues with scholars from diverse fields, constitutional scholars broadened their horizons during this period. Many long-time students of constitutional law were prepared to breach traditional boundaries and venture into related areas of inquiry. They even took the initiative to organize multi-disciplinary conferences, such as the symposium on "dialogues between jurisprudence, constitutional law and administrative law" held on April 28, 2005, the symposium on "dialogues between criminal jurisprudence and constitution" on December 10, 2005, the symposium on the "academic dialogue between science of civil law and constitutional law" on May 25, 2006, the symposium on "academic dialogues between constitutional law and social jurisprudence" on December 29, 2007, "including litigious right into the constitution—dialogue between constitutional law and science of procedure laws" on April 9, 2008, and "academic symposium on public finance and constitutionalism construction—academic dialogue between constitutional law and finance and taxation jurisprudence" held in Guangzhou on May 24–25, 2008 and so forth. At the symposium on constitutional issues in

[17]The recorded numbers of participants in each annual meeting was all approximate numbers by using such words as "about," "nearly" and "more than," but concrete numbers are required for making the graph, so integers are used hereby.

[18]Zhang [12].

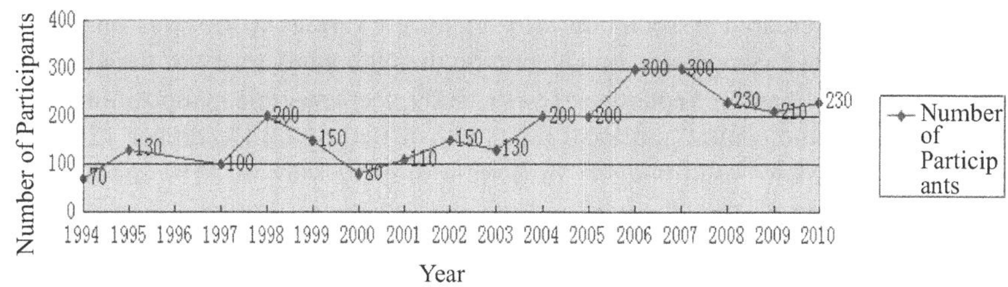

Fig. 2 Number of participants in annual meetings between 1994 and 2010

amending the three major procedure laws held on September 17, 2011, more than 40 scholars of constitutional law, procedural laws and administrative law engaged in in-depth discussions on constitutional issues in amending the criminal procedural law, civil procedural law and administrative procedural law.

This was also a time during which constitutional researchers became more critically reflective of methodological issues inherent to the discipline. The series of meetings on "The Chinese Constitution: Scope and Methodology" was one example. Faced with wide disagreements on these issues among constitutional scholars, relevant professional societies felt it necessary to meet specifically on these topics. To that end, seven meetings were held between 2005 and 2011 at different locations, including Zhejiang University, Shandong University, Nanjing Normal University, Wuhan University, Pingtan of Fujian, Xiamen University and Yunnan University. These meetings were quite fruitful, generating broad agreements on some foundational issues. The meetings became something of an academic name brand created by the constitutional community, in many ways similar to the annual meeting on the Constitution. The importance of the basic constitutional scope and constitutional study method attracted more attention to the constitutional community. More and more scholars realized that correctly understanding the historical position of China's constitutional law, defining the basic scope of constitutional law and carrying out studies on this basis were the key to recap the constitutional knowledge system.

During this stage, the exchange platforms available for constitutional scholars became more diversified. The number of panels at the Annual Meeting of China Constitutional Research Association grew, and keynote speeches were introduced, as were concluding remarks at the end of panel sessions. The executive committee of the Constitutional Research Association of China Law Society approved the establishment of the Research Committee for the Teaching of Constitutional Law in 2007, the establishment of the Research Committee on the Legal System of China's Mainland, Taiwan, Hong Kong and Macao in 2009 and the establishment of the Research Committee for the People's Congress System in 2010. These moves helped to bring all teaching under a uniform set of pedagogical standards and promote resource sharing and improvements in research and teaching practices. Apart from holding exchange meetings by these specialized committees,

Constitutional Research Association also organized various workshops on special topics, such as the "symposium on celebrating the 60th anniversary of the *Common Programme*" in Jinan on September 18–19, 2009, the academic symposium on the "legalization of the central and local relations" in Beijing on December 12, 2009, the seminar on "law-based budget" in Beijing in early May in 2010 and the academic symposium on the "theories and practices of the institutional innovation of special administrative regions" in Guangzhou on December 19, 2010. Other examples included the organization of international symposiums, such as the 24th World Congress of Philosophy of Law and Social Philosophy held in Beijing on September 15–20, 2009, the Second Asian Constitutional Law Forum held in Harbin on August 21–22, 2009, the Fourth International Forum on the Status and Future of Public Law in East Asia held in Jinan on April 24, 2010, and the Second Symposium on the Succession and Evolution of Western Constitutionalism in Asia held in Yunnan on August 25, 2011.

2.5 Greater Independence and Openness: 2011 Till Now

To guarantee and regulate the organizations and activities of national law societies, China Law Society formulated *Rules for Legal Social Groups* in June 2011 based on the *Regulation on Registration and Administration of Social Organizations* and *Bylaws of China Law Society*, which have provided an important basis for China's law societies to carry out professional activities. On October 22, 2011, Constitutional Research Association of China Law Society held its first membership conference in Xi'an. The conference brought together 248 representatives and adopted the regulations on the election of the first session of the council of Constitutional Research Association of China Law Society. Based on the regulations, all representatives attending the first plenary session of members of Constitutional Research Association elected the directors of the first council by secret ballot.[19] Since then, the community of constitutional researchers began to exist in the form of a distinct and independent legal body of mass organization. The establishment of Constitutional Research Association, as a national legal social group of the community of constitutional scholars, signaled that lawfully established self-governed academic social groups would conduct autonomous academic activities based on the *Regulation on Registration and Administration of Social Organizations*, *Bylaw of China Law Society*, *Rules for Legal Social Groups* and their respective bylaws. Constitutional Research Association will keep playing an irreplaceable organizational role in training constitutional talents, organizing academic meetings on the constitution, guiding the constitutional study focus and communicating on constitutional law.

---

[19]"2011 Work Summary and 2012 Work Focus of Constitutional Research Association of China Law Society," refer to the website of China Law Society.

In addition to becoming more independent on the strength of support of the law, the Constitutional Research Association was also becoming increasingly open. A brief review of the background and institutional affiliation of its 248 members and panel presenters shows considerable diversity. Some worked primarily in other areas but were interested in constitutional studies. These other areas covered a broad range, including jurisprudence, administrative law, history of legal systems, civil law, just to name a few. Belying such incredible diversity is the fact, perhaps somewhat unexpected that these researchers all shared one common goal, which was to promote constitutionalism in practice in China. They were all striving to make theoretical research in the area more applicable.

3 Current Conditions of the Community of Constitutional Scholars

Given a large number of constitutional scholars in China, accurate data collection about them is difficult. So we shall instead attempt to offer a group profile by reference to three sources of information. First, we use data from executive committees of professional societies and basic information on articles published in academic journals. Second, we try to identify different types of entities engaged in constitutional law studies. Third, we resort to the first-hand experience with members of this vast group.

3.1 Group Portrait Based on Pertinent Data

1. An overview of the makeup of the first six executive committees of Constitutional Research Association of China Law Society and the first executive committee of Constitutional Research Association (see Table 1).
   Generally speaking, executive committee members are coming from more diverse institutions and background, providing a better representation of constitutional scholars. However, there has been little increase in recent years in the number of participants from people working on the frontline of legal practices. There may be three reasons for this. First, some theoretical studies may be too esoteric to have ready practical applications, making fruitful exchanges difficult among participants. Second, theoretical studies of the constitution can often be quite creative, while legal workers on the frontline tend to be more conservative, making it hard for the two groups to find common ground. The third reason may have to do with changes in the way annual meetings are organized. Until 1995, the Constitutional Research Association mainly relied on law practitioners to organize the annual meeting, in which practical issues tended to dominate. But

Table 1 Memberships of first six executive committees of Constitutional Research Association of China Law Society and of the first executive committee of Constitutional Research Association

Session number	Number of directors	Number of female	Number of minorities	Number of directors from practical sectors	Number of units	Average age	Proportion of professors
First session in 1985	53	5	4	9	40	50.08	3
Second session in 1989	75	8	2	20	57	50.71	13
Third session in 1993	83	5	6	28	64	51.98	20
Fourth session in 1998	88	5	5	30	62	51.12	29
Fifth session in 2002	92	17	4	17	67	43.76	46
Sixth session in 2007	150	28	5	14	93	43.34	67
New session in 2012	185	36	5	18[a]	108	46.46	102

[a]Including full-time editors of publishing houses and periodical offices

after 1995, colleges and universities largely took over this role, resulting in a shift toward greater emphasis on purely academic topics.

2. Analysis of the first executive committee of Constitutional Research Association and of the Constitutional Research Association, established in 2011. See Tables 2, 3, 4, 5, 6 and 7.
3. Number of publications and topics.
   See Table 8.

3.2 *Types of Researchers*

To really appreciate who these individuals are who make up the community of constitutional scholars, we need more than a general description. While identifying different types of something does not meet the highest standards of scientific rigor,

Table 2 Gender breakdown of membership of first executive committee of Constitutional Research Association

Gender	Number of people	Proportion in the total number of people (%)
Male	149	80.54
Female	36	19.46

Table 3 Nationality breakdown of membership of first executive committee of Constitutional Research Association

Nationality	Number of people	Proportion (%)
Han	176	95.14
Ethnic minorities (Korean, Tujia, Tibetan, Miao)	5	2.70
Unclear	4	2.16

Table 4 Age breakdown of membership of first executive committee of Constitutional Research Association

Age	20–29	30–39	40–49	50–59	60–69
Number	0	29	107	45	4
Proportion (%)	0	15.68	57.84	24.32	2.16

Table 5 Professional ranking breakdown of membership of first executive committee of Constitutional Research Association

Title	Professor	Associate professor	Lecturer	Having no title but having post or academic degree
Number	102	59	2	22
Proportion (%)	55.14	31.89	1.08	11.89

Table 6 Regional distribution of members of Constitutional Research Association

Region	North China	Northeast China	East China	Southern China	Northwest China	Central China	Southwest China
Number	61	8	52	22	7	25	10
Proportion (%)	32.97	4.32	28.11	11.89	3.78	13.51	5.41

(*Note* China's regional division: North: Beijing, Tianjin, Hebei Province, Shanxi Province and Inner Mongolia Autonomous Region; Northeast: Liaoning Province, Jilin Province and Heilongjiang Province; East: Shanghai, Shandong Province, Jiangsu Province, Zhejiang Province, Anhui Province and Jiangxi Province; South: Fujian Province, Hainan Province, Guangdong Province, Taiwan Province, Hong Kong and Macao; Northwest: Shaanxi Province, Ningxia Hui Autonomous Region, Gansu Province, Qinghai Province and Xinjiang Uygur Autonomous Region; Central China: Henan Province, Hubei Province and Hunan Province; Southwest: Guangxi Zhuang Autonomous Region, Sichuan Province, Guizhou Province, Yunnan Province, Chongqing Municipality and Tibet Autonomous Region. *Data source* baidu.com)

Table 7 Number of on articles on the constitution in 13 law journals between January 2011 and June 2012

Journal name	Number of articles on the constitution
Law Science	35
Law Review	30
Studies in Law and Business	20
Science of Law	16
Modern Law Science	13
Law and social development	13
Global Law Review	11
China Legal Science	8
Tribune of Political Science and Law	8
Journal of Comparative Law	8
Peking University Law Journal	7
Chinese Journal of Law	6
The Jurist	4

Table 8 Topic analysis (statistical analysis of 179 papers published in more than 13 journals)

Classification item	Basic theory of constitution	Human rights, basic rights	On constitutional guarantee system	On national basic system	Research overview, etc.
Study field	53	54	16	54	2
Proportion (%)	29.6	30.17	8.94	30.17	1.12

it can be helpful toward uncovering key features and arriving of some basic shared understanding.

Researcher Zhang Qingfu once offered a systematic description of China's constitutional research and teaching institutions. He identified three major systems, namely specialized research institutes, teaching units and membership-based professional societies and associations. Specialized research institutes are the constitutional teaching and research offices of Institute of Law, Chinese Academy of Social Sciences and the institute of law of provincial, regional or municipal academies of social sciences. By teaching units, he is referring to the constitutional teaching and research offices of departments of law in colleges and universities nationwide. Membership-based professional societies and associations include such organizations as the Constitutional Research Association of China Law Society and constitutional research associations of law societies of provinces, autonomous regions and municipalities directly under the central government.[20] Based on this kind of classification, the first two classes are basically targeting researchers

[20]Zhang [5].

attached to units, while the third class is a self-governing group, members of which are frequently overlapped with the first two classes of people.

Constitutional scholars can be found in four large types of professions: (1) those who teach and conduct research in colleges and universities; (2) professional researchers (including many who work as career editors, often in senior positions) in research institutes; (3) researchers who study issues of application in people's congresses, courts and procuratorates and public intellectuals who regularly comment on public events. The American Federal Judge Posner believes that public intellectuals are individuals who speak to the public on political or ideological issues.[21] Some others believe that public intellectuals are "gadflies" of the society, who should, as Socrates did, raise questions about the status quo, speak truth to power and hold those in the position of authority to account.[22] Professor Su Li conducted a study on and criticized Chinese public intellectuals. Anyway, we should acknowledge that the role they have played in raising public awareness and building the discipline should not be overlooked. They are professional researchers that occupy their own academic niche, but what they do also serves the general public, something they take very seriously.[23]

By age, we can roughly divide the community into three groups: senior researchers from the old generations, middle-aged researchers and junior researchers. Theoretical studies are inseparable from the practical development on the ground. In China, those who are now senior members of the community, who belong to the older generations, mostly got into the field around 1954, when the constitution was passed and officially adopted. At the time, the country was in an acute need for individuals with expertise in the constitutions (many older scholars in the field were, in their own recollection, placed by the authorities in their jobs as teachers or researchers). Second, developing a country's political institutions calls for guidance from the constitution. Most of the middle-aged constitutional scholars began their career around 1982, when the updated Constitution was approved and adopted, many of them are still working actively. It would be fair to say that since work began to amend substantially the constitution after the Third Plenary Session of the 11th Central Committee of the CPC held in 1978, the academic status of the field has been significantly elevated, attracting a considerable number of young legal scholars. The junior scholars in this age-based classification include those who have been working in this field, often with innovative ingenuity, while the constitution itself has been undergoing the latest round of revision. By our reckoning, the year 1993 was the year in which there was a notable increase in the number of professional researchers in this field. Since then, more and more young people have driven by both academic interest and a sense of civic responsibility, chosen this field as their career path.

[21]Quoted from Lu [13].

[22]Su [14].

[23]Chen [15].

We can identify a number of quasi-schools of thoughts in this field, including political constitutionalism, normative constitutionalism, hermeneutic constitutionalism and sociological constitutionalism.[24] Some scholars use the research approach and methodology as the criteria for classification. According to them, China's constitutional studies have been built on the basis of what may be called "political doctrinal constitutionalism" and has branched off in the last decade into three subfields each with its own methodology: sociological constitutionalism that stresses scientific rigor; hermeneutics/normative constitutionalism that stresses explanatory clarity; and politico-philosophical constitutionalism, whose emphasis is on the political dimension.[25] Here, we use the "quasi" qualifier advisedly. Any school of thought has to have a number of essential properties: a set of ideas, a group of scholars who subscribe to those ideas and somebody or persons who can be regarded as the figurehead of the school.[26] A mature school of thought, let us say, should have (1) representatives, (2) distinct set of ideas or body of theories associated with it and (3) a group of scholars that are committed to these ideas and theories and to working toward disseminating them. Or, in the words of Xu Jintang, a school of thought can be identified with a shared set of presuppositions, research methodologies and basic postulates.[27] [But] in the case of constitutional law studies, there is as of yet no such school of thought, the classification above is mostly based on methodology.

In sum, the community of constitutional scholars is not static, but is constantly changing. In addition, each type of researchers has their representative figures and does work that reflects the time we live in.

3.3 *Key Features of Today's Constitutional Scholars (p. 45)*

1. More people have chosen to enter the field. On the one hand, there is growing need, as the government resolves to strengthen the rule of law, for academic research to support that effort insofar as it can help answer some foundational questions about institutional building and the role the constitution can and should play in it. On the other hand, a notable number of people have opted for this career path to answer a calling, i.e., contributing toward the strengthening of the rule of law in this country.[28] At the same time, long-time students of the constitution continue to play a leadership role.

---

[24]Gao [16].

[25]Lin [17].

[26]*Philosophy Dictionary* (Volume of Marxist Philosophy), Shanghai Lexicographical Publishing House, 1990 edition, page 720–721.

[27]Xu [18].

[28]Refer to Lin [19]. "Just quoting Hegel's words describing philosophy (philosopher), constitutional law studies are 'an animal eating withered grass on prairie'."

2. The structural makeup of the community of constitutional scholars has been optimized. First, there are outstanding constitutional scholars in all adult age groups. Attendees at annual meetings include junior lecturers and doctoral degree holders in their 30s and senior researchers in their 70s. Second, researchers now come from just about every province or autonomous region in the country, and not just bastions of academic research such as Beijing, Shanghai and Wuhan. Third, the number of constitutional scholars who have studied abroad for at least a year has increased. Of course, despite these trends, there is room for further improving the makeup of the constitutional study community. For example, within legal practices, i.e., service providers, the size of their research staff has changed little over the years.
3. p. 45 The scope of constitutional research has broadened and there is growing attention to issues of application. These trends cover not only basic theories but also specific issues related to constitutional government; not only theories of the Chinese constitution but also those of constitutions in other countries, including how specific clauses should be interpreted; not only the current state and cultivation of basic constitutional awareness but also the factors behind that awareness; not only studies about the constitutional system itself but also those that look at how actors within those systems conduct themselves; not only interpreting legal classics but also constitutional analysis of government policies, reports to the congress of party representatives and decisions; even cutting-edge research into various technical and procedural issues related to constitutionality review. Constitutional scholars also study the development of the constitutional system in depth and breadth while highlighting traditional and grandly narrative constitutional studies, which can be evidenced by studies on special topics in recent years.
4. Methodologically, constitutional studies show both a respect for tradition and a receptiveness toward innovative ideas, and a methodological framework for studying constitutional issues in the Chinese context has begun to take shape. In the process of exploring the constitutional theory system with Chinese characteristics, Chinese constitutional scholars have taken note of the important role methodology plays in constitutional studies and been engaging in discussions on this topic. After many years of research, a certain consensus has been reached on this issue and branches including hermeneutic constitutionalism, normative constitutionalism, sociological constitutionalism, constitutional policy studies and the economics of constitutionalism now can claim to have their own methodological approaches.
5. Chinese constitutional scholars have been very active in their research endeavors. On the one hand, constitutional scholars disseminate ideas and share their learning by publishing articles and books; on the other hand, they exchange ideas with others in the community and promote the growth of the field by attending conferences. At annual conferences in recent years, one almost never hears things like “this year, little notable happened in this field.” In fact, constitutional scholars are making themselves seen and heard in a growing number of places and ways, including the legislative process, administrative law

enforcement, "constitution" petition, incidents involving members of the public defending their rights and interests, release of judicial interpretations, amendment to criminal law, amendment to procedural law, academic conferences, expert testimonies and televised public lectures. A new generation of constitutional scholars who are well-rounded in research competence, more innovative and full of energy is coming of age.

6. Constitutional scholars have been setting examples for others in following constitutional principles in their own conduct, effectively raising the profile of the field in the minds of the public. Insofar as they are professionally expected to help raise public awareness about the importance of the constitution, constitutional scholars inform their daily activities with their understanding of and reverence for the constitution. As people who practice what they believe in, they are showing others around them the choice worthiness of this way of life. Some scholars have worked to increase the visibility of constitutional issues. All of these efforts have helped to build an image of constitutional scholars as guardians of public interest. In the meantime, constitutional scholars have played an important role in bringing together different levels of understanding of the constitution so as to improve coordination among groups with diverse interests and objectives when it comes to their efforts to make use of the constitution.

Constitutional studies are becoming more influential, whose impact is increasingly being felt in related fields, including the broader area of legal studies. In the field of policy-making, the voice of some individuals and group of individuals has grown loud enough to render their input almost indispensable. In terms of current affairs, symposiums and press conferences on events with constitutional dimension are attracting more attention from agencies and other organizations that are charged with making decisions and formulating policies. Within academia, more prestige is being associated with constitutional studies, and those who work in the field are accordingly held in higher regard than before, at least insofar as this can be measured by the rise in the number of funded studies, invited talks or topical seminars organized by the government on topics related to the constitution.

4 Contributions by and Existing Problems with the Community of Constitutional Scholars

4.1 Contributions

Depending on the kind of research one does, any constitutional scholar contributes to the field in different ways. Some have helped educate the public about the constitution, others engage in advocacy about reform, some advance the field and its cultural impact through publishing, still others work on the frontline of teaching and training. On the whole, China's constitutional scholars have made significant contributions toward the theoretical and practical development of the constitution.

4.1.1 Theoretical Framework

Constitutional studies are a comprehensive theoretical system encompassing all aspects of the constitution. Textbooks and other publications in this field reflect the state of constitutional studies in a country. After the passage the 1982 Constitution, *Constitutional Law*, an experimental textbook edited by Mr. Wu Jialin in 1983, was designated as the official textbook on this subject to be used by all higher education institutions across the country.[29] But since then both the type and the number of available teaching materials in this field have grown considerably. Apart from those compiled by the Ministry of Justice, the Ministry of Education, and those compiled specifically for examination preparations and for continuing education, more universities are producing their own textbooks. These go some distant toward showing how much is being done by constitutional scholars to establish a workable theoretical framework for the field. Having said this, it is worth noting that, behind the rapid growth in quantity lies a serious problem, namely substantive homogeneity among the different textbooks, most if not all of which having been based on the 1982 Constitution.[30] Efforts have been made in recent years to address this. For example, textbooks such as *Principles of Constitutional Law and Case Tutorial* and *Introductory Theory of Constitution* break from that mold and include a larger number of case studies and target students at different levels.

4.1.2 Teaching, Training and Studying

Within the community of constitutional scholars those who teach, and there is a large number of them, tend to stay in their jobs longer. The same individuals also, insofar as they also conduct research, show long-term commitment. While the field has lost some top talents to other fields, the number of people that join it is large enough to more than make up for it. At present, constitutional law studies are one of the fourteen core required courses offered by universities or colleges specializing in law. Published works in constitutional studies disseminate ideas by means of printed words, classes in which the subject is taught does it by means of spoken words. Neither is sufficient by itself as a way to improve the constitutional awareness among the public in any country. It would indeed be difficult to imagine how people who are illiterate about the constitution can be expected to have a general appreciation for the importance of the law and its compliance in modern society.

---

[29] Chief Editor Wu [20].

[30] Han [21].

4.1.3 Theoretical Support for Frontline Practices

Instead of doing research for its own sake, constitutional scholars are always mindful of the practical implications of their studies for those who work on the frontline of providing legal and other professional services.[31] As Fichte once noted, scholars are responsible not only for understanding how humanity's developmental history unfolds but also for facilitating it.[32]

First, they bring their expertise to policy formulation and decision-making. Constitutional scholars are always paying close attention to the development process of democratic politics and legal system, trying to address key issues facing the country at the time. They strive to provide answers to major theoretical and practical questions related to reform and opening up and the modernization process; they make their voices heard in public discourses on issues that the Chinese people care deeply about and show how the constitution and the laws more generally are not just relevant but critical in the government's effort to build China into a country that is modern economically, politically, culturally and socially. A good number of constitutional scholars also take part in national and local legislative activities, and some are entrusted to draft laws, administrative regulations, local regulations, local government rules and other official documents, others have written and submitted high-quality research reports on legislative topics. Some professional groups have been involved in practical activities in the area of rule of law. For instance, China Constitutional Research Association has submitted a number of legislative suggestions and policy proposals to state legislative organs and other related departments. In 2004, when the constitution was being amended, the association submitted "Suggestions of the Constitutional Research Association of China Law Society on Several Issues Related to Amending the Constitution" to the constitution amendment task force. Some of the suggestions were adopted during the fourth round of constitutional amendments.

Second, constitutional scholars provide expert analysis of cases involving the constitution.[33] In doing, so they not only synthesize theory and practice but also create new opportunities for further improving compliance and implementation. Since 2005, Law Press China has been publishing *Chinese Constitutional Case Studies*, one volume every year, consecutively. Since 2006, an official list is published each year in which the most significant events related to the constitution are ranked. The list is suggestive of new ideas about how to improve education about the constitution and the laws. This can be clearly evidenced by the relations between important constitutional cases and institutional innovation in recent years.[34] For instance, the case of Sun Zhigang in 2003 involved the protection of the right of personal freedom and finally led to the abolition of the sheltering for

[31]Hu [22].

[32][Germany] Fichte [23].

[33]Fan [24].

[34]Han [25].

investigation system and the establishment of the social relief system. The "case of hepatitis B discrimination" involved citizens' right to equality and finally resulted in the reform of civil servant recruitment examination standards.

4.1.4 Raising Constitutional Awareness

China's constitutional scholars have also been working to educate the public about the constitution through mass media, such as TV, broadcast, newspaper and the Internet. Appearances on shows like *Topics in Focus*, interviews with Sun Media International, articles published in *People's Daily*, *Guangming Daily*, *Legal Daily*, *Southern Weekly* and other newspapers and journals have all contributed greatly toward helping more people understand and appreciate the constitution. Citizens keep discovering constitutional issues, pursue questions related to the constitution and some have even tried to make use of the constitutionality review procedures. All of this goes to show the degree to which awareness about the constitution has taken roots in public consciousness. At the same time, famous professors in constitutional law are often invited to take part in lectures on the legal system attended by central and local government officials. The fact that more government officials would invoke or otherwise make reference to the constitution in their official remarks and speeches is a testament to the effectiveness of constitutional law professors' work over the years in raising awareness. After the Sixteenth National Congress of the CPC, the first group seminar organized by the Political Bureau of CPC Central Committee was on the constitution. General Secretary Hu Jintao pointed out the need to further strengthen the promotion and education of legal system with the constitution at the core and increase awareness about the constitution and the law in general among the public as well as cadres and staff of government agencies and developments. In the speech delivered in 2002 at the 20th anniversary of the passage of the Constitution, Hu Jintao pointed out the need to examine and improve the constitution supervision system, clarify the procedures to timely correct all behaviors violating the Constitution.

5 Problems in the Development Process of China's Constitutional Studies Community

At any given time in history, we try to identify problems facing any group of individuals by reference to one or more sets of parameters. [In the case of China's constitutional scholars at the present time,] we can refer either to the overall performance of constitutional researchers of other countries, or the overall performance of the researchers in other disciplines in the same the country, or the group's own historical track record. We have identified a number of issues facing China's constitutional studies community.

How to strengthen constitutional studies by raising the academic standards and how to make the results more relevant to those working to apply theoretical knowledge are the most important issues facing constitutional scholars today.

1. For the researchers, the following problems need urgently to be solved. (1) Many still do not quite seem themselves as intellectuals working in an established field of scholarly pursuit; their level of general knowledge should be increased and better professional trainings (including those about compliance with professional norms and standards) should be made available to them. (2) Mature schools of thought in constitutional studies have yet to be established, and much room still exists for improving communications and coordination among researchers. (3) Seasoned and junior researchers face obstacles as the former try to pass the baton to the latter. Although constitutional studies can claim to have a more effective mentor system than other disciplines, intergenerational communications among scholars of different ages are sometimes complicated by the fact all do not use the same discourse.
2. (p. 48) In terms of motivations and objectives, there are few agreements among constitutional scholars. For example, some works are produced purely for utilitarian reasons. Against the backdrop of social transformation, in which constitutional scholars face plentiful temptations, poorly designed assessment systems and sometimes vicious competition among different disciplines, it can be a genuine challenge to follow one's moral compass and to maintain a clear conscience.[35] Those constitutional studies often end up with a disproportionally small share, both in the allocation of academic resources and the distribution of economic benefits, put to test the integrity of all members of the community. Some continue to treat what has been produced in the Western tradition as ultimately authoritative. But blindly following the West deprives constitutional studies of concrete substance and prevents them from taking roots in the Chinese context.
3. Greater methodological diversity is needed. It is not uncommon for researchers to lose track of the right reason for doing what they do, too much emphasis is placed on policy interpretation, and many uncritically adopt methodology used in the West. Especially when it comes to the question about the relationship among methodology, knowledge and paradigm, Chinese constitutional scholars still have a long way to go before accumulating enough foundational theoretical insights either to engage in methodological discussions about paradigm or to develop the necessary sensitivity for problematization. There are as of yet no established schools of thought in the field of constitutional studies, and most disagreements that exist today are little more than differences in perspective and

[35]A doctor in physics once asked outstanding young scientists returning from abroad about the differences between domestic young talents and foreign talents and about restrictions on the innovation ability of Chinese young talents. They said that domestic young talents may consider specific issues in life, such as house, salary, kid's schooling, while foreign young talents consider major scientific issues and how to creatively accomplish research projects. Refer to Guo [26].

do not amount to substantive differences in basic tenets or core beliefs. While everybody is keen to making sure the Chinese constitution is treated holistically in theoretical studies, there are clear variations in terms of points of view, original methodology, level of maturity of the discourse and explanatory power of the theory.[36]

4. Ample room for strengthening practical applications of research findings. Better cooperation and coordination between those doing academic research and those working in practical applications are urgently needed. No research is sustainable unless its results can be turned into something that makes a difference in the real world. For any academic field of study, a disconnect between theories and practice should not be allowed to become the norm. In the preface to *Discussions of Several Issues related to the Chinese Constitution: An Overview*[37] He Huahui noted the importance of this point. He wrote that it is a unique feature of constitutional studies that many individuals engaged in it are themselves deputies to provincial, municipal and county-level people's congresses or standing committee members. They are an important part of the community and make significant contributions to this field, thanks to the combination of deep learning and first-hand experience working on the frontline.
5. The research platform needs to be further expanded and international outreach capacity strengthened. Constitution is a key element in the development of political civilization, so it is important to make sure it enjoys as broad a research platform as possible that can maximize the practical value of the research. Right now, the number of study-abroad returnees in this field is quite limited, and even fewer are able to engage competently in exchange of ideas between Chinese and other scholars from around the world. In subfields such as comparative constitutional studies and the constitution of other countries, there is a notable shortage of junior researchers. Chief among the many problems facing constitutional studies today are: how to educate the general public about the constitution and issues related to it, how to get researchers to speak to one another in a way that can be understood by all, how to keep up with and become involved in international constitutional studies. Making constitutional studies truly internationally oriented is possible only with the participation of highly trained researchers in the field who are both excellent academically and outstanding in their mastery of the English language.[38]
6. The social status of constitutional scholars should be raised. The field is still relatively weak in terms of impact on both other fields of studies and public discourse. In any country with developed rule of law constitutional scholars are held in high regard by all. Conversely, not taking legal scholars seriously hurts a country's chances of achieving the rule of law; not taking constitutional scholars

[36]Gao and Tian [16].
[37]Lu and Xu [27].
[38]Han [28].

seriously hurts a country's chances of becoming a constitutional republic. It is also noticeable that dialogues between constitutional researchers and those specializing in other areas in legal studies have tended to be initiated by the former. Difficult questions such as how constitutional studies can become more influential, especially in relation to other fields of legal studies, and be protected from being reduced to them still need to be answered. For instance, almost no attempt was made to seek input from constitutional scholars when property law, which is part of civil laws, was being drafted. In 1999, China renamed "crime of counter-revolution" as "crimes against public security" in a constitutional amendment. Those working in criminal law were convinced that this amounted to the criminal codes' contribution to the constitution since the same revision had already been made in the former in 1997. Most people engaged in research on land tenure system are experts in civil law, and very few constitutional scholars are involved.

6 Future Development of the Community of Constitutional Legal Scholars

Insofar as it is true to say that the legal studies scene in China has seen the dominance of criminal law and the robust growth of civil law, then the status of constitutional law must be appropriately elevated to support the government's efforts to establish the rule of law in the country. The constitution is held in highest regard in all countries in which the rule of law prevails. On the basis of this general presumption, we hope to see progress in the following areas in the future development of Chinese constitutional law studies:

6.1 Respect for Individual Scholar's Independence and Sense of Agency and Advocacy for Academic Freedom

While constitutional scholars are members of a community, they are also individuals in pursuit of ideals of academic excellence. We consider constitutional scholars intellectuals, and in that role, they are first and foremost learned individuals and then secondarily as people with intellectual integrity and independence. Without such integrity and independence, whatever knowledge one possesses be subject to permutation. Only when their "free will and independent spirit" are respected can intellectuals be fully creative and academic studies and research thrive.

Constitutional scholars' sense of agency refers to their being cognizant of their role in making the society and the world a better place. They know how to bring to bear not only their knowledge but also their spiritual strength while trying to strengthen social conscience among the general public and to bring about changes in society. In addition to studying objective facts, constitutional scholars also seek to uncover patterns behind the facts and evaluate what facts they find. But whatever it is they do, they must do it of their own volition and in a way that is consistent with principles they hold fast. Otherwise, their studies would lack merit.

The importance of academic freedom and independence is self-evident and a consensus among scholars. Relative independence and autonomy is paramount to the field of constitutional law and should govern the research conduct of those in this field. Failure to do so threatens the credibility of what they do. Being unscrupulous and subservient to political objectives fundamentally weakens constitutional studies. In some countries, protection of academic freedom for universities and for teaching is clearly stipulated in the constitution. For instance, the basic law of Germany stipulates in Article 5 that: "Arts and sciences, research and teaching shall be free, The freedom of teaching shall not release any person from allegiance to the constitution." Article 23 of the constitution of Japan guarantees academic freedom. Article 33 of the constitution of Italy calls for protecting freedom for the arts and sciences and the teaching thereof. Of course, constitutional scholars should pay attention to the normative autonomy and logical self-sufficiency of the field and retain what makes it academically distinct.

6.2 *Facilitating the Growth of Constitutional Studies as a Self-standing Discipline, Adopting Improved Professional Standards and Increasing Researchers' Sense of Social Responsibility*

Constitutional researchers mostly work in their own professional niche. As professional researchers and intellectuals, more than anything else they need to cultivate their own work ethic and professional capabilities. Max Weber pointed out in *Science as a Vocation* that a scholar can make long-lasting achievements in the production knowledge only if they adhere to the highest of professional standards. The study of constitutional law studies is methodologically improved by the establishment and adoption of a distinct discourse suitable specifically for the field.[39] While it is important for constitutional studies to be a self-standing field of study, it should not be placed in a disciplinary straitjacket. It should be open to penetration from and enrichment by other fields of inquiry, as such exchange that transcends disciplinary boundaries invariably benefits all involved fields.

At the same time, academic studies should aim at audiences beyond peer researchers. Those engaged in constitutional studies in particular should take seriously the impact of their work on the general public, who stands to benefit when the society as a whole adopts a reverential attitude toward the constitution and what

[39]Refer to [US] Max [29].

it represents. Confining one's thinking within the narrow scope of esoteric subject matters would impose limits on one's vision, render one's methods less effective and makes it hard to solve a problem.[40] It is up to modern intellectuals to demonstrate their value for society by staying on top of, getting involved in and providing explanations for and guidance about social affairs. Intellectuals can only stay relevant if they work to keep memories of the past alive and are critical of reality, try to explain general issues and lead the way toward universal norms, reflect on common phenomena and social justice issues, get involved in social activities and show concern for how people think and feel. In this sense, for intellectuals, fulfilling their social responsibility toward the public is imperative given the role they play in modern society.[41] We should also recognize that how effective intellectuals can be in these roles is importantly determined by how much political space they are given and how competently they can make use of the media.

6.3 Constructing a Distinctly Chinese Discourse on the Rule of Law and a Sound Theoretical System for Studying the Chinese Constitution

While the Chinese government has declared its determination to build a socialist country under the rule of law, the discourse surrounding the issue is still very much something foreign that was only recently introduced. This is why, at a meeting of the China Law Society held in 2012, Chen Jiping called upon the organization to "encourage legal scholars and practitioners to get involved in efforts to construct a discourse on socialist rule of law on the basis of Chinese legal theories, because few things are more important for Chinese legal scholars and for the organization than being able to apply such a discourse when examining China's own legal experience."[42]

The same is true for constitutional law studies. As the field emerged relatively late in China compare with other countries, we are still climbing a steep learning curve, constantly borrowing from those who have been studying the topic for much longer in countries that have more mature systems of rule of law. In specific studies, references are often made to "some other country," and in some cases, little thought is given to the theoretical possibility, legal justifiability and practical feasibility of transplanting some foreign system into the Chinese context. This kind of discussion is both irrelevant and wasteful. Instead, constitutional studies should be aimed at a common goal, namely to adapt constitutional law studies to this country, so that they are at once based on universal principles and informed by China's own

[40] [US] Russell [30].

[41] Refer to Ren [31].

[42] "Convocation of the Meeting of Leaders of Research Associations of China Law Society in Beijing," iolaw.org.cn, July 15, 2012.

experiences. There are multiple dimensions to the idea of adapting constitutional law studies to the Chinese context. By synthesizing internationally applicable general principles with an understanding of conditions on the ground in China, the goal is to fashion a field of inquiry that can claim some theoretical independence and that can help us make better sense of China's own constitutional experiences and situation.

Properly managing the relationship between drawing on overseas resources and preserving local ones is, therefore, crucial. Only then can China's constitutional studies develop in a way that is truly unique, i.e., different not only from Western countries such as those in Europe but also from non-Western countries. In essence, it will be a development path that is fundamentally China-centered in its motivations, orientation and commitments. In fact, when Chinese constitutional law studies are responsive to China's own problems, the field is more dynamic and the people who conduct such studies are more dedicated and creative.

6.4 Encouraging Diversification of Research Methods and Forming a Self-consistent Methodological System

As the political, economic and cultural conditions in China continue to evolve, questions to which constitutional studies are expected to provide answers have become increasingly difficult and challenging. When traditional research methods are no longer adequate for the task, deep reflections and innovations become especially important. For a long time, the default analytical method used by constitutional scholars was centered on the notion of class. For understanding society in transition, in which class divisions are fluid and defy clear definition, that method has proven to fall short. Neither can value absolutism support an analysis that meets the need to evaluate the institutions themselves. The problem with the static analysis is its inability to forecast or help shape changes in people's wants and desire. Purely theoretical analysis has yet to confront institutional deficiencies in constitutional practices. The current logical system underlying constitutional law studies ill suits the purposes of evaluating the de facto constitution and adjusting legislative relations.

With regard to research methods, apart from being reflective and self-aware, we should also strengthen research, encourage pluralism and be open and tolerant of differences. For any serious academic discussion and academic argument can help correct prejudices and defects, while improving existing theories.[43] The best way to increase methodological diversity is by encouraging debates and getting involved in them. This process brings about progress and can lead eventually to a comprehensive and self-consistent methodological system for studying the constitution.

[43]Yu [32].

6.5 Increasing the Range of Application and Practical Value of Constitutional Law Studies

In response to multi-dimensional social transformation, constitutional law studies have also been evolving in its theory, methods and focus.[44] Just like scholars in other social sciences and humanities, constitutional scholars need to adjust their thinking so that their knowledge and theories can be used toward constitutional analyses in support of social transformation. Increased capacity for problematization is of particular importance, insofar as it is a prerequisite for looking for solutions.

If requirements formulated on the basis of the de facto constitution cannot be formally codified into a constitutional theory, thereby compromising the evaluative efficacy of the theory, the relationship between the constitution at the de facto, the conceptual and the institutional levels would be adversely affected. This would in turn impede progress toward the full establishment of constitutional order. It was Lenin who said that when the law and reality are disconnected from each other, the constitution becomes specious, but when the law is in agreement with reality, that gives the constitution credibility.[45] Constitutional scholars play a crucial role in building the constitution at the conceptual level. At the same time, they also contribute toward narrowing the gap between the published and the de facto constitution. It is incumbent upon Chinese constitutional scholars to bring their expertise to bear as they try not only to understand but also to change the society and to improve the conditions for every individual member thereof.[46] For instance, they can be instrumental in helping the general public understand better the constitutional significance and implications of current affairs, including social problems new and old, as well as government policies and legislations.

6.6 Strengthening Professional Organizations and Sustaining the Community

Talent recruitment plays a key role in sustaining and expanding the community of constitutional scholars. Han Zhubin, president of China Law Society noted that the organization's strong capability for organizing, campaigning for and leading professional conferences makes it a *bona fide* mainstay of constitutional studies in the country.[47] Sustaining the community calls for the establishment of a coherent system in which universities, academies of social sciences at the national, provincial

---

[44]Zhang [33].

[45]*V.I. LENIN Selected Works*, Volume 15, page 309.

[46]Hu and Chen [34].

[47]See Footnote 42.

and municipal levels and legal service providers work in concert to attract talents to the field and educate and train them to become young scholars.

In addition, more should be done to facilitate productive interactions among scholars in different age groups, so that senior scholars can more effectively help junior scholars grow and mature professionally. Regional and international differences should also receive attention from professional associations, who should find ways to promote dialogue and exchange among scholars from different countries and different places within China. Last but not least, local chapters of professional associations devoted to promoting constitutional law studies should be given what support they need to organize conferences, seminars and other activities.

6.7 Increasing the Clout of Constitutional Law Studies

Both its intrinsic merits and strength and public opinion can help elevate the status of constitution law studies within academia. For instance, greater legislative and policy-making involvement among constitutional scholars would have the effect of making the importance of the field more visible and widely appreciated. In both the West and China, the idea of getting involved in public life while staying emotionally detached is widely endorsed, and individual emancipation is seen as the ultimate aim of our care and compassion directed at fellow human beings. On the question of whether it is better to be holed up in the proverbial ivory tower thinking and writing or to participate actively in efforts to make the world a better place, the answer has already been given to us by our ancestors. In this day and age, the former is the wrong choice. For constitutional law studies in particular, as a purely academic or intellectual pursuit, they are unlikely to make any difference to the real world. Of course, we must also guard against the danger of technical and instrumental rationality taking over our thinking, to the point of reducing us to playing a subservient role relative to the "needs of society." The proper aim is to help strengthen the normative function of the constitution in Chinese society as a whole so that it is no longer seen as a document that is largely ornamental and useless. Constitutional scholars should contribute toward improving the level of constitutional literacy among the citizens and allowing it to function as the foundational law as it is meant to be.

References

1. Zhou Yezhong: *Supremacy of Constitution: Soul of China's Law-based Road*, *Law Review*, 1995, Issue 6.
2. Liu Maolin: *An Introduction to China's Constitution*, Peking University Press, 2009 edition, page 31.
3. Dong Chengmei: *Historical Review of Constitutional Law*, published in *Legal Study and Research*, 1988, Issue 3.

4. Zhang Baogui: *Summary of the Symposium Marking the 20th Anniversary of the Convocation of the Third Plenary Session of the 11th Central Committee of the CPC & the 16th Anniversary of the Promulgation of the Constitution*, published in *China Legal Science*, 1999, Issue 1.
5. Zhang Qingfu: *A Brief Introduction to Constitutional Law Research*, Tianjin Education Press, 1989 edition, page 258.
6. Han Dayuan and Hu Honghong: *Academic Community of Constitutional Scholars – Marking the 20th Anniversary of the Establishment of Constitutional Research Association of China Law Society, 2005 Chinese Yearbook of Constitutional Law*, China Law Press, 2006 edition, page 4–14.
7. Dong Fanyu: *Chinese Constitutional Law in the Last Forty Years*, published in *Tribune of Political Science and Law*, 1989, Issue 5.
8. Han Dayuan: *China's Constitutional Law: Review of the 20th Century and Outlook on the 21st Century*, published in *Constitutionalism Review*, Volume 1, China Law Press, 1998 edition.
9. Zhang Youyu: Author's preface of the *Collections of Academic Works of Zhang Youyu*, Beijing Normal University Publishing House, 1988.
10. Wen Zhengbang: *Chinese Constitution moving towards the 21st Century*, Chongqing People's Publishing House, 1993 edition, page 153.
11. Han Dayuan: *Academic Mission and Functional Evolution of China's Constitution Law-Reflection on the 30-year Development of China's Constitution Law, Northern Legal Science*, 2009, Issue 2.
12. Zhang Zhen: *Brief Review on the Development Course and Academic Prospect of Chinese Constitution in 1990s, Tribune of Constitution and Administrative Law*, volume 4.
13. Lu Xiansheng: *Are Public Intellectuals Gadflies of the Society?, Yangcheng Evening News*, January 19, 2003.
14. Su Li: *Social Construction of Chinese Public Intellectuals*, published in *Sociological Study*, 2003, Issue 2.
15. Chen Lai: *Confucian Tradition and Public Intellectuals – On the Public Nature and Specialty of Modern Chinese Intellectuals*, published in *Inheritance Collection: Selected Works Marking the 20th Anniversary of Sinological Research Institute of Shenzhen University (1984–2004)* by Jing Haifeng, Peking University Press, 2004 edition.
16. Gao Quanxi and Tian Feilong: *Issues, Positioning and Method of Political Constitutional Law, Journal of Soochow University* (Philosophy & Social Science Edition), 2011, Issue 3.
17. Lin Laifan: *Present Situation and Outlook of Chinese Constitution, Chinese Journal of Law*, 2011, Issue 6.
18. Xu Jintang: *Several Points of Thinking on Building and Developing Chinese Academic Schools*, edited by Li Shuangyuan, *International and Comparative Law Review (Volume 18)*, China Procuratorate Press, 2010 edition.
19. Lin Laifan: *On the Fundamental Method of Constitutional Law – Investigations from the Aspect of Nomology*, published in *Legal Articles*, 2001, Issue 2.
20. Wu Jialin: *Constitutional Law*, Masses Publishing House, 1983 edition.
21. Han Dayuan: *China's Constitutional Law Research in Thirty Years*: 1978–2008, *Social Sciences in Hunan*, 2008, Issue 4.
22. Hu Honghong: *On the Present Mission of Constitutional Scholars, Studies in Law and Business*, 2007, Issue 3.
23. Fichte: *The Vocation of the Scholar*, translated by Liang Zhixue and Shen Zhen, The Commercial Press, 1980 edition, page 37.
24. Fan Jinxue: *Evaluation and Analysis of Constitutional Cases*, published in *Shandong Social Sciences*, 2007, Issue 11.
25. Han Dayuan: *Humanistic Spirit of Constitution*, published in *Studies in Law and Business*, 2012, Issue 3.
26. Guo Lianjie: *Professionalism Is Our Only Way, China Basic Science*, 2002, Issue 4.
27. Lu Deshan and Xu Weidong: *Summary of Discussions about Several Issues in Chinese Constitution*, preface, Jilin University Press, 1992 edition.

28. Han Dayuan: *Review and Outlook of China's Constitutional Research*, published in *Research Reports on Constitutional Development* of *China* (1982–2002), China Law Press, 2004 edition, page 435.
29. Max Weber: *Wissenschaft Als Beruf Politik Als Beruf*, translated by Feng Keli, Beijing SDX Joint Publishing Company, 1998 edition, page 17–48.
30. Russell Jacoby: *The Last Intellectuals*, translated by Hong Jie, Jiangsu People's Publishing House, 2002 edition.
31. Ren Jiantao: *Professional and Public: Aspiration and Choice of Intellectualsin a Transforming Society*, *Century Weekly,* January 11, 2003.
32. Yu Keping: "Right-oriented Politics, or Public Interest Politics", http://www.tszz.com/scholar/ykp/yukeping022.doc.html, lastly visited on April 7, 2014.
33. Zhang Qianfan: *From People's Sovereignty to Human Rights – Evaluations of the Changes of Mode of Chinese Constitutional Studies*, published in *Tribune of Political Science and Law*, 2005, Issue 2.
34. Hu Jinguang and Chen Xiong: *Thinking about Chinese Constitutional Research Methods*, published in *Zhejiang Academic Journal*, 2005, Issue 4.

Continuous Growth in Reform and Opening-up: Three Decades of Development of Constitutional Law Studies in China

Jihong Mo and Guoqiang Zhai

1 Current Status and Development Trend of Constitutional Law Studies in China

1.1 Main Achievements in Constitutional Research

Since the promulgation and enforcement of the current constitution in 1982, focusing on the publicity and education of current constitution, the subject status of constitutional law studies as an independent subject of law science has been fully recognized. At the same time, the subject construction of constitutional law studies has gradually got onto the right track. In addition, as a special law science studying constitutional phenomena, constitutional law studies have played a very important role in booming the undertaking of socialist law science with Chinese characteristics. Especially during the "10th Five-year Plan" ("10th FYP") period, China's constitutional studies witnessed significant development and made remarkable achievements, which can be demonstrated in the following aspects.

1.1.1 Publication of Quality Works on Constitutional Theories

During the "10th FYP" period, the community of constitutional scholars with young and middle generations of researchers as the main body applied new research methods on the basis of summarizing traditional constitutional study results. They

This part was first published in the *New Development of Legal Studies* (China Social Sciences Press, October 2008, 1st edition) compiled by Mo Jihong et al., and the contents contained herein are both added and deleted.

J. Mo (✉) · G. Zhai
Institute of Law of Chinese Academy of Social Sciences, Beijing, China
e-mail: 13263169197@163.com

L. Li et al. (eds.), *Constitutional Development in China, 1982–2012*,
Research Series on the Chinese Dream and China's Development Path,
https://doi.org/10.1007/978-981-32-9261-1_3

published some new academic research works on constitutional law and came up with some constitutional theories with greater social influence through expanding the research scope of constitutional theories. Some representative works included Tong Zhiwei's *Legal Rights and Constitutionalism*,[1] Mo Jihong's *Logical Foundation of Modern Constitution*,[2] Lin Laifan's *From Constitutional to Normative Constitution*[3] and Zhang Qianfan's *Western Constitutionalism System*,[4] etc. All these works on constitutional theories went beyond the traditional constitutional research framework, or made some innovations in research method, or made greater breakthroughs in the field of constitutional research subjects. The publication of these works changed the simplifying trend of studies on constitutional theories in China. The research achievements of the constitutional circle began to attract the overall attention of the law circle.

1.1.2 Translated, Published or Introduced a Batch of Influential Foreign Works on Constitutional Law or Constitutional System

During the "10th FYP" period, the constitutional circle made tremendous achievements in translating and publishing foreign constitutional works and in publishing and introducing foreign works on constitutional system. In terms of translating foreign constitutional works, a batch of quality translation works emerged in China, including *Constitutional Law in Practice* ([Japan] by Takashi Miura) translated by Li Li and Bai Yunhai,[5] *Freedom's Law* ([U.S.] by Ronald Dworkin) translated by Liu Lijun,[6] *The Parliamentary Ombudsman in Sweden* translated by Cheng Jie,[7] *The Right of Existence* ([Japan] Osuga Akira) translated by Lin Hao,[8] the second edition of *Introduction to the Study of the Law of the Constitution* ([Britain] A.V. Dicey) translated by Lei Binnan,[9] etc. These translations filled the gap in China's constitutional research materials and enriched the comparative research data about constitutional law. In addition, during this period, some constitutional works were published for introducing foreign constitutional systems. The most influential ones were the series of books about parliaments system of countries in the world, which were compiled under the organization of the Research Office of the Standing Committee of the NPC Standing Committee,

---

[1]Shandong People's Publishing House, March 2001, 1st edition.

[2]China Law Press, December 2001 edition.

[3]China Law Press, May 2001 edition.

[4](Volume I, Constitution of the United States), China University of Political Science and Law Press, July 2007 edition; (Volume II, European Constitution), China University of Political Science and Law Press, May 2001 edition.

[5]People's Public Security University of China Press, July 2002 edition.

[6]Shanghai People's Publishing House, September 2001 edition.

[7]Tsinghua University Press, November 2001 edition.

[8]China Law Press, March 2001 edition.

[9]China Legal Publishing House, April 2001 edition.

including *The National Assembly of Republic of Korea* by Han Dayuan, *The Parliament of Germany* by Gan Chaoying, *The Parliament of France* by Xu Zhenzhou et al., *The Parliament of Japan* translated by Yang Jianshun and *The Parliament of Singapore* by Wang Ruihe,[10] etc. Some scholars also further reinforced in-depth studies on foreign constitutional law and published relevant works on comparative constitutional law or country-based constitutional law, which enriched China's theoretical research results in comparative constitutional law. The main accomplishments in this aspect included *Comparative Research on Constitution of the Commonwealth of Independent States* by Ren Yunzheng and Ding Hongjun[11] and the *Comparative Constitution—a Comparative Study of the Constitution of Eight Countries* by Shen Zongling,[12] etc.

1.1.3 Strengthened the Compilation of Textbooks on Constitutional Law for Higher Education

During the "10th FYP" period, the compilation of teaching materials on constitutional law was further deepened for higher education. The compilation of constitutional textbooks showcased a booming landscape with the expanding types and improving system and contents of teaching materials. Some distinctive teaching materials on constitutional law included *Constitution: Theories and Practice* by Zheng Xianjun,[13] *Constitution*[14] by Wei Dingren, Gan Chaoying and Fu Siming, *Constitutional Law*[15] by Yang Haikun, *Institutiones Novae*[16] by Zhang Qianfan, and LLM(master of law) textbook *Constitutional Law*[17] by Mo Jihong and Li Zhong, etc. These books made further explorations in the teaching material system, made more introductions about new subjects of constitutional law, played a better demonstration role and was well received by students.

1.1.4 Published a Large Number of Papers on Constitutional Law with Tremendous Social Influence

During the "10th FYP" period, the constitutional community made beneficial innovations and attempts in discussing the basic theories of constitutional law and

[10]The series of books about parliaments of countries in the world, published by Huaxia Publishing House, January 2002 edition.

[11]China Social Sciences Press, January 2001 edition.

[12]Peking University Press, January 2002 edition.

[13]Peking University Press, November 2002 edition.

[14]Peking University Press, March 2002 edition.

[15]China Human Resources Publishing House, August 2002, edition 1.

[16]China Law Press, January 2004 edition.

[17]Social Sciences Academic Press, October 2004 edition.

building socialist constitutional government, etc. There were not only greater changes in research method but also substantive development in research content. Moreover, the studies paid more attention to the combination with constitutional practices. Many influential academic thoughts were presented through papers on the constitution published on all kinds of legal theory publications. In this aspect, some academic papers on constitutional law with great academic influence included: *On the Limits of Constitutional Interpretation*[18] by Han Dayuan and Zhang Xiang, *The Case of Qi Yuling and Judicial Application of the Constitution*[19] by Hu Jinguang, *Judicatory Actualization of Constitution Is Theoretical Misunderstanding of Constitutional Law*[20] by Xu Chongde and Zheng Xianjun, *Reflections and Reconstruction of Constitutional Theory System*[21] by Zhou Yezhong and Zhou Youyong, *Basic Issues in Economic Constitution*[22] by Zhao Shiyi, *On Constitutional Principles*[23] by Mo Jihong, *An Examination of "Ought to Be"–A Field of Vision of Constitutional Logic*[24] by Mo Jihong, *On the Fundamental Methods of Constitutional Law*[25] by Lin Laifan, *New Constitutional Research Topics in the Internet Age*[26] by Han Dayuan and *Questioning the Report of Work by Courts to People's Congresses*[27] by Jiao Hongchang and Yao Guojian, etc. The most important feature of these papers on the constitution was the breakthrough made in constitutional research method. At the same time, they raised a whole new perspective of the way of thinking on basic constitutional concepts and problems, which exerted great social influence and improved the academic status of constitutional law in the entire legal theoretical field.

1.1.5 Reformed the Traditional Research System for Constitutional Theories

China's traditional constitutional law had two obvious characteristics in research system. First, the subject system of constitutional law was basically arranged based on the contents and structure of the constitutional code. Constitutional studies were carried out mainly by centering on the contents provided in the constitutional code. Therefore, constitutional law was more like constitutional code hermeneutics in a way. Second, the main points of constitutional law in content were typically about

---

[18]*The Jurist*, 2001, Issue 1.

[19]*Renmin University Law Review*, 2001, Issue 1.

[20]*The Jurist*, 2001, Issue 6.

[21]*Chinese Journal of Law*, 2001, Issue 4.

[22]*Chinese Journal of Law*, 2001, Issue 4.

[23]*China Legal Science*, 2001, Issue 4.

[24]*Social Sciences in China*, 2001, Issue 6.

[25]*Legal Articles*, 2001, Autumn Issue.

[26]*Global Law Review*, 2001, Spring Issue.

[27]*Yuelu Law Review*, 2001, Issue 2.

the political system of the state, lacked the characteristics of law, especially lacked attention to constitutional issues, constitutional disputes and the legal mechanism for handling constitutional issues and constitutional disputes. There are more evident duplications of constitutional law and political science in subject system.

For example, Mr. Wu Jianlin wrote a trial textbook on legal science for institutions of higher learning, which was titled *Constitutional Law*.[28] This textbook used to be taken as a primary textbook on constitutional law by institutions of higher learning in China in 1980s and early 1990s. This teaching material was published after the promulgation of the current constitution (1982 Constitution). Its system basically reflected the content arrangement of China's current constitution. The book was composed of five chapters, namely the introduction, state system, economic system, basic rights and obligations of citizens and state institutions. However, the book virtually had no mention of the legal issue that constitution is a fundamental law. Regarding how to handle constitutional disputes, it even failed to enter into the research scope of the textbook. Therefore, it can be said that the basic characteristic of the textbook in content is that it is a book of political science with the content from the current constitution and added some principles of scientific socialism to it, rather than constitutional law addressing constitutional issues and disputes as the core in a strict sense. Mr. Xu Chongde made a lot of efforts in making breakthroughs in the constitutional code interpretation model in his *Constitution of China*[29] written for institutions of higher learning as a textbook of arts in late 1980s. This textbook was divided into 11 chapters, including the introduction, basic theory of constitution, historical development of constitution, state nature, state form, central state organs, local systems, judicial and procuratorial system, electoral system, political party system, and citizen's basic rights and obligations, etc. Obviously, this textbook had laid emphasis on arranging its logical system from the basic systems established by the constitution rather than being limited to the content system of the current constitutional code. However, this textbook still failed to get rid of the influence of political science, and its basic contents were similar to or the same with China's political system. It still failed to accomplish the division of subject functions between constitutional law and political science.

Some constitutional works published in recent years have begun to focus on studies on constitution itself. The constitutional subject system and research methods have gradually broken away from the traditional "pan-politics" and have had their independent value judgment system. Taking Zhou Yezhong's *Constitution* (teaching textbook for the 21st century)[30] as an example, this textbook highlights studies on constitutional issues. This textbook included 25 chapters of 3 sections. The first section is the "basic theories of constitution", involving the concept of constitution, historical development of constitution, formulation of constitution,

[28]Masses Publishing House, November 1983, 1st edition.

[29]China Renmin University Press, April 1989, 1st edition.

[30]Higher Education Press, Peking University Press, December 2000, 1st edition.

basic principles of constitution, constitutional form and constitutional structure, constitutional norms, constitutional relations, value and function of constitution, constitutional concept and constitutional culture, constitution and constitutionalism. The second section is the "basic system of constitution", involving nature of state, form of state, basic rights and obligations of citizens, electoral system, state organs and political party system. The third section is the "implementation of constitution", including the conditions for constitutional implementation, constitutional implementation process, interpretation of constitution, amendment of constitution, constitutional implementation assessment and review for constitutionality, and constitutional order, etc. Apparently, the most important characteristic of this textbook is the continuous focus on taking constitution as the clue to firmly uphold the research object of constitution while arranging constitutional law system. However, we should also notice that "basic system of constitution" as the main part of the book still fails to get rid of the constraints of traditional political research methods although it has expanded studies on the basic theories and implementation of constitution. In this sense, the textbook is featured by narrowness. For instance, in terms of the basic rights and obligations of citizens, constitutional rights and ordinary legal rights are not distinguished based on the basic characteristics of legal rights. Instead, the book makes political elaborations based on the citizens' basic rights and obligations as stipulated by the constitution. In this case, this textbook can be further developed in terms of research method.

It is noteworthy that, in the *Basic Theory of Modern Constitution*,[31] Xu Xiuyi and Han Dayuan applied a unique research method to replace conventional methods of theoretical research on constitution. The most important characteristic of the book is multi-angle discussions and studies on some most elementary categories of constitution and the deepened subject system of constitutional law. This book is divided into two parts. The first part is the "basic concept of constitutional law", including the concept of constitution, constitution-making power, constitutionalism, structure of constitution, origin of constitution, constitutional relations, constitutional norms, constitutional principles, constitutional value, constitutional functions, constitutional culture, interpretation of constitution, revision of constitution, constitutional convention, judicial applicability of constitution and constitutional cases, etc. The second part is the "constitutional law in the academic community", including the history and future of constitutional law, method of constitutional law, constitutional law and science of civil law, constitutional law and science of criminal law, constitutional law and science of administrative law, constitutional law and science of international law, constitutional law and science of military law, constitutional law and science of criminal procedural law, constitutional law and science of labor law, constitutional law and philosophy, and constitutional law and political science, etc. This work not only focuses on discussing theoretical issues of constitution but also studies theoretical issues of constitution. This book had already focused on drawing a line between constitutional law and studies of

[31]People's Public Security University of China Press, January 2001 edition.

constitutional law and realized the significance of the development of studies of constitutional law in the development of constitutional law.

Of course, constitutional issues must be taken as the core of constitutional law in order to get rid of the influence of politics. Besides, the discipline levels of constitutional law must be clear-cut. At the moment, China's constitutional law studies are basically the one between its first and second generations. Currently, China's constitutional law pays more attention to the basic theories of early modern constitution and starts to introduce the knowledge system of modern constitutional law. But, it covers little subject contents and research methods of the third generation of constitutional law that reflects the constitutional development trend of modern countries. Therefore, China's studies on constitutional theories must start from solving constitutional issues in development so as to truly get rid of the bad influence of political constraints on traditional constitutional law in both concept and category and truly have the own theoretical characteristics of constitutional law.

During the "10th FYP" period, China's constitutional research system witnessed further development. Taking several constitutional teaching materials published in recent years as examples, they have realized better innovations in research system, especially expanded the research scope of traditional constitutional law. The *Constitutional Law* edited by Yang Haikun divides the constitutional research system into four parts, including the constitutional foundation theory, constitutional right theory, constitutional power theory, and constitutional operation theory. In the part of constitutional foundation theory, constitutional relations, constitutional effectiveness, and constitutional culture are taken as the basic concepts of constitutional law for in-depth studies. In the part of constitutional right theory, constitutional rights are stated by new classifications, including personal rights, political rights, social rights and rights of vulnerable groups, etc., which has effectively amplified the meaning of constitutional rights. In the part of constitutional power theory, it is classified statements of the relations between constitution and state power. In the part of constitutional operation theory, it is about the theory of constitution applicability, etc. Above contents have made breakthrough in the traditional constitutional research field and expanded the constitutional research system. In *Institutiones Novae*, Zhang Qianfan placed particular emphasis on analyzing constitutional cases and systematically introduced constitutional issues valued in foreign constitutional theoretical studies and practices. He introduced the constitutional research system with a method that is totally different from traditional constitutional research methods and has a very outstanding system innovation spirit. In the textbook *Constitutional Law*, Mo Jihong and Li Zhong systematically elaborated constitutional research methods and theoretical issues related to the establishment of constitutional subjects. They also defined the status of constitutional law in the entire legal subject and the relations between constitutional law and other branches of law. Besides, they added many new concepts and categories to the basic theories of constitution, such as constitutional disputes, constitutional relief, constitutional litigation, among other special topics. They also divided the normative system of constitution into two different levels, namely basic state policy and basic system and stressed the guiding role of constitutional policy in constitutional system.

In short, during the "10th FYP" period, China's research system for constitutional theories was moving towards comprehensive and diversified development. The conceptual system and category system of constitutional law realized substantive development. The subject area of constitutional law became wider and wider, involving social, political, economic and cultural lives.

1.1.6 Achieved Some Quality Academic Results in Research on Constitutional History

During the "10th FYP" period, an essential feature of China's theoretical studies on constitution was the important breakthroughs made in studies on constitutional history. Several influential academic works were published during this period, which filled the gap in China's studies on constitutional history. The most remarkable achievements were the *Constitutional History of the People's Republic of China*[32] written by professor Xu Chongde and *1954 Constitution and Constitutionalism of the People's Republic of China*[33] compiled by professor Han Dayuan. In these two works on constitutional history, the authors systematically studied the development history and features of Chinese constitution and summarized the experience and lessons of the PRC in constitutional development. These two works have very important academic reference values in understanding and comprehending the characteristics of China's current constitution and the basic meaning and spiritual essence of China's constitutional system. *The Constitutional History of the People's Republic of China* by professor Xu Chongde systematically introduced and analyzed the first-hand data about the evolution process of China's constitution, especially the emergence of the 1982 Constitution from a macro perspective. It can be said that this is the most authoritative research result in domestic constitutional community. *The 1954 Constitution and Constitutionalism of the People's Republic of China* written by professor Han Dayuan made all-round studies on the 1954 Constitution with a plenitude of the first-hand data. It is a work on constitutional history with high academic quality and filled the gap in China's studies on the 1954 Constitution.

1.1.7 Presented the Phenomenon of Contention of Many Schools of Thought in Constitutional Research Method

During the "10th FYP" period, China made greater breakthroughs in constitutional research method, especially in theories explaining the origin of constitution. The

[32]Fujian People's Publishing House, April 2003, 1st edition.

[33]Hunan People's Publishing House, August 2004, 1st edition.

most influential research methods included the social right theory put forward by Tong Zhiwei in his book titled *Legal Rights and Constitutionalism*, the people's sovereignty theory raised by Zhou Yezhong and Zhou Youyong in the article titled *Reflections and Reconstruction of Constitutional Theory System*, the economic constitutional law theory proposed by Zhao Shiyi in *Basic Issues in Economic Constitution*, the constitutional logics raised by Mo Jihong in *Logical Foundation of Modern Constitution* and the normative constitutional research method proposed by Lin Laifan in the book titled *From Constitutional to Normative Constitution.*

Lin Laifan deeply probed into constitutional research methods and proposed many inspirational opinions in the book titled *From Constitutional to Normative Constitution-A Preface of Normative Constitutional Law*. According to him, constitutional research methods can be divided into three levels, including fundamental methods, general methods, and specific methods. The so-called fundamental method refers to positioning the value orientation of China's constitution in the twenty-first century at some point similar to aesthetic "golden section point" between early modern subject and modern subject of constitution on the basis of differentiating value and fact, and existence and intention.[34] The so-called general method refers to the methods commonly used in traditional constitutional law studies, such as combining theory with practice, essential analysis (or class analysis), historical analysis, comparative analysis, and systematic analysis. Also, the general methods include the application of legal philosophy, jurisprudence, sociology, and politics, among others. The so-called specific method refers to the specific methods or skills reflected in implementing the fundamental methods and general methods in constitutional research process. Specific methods intuitively present academic styles, tastes, and features. For instance, Chinese constitutional scholars attach more importance to making direct conclusions while their Japanese counterparts pay more attention to the process of argumentation.[35] Lin Laifan had his rationality in revealing the levels of constitutional research methods. What's worth praising was the taking of fact and value, existence and intention as the primary research method. The fundamental role of philosophical methods was actually highlighted here. That is to say, if theoretical studies on constitutional law no longer focus on the basic philosophical method, it would be impossible to study constitutional law in normative and scientific sense, and the research conclusions would have a far cry from the requirement of normative constitution. However, lowering historical analysis and comparative analysis down to general methods corresponding to fundamental methods seems to fail to accurately reclassify the own value of methods. This implies that history is subordinate to philosophy. It is worthy of vigilance in this kind of preference in methodology. The statements of Lin Laifan about reevaluating constitutional research methods have attracted extensive attention of the constitutional circle and become a hot topic in theoretical studies on constitutional law in recent years.

---

[34]Lin [1], p. 26.

[35]Lin [1], p. 54.

1.1.8 Constitutional Studies Timely Followed and Reflected the Latest Development Trend of Constitutional Studies in Modern World

During the "10th FYP" period, the Chinese constitutional circle had special focus on the latest development trend of constitutional studies in modern world and introduced the latest dynamics of foreign studies on constitutional theories. In addition, the Chinese constitutional circle also cooperated with International Association of Constitutional Law (IACL) and co-organized an international academic workshop on market economy and constitutional government construction in Beijing in November 2002. Nearly 100 constitutional experts and scholars from 20 countries participated in this international academic workshop. This international academic workshop on market economy and constitutional government construction was the first international academic meeting undertaken by China Law Society. The IACL is an international non-governmental academic organization founded in September 1981 with the purpose of promoting extensive academic exchanges among global constitutional experts and scholars, constantly deepening theoretical studies on constitutional law and facilitating the development of constitutionalism of countries in the world. Since the foundation of IACL, the Chinese constitutional community has actively participated in various academic exchange activities convened by this organization. Chinese famous constitutional experts Zhang Youyu, Wang Shuwen, and Pu Zengyuan used to serve as executive committee members of IACL. The Constitutional Research Association of China Law Society joined IACL as a group member in 1986 and has played a pivotal role in the association and received respect from constitutional communities of the countries of the world.

This international workshop had in-depth discussions by centering on the relations between market economy and constitutional government construction. The discussions focused on constitutionalism against the background of globalization, constitutional protection of economic rights, restrictions on government regulations on private property rights, judicial review and legal control over the legitimacy of administrative behaviors. Eight Chinese and foreign constitutional experts and scholars delivered special reports on above contents. The attendees from across the world also actively took part in academic discussions on these special topics. The participants freely spoke out and fully presented their academic opinions, exchanged viewpoints on above topics, formed many consensuses and showcased full understanding of and respect for different viewpoints in discussions. This international workshop provided an absolutely good opportunity for the Chinese constitutional community to have academic exchanges with their foreign peers. In the meantime, this event enabled international constitutional circles to better understand China's achievements in building the socialist market economy and strengthening the building of socialist legal system ever since the reform and opening up. This international gathering also enabled international constitutional circles to have a correct understanding of the situation and features of China's socialist constitutional government construction. This international workshop is bound to have a far-reaching significance for boosting China's constitutional government construction and improving China's level of research on constitutional theories.

1.1.9 Proposed the Proposition of Governing the Country and Exercising Power in Accordance with the Constitution Based on Actual Conditions

During the "10th FYP" period, the great contribution of the constitutional community to China's legal system building theories was the proposal of the proposition of governing the country and exercising power in accordance with the Constitution. This proposition was adopted by the top decision-making level and affirmed by the top leaders in speeches. This proposition has become an important theme guiding China's building of the socialist legal system. The proposition of governing the country by constitution was first raised by professor Mo Jihong in 1996. Later, it was accepted by the constitutional community and has been acknowledged by leaders and decision-making departments. In early 2004, Premier Wen Jiabao made clear at a legal lecture of the State Council that the core of governing the country by law is governing the country by constitution. In September 2004, General Secretary Hu Jintao reiterated the importance of governing the country and exercising power in accordance with the Constitution in an important speech delivered at the meeting commemorating the 50th anniversary of the people's congress system. Therefrom, governing the country and exercising power in accordance with the Constitution has become an important guiding thought recognized by the legal community for the building of China's socialist legal system.

1.1.10 Made Key Breakthroughs in Studies on the Theory of Constitutionality Review System

During the "10th FYP" period, China made major breakthroughs in studies on review for constitutionality theories. In particular, the Chinese constitutional community started from implementing the review for constitutionality provisions established by the legislation law and took the "8·13" judicial interpretation of the Supreme People's Court in 2001 and the "Sun Zhigang Case" in 2003 as the opportunities to carry out full studies on how to improve and perfect the review for constitutionality system in China. A number of very influential academic works were produced during this period. First, the judicatory actualization of constitution became a hot topic of the constitutional community. The constitutional community conducted extensive discussions on the applicability of constitution in judicial judgment, which not only filled the gap in China's studies on the issue but also introduced China's studies on constitutional theories to the practical level of legal system building. Constitutional cases were highly valued in constitutional studies. Second, the constitutional community laid emphasis on in-depth studies on constitutionality of laws and regulations and put forward a whole set of ideas for the theoretical building of the review for constitutionality system. Lastly, the constitutional community started to publish and introduce foreign constitutional procedural theories and review for constitutionality theories by combining comparative law research. In this aspect, the quite influential works included Hu Xiaohua's *Original Theory of Constitutional Lawsuit*, Zhang Qianfan's *Western Constitutionalism System* and Wang Zhenmin's *China's Review for constitutionality System*, etc. The theory of review for constitutionality system has become an essential category of China's studies on constitutional theories.

1.1.11 Had Rather Systematic Legal Principles for the Interpretation of the Basic Law

During the "10th FYP" period, China's constitutional community enhanced studies on the interpretation of constitution, especially made systematic and special studies on general theories of legal interpretation. Some monographs on constitutional interpretation appeared during this period, such as Fan Jinxue's *Theoretical Construction of Constitutional Interpretation*.[36] There also emerged some research works on legal interpretation based on the interpretation of basic law. On April 6, 2004, the Eighth Session of the 10th Standing Committee of the National People's Congress deliberated and adopted the proposal on interpretations of Article 7 of Appendix I and Article 3 of Appendix II of *the Basic Law of the Hong Kong Special Administrative Region of the People's Republic of China*. This proposal gave the second interpretation of the implementation of the basic law after the "case regarding the residency rights" in 1999. While the Standing Committee of the NPC giving the second interpretation of the basic law, experts and scholars of China's constitutional community extensively took part in the discussions and argumentations about the proposal for legal interpretation and took this occasion as the opportunity to extensively and profoundly discuss the basic legal theories and features of China's legal interpretations and provided a better research environment and background for establishing and improving China's constitutional interpretation mechanism.

1.1.12 Paid Attention to the Relations Between Theoretical Studies on Constitutional Law and Other Branches of Law

During the "10th FYP" period, China's constitutional law also laid emphasis on the inter-disciplinary connections and communications with branch law subjects. Not just in academic activities, the constitutional circle also cooperated with other branch law circles and organized several cross-disciplinary academic dialogues. In addition, the constitutional circle also demonstrated the integration between constitutional law and branches of law in research results. The dialogues between constitutional law and other subjects, including litigation law and criminal law led

[36]Shandong People's Publishing House, February 2004, 1st edition.

to the emergence of some cross-disciplinary research results, constitutional criminal law.[37] The relations between constitution and criminal law, between constitution and ecology, between constitution and network, between constitution and clone man, among other comprehensive social topics, attracted the attention and emphasis of the constitutional circle and other branch law circles.

1.1.13 The Importance of Constitutional Philosophy Received the Attention of the Constitutional Circle

During the "10th FYP" period, constitutional philosophy started to attract the attention of the constitutional circle. Some works on studying and discussing constitutional philosophy appeared. In the book titled *Logical Foundation of Modern Constitution*, Mo Jihong mentioned three levels of constitutional philosophy, namely constitutional morality, constitutional culturology, and constitutional sociology, and constitutional logics. He also pointed out that establishing scientific constitutional philosophy is the precondition for China's theoretical development of constitutional law in the twenty-first century.[38] Beyond that, some young constitutional scholars also discussed the basic thinking of constitutional philosophy from the perspective of general philosophical knowledge. For instance, Dr. Jiang Guohua systematically discussed the important role of constitutional philosophy in building the theoretical system of constitutional law with *Critics of Constitutional Philosophy* as the title.[39] The construction of constitutional philosophy has become a theoretical hot topic among middle-aged and young constitutional scholars in recent years.

In brief, during the "10th FYP" period, China's theoretical studies on constitutional law witnessed more substantive development than ever before either in mastering and recapping constitutional documentation or in observing and summarizing constitutional practices. In particular, as young and middle generations of constitutional scholars grew, there were constant innovations in constitutional research method. The traditional constitutional research framework and structural system also developed and changed. Compared with traditional constitutional law, there were also further expansions in both constitutional problem areas and constitutional concept and category system. Theoretical studies on constitutional law began to develop towards normative and scientific academic argumentation in the process of enhancing the disciplinary relevance with branches of law.

[37]Liu [2].

[38]Mo [3].

[39]Jiang [4].

1.2 Main Problems in Constitutional Research

Many problems exist in China's constitutional research and need to be taken seriously. These problems include:

1.2.1 The Basic Concepts and Categories of Constitutional Law Remain Confounding

China's constitutional law was developed on the basis of the national law of the former Soviet Union. In this connection, the conceptual system and category system applied by China's traditional constitutional law studies are basically the same with or similar to the national law theory of former Soviet Union. The concepts and categories in constitutional law are quite similar to the scientific socialism theory and some were directly borrowed from the scientific socialism theory. Besides, the conceptual and category system of constitutional law studies have little sense of laws and has no effective division of subjects with the conceptual and category system of politics. There is no differentiation in value and fact between constitutional research objects and the social relations adjusted by constitutional research objects. Constitutional issues and political issues are mixed together.

In addition, constitutional law studies are a law subject studying the fundamental law, but there is a lack of in-depth and systematic studies on the relations between constitution and other branches of law. This has made the constitutional research results unable to guide studies on other branches of law. Special concepts and categories of constitutional law have not yet taken shape for guiding the development of other branches of law.

1.2.2 Constitutional Issues Have not Been Taken Seriously in Constitutional Law

For quite some time, the principal constitutional research methods have been typically based on certain intuitive experiences to positively describe the mutual relations between constitutional concepts. There are many constitutional propositions, but there is a shortage of rational verifications of constitutional propositions, especially the lack of constitutional problem consciousness. Necessary academic connection has not yet been established between constitutional issues and constitutional propositions, resulting in a very strong subjective sense of constitutional propositions. In the part of basic theories of constitutional law, the concepts including nature of state, form of government, sovereignty and human rights directly set relevant constitutional propositions in most cases. In particular, many relevant constitutional propositions have been affected by some classical conclusions of scientific socialism theory. Some have been even directly copied and imitated from these conclusions. Due to the lack of consciousness of constitutional issues, there is a lack of public theory platform for building a constitutional concept and category system. There have also been no academic critics in real sense in the constitutional community. Most of the constitutional research results are basically at the stage of constitutional scholars' individual production. A public theory system with scientific features has not yet taken shape. This problem was not effectively addressed during the "10th FYP" period.

1.2.3 Lack Normative Constitutional Research Methods

During the "10th FYP" period, the constitutional circle paid more attention to scientific and theoretical innovations in constitutional research method as a whole. However, many scholars showcased obviously subjective fabrications in applying new research methods to study constitutional issues due to the shortage of normative academic research traditions. Many research methods were novel in form, yet, there were few methodological bases. Some scholars were imprudent in choosing the research method and often revised the drawbacks of research method. That said, they didn't master the objective law of new methods in essence. In this sense, the so-called innovations in research method had little scientific significance in effect.

From the perspective of the overall innovation of the entire constitutional circle in constitutional research method, many new research methods which emerged under the premise of lacking necessary normativity were not accepted by many constitutional scholars as innovations in research method were mainly the creations of individual scholars and lacked publicness. In this case, these research methods failed to play a substantively promoting role in academic development.

1.2.4 Constitutional Law Fails to Properly Absorb the Results of Theoretical Studies on Branches of Law

At present, the overall situation of China's constitutional studies is that the limitation of concepts and systems contained in the constitutional code has not been gotten rid of and there have been no in-depth discussions about the relations between constitution and other legal forms. The constitutional community strengthened its academic connection with other branch law circles during the "10th FYP" period, but there were no presentable theoretical results when it comes to the organic connection between constitutional law and other branches of law in research content and research system. Xu Xiuyi and Han Dayuan made tentative studies on the relations between constitutional law and other branches of law, such as philosophy, science of criminal law, science of civil law, science of procedure law and international jurisprudence in the book titled *Basic Theory of Modern Constitution*, and achieved certain research results. However, in the theoretical system of branches of law, there basically was no mention of the guiding role of constitutional law and the relations between the branch of law and constitutional law. The research results of constitutional law and other branches of law are still isolated and are not shared and commonly developed.

1.2.5 Comparative Constitutional Research Lags Behind Relatively

Comparative constitutional law focuses on the materials of comparative constitutional law to discuss the common features or unique features of constitutional awareness and systems of countries in development. Studies on comparative constitutional law are conducive to referring to foreign and domestic constitutional research results and provide necessary references for building the constitutional law with Chinese characteristics. Looking from the comparative constitutional research situation of China's constitutional circle during the "10th FYP" period, issues existed in two aspects. First, China's constitutional circle failed to summarize the commonality of constitutional systems of different countries and extract constitutional theories with commonality. Second, China's constitutional community paid little attention to the constitutional development history and constitutional thought development history of foreign countries, which resulted in the low comparative constitutional research level as a whole. The only available scientific research results still appeared in the form of country-based constitutional law and failed to truly embody the subject characteristics of comparative constitutional law.

1.2.6 Constitutional Law Studies Are Inapplicable to the Actual Life

The framework of China's current constitutional law was established based on the basic framework and system of the current constitution. The current constitution has no provisions on how a sound constitutional system shall apply constitution, so the constitutional law with constitutional research as the central task has not paid necessary attention to the applicability of constitution. This has resulted in the fact that theoretical studies on constitutional law have been basically established on principle research or principle statement, or mainly focus on purely theoretical issues. Theoretical studies on constitutional law have no in-depth studies on how to give play to the role of constitution in the real life, especially how to give play to the legal function of the fundamental law. In this case, the results of theoretical studies on constitutional law fail to effectively guide social reality.

1.2.7 There Are Insufficient Theoretical Studies on the Implementation of the Basic Law

In recent years, with the establishment of Hong Kong and Macao special administrative regions, the basic law has been implemented in the two special administrative regions. The basic law was enacted before the establishment of special administrative regions, so it is impossible to be so perfect for all systems and inevitable to meet some new problems that were not taken into consideration at the time of enactment. As a matter of fact, after the return of Hong Kong and Macao to the motherland, the Standing Committee of the NPC made two legal interpretations of the basic law and the appendix of the basic law respectively in 1999 and 2004 for the implantation of the Basic Law of Hong Kong SAR. Relative to the requirement for legal safeguard for the implementation of the basic law, China's constitutional community has insufficient attention to the theoretical issues in the implementation of the basic law. Constitutional scholars haven't paid necessary attention to studies on the basic law. In addition, the entire legal community hasn't proposed some influential works targeting some issues that possibly occur in the implementation of the basic law. Therefore, the constitutional community cannot provide an effective theoretical support for the implementation of the basic law as a whole.

1.2.8 There Are no in-Depth Theoretical Studies on the Reform of Judicial Adjudication System in Terms of Constitutional Law

The reform of judicial adjudication system is a hot topic in China's building of the legal system in recent years. However, the theoretical support for the reform of judicial adjudication system mainly comes from the litigation law circle and the jurisprudence community, or from procuratorial organs or judicial organs and judicial administrative departments. This research situation has resulted in the shortage of constitutional theory guidance in the reform of judicial adjudication system. Many suggestions for the reform of judicial adjudication system fail to correctly comprehend the features of the people's congress system in China at the moment and fail to correctly handle the relations among all powers involved in the reform of judicial adjudication system. The constitutional circle has also touched upon some individual issues related to the reform of judicial adjudication system, but it fails to provide an effective thought and constitutional basis for the reform of judicial adjudication system as a whole.

1.2.9 There Is a Lack of Weighty Results of Studies on the Role of Legislative Power in Constitutional Law

Legislative power is an important state power and an important power system of China's people's congress system. However, China's traditional constitutional law failed to value the nature of legislative power but mainly focused on legislative system and legislative institution. Therefore, the basic constitutional relations related to legislative power are not very clear and lack cogent works. During the "10th FYP" period, many cases related to the nature of legislative power occurred in China's constitutional practices. For example, *Measures for Sheltering and Sending away Vagrants and Beggars in Cities* was replaced by *Measures for Assisting Vagrants and Beggars with No Means of Support in Cities*, which was triggered by the "Sun Zhigang Case" in 2003. Both practical departments and theoretical departments mainly focused on human rights protection in argumentations of this change and failed to consider legal issues brought about by this change from the perspective of legislative power. The cause for this is that China's constitutional theories have not formed effective analytic thinking of legislative issues and there are inadequate systematic and mature constitutional theories.

1.2.10 There Are not Enough Introductions of the Development Trend of the Constitutional Procedural System of Other Countries in Constitutional Law

The constitutional litigation system is an important part of modern constitutional systems of countries. A subject branch, constitutional litigation law science, has been gradually separated from the constitutional law with constitutional litigation system as the research object. The establishment of constitutional litigation law science has effectively made up for the deficiencies of civil action, criminal action and administrative action in realizing judicial remedy of civic rights in legal theories and further enriched the meaning of the rights of action protected by the constitution.

China has not yet established a formal constitutional litigation system. In terms of theoretical studies on constitutional law, there are only fragmentary results in studies on the constitutional litigation system and no formation of systematic and comprehensive thoughts and theories. In addition, there have been no in-depth introductions of foreign constitutional litigation systems due to language barriers. Up to now, domestic constitutional community's knowledge about foreign constitutional litigation systems still stays at a superficial level. This kind of backwardness has also seriously affected the improvement of the overall research level of the constitutional community in the aspect of constitutional litigation system.

In short, during the "10th FYP" period, the problems existing in theoretical studies on constitutional law were mainly the rotten legacy from traditional constitutional law. Or we should say, the studies on a host of constitutional issues were still at a superficial level as a result of inadequate constitutional practices. Therefore, to fundamentally change China's backwardness of theoretical studies on constitutional law and comprehensively improve the level of theoretical studies on constitutional law, we must make effort in various aspects, such as research method, research means, and research environment. It is necessary to attract more research forces to engage in basic theoretical studies on constitutional law. At the same time, theoretical studies on constitutional law should also be constantly combined with constitutional practices. The constitutional circle should actively put the fruits of theoretical studies on constitutional law into social practices and provide timely theoretical guidance of constitutional law in the practices of building the legal system. Therefore, a good interaction between theoretical studies on constitutional law and practices in building constitutional system could be established.

1.3 Development Trend of China's Constitutional Research

During the "11th FYP" period, China's theoretical studies on constitutional law further improved in countermeasures and suggestions in basic theoretical studies and practices on the basis of the important achievements made in theoretical studies on constitutional law during the "10th FYP" period. This is to improve China's theoretical research system for constitutional law, build the core position of constitutional law in the legal science system and apply constitutional theories to guide China's practices in building the socialist constitutionalist. Constitutional studies will showcase the following development trend.

1.3.1 The Theoretical System of Constitutional Law Will Keep Absorbing Foreign Constitutional Research Results and Form the Theoretical System of Constitutional Law with China's Own Characteristics

Theoretical studies on constitutional law need to adapt to the requirement for the implementation of constitution in China. First and foremost, there is a must to establish a normative and scientific concept and category system. We should not randomly create concepts or those constitutional viewpoints without any guiding significance for theoretical studies and constitutional practices. To this end, we must sum up constitutional research achievements of other countries and absorb the latest results of development in constitutionalism civilization. Second, there is a must to strengthen comparative constitutional studies, which can help regulate China's constitutional research methods and research systems. In particular, it could help draw on relatively mature constitutional research ideas of other countries to avoid detours in theoretical innovations. Lastly, during the "11th FYP" period, many educated young and middle-aged constitutional scholars returned from abroad gradually came to the fore of the academic study, strengthened the competence of constitutional community and foreign language ability in comparative constitutional studies. These returnees could comprehensively boost China's development in comparative studies on constitutional law within a short period of time through translating and introducing foreign constitutional research contents and research dynamics.

1.3.2 Constitutional Law Will Develop from Concept-Oriented Constitutional Law to Issue-Based Constitutional Law

While building the theoretical research system, China's traditional constitutional law usually just laid emphasis on the description of some basic constitutional concepts, or put forward some more subjective constitutional propositions without strict demonstrations and lacked consciousness of constitutional issues.

Constitutional scholars studied constitutional law usually from concepts or some available notions or principles but not from common constitutional issues. The result is that theoretical studies on constitutional law lacked public knowledge base and a wild variety of research systems. In recent years, the consciousness of constitutional issues has attracted the attention of constitutional scholars and become a development direction of normative constitutional studies. Issue-based constitutional law studies are expected to become an essential feature of theoretical studies on constitutional law.

1.3.3 Constitutional Law Will Focus on Building a System of Complete and Scientific Concepts and Categories

The scientific nature and guiding role of constitutional law in social practices depend on the scientific nature and order of the constitutional knowledge system. Traditional constitutional law arranges constitutional knowledge contents and research system based on the formal structure of constitutional code, but there has not yet formed a system of complete and scientific concepts and categories. In particular, there have been no serious studies on the relations between concepts, and some relations have even been intentionally omitted sometimes. In recent years, the constitutional community has begun to reflect on the drawbacks of traditional constitutional research system and focused on improving the overall research level of the constitutional community from the perspective of establishing a system of scientific and complete concepts and categories.

1.3.4 Theoretical Studies on Constitutional Law Have Been Further Standardized

For quite some time, due to the lack of scientific guidance in constitutional research method, different authors of constitutional law have caused big differences in theoretical research contents and research systems. Particularly, the train of thought of elaborations of basic principles of constitution has been more often than not affected by life experience and lacks standardized theoretical research platforms. As China's constitutional community begins to pay attention to strengthening studies on constitutional research methods, constitutional theory studies will become more and more standardized. The normativity of constitutional theory studies will demonstrate two development trends. First, some scientific research methods will be widely accepted by the constitutional circle and become general constitutional research methods. Second, constitutional law will see the formation of some common fields of constitutional issues under the influence of strict academic criticism mechanism for constitutional law, and there would be discussions about the standardization of constitutional concepts and concept systems under the guidance of scientific research methods. On this basis, an academic community of constitutional law will be formed in real sense.

1.3.5 Theoretical Studies on Constitutional Law Pay More Attention to Studies on Constitutional Cases

China's traditional theoretical studies on constitutional law generally lay emphasis on the description of constitutional concepts and the statement of constitutional principles while paying little attention to the application of constitutional cases to explain constitutional principles, or discovering constitutional issues from the perspective of constitutional cases. Constitutional law usually develops from theory to theory. Constitutional knowledge education also places particular emphasis on reasoning but not solving specific constitutional issues. As some young and middle generation constitutional scholars collect and sort out foreign and domestic constitutional cases in recent years, teaching materials and works on constitutional law have gradually incorporated the contents of constitutional case studies. Constitutional cases have entered into the sight of constitutional researchers, which will help deepen constitutional research contents and improve the effectiveness of theoretical studies on constitutional law and further highlight the social service function and theoretical guiding role of constitutional law.

1.3.6 Constitutional Law Studies Have Closer Connections with Socialist Constitutional Government Practices

Constitutional law studies are a legal subject with constitution as the research object, so the source of its theoretical concepts and theoretical systems is closely linked to constitutional government practices. Essentially, the basic theories of constitutional law have developed constantly by constitutional practices as the driving force. Constitutional law studies have never been a purely theoretical subject developing behind closed doors but an applied science of law combining theories with practices. The constitutional knowledge system must directly serve constitutional government practices, especially be capable of solving all constitutional issues raised in practices. China's constitutional community has begun to focus on applying constitutional theories to analyze and study important issues which occurred in constitutional government practices in recent years. Against this backdrop, the practical characteristics of constitutional law will become more and more evident. At the same time, practical constitutional law studies are about to become a development emphasis of branch subjects of constitutional law.

1.3.7 There Will Be Further Emphasis on Studies of the History of Constitution and History of Constitutional Theories

During the "11th FYP" period, China's constitutional circle paid more attention to studies on the history of constitution and history of constitutional theories. In particular, as normative constitutional law keeps improving, studies on the history of constitutional theories and history of constitutional ideas are expected to become a hot topic and focus of the constitutional community in theoretical studies. In the past studies on the history of constitution, the constitutional circle paid more attention to the history of constitutional systems but little attention to studies on constitutional ideas and constitutional theories, the research results in this aspect was even less. This is a new constitutional research field that merits further explorations and development.

1.3.8 Studies on Country-Based Constitutional Law Will Be Further Deepened and Systemized

In traditional constitutional law, studies on country-based constitutional law have been a field that got more attention still there were many drawbacks. The principle drawback was the poor country-based categories, which was mainly concentrated on the constitutions of several developed countries, such as the United States, Britain, France, Germany, and Japan. Studies and introductions of constitutions of other countries were inadequate. A lot of results of studies on country-based constitutional law were duplicated. During the "11th FYP" period, studies on country-based constitutional law will keep expanding in scope and will shift the focus on studies on country-based constitutional law from western countries to non-western countries. Moreover, there will be more emphases on studies on regional constitutions like the constitution of the EU and studies on country-based constitutional law under the influence of different legal cultural traditions.

1.3.9 Constitutional Law Will Focus More on New Technological and Ethical Issues Which Occurred in Human Society

With the development of human society, there have emerged many new legal issues beyond the scope of traditional constitutional law. In particular, the challenges brought about by scientific and technological revolution to social ethics and moral codes as well as social legal system have also directly affected the development of constitutional concepts and constitutional systems. Therefore, during the "11th FYP" period, constitutional law will keep focusing on some new legal issues raised by new technological revolutions to constitution, including the legal status of clone men and the legal application of cloning technologies, right protection system in the Internet era, and so on and so forth.

1.3.10 Researches on Studies of Constitutional Law Will Be Valued by the Theoretical Community

Studies of constitutional law have been valued by the constitutional community with the development of constitutional research methods. In recent years, China's constitutional community has begun to invest energies in studying some scientific issues in the development of constitutional law while studying constitutional theories.

Studies of constitutional law are expected to become a science subject gradually valued on the basis of continuously improved and developed constitutional law.

1.3.11 Theoretical Studies on the Formulation of New Constitution Will Attract Extensive Attention of the Constitutional Community

China's current constitution was promulgated in 1982 and has developed for 30 years. In the past three decades, China has amended the current constitution for four times in order to adapt to the need of building a socialist legal system, which has improved the constitutional system. However, as China's socialist democratic system and legal system become increasingly better and China's socialist human rights protection undertaking keeps developing, there will be more and more demands for further improving the constitutional system to meet theoretical and practical requirements. In this connection, during the "11th FYP" period, theoretical studies on the formulation of constitution will be intensified.

1.3.12 Constitutional Law Will Give Prominence to the Important Position of Constitutional Interpretation

Modern constitutional law studies are, in a manner of speaking, the constitutional hermeneutics. The entire constitutional knowledge system has been actually established on how to apply a set of self-justifiable theoretical system to explain constitutional phenomena and providing essential theoretical bases for constitutional practices. Therefore, there is a need to constantly improve the authoritative position of constitution as the fundamental law and give full play to the guiding role of constitution in practices of building the legal system. Also, there is a must to take studies on the interpretation of constitution as the focus of the theoretical studies on constitutional law for a period to come. Only when the theoretical research level on the interpretation of constitution is improved, the entire constitutional knowledge system could be improved in the sense of science and standard.

In brief, during the "11th FYP" period, the general trend of China's theoretical studies on constitutional law is more normatization will take place. The core and priority of studies on constitutional law will be constitutional issues and the interpretation of the constitution respectively.

1.4 Key Direction and Issues in China's Constitutional Research

China's constitutional research focus will be put on the basic theoretical construction of constitutional law and studies on several important theoretical issues in socialist constitutional government practices. Specifically speaking, the studies will be on the following several key issues.

1.4.1 Improve and Perfect the Basic Theoretical Framework of China's Constitutional Law

For a long time, the basic theoretical framework of China's constitutional law studies has been arranged based on the form and system of the current constitution. As the chapter and section system of the current constitution mainly reflects the features of the people's congress system as China's fundamental political system. Therefore, the theoretical system of China's constitutional law studies has basically focused on introducing the contents of China's people's congress system. Constitutional law studies have a weak legal sense and a strong sense of such subjects as politics, sociology, and scientific socialism. In this sense, retransforming and improving the basic theoretical framework of China's constitution based on the legal features and functions of the current constitution is bound to fundamentally change the disciplinary orientation of China's constitutional law, strengthen the legal sense of China's constitutional law, separate China's constitutional law from politics, people's congress system theories and related disciplines, and make it become an independent branch subject of the constitutional law subject system.

1.4.2 Further Reinforce the Theoretical Studies on the Relations Between Human Rights and Constitution

Human rights have always been a key point of theoretical studies on constitutional law. However, under the influence of the system of basic rights of citizens as stipulated by China's current constitution, China's traditional constitutional law was basically concentrated on studies on citizens' basic rights while studying issues related to human rights and failed to deeply emphasize general theories of human rights. In particular, there have been no serious studies on the relations between human rights and constitution as well as the position of human right concept in the entire constitutional theoretical system. Human rights have become a legal issue having the farthest distance with the constitutional subject system. To change this abnormal research situation, there should be whole-new studies on the relations between human rights and constitution. There is also a need to incorporate issues related to human rights into the categories of constitutional issues, correctly handle the relations between human rights and citizens' basic rights, and establish a rather rational and scientific constitutional rights system.

1.4.3 Further Deepen Studies on Theories of Constitutional Interpretation

Constitutional interpretation is an essential part of China's traditional theoretical studies on constitutional law. That said, the constitutional interpretation system defined by China's current constitution is imperfect, the constitutional interpretation procedure has never been launched in practice, and there is a lack of constitutional interpretation case in real life, so constitutional studies on constitutional interpretation theories have been the elaborations of terminologies related to constitutional interpretation, or the introductions of foreign constitutional interpretation systems. Constitutional interpretation has not become an effective constitutional issue of constitutional law. Therefore, there is a must to take constitutional interpretation as the focus of China's constitutional studies down the line.

1.4.4 Carry Out Studies on Constitutional Litigation Theory

Constitutional litigation represents a constitutional arbitration system with constitution dispute as the basis, the most important legal form of constitution applicability, and a key legal mechanism for constitution to play the role of standard regulation of behaviors in social life. In modern law-based society, there is a must to establish a constitutional litigation system to truly implement the system of constitutionalism. Up to now, China has not yet established a formal constitutional litigation system and constitution still cannot be taken as the juridical rules for addressing specific constitutional disputes. Constitution has not been valued as a standard for judging whether human behaviors are correct or wrong. In order to implement the law-based ideas of governing the country by constitution and building a socialist country under the constitutionalism, establishing a constitutional litigation system must be taken as the supreme goal of China to improve the constitutional system. For that matter, there is a must to reinforce studies on constitutional litigation in theory, especially explore a theoretical basis for building a constitutional litigation system with Chinese characteristics in line with China's specific national conditions of China's constitutional system. In this connection, studying the legal features of constitutional litigation systems of global countries from the perspective of carrying out studies on the basic theories of constitutional litigation and from the perspective of comparative constitutional law represents an important academic guarantee for establishing and improving China's litigation theory.

1.4.5 Reinforce Studies on Theories and Countermeasures of Exercising Power in Compliance with the Constitution

As the core content of governing the country by law, exercising power in accordance with the constitution has been generally accepted by both the government and the public. Exercising power in compliance with the constitution is an important guarantee for improving the ruling party's ruling ability and ruling level. To realize a full development and improvement of the theory of exercising power in accordance with the constitution and make it become the basic starting point in guiding the ruling party to develop various lines, principles, and policies, the constitutional community should focus on studying the legal basis and the form of exercising power in compliance with the constitution. The constitutional community should also focus on studying the relations between exercising power in accordance with the constitution and governance by law and the relations between exercising power in compliance with the constitution and building a socialist country under the rule of law, and so on and so forth. This is to provide an essential theoretical basis for the Party and the state to stay committed to and implement the program of action of governing the country and exercising power in compliance with the constitution.

1.4.6 Carry Out Studies on the Theoretical Framework of Socialist Constitutionalism

Constitutionalism is a modern democratic political system established with constitution as the basis and a concentrated reflection of modern law-based principles. In modern countries with rather developed rule of law, constitutional government issues have attracted high attention. China is a socialist country and constitution is the fundamental law of China. In this sense, the characteristic of China's political system should be the democratic political system established with constitution as the basis. However, different from the constitutionalism of capitalist countries, what we have established is the socialist constitutionalism and the socialist system established on the basis of the constitution with socialist nature for guaranteeing the ruling status of the Communist Party of China. In addition, the constitutionalism we've established is closely related to the people's congress system as stipulated by China's constitution. To some extent, the people's congress system is the core content of China's socialist constitutionalism and the most important feature of the socialist democratic politics. Of course, in addition to people's congress system, socialist constitutionalism also includes law-based principles of governing the country by law and building a socialist country under the rule of law, and the principle of the supremacy of constitution, such as governing the country and exercising power in accordance with the constitution. For some period to come, China's constitutional community should focus on strengthening studies on the socialist constitutional government theories to obtain the theoretical basis for the constitutional government that is different from capitalist constitutionalist governments.

1.4.7 Carry Out Studies on the Legal Theories for Reunification Between the Two Sides of the Taiwan Straits

As early as when the current constitution was being formulated, the special administrative region system was provided in Article 31 of the current constitution per the legal requirements for the reunification between the two sides of the Taiwan Straits. Pursuant to the provisions of Article 31 of the current constitution, China successfully regained sovereignty over Hong Kong and Macao and established the Hong Kong Special Administrative Region (Hong Kong SAR) and Macao Special

Administrative Region (Macao SAR). Since their establishment, Hong Kong SAR and Macao SAR have maintained their original capitalist system and economic prosperity and stability on the basis of the basic law and under the guidance of the "one country, two systems" principle, which has become a good sample for solving Taiwan issue. For that to happen, the constitutional community should have in-depth studies on how to solve the issue of peaceful reunification of Taiwan based on the "one country, two systems" principle and successful experience of Hong Kong and Macao, thus providing a series of effective theoretical bases for relevant departments to enact policies and related laws correspondingly. The constitutional community should put a high premium on the application of socialist constitutional theories to address many existing constitutional issues for the reunification between the two sides of the Taiwan Straits.

1.4.8 Further Deepen Theoretical Studies on the Reform of Judicial Judgment System

The reform of judicial judgment system is an important practical issue in China's socialist legal system building and a theoretical issue in establishing the socialist constitutional government. Judicial judgment system has bearings on the legal status of state procuratorial organs and state adjudicatory organs in the people's congress system. Judicial judgment system also involves the status of state procuratorial authority and adjudicatory authority in the entire state power system and the legal relations between legislative power and administrative power. In order to provide adequate constitutional basis for the ongoing reform of the judicial judgment system, it is necessary to have in-depth studies on the basic theoretical issues related to the reform of the judicial judgment system. Particularly, it is necessary to start from the state power structure designed by the people's congress system of China to provide necessary guidance of all kinds of constitutional principles for China's judicial judgment system reform.

1.4.9 Strengthen Studies on the Relations Between Constitutionalism and Globalization

With the continuous development of global economic integration, what's in conformity with economic globalization is the popularization of constitutionalism value. Looking from the origin of modern constitutionalism, the generation of constitutionalism value depends on the development of the market economy. Under the mature market economic system, government is bound to appear in the image of a law-based government and manage the economy and adjust various economic relations by law-based administrative means. China joined the World Trade Organization (WTO) in 2001. The accession to the WTO means not only opportunities but also challenges. WTO takes mature market economy as the premise and takes modern law-based principle and modern legal system as the conditions for institutional guarantee. Economic globalization has inevitably triggered the transmission and popularization of constitutionalism value in conformity with economic globalization. Therefore, there is a must to reinforce studies on the relations between constitutionalism and globalization. Currently, China's constitutional community needs to first study how to meet the requirement of International Human Rights Protection to enable China's legal system for human rights protection to conform to international human rights protection systems. On this basis, there is still a long way to go for the constitutional law to regulate government management of market behaviors according to the requirement of a law-based government, put in place an effective mechanism for realizing human rights protection, comprehensively boost the social development and progress, further expand the fields and scope of foreign exchanges, integrate with the international community while better protecting China's own characteristics, and orderly develop socialist modernization.

1.4.10 Improve Studies on the Basic Theories of the Socialist Democratic System

Democratic issues are closely connected with constitutionalism theories. China's people's congress system is the socialist democratic political system established on the basis of the people's democratic system. Over the past 5 decades since the establishment of the people's congress system, we have made great achievements in building the democratic system. There are certain deficiencies, especially in the electoral system where people feel disappointed in many ways. In this connection, there is a must to take developing socialist democracy as the top priority in building a socialist constitutional government. At the same time, there is also a need to closely link democratic system building with the socialist modernization. There would be no modernization without democracy. China's traditional constitutional law had in-depth studies on the socialist democratic system with the people's congress system as the basis, and a set of rather mature democratic theories have taken shape. However, in face of the new issues and new situation of the socialist modernization, there is a must to re-understand the feature of socialist democratic value and the function of the socialist democratic system, explore a new democratic form in conformity with modern democratic political practices. In particular, there is a must to deeply study the democratization of the electoral system and further develop the legitimacy theory and democracy theory in China's constitutional law.

1.4.11 Enhance Theoretical Studies on the Relations Between the International Law and Constitution

The relations between international law and constitution have also been a basic constitutional category neglected by traditional constitutional law. With the further development of the opening up and the accelerated integration of China with the international community, studies on the relations between international law and constitution can organically combine international principle of rule of law with domestic principle of rule of law and establish an international law protection system and domestic law guarantee system with human rights protection as the core. Strengthening studies on the relations between the international law and constitution can further expand and enrich traditional law-based theories, organically unite the legitimate theory of domestic laws and the legitimacy theory of international law, maximally safeguard national interests, guard national sovereignty, and explore a new legal order of the international community in conformity with today's international relations.

1.4.12 Deepen Theoretical Studies on the Relations Between Constitution and Branch Laws

The relations between constitution and branch laws come as a basic theoretical issue that has long been overlooked by China's law circle. Just the lack of necessary scientific and rational value connections between constitution and branch laws has long separated the constitutional law and branch laws in terms of theories and resulted in the lack of organic connections between the two. Both constitutional law and branch laws have rarely probed into issues of each other, which have caused the disconnection between theoretical features and actual functions of constitution. From another point of view, due to the lack of theoretical guidance of constitutional law, the legal principles of branch laws have failed to be effectively established, the basic theories of branch laws are less scientific and narrowly applied. Therefore, there is a must to carry out in-depth, meticulous and effective studies on the relations between constitution and branch laws so as to fundamentally reverse the weak position of constitutional law in the entire legal theory research field.

In summary, during the "11th FYP" period, China's theoretical studies on constitutional law not only need to highlight major issues and new issues but also focus on basic issues of traditional constitutional law, and enrich the constitutional knowledge system and improve the guiding function of constitutional law in branch laws and constitutional practices through constantly expanding the issue field of constitutional studies.

2 Building and Development of China's Constitutional Law Theory Research System Over the Past Three Decades

Constitutional law studies are the science with constitution as the research object. In a strict sense, constitution didn't exist in China in the ancient times. Forced by the situation, the Qing Government decided to reform the political system in the aftermath of the Opium War. The Qing Government sent five ministers abroad for observing the constitutionalism of various countries. Soon afterwards, the Qing Government issued an imperial decree on preparations for constitutionalism. The Qing Government promulgated *the Constitutional Outline Made by the Imperial Order* on September 2, 1908. It is China's first legal document with constitutional significance and symbolizes the 100-plus years of history of China's constitutionalism. China's history of constitutionalism was also the process of the Chinese people's fight for democracy and freedom and gradual realization of being masters of the country. Along with the reform of constitution and the change of concepts, China's constitutional theories have also seen gradual improvement ever since its emergence. As early as in late nineteenth century and early twentieth century, Chinese scholars started to translate and introduce western works on constitutional law, including constitutional law books of such western constitutionalists as Montesquieu, Duguit, Dicey, and Tatsukichi Minobe. While introducing western constitutional theories, many scholars began to explore China's constitutional studies. Liang Qichao was an important representative. Liang Qichao wrote many works, including works on constitutional law. His works on constitutional law include *On Similarities and Differences among Constitutions of Various Countries*, *Three Major Spirits of Constitution*, *Private Discussions on Chinese Congress System*, *On Constitutionalism*, *Brief Introduction to Constitutionalism*, *Constitutional Government and Political Morality*, *Duty Cabinet Interpretation* and *On Enlightened Despotism*, etc.[40] Liang Qichao made systematic introductions and comprehensive comparative studies on major academic issues, including western theories on nature of state and form of government, "tripartite" political system, duty cabinet system, congress, and constitutionalism system, electoral system, local autonomy system, rule of law and law of utilitarianism, etc. in *On Similarities and Differences among Constitutions of Various Countries*, *On Legislative Power*, *Three Major Spirits of Constitution*, *Private Discussions on Chinese Congress System*, *Theories of Jurist Master Montesquieu*, *Theories of Political Master Bluntchli* and *Theories of Leading Utilitarian Scholar Bentham*, etc. His study objects included almost all leading countries that had established constitutional system back then, such as the United States, Britain, Germany, France, Japan, Italy, Austria, the Netherlands, Belgium, Sweden, Spain Portugal, etc. These studies established the position of Liang Qichao as the earliest founder of constitutional law in China.[41] In early twentieth century, Sun Yat-sen put forward the "Five-power Constitution" theory. He divided state political power into two parts, namely political power and governing power. According to him, political power includes four civil rights, namely the right to vote, the right to recall, the right of initiative and the right to revote, and the people rely on these four rights to manage the government. Governing power refers to the complete government authority organized under the "Five-power Constitution". The so-called five-power refers to administrative power, legislative power, judicial power, procuratorial power and

[40] Fan [5].

[41] Fan [6].

examination power that independently operate and mutually supervise for counterbalance. During the period of the Republic of China, a great number of constitutional research achievements were presented, such as *Comparative Constitution* written by Wang Shijie and Qian Duansheng and *Constitutional Law* by Zhang Zhiben, etc. Taking Shanghai back then as an example, constitutional studies were extensive and rich in contents and nearly 200 types of books were published. Some books propagated the "Five-power Constitution" theory of Sun Yat-sen. Some criticized the provisional constitution, constitutional draft, and constitution of the government of the Northern Warlords and the Kuomintang government. Some mainly introduced and discussed the new-democratic constitutional movement led by the Communist Party of China. There were also quite many papers discussing constitution and human rights. *The Eastern Miseellany* and *Xin Yue* were the strongholds. Shanghai scholars started to publish their works on constitutional studies and began to attach importance to studies on comparative constitution in late 1920s and early 1930s. In 1940s, constitutional studies mainly focused on the formulation and promulgation of the constitution of the Republic of China and arguments over different opinions.[42]

After liberation, China's constitutional studies completely abandoned previous constitutional theories. At the same time, constitutional theories experienced the baptism of Marxism, and the constitutional law with class analysis as the fundamental method was created. However, the constitutional law was heavily influenced by the Soviet theory of state and even accepted it completely and uncritically. The constitutional community during this period translated and introduced a large number of works on Soviet constitutional system and theories. Yet, China's constitutional law studies are still unconsciously influenced by those general principles of constitutional theories in the period of the Republic of China. After all, many Chinese constitutionalists in early days went through the period of the Republic of China, including Qian Duansheng and Zhang Youyu who had written many papers on the constitution and works before liberation. Many of their standpoints were based on the constitutional theories of that period of time. Many subsequent constitutionalists felt their influence somewhat due to their mentoring relationship and inherited some of their general principles related to constitutional law. During the Cultural Revolution period, constitutional teachings and studies in the real sense were almost completely brought to stagnation. As forced by the political situation, discussions on the constitution were restricted in many ways. Constitutional law suffered grave political influence, so it is far from being significant in academy.

After 3 decades of reform and opening-up, China's constitutional studies are experiencing the period of recovery and prosperity.[43] China's constitutional research quality has been constantly improved, and there are increasingly more research achievements in papers on the constitution, works, and comments.

[42]Shanghai Social Science Records edited by Shanghai Social Science Records Compilation Committee: Shanghai Academy of Social Sciences Press, 2002 edition.

[43]Han [7].

Besides, constitutional research contents are also being enriched and refined. The Fifth Session of the National People's Congress held in September 1980 adopted the resolution on the amendment to the constitution. The current constitution was issued on December 4, 1982. Afterwards, interpreting the current constitution has become an important proposition of the academic circle and constitutional theories have continuously developed. After the promulgation of the current constitution, some senior constitutionalists who took part in drafting the constitution, such as Zhang Youyu, Wang Shuwen, Xu Chongde, and Xiao Weiyun emancipated their minds, blazed new trails in a pioneering spirit and took the promulgation of the new constitution as the opportunity to build and improve the framework of constitutional law system. They laid a solid foundation for China's constitutional development. In 1983, *Constitutional Law*, a trial textbook on legal science edited by Mr. Wu Jialin for institutions of higher learning was published.[44] This book was the first textbook after the promulgation of the new constitution. The book systematically stated the basic principles of constitution and comprehensively and amply stated and interpreted the basic principles and specific norms of the 1982 Constitution. Since then, constitutional teaching books mushroomed on the scene and strongly boosted the development of China's legal education undertaking and constitutional studies.

Constitutional Research Association of China Law Society was founded on October 12, 1985 as a national academic organization under the leadership of China Law Society. The association has facilitated the development of China's constitutional research through various forms, such as organizing annual meetings and academic workshops, taking part in international exchanges and publishing collected works on constitutional law. Apart from 1988, 1989 and 1996, the association held its annual meeting on constitutional law every year. The annual meetings had discussions by centering on specific themes and provided wisdom and knowledge supports for solving theoretical and practical issues faced currently, such as the implementation of constitution, the improvement of the people's congress system, the guarantee of citizens' basic rights, and changes of constitution in the constantly reforming society. The association has also published proceedings of the annual meeting from time to time to summarize the current research results and provide the latest academic information. Furthermore, as the number of participants keeps increasing, the annual meeting has become an important platform for domestic constitutional scholars to exchange views and share insights and has boosted the development of constitutional studies.[45] Chinese constitutional scholars have also attended international constitutional exchanges and dialogues organized by International Association of Constitutional Law for many times with the purpose of offering experiences and lessons for China's constitutional studies and practices, thus promoting the progress of China's democratic rule of law.[46]

[44]Chief Editor Wu Jialin: Constitutional Law, Masses Publishing House, 1983 edition.

[45]Han and Hu [8].

[46]Mo [9].

As constitutional studies keep developing and deepening, the constitutional educational undertaking has also developed rapidly. In November 1981, the Department of Law of Peking University was authorized to confer a master degree. Since then, the number of constitutional master education bases has gradually increased. At present, there are 88 constitutional master education bases nationwide (including directly approved level-2 master education bases). The Institute of Law of Chinese Academy of Social Sciences (CASS) was the first doctor station in China. Mr. Zhang Youyu, a famous legist and one of the founders of constitutional law of the People's Republic of China (PRC) and Mr. Wang Shuwen are the first batch of doctoral supervisors of the station. Afterwards, Peking University, Renmin University of China, Wuhan University, Zhejiang University, Jilin University, Zhongnan University of Economics and Law, Xiamen University, Zhengzhou University and East China University of Political Science and Law, etc. have also been successively authorized to confer constitutional doctor degree. The continuous development of constitutional education has also facilitated the expansion of the community of constitutional scholars and the improvement of constitutional research level. Many excellent young and middle-aged constitutional scholars have come to the fore. Constitutional research development has also boosted the improvement of the constitutional education level and thus the forming of a virtuous cycle, making constitutional law become a popular subject from a byway of learning in the legal subject system.

2.1 Development of Basic Constitutional Theories Over the Past Three Decades

2.1.1 What Exactly Is Constitution?

In the early years of the twentith century, Liang Qichao had already given the answer for what constitution is. According to him, constitution is an unchangeable constitutional code and the source of all laws, and all people of a country, including state leader, officials and all citizens should abide by the constitution. He said that all new orders and laws should conform to the constitution. Besides, he also pointed out his opinions on the relations between constitution and civil rights. As he said, constitution and civil rights are inseparable, which is a timeless truth and also the experience of all countries.[47] This basic judgment of constitution became the general theory of constitutional law later on. After liberation, most of China's constitutional theories defined the concept of constitution from the perspective of "class will". Since the reform and opening up, the mechanical and single "class analysis method" gradually faded out of the field of constitutional research. This change was reflected by the answer of scholars for this fundamental question of

[47]Liang Qichao: *On Constitutionalism.*

what constitution is. In earlier constitutional studies, the source of the meaning of the word "constitution" was a basic question of constitutional research. Some scholars had detailed discussions on the origin of constitution from three different angles, namely English, Japanese and Chinese. The final conclusion was that constitution was a vocabulary in ancient Chinese, and was later introduced to Japan and added with new meanings and denotations introduced from the West after Meiji restoration. Then, it was reintroduced into China amid the ideological trend of reformation in late Qing Dynasty. As such, constitution completed the transformation from institutional system to fundamental law.[48] So far, there is still no final conclusion on when the word constitution was introduced to China, when and by whom it was first used in China, and what kind of Chinese document first used it. With regard to defining the meaning of constitution, China's constitutional community has different understandings. As affected by the Soviet constitutional theories, China's constitutional theories on the concept and essence of constitution in early days were still limited to class struggle theories. For instance, Chinese famous constitutionalist professor Wang Shuwen pointed out that we must take the essence of constitution into consideration when speaking of the concept of constitution because concept in philosophy needs to reflect the essential, primary and defining connections and features of an object. Therefore, we must know the essential feature of constitution besides knowing it as the fundamental law and fundamental system of a state when comprehending the concept of constitution. The essential feature of constitution is that it is the superstructure with a certain economic foundation, the concentrated reflection of the wills and interests of the ruling class, and reflects the contrast correlations of class forces.[49] Constitutional law with class analysis as the fundamental method emphasizes that constitution is the concentrated reflection of the wills and interests of the ruling class, and believes that "constitution is the fundamental law of a state with concentrated demonstration of the wills of the ruling class".[50] Constitution is the fundamental law of a state, the legalization of democratic system and the demonstration of the contrast correlations of class forces.[51] Comprehensions as such also include that constitution is the basic principles reflecting the wills and interests of the ruling class and regulating national system and social system and the fundamental law with the supreme legal authority.[52] Constitution is the basic principles reflecting the class wills and interests of the ruling class and defining and regulating national system and social system, and the fundamental law with the supreme legal authority.[53]

Being influenced by the Soviet constitutional law for some time, that "constitution is the fundamental law" has almost become the general theory of China's

---

[48]Hu and Zang [10].

[49]Wang [11].

[50]He [12].

[51]Chief Editor Wu Jialin: Constitutional Law, Masses Publishing House, 1983 edition, page 46.

[52]Xu [13].

[53]Tian [14].

constitutional theory. professor Zheng Xianjun believes that constitution is the mother law while laws are branch laws, and the relations between the constitution and laws can be understood in two ways: laws are born from constitution; laws should not defy the constitution. The former way of understanding embodies the "reproductive function" of constitution while the latter reflects the "monitoring function" of constitution. The reproductive function of constitution refers to the function of constitution as the legislative foundation of common laws. The monitoring function of constitution refers to the constitution's function of protecting branch laws and restricting the implementation of branch laws. Therefore, if focusing on the monitoring function of constitution while putting aside the reproductive function of constitution, then the viewpoint upholding constitution as the mother law has a very positive significance.[54] To this issue, professor Xie Weiyan pointed out that mother law is a key vocabulary for understanding China's constitution. According to him, the concept of mother law used to play a positive role in building democratic legal system, but it has showcased a negative influence on the building of China's current constitutionalism and rule of law, especially on the revision of constitution. Therefore, he proposed to eliminate the negative influence of the concept of mother law.[55] As a matter of fact, the arguments over "constitution is the mother law" are actually over the semantic interpretation of the concept of mother law. As interpreted by supporters of the concept, the concept of mother law contains the monitoring function of the system of law. According to the interpretation of naysayers, the concept of mother law easily neglects the implementation mechanism required by constitution.

With the development of the times and the further emancipation of academic thoughts, taking "contrast relations of political forces" as the essential feature of constitution has gradually replaced the class theory and become the new theory. This theory emphasizes that constitution reflects the contrast relations of political forces and represents the legalization of democratic system. Constitution reflects the contrast relations of various kinds of political forces, defines revolutionary victory and realistic democratic politics, stipulates national basic system and basic tasks and is the fundamental law with the supreme legal authority.[56] Constitution is a state's fundamental law regulating the rules for democratic governance; the generic term of the rules for state power and democratic operation, national basic policies, and legal norms for the fundamental rights and obligations of citizens; the concentrated reflection of contrast relations of forces and existing social and economic structural requirements.[57] Constitution is a state's fundamental law adjusting the fundamental social relations of the state, regulating the basic system and tasks of the state, reflecting the contrast relations of various political forces, and having the

[54]Zheng [15].
[55]Xie [16].
[56]Yu [17].
[57]Dong et al. [18].

supreme legal authority.[58] This core of social relations formed by centering on state power takes "state power formation" as an important concept showing the central meaning of constitution. According to this standpoint, the object of adjustment for constitution is the social relations formed by the people by revolving around state power. Therefore, it should be defined as such: constitution is a legal norm system adjusting a narrow sense of political relations that is the relations between people in taking part in, organizing and striving for state power." Based on this understanding, the concept of "state power formation" is used to represent people's behaviors and activities of taking part in, organizing and striving for state power and the relations thus formed would be "relations in state power formation", "subject of state power formation", "power of state power formation", "way of state power formation" and "procedure of state power formation", etc. which are all derived from this core concept of "state power formation". In this connection, constitution can be further defined as a legal norm system for adjusting relations in state power formation that is the interpersonal relations formed in the process of establishing important state systems and determining major state affairs.[59]

Different from those holding the view that constitution is the reflection of contrast relations of forces, some scholars reveal the characteristics of constitution from the relations between constitution and common laws. They observe that, as a state organic law, constitution is a kind of law and a state's fundamental law outmatching all other laws in both content and form.[60] This viewpoint attaches more importance to the universality of constitution and defines the concept of constitution from the perspective of the fundamental law. This point of view avoids the argument over whether constitution belongs to socialism or capitalism in constitutional studies. It is conducive to comparative studies on constitutions of countries in the world and provides a reference for China's constitutional studies.

As the constitutional community gradually reaches the consensus on taking constitutional rights as the core value of constitution, scholars start to comprehend constitution from the relations of the state and citizens and believe that constitution is the fundamental law adjusting the relations between the state (power) and citizens (right). Constitution is the fundamental law of a state that stipulates the national basic system and people's basic rights and obligations and reflects in concentration the fundamental interests of the class or group holding the state power.[61] Constitution is a state's fundamental law adjusting the relations between state organs and citizens in rights and obligations and the relations between state organs.[62] Constitution is the fundamental law stipulating how state power should serve civic rights.[63] The contents of constitution are actually the unity of opposites

[58]Yin and Wang [19].

[59]Yu [20].

[60]Zhu [21].

[61]Li [22].

[62]Zhu [23].

[63]Lyu [24].

of the two aspects, namely civic rights and state power.[64] Constitution should be defined as a branch law adjusting the basic relations between civic rights and state power and the fundamental law of a state. Civic rights give rise to state power and state power serves civic rights. In turn, civic rights restrict state power. The current constitutional studies lack the focus on the attribute of constitution as a law, making it difficult to implement the constitution just like other laws.[65]

As the extension of this kind of theory, some scholars have continuously abstracted the common attribute of interests of state power and civic rights, put forward the concept of social rights and comprehended constitution from the perspective of social rights.[66] The so-called social rights refer to the sum of all rights and powers of a certain society.[67] The relations between social rights have reflected the common attribute of all constitutional phenomena and the inner connections between each other, which can be mirrored by all stages of constitution, from its emergence to its development. It can be said that all constitutional principles and constitutional norms are established for the sake of distributing social rights and regulating social right application procedures. The review of national destiny and country history in the preface of constitutions of many countries was arranged for demonstrating the fairness and rationality of the social rights allocation plan in the body text of the constitution. Therefore, social rights are the direct object for the common adjustment of all constitutional principles and norms and almost the only basic issue commonly faced by all constitutional categories.[68]

On the basis of realizing the characteristic of constitution as the fundamental law, some scholars have tried to go beyond the constitution in the sense of form while including constitutional order in the categories of constitution in recent years. When it comes to the question of what exactly constitution is, professor Liu Maolin raised the rule of community theory. According to this theory, constitution is the rule for people to consciously organize a political community for survival and development and the social order built by this rule.[69] People's survival and development are the purpose and ultimate pursuit of constitution. Constitution is not necessarily connected with the state and state is nothing but a political community organized by constitution. Human beings are social beings and political community makes us truly human. Therefore, the rules for organizing a political community are fundamental. Constitution as a rule is a fundamental normative system of laws, and this system can be interpreted using the constitutional structure of idealistic constitution and practical constitution. Constitution is not only a norm but also a social order, i.e., constitutional order. Only the unity of constitution as a rule and the constitution as social order conforms to the existence of constitution in

64Liu [25].

65Wang [26].

66Tong [27].

67See Footnote 66.

68Tong [28].

69Liu [29].

concept.[70] According to this theory, constitution is not only the constitution in writing or the constitution in an ideal sense. The theory believes that constitution of a state should also include the constitutional order formed according to the constitution, and even the existence of a written constitution would mean the absence of constitution without this kind of constitutional order. When it comes to the point of emphasizing the effectiveness of constitution, the theory of community rule naturally has its positive significance.

2.1.2 Methods and Basic Categories of Constitutional Law

Defining which concepts belong to the basic categories of constitutional law depends importantly on one's methodological commitments. In this sense, method comes before category. China's constitution law used to be long affected by the Soviet constitution in method and strictly followed the so-called Marxist class analysis method in fundamental method. While analyzing specific issues, political words are commonly used to interpret articles on the constitution. Even just the opposite, articles on the constitution are directly taken as the basis for demonstrating the legitimacy of political decisions. Some scholars called the constitutional law method in early days the constitutional method of "no specificity" state.[71] Constitutional research methods are no different from the methods of general social science. The methods of philosophy, sociology politics, etc. are directly and widely applied by constitutional law. There is no independence to speak of in terms of the methods of constitutional law. Entering the twenty-first century, most constitutional scholars believe that constitutional law should be independent of other proximate subjects, especially politics in methodology.[72] Professor Lin Laifan is one of the pioneers of the constitutional community to pay attention to the methods of constitutional law. He raised his unique insights into the basic and special methods that should be applied by China's constitutional law. He noted that constitutional law indeed contains the sense of science and has the ability to reveal "facts" in terms of the basic method, but it also contains the elements of "knowledge" and engages in various kinds of complex value judgments. Therefore, there is a must to envisage the strained relations between facts and values and the specific value orientation of constitution. Specific methods of constitutional law actually refer to the methods of interpretation of constitution. However, in today's China, people despise the annotation of constitution and the methods of constitutional law are in a "no specificity" state.[73] Professor Tong Zhiwei also agrees that the theoretical part of China's constitutional law "from special subject analysis method to language system" is obviously the mechanical extension of the subject of historical

[70]Liu [29].

[71]Lin [30], p. 28.

[72]Zheng [31].

[73]Lin [30], pp. 7–40.

materialism, such as class analysis method, and nature of state, form of government, class, revolution, economic foundation, superstructure, productivity, productive relations and other terms. That means China's constitutional law studies are still lagging behind as it uses the methods of world view level to replace the specific subject analysis method that should be but has not yet been available, and its own specific subject analysis method has not yet been created.[74] Prof. Zheng Xianjun also agrees that the methods of constitutional law should be independent. She believes that one of the ways to make constitutional law become an independent subject is methodology, so there is a need to establish a method that is relatively independent from politics, even traditional philosophy, and history so as to make it become an irreplaceable and professional attempt in responding to constitutional issues and to build its subject autonomy.[75] To this issue, professor Miao Lianying tends to believe that traditional constitutional law studies are far enough from other methods, China's current constitutional law must refer to the methods of other subjects and the key is the capability of solving actual constitutional issues.[76]

Even so, most scholars have the consensus that constitutional law should have a specific method. However, scholars remain divided in how to establish China's constitutional research method at this point. professor Lin Laifan proposed the method for regulating constitutional law and believes that constitutional law studies are a subject with constitutional phenomena as the research object and constitutional norms are the axis of constitutional phenomena. Given the current situation of China's constitutional studies, constitutional law must be brought back to normativity and constitutional studies must be carried out by centering on the norms. Specifically speaking, that is to return back to moderately approximate normativity, but not completely back to the stance of traditional legal positivism.[77] Normativity-centered constitutional studies dare to speak of the important value of constitutional hermeneutics. This viewpoint taking constitutional hermeneutics as the core of constitutional law studies are also the consensus of many constitutional scholars. professor Han Dayuan is one of the scholars who first raised constitution hermeneutics. He believes that the development of modern constitutional theories and systems relies on the development and improvement of constitution hermeneutics to a large extent. He also believes that modern constitution hermeneutics has reflected the basic direction of modern constitutional development. At the same time, he has continuously advanced the research and application of constitution hermeneutic method and published a series of papers on constitution hermeneutic method.[78] The technology-based constitutional hermeneutic method easily makes constitutional law satisfied with the myth of value neutrality and become merely formalistic. Young scholar Zhang Xiang has realized that

74Tong [27].

75Zheng [31].

76Lin et al. [32].

77Lin and Zheng [33].

78Han and Zhang [34]; refer to Han and Zhang [35].

constitutional hermeneutics must pay attention to the value orientation of interpretation method. He pointed out that it is inevitable to include politics in constitutional interpretation. For the same articles on the constitution, there would be totally different interpretations under the guidance of different political theories. He also argued that constitutional interpretation must take root in the country's history of constitution formulation, normative environment and texts of constitution to accommodate "external argumentation", i.e., political theory argumentation and dispel its damage to the definition of constitutional interpretation.[79]

Prof. Zheng Xianjun summarized the main constitutional research methods in recent years and divided existing studies into three levels. First, it remains at the spiritual level of constitution. Second, it is research on constitutional principles. Third, it is normative research. We should break the categories of spirit, ideology and principle, and enter into the rules. We shouldn't stay inside the ivory tower of spirit for too long. We must always take norms as the basis and face the reality without overlooking spirit and let justice return back to the world.[80] For this point, professor Fan Jinxue raised a different point of view. Prof. Fan argued that constitutional studies should be based on three levels, namely value-based constitutional law, normative analysis of constitutional law and constitutional hermeneutics. Studies at these three levels respectively point to value jurisprudence, analytical jurisprudence and expository jurisprudence. The theoretical basis of value jurisprudence is natural jurisprudence. The theoretical basis of analytical jurisprudence is analytical-positivist jurisprudence. The theoretical basis of expository jurisprudence is philosophical and language hermeneutics. Value-based constitution studies and emphasizes the proposition of "what constitution should be". Normative analysis of constitutional law studies and emphasizes the proposition of "what constitution is". Constitution hermeneutics studies and emphasizes the proposition of understanding and interpreting the methods and skills of constitution normative significance. Different research objects and research methods mean different propositions emphasized. Professor Fan further noted that most scholars currently belong to the camp of value-based constitutional law and simply remain at the metaphysical level in various so-called interpretation activities. For that matter, he called on the shift of focus of constitutional law to studies on constitutional hermeneutics.[81]

While some accept traditional methods for studying the constitution, others have tried to build new ones. A case in point is Tong Zhiwei's proposal to fundamentally transform the original class analysis method and related basic theories of constitutional law. The specific practice is to use social rights as the core concept or fundamental category to establish social right analysis method as specific subject analysis method of constitutional law, and then use this new method as the core to reform and improve existing basic theories and form more systematic and scientific

---

[79]Zhang [36].

[80]Zheng [36].

[81]Fan [37].

professional basic theories.[82] As an analysis method, social right analysis method refers to the theoretical method starting from analyzing social rights to comprehending the basic social attribute, especially explaining and cognizing constitutional phenomena on the basis of the law of decomposition and re-decomposition.0[83] Corresponding to the social right analysis method of Tong Zhiwei, Zou Pingxue believes that constitutional research should introduce in economic analysis methods. The introduction of economic analysis methods means understanding the economic nature of constitutionalism and the economic logic contained with an all-round thinking from economy to constitutionalism from the perspective of economic category. The introduction of economic analysis methods also means exploring the interactive relations and integrated mechanism between economy and constitutionalism to find out the internal law of constitutional government development. The methodological foundation of economic analysis methods is Marxist economic philosophy, and the objective basis is laid by the deep and close relations between economy and law and between economy and politics. The theoretical basis is economics, constitutional law, and politics. He also observes that the existing economic philosophical view and theoretical basis have provided the guiding thoughts and necessary conditions in methodology for economic analysis of constitutionalism. Existing knowledge has not yet taken this topic as a systematic theme for studies, so the understandings and conclusions are sporadic and scattered. The relationship between constitutionalism and economy exists objectively, and they are also united inherently. We should reflect and represent the unity of objective objects through the logical and historical unity of research methods and research objects.[84] Constitutional studies should introduce in economic analysis methods and use an all-round thinking from economic to constitutionalism to comprehend the economic nature of constitutionalism and the economic logic contained.[85]

Hu Jinguang and Chen Xiong stand for studying China's constitutional research methods. They also propose to pay attention to distinguish the differences and connections between constitutional research methods and general legal research methods, political research methods, and constitutional interpretation methods. At the same time, they believe that China's constitutional research methods should also have the consciousness of Chinese problems and a relatively "neutral" stance towards China's constitutional text. They also propose to better handle the relations between the value of universality and Chinese characteristics in constitutional studies and correctly handle "time difference".[86] Professor Li Shuzhong further pointed out that the biggest challenge faced by China's constitutional law studies are "the particularity of China's problems". For a long time, our studies have been

[82]Tong [27].

[83]See Footnote 82.

[84]Zou [38].

[85]See Footnote 84.

[86]Hu and Chen [39].

mainly focusing on absorbing foreign advanced theoretical achievements but lacking the habit of solving China's problems from the perspective of China's history and China's social background. Modern China introduced in constitution with the initial purpose of making China rich and strong. Even today when citizens' freedom and rights are being protected, the pursuit of national prosperity and strength remains to be an important mission of constitution. Under this value orientation, the top priority of current constitutional studies should be how to build a constitutional theory system different from that of western capitalist countries and that of the former Soviet Union, how to understand the relations between the ruling party and constitution, how to look at the people's congress system and how to comprehensively interpret China's constitutional text.[87] Professor Liu Maolin believes that the Scientific Outlook on Development has a methodological significance for China's constitutional law to walk out of difficulties. He pointed out that constitutional law studies are the superstructure of thought according to Marxist social structural theory and comprehensive, coordinated and sustainable development cannot happen without the development of constitutional law. He also noted that constitutional law must follow up with social development and change with the times, which is also the requirement of Scientific Outlook on Development and the only way for China's constitutional law to break through the dilemma. According to him, Scientific Outlook on Development is the scientific outlook on social development and the scientific outlook on scientific development and requires China's constitutional law to follow the spirit of "putting people first" and take people's all-round and free development as the basic principle. Scientific Outlook on Development requires integrating the social philosophical theory of constitution and the interpretation theory of constitution so as to realize comprehensive, coordinated and sustainable development.[88]

2.1.3 Basic Categories of Constitutional Law

Along with the deepening studies on the basic categories of the science of law, the constitutional law studies have also been following the basic categories of constitutional law. professor Zhang Guangbo had already touched upon this problem as early as in the 1980s.[89] Some scholars observe that the basic categories of constitutional law represent the most basic concept running through the entire constitutional law and the pillar of the entire constitutional theory system.[90] Both improving the existing constitutional theory system and rebuilding a new theoretical framework are inseparable from this important basic research on establishing and defining the basic categories of constitutional law. Due to the lack of studies on

[87]Liu [40].
[88]Liu [41].
[89]Zhang [42].
[90]Li and Zhou [43].

the basic categories of constitutional law, China's constitutional community has not yet reached a consensus on the contents of the basic categories. Prior to the reform and opening-up, China's constitutional theories mostly took the nature of state, form of government, among other basic categories of politics as the basic categories of constitutional law. With the improvement of the overall legal research level, the science of law gradually became a subject with unique methods over time, so did the constitutional law. Thereupon, many political concepts were marginalized by constitutional law and constitutional law became gradually independent from politics and became a member of the law family. Many constitutional scholars started to define the basic categories of constitutional law, such as professor Li Long and professor Zhou Yezhong. They believe that constitutional law includes five pairs of basic categories, namely constitution and constitutionalism, sovereignty and human rights, nature of state and form of government, basic rights and basic obligations, and state power and state organ. professor Han Dayuan thinks that China's constitutional law should gradually abandon those obsolete categories and establish its own category system, and category is more abstract than concept. The categories of China's constitutional law should first belong to China. China's constitutional law should establish its own word system. Consensus formation is the gradual accumulation process. China's constitutional law should have its own category system as an independent category system is a significant symbol of the formation of an independent subject character. The professor further believes that the basic principle of "unity of history and logic" should be upheld in the process of building the basic categories of China's constitutional law. This principle unveils the constitutional development process and logic relations through various analyses of constitutional phenomena and represents the historical environment of the formation of constitutional society. Given this, the elements which constitute the basic categories of China's constitutional law include state-society; constitution-law; constitutionalism-democracy; human rights-basic rights; sovereignty-international community.[91]

Constitutional theories can be roughly divided into two major parts, namely state organs and basic rights. The logical starting point of the part of state organs is sovereignty concept. What's relative is the concept of human rights or basic rights. Constitutional theories before the reform and opening up principally took popular sovereignty as the core category of constitutional law. After the promulgation of the 1982 Constitution, constitutional scholars took the basic right articles of constitution as the starting point to elaborate the value of basic rights in detail. Basic rights have become the core category of constitutional law. In particular, theoretical studies on the basic categories of rights and obligations have also promoted the constitutional community to pay attention to the basic rights. Some scholars even take human rights as the most central basic category of constitutional law. professor Liu Wanghong believes that the basic categories of constitutional law belong to the ontology in legal philosophy, and there is only one core of the constitution, which is

[91]Han [44].

human right. All constitutional norms are centered on this core and on guaranteeing and realizing people's basic rights. He pointed out that the categories of constitution can be divided into three levels. First, it is the core category which should be connected with the ultimate goal to be adjusted and realized by the science of law. Second, it is the basic category which is determined by the basic relations and basic contradictions in the process of adjusting the social relations by a law. Third, it is the general category under the basic category, which is the extension of the basic category. As such, professor Liu observes that centering on the core category of human rights, the three main pairs of contradictions in constitutional relations are interpersonal relations, or the relations between ordinary citizens, the relations between the state and the society, and the relations between powers. Professor Lin Laifan upholds stability. He believes that the core category of constitutional law should be human rights-sovereignty. The two are just like the two centers of an ellipse, which are mutually contained and connected and form the inner tension structure of constitutional norms and constitutional theories. He pointed out that the concept of sovereignty overwhelms the concept of human rights and the tide of democracy overwhelms the tide of liberalism in the process of constitutional development in China. Both the concept of sovereignty and the concept of human rights are very important, but there is a value sequence relationship between them. From the perspective of both the traditional constitutionalism and China's constitutional government history, the concept of human rights comes before the concept of sovereignty. That is to say the mastering of public rights matters a lot, but this is not necessarily more important than how to exercise public powers.[92]

Constitutional theories generally believe that constitutionalism is dynamic constitution and the concept of constitutionalism is also a basic category of constitutional law. In 1992, the Institute of Law of CASS and China Association of Oriental Cultural Studies jointly organized a special academic workshop with the concept of constitutionalism as the theme. Most scholars believed that constitutionalism and constitution are both connected and different. Constitutionalism is the pillar, driver, and soul of constitution. Constitution would lose its authenticity without constitutionalism. For this point, professor Dong Heping further pointed out that the core and essence of constitutionalism are a high degree of unity of "governance by the people" and "governance by constitution" and a high degree of unity of "civic right supremacy" and "constitutional supremacy". To understand the concept of constitutionalism, there is also a must to correctly understand the relations between "governance by the people" and "governance by constitution". The elements of constitutionalism include "the element of governance by the people" and "the element of governance by constitution".[93] The element of governance by constitution refers to the necessary conditions for realizing governance by constitution, including constitution, review for constitutionality, constitutional litigation,

[92]Lin et al. [32].

[93]See Footnote 92.

and rule of law. Only the possession of these four elements together could realize governance by constitution and then form the exterior regularity of constitutionalism state. The latter refers to the necessary conditions for realizing governance by the people, including power restriction, power separation, and human rights, which is the inner regularity of constitutionalism state. Only demonstrating these three major elements, governance by constitution could be called constitutionalism.

In China's constitution, citizens are the subject of basic rights. According to most constitutional theories, the concept of citizen should be taken as a basic category of constitutional law for studies and promotion and should be particularly differentiated from the concept of people. This is because the concept of people has been politicized. In China, "people" is a political concept and was once thought to be an opposite concept of "enemy" and "object of dictatorship". As the legal attribute of constitution is underlined by the academic community, the politicized concept of people has been excluded from the basic categories of constitutional law. For example, professor Wang Guanghui believes that the concept of citizen is the basic category of constitutional law and using the concept of citizen in constitutional law quite appropriately and vividly expresses the identity and status of individuals in the state. However, regarding the comprehension of the concept of citizen, we commonly describe it as the people with the nationality of a country. In fact, the meaning of the concept of citizen is richer in content than the definition of the concept of citizen. Citizen is a concept representing human attribute and reflects the relations between individuals and the state and between the society and the state. Citizen is a legal statement of the role of man. The establishment of the concept of citizen is actually the legal confirmation of the subjectivity of human being. The most fundamental significance of unveiling the rich meaning of the concept of citizen for China to build a law-based country is the cultivation of individuals' consciousness of equality in the society. Young scholar Hu Honghong also agrees that the concept of citizen is a basic category of constitutional law, so he proposes to pay particular attention to the cultivation of civic consciousness and strengthen citizenship education in China at this point.[94]

On the basis of recognizing the attribute of constitution as "a national law", some scholars firmly believe that the form of government is also a basic category of constitutional law. professor Yu Depeng is an example. He believes that the form of government is basic category of constitutional law, and form of government includes three aspects in a general sense. The first element is the attribution in sovereign form and many countries directly stipulate the form of government. Second, it is the way of exercising sovereignty, which is an element that cannot be overlooked by the form of government. For some people, the representative system is not the form of government and there is no such statement even in teaching books. Yet, constitutions of many countries stipulate that representative system is

[94]Hu [45].

the form of government. Third, it is the relations between state organs.[95] Given this theory, some scholars pointed out that the concept of the form of government is in essence a political concept but not the concept of constitutional law and it is the category which already existed in constitutional law in 1950s. They also noted that the form the concept of the form of government has its special historical conditions, has already accomplished its historical missions, and shall not be taken as the basic category of constitutional law in politics at the current stage.

The constitutional community has convened two special workshops on issues related to the basic category of constitutional law but has not yet reached a rather consistent consensus in the contents of the basic categories. Regarding the development of the basic categories of China's constitutional law, professor Han further pointed out that Chinese constitutional law studies are different from China's constitutional law, and the process of building Chinese constitutional law studies are bound to be accompanied by the stage of China's constitutional law. He added that in the process of building Chinese constitutional law, there might be the possibility of using terms in the grey belt between political phenomena and constitutional phenomena, but Chinese constitutional law should gradually abandon these obsolete categories when it could be established and become mature.[96]

2.1.4 Theoretical System of Constitutional Law

During the period of the Republic of China, the constitutional law system could be basically divided into two parts, namely people's rights and obligations and state organs' organization, functions, and powers. The former included the types and meanings of all basic rights. The latter included state legislative organs, judicial organs, administrative organs, and local systems, etc.[97] With the formulation of the state constitution, the constitutional law system was basically studied based on the structure of constitutional code. This situation remained till the period after the reform and opening up. A mainstream version of teaching books on constitutional law used to take the system of constitutional code as the basis. Apart from the introduction, the teaching books mainly covered seven chapters, namely the pandect of constitution, emergence and development of constitution, state nature, state form, basic rights and obligations of citizens, electoral system and state organs.[98] The teaching books on constitutional law in recent years have generally applied the binary pattern of citizens' basic rights and obligations and state organs in system arrangement. Some examples include *The Chinese Constitution* compiled by Hu Jinguang and Han Dayuan. This book is composed of three parts, namely overview

95Lin et al. [32].

96See Footnote 95.

97Zhang [46].

98Xu [47].

of constitution, basic rights and basic obligations of citizens, and state organs.[99] With the constantly deepening reflections and studies on China's constitutional research methods and basic categories of constitutional law, scholars have started to be committed to building a new system of constitutional theories. professor Wang Guanghui pointed out that, for a long time, China's law community has various opinions on defining constitutional research objects, which have not only affected our confirmation of constitutional research objects but also led to the failure in building a theoretical constitutional theory system and thus fundamentally affected our understandings of the spirit and core value of constitution. Anyhow, the meaning of constitutional research objects should be comprehended based on the adjustment objects of constitution without deviating from the theme which is relations between state powers and civic rights. Hereby, the theoretical system of constitutional law should be composed of original theories, theory of state power, theory of civic rights and theory of coordination.[100] Prof. Tong Zhiwei also holds the view that China's constitutional law teachings and studies since 1970s have been centering on the formation, interpretation, implementation, and revision of the 1982 Constitution reflecting the social and economic development, which were, of course, limited by the development situation of the latter to a large extent. Having developed rapidly, but China's constitutional teachings and studies still remain at a lower level as a whole. The principal reason lies in China's relatively backward political system reform. Besides, constitutional government practices still cannot provide necessary and enough research resources, and constitutional teachings and studies lack realistic driving force. In recent years, China's constitutional teachings and studies have witnessed some new development trends. These new development trends have adapted to the requirement of China's social and economic development of the current stage and have led China's constitutional research teachings and studies in a new direction.[101] Zhu Fuhui believes that China's current constitutional law system is rather obsolete and doesn't adapt to governance by law and to the need of building a socialist country under the rule of law. Zhu Fuhui proposes to take the theory of the mutual relations between civic rights and state powers as the principal line of constitutional law system. Zhu Fuhui also proposes to divide the contents of constitutional law into four parts, namely general introduction, theory of state, theory of citizen and typical case analysis. He takes regulating state powers and safeguarding civic rights as the guiding ideology of all theories. This is an important thought of constitutional law system innovation.[102] Zhou Yezhong and Zhou Youyong also believe that rebuilding the constitutional law theory system should first and foremost correctly address such problems as ethical basis, social basis, and logical starting point. According to them, human supremacy and weakness are the ethical basis of constitutional law; the duality of state and society

[99] Hu and Han [48].
[100] Wang [49].
[101] Tong [50].
[102] Zhu [51].

is the social basis of constitutional law; popular sovereignty is the logical starting point of constitutional law; civic rights and state powers are the basic contradiction of constitutional law. The constitutional law theory system built with the relations between civic rights and state powers as the principal line includes four interlinked components. First, it is the basic theory of constitution, including the theoretical foundation and basic phenomena of constitution. Second, it is the theory of civic rights including such contents as citizens, human rights, civic rights, citizens' constitutional rights, and obligations. Third, it is the theory of state power including state power and state nature, structural system of state power, state power exercising organizations and state power operating procedures. Fourth, it is the theory of constitutional operation, including constitutionalism, formulation, and revision of constitution, constitutional implementation and interpretation, and constitutional government procedures and constitutional litigation.[103]

Some other scholars stand for building the theoretical system of constitutional law with right or power as the cornerstone. Lyu Taifeng is an example. He thinks that the constitutional law system should be rebuilt with rights and powers as the center, and should include five parts after being rebuilt, including the basic principles of constitution, guaranteeing the basic rights of citizens, monitoring state powers, restricting party rights and monitoring constitutional implementation.[104] Prof. Chen Baoyin considers that China's constitution affirms the socialist democracy in the primary state of socialism in the form of law and the essence of socialist democracy is the people's role as masters of the country. According to the requirement for people's exercise of state powers, China's constitutional law system should be composed of seven specific legal systems. These seven legal systems are constitutional theory, civil status, nature of state and form of government, state structure, state agency, electoral system, and political party system.[105] Professor Zhao Shiyi believes that property right is the historical starting point of constitution and the cornerstone of the entire constitutional government system. He proposes to use property right as the footstone category to build the theoretical system of economic constitutional law. This system falls into three major parts, namely general theory of economic constitution, theory of economic rights and theory of economic power. In the general theory of economic constitution, the relations between citizens and the state can be understood as the conflict between individual property rights and state's financial rights. As such, we can make clear that market economy is the economic neutrality principle of the economic constitution under constitutionalism, the law from resource allocation to right allocation, among other constitutional propositions. When it comes to theory of economic rights, property right is taken as the starting point of rights to study the right system featuring the dualistic confrontation of economic freedom and economic rights in the logic of the conflict and coordination between contract freedom and labor right. As regards the

[103]Zhou and Zhou [52].
[104]Lyu [53].
[105]Chen [54].

theory of economic power, financial power is taken as the core content to build the national economic power system. The train of thought is that state is maintained by taxation and financial power is the foundation of all state powers. Economic constitutional law studies are a key part of the constitutional subject group and belong to an inter-discipline between constitutional law and economics.[106]

Prof. Tong Zhiwei built the constitutional law system with "legal rights" as the core category and came up with the legal rights-based constitutional theory. In his opinion, the interests behind rights and powers have common characteristics and connecting rights and powers forms this category of "legal rights" (or, "social rights") as the core category of the legal rights-based constitutional theory. Given the two extremes in terms of the basis of law, namely individual basis and state basis, the author pointed out that constitution and even all laws should neither take rights as the basis nor take powers as the basis. The author proposed to take legal rights as the basis and pursue maximized legal rights.[107] Prof. Tong's constitutional theory with legal rights as the core has had greater influence in the constitutional community and the legal community at large but failed to be widely accepted. This theory has been even questioned by some scholars. Some researchers pointed out that there are drawbacks in proposing the concept of social rights and taking it as the constitutional research method and the logical starting point of constitutional law system. The drawbacks are that the concept of social rights is more abstract and includes fewer categories compared with the theory focusing on the relations between civic rights and state powers, and there is no basis for taking it as the logical starting point of constitutional law subject. Also, social rights are neither summarized from practices of constitutionalism nor deduced from constitutional theories. Instead, social rights are concluded by simply adding state powers and civic rights.[108]

Some scholar pointed out that Mr. Tong Zhiwei tried to unite such categories as right and interest, wealth and freedom, power and right from the perspective of the definition of social rights, and social rights are the footstone category of the unity of above categories. However, Mr. Tong Zhiwei didn't make necessary academic statements of a series of questions, including whether individual right could definitely direct single specific interest; whether the entire rights correspond to the entire social interests; whether rights can be taken as a kind of independent interests; whether rights as interests are identical with interests relative to rights. Therefore, the academic structure simply unifying rights and interests in form and content is rather offhand logically and features forced logic. Moreover, whether freedom can be seen as the wealth dominated by ownership relations? Whether definitive wealth could reflect the essence of the concept of freedom? In what sense of interest does freedom mean? What most puzzling is that civic rights and state powers become the categories that can be totally added in nature in the logical

[106]Zhao [55].

[107]Tong [56].

[108]Zhao and Zou [57].

group of Mr. Tong Zhiwei. However, the correlation of identity and subordination still exists in the additive relations. Mr. Tong Zhiwei directly adds the two categories, namely civic rights, and state powers together through identical logics without detailed analysis of above relations and without any explanation of the possibility of other relations. Anyway, this kind of inference method lacks preciseness academically.[109]

Prof. Liu Maolin divides the theoretical system of constitutional law into three aspects. First, it is the social philosophy theory of constitution (including constitutional politics, constitutional philosophy, constitutional sociology, constitutional history, and constitutional economic analysis, etc.). Second, it is explanatory theory of constitution. It is the legal theory of pure constitution with the constitution as the practical law as the research object. In terms of its scientific value, task, and function, the explanatory theory of constitution needs to resolve questions about constitution law in the legal development process. These questions include what constitution as a law is; how constitution was formed and constructed, how constitution allocates and regulates state powers, how constitution confirms and protects civic rights, and so on and so forth. Looking from the operation process of law, the explanatory theory of constitution is committed to providing theoretical interpretations and technical assistance for the enactment, revision, interpretation, and application of constitution so as to realize and give play to the role and function of constitution as the supreme law. Third, it is the relations between the social philosophy theory of constitution and the explanatory theory of constitution. The professor believes that it is simply the integration of the social philosophy theory of constitution and the explanatory theory of constitution that has built up the theoretical quality and application value of constitution as a branch subject of independent science of law. The social philosophy theory of constitution makes constitution become a science. The explanatory theory of constitution makes constitutional law become a science of law that is different from general theories and branch laws, such as science of criminal law and science of civil law.[110]

2.2 *Development of Branch Subjects of Constitutional Law*

As more and more scholars have paid attention to and remained dedicated to the establishment of branch subjects of constitutional law, constitutional studies have presented multiple branches since 1990s. Among these branches, those holding a dominant position include studies on the constitutional theory system (constitutional philosophy), studies on constitutional text (constitutional hermeneutics) and studies on constitutional politics from the perspective of state-building (constitutional politics). Their common characteristics are normative studies on constitution

[109]Mo [58].

[110]Liu [41].

and the focus on the question of what constitution is. In addition to these branches, there are also constitutional economics, constitution, and literature, constitutional sociology, constitutional anthropology, etc.[111] Thanks to the efforts of scholars, China's constitutional studies have received fruitful results in many areas, including constitutional philosophy, constitutional sociology, comparative constitutional law, basic right theory, and Chinese constitutional history, etc.

2.2.1 Constitutional Philosophy

Entering the new century, the so-called research on constitutional philosophy appeared in China's constitutional law. Actually, in foreign constitutional theories, it is relatively rare to see the concept as an alleged subject strictly corresponding to constitutional philosophy, but there are similar concepts, such as constitutional philosophy or constitutional law's philosophical foundations. What needs to be pointed out is that there are abundant related studies, and the fields involved are rather broad, even involving the categories of political philosophy and moral philosophy. No final conclusion has yet been made on whether the concept of constitutional philosophy can be called a kind of knowledge with independent character. However, studies in this field are indeed necessary for constitutional law. Some scholars also call constitutional philosophy as constitutional logics.[112] Professor Mo Jihong believes that China's constitutional law must focus on the most fundamental logical issues and build the constitutional philosophy conforming to the requirement of the socialist constitutionalism with Chinese characteristics based on the respective scientific features of moral philosophy, cultural philosophy, and logical philosophy in order to get out of the dilemma.[113]

However, there is a need to demonstrate whether constitutional philosophy can be established as a branch subject of constitutional law. To this, professor Li Qi observes that constitutional law studies have to answer a basic question: what is constitution? This question can be further translated into three specific questions: why does human life need constitution; what kind of constitution does human life need; in what way does human life realize our purposes through constitution? These are three elementary questions related to constitution and they involve the legitimacy of constitution, so there is a reason to understand it as constitutional philosophy.[114] Certainly, constitutional philosophy has philosophical temperament, but it still needs philosophical tests. However, it is not philosophy in itself. Instead, it belongs to the scope of constitutional law. Wen Zhengbang thinks that constitutional philosophy is a theoretical subject of constitutional law that uses philosophical opinions and methods to think and study theoretical and practical problems

---

111 Hou [59].

112 Mo [60].

113 Mo [61].

114 Li [62].

of constitution from philosophical perspective. Constitutional philosophy is the highest level of theoretical constitutional law and one of the very important philosophies in-branch laws. Constitutional law summaries and generalizes the contents and issues with world views and the importance of methodology through rethinking and recognizing existing theoretical results of constitutional law, that is philosophical reflection, and through philosophical review, cognition and analysis of constitutional practices. This is to reveal the deepest essence and most common regularity of constitutional and constitutional government phenomena, thus providing direct philosophical guidance and basis for the development of constitution and constitutionalism. That is to say constitutional philosophy is a theoretical and systematic knowledge of world outlook and methodology for issues related to constitution and constitutionalism. In general, it is the theory of legal philosophy for issues about constitution and constitutionalism. It helps us look far ahead and aim high and grasp the overall, macroscopic and strategic issues in developing constitution and building constitutionalism. It also helps us better understand the essence and foundation of numerous and complicated issues related to constitution and constitutionalism.[115] Professor Xie Weiyan believes that constitutional philosophy is to explore and build a subject of idealistic constitution from the perspective of human rationality and on the basis of introspecting and criticizing the science of constitution. Introspection and criticism are not suspicion or denial of constitutional science. It is simply unsatisfied with the knowing of the state of practical constitution but rather explore the root cause. It sticks to going deep into the bottom of the science of constitution and seeking for the ultimate basis. Constitutional philosophy is a form superior to the science of constitution. Therefore, constitutional law should develop towards constitutional philosophy from constitutional science.[116] Professor Liu Zhigang also holds the view that constitutional philosophy is a subject upgraded from legal theory contained in constitution to philosophy for studies. Constitutional philosophy as a basic theory of constitutional law studies is highly relevant to the development of constitutional law. In China's constitutional law field, constitutional philosophy remains to be filed not yet being explored.[117]

Discussing the philosophical foundation of constitutional interpretation also belongs to the category of generalized constitutional philosophy. Xu Zhendong has studied the history and schools of constitutional interpretation on the basis of probing into philosophical hermeneutics and legal hermeneutics and come up with his opinions on constitutional interpretation. He had systematic and comprehensive investigations into the relations between constitutional interpretation and philosophical hermeneutics and revealed the philosophical basis for the historical development and constitutional interpretation philosophy. He has also studied and recapped various kinds of active methodologies and hermeneutic thoughts in contemporary legal field, such as anti-foundationalism, deconstructivism,

[115]Wen [63].

[116]Xie [64].

[117]Liu [65].

neo-pragmatism, construction of explanatory theory and proceduralism, etc. On top of that, he has probed into the possibility of establishing the norms for the legitimacy of constitutional interpretation.[118]

2.2.2 Constitutional Sociology

Constitutional sociology is a branch subject of constitutional law by using sociological method to study and identify the subject characteristics of constitutional law.[119] Professor Dong Fanyu was one of the scholars who first proposed the concept of constitutional sociology. He pointed out that constitutional sociology is an empirical science taking constitutional process as social process and connecting constitutional phenomena like constitutional norm, constitutional system, constitutional consciousness, constitutional relations and constitutional operation with social phenomena like politics, economy, and society for empirical studies.[120] Professor Han Dayuan also pointed out that the concept of constitutional sociology emphasizes the connections between constitutional phenomena and other social phenomena and highlights the social foundation for the existence of constitution. He also noted that, under the framework of constitutional sociology, constitutional law as a social science could establish a corresponding relationship with the constitutional law as a normative science. According to him, constitutional sociology is a dynamic system with historical nature. He said that the core of the concept of constitutional sociology is the practical function of constitution and plays its academic influence through the social life evaluation system.[121] At the same time, there are also preliminary statements on the objective, function, basic framework and methodology of constitutional sociology. Constitutional sociology is a subject using sociological method to study constitutional law. The constitutional structure with sociological significance is based on the relations between public authorities safeguarding freedom and economic society organized in accordance with private laws. The separation between state and society is the precondition for the establishment of constitutional relations. The demarcation between public and private areas is the foundation for the existence of limited power government. The confrontation between public power and private power is the constitutional demonstration of classical basic rights. Social rights are the products of mutual penetration of state and society.[122]

Constitutional sociology is obviously in its initial stage for China's constitutional law. When it comes to its independence as a subject, the question and challenge first faced are probably the difference between constitutional sociology and politics or

[118]Xu [66].

[119]Zheng [67].

[120]Dong [68].

[121]Han [69].

[122]See Footnote 119.

political sociology, especially when they all feature the characteristic of applying sociological method, making it difficult to define the subject research scope. For example, constitutional system in sociological sense and political system have no essential difference. Constitutional concept and political concept are duplicated in many aspects. Under the premise that many constitutional phenomena are also political research objects, probably only the studies maintaining certain distance with constitutional norms while applying sociological method could be classified as studies on constitutional sociology. This kind of delimitation method might be promoted to the delimitation between legal sociology and sociological jurisprudence.

2.2.3 Comparative Constitutional Law

Comparative studies on constitutional systems of countries in the world have a vital referential significance for China's constitutional practices and building of the rule of law. To this, professor Lin Laifan pointed out that, if we can at least refer to some foreign jurists' research methods, especially empirical research methods, and establish a set of rigorous and scientific academic norms in China's constitutional theory studies, then we could accordingly improve China's constitutional theories and facilitate gradual and calm settlement of ideological research problems. Finally, we could integrate them with international constitutional theories even at the stage when political ideology still profoundly affects the research status of constitutional theories.[123] Before the reform and opening-up, China's constitutional studies were basically limited to political analysis and typically referred to the Soviet constitutional theories but ignoring and criticizing the constitutional law of other countries. So, comparative constitutional studies were still at the level before the founding of the RPC. In mid-1980s, the name of comparative constitution began to be widely used in China's legal community. At the same time, some influential works on comparative constitutional law were published, including *Comparative Constitution and Administrative Law* by professor Gong Xiangrui, *Outline of Comparative Constitution* by professor Zhang Guangbo, *Comparative Constitutional Law* by professor He Huahui and *Constitution and Government of Western Countries* by professor Zeng Guangzai. These works inherited the research achievements of predecessors, absorbed many new ideas and made innovations in system content and opinion. These works also laid a foundation for in-depth studies on comparative constitutional law and played a powerfully promoting role.[124] Since then, works on comparative constitutional law have kept cropping up. The representative works include *Collected Works on Constitutional Comparative Studies*[125] edited by

[123]Lin [70].
[124]Wang [71].
[125]China Democracy and Legal System Publishing House, 1993 edition.

professor Li Buyun, *Comparative Constitution*[126] by professor Wang Guanghui, *Western Constitutionalism System (Vol. I, Vol. II)*[127] by professor Zhang Qianfan, *Comparative Constitution—a Comparative Study of the Constitution of Eight Countries*[128] by professor Shen Zongling and *Comparative Constitutional Law*[129] by professor Han Dayuan, etc. As constitutional studies keep deepening, the status of comparative constitutional law as an independent subject has been widely acknowledged; the research results of comparative constitutional law have begun to exert an academic influence on legislative and national major decisions; comparative constitutional law studies have provided a knowledge and theoretical foundation for improving the constitutional subject system; comparative constitutional law offers knowledge and analytical tools for dialogues and communication between subjects; comparative constitutional studies have created good environmental conditions for China's constitutional law to move towards the world, for global constitutional circles to understand China's constitutional law and for the development of China's constitutional government system.[130]

With respect to the purpose of comparative constitutional law, professor Dong Heping believes that comparative constitutional law studies are not for comparing the "goodness or badness" of constitutions of different countries in the world but for finding out their differences. The comparative constitutional law seeks to find out whether some specific system plays a promoting role in China's building of the rule of law under a specific environment. In summary, it is for comparing the differences, figuring out the law, summarizing experiences for our own purposes. professor Zheng Xianjun further pointed out that foreign laws will exert influence on the constitutional judgment and constitutional interpretation of a state with the globalization. For instance, some individual judges of the Supreme Court of the United States lately tried to quote the constitutional judgment cases of the EU, which was severely criticized by some conservative judges of the Supreme Court of the United States. However, this attempt indeed showcased the trend of referring constitutional values. Some scholars raised the question of whether globalization in Asian and African countries will be manifested as the strong influence of Europe and the United States. They also believe that reference should be mutual; otherwise, it would become another kind of cultural aggression.[131] With regard to comparative constitutional method, professor Ma Ling pointed out that we have always been emphasizing the differences while neglecting the commonalities of comparative constitutional methods. On the one hand, the so-called commonalities include the analysis of similar constitutional phenomena and laws under the same and similar

---

[126]Wuhan University of Hydraulic and Electrical Engineering Press, 1998 edition.

[127]China University of Political Science and Law Press, 2000 edition, China University of Political Science and Law Press, 2001 edition.

[128]Peking University Press, January 2002, 1st edition.

[129]Higher Education Press, 2003 edition.

[130]Han [72].

[131]Liu [40].

social and cultural backgrounds. For example, we talked much about the constitutions of countries like the United States, Britain, Germany, France, and Japan that have quite different system backgrounds with that of China, but we overlooked studies on constitutions of Russia (and former Soviet Union) and eastern European countries. On the other hand, the commonalities also include the analysis of constitutional values and constitutional systems generally applicable to some transnational constitutions. The most typical one is the system of basic rights of citizens.[132] Globalization has raised many new topics to comparative constitutional studies. To this issue, professor Mo Jihong believes that the development of globalization has resulted in the absence of corresponding new vocabularies in traditional constitutional theories. For example, the concept of the right to choose law emerged in foreign countries. That means individuals have the right to choose the applicable laws at will in case of the occurrence of some specific conflict. This concept is different from the concept of conflicting law in international private laws. Another example is that Toronto of Canada stipulates that Islamic citizens of different communities may choose to apply Sharia in family disputes. Vocabulary innovation in constitutional law studies is not the patent of foreign countries. China may also summarize or propose new constitutional concepts in line with its national conditions and practices and make contributions to the development of global constitutional law.[133]

2.2.4 Studies on Basic Right Theory

Constitutional right is the core value of constitution. Liang Qichao, the renowned thinker and reformer of late Qing raised his opinions on this point. In his view, without civic rights, even a perfect constitution would become a mere scrap of paper and useless. He also observed that constitution and civic rights were inseparable, which couldn't be changed and also represented global experiences of countries.[134] Research on basic rights has always been a principal content of constitutional law. That being said, most studies on basic rights in early days were carried out from the perspective of political philosophy or legal philosophy and focused on the legitimacy of basic rights and the guarantee of basic rights. For example, China's studies on constitutional rights in early 1980s mainly focused on the meaning and value of basic rights, such as the behaviors protected by constitutional basic rights and the significance and value of a specific basic right. Beyond that, there were also more studies on the basic rights from the perspective of legal philosophy and moral philosophy, such as the characteristics and legitimacy of constitutional basic rights, and the moral, historical and cultural basis of the basic rights confirmed by constitution. As constitutional studies become further refined,

---

[132] Liu [40].

[133] See Footnote 132.

[134] Liang [73].

constitutional scholars have paid more attention to the specific applications of constitutional basic rights. In other words, it is to take the basic right norms of constitution as legal norms for studies rather than merely study the moral basis and legitimacy of constitution. The starting point of this kind of studies is based on how to protect basic rights in the implementation of constitution. The principal method is comparative constitutional research method. It is to study by referring to the theories of countries with rather mature constitutional protection system for basic rights, such as Germany, the United States, and Japan. This kind of studies is quite popular among Chinese young scholars, such as Zhang Xiang. Zhang Xiang tried to establish a set of law hermeneutics for basic rights to conform to China's reality and the basic right articles of China's constitution while referring to the basic right theory of Germany in his studies on basic rights.[135] He Yonghong carefully and meticulously compared the review standards for basic right restriction between the United States and Germany and tried to establish a set of review benchmark system applicable to China's basic right system in studies on the constitutionality review standards for basic right restriction.[136] Wang Shucheng made comparative analysis of the basic right guarantee models of Germany and the United States and abstracted the universal laws, which have demonstrated the development direction of theoretical studies on basic rights.[137]

An overview of China's constitutional circle's research on basic rights indicates that it roughly experienced the process from value research to normative research. Studies in early days chiefly demonstrated the legitimacy of basic rights from the perspective of legal philosophy. With the wide recognition and acceptance of the concept of basic rights, the constitutional circle gradually refined the studies on basic rights and laid emphasis on the meaning of specific basic rights. That was to define what behaviors and interests belong to the scope of basic rights for protection. This can be seen as a kind of normative studies. In recent years, the constitutional circle has differentiated the rights protected by constitution from the rights protected by laws on this basis and has studied the basic rights under the framework of constitutionality review. These studies have boldly mirrored the research results of countries that have entered the stage under the rule of law to analyze the normative structure of constitutional basic rights and proposed the protection framework of "protection-restriction-restriction on restriction" of basic rights.[138]

2.2.5 Studies on the History of Constitution

Constitutional studies include studies on the history of constitution. Studies on the history of constitution can promote constitutionalists to accumulate profound

---

[135]Zhang [74].
[136]He [75].
[137]Wang [76].
[138]Lin and Ji [77].

cultural heritage. In this case, constitutionalists could observe the relations between constitution evolution and social development and deepen the understanding and comprehension of the current constitution and constitutional system in the historical development process from a strategically advantageous perspective. After the founding of the PRC, studies on the history of China's constitution have actually broken away from the development and the development degree already reached in the period of the Republic of China due to the change of state nature and the influence of ideology. Particularly, after the extension of the anti-rightist struggle and during the 10-year turbulent period of Cultural Revolution, it is naturally impossible to have normal studies on the history of constitution under the circumstance that legal educations and studies were almost all paralyzed.[139] Along with the recovery and development of legal education, China's studies on the history of constitution began to attract attention. Earlier research works on constitutional history included *Brief History of the Constitution of China* written by Zhang Jinfan and Zeng Xianyi. With China's reformist constitutional government movement in modern times and the constitutionalism fraud and constitution promulgation of the Qing Government as the starting point, this book respectively studied the development process of the constitutional system of Republican period and the constitutional system after the founding of the PRC. On this basis, the authors also historically classified the development of constitutional system.[140] *The Brief History of the Constitutionalism and Constitution in Contemporary China* written by professor Jiang Bikun was also one of the first books on studying the history of China's contemporary constitution. It is also one of the first works of constitutionalists on Chinese constitutional history.[141] The contents of the book with the history of constitutionalism and constitution in modern China as the theme involved the reformist reform movement, constitutional issues in late Qing Dynasty, interim constitution of the Republic of China, constitution of the period under the reign of the Northern Warlords, constitutional documents of Guangzhou and Wuhan national governments, constitutional issues of the Kuomintang government and the new-democratic constitutional government movement, among other aspects. The book comprehensively analyzed and assessed major historical events and figures related to the history of constitutionalism and constitution in China's modern historical development process. The book particularly analyzed the contents as stipulated by constitutional documents by persisting in the basic stance of Marxism–Leninism and class analysis method. The book used abundant historical documents as evidence in revealing the fake democracy and real despotism of the Qing Government, the Northern Warlords and the reign of the Kuomintang, explaining the democracy of constitutional documents of the revolutionary base areas led by the CPC, and comparing the new and old democratic constitutional government. The book integrated the history with theories and demonstrated

[139]Wang [78].

[140]Zhang [79].

[141]Jiang [80].

professor Jiang Bikun's profound academic background and rigorous scholarship. Professor Xu Chongde compiled the book titled *Constitutional History of the People's Republic of China* with his personal experience in taking part in the formulation of the constitution.[142] In this book, the author provided a great deal of first-hand data about constitutional history and vividly presented the process of amending the constitution, made analysis and evaluation in line with constitutional theories, and provided abundant materials for studying history and seeking the original meaning of constitutional norm. In this academic development history, many young constitutional scholars have also started to pay attention to studies on the history of constitution and written numerous related books.[143]

2.3 Studies on Hot Issues Related to Specific Constitutional Systems

2.3.1 Research on the People's Congress System

Over the past three decades, one of the most important theoretical studies on the people's congress system is whether the combination of legislative and executive powers is a matter of principle of China's people's congress system. The Chinese constitutional circle used to regard the combination of legislative and executive powers as a universal principle of the state power of socialist countries and make it contrast to capitalist "tripartite" political system to embody the system or principle with the superiority of socialist system. China's constitutional circle took it as the standard for differentiating the capitalist and socialist natures. The so-called combination of legislative and executive powers refers to the combination of legislative organs and administrative organs, and the organs making laws also take charge of the enforcement of laws.[144] Some scholars holding positive views think that the combination of legislative and executive powers as the organization principle of the people's congress is capable of integrating powers of state and wills of people to the people's congress and helping the building of China's democratic politics.[145] The combination of legislative and executive powers is the specific embodiment and new development of democratic centralism in China.[146] In 1989, Wang Yuming clearly pointed out that the combination of legislative and executive powers is not the organization principle of China's state organs.[147] Wu Jialin published an article on *China Legal Science* in 1992 to profoundly introspect the theory of

142Xu [81].
143Yin [82].
144Cai [83], pp. 92–93.
145Zhao [84].
146Zeng [85], Fan [86], Xu [87], Du [88].
147Wang [89].

"combination of legislative and executive powers" and clearly raised the proposal of separating legislative and executive powers. Mr. Wu demonstrated from six aspects that it is inappropriate to combine legislative and executive powers. First, how did the Paris Commune implement the theory of combining legislative and executive powers? Second, why did the Paris Commune implement the theory of combining legislative and executive powers? Third, how did Marx and Lenin affirm the theory of combining legislative and executive powers? Fourth, what's the disadvantage and disadvantages of the theory of combining legislative and executive powers? Fifth, which of the democratic centralism or the combination of legislative and executive powers is the organization principle of China's state power? Sixth, whether the theory of combining legislative and executive powers is the same with the theory of uniting legislative and executive powers? Mr. Wu emphasized that the theory of combining legislative and executive powers is neither applicable to China nor applicable to other socialist countries. Combining legislative and executive powers is an institutional centralization system, an obsolete political system and the basic principle of state power structure of feudal states. This theory should not be advocated and promoted. More than one hundred years of practical experiences demonstrate that this is not a way out. Partial experiments are also unsuccessful, and it is not good to repeat this slogan. The demonstrations of Mr. Wu were careful and detailed analyses, interlinked, progressive, rigorous in logic and strongly persuasive. This innovative theory has been deemed as a major development in China's theoretical studies on constitutional law.[148] This point of view has been agreed by many scholars. In 1992, Liu Zheng who worked in the General Office of the National People's Congress wrote an article pointing out that the theory of combining legislative and executive powers is not the characteristics of China's people's congress system.[149] Professor Zhou Yongkun also believes that this theory doesn't comply with the socialist reality as a concept describing the power structure of the socialist political power, and it is even harmful as an ideal model of power structure. In the socialist history, the theory of combining legislative and executive powers only temporarily existed in abnormal times. Except for the war times, it brought about disasters rather than benefits to humanity. Therefore, this theory and principle should be thoroughly abandoned.[150] Tong Zhiwei et al. also believe that people have vague and skeptical understanding of power separation within state organs due to the existence and dissemination of the theory of combining legislative and executive powers. This has misled the basic development direction of the people's congress system and caused adverse consequences in practices. Therefore, we should thoroughly abandon this theory and replace it with the theory of allocating statutory powers in accordance with the law.[151] Cai Dingjian also agreed and emphasized that the theory easily overlooks

148 Han et al. [90].

149 Liu and Cheng [91].

150 Zhou [92].

151 Tong et al. [93].

rational labor division and restriction between state powers, which goes against guaranteeing state organs to exercise duties and powers by law. In addition, its actual proposition of part-time works of deputies to the NPC and members of the NPC Standing Committee also goes against the strengthening of the NPC's monitoring role.[152] After some disputes, the theory of combining legislative and executive powers gradually faded out of China's theoretical studies and practices.

Over the past three decades, China's studies on the people's congress system have always been revolving around two major themes, namely, adherence and improvement. Disputes over theories have usually centered on the specific building of the people's congress and giving play to the role of the legitimate authority of people's congress. In particular, the NPC supervisory system has always been the focus of attention of the constitutional circle along with the drafting and promulgation of the *Supervision Law*. Given the NPC individual case supervision, the academic community has had heated discussions and had mixed evaluations.[153] Some scholars believe that individual case supervision by the NPC is the embodiment of full exercise of functions and powers by the authority. Individual case supervision is good for guaranteeing judicial justice and symbolizes the continuous improvement of the people's congress system. There are clear legal bases for people's congress to exercise the right of supervision. The people's congress must exercise the right to supervision through individual cases. Without intervening in individual cases, supervision is only a meaningless term. Individual case supervision and judicial independence are not contradictory because judicial independence is not unlimited and judicial injustice shall be restricted. The necessity and value of supervision lie in the prevention of judicial organs' misuse of authority on the pretext of independence. The subsequence of individual case supervision needs to be defined. The occurrence of allowance of law-breakers not being punished, failure in full observation of laws and denial of justice should be regarded as subsequence and should be included in the scope of supervision of the people's congress. Some scholars think that accepting the supervision of the people's congress can help urge people's courts to handle cases in accordance with the law and represents a necessary approach for judicial justice of courts. In addition, there are sufficient constitutional bases for the people's congress to carry out individual case supervisions targeting people's courts.[154] Some scholars have a positive attitude towards individual case supervision of the people's congress, but they think that the supervisions are inadequate in method application and strength. Therefore, the following aspects should be emphasized. First, it is to correctly define the scope of individual cases and key cases for supervision. Second, it is to correctly define the position of supervision departments in individual case supervisions. Third, it is to define the method to carry out individual case supervisions without handling cases. Fourth, it

[152]Cai [83], pp. 88–91.

[153]For related arguments and summaries, please see Han and Liu [94].

[154]Refer to *Explorations into New Issues related to Individual Case Supervision of the People's Congress*, *Political Science and Law*, 2000, Issue 2.

is to correctly understand the relations between supervision and support in individual case supervision. Fifth, it is to correctly define the targets pursued by individual cases.[155]

However, many other scholars oppose this point of view. They argued that individual case supervision will not only damage judicial independence and lead to unbalanced power but also give rise to the following insurmountable difficulties and obstacles. First, the individual case supervision of the people's congress will trigger mutual conflicts between laws and conflicts between legal systems within the system of law. Second, the individual case supervision of courts by the people's congress is costly.[156] Third, the people's congress winks at the refusal of parties involved in a case to execute court judgment, demonstrating serious local protectionism. The legal representatives of the complaining party intervene in the supervision procedures as deputies to the NPC, making the people's congress become the representative of some individuals and units. This is likely to lead to deputies' misuse and abuse of powers and thus the occurrence of new power corruptions. Moreover, this can also easily give birth to local protectionism, thus exerting negative influence on judicial authority and impartiality of courts. Fourth, the individual case supervision of the people's congress seriously violates the judicial authority of courts. Courts may retry a case many times and may be forced to change the judgment, making their independence exist only in name. People's Congress may propose specific opinions on the handling of a case being tried and demand the settlement of the case within a limited time period, making it become the judge in real sense. This not only makes it difficult to meet the requirement for judicial independence in system but also contradicts the modern proceeding system in procedural principle, which will exert much negative influence on the normal trial procedures of people's courts.[157]

Legislation is the principal function of the people's congress. Toward currently existing reversing legislative behaviors in practices, constitutional scholars have two different attitudes. The positive attitude believes that social relations are unstable in the process of reform and opening up, so it is impossible to find a rather stable bonding point in law for both defining civic rights and regulating government powers. In this connection, we should allow the legislative principle of adopting rules and regulations first and then enacting laws in the fields featuring stronger policy factors. The premise for making laws should be mature and stable and we must avoid acting in haste. The opposite attitude believes that the theme of China's current socialist modernization is governing the country by law. Governance by law is to build the authority of constitution and laws. If we allow abandoning the principle of unified socialist legal system in practices and implementing the legislation model of making regulations first and then enacting laws, first, it would easily cause the conflict between laws for one part and regulations and rules for

[155]Sun [95].
[156]Li and Feng [96].
[157]Liu [97], Shen [98].

another. Second, it would easily mix the different legal forms and functions undertaken by laws for one part and regulations and rules for another.[158]

China's constitution stipulates that deputies to the people's congress will not be called to legal account for their statements made at meetings of all kinds. The academic community generally believes that this immunity of speech system is conducive to ensuring sufficient expression of people's wills. Some scholars compared the "immunity of speech" for people's representatives as stipulated in Article 75 of the current constitution with the privilege of freedom of speech of senators as provided in western constitutions. After comparison, they pointed out that, in western countries, this constitutional system was closely linked with the sovereignty principle and representative principle of the constitutionalism in modern times. For that matter, under the premise of modern constitutionalism, western constitutional theories generally conclude that the privilege of freedom of speech cannot be applied by each political party to impose constraints on members of the party. If this modern constitutional theory is introduced into China, then this kind of "connection" with "fault" in history may have certain risks.[159]

2.3.2 Studies on the Regional National Autonomy System

The regional national autonomy system is a crucial part of China's socialist democratic politics. The constitutional circle has made in-depth studies on the improvement of the regional national autonomy system. Constitutional scholars have elaborated the concept, meaning, type, autonomous function, among other theoretical issues of the regional national autonomy system from the perspective of constitutional law. They have also put forward many feasible countermeasures for issues in reality. Some scholars have also analyzed the regional national autonomy system by applying the institutional change theory of neo-institutional economics and come to the conclusion of the institutional changes of the regional national autonomy system from mandatory-oriented system to the combination of mandatory and induced system.[160] Some scholar considered that a perfect legislative system should be established for improving the regional national autonomy system. In particular, there is a need to solve supporting legislative problems for the Regional National Autonomy Law. This scholar proposed a pyramid-shape supporting legislation model system after studying the background of the regional national autonomy and on the basis of the existing legislative system in an attempt to break the bottleneck of traditional thinking.[161]

Some scholars believe that the Regional National Autonomy Law lacks specific stipulations on guaranteeing the human rights of ethnic groups. First, as a special

158Mo [99].
159Lin [70].
160Xu [100].
161Zhang [101].

law for national relations and national autonomous regions, *the* Regional National Autonomy Law should have provisions for autonomous organs to guarantee the human rights of ethnic groups, which is not only the embodiment of articles on the constitution but also the must for guaranteeing the civic rights of ethnic groups. Article 52 of *the* Regional National Autonomy Law stipulates that autonomous organs of national autonomous areas should guarantee that local citizens of all nationalities enjoy civic rights as stipulated by the constitution, but there is need to make clear the human rights of ethnic groups due to the national characteristics. One clause may be added to Article 52: autonomous organs of regional national autonomous areas should respect and protect the human rights of local citizens of all nationalities. Second, there should also be stipulations on the social security system for national autonomous areas. As mentioned before, people in national autonomous areas live in poverty, and some even find it difficult to maintain their basic living needs. Social security is the system offering material assistance to aged, sick, handicapped and unemployed social members and members facing disasters or life difficulties. In this sense, the Autonomy Law may stipulate the system. A provision may be added to Clause 2 of Article 6 of the Regional National Autonomy Law: establish and improve a social security system adapting to local economic development level of national autonomous regions. This is highly relevant to the realization of social equity and maintenance of social stability. Third, citizens of areas inhabited by ethnic groups should be protected from being encroached in terms of private property. Autonomous organs have the right to autonomously manage local economic affairs and enjoy greater autonomy under the condition of having limited resources, so the protection of the legal private property of citizens of areas inhabited by ethnic minorities is very important. Fourth, from the perspective of human rights protection, the Regional National Autonomy Law should be added with a mechanism for punishing lawbreakers. As the basic law for implementing the regional national autonomy system as stipulated by constitution, the Regional National Autonomy Law in itself has many prohibiting and obligatory stipulations, but it has no stipulation on the liabilities for violating these regulations. In order to better protect the rights of citizens of ethnic groups and prohibit the occurrence of illegal phenomena, there should be an illegal sanction system.[162]

The autonomous organs, i.e., people's congresses of most national autonomous areas in China, developed autonomous regulations. Autonomous regulations are generally composed of general principles, composition of autonomous organs, autonomy, national relations, and supplementary provisions, etc. Autonomy commonly includes autonomy in personnel, autonomy in legislation, autonomy in economy, and autonomy in education, science, culture, and health. Some scholar pointed out that autonomous regulations have received great achievements in implementation, but some issues still exist, such as lacking ideas of autonomy, misunderstanding, lacking scientific systems for coordination, and among other drawbacks of autonomous regulations. Therefore, there is a need to foster correct

[162] Yang [102].

ideas of autonomy in regional national autonomous areas, correctly handle several major relations and improve the specific systems for autonomous regulations and the structure of autonomous regulations. There is also a need to compile legislation programs and plans, strengthen the applicability and innovative building of the contents of autonomous regulations and improve the legal environment for the implementation of autonomous regulations.[163]

2.3.3 Studies on the Basic Law of Special Administrative Regions

Some constitutional scholars who directly took part in drafting the basic law first carried out studies on the basic law of special administrative regions. For instance, professor Wang Shuwen took part in drafting the basic law of Hong Kong SAR and the basic law of Macao SAR. After drafting the basic law, Wang Shuwen and some relevant experts together organized the compilation of *the Introduction to the Basic Law of Hong Kong Special Administrative Region* and *the Introduction to the Basic Law of Macao Special Administrative Region.*[164] These two works systematically introduced the legislative spirit of the basic law and different opinions in the legislative procedures and provided rich, detailed and accurate data for studies on the basic law of Hong Kong SAR and the basic law of Macao SAR. With regard to the basic rights of citizens of Hong Kong SAR, he pointed out that the basic law has not only great features in the subject of rights but also many features in content of rights in stipulations on the rights and freedom of citizens. The main features include extensiveness in content and the guarantee of rights and freedom in multiple levels.[165] He also compared the differences between the stipulations of the basic law of Macao and that of Hong Kong and pointed out that the legal system and rights protection method in Macao are somewhat different from that of Hong Kong. Therefore, in the basic law of Macao, there are clear stipulations on legal identification of crimes, the protection of the legitimate rights and interests of women, the elderly and children. The basic law of Macao also includes clearer stipulations on the right of reputation and right of privacy. These stipulations have completely met the requirement for maintaining the basic legal system of Macao unchanged after its return to the motherland, and are quite innovative.[166] Other constitutionalists taking part in drafting the basic law also included Xiao Weiyun and Xu Chongde. They also wrote many books, which have laid a theoretical foundation for studies on the basic law of special administrative regions.

In the constitutional circle, professor Wang Zhenmin represents one of the scholars who have paid more attention to the basic law theory. He has probed into the basic theory and framework for handling the relations between the central

---

[163]Cheng [103].

[164]Wang [104, 105].

[165]Wang [106].

[166]Wang [107].

government and special administrative regions under the circumstance of implementing the "one country, two systems" policy from law-based, especially constitutional perspectives. He has also probed into the basic principle and method followed in dividing powers between the central government and special administrative regions. He has also made in-depth studies from an empirical perspective on some technical and operational issues in handling the relations between the central government and special administrative regions, especially the practices and the application of *the Basic Law* in handling the relations after the establishment of special administrative regions, including China's unconstitutional inspection system and its influence on special administrative regions.[167] Regarding new issues occurred in judicial practices and in the implementation of the basic law of special administrative regions, some scholars have made systematic theoretical analyses by centering on the disputes over the interpretation of the basic law under the policy of "one country, two systems". Some other scholars have also made reflections on the interpretation of the basic law ever since its implementation and proposed to fully realize the local legislation of Hong Kong from the perspective of the stipulation of constitutional government on power relations. According to the reflections, there is a lack of effective counterbalance between administrative and judicial powers, which leads to the dual-track interpretations of the Basic Law of Hong Kong. Under the framework of the basic law, the response to the dual-track system is differentiating political issues from legal issues.[168]

Many constitutional scholars consider that the basic law of special administrative regions is a special law, a constitutional law, and a national law. It is enacted in accordance with the constitution of the People's Republic of China and in line with the specific condition of the special administrative regions. The Standing Committee of the NPC has the power of interpretation of the basic law. Professor Jiao Hongchang holds the view that the basic law of Macao SAR is a special law, a constitutional law, and a national law. It is enacted in accordance with the constitution of the People's Republic of China and in line with the specific condition of Macao. The power of interpretation of it belongs to the Standing Committee of the NPC. With the social, economic and cultural development of Macao SAR, the basic law will be revised in line with the actual condition and needs of Macao going forward to adapt to the times. The original law of Macao is an important legal concept within the transition period of Macao and has a very close relation with the basic law. The contents of the original law should not conflict with the basic law but conform to the actual social condition of Macao.[169] Prof. Li Qi believes that the basic law of special administrative regions is a "minor constitution" but not a statute law of a representative organ. Instead, it is a special law of constitution. This depends on the contents, functions, name, legal effects, etc. of the basic law of special administrative regions. The definition of the legal nature of the basic law of

---

[167]Wang [108].
[168]Cheng [109].
[169]Jiao [110].

special administrative regions is not only an academic issue but also an issue directly involving the actual operation of the special administrational region system but also the actual operation of the constitution. The nature of the basic law of special administrative regions as a special law of constitution is not invalid due to its conflict with the constitution. The efficacy of constitution in special administrative regions is realized through the special law, namely the basic law of special administrative regions. The interpretation of the basic law by the Standing Committee of the NPC accordingly belongs to constitutional interpretation and thus can change the "precedent" of the court of final appeal of special administrative regions.[170] However, some other scholars believe that the basic law of Hong Kong SAR is simply a law formulated by the NPC, and if the basic law conflicts with the legislation behavior of the NPC, then Hong Kong courts should apply the constitution, the basic law and the laws admitted by China to resolve the issue of general applicability of laws rather than regarding the basic law as China's constitution and advocating the so-called constitutional right of jurisdiction. The NPC has the right of investigating the unconstitutional legislation behaviors of the NPC or the Standing Committee of the NPC.[171]

The interpretation of the basic law by the Standing Committee of the NPC used to attract widespread attention of the constitutional circles of the mainland, Hong Kong and Macao. In response to this question, professor Qiang Shigong analyzed the legal interpretation methods applied in the three interpretations of the basic law of Hong Kong SAR by the Standing Committee of the NPC since the return of Hong Kong to China. These three methods included text interpretation, structure interpretation, and legislation purpose interpretation. He pointed out that, in the case regarding the residency rights, the principal divergence between the Court of Final Appeal of Hong Kong SAR and the NPC in legal interpretation method is which of the procedural formal examination and substantive intention presumption should be adopted in the process of determining the authoritative texts demonstrating the legislation purpose. It is not only the divergence in legal interpretation but also the difference in legal theories and political stance. In the meantime, the scholar also criticized the popular prejudice that it is inappropriate for legislators to interpret laws and called for the inclusion of the basic law in the national constitutional government system for comprehension.[172] This theory studies the basic law of special administrative regions under the theoretical framework of Chinese constitutional law and well connected the studies on the basic law and studies on constitutional theories, which are undoubtedly of great significance to China's constitutional theory system.

---

[170] Li [111].

[171] Ling [112].

[172] Qiang [113].

2.3.4 Studies on the Village Self-Governance Theory

The emergence and development of villager autonomy as a historical process should be studied under specific historical background. It is unable to establish a village governance system with farmers as the main body only by relying on top-down external forces. After empowering villages in politics and organizing rural organizations by party members, the emergence of villager autonomy with peasants as the subject became a historical inevitability. After the abolition of the commune system, the essence of the villager autonomy system was the Party's support for farmers to be masters and establish their subject position in their active involvement. Scattered farmers were included in the state system to establish their recognition of the state, realize the coordination of state governance and villager self-management and thus boost the development of Chinese socialist democratic politics. Looking from the perspective of modern state construction, China's village governance system also needs corresponding transformation, integrating various power resources and governance mechanisms, implementing state and village co-governance and boosting the development of village self-governance in this process.[173] Lin Shangli believes that grassroots autonomy is an important logical starting point and realistic basepoint of development under China's democratic politics in the new century. The author overviewed the development process of grassroots autonomy and its legal basis ever since the founding of the PRC and pointed out that grassroots autonomy was first born in urban areas, but it has developed in the interactions between urban areas and villages in grassroots autonomy. According to him, grassroots autonomy has entered the stage of functional realization after organization building and system formation. Grassroots autonomy must go through three political development procedures before realization. First, it is the state power's moderate social intervention. Second, the Party's grassroots organizations strengthen their influence in grassroots society. Third, grassroots democracy and autonomy realize substantive development. In the development of grassroots autonomy, there is a must to properly handle the relations among the government, political party and autonomous organization and the relations between the autonomous organization for one part and grassroots organizations and interest organizations for another. There is also a must to properly handle the relations between institutional innovation and acting by law, between international experiences and China's national condition and between reform and development for one part and stability for another.[174] Cui Zhiyou positioned the villager autonomy system from the legal point of view. He concluded that villager autonomy is neither individual autonomy of villagers nor autonomy of villager committees. Instead, it is the autonomy of all villagers as the autonomous subject. When the conditions are there, the autonomy system can be taken as an independent chapter of constitution for explicit stipulation. Within the autonomous community

[173]Xu [114].

[174]Lin [115].

composed of all villagers, villager meeting is the organization of supreme power of the village community. Villager Committee is the executive organ of the villager community, but it cannot be called autonomous organization. Villager autonomous community should possess the autonomy and have the legal person capacity. According to the statutory principle of legal person form, villager autonomous community can be classified as an autonomous legal person.[175]

Some scholar analyzed the phenomenon of "two skins", namely party branch and villager committee of some villages under the background of villager autonomy based on empirical data. The scholar thought that the "two skins" phenomenon is extremely harmful to the current social stability, villager autonomy and economic development of rural areas and influential to the implementation of the Party's rural policies. This phenomenon is related not only to village families and sectarian factors but also to the defects of the electoral system and the quality of cadres. The scholar concluded that the basic idea of solving this issue is to strengthen education, deepen rural reform, improve the electoral system and clarify the authority-responsibility relationship between two leading groups.[176] Some scholar pointed out that irrationality in the operation of villager autonomy has become a prominent issue restricting the healthy development of villager autonomy. To solve this issue, the basic idea is to build a normalized and benign township government–village governance interaction model and maintain the dynamic balance of inherent tensions within the village public power system. The basic idea is to eliminate the conflicts between villager autonomous authority and the political authority of village party organization and build a unitary public authority of village grassroots society under the leadership of the Party. The basic idea is to accelerate the modernized transition of farmers in the process of transforming the traditional agricultural society and cultivate mature and rational subjects of villager autonomy. The basic idea is also to establish and improve a legal system and efficient social integration mechanism and build a good social eco-environment for villager autonomy.[177]

The relationship between villager autonomy and township government is very important for improving the villager autonomy system. To this, some scholar thought that township governments administer by law as a new state power at the grass-roots level pursuant to the institutional arrangement of *the Organic Law of the Villagers' Committees of the People's Republic of China* (hereinafter referred to as *Organic Law of the Villagers Committees*). The scholar also noted that villagers committees implement autonomy in accordance with the law as villager autonomous organizations. Townships (towns) and villages are no longer the superior and subordinate under direct leading-subordinating relations in administration in legal sense. Or rather, township-village relations are transforming from "leading-subordinating relationship" to "guidance relationship". The two are gradually

[175]Cui [116].
[176]Gao [117].
[177]Wang [118].

entering into the run-in period. But, many believe that it is still the administration-dominated township–village relations and villager autonomy remains insufficient although it is in the middle of development. They also pointed out that the township-village relation is the relation between state and farmers in essence. Some other opinions hold that the current township-village relations reflect the traditional superior-subordinate inter-governmental relations in China. There is also an opinion that the township-village relations are featured by three natures, namely guiding and being guided, leading and being led, and managing and being managed relations. The difference is that the relations of some nature or some two natures are more evidently presented in different areas or different periods. In addition, some people believe that the township–village relations are featured by quasi-administrative nature and quasi-contractual nature. The quasi-administrative nature refers to weakened administrative control and demonstrates a non-administrative trend, but it is still administrative in content currently and it is simply weakened in administrative power.[178]

2.3.5 Theories on Constitution-Making Power and Amending Power

The theories on constitution-making power in foreign constitutional law can be traced back to French constitutionalist Sieyes's *What is the Third Estate?* Since then, the concept of constitution-making power has been gradually accepted by constitutional law and become an important category of constitutional law in various countries. Chinese earlier studies on constitution-making power theories were made by professor Xiao Weiyun.[179] But, it is professor Han Dayuan who made more comprehensive and systematic studies on the concept and origin, legitimacy and nature, and function and value of constitution-making power, constitution-making organ, procedures, etc.[180] Some scholar also pointed out that constitution-making power is the power of all people of a country to make constitution by themselves or via a certain organization according to the preset constitutional procedures, and features originality, paramountcy, and politics.[181]

The theories on constitutional law generally support the separation of constitution-making power and amending power, namely the so-called power of making constitution and power of being made by constitution. The application of amending power is not random amendment of contents of the constitution.[182] Similarly, some Chinese scholar observes that the amending power is not an absolute power and features internal and external limits objectively. The limits of

[178] Tan [119].

[179] Xiao [120].

[180] Han et al. [121].

[181] Refer to Zhang [122].

[182] Han [123].

amending power are reflected in the restriction of the basic spirit and principle of constitution, natural laws and international laws and the restraint on amending power in positive laws.[183] In recent years, some scholars have made systematic studies on the theory of amending power and concluded that the amending power is an important concept in constitutional theory and its meaning cannot be described by functions and powers. They also observe that the analysis of the concept of amending power may discover that the amending power is not simply a single function and power but a concept mixing obligation, freedom, power, and incompetence.[184]

2.3.6 Development of Constitutional Supervision Theory

Constitutional supervision has always been a focus of the constitutional circle. China's constitution stipulates the non-contravention principle and the supervision system of the people's congress over the government, courts, and procuratorates. Other relevant laws also stipulate the record review system and legislation interpretation system, etc. However, it is still difficult to guarantee the legislative legitimacy principle due to the absence of a specific review for constitutionality and supervision system. To this issue, some scholar pointed out that unconstitutionality is the most serious violation of law and governance by law is governance by constitution in the first place. In this connection, constitutional supervision has become the core and top priority of the supervision of people's congress. The function of china's constitutional supervision has not yet been effectively exercised. One of the reasons is that the constitutional supervision mechanism and procedures need to be further improved.[185] Constitutional studies in early days mainly focused on how to establish a constitutional supervision system under the people's congress system, especially on how to establish a constitution supervisory organ. Regarding the necessity of establishing a constitution supervisory organ, the constitutional circle used to propose two totally different opinions. One is that constitutional supervision exists to adapt to the needs of diversified democratic politics in capitalist countries and constitutional supervision is frequently proposed by the out-party and is the democratic form of out-party's restriction on the ruling party. China doesn't implement the multi-party system, so it is unnecessary to establish a constitutional supervision system. Another opinion is that the existence of constitutional supervision is determined by the legal characteristics of constitution and there would be no constitution without constitutional supervision.[186] As the concept

[183] Dou [124].
[184] Du [125–127].
[185] Cheng [128].
[186] Mo [99].

of constitution applicability is gradually accepted, the latter concept has become the mainstream theory of the constitutional circle. Most scholars support the establishment of a constitution committee or constitution supervisory committee, and its status may be affiliated or parallel to the Standing Committee of the NPC. Of course, some scholars observe that constitutional supervision can be implemented without the establishment of a constitution supervisory institution.[187] This point of view has overlooked that the core of constitutional supervision is to supervise the constitutionality of laws, so it has been criticized by many scholars.

There are certainly scholars opposing the NPC's supervision of the constitutionality of its own behaviors. They have raised the topic about the so-called judicatory actualization of constitution or judicatory actualization of constitutional supervision. Some other scholars observe that, in China, it is impossible to realize judicatory actualization of constitutional supervision. This is because the current constitution stipulates that only the NPC and the NPC Standing Committee have the power to supervise the implementation of constitution, constitutional supervision organ must be established under the NPC or the NPC Standing Committee rather than the Supreme People's Court. To this issue, some scholar pointed out tit for tat that constitutional supervision was raised from judicial perspective in essence because, if constitution is created and supervised by a legislative organ, then it would mean affirming the legitimacy of unconstitutional self-supervision behaviors in system.[188]

Scholars have made full comparative studies on the constitutional supervision systems of global countries and summarized the models and types of constitutional supervision system since 1990s in a bid to provide references for China's constitutional supervision system. Some scholar noted that China should learn from the German model of constitutional court or the French constitutional council system to build China's constitutional supervision system, and first establish an institution similar to constitutional court to exercise constitutional supervisions.[189] However, some other scholar proposed the implementation of the system that judicial organs supervise constitutional implementation and the Supreme People's Court interprets and supervises the constitution.[190] Of course, some scholar suggested the establishment of a dual double-checking model, under which the organ of supreme power and judicial organ jointly assume the responsibility of constitutional supervision. This point of view is the product of the former two opinions.[191]

The Supervision Law that has been adopted doesn't involve constitutional supervision. The Office for Recording and Examining Laws under the Legislative

---

[187]For the summary of related theories, please see Hu [129].

[188]Mo [99].

[189]Fei [130], Zhao [131].

[190]Wang [132], refer to Bao [133].

[191]For related summaries, please see Hu Jinguang's *Comparative Studies on constitutionality review Review for constitutionality,* China Renmin University Press, 2006 edition, page 368–370, the part written by Wang Kai.

Affairs Commission of the Standing Committee of the NPC handles the conflict of administrative laws and regulations, local laws and regulations and departmental rules, etc. with the Constitution and laws. This approach certainly has a positive significance for maintaining the unity of national legal system and safeguarding the constitutional rights of citizens. But ever since its establishment, the Office for Recording and Examining Laws has not yet made any decision on compliance with or violation of the Constitution. Currently, Chinese society has no lack of applications by citizens to the NPC for examining violations of the Constitution. We believe that constitutional decisions can be made for state acts of these applications that do not collide with the Constitution. On the one hand, these constitutional decisions can remove the doubts of all walks of life about the constitutionality of state acts. On the other hand, these constitutional decisions can help provide a legitimate basis for state acts in Constitution and establish the authority of law-based government. Therefore, constitutional law should study the way of making decisions on constitutionality so as to provide technical and mental support for China's constitutional supervision.

2.3.7 Studies on Constitution Applicability in Specific Cases

An academic strategy commonly adopted by the constitutional circle is to boost constitution applicability through studying and interpreting the cases or examples currently happening in the society. In recent years, the constitutional circle has paid more attention to the implementation of constitution, such as the Law School of Renmin University of China. The Constitutionalism and Rule of Administrative Law Research Center of Renmin University of China released the 2006–2007 "Annual Top10 Constitutional Cases in China" and took the case selection as an opportunity to organize symposiums on studying the theory of constitution applicability. As a matter of fact, this tendency can be traced back to the so-called "No. 1 case on judicatory actualization of constitution" at the turn of the century.[192] The reply of the Supreme People's Court on this case triggered the discussions of the constitutional circle and the entire law circle at large on constitution applicability. The Supreme People's Court pointed out in the reply that Chen Xiaoqi et al. infringed upon the basic right of Qi Yuling to education as stipulated by the Constitution by means of infringing upon her right of name, which has caused specific harmful consequences, so they shall bear corresponding civil liabilities. The law community raised different opinions on this reply. There was one viewpoint disagreeing judicial organs' direct application of articles on the constitution on the ground that constitution is a behavior rule but not a judgment rule. Articles on the constitution have no logical structure of judgment rules that is simultaneous stipulations on key components and legal effects. After all, the task of constitution is to

[192]Refer to *No. 1 Case on Judicatory Actualization of Constitution Triggered by Assuming the Identity of Another Student for Going College*, *Southern Weekly*, report on August 16, 2001.

define the basic principle and basic system for national life rather than establishing the benchmark for courts to judge civil cases.[193] Especially in civil trials, the cases on private encroachment of basic rights are adjusted by the civil law, so using the Constitution to adjust cases on right encroachment between citizens is obviously beyond the adjustment scope of the Constitution. In fact, it is the generalization of the concept of unconstitutional behaviors. It doesn't help maintain the authority of the Constitution and may just cause just opposite effects.[194] Many opponents believe that it is the application of the Constitution by representative organs in China and there is no space for judicial organs to apply the constitution in system. However, some other scholars observe that the right of Qi Yuling to education doesn't belong to the rights that could be included in the civil law theory but obviously belongs to the basic rights of citizens as stipulated by the Constitution. Without direct application of constitutional stipulations, it would be unable to realize judicial relief. Therefore, we should set a precedent that Chinese courts guarantee the basic rights of citizens in constitutional sense through judicial reviews. We should also explore the approach of judicial relief of constitutional rights of citizens and blaze a trial indirectly using the constitution as the legal basis for Chinese courts to judge cases. In essence, there is a need to realize judicatory actualization of constitution and make the Constitution enter judicial procedures.[195] Liu Liantai also agrees to directly apply constitutional norms in trials and boldly quote constitutional norms in legal documents.[196] The different opinions of different constitutional scholars on this case can be seen as their furious debates and directly reflect the confrontations between different legal theories. The Qi Yuling case has become a media and platform for communications between different legal theories. In this connection, the analysis of the case from the constitutional perspective can also be taken as a dialogue among constitutional scholars. In this process, constitutional theories on constitution applicability and basic rights have well developed in their dialogues and confrontations.[197]

2.3.8 Studies on Constitutional Theories of the People's Political Consultative Conference

The people's political consultative conference is an organization of the united front with extensive representativeness. It is also an important organ for the development of multi-party cooperation and political consultation under the leadership of the CPC. It is a constituent part of China's political system and plays an irreplaceable and critical role in developing socialist democracy and building the socialist

[193]Liang [134].
[194]Yin [135].
[195]Wang [136].
[196]Liu [137].
[197]Lin and Zhu [138].

political civilization. According to the stipulations of China's constitution, the Chinese People's Political Consultative Conference is an organization of the united front with extensive representativeness and played an important role in the past. As the Constitution stipulates, the CPPCC will further play its important role in national political life, social life and friendly foreign activities, socialist modernization and struggles safeguarding national unification and solidarity. The Constitution stipulates that the multi-party cooperation and political consultation system led by the Communist Party of China will exist and develop for a long time. Thus it can be seen that its positioning by the Constitution is an organization of united front and an organization form of democratic parties and other patriotic democratic personages for political consultation under the leadership of the CPC. That said, some scholar pointed out that it is simply the principle provision of the Constitution that has made some scholars believe that the status and identity of the CPPCC are unclear and inconsistent with its actual status and identity. The scholar proposed to clearly stipulate in the Constitution that the CPPCC is a state organ or public opinion organ with certain powers.[198]

In practice, the people's political consultative system is an important part of China's political system. CPPCC organizations at all levels have played the function of democratic supervision and participating in the administration and discussions of state affairs. The CPPCC has a pivotal role in national political life and social life and is similar to some state organs in some aspects. Many people have been used to paralleling the CPPCC with Party committee, government, and the people's congress. The expenses of the CPPCC are covered by state finance. The CPPCC participates in foreign activities and members of the CPPCC may go to grassroots units for inspections. China's constitution stipulates the status and nature of the people's political consultative system, but there is no specific law on fixing the CPPCC's organization and carrying out of work. For that matter, some scholars propose the legalization of the CPPCC that is to specifically stipulate the status, nature, function, power, organization, etc. of the CPPCC in the constitution and laws.[199] Fan Zhongxin and Wang Yibai believe that the people's political consultative system is a vital part of China's political system. Currently, the maintenance of this system is mainly relying on political party policies, political conventions and the internal constitution of the CPPCC. The system has not yet been incorporated into the national legal system and it has not become formal written articles of law. This situation is particularly detrimental to the full guarantee of the CPPCC's status as a united front of multi-party cooperation and giving full play to its function of representing all people's opinion. This situation also goes against the principle of governance by law. The CPPCC should departmentalize and legalize public opinions, which is one of the key projects for building socialism with Chinese characteristics.[200] Some scholar pointed out that we can include the

---

[198]Liu and Cheng [139].

[199]See Footnote 198.

[200]Li [140], Fan and Wang [141].

CPPCC in the people's congress system and make it part of the people's congress while staying committed to the people's congress system. The scholar also pointed out that the CPPCC could have its independence within the people's congress system, share part of the legislative power, and make its state organ supervision truly become a part of the statutory supervision of public representative organs. The specific steps of this kind of legalization are as follows: first, it is to reform the way of election and recommendation of the CPPCC to make it have more natures of public representative organs and the legitimacy of mastering the state power; second, it is to gradually grant all powers to the CPPCC, promote works in all areas by drawing upon the experience gained on key points, and gradually improve the deserved powers and functions of the CPPCC through tentative legislative; lastly, it is to make an overall and fundamental regulation on the development of the CPPCC towards the so-called upper house in constitution and laws and promote its final accomplishment of legalization.[201] To this point, some scholars have different point of views and believe that all activities of the CPPCC are not beyond the scope of constitution and laws, so we shouldn't give it a so-called identity for the specialty of its status and function, and level it up to the status as a state organ. Looking from the actual situation, there are foundations for its existence.[202] In addition, bicameralism is commonly rejected in political theories and constitutional theories in China at the current stage.

The problem is whether our rejection of bicameralism and denial of the legalization of the people's political consultative system mean that the people's political consultative system stays out of the framework of the Constitution and rule of law. The answer is negative because constitution is not just composed of texts according to the conventional theories of constitution. Generalized constitutional norms should also include the special form of constitutional conventions. It is generally believed that constitutional conventions are formed in the long-term political life and practices of the state and the contents involve the fundamental issues of the state and are recognized by the state or the public. They are major principles and systems without formal legal form. Constitutional conventions mainly exist in countries without a written constitution, but they also exist in some countries with a written constitution, and the difference is simply in the status and function. In countries without a written constitution, it is an important part of the constitution. In countries with a written constitution, it plays a supplementary role in the constitution.[203] China is a country with a written constitution and the constitutional conventions also play a pivotal role in the political life. In today's China, the people's political consultative system just belongs to one of the specific expressions of constitutional conventions. For instance, in terms of making national major decisions, the convention is that the CPPCC, democratic parties and mass organizations hold consultations and discussions first and then a state organ makes the

---

[201] Fan and Wang [141].

[202] See Footnote 198.

[203] See Footnote 198.

decision in accordance with the law. This is a typical convention. These constitutional conventions are not laws in themselves, so they have no legal form and no legal restrictions, but they have already had the inherent spirit of laws- regularity. These conventions have no legal force, but they have constraints in both politics and morality. Violating these conventions would not cause legal sanctions but go against the political stability, the development of democratic politics and the realization of a law-based country.[204]

2.4 *Conclusion: Focus on Practice*

Social development comprises all kinds of facts and interpretations of these facts from different angles have formed into different subjects. Given these social facts, raising questions and giving interpretations and answers by means of constitutional law and making analysis and explanations in constitutional words have constituted the subject system of constitutional law. In this sense, the development history of constitutional law studies are composed of constitutional statements of countless facts.

Words makeup thoughts and thus affect our actions. Sometimes, people's actions frequently depend on what they say, which is the "symbolic power" theory of Pierre Bourdieu.[205] If we hold the standpoint of nominalism, we can even say that language has shaped the facts and the one who owns a language owns the world. The one that can be called a thing can be given a meaning and thus can be controlled. Law is also a world, or we can say, when a law is used and realized, it usually links two worlds, namely law-related facts in life—a world with daily facts and a legal world with idealistic norms as the content.[206] Narrating facts in social life by using constitutional words enables the connection between idealistic constitutional values and facts in actual social life. Therefore, only by narrating facts in life in the first place could constitutional theories change the social reality. In a specific case, the explaining process combining constitutional theories and practices is the process for the constitution to develop towards practice and towards life.

Given the fact that constitution always has a superior position, many scholars demonstrate the "supremacy of constitution and laws", "maintenance of the authority of constitution" and "taking constitution seriously". Of course, we do not deny the significance of these slogans in building Chinese constitutional government at this point. However, the speaker of these slogans is inappropriate. After all, we are living in a society with increasingly intensifying division of labor based on specialization. Our constitutionalists are different from politicians. It is not the responsibility, at least not the principal responsibility of jurists for shouting slogans.

---

[204] Liu and Cheng [139].

[205] Refer to [France] Bourdieu [142].

[206] [Germany] Kaufmann [143].

We need to demonstrate and prove why we should take constitution (authority of constitution) seriously, but more importantly, how we should take constitution seriously. What merits our reflections is that, over the past three decades, Chinese constitutional law used to be satisfied with this slogan-based preaching. While being called for taking constitution seriously, Chinese constitutional law studies have just failed to take China's constitution seriously. When we are promoting "constitutionalism" which is said to be a quality product of western society, we as constitutional scholars are the ones being convinced. Constitution is not the text simply composed of words. It is more like a value system. Narrating facts in social life by using constitutional words enables the connection between idealistic constitutional value and the facts of actual social life. Therefore, in China's constitutional community, more scholars have started to focus on China's constitutional practices, call for the practical character of constitutional law and promote a constitutional law with more explanatory power.

We can see from the historical development of constitutional law over the past three decades that China's overall theoretical research system for constitutional law studies have got rid of the influence of the national law model learned from Soviet teaching books and started to focus on how constitution as the fundamental law could play its legal function and role in the realistic society. However, the current constitutional theories, viewpoints, and doctrines have not completely adapted to China's practical needs of building the rule of law. Studies of constitutional law are too theoretical, but there is still a lack of analyses and studies of constitutional issues in real life. Existing constitutional theories fail to better interpret the constitutional phenomena in practices, still less providing an effective theoretical support in resolving practical constitutional issues. Therefore, there is a must to make the constitutional knowledge system more effective, reliable and scientific in order to get out of the traditional constitutional research framework. Specifically speaking, for some period to come, theoretical studies on constitutional law should prioritize the normative and scientific nature of constitutional texts and norms, the relations between constitution and specific legal forms and between constitution and branch laws, and the status and function of constitution in the system of law with Chinese characteristics. Going forward, theoretical studies on constitutional law should also emphasize the relations between constitution and international laws, civic system in constitution, national system in constitution, constitutional authorization and constitutional entrusting system, constitutional authority system, constitutional responsibility system, constitutional right system, constitutional obligation system, constitutional prohibition system, constitutional interpretation system, constitutional change system, emergency state system, constitution applicability system, constitutional dispute handling system, review for constitutionality system and constitutional supervision system. Theoretical studies on constitutional law should also lay stress on the relations between globalization and constitutionalism, social autonomy and constitutionalism, the basic constitutional relations between individuals and the state, relations between constitution and politics, relations between constitution and society, etc. There is a need to make constitutional theories more targeted and effective. Particularly, there is a need to realize the unity of legislative system based on various written provisions of constitution. There is a need to study the applicability of constitution in legislation, law enforcement and judicature and the feature of constitution with legal effect. There is a need to enable constitutional theories to effectively interpret the currently existing constitutional phenomena of various kinds in China through theoretical studies. There is also a need to provide a fundamental theoretical support for realizing China's law-based reform and improving the constitutional system.

References

1. Lin Laifan: *From Constitutional to Normative Constitution-A Preface of Normative Constitutional Law, China Law Press*, May 2001, 1st edition.
2. Liu Shude: *The Constitutional Research to Criminal Law*, China Law Press, June 2002, 1st edition.
3. Mo Jihong: *Logical Foundation of Modern Constitution*, chapter one, "methodology of constitutional logics", China Law Press, December 2001 edition.
4. Jiang Guohua: Critics of *Constitutional Philosophy*, Vol. 4 of *Constitutionalism Review* edited by Zhang Qingfu, China Law Press, June 2004, 1st edition.
5. Fan Zhongxin: *Getting to Know Legist Liang Qichao, Political Science and Law*, 1998, Issue 6.
6. Fan Zhongxin: *Legal Achievements of Reformists*, *Legal Daily*, January 7, 2001.
7. Han Dayuan: *Research on Chinese Constitutional Law during the society—transforming period*, *The Jurist*, 2002, Issue 6.
8. Han Dayuan, Hu Honghong: *Academic Community of Constitutional Scholars – Marking the 20th Anniversary of the Establishment of Constitutional Research Association of China Law Society*, Zhang Qingfu, Han Dayuan: *2005 Chinese Yearbook of Constitutional Law*, China Law Press, 2006 edition.
9. Mo Jihong: *Constitutionalism, Universalism and Democracy, Foreign Law Translation and Review*, 2000, Issue 1.
10. Hu Jinguang, Zang Baoqing: *Exploration of the Origin of the Meaning of Constitution*, published in *Zhejiang Social Sciences*, 1999, Issue 4.
11. Wang Shuwen: *Constitution*, Sichuan People's Publishing House, 1988 edition.
12. He Huahui: *Comparative Constitutional Law*, Wuhan University Press, 1988 edition, page 17.
13. Xu Qing: *Constitutional Law*, China University of Political Science and Law Press, 1995 edition, page 4.
14. Tian Jun: *Principles of Constitutional Law*, Nanjing University Press, 1991 edition, page 25.
15. Zheng Xianjun: *What Law Is Constitution*, published in the *Studies on Constitution and Administrative Rule of Law-Collected Works for Celebrating the 50th Anniversary of Teaching of Professor Xu Chongde* edited by the Research Center of Constitutionalism and Rule of Administrative Law, Renmin University of China, China Renmin University Press, 2003 edition, page 65.
16. Xie Weiyan: *Interpretation of the Concept of "Mother Law"- New Interpretation of the Relations between Constitution and Laws, Journal of Sichuan University (Social Science Edition)*, 2005, Issue 05.
17. Yu Ziqing: *Constitution*, China University of Political Science and Law Press, 1999 edition, page 10.
18. Dong Heping, Han Dayuan, Li Shuzhong: *Constitutional Law*, China Law Press, 2000 edition, page 39.

19. Yin Xiaohu, Wang Yueming: *Constitutional Law*, China Legal Publishing House, 2001 edition, page 9.
20. Yu Depeng: *Legal Norm System: A New Definition of the Concept of Constitution*, Political Science and Law, 1998, Issue 6.
21. Zhu Guobin: *Constitution and Political System of China*, China Law Press, 1997 edition, page 5.
22. Li Buyun: *Comparative Study on Constitution*, China Law Press, 1998 edition, page 23.
23. Zhu Fuhui: *New Edition of Constitutional Law*, China Law Press, 1998 edition, page 9.
24. Lyu Taifeng: *What Is Constitution, Studies in Law and Business*, 1999, Issue 6.
25. Liu Jinghai: *Civic Rights and State Power --Cognition of Basic Constitutional Issues, Jilin University Journal: Social Sciences Edition,* 1990, Issue 6.
26. Wang Lei: *On the Concept of Constitution*, published in *Law Science Magazine*, 1999, Issue 5.
27. Tong Zhiwei: *Constitutional Research Method Modification, Law Science*, 1994, Issue 9.
28. Tong Zhiwei: *Using the Social Right Analysis Method to Reconstruct the Constitutional Law System, Chinese Journal of Law*, 1994, Issue 5.
29. Liu Maolin: *What Exactly Is Constitution*: *China Legal Science*, 2002, Issue 6.
30. Lin Laifan: *From Constitutional to Normative Constitution*, China Law Press, 2001 edition.
31. Zheng Xianjun: *Why Does Constitutional Law Require Consciousness in Methodology? - Discussions on Constitutional Methodology, Zhejiang Academic Journal*, 2005, Issue 2.
32. Lin Laifan, Zheng Lei et al.: *Fantasy of Dialogues and Agreements-Summary of A Round-table Academic Meeting on China's Constitution, Zhejiang Social Sciences*, 2005, Issue 3.
33. Lin Laifan, Zheng Lei: *So-called Centering on Normativity* published in *Zhejiang Academic Journal*, 2005, Issue 4.
34. Han Dayuan, Zhang Xiang: *On Objectivity and Subjectivity of Constitutional Interpretation, Science of Law*, 1999.
35. Han Dayuan, Zhang Xiang: *On the Limit of Constitutional Interpretation*, published in *Law Review*, 2001, Issue 1.
36. Zhang Xiang: *Disenchantment and Self-containment: Influence and Limitation of Political Theories on Constitutional Interpretation*, published in *Tribune of Political Science and Law*, 2007, Issue 4.
37. Fan Jinxue: *Constitutionalism and Method: Interpretation Moving towards the Text of Constitution - Analysis of the Significance of Constitutional Hermeneutics, Zhejiang Academic Journal*, 2005, Issue 2.
38. Zou Pingxue: *Humble Opinions on the Introduction of Economic Analysis Methods to Studies on Constitutionalism, Law and Social Development*, 1996, Issue 1.
39. Hu Jinguang, Chen Xiong: *Thinking about Chinese Constitutional Research Methods, Zhejiang Academic Journal*, 2005, Issue 4.
40. Liu Hui: *Modern Constitutional Development Challenge and Trend, Procuratorate Daily*, November 10, 2006.
41. Liu Maolin: *Dilemma and Outlet for China's Constitutional Law, Studies in Law and Business*, 2005, Issue 1.
42. Zhang Guangbo: *Recognition of the Basic Categories of Constitutional Law, Chinese Journal of Law*, 1987, Issue 3.
43. Li Long, Zhou Yezhong: *Brief Introduction of the Basic Categories of Constitutional Law, China Legal Science*, 1996, Issue 6.
44. Han Dayuan: *Analysis of and Reflection on the Basic Categories of China's Constitutional Law in 1950s, Contemporary Law Review*, 2005, Issue 5.
45. Hu Honghong: *Brief Introduction of Differences between Human Rights and Civic Rights, Proceeding of the 2005 Annual Meeting of China Constitutional Research Association of China Law Society (Vol. A)*, page 504.
46. Zhang Zhiben: *On Constitution*, China Fangzheng Press, 2004 edition, (edition of collation of ancient books, proofed by Yin Xiaohu, Li Li).

47. Xu Chongde: *Constitutional Law*, China Renmin University Press, 1999 edition.
48. Hu Jinguang, Han Dayuan: *The Chinese Constitution*, China Law Press, 2004.
49. Wang Guanghui: *On Adjustment Objects of Constitution and Theoretical System of Constitutional Law*, *The Jurist*, 2007, Issue 6.
50. Tong Zhiwei: *Constitutional Teaching and Research of China over the Past Three Decades*, *Science of Law: Journal of Northwest University of Political Science and Law*, 2007, Issue 6.
51. Zhu Fuhui: *On the Innovation of the Constitutional Law System of China*, *Journal of Yunmeng*, 2002, Issue 5.
52. Zhou Yezhong, Zhou Youyong: *Reflections and Reconstruction of Constitutional Theory System*, *Chinese Journal of Law*, 2001, Issue 4.
53. Lyu Taifeng: *Rebuild the Constitutional Law System with Rights and Powers as the Center*, *The Jurist*, 2000, Issue 5.
54. Chen Baoyin: *Thinking of the Constitutional Law System of China*, *The Jurist*, 2000, Issue 3.
55. Zhao Shiyi: *Basic Issues in Economic Constitution*, *Chinese Journal of Law*, 2001, Issue 4.
56. Tong Zhiwei: *Legal Rights and Constitutionalism*, Shandong People's Publishing House, 2000 edition.
57. Zhao Shiyi, Zou Pingxue: *Questioning of Using Social Right Analysis Method to Rebuild Constitutional Law System*, *Chinese Journal of Law*, 1995, Issue 5.
58. Mo Jihong: *Logic Foundation of Modern Constitution*, China Law Press, 2001 edition, page 48–51.
59. Hou Meng: *Building of Branch Subject System and Development of Constitutional Law of China*, *Jianghai Academic Journal*, 2006, Issue 3.
60. Mo Jihong: *An Examination of "Ought to Be"–A Field of Vision of Constitutional Logic*, *Social Sciences in China*, 2001, Issue 6.
61. Mo Jihong: *Research Target and Task of China's Constitutional Law in the 21st Century*, *The Jurist*, 2000, Issue 3.
62. Li Qi: *Constitutional Philosophy: Questioning the Legitimacy of Constitution*, *Journal of Xiamen University*, 2005, Issue 3.
63. Wen Zhengbang: *Constitutional Philosophy - New Vision of Deepening Constitutionalism Theory*, website of *Procuratorate Daily*, www.jcrb.com.
64. Xie Weiyan: *Direction of Constitutional Law: from Constitutional Science to Constitutional Philosophy*, *Journal of Sichuan Normal University*, 2006, Issue 1.
65. Liu Zhigang: *Philosophical Dimension of Constitution*, *Political Science and Law*, 2003, Issue 3.
66. Xu Zhendong: *Philosophy of Constitutional Interpretation*, China Law Press, 2006 edition.
67. Zheng Xianjun: *Sociological Concept of Constitution*, *Science of Law*, 2002, Issue 3.
68. Dong Fanyu: *Chinese Constitutional Law over the Past 14 Years*, *Tribune of Political Science and Law*, 1989, Issue 5.
69. Han Dayuan: *On the Basic Framework and Method of Constitutional Sociology*, *Zhejiang Academic Journal*, 2005, Issue 2.
70. Lin Laifan: *Comparative Studies on the Features of Chinese and Japanese Constitutional Studies*, *The Jurist*, 1997, Issue 4.
71. Wang Guanghui: *Comparative Constitution*, Peking University Press, 2007 edition, Preface.
72. Han Dayuan: *Development and Major Trend of Contemporary Comparative Constitutional Law*, published in *Exploration into Constitution and Administrative Rule of Law: Collected Works for Celebrating the 50th Anniversary of Teaching of Professor Xu Chongde*, China Renmin University Press, 2005 edition.
73. Liang Qichao: *On Constitutionalism*, published in *Collected Legal Works of Liang Qichao*, China University of Political Science and Law Press, 2000 edition.
74. Zhang Xiang: *Double Characters of Basic Rights*, *Chinese Journal of Law*, 2005, Issue 3.
75. He Yonghong: *Constitutionality review for Basic Right Restriction*, doctoral dissertation in 2007 at Zhejiang University.

76. Wang Shucheng: *Difficulties in Regulating Proportionality Principles and Countermeasures*, *Contemporary Law Review*, 2007, Issue 6.
77. Lin Laifan, Ji Yanmin: *Human Rights Protection: Significance as Principle*, *Studies in Law and Business*, 2005, Issue 4.
78. Wang Guanghui: *Destiny and Historic Responsibilities of Constitutionalists*, publaw.znufe.edu.cn, last visited on April 5, 2008.
79. Zhang Jinfan, *Zeng Xianyi: Brief History of the Constitution of China*, Beijing Publishing House, 1979 edition.
80. Jiang Bikun: *Brief History of the Constitutionalism and Constitution in Contemporary China*, published by China Law Press, 1988 edition.
81. Xu Chongde: *Constitutional History of the People's Republic of China*, Fujian People's Publishing House, 2003 edition.
82. Yin Xiaohu: *the History of Modern Constitutionalism in China*, Shanghai People's Publishing House, 1997 edition; Wang Renbo: *Modern China and Its Constitutional Culture*, China Law Press, 1997 edition.
83. Cai Dingjian: *The People's Congress System of China*, China Law Press, 2003 edition.
84. Zhao Shichen: *Brief Comments on the People's Congress System of China*, *Journal of Northeast Normal University*, 1998, Issue 1; Long Taijiang: *Analysis of Several Issues related to the Combination of Legislative and executive Powers*, *The Journal of Yunnan Administration College*, 2000, Issue 5.
85. Zeng Jun: *On the Combination of Legislative and Executive Powers*, *Theoretical Study Monthly*, 1995, Issue 7.
86. Fan Yi: *The Combination of Legislative and Executive Power of China's People's Congress System Has Chinese Characteristics*, *Journal of Yiyang Teachers College*, 1995, Issue 2.
87. Xu Chongde: *Encyclopedia of Chinese Law-Constitution*, China Procratorate Press, 1995 edition, page 749.
88. Du Gan: *Analysis of Several Issues in Studying the Theory of People's Congress*, *Social Science Research*, 2001, Issue 3.
89. Wang Yuming: *The Combination of Legislative and Executive Powers Is Not the Organization Principle of China's State Organs*, *Tribune of Political Science and Law*, 1989, Issue 4.
90. Han Dayuan, Zhu Fuhui, Xu Zhendong, Chen Junjun: *Development Course of the Constitutional awareness of Mr. Wu Jialin*, www.calaw.cn, June 3, 2005.
91. Liu Zheng, Cheng Xiangqing: *Theory and Practice of the People's Congress System*, page 108–115, China Democracy and Legal System Publishing House, 2003 edition.
92. Zhou Yongkun: *The Principle of Combining Legislative and Executive Powers Should Be Thoroughly Abandoned*, *Science of Law*, 2006, Issue 1.
93. Tong Zhiwei, Wu Jin, Zhu Meiquan: *Introspection and Reevaluation of the Law Community on the Theory of Combining Legislative and Executive Powers*, Jianghai Academic Journal, 2003, Issue 5.
94. Han Dayuan, Liu Zhigang: *Review and Outlook of Studies on Constitutional Law* in 2000, *The Jurist*, 2001, Issue 1.
95. Sun Hengsan: *Thinking on Difficult Problems in the Individual Case Supervision of the People's Congress*, *Law and Social Development*, 2000, Issue 31.
96. Li Guozhi, Feng Xiaoqin: *Reverse Thinking of the Individual Case Supervision of Courts by the People's Congress*, *Law Science*, 2000, Issue 5.
97. Liu Liping: "Questioning of the Constitutional Basis for Individual Case Supervision of the People's Congress", *Law Science Magazine*, 2005, Issue 4.
98. Shen Qingzhong: *Thinking on the Exercise of Supervision by the People's Congress*, *Journal of Law Application*, 2000, Issue 6.
99. Mo Jihong: "Give Play to the Role of Constitution and Staying committed to Governance by Law," *Legal Daily*, September 20, 1997.
100. Xu Hang: *Simple Analysis of the Regional National Autonomy System by Using the New Institutional Economics*, *Modern Business*, 2007, Issue 26.

101. Zhang Wenshan: *Studies on Issues Concerning Supporting Legislation for Regional National Autonomy Law*, China Law Press, 2007 edition.
102. Yang Linhong: *Improve China's Regional National Autonomous System under the Guidance of the Concept of Constitutionalism*, *Yunnan People's Congress*, 2005, Issue 4.
103. Cheng Jian: *Empirical Analysis of Autonomous Regulations of Regional National Autonomous Areas*, *Proceeding of the 2007 Annual Meeting of the Constitutional Research Association of China Law Society*.
104. Wang Shuwen: *Introduction to the Basic Law of Hong Kong Special Administrative Region*, Press of Party School of the Central Committee of C.P.C, 1997 edition.
105. Wang Shuwen, Zheng Chengsi: *Introduction to the Basic Law of Macao Special Administrative Region*, Press of Party School of the Central Committee of C.P.C, 2001 edition.
106. Wang Shuwen: *On the Basic Rights and Obligations of Citizens of Hong Kong Special Administrative Region*, *Science of Law*, 1990, Issue 5.
107. Wang Shuwen: *Characteristics of the Rights and Obligations of Citizens of Macao*, *Macao Daily News*, 1999, March 30.
108. Wang Zhenmin: *Relations between the Central Government and Special Administrative Regions: a Law-based Structural Analysis*, Tsinghua University Press, 2002 edition.
109. Cheng Jie: *Judicial Power of Hong Kong under the Dual Track System*, *China Legal Science*, 2006, Issue 5.
110. Jiao Hongchang: *Studies on Several Issues Concerning the Basic Law of Macao Special Administrative Region*, *Tribune of Political Science and Law*, (Journal of CUPL), 1999, Issue 1.
111. Li Qi: *Nature of the Basic Law of Special Administrative Regions: Special Law of Constitution*, *Journal of Xiamen University: Philosophy and Social Sciences*, 2002, Issue 5.
112. Ling Bing: *Limit of the Basic Law of Hong Kong Special Administrative Region and the Legislative Power of the National People's Congress-Constitutional Thinking on the Judgment of the Residence Right by the Court of Final Appeal of Hong Kong Special Administrative Region*, *The Rule of Law Forum*, 2003, Issue 1.
113. Qiang Shigong: *Text, Structure and Legislation Purpose-Legal Skills of the National People's Congress' Interpretations of the Basic Law*, published in *Social Sciences in China*, 2007, Issue 5.
114. Xu Yong: *Building of Modern Country and Growth of Villager Autonomy-Interpretation of the Emergence and Development of Village Autonomy in China*, *Study and Exploration*, 2006, Issue 6.
115. Lin Shangli: *Grassroots Autonomy: China's Practices in Building Democracy*, *Cass Journal of Political Science*, 1999, Issue 4.
116. Cui Zhiyou: *Legal Reflection on Villager Autonomy in China*, *Social Sciences in China*, 2001, Issue 3.
117. Gao Wang: *Studies on Issues Related to the "Two Skins"- Party Branch and Villager Committee of Villages under the Background of Village Autonomy*, *Material in the Copy Press: Chinese Politics*, 2002, Issue 11.
118. Wang Zhenya: *Several Reflections on the Rationalization of Villager Autonomy*, *Journal of Shaanxi Normal University: Philosophy and Social Science Edition*, 2002, Issue 9.
119. Tan Tongxue: *Summary of the Academic Workshop on the Township-Village Relations in the Process of Villagers Autonomy*, *Open Times*, 2002, Issue 1.
120. Xiao Weiyun: *On the Constitution-making Power of the PRC*, *China Legal Science*, 1984, Issue 1.
121. Han Dayuan, Lin Laifan, Zheng Xianjun: *Study on the Subject of Constitutional Law*, China Renmin University Press, 2004 edition, the part written by Han Dayuan.
122. Zhang Jiansheng: *On Constitution-making Power*, published in *Soochow Law Review*, 2001 edition.
123. Han Dayuan: *On the Nature and Limit of Constitution Amending Power*, *The Jurist*, 2003, Issue 5.

124. Dou Xingxing: *On the Limit of Constitution-amending Power, Journal of Southwest University of Political Science and Law*, 2006, Issue 1.
125. Du Qiangqiang: *Analysis of the Concept of Constitution-amending Power, Journal of Henan Administrative Institute of Politics and Law*, 2005, Issue 1.
126. Du Qiangqiang: *"Basic Framework Restriction" of Constitution-amending Power, Studies in Law and Business*, 2006, Issue 3.
127. Du Qiangqiang: *Implicit Limit of Constitution-amending Power, Global Law Review*, 2006, Issue 4.
128. Cheng Xiangqing: *On the Improvement of the Supervision System of People's Congress*, National People's Congress of China, 2004, Issue 8.
129. Hu Jinguang's *Studies on Chinese Constitutional Issues*, Xinhua Publishing House, 1998 edition.
130. Fei Shancheng: *On China's Selection of the Model of constitutionality review Review for constitutionality System, Tribune of Political Science and Law*, 1999, Issue 2.
131. Zhao Xiaoli: *Judicial Process and Democratic Process, Chinese Journal of Law*, 2004, Issue 4.
132. Wang Lei: *On China's Constitutional Interpretation Agency, Peking University Law Journal*, 1993, Issue 6.
133. Bao Wanchao: *Establish the Double-checking System of the Constitutional Council Collateral with the constitutionality review Review for constitutionality Court of the Supreme People's Court, Law Science*, 1998, Issue 4.
134. Liang Huixing: *Why should the case involving a girl being deprived of education be judged by constitution – calm thinking of judicatory actualization of constitution, World Journal of Law*, 2002, Issue 04.
135. Yin Xiaohu: *Several Queries and Thinking of Judicatory Actualization of Constitution, Material in the Copy Press: Constitutional Law and Administrative Law*, 2002, Issue 2.
136. Wang Lei: *Judicatory Actualization of Constitution – Basic Ideas of China's Constitutional Research in the 21st Century, The Jurist*, 2000, Issue 3.
137. Liu Liantai: *Empirical Analysis and Comments on Direct Application of Chinese Constitutional Norms in Trials in China, Chinese Journal of Law*, 1996, Issue 6.
138. Lin Laifan, Zhu Yuxia: *Malposition and Coincidence – On the Four Thinking Trends of the Current Relations between Constitution and Civil Law, Zhejiang Social Sciences*, 2007, Issue 1.
139. Liu Siyuan, Cheng Jianfeng: *Studies on Several Theoretical Issues Related to the CPPCC, Public Administration & Law*, 2004, Issue 11.
140. Li Bing: *On the Normalization and Legalization of the People's Political Consultative System*, Socialism Studies, 1998, Issue 3.
141. Fan Zhongxin, Wang Yibai: *On the People's Representative Organs and Legalization of the People's Political Consultative Conference, Studies in Law and Business*, 2001, Issue 6.
142. Bourdieu: *Language and Symbolic Power*, translated by Wu Fei, *Academic Thought Review* (Vol. 5), Liaoning University Publishing House, 1999 edition, page 116–117.
143. Kaufmann: *Rechtsphilosophie*, China Law Press, 2003 edition, page 170.

The International Perspective: Thirty Years of International Outreach and Exchanges (1981–2012)

Jihong Mo

Founded in September 1981, the International Association of Constitutional Law (IACL) is an international non-governmental academic organization uniting global constitutional scholars to conduct constitutional studies and exchanges. Being elected as an executive member of the IACL at the First World Congress of Constitutional Law held in Belgrade, Yugoslavia, in 1983, Chinese famous constitutionalist Mr. Zhang Youyu became a member of the leadership of this international organization for the first time. At the Second World Congress of Constitutional Law convened in Paris, France, in 1987, Mr. Zhang Youyu was reappointed as an executive member of the IACL. Notable constitutionalist Mr. Wang Shuwen was elected as an executive member of the IACL at the Third World Congress of Constitutional Law in Warsaw, Poland, in 1991 and was reelected at the Fourth World Congress of Constitutional Lawin Tokyo, Japan, in 1995. Mr. Pu Zengyuan, an eminent constitutionalist of Shanghai Academy of Social Sciences, became an executive member of the IACL at the Fifth World Congress of Constitutional Law in Rotterdam, the Netherlands, in 1999 and won a second term at the Sixth World Congress of Constitutional Law in San Diego, Chile, in 2004. As an international academic organization, the IACL has witnessed continuous development and growth in recent years, so it has gradually opened itself to more international and regional constitutional research groups from taking national constitutional associations as the basis. Accordingly, global different geographical and cultural areas have become the targets for selecting members of the Executive Committee as an important leading organization of the IACL. Executive members of the IACL no longer represent the interests of their respective member states. Instead, the IACL nominates those recommended by the Nominating Committee within the global reach according to its own development requirements. At the Seventh World Congress of Constitutional Law held in Athens, Greece, in June

J. Mo (✉)
Institute of Law of Chinese Academy of Social Sciences, Beijing, China
e-mail: 13263169197@163.com

L. Li et al. (eds.), *Constitutional Development in China, 1982–2012*,
Research Series on the Chinese Dream and China's Development Path,
https://doi.org/10.1007/978-981-32-9261-1_4

2007, Mo Jihong, Executive Vice President of Constitutional Research Association of China Law Society and researcher of the Institute of Law of Chinese Academy of Social Sciences (CASS), was successfully elected as an executive member of IACL. His election indicated IACL executives' full acknowledgment of the achievements of Chinese constitutional scholars in advancing and promoting the communication and cooperation between the Chinese constitutional circle and the IACL in recent years. His election also demonstrated that China's accomplishments in studying constitutional theories and building the rule of law have received more and more attention of international constitutional circles.

The IACL was founded in 1981. It is an international non-governmental academic organization under the guidance of the United Nations Educational, Scientific and Cultural Organization (UNESCO). Its main purpose is to unite global constitutional scholars to carry out comparative studies on the development of constitutional systems of different countries, strengthen mutual academic exchanges and promote the development of different countries in theoretical research on constitutional law. China Law Society has been a group member of the IACL ever since the association's establishment. China Law Society has been actively exercising its rights as a state member and positively participating in academic exchange activities organized by the association. China Law Society has made use of all occasions to introduce China's achievements in building the constitutional system and latest results in constitutional law research to its constitutional peers worldwide. As a consequence, China Law Society has gained some ground in the IACL.

The IACL typically organizes academic activities in the form of quadrennial World Congress of Constitutional Law and several roundtable meetings on constitution every year. Up to now, the IACL has organized eight sessions of the World Congress of Constitutional Law and nearly 40 roundtable meetings. Ever since the foundation of the IACL, China Law Society has been active in organizing domestic constitutional scholars to attend all academic activities of the association. China Law Society has organized delegations to the IACL's all eight sessions of World Congress of Constitutional Law and most table meetings. In order to further expand its organization influence in the IACL, China Law Society held a roundtable meeting of the IACL in Beijing in October 2002. The meeting invited nearly 30 foreign experts affiliated to the IACL for academic exchange and ended with a great success.

With the growingly expanding influence of the IACL in constitutional circles in the world in recent years, member units of the IACL have actively bid for organizing its roundtable meetings besides the quadrennial World Congress of Constitutional Law. By doing so, they wish to expand the academic influence of constitutional research results of their respective countries in international constitutional circles through the roundtable meetings. In recent years, China's social security problems have become increasingly prominent and the building of legal system in the field of social security has also been highly valued by the Chinese government and academic circle. To better learn and draw on other countries' achievements in building the legal system and academic research results in the field of social security, IACL's executive member Mo Jihong submitted a formal application to the Executive Committee of the IACL with the consent of China Law Society for holding an IACL roundtable meeting under the theme of "constitutional protection of the right to social security" in Xi'an, Shaanxi Province, in October 2011. This application was formally approved at a meeting of the Executive Committee of the IACL in Mexico on December 10, 2010.

For holding a successful roundtable meeting of the IACL, China Law Society organized domestic constitutional experts and scholars to seriously prepare for the event and won great support from various aspects. All organizational works were carried out smoothly.

To further enhance the connections between the IACL and the Chinese constitutional community, China Constitutional Research Association, which was just established at Northwest University of Political Science and Law, invited two executive members who would attend the roundtable of the IACL in Xi'an in 2011 to make reports at the closing ceremony of its Annual Meeting before the roundtable meeting. The two executive members were Mr. César Landa, former President of the Constitutional Court of Peru, and Mrs. Christina Murray, current Vice President of the IACL. The two experts mainly introduced the important role of Constitutional Court in safeguarding human rights and maintaining the authority of constitution and the implementation of the constitution of South Africa since its formulation. Their reports were highly appraised by experts and scholars attending the Annual Meeting of China Constitutional Research Association. Besides, during the Xi'an Roundtable Meeting of the IACL, Northwest University of Political Science and Law, one of the undertakers of the roundtable meeting, especially invited three foreign constitutionalists participating in the event to give academic lectures at the university. They introduced to the faculty and students the current constitutional issues attracting the attention of international constitutional circles and the latest development of the constitutional system in various countries. Their introductions broadened the vision of the faculty and students of the university and produced fruitful results. Before the conclusion of the roundtable meeting, President Jia Yu of Northwest University of Political Science and Law especially invited all foreign participants of the 2011 Xi'an Roundtable Meeting to visit the new campus and had informal discussions with principal leaders of the IACL. The host and the guests exchanged gifts and expressed their wishes for academic communication and cooperation.

After the conclusion of the Xi'an Roundtable Meeting, foreign attendees led by Chinese executive member Mo Jihong visited Macao Polytechnic Institute (MPI). They had an extended meeting of the Xi'an Roundtable Meeting at the "One Country Two Systems" Research Center of MPI. At the extended meeting, the participants focused on discussing the achievements of Macao Special Administrative Region (Macao SAR) in the implementation of the Basic Law after its return to the motherland, especially its experiences in guaranteeing the social rights of citizens of Macao.

Following the trip to Macao, foreign delegates of the 2011 Xi'an Roundtable Meeting also visited Hong Kong Special Administrative Region (Hong Kong SAR) and personally felt the economic achievements of Hong Kong SAR in a dozen of years after its foundation. After field visits to Macao and Hong Kong, all foreign representatives of the Xi'an Roundtable Meeting expressed their impressiveness of and gratitude for the trip to China. Many experts also expressed their wishes for strengthening the communication and cooperation with the Chinese constitutional community.

Ever since its foundation in 1981, the IACL has organized eight sessions of World Congress of Constitutional Law.[1] All the themes of the eight sessions were designed in line with the development situation of constitutionalism in modern countries worldwide. At the same time, the eight events had extensive academic discussions about the latest constitutional issues attracting widespread attention of global countries on the basis of the results of traditional theoretical studies on constitutional law. Also, under the organization of the IACL, 20-plus roundtable meetings have been held in member states to have in-depth discussions about some hot constitutional issues.[2] It can be said that the academic activities conducted and constitutional issues discussed by the IACL in the past 27 years have basically reflected the frontier issues and development trend of theoretical studies on constitutional law in today's countries worldwide. These academic activities and discussions are of great significance to the deepening of China's theoretical research on constitutional law.

The First World Congress of Constitutional Law was held in Belgrade, former Yugoslavia, in August 1983. Chinese famous constitutionalist Professor Xiao Weiyun attended the great event on behalf of executive member Zhang Youyu. This World Congress of Constitutional Law brought together 160 delegates from 28 countries. The Congress had panel discussions on 5 topics: (1) concept of modern constitution; (2) issues related to constituent power; (3) interpretation of constitution; (4) applicability of constitution; (5) constitutionality of laws.

The Second World Congress of Constitutional Law was convened in Paris and Aix-en-Provence of France between August 31 and September 4, 1987. Professor Zhang Youyu, well-known constitutionalist and IACL executive member, led a Chinese delegation of 4 members attended the event on behalf of China Law Society. This session brought together 350 constitutionalists from 47 countries. This grand gathering discussed the concept of human rights and relevant tasks, the third generation of human rights, constitutional guarantee of human rights, relations between constitution and international laws, strengthening of constitution and property rights and administrative rights, etc. Chinese delegates submitted and distributed the report titled *Development of China's Current Constitution in the Basic Rights and Freedom of Citizens* to the Congress. Professor Xiao Weiyun presided over a panel discussion on "the form of citizens' participation in national

[1]As determined by the Executive Committee of the IACL, the Ninth World Congress of Constitutional Law was planned to take place in Oslo, capital of Norway in early June 2014.

[2]For the round tables organized by the IACL in recent years, please visit the website of the IACL: http://www.iacl-aidc.org.

management” as a subgroup chairman and introduced the current situation of Chinese citizens’ participation in national management.

The Third World Congress of Constitutional Law took place in Warsaw, Poland, between September 2 and 5, 1991. Chinese distinguished constitutionalist Wang Shuwen led a delegation to the conference. This session attracted more than 400 participants, two-thirds of whom came from Europe and America and the other one-third from other regions. The theme of this occasion was “the Constitutional development on the eve of the Third Millennium.” The Congress had in-depth discussions on four special topics. First, it is commemoration of the 1791 Constitution of Poland and 1791 Constitution of France and the significance. Second, it is the development of the constitutional system of East Europe and Central Europe. Third, it is the generation of democracy in the Third World. Fourth, it is the strengthening of constitutional implementation in Western countries. The panels also had full discussions on constitution and communication, constitution and scientific progress, economic and social development challenges faced by constitution, constitution and legislative requirement, constitution and local autonomous requirement, etc. Professor Wang Shuwen delivered a special speech titled “the role of China’s constitution in guaranteeing and promoting the reform and opening-up” at a panel meeting. Chinese scholars’ introductions of China’s achievements in building the constitutional system and the legal system since the reform and opening-up were highly valued and appraised by the participants.

The Fourth World Congress of Constitutional Law was held in Tokyo, Japan, between September 25 and 28, 1995. The theme of this session was “Five Decades of Constitutionalism—Reality and Perspectives.” This congress centered on the following eight aspects for full discussions. These eight aspects included development and crisis of constitutionalism; constitution: interpretation and interpreters; constitution and peace within a country; the minority, human rights and welfare state; constituent power and birth of a new state; function and development of parliament; evolution of federalism, regionalism and separation of powers; political party and constitutional system.

The Fifth World Congress of Constitutional Law hosted by the IACL took place at Erasmus University of Rotterdam, the Netherlands, between July 12 and 16, 1999. This congress took “Constitutionalism, Universalism & Democracy” as the theme. The organizing committee of the Congress shortlisted a dozen of important issues centering on the theme of the Congress for discussions among participants. The theme of the Congress involved constitutional legitimacy in judicial judgment and democracy, universality of the basic human rights and cultural pluralism, and constitutionalism of national state undergoing changes. The themes of panel discussions included selection of the model, concept and practice of constitution; constitutional framework of representative democracy; constitutional rights of the minority, including localism; constitutional rights and weakening countries; constitutional rights of stateless persons; constitution, democracy and corruption; religion and state; individual and collective equal rights, including confirmatory action; rule of law and law-based country, constitution and bioethics; and education of constitution. The participants had heated discussions on each special topic organized by the Congress in the light of the constitutional government development practices of different countries, which promoted their mutual learning and understandings. The Chinese delegation spoke enthusiastically at the Congress and panel discussions, actively introduced China's achievements in building the legal system and the NPC's amendment to the constitution of the current year to the attendees, which attracted widespread attention of the participants.

The Sixth World Congress of Constitutional Law hosted by the IACL was held in San Diego, capital of Chile, between January 11 and 17, 2004. Nearly 500 representatives from 62 countries were presented at the Congress, making it the session with the most attendees. China Law Society sent to the Congress a delegation of 6 members with Liu Fahe, Vice President of China Law Society and Mo Jihong, Vice President of Constitutional Research Association of China Law Society as the head and deputy head respectively. At the sixth meeting of the Council of the IACL, Professor Pu Zengyuan was elected as a member of the Executive Committee of the IACL. Professor Mo Jihong and Professor Dong Heping were elected as directors of the IACL. The theme of this congress was "Constitutionalism: Old Concepts, New Worlds." The organizing committee of the Congress chose a dozen of important issues centering on the theme of the Congress for discussions among the participants. Subthemes of the Congress involved rights, state, the minority and indigenous peoples; external influence on the emergence of constitution of a national state; freedom of expression, privacy and the Internet. The subthemes also involved human rights and private laws; right to self-determination; social and economic rights; and constitution. Other subthemes included local democracy and representative system; transnational rights of citizens; international restrictions on the formulation of constitution; constitution, rule of law and migration; comparison of constitutionality review models; and rules and principles of unwritten constitution. The Congress also included key speeches and discussions on the nature of state; changing constitutional models; formulation and revision of constitution and democracy; and constitutional comparison in practice. The participants had heated discussions on all special topics organized by the Congress based on the practical experiences of different countries in constitutional government development and in line with the influence of globalization on modern constitutionalism. This Congress enabled the participants to enhance their mutual understandings of many issues and reached certain consensuses. The Chinese delegation actively took part in the plenary conference and panel discussions, actively introduced China's achievements in building the legal system and revising the Constitution to the participants and received their extensive attentions.

The IACL organized its Seventh World Congress of Constitutional Law in Athens, capital of Greece between June 11 and 15, 2007. This Congress brought together nearly 600 delegates from 70 countries, making it the session with the most participants ever since. China Law Society sent to the Congress a delegation of 8 members headed by Mo Jihong, Vice President of Constitutional Research Association of China Law Society. At the seventh meeting of the Council of the IACL, Professor Mo Jihong was elected as a member of the Executive Committee of the IACL. Professor Dong Heping and Dr. Dai Ruijun represented China Law

Society to attend the plenary meeting of the Council. This session of the World Congress of Constitutional Law was themed by "Rethinking the Boundaries of Constitution." The participants had heated discussions on the fourth themes and sixteen subthemes organized by the organizing committee of the Congress. The four themes included "constitution between conflict and stability," "philosophy of constitutionalism under threat," "religion, state and society" and "internationalization of constitution." The sixteen subthemes involved "public engagement in the formulation of constitution," "constitution and state of emergency," "electoral system: reach balance between legitimacy and political instability," "European constitution and modern constitutionalism," "judicial review on sensitive political issues," "the role of constitutionalism mechanism in resolving the conflicts within a state," "latest development of constitutional theories and principles," "constitution and global terrorism," "restriction on constitution-amending power," "privatization-based constitutional guarantee," "state constitution of a federal constitutional state," "secularism and constitutionalism," "legitimacy of social rights," "gender equality, religious freedom and culture," "balance and proportionality principle in review for constitutionality" and "constitution, corruption and good governance." The participants had heated discussions on all special topics organized by the Congress based on the practical experiences of different countries in constitutional government development and in line with the influence of globalization on modern constitutionalism. This Congress enabled the participants to enhance their mutual understandings of many issues and reached certain consensuses. The Chinese delegation actively took part in the plenary session and panel discussions. Professor Mo Jihong chaired the discussions of the second panel on "constitution and state of emergency." Dr. Wang Zhenjun delivered a keynote speech titled "On Non-derogable Rights" in the discussions of panel two. The delegation of China Law Society actively briefed the Congress on China's accomplishment in building the legal system and theoretical studies on constitutional law, which received widespread attentions.

At the Seventh World Congress of Constitutional Law, the topics raised by the representatives voluntarily for discussions included: democratic control of national resources, state constitution, teaching of constitution, social rights, constitutional court, constitutional response to terrorism, human rights, mediation, comparative studies on constitutional and judicial rights, European constitution, constitution in text, output and input of laws; legal philosophy structure of constitution; education and constitution.

The Eighth World Congress of Constitutional Law was convened in the Palacio de Minería of Mexico City between December 6 and 10, 2010. This congress was organized by the IACL and undertaken by the Law Institute of the Universidad Nacional Autónoma de México. This event attracted nearly 600 representatives from 70 countries and received nearly 400 papers submitted by the participants to the organizing committee. This session of World Congress of Constitutional Law received the most papers compared with all previous sessions. China Law Society sent to the Congress a delegation of 12 members headed by Yin Baohu, Deputy

Director of the International Liaison Department of China Law Society, and Mo Jihong, researcher of the Institute of Law of CASS.

"Constitutions and Principles" was taken as the theme of the Congress which was divided into 4 theme units and 18 subtheme units. The topics of the 4 theme units were philosophical perspective of constitutional principles, formation and usage of constitution and principles, general or specific principles, constitutional principles and judges. The topics of the 18 subtheme units included: electoral system and constitutional principles, old authoritative constitution and new democratic constitution, media and constitutional principles, society under decentralization and principles, substate constitution, rule of law in the era of anti-terrorism, multi-culture and rights of indigenous residents, whether federalism is a constitutional principle, proportionality principle, inalienability of human rights, religion and state, foreign law: nutrient of legal philosophy, new trend of constitution of Latin America, revised power separation principle, influence of international laws on constitutional principles, constitutional principles and democratic transition, how to make comparison in comparative constitution, constitutional implications of regional integration, etc. The delegation of China Law Society participated in all academic activities on the 4 major themes and 18 subthemes. Researcher Mo Jihong chaired the workshop of the subforum 5 on "substate constitution." Other Chinese delegates made keynote speeches on themes and subthemes of the Congress, including Associate Professor Wang Zhenjun from CPC Dalian Municipal Committee Party School, Associate Researcher Han Bing from the Institute of World Economics and Politics, CASS, Associate Professor Wang Xiuzhe from Shandong Technology and Business University, Associate Professor Ding Wei from Harbin Engineering University and Associate Professor Zhang Yiqing from Xiangtan University, which received widespread attention of the participants.

The IACL held a roundtable to mark the 30th anniversary of the founding of the association and international seminar on main developments in constitutionalism and constitution between 1981 and 2011 in the Congress Hall of Belgrade, capital of Serbia, between May 4 and 5, 2012. Nearly 100 constitutional scholars from nearly 30 countries appeared at the Congress. This congress invited several founders of the IACL, including Nikolic, President of the Association of Constitutional Law of former Yugoslavia, French Senator Gérard, Starck from the University of Gottingen, Germany, Klein from Hebrew University of Jerusalem, Israel, and Thomas Fleiner from Swiss Federal Research Institute WSL, etc. These founders particularly introduced the specific information on the founding of the IACL in Belgrade, capital of former Yugoslavia, in September 1981. French Senator Gérard also mentioned the role of Mr. Zhang Youyu, a deceased Chinese famous constitutionalist, in the founding of the IACL. Over the past 30 years, the IACL has been actively organizing academic exchange activities under the organization and advocacy of all previous presidents of the Association, including Professor Gérard of Paris University, Professor Amor of Morocco University, Professor Fleiner of Swiss Federal Research Institute, Professor Rosenfield of Yeshiva University of New York, the USA, Professor Saunders of the University of Melbourne, Australia,

Professor Mauss of Paris University, France, and the current president Martin Scheinin of the IACL, Professor of European University as well as other international prestigious constitutional experts. The IACL has made its best efforts to serve as a platform for the global interactions of constitutional scholars and has the permanent residence of its Secretary-General at the University of Pretoria, South Africa. Since the foundation of the IACL 30 years ago, the academic exchange activities organized by the IACL have attracted the involvement of constitutional scholars from nearly 100 countries, and IACL has become the most extensively influential non-governmental academic organization within the global reach.

The Chinese Constitution as the Fundamental Law and Supreme Law of the Land: Marking the 30th Anniversary of the Adoption of the 1982 Constitution

Jinxue Fan

The Constitution of the People's Republic of China was adopted at the Fifth Session of the Fifth National People's Congress held on December 4, 1982. It has been 30 years since the promulgation of the Constitution. The Preamble to the Constitution contains the following statements in the last paragraph. "This Constitution affirms the achievements of the struggles of the Chinese people of all nationalities and defines the basic system and basic tasks of the state in legal form; it is the fundamental law of the state and has supreme legal authority. The people of all nationalities, all state organs and armed forces, all political parties and public organizations and all enterprises and undertakings in the country must take the Constitution as the basic norm of conduct, and they have the duty to uphold the dignity of the Constitution and ensure its implementation." However, over the past three decades, the procedure guarantee mechanism for the implementation of the Constitution has been bogged down. As declared in the Preamble to the Constitution, the Constitution is the fundamental law and higher law of China, which has not become a reality. What's the reason? How to interpret the statement that the Constitution is the fundamental law and higher law of China? How to choose the constitutional implementation path? For these questions, the author tried to make an initial research for advices of colleagues.

J. Fan (✉)
Koguan School of Law, Shanghai Jiao Tong University, Shanghai, China
e-mail: 13263169197@163.com

L. Li et al. (eds.), *Constitutional Development in China, 1982–2012*,
Research Series on the Chinese Dream and China's Development Path,
https://doi.org/10.1007/978-981-32-9261-1_5

1 What Is "Fundamental Law"? Why Is China's Constitution "The Fundamental Law of the State"?

What is "fundamental law"? According to *the Oxford Companion to Law*, fundamental law was a term commonly used in England in the seventeenth century. This term generally refers to the legal rules that shall not be violated by parliaments or courts. Sometimes, common law is said to be fundamental law, and so is *the Magna Carta*, or natural law, or natural reason. Yet, there is not any specific case to illustrate that a court sets aside or ignores the regulations or rules of common law on the ground of their violation of natural law or natural reason. This notion had already been abandoned in the eighteenth century.[1] Actually, the interpretation by Walker was still incomplete as it is simply a cycle of definition, meaning that the fundamental law is common law or natural law and common law or natural law is fundamental law. As such, we can further ask the following questions. Why is common law or *the Magna Carta*, or natural law or natural reason called the legal rules that shall not be violated by parliament or courts, or fundamental law? What's implied by them? Only after revealing their metaphors, we could understand the essence of fundamental law.

The true starting point of the history of English Common Law was the central trial system of "Justices in Eyre" established by King Henry II in the second half of the twelfth century. In the hearing of a case, unless there was a decree for pardon from the King, the justice typically analyzed Germanic laws and habits of different areas by referring to the common law of Germanic people and from the perspective of the interests and needs of foreign conquerors. After analyses, those thought to be correct and rational and consistent with the legislations of the King were taken as the basis for judgment. In this sense, Corwin believed that common law was established based on habits from the very beginning, but it is not merely habits because justices had actually applied "rationality" as the standard for verification when they chose to admit some habits and made them have effectiveness nationwide and to prohibit some habits for enforcement. Right reason as the cornerstone of common law was the correct reason of justices.[2] In other words, common law was discovered by justices in using their knowledge and reason, so it is nationally enacted and widely applicable across the nation. Therefore, common law had reflected the right reason of justices. Just because its concept as "right reason," common law was deemed as the higher law restricting the King as the supreme authority in the fourteenth century. Against this background, Justice Bracton of the Court of King's Bench under the reign of Henry III put forward the proposal, "the

[1] [Britain] Walker [1], p. 364.

[2] [U.S.] Corwin [2], pp. 19–20.

King ought to be under no man, but under God and the law because the law makes him King."[3] As the source of the King's power, common law is featured by fundamentality[4] and represents a fundamental law.

British aristocrats forced King John to sign *the Magna Carta* in 1215 with the main purpose of defending their liberties as free men. Later, *the Magna Carta* was regarded as the certificate of their liberties. Coke even regarded it as the renaissance and declaration of the ancient common law. In this sense, *the Magna Carta* is also known as *the Great Charter of Liberties*. According to Article 39 of *the Magna Carta*, "No freemen shall be taken or imprisoned or disseized or exiled or in any way destroyed, nor will we go upon him nor send upon him, except by the lawful judgment of his peers or by the law of the land."[5] This stipulation is taken as the source of due process of law in modern times. *The Magna Carta* is deemed as the fundamental law on the ground of two points. First, *the Magna Carta* implies the basic liberties of English free men. The concept of fundamental law raised by Prynne in the seventeenth century was the traditional individual liberties and property rights, especially those stipulated in *the Magna Carta*, which are basic, permanent and unalterable.[6] Second, *the Magna Carta* implies the notion of higher law under which the sovereignty is subject to the law. As stipulated in Article 61 of *the Magna Carta*, a council of 25 barons was established to monitor the implementation of *the Magna Carta*. If the king, or the king's justice, executive officer or any other servant violated the rights or destroyed any peace clause in any aspect, which was discovered by 4 of the 25 barons, it would be informed to the king for rectification within 40 days. Otherwise, the 4 barons would make the decision based on other barons. Together with all the people, the 25 barons must bring restraint and pressure to bear on the king, such as seizing the king's castle, land and properties, etc., till the correction of the error. Article 61 is the seed of the provisions of modern constitution for the implementation of constitution by constitutional courts. No wonder King John angrily said that the 25 barons were all his fathers. The former is "the most important part of a thing" in the sense of "fun damentality". The latter is the concept that the sovereignty of a secular state was rooted in the law.[7]

---

[3][U.S.] Corwin [2], p. 21.

[4]*Xinhua Dictionary* explains "fundamentality" as "the source or the most important part of a thing" (revised by Dictionary Research Center of Commercial Press: *Xinhua Dictionary*, the Commercial Press, 2001 edition, page 320; edited by the Dictionary Editorial Office of the Institute of Linguistics, CASS: *Contemporary Chinese Mini-Dictionary*, the Commercial Press, 1980 edition, page 175).

[5]Shilin et al. [3], p. 1262.

[6]Huntington [4], p. 93.

[7]By the fourteenth century, *the Magna Carta* was likely to be seen as a written constitution similar to what is understood in modern times. At the end of the thirteenth century, Edward I of England ordered all justices, sheriffs, mayors and other ministers to treat *the Magna Carta* as the common law in handling all lawsuits. Any judgment conflicting with it should be declared null and void. In 1368, Edward III of England who was in his late reign announced in written law that all written laws and regulations violating *the Magna Carta* must be invalid. Afterwards, *the Magna Carta*

The British theory of natural law or natural reason is Locke's natural law theory in the second half of the seventeenth century. In 1689, Locke wrote *the Second Treatise of Government* for defending the Glorious Revolution. The prominent characteristic of Locke's natural law theory is the integration of the concept of natural law into the natural rights of individuals. Locke pointed out, "The state of nature has a law of nature to govern it, which obliges every one: and reason, which is that law, teaches all humanity, who will but consult it, that being all equal and independent, no one ought to harm another in his life, health, liberty, or possessions."[8] Natural law is the rule for respecting and protecting people's natural rights of life, liberty and possessions from being harmed and encroached by others.[9] These natural rights contained in the natural law are prior to the government and still exist after the establishment of the government, and government could not create man's natural rights and its main purpose is to protect man's possessions for the sake of the peace, safety and public good of the people.[10] Therefore, "The law of nature stands as an eternal rule to all men, legislators as well as others. The rules that they make for other men's actions must, as well as their own and other men's actions, be conformable to the law of nature: i.e. to the will of God, of which that is a declaration, and the fundamental law of nature being the preservation of humanity, no human sanction can be good or valid against it."[11] Thus, it can be seen that the theory of seeing natural law or natural reason as the fundamental law also lies in two points. First, natural law implies the natural rights prior to and higher than the government, including such basic rights as life, liberty and possessions. Second, natural law is a higher law and the basis and source of government legislation In this sense, Walker observed that fundamental law actually indicated such principle that politics is subject to morality and individual rights, especially the guarantee of their liberties and possessions.[12]

As natural rights, i.e., human rights, are prior to and higher than government and are taken as the background of higher law, so the common law, or *the Magna Carta*, or natural law, or natural reason is regarded as a fundamental law, meaning the legal rules that should, by no means, be violated by parliament or courts. This is the basis for taking modern constitutions as the source of the fundamental law and higher law. The interpretation of fundamental law in *Black's Law Dictionary*—"the organic law defining the ruling principles of a nation or state, especially the constitution, which is also called organic law"[13]—is built on this concept. Basic rights represent the principal source of constitution defining the scope and mode of

---

was gradually absorbed to the mainstream of the common law and most of its contents were actualized in daily practices of courts. In this case, the British began to shift their worship from *the Magna Carta* to the common law (refer to [U.S.] Corwin [2], pp. 28–29).

[8]Locke [5], p. 6.

[9]Locke [5], p. 53.

[10]Locke [5], p. 80.

[11]Locke [5], p. 84.

[12]Walker [1], p. 364.

[13]Black's law Dictionary, West Group, ST PAUL, MIN., 1999, p. 683.

government power operation. After the USA took *the Bill of Rights* as an essential content of constitution in 1791, almost all countries' written constitutions have clearly stipulated the basic rights as the target that must be respected and protected by state government.

Even lacking the heritage of historical and cultural traditions of natural law or natural reason, China accepted the concept of natural rights, i.e., human rights in the fourth amendment to the Constitution in 2004. In this amendment, China included "respecting and protecting human rights" in the Constitution, making human rights become part and parcel of the Constitution of China. The acceptance of the human right concept in Western traditional culture was actually the inheritance of the concept of fundamental law. According to the text rules of China's constitution, the reason for taking the Constitution as the fundamental law of the state was that, firstly, "it affirms the achievements of the struggles of the Chinese people of all nationalities"; secondly, "it defines the basic system and basic tasks of the state".

First, what are the achievements of the struggles of the Chinese people of all nationalities? The Preamble to the Constitution pointed out, "the Chinese people waged many successive heroic struggles for national independence and liberation and for democracy and freedom". The author believes that this sentence fully expresses "the achievements of the struggles of the Chinese people of all nationalities," which are national independence and liberation, democracy and freedom. China descended to a semi-colonial and semi-feudal state after the Opium War in 1840. The Chinese people waged unyielding and heroic struggles for national independence and liberation. The Chinese people of all nationalities led by the Communist Party of China with Mao Zedong as the leader finally overthrew the rule of imperialism, feudalism and bureaucratic capitalism and founded the People's Republic of China in 1949. Ever since, the Chinese people have taken control of the state power and become masters of the country. In this connection, "national independence and liberation, democracy and freedom" being boiled down to one point is that the Chinese people of all nationalities have won democratic rights and liberties, including political, economic, cultural and social basic rights. Without national independence, there would be no right to survival and development of the people of a state; i.e., there would be no human rights. Without national liberation, there would be no liberties and equality of all nationalities and no basic rights of people of all nationalities. National independence and liberation is the precondition and guarantee for the realization of democracy and freedom. Therefore, the achievements of the struggles of the Chinese people of all nationalities as stated in the Constitution are the affirmation that "all powers of the People's Republic of China belong to the people" and "basic rights of citizens".

Second, the "fundamental system of the state" as stipulated in the Constitution is the socialist system. Article 1 of the Constitution stipulates, "The socialist system is the basic system of the People's Republic of China. Sabotage of the socialist system by any organization or individual is prohibited." The fundamental system, i.e., the socialist system, includes the socialist economic system, socialist cultural and educational system, socialist political system, socialist social system, etc. "The basic task of the state" as stipulated by the Constitution is "to concentrate its efforts on socialist modernization by following the road of building socialism with Chinese characteristics". The core of the socialist system is democracy and equality and socialist economic system, cultural and education system, political system and social system respectively correspond to the economic rights, cultural and educational rights, political rights and social rights. The basic tasks of the state include socialist modernization, and the basic target of socialist modernization is to improve and enhance the people's right to survival and development, improve people's livelihood and protect civic rights.

Analysis of the contents of the Preamble to the Constitution of China indicates that the Constitution "affirms the achievements of the struggles of the Chinese people of all nationalities and defines the basic system and basic tasks of the state," so it is "the fundamental law of the state and has supreme legal authority". In the final analysis, China's Constitution is the fundamental law of the state because it affirms the popular sovereignty and citizens' basic rights and stipulates the state's respect and guarantee of human rights.

Chen Duanhong used to talk about the Constitution as the fundamental law of China and decomposes it into five basic laws. According to the order of priority, it comes down to "the Chinese people under the leadership of the Communist Party of China (CPC)," socialism, democratic centralism, modernization construction and guarantee of basic rights.[14] Not to mention the rationality of this priority ordering but simply talking about the core value, the most fundamental point of these five basic laws should be the guarantee of basic rights, while the other four are all its derivatives in the author's opinion. Specifically speaking, the fundamentality of the Chinese people under the leadership of the CPC is people, so there would be no Communist Party to speak of without the Chinese people and the most fundamental achievement in terms of people's survival after liberation is human rights and basic rights in the science of law. The fundamentality of the socialist system is democracy and equality which are translated into democratic rights and equal rights in law. The fundamentality of modernization is improving people's livelihood and realizing civic rights which are finally translated into human rights, including political, economic, social and cultural rights. The fundamentality of democratic centralism is democratic rights because democracy is centralism in real sense. Therefore, the CPC, socialist system, modernization construction or democratic centralism would lose its target and direction without guaranteeing the basic rights of citizens. In this sense, the most fundamental nature of the Constitution of China is the guarantee of the basic rights.

No matter being called the fundamental law or the basic law, constitution is significant in the fundamentality, essentiality, inalterability and permanency of human rights. Article 16 of *the Declaration of the Rights of humanity and of the Citizen* of France in 1789 declares, "Every community in which a separation of powers and a security of rights is not provided for, wants a constitution." This is because the French see human rights of humanity as "natural, inalienable and

---

[14]Duanhong [6], p. 256.

sacred" and "the purpose of all political association is the preservation of the natural and imprescriptible rights of man". Therefore, its purpose is not to determine the separation of powers but to never overlook or despise human rights through "separation of powers" rather than "centralization of powers". The 1949 Constitution of Germany is called "the Basic Law of the Federal Republic of Germany (GFR)" because of the clear stipulation of the first article of the "Basic Law," which was "Human dignity shall be inviolable. To respect and protect it shall be the duty of all state authority." The German people therefore acknowledge inviolable and inalienable human rights to be the basis of every community, of peace and of justice in the world. *The Declaration of Independence* of the USA asserts that human rights are unalienable and sacred rights endowed by nature. Almost all written constitutions declare the sacredness of human rights, which is also the general rule of all countries in the world. China's Constitution is a component of constitutions across the world, and it is impossible to stay outside of the universal value of world human rights. China has signed *the International Covenant on Economic, Social and Cultural Rights* and *the International Covenant on Civil and Political Rights*. Both the two covenants claim the inherent dignity and the equal and inalienable rights of all members of the human family, and these rights "derive from the inherent dignity of the human person". Therefore, as China acknowledges and accepts the idea and spirit of human rights, the constitution's assertion that "the state respects and safeguards human rights" is the recognition of the universal truth of human rights. It may well be asked, if the Constitution of China does not affirm and stipulate "respecting and safeguarding of human rights" and "basic rights of citizens," could it be called the fundamental law? In the view of the author, the essence of constitution is the essence of human rights because constitution as the carrier of human rights is sacred because of the sacredness of human rights and is fundamental because of the fundamentality of human rights. It is just like a beggar wearing an imperial yellow robe. The beggar is still a beggar but being worshiped as an emperor because of the yellow robe. People simply worship the "yellow robe" but not the beggar. It is the same with constitution. Constitution becomes fundamental because of the yellow robe of human rights. Without the essence of human rights, how could the constitution be fundamental? No matter it is in ancient China or in ancient Greece, there were words like constitution, but how did it become fundamental? It is simply because that the common people have taken the form of constitution as the essence of human rights in modern times, the constitution has become the fundamental law.

2 What Is Higher Law? Why Does China's Constitution Have Supreme Legal Authority?

What is higher law? According to *the Oxford Companion to Law*, higher law refers to the concept of those rules more authoritative than the simple regulations of positive laws. It includes inherent law and the natural law championed by Aquinas.[15] In brief, higher law, in terms of the theory of legal hierarchy, means a law with higher effectiveness and above national laws. German constitutionalist Dieter Grimm pointed out that the legal hierarchy theory was familiar to people in the Middle Ages and was later preserved through the concept of basic law rule contract. Afterward, the legal order was divided into two basic parts based on the hierarchy theory. The first part is traditional laws enacted by the state to restrain individuals. The second part is new type of laws enacted by the sovereign to restrain the state. Still later, the second part of laws was called constitution and this concept has been given its modern meaning with the development of history.[16]

The concept of higher law was rooted in the dualism of law in Western legal culture and began in ancient Greece. *Homer's Epic* written around 750 BC used the concepts of Dike and Themis in Greek myths.[17] Themis and Dike are two vague notions but demonstrate that people in the Homeric Age had distinguished justice and common law, and justice was the absolute basis and principle of common law while common law was the specific manifestation of eternal justice. The dualism of two types of laws and orders running through the entire Western legal philosophy made its first appearance hereby. Back then, laws were considered being promulgated by the God and humanity learns about laws through the inspirations of the God. In the fifth century BC, the Sophocles' tragic character Antigone disobeyed the edict of Creon and resorted to the divine law, making the divine law above the laws enacted by man. The meaning of law in ancient Greece referred to the law with higher contents or the law with lower contents. Higher law—divine law or natural law and lower law—state law are all included in the law. Therefore, when it is unable to win a lawsuit by referring to the state law, there would be a need to resort to the natural law. In the opinion of Antigone et al., unjust laws are not laws. The tragedy of Socrates has interpreted the conflicts between secular law and divine law from a different aspect. Socrates merely chose state law rather than divine law. In his view, the stateliness overweighs the rightness and wrongness of individuals and state governance and justice must maintain a consistent effect. Aristotle raised the "natural justice" concept in his *Ethics*. He pointed out, "Of political justice part is natural, part legal, natural, that which

[15]Walker [1], p. 410.

[16]Grimm [7], p. 14.

[17]They are goddesses in Greek myths. Dike is a goddess of justice while Themis is a goddess of sanction and punishment. According to Coustellet, Themis is a divine law while Dike is a secular law copied from it. The former relies on the system of God, but the latter relies on the instructions of statute laws, so it is the law derived from the decision of judges. (refer to [Ireland] Kelly [8], p. 7).

everywhere has the same force and does not exist by people's thinking this or that; legal, that which is originally indifferent, but when it has been laid down is not indifferent."[18] Aristotle thought that natural law was unchangeable, while state law was changeable and might be discovered from natural law. If we say that Aristotle's natural justice is principally a norm and guide followed by legislators, then the natural law of the Stoic School is the royal road to happiness of the humanity. The Stoics think that the universe is a single whole with humans being as an integral part of this single whole. The Stoics also think that human rationality is also part of the universal reason of the universe and the reflection of universe reason in humans, so humans are also controlled by this law of universal reason and constitute part of the harmonious natural order. This "God" or "reason" controlling the universe and humanity is natural law which exists in all things and represents the highest rule for human behaviors. This kind of rational natural law is universally effective in this entire universe and has a binding force for everyone in the world. Its principles are unchangeable for both the rulers and the subjects because it is the law of God.

The concept of natural law as higher law was developed into a worldwide legal and political concept by Cicero from the expanded and supplemented Stoic conception of natural law. In Chapter 22 of Volume III of his *De Re Publica*, Cicero raised his concept of natural law:

> "True law is right reason in agreement with nature; it is of universal application, unchanging and everlasting; it summons to duty by its commands, and averts from wrong-doing by its prohibitions. And it does not lay its commands or prohibitions upon good men in vain, although neither have any effect on the wicked. It is a sin to try to alter this law, nor is it allowable to attempt to repeal a part of it, and it is impossible to abolish it entirely. We cannot be freed from its obligations by Senate or People, and we need not look outside ourselves for an expounder or interpreter of it. And there will not be different laws at Rome and at Athens, or different laws now and in the future, but one eternal and unchangeable law will be valid for all nations and all times, and there will be one master and ruler, that is, God, over us all, for He is the author of this law, its promulgator, and its enforcing judge. Whoever is disobedient is fleeing from himself and denying his human nature, and by reason of this very fact he will suffer the worst penalties, even if he escapes what is commonly called punishment…"[19]

These wonderful words have been spread to this day. Almost all related important works have quoted this paragraph. It is actually the most complete and systematic generalization and summary of the Stoic conception of natural law. It has exerted far-reaching influence on the theories of rule of law and constitutionalism of later generations. "While not enforced or strictly enforceable by any human agent, the commands of this law cannot be ignored with impunity." For individuals, going against these commands means the abandoning of the best thing in human nature, and inevitable suffering from the spiritual torture of self-abasement and consciousness. For a state, going against these commands would eventually result

---

[18]Kelly [8], p. 20.

[19]Cicero [9], p. 120; [U.S.] Strauss and Cropsey [10], p. 181; [U.S.] Bodenheimer [11], p. 14; [U.S.] Corwin [2], p. 5; [U.S.] Sabine [12], p. 204

in destruction.[20] Cicero frequently quoted "law" to object the making of laws and suggested that divination officers and the Senatus should have the right to abolish those laws enacted without legal basis. He said that all what declared by divination officers as unjust, profane, villainous and filthy would be invalid and not be enforced, and nonconformists would be extremely punished.[21] In a speech delivered at the Senatus, Cicero directly resorted to "just theory" to oppose "written law". Even Cicero did not play a direct role in the establishment of judicial review system, but he, at least, played an indirect role through integrating some of his thoughts into the just causes defending this system.[22] His basic thought was that the violation of "law" is violation of "law" in the essence of law, meaning that a law does not become a law because of the announcement by an authoritative organ and the violation of "law" is not because of announcement by an authoritative organ. It is the violation of "law" in itself.

The Middle Ages was awash with the concept of higher law. For the priests in Early Middle Ages, they valued the similarity between Stoic form of natural law and the law of God. This similarity provided them with tremendous convenience. St. Paul wrote in a letter that God's law was written in their hearts. Origen said that natural law was the God's law inscribed in man's heart and demonstrating rational forces. He also proposed all state laws going against the natural law should be invalid.[23] Theologian Augustinus clearly distinguished the two types of laws, namely eternal law and secular law or human law. According to him, eternal law is that law in virtue of which it is just that all things exist in perfect order, and this kind of law equals the God's will and wisdom guiding all things to reach their respective purposes. He said that eternal law constitutes the common and sacred source of justice and impartiality, the highest standard of justice. He noted that the God has already imprinted this law in human spirit, all people could know it and obey it at any time, and it is the basis for praising virtue and punishing vice. He added that secular law changes with the time and place, and safeguards, as a law, public benefits and represents a just law as unjust law is not a law. Augustinus thought that if a state law failed to conform to the natural law and justice, it would not have the features of true laws and the state would not be a true state. It can thus be seen that there would be no law and state without justice. Augustinus said, "Justice being taken away, then, what are kingdoms but great robberies?"[24] German historian Otto von Gierke especially emphasized the superiority and stateliness of the concept of higher law in the Middle Ages and thought that natural law restricted the supreme power of humanity, ruled the Pope and emperor, and also ruled the ruler and the people with sovereignty. He thought that natural law actually ruled the entire human society. Anything, so long as being in conflict with the eternal

---

[20]Strauss and Cropsey [10], p. 181.

[21]Cicero [9], p. 225.

[22]Corwin [2], p. 8.

[23]Kelly [8], p. 97.

[24]Morrison [13], p. 67.

principle of natural law, is invalid and thus unable to restrict anyone.[25] In medieval England, common law was seen as higher law. Worthy of the name, *the Great Charter of Liberties* adopted in 1215 became the higher law. The birth of *the Great Charter of Liberties* was a great event in the English history in the thirteenth century and has become the certificate of British liberties from the very beginning. It is the first legal form of restriction and constraint of the power of king, so it is thought to be the start of the rule of law. As stated before, in the fourteenth century, *the Magna Carta* had been basically seen as a written constitution as cognized in modern times. In particular, in 1368 when it is the late reign of Edward III, beyond the Royal confirmation, there was announcement in written form: The adoption of any written law that is in conflict with *the Magna Carta* is bound to be invalid. *The Magna Carta* became the British higher law. Huntington pointed out, "In late medieval Europe, law was variously defined in terms of divine law, natural law, the law of reason, common law, and custom." All these statements took laws as relatively unchangeable external authority controlling human behaviors. Especially in England, what taking the dominant place was this kind of typical feudal concept that all authorities came from the law. Since the law is supreme, the authorities in the world could be diversified as no single authority is the only source of law. The humanity must comply with authorities, but authorities are contained in many organizations, including the king, parliament, court, common law, custom, church and common people. He quoted Figesas saying that for people in 1600, laws are truly supreme without taking into account whether the ultimate authority of a state is the king, or nobility, civilians or both together.[26]

European classical natural law existed in the seventeenth and eighteenth centuries. Dutch Hugo Grotius reformed the medieval theological natural law into secular natural law. He took secular habits and contracts as the source and contents of natural law, symbolizing the start of the secularization of natural law. Grotius' natural law theory regarded natural law as proper rational principles. He thought that natural law was different from human law and theological law, capable of prohibiting people's illegal behaviors and supporting people to do what they must do, and natural law was unchangeable.[27] In particular, Locke's natural law theory took natural rights—life, liberty and property as prior to and higher than government rules. He advocated, "The law of nature stands as an eternal rule to all men, legislators as well as others." He also proposed that the laws enacted by state governments for regulating the actions of others, and the actions of themselves and others, must conform to natural law, and all human sanctions going against it would not be right or effective.[28] As such, he established the supreme status of natural law, which is the background of constitution as higher law.

---

[25]Corwin [2], p. 12–13.

[26]Huntington [4], pp. 92–93.

[27]*The Rights Of War And Peace*, quoted from *Selected Data of History of Western Legal Thoughts*, Peking University Press, 1983 edition, page 139.

[28]Locke [5], p. 84.

The USA in the eighteenth century refused to take political authority as the source of law but still took natural law or basic law as the ultimate authority for regulating human behaviors and believed in the supremacy of the law. For them, the law was irresistible external orders or restrictions and the people could only discover but not enact laws. Even by the nineteenth century, the popular concept remained to be "law announcement theory" that was to believe that laws were destined to be announced and established by justices rather than the thought of "enactment". Thomas Jefferson wrote in *the Declaration of Independence*:

> We hold these truths to be self-evident, that all men are created equal, that they are endowed by their Creator with certain unalienable Rights, that among these are Life, Liberty and the Pursuit of Happiness. That to secure these rights, Governments are instituted among Men, deriving their just powers from the consent of the governed, — That whenever any Form of Government becomes destructive of these ends, it is the Right of the People to alter or to abolish it, and to institute new Government, laying its foundation on such principles and organizing its powers in such form, as to them shall seem most likely to effect their Safety and Happiness.

This paragraph has five implications. First, all men are created equal that they are endowed by their creator with certain unalienable rights, including life, liberty and the pursuit of happiness. It is to prevent these rights from being revoked with the rise and decline of government powers, and man's such basic rights as life, liberty and pursuit of happiness should be higher than the government. Second, governments are instituted among men to secure the natural rights of man, i.e., human rights, which demonstrate the essence and target of governments. Third, governments are instituted among men, deriving their just powers from the consent of the governed. This is to point out that government powers must have the consent of men for legitimacy and government powers come from the consent of men. Fourth, any arbitrary government power would destruct the guarantee of human rights and the content of men. Whenever it happens, it is the right of the people to alter or to abolish it, and to institute a new government. This indicates that the people reserve the final power and government is simply the tool for serving the people. The people are masters of government. Government is always and must be servant of the people. Fifth, the organization of a new government and government power must be based on the basic principle of maximizing the realization of people's safety and happiness. This principle has defined the intention and target of government and power organization. In short, guaranteeing the natural rights of man, i.e., human rights and restricting the powers of national government is the only reason for the formulation and promulgation of constitution.

The Constitution of the USA was formulated based on the theory of natural rights. The symbol of the legalization of natural rights is the inclusion of natural rights in constitution. Antieau pointed out in 1968 that the Constitution of the USA was not only drafted by the jurists actually all believing in natural rights, but also approved by the generation of people who equally admitted these points of view.[29]

---

[29]Antieau, Rights of Our Fathers (Coiner, 1968).

James Wilson who was a principal drafter of the Constitution of the USA and was appointed as Chief Justice of the Supreme Court of the USA by George Washington in 1789 once said, "Government, in my humble opinion, should be formed to secure and to enlarge the exercise of the natural rights of its members; and every government, which has not this in view, as its principal object, is not a government of the legitimate kind."[30] In the process of formulating and approving the Constitution of the USA, the representatives of the Constitutional Convention were most concerned by how to protect natural rights. Sherman pointed out, "The question is not what rights naturally belong to men; but how they may be most equally and effectually guarded in Society."[31] Yates also explained, "The first principle of government is founded on the natural rights of individuals, and in perfect equality."[32] The Bill of Rights was not included in the 1787 Constitution, but it is the most important part of the final constitution. The Bill of Rights contains not only provisions on the protection of natural rights but also several stipulations on safeguarding common law rights. However, the protection of natural rights is undoubtedly the center of the Bill of Rights. All essences of the theory of natural rights are contained in the Bill of Rights. When the Supreme Court spoke of the basic rights in modern version, it understood that it is the constitutional legalization of the natural rights of the Americans in early days. The court realized that the rights called "basic rights" are what used to be called "natural rights" of an individual.[33] Therefore, in the interpretation of the Constitution of the USA, a consistent and long-term judicial practice of courts is to interpret the constitution based on the political philosophy of natural rights.

As the earliest written constitution in the world, the Constitution of the USA has become the constitutional target of all countries. Its mode is nothing but directly including the articles of "basic rights" in the constitution, or attaching it to the contents of the constitution in the form of "human rights act" and "bill of rights". The four constitutions after the founding of the PRC all adopted the former model, which was directly writing the articles of basic rights in the constitution so as to make constitution become the higher law of China.

The preamble to the current constitution of China clearly states, "The Constitution…has supreme legal authority." Yet, people still need to ask why. There are two reasons. First, it is based on the stipulation that the Constitution is the fundamental law of the country. Since the basic system and tasks of the state are boiled down to human rights and basic rights, they are most fundamental and represent the source of government powers. The deceased Mr. Wu Jialian believed that the characteristic of the Constitution as the fundamental law of the state in

[30]Works of James Wilson (Wilson ed., 1804) II, p. 466.

[31]Farrand, ed., Records of the Federal Convention, vol. 1, p. 147 (remarks of Roger Sherman).

[32]Ibid. vol. 1, p. 440 (remarks of Robert Yates). At the Constituent Assembly, other representatives also made the same point of view, including Alexander Hamilton, Rufus King, and Luther Maetin.

[33]Chase Securities Corp. v. Donaldson (1945) 325 US 304, 314, 89 L Ed 1628, 65 S Ct 1137.

content determines that the Constitution has a higher legal status than common laws, the supreme legal authority and legal effect. Constitution is the basis for making common laws, and the contents of common laws must be in conformity with the provisions of the Constitution. All laws conflicting with the contents of the Constitution are invalid.[34] Second, the Constitution is the higher law. The basic rights provided in the Constitution are not endowed by the state or government but people's inherent rights. In this case, the basic rights are prior to and higher than the government. The basic rights were not defined after the founding of the PRC but announced and confirmed in legal form with the Constitution as the carrier after the founding of the PRC. The status of the Constitution of China as the higher law is not only an announcement by preamble but also evidence-based in the form of legal norms. Article 5 of the Constitution stipulates, "No law or administrative or local rules and regulations shall contravene the Constitution. All acts in violation of the Constitution and the law must be investigated." Article 78 of *the Legislation Law* stipulates, "The legal effect of the Constitution is the highest, and no laws, administrative regulations, local regulations, autonomous regulations, separate regulations or rules whatever may contradict it." Therefore, "The Constitution has supreme legal authority" is no longer an empty phrase but a clear stipulation and affirmation of the Constitution and the law.

3 Constitution as the Fundamental Law and Higher Law and Constitutionality Review

Both the Constitution and *the Legislation Law of the People's Republic of China* affirm the Constitution's status as the fundamental law and effect as the higher law. In this connection, the Constitution as the fundamental law and higher law has become the ultimate standard for China's constitutionality review. China has also progressively established the Chinese model of constitutionality review system.

The so-called Chinese model of constitutionality review system refers to the system with the Standing Committee of the NPC as the subject and administrative regulations, local regulations, autonomous regulations and separate regulations as the objects. Under this system, state organs, social groups, enterprises and public institutions and citizens submit the requirements or suggestions for constitutionality reviews. This is to examine whether regulations contradict the Constitution, which are recorded, and to abolish administrative regulations, local regulations, autonomous regulations and separate regulations contradicting or violating the Constitution. In short, the Chinese model of constitutionality review system is the

[34] *Encyclopedia China-Jurisprudence*, the Encyclopedia of China Publishing House, 1984 edition, page 639.

unconstitutional recording and review system implemented by the Standing Committee of the NPC targeting regulations,[35] and its basic features are as follows.

First, the subject of review for constitutionality is only limited to the Standing Committee of the NPC. No other state organ has the constitutional and legal basis for review for constitutionality.

Second, the main objects of review for constitutionality are administrative regulations, local regulations, autonomous regulations and separate regulations. Laws, rules and specific actions of governments of all levels are excluded from the objects of review for constitutionality. The reasons for calling "main" objects but not "all" objects are as follows. China's Constitution stipulates in the seventh and eighth clauses of Article 67 that the objects of the review for constitutionality of the Standing Committee of the NPC include not only administrative regulations and local regulations but also the decisions and decrees of the State Council and the resolutions developed by state organs of provinces, autonomous regions and municipalities directly under the Central Government. Article 88 of *the Legislation Law* adopted at the Third Session of the Ninth National People's Congress held on March 15, 2000 only takes administrative regulations, local regulations, autonomous regulations and separate regulations as the objects of the review for constitutionality of the Standing Committee of the NPC. The *Legislation Law* has no

[35]Administrative regulations, local regulations, autonomous regulations and separate regulations are together called "regulations" on the basis of*the Working Procedures for the Recording and Review of Administrative Regulations, Local Regulations, Autonomous Regulations and Separate Regulations, and Laws and Regulations of Special Economic Zones*adopted at the 34th Meeting of Chairmen of the Standing Committee of the Ninth National People's Congress held on October 16, 2000 and *the Regulations on Putting Laws and Regulations on Record* (No. 337 Decree of the State Council) issued on December 24, 2001. According to the second provision of *the Working Procedures for the Recording and Review of Administrative Regulations, Local Regulations, Autonomous Regulations and Separate Regulations, and Laws and Regulations of Special Economic Zones*, administrative regulations formulated by the State Council, local regulations formulated by the people's congresses and their standing committees of provinces, autonomous regions, municipalities directly under the central government and larger cities, autonomous regulations and separate regulations formulated by autonomous prefectures and autonomous counties, and laws and regulations formulated by special economic zones as authorized (hereinafter referred to as "regulations") shall be reported to the Standing Committee of the NPC for record within 30 days after issuance. According to the stipulation of Article 2 of *the Regulations on Putting Laws and Regulations on Record*, the regulations as stated in this Ordinance refer to local regulations formulated by the people's congresses and their standing committees of provinces, autonomous regions, municipalities directly under the central government and larger cities in accordance with the statutory functions and powers and procedurals, laws and regulations of special economic zones enacted by the people's congresses and their standing committees of the provinces and cities of special economic zones in accordance with the statutory functions and powers and procedurals, and autonomous regulations and separate regulations formulated by the people's congresses of autonomous prefectures and autonomous counties in accordance with the statutory functions and powers and procedurals. Thus it can be seen that both *the Working Procedures for the Recording and Review of Regulations* adopted by the Standing Committee of the NPC and *the Regulations on Putting Laws and Regulations on Record* issued by the State Council call administrative regulations, local regulations, autonomous regulations and separate regulations as "regulations".

provision on the contradictions of decisions and decrees of the State Council and resolutions of state organs of provinces, autonomous regions and municipalities directly under the Central Government.[36] The local regulations as stipulated in *the Legislation Law* expanded the scope of the "local regulations" as defined in Article 67 of *the Constitution*. According to the eighth clause of Article 67 of *the Constitution*, "local regulations" simply refer to those formulated by state organs of provinces, autonomous regions and municipalities directly under the Central Government. According to Article 63 of *the Legislation Law*, "local regulations" refer to not only those formulated by state organs of provinces, autonomous regions and municipalities directly under the Central Government but also those formulated by people's congresses and their standing committees of larger cities in line with the specific conditions and actual requirements of their respective cities under the precondition of not contradicting the Constitution, laws, administrative regulations and local regulations of their provinces or autonomous regions. At the same time, according to the second provision of Article 88 of *the Legislation Law*, the Standing Committee of the NPC has the right to abolish local regulations contradicting the Constitution, laws and administrative regulations without proviso, and the local regulations formulated by the people's congresses and their standing committees of larger cities are not excluded. Therefore, local regulations for review for constitutionality should include the local regulations formulated by the people's congresses and their standing committees of larger cities.

Third, the subjects raising the requirements or suggestions for review for constitutionality are state organs, social groups, enterprises and public institutions, and individual citizens. Article 90 of *the Legislation Law* stipulates, "When the State Council, the Central Military Commission, the Supreme People's Court, the Supreme People's Procuratorate or the standing committees of the people's congresses of the provinces, autonomous regions and municipalities directly under the Central Government consider that administrative regulations, local regulations, autonomous regulations or separate regulations contradict the Constitution or laws, they may submit to the Standing Committee of the National People's Congress written requests for examination, and the working offices of the Standing Committee shall refer the requests to the relevant special committees for examination and suggestions. When state organs other than the ones mentioned in the preceding paragraph, public organizations, enterprises and institutions or citizens consider that administrative regulations, local regulations, autonomous regulations or separate regulations contradict the Constitution or laws, they may submit to the Standing Committee of the National People's Congress written suggestions for examination,

[36]The second provision of Article 88 of *the Legislation Law* stipulates that the Standing Committee of the National People's Congress has the right to abolish administrative regulations contradicting the Constitution and the law, abolish local regulations contradicting the Constitution, laws and administrative regulations, and abolish autonomous regulations and separate regulations approved by the standing committees of people's congresses of provinces, autonomous regions and municipalities directly under the central government but violating the Constitution and the second provision of Article 66 of *the Legislation Law*.

and the working offices of the Standing Committee shall study the suggestions and shall, when necessary, refer them to the relevant special committees for examination and suggestions." This is also clearly stipulated in Article 7 of *the Working Procedures for the Recording and Review of Administrative Regulations, Local Regulations, Autonomous Regulations and Separate Regulations, and Laws and Regulations of Special Economic Zones* adopted at the 34th Meeting of Chairmen of the Standing Committee of the Ninth National People's Congress held on October 16, 2000.[37] Thus, it can be seen that *the Legislation Law* and *the Working Procedures for the Recording and Review of Regulations* make a clear classification of the subjects raising the requests or suggestions for review for constitutionality. The subjects raising requests for review for constitutionality to the Standing Committee of the National People's Congress must be the State Council, the Central Military Commission, the Supreme People's Court, the Supreme People's Procuratorate and the standing committees of the people's congresses of provinces, autonomous regions and municipalities directly under the Central Government. The subjects proposing review for constitutionality suggestions to the Standing Committee of the National People's Congress are state organs, social organizations, enterprises and public institutions and individual citizens other than the ones mentioned in the preceding paragraph.

Fourth, review for constitutionality is a kind of post-recording and review. The recording system for review for constitutionality was preliminarily established after the issuance of *the Notice on the Recording of Regulations of Local Governments and the State Council* by the General Office of the State Council in 1987 and *the Notice on the Recording of Local Regulations* by the General Office of the Standing Committee of the National People's Congress and the General Office of the State Council.[38] With the implementation of *the Regulations on Recording Regulations and Rules* issued by the State Council on February 18, 1990, and *the Regulations on Putting Laws and Regulations on Record* issued by the State Council on December 4, 2001, China has phased in a rather perfect system for the recording and examination of regulations and rules. However, the system for the recording and

[37]The stipulations of this article are: "When the State Council, the Central Military Commission, the Supreme People's Court, the Supreme People's Procuratorate and standing committees of the people's congresses of provinces, autonomous regions and municipalities directly under the Central Government consider that regulations contradict the Constitution or laws, they may submit to the Standing Committee of the National People's Congress written requests for examination, and the working offices of the Standing Committee of the NPC submit it to the Secretary General for approval, and the Secretary General refers them to the relevant special committee for examination. When state organs other than the ones mentioned in the preceding paragraph, public organizations, enterprises and institutions or citizens consider that regulations contradict the Constitution or laws, they may submit to the Standing Committee of the National People's Congress written suggestions for examination and the working offices of the Standing Committee shall organize relevant personnel to study the suggestions. When necessary, the General Office of the Standing Committee shall submit them to Secretary General for approval, and the General Secretary shall refer them to relevant special committees for examination after approving them."

[38]Kangtai [14], p. 192.

examination of regulations was established with the promulgation of *the Legislation Law*. As stipulated by Article 89 of the law, administrative regulations shall be reported to the Standing Committee of the National People's Congress for the record; local regulations formulated by the people's congresses or their standing committees of provinces, autonomous regions and municipalities directly under the Central Government shall be reported to the Standing Committee of the National People's Congress and the State Council for the record; local regulations formulated by the people's congresses or their standing committees of the comparatively larger cities shall be reported by the standing committees of the people's congresses of the relevant provinces and autonomous regions to Standing Committee of the National People's Congress and the State Council for the record; autonomous regulations and separate regulations formulated by autonomous prefectures and autonomous counties shall be reported by the standing committees of people's congresses of the relevant provinces, autonomous regions or municipalities directly under the Central Government to the Standing Committee of the National People's Congress and the State Council for the record. In China, a review for constitutionality on a regulation shall be conducted after the regulation is reported to the organ concerned within 30 days from the date of promulgation of the regulation, so this kind of examination shall be a typical post-examination. Apart from the reporting procedures stipulated in Article 89 for review for constitutionality and the procedures of raising an examination request or suggestion stipulated in Article 90 of *the Legislation Law*, Article 91 provides specific procedures for the implementation of examination.[39] The Meeting of the Standing Committee of the Ninth National People's Congress held in October 2000 adopted *the Working Procedures for the Recording and Review of Administrative Regulations, Local Regulations, Autonomous Regulations and Separate Regulations, and Laws and Regulations of Special Economic Zones*, which makes more detailed stipulations on the working procedures for unconstitutional recording and examination of regulations on the basis of *the Legislation Law*. Accordingly, China's unconstitutional recording and examination procedures are defined as follows. Firstly, it is to report to the state organs concerned within

[39]As stipulated in Article 91 of *the Legislation Law*, when, after examination, a special committee of the National People's Congress considers that administrative regulations, local regulations, autonomous regulations or separate regulations contradict the Constitution or laws, it may submit written suggestions to the organ that has formulated the regulations for examination; or the Law Committee and other relevant special committees may convene a joint meeting for examination and request the said organ to attend the meeting and give an explanation, and then after examination submit to the organ written comments and suggestions. The organ that has formulated the regulations shall, within two months, study and put forth suggestions as to whether to revise the regulations, and shall give feedback to the Law Committee and other relevant special committees of the National People's Congress. If, after examination, the Law Committee and other relevant special committees of the National People's Congress consider that administrative regulations, local regulations, autonomous regulations or separate regulations contradict the Constitution or laws and the organ that has formulated such regulations refuses to make revision, they may submit written comments and suggestions on the basis of their examination and propose a motion for annulment of the regulations to the Meeting of Chairmen, which shall decide whether to submit the motion to a meeting of the Standing Committee for examination and decision.

30 days from the date of promulgation of regulations for the record. Secondly, it is to raise the requests and suggestions for examination, namely the examination requests or suggestions raised by the State Council, the Central Military Commission, the Supreme People's Court, the Supreme People's Procuratorate or the standing committees of the people's congresses of the provinces, autonomous regions and municipalities directly under the Central Government, or state organs other than the ones mentioned above, social groups, enterprises, public institutions and individual citizens to the Standing Committee of the NPC. Thirdly, it is to implement the examination procedures. That means if a special committee, after examination, considers regulations as consistent with Constitution or laws, it should notify the General Office of the Standing Committee in written form. If the special committee considers that regulations contradict the Constitution or laws, it shall submit written examination suggestions to the organ that formulated the regulations. When two or more special committees take charge of the examination, the special committees concerned shall exchange views. If they consider that regulations are consistent with the Constitution or laws, they may jointly or separately notify the General Office of the Standing Committee in written form. If they consider that regulations contradict the Constitution or laws, they should jointly raise the written examination suggestions to the organ that formulated the regulations. If the special committees consider that it is necessary to jointly convene an examination meeting with a legal committee, it should be reported by the General Office of the Standing Committee to the Secretary General for approval, and then the legal committee and other relevant special committees may convene a joint meeting for examination and request the organ that formulated the regulations to attend the meeting and give an explanation, and then after examination submit to the organ that formulated the regulations written comments and suggestions. If, after examination, the legal committee and relevant special committees consider that regulations contradict the Constitution or laws, and the organ that formulated such regulations refuses to make revision, they may submit written comments and suggestions on the basis of their examination and propose a motion for annulment of the regulations to the Meeting of Chairmen, which shall decide whether to submit the motion to a meeting of the Standing Committee for examination and decision. Fourthly, it is the notification procedures in writing. That means, after examination, the General Office of the Standing Committee is responsible for notifying the unit or individual that has raised the examination requests and suggestions of the examination results.

Fifthly, the consequence of review for constitutionality is the abolition of the administrative regulations, local regulations, autonomous regulations and separate regulations contradicting the Constitution, excluding the case of abolishing or terminating articles or contents contradicting the Constitution. Implementing review for constitutionality by means of abolition signifies that so long as a regulation contradicts or goes against the Constitution, it shall be completely abolished and no longer have any legal effect.

The objects of Chinese model of constitutionality review system are mainly regulations, and the mode of review implementation is the recording and examination system. In this sense, the author calls this kind of constitutionality review system with Chinese characteristics "the system for recording and examining unconstitutional regulations". Zhai Xiaobo raised the proposition that the 1982 Constitution has established the unitary unconstitutional regulation review system.[40] The author basically agrees with this proposition. But, the following points need to be clarified and emphasized. First, it is not absolutely "unitary" but mainly involves regulations. Second, the mode of examination is recording. Third, the regulations for unconstitutional recording and review refer to all regulations but not simply the regulations directly applicable to the Constitution while excluding the regulations indirectly applicable to the Constitution. The reason for saying that objects of China's constitutionality review are all regulations is that neither the current constitution nor the law classifies the regulations for review for constitutionality into the regulations directly and indirectly applicable to the Constitution, and all regulations shall be reported for constitutionality review so long as they contradict or go against the Constitution. Zhai Xiaobo excludes regulations indirectly applicable to the Constitution, i.e., local regulations formulated for the enforcement of laws and administrative regulations in line with the actual condition of the administrative region, administrative regulations formulated for the enforcement of legal provisions, the judicial interpretations and judgments of the Supreme People's Court and the Supreme People's Procuratorate, administrative rules and other normative documents, etc., from review for constitutionality. Zhai Xiaobo also asserted that they are unlikely to contradict the Constitution. He added that, even they contradict the Constitution, they should be firstly judged by the superior regulations. He also noted that if they conform to the superior regulations, but the review subject still considers it unconstitutional, the legitimacy of the regulations would be whether the superior regulations conform to the even superior regulations.[41] This seems justified, but it is actually an ex parte statement. Even it is an administrative regulation formulated for the enforcement of laws or a local regulation formulated for the enforcement of provisions of laws and administrative regulations, once it contradicts the Constitution and laws, it shall be subject to Constitutional and legal review. Only at the constitutionality review level, we could safeguard the unity and dignity of the legal system. However, if they do not directly contradict laws but directly contradict the Constitution, it would be difficult to resolve unconstitutional issues even at the legal review level, and it would finally go back to the constitutionality review level for correction.

[40]Xiaobo [15], p. 52.

[41]Xiaobo [15], p. 58.

4 Selection of Constitutional Implementation Path

Before the promulgation of the 1982 Constitution, scholars, officials, the masses and overseas media all worried that the Constitution, even it is perfect, would not play its role without implementation. Some people said that the Constitution was good, but it would be another story when it comes to the implementation, and laws would be ineffective after the occurrence of a movement, and articles on how to guarantee correct implementation should be added to the Constitution. Some other people said that it would not work without implementation even it is perfect. *Sin Chew Daily* of Singapore pointed out that it is easy to make constitution but difficult to implement it. In China, the rule of law has always been covered by the rule of man. Therefore, it is a big issue in terms of how to learn lessons to strengthen the rule of law. *Overseas Chinese Daily News* of Hong Kong noted that the key is the implementation of constitution and turning articles into actions no matter how magnificent and solemn it looks. *Ming PaoDaily News of* Hong Kong also pointed out that constitution is simply the black letters on a white paper, its effectiveness lies in whether the person holding powers respects it or not.[42]

The worries of people about constitutional implementation 30 years ago have become a reality today. Just as the deceased Cai Dingjian said 10 years ago that, in China's reality, the status and supreme authority of the Constitution as the fundamental law had not been established for its resolute and decisive announcement, and the supreme law is still left out today when governance by law is emphasized. He said that just saying it in words without implementing it as the fundamental law and the highest law would look like a balloon flying in the sky for commercial advertisement. It is high in the sky and looks good, but it has no effect on people's behaviors except for the promotional function. He added that it would become an insignificant thing standing high above the masses as a result.[43] Eight years ago, Professor Wang Zhenmin pointed out that, in China, all other laws could enter lawsuit procedures except for the Constitution as the fundamental law and the law with the supreme authority in the country, and it had been the case since the 1954 Constitution. He said that this gave rise to a marvelous spectacle in Chinese and foreign legal history: China has a law called constitution with the supreme authority compared with all other laws, but it was formulated not for entering lawsuit procedures.[44] This situation has lasted for another eight years till today. As such, the implementation of the Constitution is the key for the unaccomplished course of building the rule of law in China. The availability of constitution without its implementation means the absence of rule of law and constitutionalism.

How to implement the Constitution is a big issue pending for solutions. Regarding the specific implementation path, we may refer to the experience of the Court of Final Appeal of the Hong Kong Special Administrative Region that

---

[42]Chongde [16], pp. 449 and 458.

[43]Dingjian [17], pp. 10

[44]Zhenmin [18], p. 169.

requested the interpretation of the Basic Law by the Standing Committee of the NPC in the case involving Democratic Republic of the Congo pursuant to the procedures stipulated in the third clause of Article 158 of the Basic Law. On June 30, 2011, the Court of Final Appeal of the Hong Kong SAR requested the Standing Committee of the NPC to interpret the 4 issues related to "foreign affairs" involved in the first clause of Article 13 and the third clause of Article 19 of the Basic Law of the Hong Kong SAR in accordance with the provisions of the third clause of Article 158 of the Basic Law. This was the first time for the Court of Final Appeal of the Hong Kong SAR to request the interpretation of laws by the organ with the power of law interpretation as required in accordance with the statutory procedures in trying cases. Given this, the 22nd meeting of the Standing Committee of the Eleventh Session of the National People's Congress held on August 26 examined and adopted the proposal by the Meeting of Chairmen on requesting the deliberation of *the Interpretation of the First Clause of Article 13 and Article 19 of the Basic Law of Hong Kong Special Administrative Region of the People's Republic of China by the Standing Committee of the National People's Congress (Draft)*. This practice has a directly referential significance for the mainland to implement the Constitution. The Standing Committee of the NPC is the organ for not only law interpretation but also constitutional interpretation. In trying cases, Chinese courts at all levels may also face the case requiring the interpretation of the Constitution by the organ with the power of law interpretation in applying the Constitution and laws. At this time, (1) if it is the Supreme People's Court, it needs to submit the request for interpreting relevant contents of the Constitution to the Standing Committee of the NPC; (2) if it is other courts, they need to firstly submit an application to the Supreme People's Court, and then the Supreme People's Court would raise the request for interpreting laws to the Standing Committee of the NPC by referring to the provisions of Article 43 of *the Legislation Law*. In this way, constitutional interpretation or constitutionality review could be established. Observing and judging the judicial reply for Qi Yuling case in 2001 from this sense, we can clearly see that this reply violated the provisions of the Constitution and *the Legislation Law* in subject and procedures alike. First, the Supreme People's Court has no power to interpret the Constitution and laws. Second, it failed to request the interpretation of laws by the organ with the power of law interpretation, namely the Standing Committee of the NPC in accordance with the stipulations of Article 43 of *the Legislation Law*. The Supreme People's Court's self-interpretation and procedures violated the law and thus triggered the questioning and criticism of the judicatory actualization of constitution. Just think, if the Supreme People's Court requested the Standing Committee of the NPC to interpret the laws or the Constitution in accordance with the procedures stipulated by *the Legislation Law*, what would it be like in building the rule of law?

At the same time, the author suggests that the National People's Congress and its Standing Committee may make some adjustments to the systems and procedures related to the implementation of the Constitution. But, the adjustments must be made under the premise of maintaining the implementation of the constitution supervision system unchanged. This is to adapt to the need of implementing the Constitution of China.

First, according to the stipulations of Article 70 of the 1982 Constitution and Article 35 of *the Organic Law of the National People's Congress*, the National People's Congress may establish the seventh special committee, i.e., constitutional supervision committee as required in work. This constitutional supervision committee may parallel with the Ethnic Affairs Committee, Law Committee, Financial and Economic Affairs Committee, Education, Science, Culture and Public Health Committee, Foreign Affairs Committee and Overseas Chinese Affairs Committee under the leadership of the Standing Committee of the National People's Congress. The establishment of the constitutional supervision committee under the National People's Congress may resolve specialized and professional issues related to constitutional supervision of the National People's Congress. All inappropriate decisions and laws of the Standing Committee of the National People's Congress contradicting the Constitution are handled, reviewed and determined by the constitutional supervision committee. When the National People's Congress is not in session, all state organs, political parties, social groups, enterprises and public institutions, and individual citizens may institute constitutional supervision procedures to the constitutional supervision committee and regulate the timeliness for acceptance, review and making decision.

Second, as provided in Article 28 of *the Organic Law of the National People's Congress*, the Standing Committee of the National People's Congress establishes a working committee for constitutional supervision as required in work so as to resolve specialized and professional issues related to constitutional supervision of the Standing Committee of National People's Congress. The working committee may take charge of handling, reviewing and determining whether administrative regulations, local regulations, autonomous regulations and separate regulations contradict the Constitution. To this, there is a need to alter Article 90 and Article 91 of *the Legislation Law*: All state organs, political parties, social organizations, enterprises and public institutions, and individual citizens may institute constitutional supervision procedures to the constitutional supervision working committee and the constitutional supervision working committee is responsible for handling, reviewing and making decision while regulating the timelessness for handling, review and making decision.

Third, it is to expand the scope of objects of constitutional supervision and incorporate specific behaviors of governments, specific behaviors of enterprises and public institutions or groups, and administrative rules, some local regulations and local administrative rules beyond the law into the objects of constitutional supervision. In case that any of the above behaviors or normative documents contradict the Constitution, all state organs, political parties, social organizations, enterprises and public institutions, and individual citizens may institute constitutional supervision procedures to the constitutional supervision working committee for acceptance, examination and making decision.

Fourth, it is to establish a constitutional appeal and relief system and its procedures pursuant to the stipulations of Article 41 of the 1982 Constitution. Individual citizens have the right to lodge complaints, make accusations or raise reports to relevant state organs regarding state organs' and state personnel's offenses and delinquencies encroaching upon their basic rights as provided in the Constitution. The relevant state organs must find out the truth and handle the complaints, accusations or reports. Individual citizens suffering losses caused by the encroachment upon their civic rights by state organs and state personnel are entitled to the state compensation according to law. The relevant state organs as stipulated by the constitution are constitutional supervision committee or constitutional supervision working committee. If the Standing Committee of the National People's Congress and its working staff encroached upon the civic rights, citizens may file complaints to the constitutional supervision committee and the constitutional supervision committee shall be responsible for handling the complaints. If state organs other than the Standing Committee of the National People's Congress and state personnel encroached upon the civic rights, citizens may file complaints to constitutional supervision working committee and the constitutional supervision working committee shall be responsible for handling the complaints.

The advantage of the above system improvements is that there is no need to revise the current constitution or change the implementation of the constitutional supervision system by the National People's Congress and its Standing Committee. The legislative system and procedures are simply supplemented and improved within the framework of the Constitution. This kind of alteration is carried out within the constitutional system, but it can greatly facilitate the implementation of the Constitution once being conducted. Its subjects are simple and concentrated, and its procedures are simplified and convenient. At the same time, it is most likely to guarantee the basic rights of citizens.

References

1. David M. Walker: *The Oxford Companion to Law*, Guangming Daily Press, 1988 edition.
2. Edward S. Corwin: *The "Higher Law" Background of American Constitutional Law*, translated by Qiang Shigong, SDX Joint Publishing Company, 1996 edition.
3. Jiang Shilin et al.: *World Constitutions*, Qingdao Publishing House, 1997 edition.
4. Samuel P. Huntington: *Political Order in Changing Societies*, translated by Wang Guanhua et al., SDX Joint Publishing Company, 1989 edition.
5. John Locke: *Second Treatise of Government*, translated by Ye Qifang, Zhai Junong, the Commercial Press, 1964 edition.
6. Chen Duanhong: *Constituent Power and the Fundamental Law*, China Legal Publishing House, 2010 edition.
7. Dieter Grimm: *Entstehung, Funktionieren und Zukunft der modernen Verfassung*, translated by Liu Gang, China Law Press, 2010 edition.
8. John M. Kelly: *A Short History of Western Legal Theory*, translated by Wang Xiaohong, China Law Press, 2002 edition.

9. Cicero: *On the Commonwealth and On the Laws*, translated by Wang Huansheng, China University of Political Science and Law Press, 1997 edition.
10. Leo Strauss, Joseph Cropsey: *History of Political Philosophy* (Vol. 1), translated by Li Tianran et al., Hebei People's Publishing House, 1998.
11. Bodenheimer: *Jurisprudence: the Philosophy and Method of the Law*, translated by Deng Zhenglai, China University of Political Science and Law Press, 1999 edition.
12. George Holland Sabine: *A History of Political Theory*, Vol. 1, translated by Sheng Kuiyang and Cui Miaoyin, the Commercial Press, 1986 edition.
13. Wayne Morrison: *Jurisprudence: From the Greeks to Post-Modernism*, translated by Li Guilin et al., Wuhan University Press, 2003 edition.
14. Cao Kangtai, *Review and Outlook of 30 Years of Building of Government Legal System*, ed., China Legal Publishing House, 2008 edition.
15. Zhai Xiaobo: *The Enforcement System of the Constitution of China*, China Legal Publishing House, 2009 edition.
16. Xu Chongde: *Constitutional History of the People's Republic of China* (Vol. II), Fujian People's Publishing House, 2005 edition.
17. Cai Dingjian: *On Constitutional Issues*, Phoenix Publishing & Media Group, Yilin Press, 2011 edition.
18. Wang Zhenmin: *China's Constitutionality review System*, China University of Political Science and Law Press, 2004 edition.

Constitutionalism and Revolution: Reflections on and Outlook for the 1982 Constitution

Xiaobing Li

1 I Could Only Say that This Is a Miracle: The 30-Year Enforcement of the 1982 Constitution

The 1982 Constitution has been continuously enforced for three decades in mainland China. For China, it is indeed a miracle, even a miracle of miracles because it has created a historical record timewise. In China's modernization process, the ruler or the people, or the ruler and the people together rolled out many constitutions or constitutional legal documents at each historical stage, but was there any one valid for more than three decades?

The late Qing Government promulgated *the Constitutional Outline Made by the Imperial Order* on August 27, 1908. At the same time, the Qing Government also announced a 9-year time limit for the preparations for constitutionalism. The document stated that the Qing emperors ruled the Qing Empire, and all emperors came from one family and must be respected forever. Under the stress of the circumstances, the Qing Government issued *the Nineteen Major Articles of the Constitution* on November 3, 1911. The first article stated that the emperors of the Qing Dynasty will rule forever. Yet, on the 25th day of the 12th month of the third lunar year of the reign of Emperor Xuantong (February 12, 1912), Empress Dowager Longyu represented the 6-year-old Emperor Puyi to announce the "Edict of Abdication," usually known as the "Imperial Edict of the Abdication of the Qing

X. Li (✉)
School of Law, Nankai University, Tianjin, France
e-mail: 13263169197@163.com

X. Li
Université de Paris I, Paris, France

X. Li
Academia Sinica, Taipei, Taiwan

L. Li et al. (eds.), *Constitutional Development in China, 1982–2012*,
Research Series on the Chinese Dream and China's Development Path,
https://doi.org/10.1007/978-981-32-9261-1_6

Emperor," then the monarchy turned to be the Republic. The constitution-making and implementation practices of the late Qing Government came to the end.[1]

Later in the early period of the Republic of China, the Nanjing Provisional Senate deliberated and passed *the Provisional Constitution of the Republic of China* on March 8, 1912. As stipulated in Article 54 of the Provisional Constitution, "The Constitution of the Republic of China shall be enacted by the National Assembly, but before the promulgation of the Constitution, the Provisional Constitution shall be as effective as the Constitution." The Beiyang Government dominated by Yuan Shih-kai especially formulated *the Constitution of the Republic of China* in 1914. As stipulated in its last article (Article 68), the constitution should come into force upon promulgation and the Provisional Constitution promulgated on March 11 of the first reign year of the Republic of China should be repealed on the date of enforcement of the Constitution. In addition, Article 64 of *the Constitution of the Republic of China* stipulated that, before the promulgation of the formal Constitution, this constitution shall be as effective as the formal Constitution." The first formal *Constitution of the Republic of China* was formulated during the presidency of Cao Kun in 1923. Its last article (Article 141) stated "The Constitution shall, under no circumstances, lose its validity otherwise than in accordance with the procedure of amendment prescribed by this chapter." However, only one year after the promulgation of the 1923 Constitution, the Second Zhili–Fengtian War broke out. At the critical juncture of the war, Feng Yuxiang staged the "Beijing Coup" and Cao Kun was forced to announce his resignation. The 1923 *Constitution of the Republic of China* became a burial object of Zhili Clique with its loss of control over the Beijing Government.[2]

During the Period of Nanjing National Government, the KMT (Kuomintang) Central Executive Committee passed a programmatic document called *An Outline of Political Tutelage* in October 1928. It was actually a national constitution text in early days of the promulgation of constitutionalism by the Nanjing National Government and stipulated the country's fundamental political system.[3] In 1931, Chiang Kai-shek put KMT senior member Hu Hanmin who had been strongly opposing the formulation of a new constitution and had resigned his post as the president of the Legislative Yuan under house arrest. Later, the National Assembly passed *the Constitution for the Political Tutelage Period of the Republic of China*.

[1]As stated in "the Imperial Edict of the Abdication of the Qing Emperor" that was issued on the 25th day of the 12th month of the third lunar year of the reign of Emperor Xuantong (February 12, 1912), almost the whole nation preferred the Republic, which was advocated firstly by southern provinces and then by northern generals, and this demonstrated that the Republic accorded the will of the people and the destiny of the nation, so there would be no necessity to go against the will of the people by staying committed to the rank and honor of the imperial family but giving the ruling power to the whole nation and turning the nature of state from monarchy to constitutional government after reviewing the situation and the public interests. At this point, the constitutionalism movement started since the thirtieth year of the reign of Emperor Guangxu ended in failure. Refer to Zou [1]. Jing [2].

[2]Bian [3], p. 129.

[3]Bian [3], p. 136.

This constitution was widely criticized, and democratic parties launched vigorous constitutionalism movement. In this case, the national government was forced to publish the "May Fifth Draft Constitution" in 1936. However, this draft constitution failed to become a formally effective constitutional document due to the intense political situation amidst transformation. Until the end of the War of Resistance and the emergence of preliminary results in the negotiations between the KMT and the Communist Party of China (CPC), the second *Constitution of the Republic of China* was passed on December 25, 1946, and was formally put into force one year later. This constitution was declared as "a bogus constitution" by the Central Committee of the CPC[4] because its formulation was solely handled by the KMT and the constitution-making procedures had critical flaws and violated the original

[4]The Central Committee of the CPC issued a statement on December 21, saying that the Chinese people would never admit the "bogus constitution" formulated by the government of Chiang Kai-shek and condemning that this constitution adopted by the "illegal national assembly" was no better than Yuan Shih-kai's Tiantan Constitution and Cao Kun's constitution. According to the statement, without abolishing the dictatorship of Chiang Kai-shek reactionary group, it is impossible for the people to realize democracy no matter how it is stated literally in the constitution. In early 1949, given Chiang Kai-shek's statement of taking the maintenance of the bogus constitution and illegally constituted authority as the condition for peace talks, Mao Zedong on behalf of the CPC published an article titled *On the War Criminals' Sue for Peace*. In the article, Mao Zedong politically criticized Chiang Kai-shek's legal right requirement article by article. Mao Zedong pointed out the intention of Chiang Kai-shek to ensure the ruling status of the Chinese reactionary class and reactionary government and the non-interruption of the constituted authority of this class and this government. In case of the interruption of this constituted authority, the KMT bandit gang would perish and all major and insignificant war criminals would be arrested and punished. On January 14, as a tit-for-tat response to Chiang Kai-shek's proposal, Mao Zedong took the "abolition of the bogus constitution" and "abolition of the bogus constituted authority" as the two conditions for peace talks with the KMT in an article titled *the Statement of Chairman Mao Zedong of the Central Committee of the Communist Party of China on the Current Political Situation*. The essence of the statement was the requirement for the thorough overthrow of the constituted authority nationwide and complete annulment of all laws enacted by the KMT government. On February 22, 1949, the Central Committee of the CPC issued *the Instructions on Abolishing the Six Codes of the KMT and Determining Judicial Principles for the Liberated Areas* according to above guiding principles put forward by Mao Zedong. The instructions clearly stated that the *Six Codes* of the KMT should be abolished under the people's democratic dictatorship led by the proletariat and based on the alliance of workers and peasants. *The Instructions* profoundly stated the fundamental differences between the old and new legal systems and pointed out the reactionary essence of the *Six Codes* of the KMT and the necessity of destroying the old constituted authority. *The Common Program of the Chinese People's Political Consultative Conference* adopted in 1949 proposed to annul all KMT reactionary government's laws, decrees and judicial systems oppressing the people, enact laws and decrees protecting the people and establish a judicial system of the people. This was the formal declaration of the demise of the old constituted authority of the KMT in legal form. Refer to *Mao Zedong's Historical Contribution to the Legal System Building of the People's Republic of China*, published in *Studies on the Socialism with Chinese Characteristics*, Issue 5 of 2006.

resolution of the Chinese People's Political Consultative Conference (CPPCC).[5] Yet, paradoxically, this constitution "being falsified" managed to survive tenaciously in history.[6] Being amended for seven major times during the short period of

[5]As early as November 16, 1946, Zhou Enlai published in behalf of the CPC *the Solemn Statement on the Convocation of the National Assembly of the Kuomintang*. He pointed out in the article that this "General Assembly" was solely convened by the single-party government, which violated the resolution of the CPPCC and the will of the whole nation, and was resolutely opposed by the CPC. He also noted in the article that the National Assembly should be convened only after the complete halt of the internal war, the implementation of the resolution of the CPPCC, the guarantee of people's liberties and rights and the reshuffle of the government, and, in this case, it could be called the National Assembly featuring the unity and participation of all political parties. As Zhou Enlai put it in the article, the National Assembly that was being convened not just violated the above-mentioned resolution and its spirit, even the meeting date or adjournment was decided by the single-party government. He pointed out that the number of deputies already released in the morning of November 15 reached 1580, which, if based on the original agreement, already appropriated 410 places of other parties, even appropriated as many as 140 of the 200 places of liberated areas. Zhou Enlai concluded in the article that this General Assembly was a completely dissociated and one-party arranged assembly.

[6]After the retreat to Taiwan, the Nanjing National Government had been holding onto the tradition of the Republic of China, which was brought from the mainland. The Nanjing National Government had frozen the implementation of the constitution text by implementing "the system of mobilization for the suppression of rebellion." Taiwan was not back to normal constitutionalism until the end of the authoritative rule. Therefore, this constitution went through so many difficulties in Taiwan. In the constitutional government reform movement of Taiwan staged in late last century and early this century, some political forces saw the 1946 Constitution stipulating the "one China principle" as a thorn in the eye and flesh and intended to abolish it. Former leader of Taiwan Lee Teng-hui delivered a speech at a "symposium on a new constitution for Taiwan" held in November 2004. In his speech, Lee Teng-hui said that this constitution of the Republic of China, no matter how to amend it, was no longer capable of adapting to and meeting the needs of Taiwan under the current situation. In addition, it had caused obstacles and barriers to the survival and development of Taiwan in the future. The issues could by no means be resolved by constitution amendment. He noted that, after six amendments which returned powers to the people, there was a need to further implement the basic human rights supporting "popular sovereignty," but this constitution of the Republic of China became the biggest obstacle. Even looking from the idea of constitutionalism and the development of democratic human rights, this constitution of the Republic of China did not conform to modern standards. Viewing from the internationally recognized documents, such as *the Universal Declaration of Human Rights*, *Charter* of *the United Nations*, *International Covenant on Economic, Social and Cultural Rights* and *International Covenant on Civil and Political Rights*, etc., this constitution could no longer keep up with the trend of the times. To formulate a new constitution, the most important reason was that the constitution being applied was not formulated for the 23 million Taiwanese. No Taiwanese participated in its formulation. Just imposing this constitution without the involvement of Taiwanese in formulation upon the Taiwanese went against the spirit of democracy and the universal value of popular sovereignty and was certainly not approved by the Taiwanese. Such a constitution incompatible with the present needs without the foundation of public opinions and inconsistent with the general idea of constitutionalism had become a shackle and a barrier for the already democratic Taiwan and seriously hindered the survival of Taiwan and restricted the development of Taiwan. Therefore, the Taiwanese had to abandon and reject it. Lee Teng-hui also added that if this improper constitution was actually imposed upon Taiwan and even prohibited Taiwan from having a new constitution of itself, it would nip the right of the Taiwanese to live. On May 20, 2004, Chen Shui-bian further pointed out in his "presidential" inauguration speech that constitution was confined to the

1980s and 1990s, the constitution remains to be a basic legal document of Taiwan.[7] That means the 1946 Constitution has been valid for more than 60 years. Apart from being modified for several times, it has been interpreted for 700-plus times by

time-and-space background of formulation, so most articles of the constitution no longer conformed to the current and future needs of Taiwan. He said that advancing the project of reforming constitutionalism and rebuilding the constitutional government order were not only the will of the people but also the consensus of the ruling and opposition parties. The project of reforming constitutionalism was for the government's good governance and efficiency improvement, for establishing the foundation of democratic rule of law and for long-term peace and order of the "state." He also said in the speech that, in order to avoid the repeat of the six amendments within ten years, the project of reforming constitutionalism should be neither dominated by one person or one party nor oriented for temporary convenience. He noted that, going forward, the ruling and opposition parties, the legal community, academic community and representatives of all areas would be invited to jointly prepare for the organization of a constitutionalism reformation committee to maximize the consensus of the society on the scope and procedures of constitutionalism reformation and to accept the supervision of the people and the public opinions. He even proposed to formulate an appropriate, suitable and compatible constitution for the Taiwanese and Taiwan before he left the office in 2008. He also proposed to accomplish the reformation of constitutionalism, abolish the National Assembly and include referendum in the Constitution at the same time so as to lay a foundation for a long-term development of democratic constitutionalism and the people's referendum for constitutional reform. Refer to Lee Teng hui's "Opening Speech at the Symposium on a New Constitution for Taiwan" on November 27, 2004, and Chen Shui-bian's "Presidential" Inauguration Speech on May 20, 2004.

[7]A thorough examination of the 1946 Constitution indicates that this constitution formulated after the World War II has the background of the KMT-CPC cooperation and was purposely retained after being brought to Taiwan by Chiang Kai-shek. Its establishment of the five-power constitutional government system and the authority of the National Assembly became the basic legal basis for Taiwan to maintain the tradition of the Republic of China. In the next 60-plus years, especially after the abolition of *the Temporary Provisions*, this constitution was amended for seven times. The constitutional government system established by this constitution changed substantially. Under the circumstance of maintaining the "one China principle," its directly applicable scope of validity was confined to Taiwan. Particularly in the recent 20-plus years, benign interactions and dynamic constitutional government order have taken shape between social changes and constitutional implementation through the interpretations of constitution by justices. The existence of the 1946 Constitution has become the basis for maintaining the basic legal ties between Taiwan and the mainland. The pro-independence groups strongly advocate the annulment of this constitution and the formulation of a new one in an effort to thoroughly cut off the inherent political and legal blood ties and bonds between the two sides of the Taiwan Straits. Against this backdrop, the mainland should reevaluate the status of the 1946 Constitution and recognize its basic values in the process of reunifying the two sides of the Taiwan Straits down the road. Refer to Li [4].

justices.[8] Changes of this constitution have responded to and driven the successful social transformation of Taiwan. It can be called another miracle in the constitutional development history of modern China. This text will not discuss it in details.

After the founding of the People's Republic of China, the mainland reformulated the constitution on the basis of annulling the *Six Codes*, from the 1949 *Common Program* to the 1954 Constitution. Afterwards, the mainland successively promulgated the 1975 Constitution on the basis of amending the 1954 Constitution, and then the 1978 Constitution and 1982 Constitution. *The Common Program* had rather comprehensive, objective and practical stipulations, but it is unworthy of the title. As a basic legal document of the newly born People's Republic of China, it is still less legitimate. In this connection, 5 years after its implementation, the first constitution of the PRC was promulgated in 1954. Yet, the 1954 Constitution was ill-fated. Apart from being ignored in various political movements, it was out of use and impracticable at the national institutional level. This constitution was completely abandoned after the outbreak of the Cultural Revolution. Thereafter, the 1975 Constitution and 1978 Constitution successively born on the basis of comprehensive amendments were both the products of political reality back then. In this case, they lacked legality and legitimacy. Thereupon, the constitution was completely modified in early 1980s. The promulgation and formal implementation of the 1982 Constitution symbolized that the mainland entered a relatively stable period. From the operational and technical perspective, the 1982 Constitution adopted the way of partial amendments in practice. This move fundamentally changed the possibility of fundamentally scraping the constitution and starting all over again. The Chinese constitutional circle generally equates the comprehensive amendment of constitution to the formulation of constitution, and partial amendment of the constitution is the amendment worthy of the name. This way of amending is more conducive to maintaining the stability of the constitution.[9] Especially in the amendments in 1999 and 2004, "the People's Republic of China implements governance by law and builds a socialist country under the rule of law" and "the state respects and safeguards human rights" were enshrined in the Constitution. The 1982 Constitution has been gradually brought back to essence, and the constitutional government practices of the Chinese mainland have gradually taken shape.

---

[8]Just in July 2012, two new interpretation documents were released by the general justice, namely Interpretation No. 701 and Interpretation No. 702. The former was "discrimination on itemized deductions of medical expenses for long-term care" (July 6, 2012). The arguments over this interpretation were whether it is unconstitutional concerning the stipulation that a deduction for expenses for an individual who is physically handicapped or is mentally defective was only applicable to medical institutions and offices designated by the tax income law. The latter was "lifetime disqualification from teaching due to conduct that is inconsistent with teachers' morals and dignity" (July 27, 2012). The arguments over this interpretation were whether it is unconstitutional in terms of the stipulation of lifetime disqualification from teaching due to conduct that is inconsistent with teachers' morals and dignity, and dismissal, appointment termination or no reappointment for those already being employed.

[9]Jiao [5].

To sum up, the 1982 Constitution has been implemented uninterruptedly for 30 years. For a country undergoing vigorous social transformation and modernization, we have to say it is a periodic victory. It is not even overemphasized to say that it is a miracle of the Chinese society in developing the rule of law. Therefore, the reflections on practices of 1982 Constitution should not simply take the Constitution itself into consideration. Instead, the constitution should be put in the process of China's modernization for reflections. If we recap by taking China's modern social development as the principle line, we may find that the 1982 Constitution is simply a staged achievement of China in developing the rule of law. Moreover, constitutional document is by no means groundless in itself. Instead, it is historical sediment rather than a mere scrap of paper without historical continuity. It reflects the historical tradition of a country and nation and responds to the realistic requirement for political, social and economic development. Even the denial of the past is also reflected in the currently available texts. Therefore, we should also make analysis by putting the 1982 Constitution in China's modernization process while drawing on lessons from successes and failures in implementing the 1982 Constitution.

2 Rethinking the "Question About Cycle": Democracy Versus Constitutionalism

With the victory of the War of Resistance in sight and in order to promote the cooperation between the KMT and the CPC, Mao Zedong especially invited five KMT senators including Huang Yanpei and Zhang Bojun to Yan'an for visit and investigations. On July 4, Mao Zedong invited Huang Yanpei and other senators to his house as guests. After a long conversation, Mao Zedong asked Huang Yanpei about his impression of the trip. Huang Yanpei thought of the vibrant scenes he saw in Yan'an and sincerely made the following statements based on his reflections on life and history. He said, "I've lived for more than 60 years. Let's not talk about what I've heard. Whatever I saw with my own eyes, it fits the saying: "The rise of something may be fast, but its downfall is equally swift." Has any person, family, community, place or even a nation, ever managed to break free out of this cycle? Usually in the initial stage, everyone stays fully focused and puts in his/her best efforts. Maybe conditions were bad at the time, and everyone has to struggle to survive. Once the times change for the better, everyone loses focus and becomes lazy. In certain cases, as it has been a long time, complacency breeds, spreads and becomes a social norm. As such, even if the people are very capable, they can neither reverse the situation nor salvage it. There are also cases where a nation progresses and prospers—its rise could be either natural or due to yearning for progression. When all human resources have been exhausted and problems crop up in management, the environment becomes more complicated and they lose control of the situation. Throughout history, there are various examples: A ruler ignores state affairs and eunuchs use the opportunity to seize power; a good system of governance ceases to function after the person who initiated it dies; people who lust for glory but end up in humiliation. None has managed to break out of this cycle. My humble knowledge shows that the Chinese Communists have always been exploring new ways to break out of this cycle." Mao Zedong replied confidently, "We've already discovered a new path. We can break out of this cycle. This new path is democracy. The government will not become complacent only if it is under the supervision of the people. If everyone takes responsibility, a good system of governance will prevail." Huang Yanpei agreed with what Mao Zedong said and further noted that only when the fundamental policy was made public, personal achievement desires would not happen. He also said that only if everything in every place is known to everyone in the place, it could make every duty be appropriately allocated and make everyone take his/her responsibility. He added that it might be effective for breaking this cycle.[10] This conversation was later called "cave conversation," representing the thinking of that generation of political elites about China's future and destiny.

Huang Yanpei's "questions about cycle" can be called as "worries deep in the history" and compelling and thought-provoking. Mao Zedong's replies can be said as sharp-witted, unique, wise and profound. This conversation went beyond the current situation while being based on the current situation. An overview of China's several thousand years of civilization history, the conversation reinterpreted and rethought the basic clue of China's historical development. The focus of the conversation was the alternate chaos and peace along with China's social development process, the turn of dynasties, the transition and cycle of old orders and new political powers, and deep-seated factors for flag changes. This "cycle" was a vicious cycle. "Flourish, people suffer! Perish, people suffer!" How to break this vicious cycle? Mao Zedong gave a prescription, which is democracy.

But what is democracy? Does democracy have its fixed form? Does democracy have its specific or personalized content or expression form in different political and cultural environments or at different political development stages? Is there a natural connection or natural gap between democracy and revolution? Is the periodic social development form of China a kind of reflection and interpretation of democracy? In his *Report on an Investigation of the Peasant Movement in Hunan*, Mao Zedong said, "A revolution is not a dinner party, or writing an essay, or painting a picture,

[10]After returning to Chongqing from Yan'an, Huang Yanpei wrote a book titled *Return from Yan'an*. After being printed and published by the Guoxun Bookstore of the China Vocational Education Association, the book was widely circulated. The book recorded a paragraph of his conversation with Mao Zedong on "cycle." For related information, refer to Wen Liming: *The Third Force and Chinese Politics in the Period of the War of Resistance*, Shanghai Bookstore Publishing House, 2004. Zhu [6]. Wikipedia, entry about Huang Yanpei: http://zh.wikipedia.org/wiki/%E9%BB%84%E7%82%8E%E5%9F%B9, lastly visited on April 7, 2014.

or doing embroidery; it cannot be so refined, so leisurely and gentle, so temperate, kind, courteous, restrained and magnanimous. A revolution is an insurrection, an act of violence by which one class overthrows another." Are revolutionary movements of this kind a manifestation of democracy? The "Cultural Revolution" launched in 1960s–1970s in mainland China advocated the theory of continuous revolution under the proletarian dictatorship. This call eventually turned into a public action. Are evolutionary movements of this kind also an expression of democracy? Is that what mentioned by Mao Zedong in his conversation with Huang Yanpei, which is, "we've already discovered a new path. We can break out of this cycle." Was the "Cultural Revolution" aimed at making the people supervise the government and take charge?[11]

In this connection, if we make a vertical historical comparison, we could find that the democracy upheld by Mao Zedong was broad in sense and rich in content. It is not necessarily the same with Western-style democracy. He had his unique observations, understandings and grasp of the requirements of the Chinese society and the general public. He also had his own designs and arrangements of China's political operation. He even took the Cultural Revolution-style "great democracy" as a manifestation of democracy. This thought and cognition was mirrored and reflected in the 1975 Constitution to some extent. This constitution stipulated in Article 13, "Speaking out freely, airing views fully, holding great debates and writing big-character posters are new forms of carrying on socialist revolution created by the masses of the people. The state shall ensure the masses the right to use these forms to create a political situation in which there are both centralism and democracy, both discipline and freedom, both unity of will and personal ease of mind and liveliness, and so help consolidate the leadership of the Communist Party of China over the

[11]Mao Zedong once said, "In the past, we waged struggles in rural areas, in factories, in the cultural field, and we carried out the socialist education movement. But all this failed to solve the problem because we did not find a form, a method, to arouse the broad masses to expose our dark aspects openly, in an all-round way and from below." He looked to find a new path and break out of the cycle, but what's the new path? "The Great Proletarian Cultural Revolution" can be called an attempt of his. Regarding this practice, someone observed that Mao Zedong's concept of history showcased some tendency of Populism (or people-centered doctrine). He unconditionally believed in "the masses" and believed that abstract group of "people" was the driving force of history. Refer to He Xin: *On the Cultural Revolution and Mao Zedong's Thought in His Late Years*. Some others thought that Mao Zedong advocated great democracy. That is to expose the dark aspects of the Communist Party and Government established under his leadership openly, in an all-round way and from below and evaluate the contributions and faults of leaders of all levels by all means including speaking out freely, airing views fully, writing big-character posters, holding great debates, choosing large-scale exposure and criticism, etc. Before the "Cultural Revolution," there had never been any democracy like this all over the world. Under this democracy, officials dare not act as tyrants and trample on the people. Therefore, officials have to serve the people wholeheartedly and become servants of the people. Otherwise, they are disqualified for being officials and would be asked for stepping down. This is the real and progressive democracy, an unprecedented democracy and a democracy opening a new era for the humanity. Refer to "*Cultural Revolution*" *was the New Path for Mao Zedong to Break out of the Cycle*, http://www.xici.net/d138636387.htm, lastly visited on April 7, 2014.

state and consolidate the dictatorship of the proletariat." Launching the Cultural Revolution meant even going as far as destroying the existing results obtained from revolutions in the past decades, including the system and tradition accumulated in national and social development. The state building constructed by the constitution could be toppled down and rebuilt. When motivating the strength of the broad masses with the revolutionary spirit of destroying the old for building the new, the revolutionary passion motivated in the end failed to break out of the cycle. Instead, more issues were created and it consequently ended up with nothing. This kind of practices received certain results within a short period of time. In the long run, it is simply a temporary relief, and inevitably caused a disaster, ended at the opposite pole, and was finally, inevitably and completely denied by the history.

In this sense, for political and intellectual elites caring for modern China's destiny, there must be an answer that is far-sighted and goes beyond the present reality for breaking the cycle. There must be the courage of abandoning individualism. To realize China's lasting stability, peace and prosperity, make the people live and work in peace and contentment and greatly rejuvenate the Chinese nation, there is a must to explore and create a set of state political systems that suit China's national conditions and conform to the basic law and historical trend. The function and value of constitution are the focus on this to a large extent that is to provide a foundation for the existence of the state building. For the prescription of "democracy," there is a need to make a careful analysis to see whether democracy could present a solution for truly breaking out of this historical "cycle." Is it a life-saving straw randomly discovered under the circumstance of simple blindness? Or, is it a rational judgment made after historical analyses and prudent comparisons? Is the judgment feasible? Could it stand the test of history?

Looking from the development process of modern political civilization, democracy is an epoch-making progress. The proposal of the principle of people's sovereignty opened a new era in human history, but it had a revolutionary complex of breaking the existing order. Especially when a state and society is in the middle of crisis, the political forces both staying at the bottom of the society and accounting for the majority of the society require expressing their interest appeals. The expression of wills like this is certainly endowed with legitimacy when the condition permits, which is revolution, continuous revolution and unceasing revolution.[12] The theory of people's sovereignty provided a direct theoretical basis for revolutions and a convincing explanation for the process from peace to disorder.

[12] After seizing the political power, was a revolution still needed? Mao Zedong gave a positive answer. Just as Huang Yanpei put it, Mao Zedong started to mobilize the people, but his democracy was to contend for cultural leadership through mass movement, Cultural Revolution, rather than voting. Just as Xiao Wu said, a basic fact was that, during the mass movement period between 1966 and 1968, the ordinary working people took part in the "revolution" only because they were tired of the previous rigid hierarchy system no matter what kind of high-level political power struggles existed. When the promise of giving the people a state of equalitarianism was unfulfilled and only when hierarchical privilege became increasingly threatening to the daily life of ordinary people, how would not they place their hopes on the Cultural Revolution and try to overthrow the establishment? Refer to Xiao Wu's *the Revolution is Dead. Long live the Revolution!*

Under the condition of lacking the restriction of order, this kind of appeals for democracy would turn into inexhaustible powers, including destructive power and destroying power. After observing the evolution of democratic theories and practices, we could find that the development process of the principle of people's sovereignty was constantly changed and enriched and gradually became the constituent power as the original power. The process towards democracy turned into the constitution-making process and into a written constitution. Then, the derivative powers formed based on constitutional stipulations have become mutually restrictive in an effective way, including the restriction of the constitution on democracy itself. This is the theoretical basis of the formation of the constitutionality review system. People's sovereignty turns into parliamentary sovereignty, and they are all expressed in constitution and under the control of the constitution. Both the US model and European model were formed under this premise. The formation of constitution order and the constitutionalism process have solved insurmountable issues for democracy, thus fundamentally addressed issues relating to the cycle generation conditions and made constitution become a social foundation. The constitutionalism process has also provided the foundation for the conflicts and updates of political forces and enabled the formation of a benign interaction between constitution and social development. Constitutionalism process has offered a carrier and expression form for social development and transformation.

As a matter of fact, if the principle of people's sovereignty is not enriched and supplemented but just being simply interpreted and the understandings of democracy are not enriched and changed, there would be space for revolutions and thus the ceaseless social cycle from peace to chaos in pure sense so long as the polarization between the rich and the poor exists, the hierarchical system still exists, the middle class is not the majority of the society, and the social security system is not rationally in place. This is because most people's requirement for overthrowing the existing social order is democracy and revolution as well. However, how to return back to normal life after a revolution? For the society, a secular life must be opened after revolution. As long as the society enters into normality, there would be differences and polarization between the rich and the poor and there would be the hierarchical system and bureaucratic system. Then, this will provide a new soil and environment for continuous revolution in some years later. After the accumulation for a certain period of time, revolution would seem to be inevitable. Judging from this, there would be continuous and ceaseless revolutions. This would not completely break out of the cycle of Mr. Huang Yanpei. Instead, we will fall into the cycle again. This is because democracy without enrichment is totally possible to become a synonym for revolution. The French Revolution that opened a new era of

---

Fei Zhengqing said that all revolutions always had a common destiny: The outbreaks were sudden just like that of a volcano, neither predictable nor controllable. Well, if we look back at them when the circumstances are different, they will be overwhelmed by landscape pictures and the cause and effect could no longer be distinguished, just like the two foots of a hill. Refer to Fei Zhengqing: *The Great Chinese Revolution*.

modern history broke out just on the basis of the pursuit for democracy. This kind of social development mode just coincides with the cycle-type development process of China over thousands of years. That is to realize social development through explosive revolutions of the bottom of society. Therefore, to completely break out of the cycle, what can be relied on is not democracy but constitutionalism on the basis of democracy.

Qin Shi Huang, the First Emperor of Qin, used to express his wish that the Qin dynasty could last for thousands of years (*The Historical Records · Biographic Sketches of Qin Shi Huang*), but the reign of Qin only lasted for two generations. Mencius said, "The influence of a sage terminates in the fifth generation. The influence of a base person does the same." (*Mencius · Li Lou Part Two*) For a modern state, a mature political system is sufficient to support the stability and existence of the state building rather than only lasting for five generations. This state building is based on democratic legitimacy to ensure the legitimacy of the existing order while carrying out various constitutional practices on this basis. The foundation for a long-lasting influence could be laid only when constitutional government practices with constitutional implementation as the main content become dynamic benign interactions between social changes and constitution.

3 Impulse Is the Devil: Constitutional Government Revolution Versus Revolutionary Constitutional Government

In China's modernization process, movements and revolutions have come one after another, demonstrating that the waves behind drive on those before. Looking from a certain period, this kind of tempest-like movements and revolutions received certain success, but in the long run they failed to bring about fundamental reforms and changes to the deeper social form of China. The repeated contests and struggles between various political forces in a radical manner failed to enable China to enter into the state featuring their interdependent benign competitions. On the contrary, it easily resulted in a zero-sum game. In the end, the interests of the entire society would not increase accordingly but even retrogress sometimes on a large scale.

At the time of making the constitution in late Qing Dynasty, the conservative political forces and radical political forces represented by both government officials and the people fought at close quarter and called war from a distance. The south and the north negotiated peace and the Qing emperor abdicated, which avoided a war that is likely to spread to the whole nation and prevented the people from plunging into an abyss of misery. Either due to the reality or due to political speculations, it is more like the result of the British "Glorious Revolution." However, it is difficult to get positive public opinions and evaluations and doubly difficult to reach a consensus from top to down.

During the period of the Beiyang Government, the murder of Song Jiaoren triggered the "Second Revolution." Sun Yat-sen stood for crusading against Yuan Shih-kai by armed forces, but the reactions were mixed within the KMT. Some leaders including Huang Xing preferred peaceful means that was to fight by legal means without breaking the Provisional Constitution. Afterwards, the "Second Revolution" ended up quickly with the retreat of the south. Beiyang troops flew into southern provinces, and the concentration of powers brought about efficient administration to the state. Yuan Shih-kai gained the support of the people through the "Second Revolution," but his justice and legitimacy were not permanent.

On December 12, 1915, Yuan Shih-kai accepted the "support" for becoming the emperor of Empire of China and ordered to change the reign title to be Hongxian in the following year. On December 25, Tang Jiyao, Cai E, et al. published an open telegram to the nation for anti-imperial restoration and declaring the independence of Yunnan. As a result, the national protection war overthrew the "Hongxian" monarchy. Yuan Shih-kai died of an illness later. Duan Qirui was forced to restore *the Provisional Constitution* and the Congress. Some scholar evaluated that the political system of the Beiyang Government had no relatively stable state as it attached little importance to political opinions, failed to follow principles and strategies and took actual gains as the basis for everything. Its inheritance of the feudal political system was out of its nature and familiarity.[13]

Between 1917 and 1922, Sun Yat-sen launched the constitution protection movements under the support of military strength, including the first constitution protection movement and the second constitution protection movement. The so-called constitution protection refers to protecting *the Provisional Constitution of the Republic of China*, overthrowing the "Republic" controlled by the Beiyang system and rebuilding the legally constituted authority of a democratic republic. Sun Yat-sen led the movement and established the military government of the Republic of China in Guangzhou to fight against the Beiyang Government. Some people also call it "the third revolution." Just as a Chinese saying goes, "The success or failure of the affair is all due to the very same person." Sun Yat-sen's two constitution protection movements ended in failure because of the change of attitude of the powerful military forces. This finally prompted Sun Yat-sen to realize the necessity of staging revolutions with his own army to achieve targets. The reality was that even leaders like Sun Yat-sen who proposed the five-power constitution and had the thought of democracy and republicanism had to build up their own armed forces to realize the unity of national politics and economic integration in armed form.

In his *Speech at the Education Meeting of Guangdong Province* on April 4, 1921, Sun Yat-sen said that there were two political trends: One was freedom trend, and the other was order trend. He also said these two forces in politics were just like the centripetal and centrifugal forces in physics… and only the balance of the two could be appropriate. He added that if freedom prevailed, there would be anarchy; if

[13]Xu [7].

order prevailed, there would be autocracy, and political changes in the past thousands of years were no more than the conflicts between these two forces. So, is it an ideal or a reality? Or, do we lack the gene of democracy, constitutionalism and republic in the cultural genes of our nation? I personally agree with the former. We have been not so devoted to the ideals and targets of democracy, constitutionalism and republic and paid little price to it. In addition, we are easily to mistake it as the reality.

In fact, except for scholars of the school of liberalism, some local powerful military forces, such as Chen Jiongming, also rejected to realize national reunification in form and essence through radical revolutions. At the time of taking charge of the administration of Guangdong, one of the contributions of Chen Jiongming was the proposition of the "joint-provinces autonomy" movement. The purpose of the movement was to establish a federal political system much like that of European and American democratic states. He especially proposed to seek permanent unification of China by means of peace and compromise due to the reality and difficulties faced by Guangdong. He extremely opposed the impractical northern expedition revolution led by Sun Yat-sen, i.e., seeking northern expedition and reunification of China by force.[14]

During the northern expedition, the KMT and the CPC completely parted ways and the state fell back into a civil war while facing the crisis of foreign invasions. After the victory of the Anti-Japanese War under the coordination, the KMT and the CPC had another opportunity to cooperate and coexist in 1945, but the confrontations between the two principles, two lines, two models and two destinies brought China back into a civil war. This war ended with the born of the People's Republic of China. That said, China lost the favorable historical opportunity for economic development and social progress upon the conclusion of World War II. It is by no means easy to form a constitutional government order against the political background of wars, revolutions, continuous revolutions and constant revolutions.

Some scholars believed that, from the point of general standards, the class evolution of modern Chinese thoughts came to the end point during the "Cultural Revolution,"[15] but realistically, this point could not be fully proved. Li Zehou once mentioned that China especially needed to cultivate a spirit of criticism which is tolerant, suspicious and rational and only this spirit could truly help judge the right or wrong and gradually abandon and avoid various emotional fanaticisms and blind political actions instigated by nationalism, moralism and populism. China paid a heavy historical price for these.[16] Today, there are still soils for radical thoughts in the evolution of China's social pattern, which can be mirrored by the expressions, public concerns, hot issues and evaluations on the Internet, especially the controversial Chongqing development model and process. The public still lacks ample

[14]Chen [8].

[15]Chief Editor Li [9].

[16]Ma [10].

immunity to radical development roads, and the rational, progressive and tolerant development path has not been fully and completely agreed with.

4 The Race Between Hare and Tortoise: Revolutionary Hare (Road) Versus Constitutional Government Tortoise (Track)

The Race between Hare and Tortoise is a famous story of Aesop's Fables. In the race, the hare ran fast, but it had a nap during the race and found that, after waking up, the tortoise had arrived at the terminal point. Comparing them in speed, the hare is faster certainly, but the tortoise has the spirit of perseverance and refuses to give up easily. As the tortoise moved towards the end point, it realized the qualitative change from quantitative change and won the race, leaving no chance for the hare to win.

In the process of China's modernization, the race between revolution and constitutionalism has been the normality, but revolution has prevailed. The grudges were finally settled in the smoke of gunpowder. As a matter of fact, in the process of China's thousand years of historical development, stories about the race between hare and tortoise have been told all the time. This is why Mr. Huang Yanpei and Mao Zedong had the famous conversation on "cycle."

In China's modernization process, the race between revolutionary hare (road) versus constitutional government tortoise (track) has been fiercer. It seems that the former is cuter and more flexible, vibrant, attractive, adorable and easily accepted by the public, while the latter seems more slow-witted and quieter, calmer, more timid, slower and not easy to become a pet.

Southern Weekly used to publish an article titled Reform and Revolution Race between Hare and Tortoise—Why "the Preparations for Constitutionalism" Failed to Save the Qing Government in 2008 marking the 100 anniversary of China's movement of constitutionalism. The article pointed out that, in the race between revolution and constitutionalism in late Qing Dynasty, the failure of the Westernization movement made the Qing Government lose the precious self-reforming opportunity. The failure of the Hundred Days' Reform was more harmful. If we say that the reform within the system and the revolution outside the system are racing, just like the race between hare and tortoise, then the government would be the half-hearted hare and the revolutionists would be the congenitally deficient but unremitting tortoise.[17] The conception of the article is good, but it

[17]Shen [11].

should not compare the results with the race of hare and tortoise and thus take government as the hare and take revolutionists as the tortoise. Analyzing from the essence, constitutionalism is more like the tortoise and revolution is more like the hare. Revolutionary storms come quickly and go quickly. The development of constitutionalism needs to be advanced progressively, little by little through accumulations and precipitations. Every move or motion needs to reflect the good intentions of constitutionalism, and there should not be the slightest negligence. In this way, China's development of constitutionalism can be said as learning step by step and must choose the process from easy to difficult progressively but not bypass. Advancing just like a jumping hare is not good for constitutionalists as it is clearly a revolutionary path (road). The road of constitutionalism should be followed steadily while making changes. There should be clear-cut targets, and the targets should be realized in a down-to-earth way. The revolutionists in late Qing Dynasty did not move slowly but quickly. They were faster than constitutionalists. Constitutionalism was not realized in China overnight. It is neither accomplished in an action. The jumping practice of the hare was inappropriate for constitutional government construction. The growth of China's constitutionalism was realized step by step. Only small steps could make a long distance.

On the one hand, today's China has witnessed nearly thirty years of rapid development and its GDP has maintained a double digit growth for many years. In addition, China has also constantly accumulated social wealth and its leading development momentum is enviable to the rest of the world. The reform and opening-up has also produced fruitful results.[18] On the other hand, the differences and differentiations between different social classes have become more prominent, and the social conflicts are becoming increasingly salient. Some local areas are rigidly maintaining the stability, which have further intensified the conflicts and contradictions, and suppressing free expression of public opinions has even strengthened the accumulation of social contradictions. At present, the social conflicts triggered by mass incidents are showcasing high frequency and high strength and attracting nationwide attentions through the dissemination of the

[18]The Chinese mainland has grown rapidly in the recent three decades. Entering the twenty-first century, China's rank in global economy keeps rising. In 2000, the GDP of the Chinese mainland surpassed that of Italy. Between 2005 and 2007, China surpassed France, Britain and Germany one by one in terms of the economic ranking and became the world's third largest economy only after the USA and Japan in GDP. When it comes to export, China even surpassed the USA to become the world's second largest exporter only after Germany in 2007. In 2010, Chinese mainland surpassed Japan and became the world's second largest economy in GDP.

network and media, thus causing strong social responses.[19] In *the Speech at the Meeting Marking the 90th Anniversary of the Founding of the Communist Party of China*, Hu Jintao summarized the four tests faced by the ruling party such as long-term, complex and severe political tests in ruling, test from reform and opening-up, test from market economy and test from the external environment; and four risks, namely slacking spirit, inadequate capacity, isolation from the people, negativity and corruption.[20]

Under these circumstances, further control of political participation would surely result in constant accumulations of negative energies. Once the public got the opportunity for political participation and the way to express their wills, it would possibly be unmanageable, just like dried firewood being ignited. If it is not controlled and prevented, the negative energies already accumulated would burst once the condition permitted and it would undoubtedly provide an opportunity for the expression of populism. Well, the efforts to resolve and fend off this great trend of

[19]For example, in July 2012, the Chinese mainland witnessed two mass incidents with greater influence. One was the Shifang incident in Sichuan, and the other was the Qidong incident in Jiangsu. The first incident happened in Shifang of Deyang City of Sichuan Province on July 1, 2012. The cause of the incident was the construction of "the project of Hongda Mo-Cu polymetallic deep processing for comprehensive utilization" launched by Shifang. This project was exposed as having significantly negative impact on local environment, which led to the rallies of a large number of people in protest. Shifang government sent police, armed police and regimental police to maintain the stability, triggering serious conflicts between the police and the people and causing many injuries. On July 3, Shifang Public Security Bureau issued a stern notice, ordering all people who instigated, planned or organized illegal assemblies and rallies, or engaged in beating, smashing and looting to turn themselves to the police within three days. On July 4, the Information Office of the People's Government of Shifang issued a notice, stating that the Public Security Bureau took away 27 personnel suspected of illegal crimes coercively according to law to calm down the incident. Afterwards, the Government of Shifang said the Mo-Cu project would not be constructed. Refer to Wikipedia, http://zh.wikipedia.org/zh/%E4%BB%80%E9%82%A1%E4%BA%8B%E4%BB%B6, lastly visited on April 7, 2014.

The Qidong Incident was also a mass incident happened in Qidong City of Jiangsu Province on July 28, 2012. This incident also caused grave influence. This incident was triggered by the approval of construction of Japanese Oji Paper's sea drainage project for papermaking by the Government of Nantong City of Jiangsu Province. In the afternoon of the incident, the incident was basically calmed down and an official notice was released in that morning to announce the cancel of the project permanently. Refer to Wikipedia, http://zh.wikipedia.org/wiki/%E6%B1%9F%E8%8B%8F%E5%90%AF%E4%B8%9C%E4%BA%8B%E4%BB%B6, lastly visited on April 7, 2014.

[20]In his *Speech at the Meeting Marking the 90th Anniversary of the Founding of the Communist Party of China*, Hu Jintao clearly pointed out that the entire party must clearly recognize that it is a long-term, complex and arduous job under the new situation of profound changes in world situation, national conditions and party conditions to improve the Party's leading and governance level, enhance the ability of refusing corruption, preventing changes and resisting risks, strengthen the Party's building of governing capacity and advancement, face up to unprecedented issues and challenges, and tests to the governance, reform and opening-up, market economy and external environment. The risks of slacking spirit, inadequate capacity, isolation from the people and negativity and corruption have become more acute to the entire party. It is more onerous and urgent to implement the tasks of self-governance and strict self-discipline of the Party than any other times. Website of the Central People's Government: http://www.gov.cn/ldhd/2011-07/01/content_1897720_3.htm, lastly visited on April 7, 2014.

populism would become very insignificant and helpless. Once the dilemma occurred, it would be the same with the historical stages we experienced. Simplified democratic practices would trigger a revolution in the end, which would make China further lose the foundation for political order legitimacy as well as precious opportunities for sustainable development. Therefore, in the process of the race between revolution and constitutionalism, revolutionary impulsions must be defused by the practices in constitutionalism so as to enable the tortoise (track) of constitutionalism to win the revolutionary hare (road).

5 Ups and Downs: Outlook for the 1982 Constitution

Mr. Tang Degang used to raise the "historical three gorges theory" based on China's several thousand years of historical development, especially the modernization process. He divided the changes of China's political and social systems over the past four millennia into three major stages, namely feudalism, imperialism and governance by the people. There were two major stages of historical three gorges, meaning two major changes of historical stages. The first change was the transition from feudalism to imperialism starting from Shang Yang (395 BC-338 BC) to Emperor Qin and Emperor Wu of Han dynasty, which lasted for about 300 years. The second change was the transition from imperialism to governance by the people which happened upon the Opium War. Since then, it is the plain sailing journey to peace and tranquility, which would last for about 200 years. By 2040, the Chinese history would accomplish the second three gorges stage and herald a new era of peaceful and happy life of people.[21] Judging from this, we can conclude that, in China's modernization process, all constitutions or constitutional laws and documents submerged in the stage of "historical three gorges." We are now in the later stage of the "historical three gorges," which happens to be the second thirty-year implementation of the 1982 Constitution. How could we walk out of the "historical three gorges" and enable the 1982 Constitution to bear this arduous task?

The 1982 Constitution just appeared at such an intersection of time and space for transformation. It had not yet had the time to accomplish the complete transformation in terms of the stance. On the one hand, it reserved some aspects of the revolutionary times. On the other hand, it opened the door for China to constitutionalism. This constitution seems rigid and clumsy in text and lacks flexibility and elasticity. Its institutional design has not yet got rid of the mechanical and simple model. Its adherence to protecting the people's sovereignty and refusal and rejection of review for constitutionality (or constitutionality review) have showcased that this constitution has not yet reached the state and realm of doing whatever one wants without making mistakes. Furthermore, the text and practices of the 1982

[21] Refer to Tang [12]. Wikipedia, entry about Tang Degang, http://zh.wikipedia.org/wiki/%E5%94%90%E5%BE%B7%E5%88%9A, lastly visited on April 7, 2014.

Constitution have manifested its natural affinity to democracy, its refusal of clear sublation of people's sovereignty and rejection to realize progressive fine-tuning with fully dynamic practices. A basic case in point is that constitutional interpretation has never been applied formally in the last 30 years after its promulgation. Well, this practice should be the most fundamental and common way of constitutional practices in countries with mature rule of law. If we look at *the Basic Law of Hong Kong Special Administrative Region*, which is called "small constitution," we can see that it has been interpreted for 4 times by the National People's Congress ever since its enforcement on July 1, 1997.[22]

Of course, there are many more unsatisfactory aspects. Furthermore, it emphasizes democracy, but it lacks power separation and restriction and also lacks restriction between powers. This regulatory principle and content have not yet been written into this constitution. The Constitution has been modified for many times and the principles of rule of law and human rights protection have been written into the constitution, but it is still congenitally deficient as lacking some basic contents, such as due process, proportionality principle and legal reservation principle. To be sure, these issues can be resolved through creative interpretations.

All these can be understood. After all, the 1982 Constitution is also a historical product. Both the 1975 Constitution and the 1978 Constitution were deeply influenced by the "left" thought. The 1982 Constitution tried to get rid of the influence of the "left" and began to turn to the "right," which was the denial of the former two constitutions. In this sense, the formulation of the 1982 Constitution was also a revolution. It is the summary and generalization of the experiences and lessons in governing the state and dealing with politics. It is the announcement and guidance of China's future political development and a "tranquil revolution" of the Chinese mainland.

Mr. Tang Degang who raised the "historical three gorges theory" had a profound and optimistic understanding of China's historical development. He wrote in his book that the nature of the one and a half-century-long turmoil in China was the bimillennial "great social and cultural transformation." No matter it is long or short in time, the historical three gorges are bound to be passed.[23] In this sense, we should also have an optimistic and positive attitude towards this seemingly imperfect fundamental law that has been with us for 3 decades. This should be the basic strategy for China's constitution to become mature in the next 3 decades. If we see constitution as the goddess in our heart, then she has been lived with us for

[22]Interpretation of the first clause of Article 13 and Article 19 of *the Basic Law of Hong Kong Special Administrative Region* by the Standing Committee of NPC (August 26, 2011); interpretation of the second clause of Article 53 of *the Basic Law of Hong Kong Special Administrative Region* by the Standing Committee of NPC (April 27, 2005); interpretation of Article 7 of Appendix I and Article 3 of Appendix II of *the Basic Law of Hong Kong Special Administrative Region* by the Standing Committee of NPC (April 6, 2004); interpretation of the fourth clause of Article 22 and the second clause (item III) of Article 24 of *the Basic Law of Hong Kong Special Administrative Region* by the Standing Committee of NPC (June 26, 1999).

[23]Refer to Tang [12].

30 years till today, which is a miracle of this oriental country in social transformation and constitutional development. If we wish to see more miracles, then this constitution is bound to bring us more miracles, just as the theory revealed by "Pygmalion Effect."[24] Our subjective understandings of and expectations for this constitution are going to determine the effect of its implementation and its future destiny.

China is still forging ahead with an all-round reform and opening-up to promote the settlement of various issues. The law-based meanings of economic system reform and political system reform are freedom and constitutionalism, respectively. We should have the reason to believe that the 1982 Constitution could realize the transformation from "nominal constitution" to "standard constitution" in the coming 3 decades. If we wish to see the life miracle of the goddess statue, then the 1982 Constitution would also become the "living constitution" under our optimistic expectations. In the 3 decades to come, the constitution could realize "constitutionalism soft landing" through rich practices and become the fundamental law knocking open the constitutionalism door worthy of the name. For that to happen, China will certainly seek for making breakthroughs in many issues in constitutional practices.

The 1982 Constitution should seek a benign interaction with the society beyond the basic development path—changes of text of the constitution. When constitution is no longer isolated from social life, constitutional interpretation would not keep missing. In the meantime, the foundation of constitutional practices—democratization of political procedures enables the public to more extensively participate in political procedures. Political development also calls for the growth of constitutional order and the coexistence of political democratization and new social order to finally promote the update of the basic concept—the transformation from democratic constitutionalism to the democracy of constitutionalism. All these would change the current situation of lacking constitutional cases. The 1982 Constitution should also realize the optimization and integration of constitutional government system through adjusting and improving the rigid constitutional government system, strengthen the constitutional government system within the regulated scope of state powers, and change its marginalized status in political life. The 1982 Constitution should boost and facilitate practices in human rights protection, realize constitution-based basic state policies and enrich the legitimacy of political practices through social welfare and security. At the same time, it should realize the

[24]Pygmalion Effect, also known as Rosenthal Effect, or "Expectation Effect," refers to the phenomenon that a person (usually referring to a kid or student) would perform better after being highly expected. Pygmalion Effect was named after a sculptor called Pygmalion in a Greek myth. He fell in love with his own ivory sculpture of a goddess and talked to it every day. Finally, that statue became a real goddess. Pygmalion Effect is a self-fulfilling prophecy development. From this point of view, those frequently having negative expectations would end up in failure, but those usually having positive expectations are bound to succeed. Refer to Wikipedia, entry about Pygmalion Effect, http://zh.wikipedia.org/wiki/%E7%9A%AE%E6%A0%BC%E9%A9%AC%E5%88%A9%E7%BF%81%E6%95%88%E5%BA%94, lastly visited on April 7, 2014.

basic target of building a harmonious society on the basis of realizing law-based social governance. The 1982 Constitution would also look to make new breakthroughs and reconciliations in national reunification in its practices. Its basic train of thought is to realize a natural and perfect integration of the target of national reunification and reshaping the order of constitutionalism across the straits.

References

1. Zou Ailian: *Imperial Edict of the Abdication of the Qing Emperor – Sign of the Ending of the Feudal Autocratic Monarchy System in China*, *China Culture Daily*, September 29, 2011.
2. Jing Zhiren, *A Constitutional History of China*, Linking Publishing, 2001 edition, page 167.
3. Bian Xiuquan: *Historical Interpretation of the Constitution Text of Modern China*, Intellectual Property Publishing House, 2006 edition.
4. Li Xiaobing: *The Mainland Needs to Correctly Look at the Values of the Constitution of the Republic of China*, *United Daily News*, January 30, 2012.
5. Jiao Hongchang: *Constitutional Law* (4th edition), ed., Peking University Press, page 77.
6. Zhu Guang: *Conversation between Mao Zedong and Huang Yanpei about Cycle*, *Guangming Daily*, January 20, 1993.
7. Xu Mao: *History of the political system of the republic of China*, Shanghai People's Publishing House, 1992 edition, page 74.
8. Chen Dingyan: *Why did I try to reverse my father's case? – public enemy and private hates can be forgotten, but historical lessons must be remembered*, Chen Jiongming research website, http://www.chen-jiongming.com/WenZi/JianJie/FanAn/FanAn.html, lastly visited on April 7, 2014.
9. Li Shitao: *Intellectuals' Position – Upheavals between Radicals and Conservatives*, The Time Literature and Art Press, 2000 edition, page 19.
10. Ma Guochuan: *Conversation between Qin Xiao and Li Zehou: China Needs to Avoid from Walking towards a Wrong Road*, *Caijing Magazine*, November 2010.
11. Shen Yang: *Reform and Revolution Race between Hare and Tortoise—Why "the Preparations for Constitutionalism" Failed to Save the Qing Government*, *Southern Weekly*, April 17, 2008.
12. Tang Degang: *The 70 Years in Late Qing Dynasty (A Comprehensive Review of Chinese Social and Cultural Transformation)*, Yuan-Liou Publishing Co., Ltd., 2011 edition.

Toward Academic Consciousness: Review of Theoretical Studies on Basic Rights Over the Past Thirty Years

Hailiang Yan and Xiaobiao Cui

The 1982 Constitution is called the best constitution ever since the founding of the People's Republic of China, which is mainly attributed to its highlight of citizens' fundamental rights and realization of the basic adjustment of the relations between citizens' fundamental rights and state organs. Looking back on the development course of the 1982 Constitution, we have very good reasons to believe that this is a process with continuously deepened understanding of the fundamental rights and constantly respected and guaranteed pursuit of the fundamental rights. During this process, the socialist market economic foundation has been established for the growth of citizens' fundamental rights, and the law-based principle has also been established for protecting citizens' fundamental rights. Accordingly, the institutional space has been enlarged for the development of citizens' fundamental rights with human rights as the principle. However, this process also indicates that the development of citizens' fundamental rights needs to be further deepened and the results of fundamental rights protection need to be further highlighted.

The development of citizens' fundamental rights since the promulgation of the 1982 Constitution can be theoretically introspected from multiple perspectives. Yet, making clear the basic development status and features of fundamental rights with the theoretical studies on the fundamental rights over the past 3 decades as the clue[1] can undoubtedly help review the gains and losses of its development, thus providing an essential theoretic basis for deepening the practices in fundamental rights.

[1]This time frame chosen by this article for theoretical studies on fundamental rights is from 1982 to late 2011. In this article, fundamental rights and constitutional rights are equivalent.

This article is one of the results of the "Projects Funded by the Priority Academic Program of Higher Education Institutions in Jiangsu Province".

H. Yan (✉) · X. Cui
Nanjing Normal University, Nanjing, China
e-mail: 13263169197@163.com

L. Li et al. (eds.), *Constitutional Development in China, 1982–2012*,
Research Series on the Chinese Dream and China's Development Path,
https://doi.org/10.1007/978-981-32-9261-1_7

Given this, this article tries to analyze the basic directions of theoretical studies on fundamental rights respectively from such aspects as the concept and nature of fundamental rights; the classification of and conflict, competition and cooperation between fundamental rights; subjects of fundamental rights; effect of fundamental rights on private activities; restriction and guarantee of fundamental rights on the basis of grasping the development of theoretical studies on fundamental rights. Then, the article proposes preliminary opinions on the future development of theoretical studies on fundamental rights. What needs to be pointed out is that this article excludes the analysis of specific categories of fundamental rights. This does not affect the general understanding of theoretical studies on fundamental rights although studies on specific categories of fundamental rights may reflect the progress and time features of theoretical studies on fundamental rights to a certain extent.[2]

1 Overall Analysis of Theoretical Studies on Fundamental Rights Over the Past Thirty Years

The revision of constitution in 1982 can be said the "constitutional moment" in the history of China's constitution. In the strict sense, China's studies on constitutional fundamental rights also started from this revision.[3] Over the past three decades since this revision, the theoretical studies on fundamental rights have produced significant progress. This progress has not only indicated China's development in constitutional law but also demonstrated the development of Chinese citizens' fundamental rights with unique theoretical languages. However, scholars have been hesitating when it comes to how to understand, in an overall and objective way, the current situation of theoretical studies on fundamental rights over the past three decades. Up to now, some studies have directly or indirectly reflected this progress, but there have been no specialized and systematic studies on it. Specifically speaking, first, on the basis of the summaries of annual meetings on constitutional law and annual summaries, some scholar generalized ten key words for studies on constitutional law between 1949 and 1999. "Right" ranks top on the list[4] while "human right" ranks the sixth. In terms of the theme of theoretical studies on "fundamental rights," it mainly involves "rights protection" and "effect of the

[2]For the general analysis of specific categories of studies on fundamental rights, please refer to Hua [1].

[3]Guoqiang [2].

[4]According to the author, "rights" principally refer to "civic rights," "fundamental rights" or "constitutional rights" rather than "human rights."

rights."[5] Studies of this scholar not only verified that the fundamental rights are always the theme of constitutional law studies but also indicated the main academic cares of constitutionalists. Second, from the methodology perspective, some scholar made some comments on the theoretical development of constitutional rights of the PRC and illuminated the basic track and trend of China's theoretical studies on constitutional rights. That is the trend from single legal philosophical studies in early days to studies on legal interpretations, which have witnessed Chinese constitutionalists' gradual maturity and consciousness in methodology.[6] Third, from the perspective of the origin and evolution of the concept of fundamental rights in China, some scholar analyzed the periodic features and progress of China's theoretical studies on basic rights since 1980s.[7] These studies have provided beneficial references for us to understand the situation of theoretical studies on fundamental rights over the past three decades as a whole.

For our part, the overall analysis of theoretical studies on basic rights needs not only to objectively reflect the law and feature of studies but also illustrate the scientific nature and rationality of the research theme against specific historical background. In modern China, it is impossible for studies on constitutional law to get rid of the basic institutional framework for the establishment of the constitution and avoid political influence. It is also the same with theoretical studies on basic rights whether they are becoming regulated and conscious or not. Based on this recognition, we try to divide the theoretical studies on basic rights into two major stages, namely the years between 1982 and 2000 and the period between 2001 and 2011. There are two reasons for taking the year of 2000 as the watershed. First, it is the features of theoretical studies on basic rights. Around 2000, China's theoretical studies on basic rights began to walk toward consciousness—from scattered studies to systematic and specialized studies, from abstract epistemology studies to practice-oriented institutional studies, from single legal philosophical studies to diversified studies with methodology of legal interpretation as the trend. Second, it is the analysis of the basic direction based on modern China's social development. If we say the reform and opening up before the year of 2000 has provided the institutional framework for human development by establishing the socialist market economic system and the governance by law as the basic strategy, then after 2000, with the establishment of the principle of "putting people first," the respect and guarantee of human rights have constantly promoted the institutional reform and improvement, and the iconic event was the establishment of "the state respects and safeguards human rights" in the Constitution in 2004.

---

[5]Hua [1].

[6]See Footnote 3.

[7]Dayuan [3].

1.1 Analysis of Theoretical Studies on Fundamental Rights Between 1982 and 2000

The amendments to the constitution in 1982 re-established the constitutional order and provided a constitutional basis for the subsequent reform, but the constitution at that time simultaneously became the object of amendments for making constant breakthroughs in reform. During this stage, the theoretical studies on fundamental rights were not the key of studies of constitutional law. Looking from the themes of the annual meetings on constitutional law and the annual summaries of constitutional law, the theoretical studies on fundamental rights involved protection of rights (1987, 1991), effect of the rights (1997) and system of rights (1995).[8] Looking from the research data, according to statistics of Chinese academic periodical net, there were only 48 papers. During this period, the theoretical studies on fundamental rights could be roughly divided into two stages: between 1982 and 1992; between 1993 and 2000.

During the period between 1982 and 1992, the academic circle generally believed that the constitution was the general program and general charter of the state and emphasized its instrumental value in economic development and social progress. Correspondingly, scholars generally paid attention to such contents as the pandect of the constitution and state system, etc. Even if there were studies on fundamental rights, most of them were interpretations centering on rights clauses provided in the constitution and elaborations on "what fundamental rights are in constitution" and "why the constitution needs to guarantee these fundamental rights" and other theses. These studies laid stress on the importance of constitutional guarantee of rights.[9] Specifically speaking, there were 35 theoretical research papers on fundamental rights during this period, which respectively involved (1) discussions about the features of China's fundamental rights and obligations on the basis of the text of the 1982 Constitution[10]; (2) interpretations of the categories of "fundamental rights and obligations," which were included in 21 papers; (3) introductions about foreign theories of fundamental rights, which were mainly manifested in those of socialist countries, such as the former Soviet Union.[11]

During the period between 1993 and 2000, there were not so many papers about theoretical studies on fundamental rights, and the number was 13 in total according to statistics of the Chinese academic periodical net. Even so, many factors consciously laid a good foundation for the deepening and direction of theoretical studies on fundamental rights.[12] Firstly, the amendment to the Constitution in 1993

---

[8]See Footnote 5.

[9]Refer to Dayuan [3], Guoqiang [2].

[10]Dexiang [4], Fangyang [5], Jialin [6], Chunsheng [7], Lansheng [8], Buyun [9], Yiwen [10], Naizhong [11], Yunsheng [12], Bikun [13].

[11]Xiangming [14], Huizhen [15], Poppe and Hermes-Epiteck [16], Shaotong [17], Shuyang [18], Friedman [19].

[12]Refer to Dayuan [3], Guoqiang [2].

established the "socialist market economy," which triggered heated discussions about "market economy is rights economy" and "is legal value based on rights or obligations," especially about jurisprudence in the law circle, and also attracted much attention of the constitutional law circle. Secondly, the restricted areas of human rights were completely broken through. Studies on human rights have promoted the constitutional circle to focus more on the theories of fundamental rights. Some works about fundamental rights theories before the liberation included *the Comparative Constitution* (China University of Political Science and Law Press, 1997 edition) of Wang Shijie and Qian Duansheng. Those works have been widely quoted and have influenced China's studies on constitutional right theories. Lastly, in 1997 and 1999, China successively resumed its exercise of sovereignty over Hong Kong and Macao, causing scholars to focus on issues related to the fundamental rights of citizens of Hong Kong and Macao.[13] On top of that, the establishment of the principle of governance by law in Constitution and the right claims triggered by urban housing demolition in the end of the twentieth century stimulated scholars to study theories about the protection of fundamental rights. In general, during this stage, theoretical studies on fundamental rights started to gradually get rid of the influence of Soviet national law theory and ideological constraints. At the same time, scholars have boldly studied and referred to the theories and practices of different countries about the protection of fundamental rights.[14] Studies on the effect of fundamental rights began to take shape.[15] The concept of fundamental rights began to be systematized.

1.2 Analysis of Theoretical Studies on Fundamental Rights Between 2001 and 2011

If we say that the top-down reforms before 2000 provided the institutional and conceptual foundation for deepening theoretical studies on fundamental rights, then the constantly emerging pursuits of personal rights after 2000 have promoted constitutional scholars to pay increasingly more attention to the protection of citizens' fundamental rights, thus making studies on theories of fundamental rights move toward consciousness.

The official reply of the Supreme People's Court for Qi Yuling Case in 2001 offered an opportunity to China's constitutional circle for using constitutional rights theories to interpret realistic cases and triggered widespread disputes over the concept and effect of fundamental rights, constitutional relief, relations between

[13]Yingjie [20]; there were documents talking about this issue even in early 1990s. Shuwen [21], Aihua [22].

[14]Guoqiang [2]; for foreign papers on the fundamental rights, refer to [ROK] Young-sung [23], Ke [24], Xisheng [25].

[15]Min [26], Yongkun [27].

constitution and private laws, etc. The "Sun Zhigang Case" in 2003 and "Blue Video Case in Yan'an" came as the analysis samples for deepening and continuous discussions of theories about constitutional rights. Centering on these topics, the results of theoretical studies on fundamental rights and related judgment cases of the USA, Germany, Japan, Taiwan and other countries and territories were substantially referred to and absorbed. Theoretical studies on fundamental rights started to show a topical, theoretical and systematic trend. In 2004, writing "the state respects and safeguards human rights" into the Constitution provided a base point for reflecting on the theories about fundamental rights. Including the concept of human rights and respecting and guaranteeing human rights in the Constitution as constitutional principles could not only guarantee that there are no deviations hindering the rule of law and constitutionalism in the transformation process from value principle to political principle and procedural principle but also help legislative and judicial organs to make interpretations and reasoning in favor of protecting human rights and civil rights when weighing up different interests.[16] At the same time, incorporating the concept of human rights into the Constitution has greatly expanded the subject scope and contents of the fundamental rights system and further triggered the thinking of the relations between human rights and fundamental rights.

From the perspective of the themes and summaries of the annual meetings of China Constitutional Research Association during this period, except for 2004 and 2006, they respectively involved the relations between fundamental rights and other rights (2001), relations between fundamental rights and human rights (2005), guarantee of fundamental rights (2001, 2002, 2003), guarantee of people's livelihood and rights (2007), practices of fundamental rights (2008), changes in guaranteeing citizens' fundamental rights (2009), fundamental rights and state system (2010), relations between constitutional government history and powers and rights (2011), and criminal law and fundamental rights protection (2011). These themes have not only reflected the deep concerns about citizens' fundamental rights in the process of social changes but also demonstrated the topical and systematic direction of theoretical studies on fundamental rights.

According to statistics of the Chinese academic periodical net, the number of theoretical studies on fundamental rights exploded during this period. In particular, the number of research papers starting from 2006 was steadily maintained at around 30 each year.[17] A large number of works about theoretical studies on fundamental rights sprang up. It can be said that, during the three decades, most works about theoretical studies on fundamental rights were published during this period. These works respectively involved deepened and systematic discussions about fundamental rights theories, fundamental rights standards, fundamental rights system,

[16]Yong [28].

[17]11 in 2001; 31 in 2002; 19 2003; 15 in 2004; 17 in 2005; 22 in 2006; 31 in 2007; 29 in 2008; 31 in 2009; 33 in 2010; 27 in 2011.

relations between fundamental rights and branch laws, effect of fundamental rights, and constitutional guarantee of fundamental rights.[18]

2 Analysis of the Basic Orientation of Theoretical Studies on Fundamental Rights

2.1 Concept and Nature of Fundamental Rights

2.1.1 Concept of Basic Rights

With regard to "basic rights," German scholars use such terms as "fundamental rights" and "essential rights" and British and American scholars prefer to use "human rights." Most Chinese scholars tend to call it "citizens' fundamental rights" according to the normative wording of the current constitution. No matter how to name it, the value meanings are basically consistent, all indicating that fundamental rights are indispensable, irreplaceable, non-assignable, stable, similar and maternal for human beings.[19] Some scholars noted that comprehending constitutional rights from the "fundamental" perspective cannot meet the requirement of constitutional theories and practices and can even easily cause misunderstandings. Compared with "basic rights," "constitutional rights" is the more normative statement.[20] However, since "basic rights" and "constitutional rights" are basically not different in value meaning, under the circumstance that "basic right" has become the consensus, it is appropriate to use the wording of constitution makers.

Regarding the meaning of fundamental rights, scholars primarily grasp from the comparisons between fundamental rights and legal rights and between fundamental rights and human rights.

(1) **Fundamental rights and legal rights**

It is generally believed that fundamental rights are created by the constitution and legal rights are enacted by legislative organs. The relationship between fundamental rights and legal rights is that the former is taken as the basis for the generation of the latter, while the latter is the refining of the former. Fundamental rights and legal rights are different in nature. The former is the root of rights, while the latter is the extension of rights; the former is the basis for the initiation of the latter, while the latter is the content presentation of the former; but the logical relations between fundamental rights and related legal rights cannot deny the independence of legal

[18]The emergence of monographs on fundamental rights during this period indicates the strengthening of topic-based studies on fundamental rights. Wei [29, 30], Xianjun [31], Ling [32] Haikun [33], Yonghong [34], Hong [35], Aolei [36], Xiuqun [37], Xiang [38], Ji'e [39].

[19]Xianming [40].

[20]Zhenglin [41].

rights.[21] Some scholars similarly differentiated the relations between fundamental rights and legal rights from the perspective of the legitimacy and legality of modern states and on the basis of the people's democratic nature of fundamental rights.[22] This point of view has certain common characteristics with the concept of the people's sovereignty of Habermas. From the perspective of the theory of constitution effect, some domestic scholars especially analyzed the homologous relationship between the principle of people's sovereignty and the principle of fundamental human rights.[23]

The comparisons between fundamental rights and legal rights in concept are specifically reflected in the following aspects.

From the perspective of the subjects of rights, it is generally believed that the two are not much different and all cover citizens, legal persons, foreigners and people without a nationality, etc. However, in terms of comprehending the nature of rights subjects, some scholars believed that the subjects of constitutional rights are integral individuals, while the subjects of legal rights are personalized individuals or the community of some individuals (legal persons). Some citizen may give up his or her legal rights, but the people could not give up the constitutional rights of all citizens. Constitutional rights are abstract rights, while legal rights are specific rights.[24] This standpoint gives prominence to the inalienability of constitutional rights, but the fundamental interests that are intended to be protected by constitutional rights might be restricted and harmed and even become impractical because they must be realized through legal rights. In fact, the abstraction of fundamental rights is relative to the specific degree of legal rights. It does not make much sense to distinguish abstract rights and specific rights because it is finally subject to the interests to be protected by rights.

From the perspective of obligation subjects, some scholars pointed out that constitutional rights correspond to state powers, while legal rights correspond to existing state powers and also individual rights.[25] Therefore, the principal obligation subject of fundamental rights stipulated by the Constitution is the state, while the obligation subjects of legal rights include not only public powers but also private subjects.

From the perspective of the nature and effect of rights, legal rights are regarded as the subjective rights that can be claimed, while fundamental rights firstly reflect the objective value order and then the subjective rights that could be claimed by individuals.[26] As such, when it comes to legal effect, many scholars observe that

[21]Zhigang [42].

[22]Dehai [43].

[23]Long and Xiaoping [44].

[24]Ling [45].

[25]See Footnote 24.

[26]See Footnote 20.

fundamental rights have not only direct effects but also indirect or the so-called third-party effects.[27]

(2) **Fundamental rights and human rights**

It is generally recognized that human rights refer to the rights that should be enjoyed by each and every human being, and moral rights that exist without relying on the laws of a state (recently, some scholar talked about the non-morality of human rights,[28] actually taking the economic and political foundation for human rights as the manifestation of non-morality of human rights). In general ideas, fundamental rights are endowed by the Constitution, representing the important status of the subjects in the rights system and the important means for realizing human rights although it is not the only way for realizing human rights. Some scholars generalized the connections and differences between the two as follows. Both fundamental rights and human rights are the rights claimed by individuals, and they are duplicated in some contents. That being said, they have many differences. Firstly, they are different in time of creation. Human rights came earlier than fundamental rights. Secondly, they have different manifestation forms. Human rights are idealistic abstract rights, while fundamental rights are the rights acknowledged by positive laws of state. Thirdly, they are different in subject. The subjects and applicable targets of human rights are all the people, while the subjects of fundamental rights are generally specific citizens of the country, and natural person with the nationality. Fourthly, they are different in content. Human rights are higher than fundamental rights in time changeability and space openness and greater than fundamental rights in content and scope. Fifthly, they are different in legal effect. Human rights are politically announced by some country and group and could become the content evaluation standard and system of fundamental rights of the country. But human rights do not necessarily have legal effect and coercive force. Fundamental rights have legal binding force.[29] Some scholars pointed out that human rights are derived from natural laws, but fundamental rights come from human rights; human rights are demonstrated as value system, but fundamental rights have specific right natures.[30]

Some scholars analyzed the similarities and differences between human rights and fundamental rights by referring to the rights structure chart in Alexy's Theorie der Grundrechte. The transformation from human rights to constitutional rights usually went through four restriction procedures: nationalization of a nation, institutionalization, scientific rationality and conventionalization.[31] Fundamental rights are not just the rights in empirical constitution. Fundamental rights also imply a wish or motivation with human rights as the standard and require the realization of

[27]Refer to the part of "effect of fundamental rights" of this text.

[28]Jihong [46].

[29]Xianjun [31, pp. 10–11].

[30]Dayuan [47].

[31]Yan [48].

human rights in constitution. From this, the three basic elements of fundamental rights can be generalized as form, essence and motivation. Of which, the element of form refers to those norms maintaining subjective basic rights. The element of essence refers to human rights. The element of motivation refers that fundamental rights always involve one proposition requiring constitutional interpretations, including legislative, judicial and theoretical interpretations, even requiring the most appropriate definition of human rights in public opinion and in legal sense, and maximized realization of human rights.

The above-said scholar tried to demonstrate the legitimacy of fundamental rights and the realization of fundamental rights on the basis of clarifying the relations between human rights and fundamental rights, which is highly relevant in the context of lacking cognitions of and institutional guarantee for fundamental rights in modern China. However, the above-mentioned scholar failed to fully cognize the legal norm attribute of human rights as an important part of international laws on the basis of the globalization of human rights and thus failed to clarify the relationship between the two from the perspective of the interactions between international human rights law and domestic constitution. In the aspect of knowledge, the scholar's studies on fundamental rights fell deep into a closed system of domestic constitution.

2.1.2 Nature of Fundamental Rights

Under the influence of German dual nature theory of fundamental rights, many domestic scholars also believe that fundamental rights are featured by both subjectivity and objective order value.[32] As "subjective rights," the primary function of the fundamental rights is to guard against the encroachment of state authorities. Specifically, it contains two meanings: First, individuals need to require the subjects of public powers to take or not take certain actions according to the fundamental rights clauses of the constitution. Secondly, individuals need to request judicial organs to intervene to meet their requirements. As "objective laws," the basic meanings of fundamental rights are that fundamental rights are the value basis of the entire social community; fundamental rights constitute the norm of all conducts of state organs; the state should provide substantive preconditions for the realization of fundamental rights; fundamental rights constitute "objective value order" as a whole and every fundamental right could be seen as an "objective value."

On this basis, some scholars pointed out that the dual nature of fundamental rights as subjective rights and objective laws refers to the legal attribute of fundamental laws. In modern society, fundamental rights also have political or constitutional government natures, i.e., democracy. Fundamental rights are the fundamental legal form of people's sovereignty. The dual nature of fundamental rights is rooted in the democratic nature of people's sovereignty. Establishing the fundamental rights by

[32] Xiang [49], Xianjun [50], Hong [51, 52].

the constitution is to carry forward democracy through guaranteeing fundamental rights.[33] Similarly, some scholars unveiled and explicated the dual nature of constitutional rights in China from three dimensions, namely the text of China's constitution, the structure of China's sovereignty and China's constitutional practices. The dual nature of constitutional rights includes: classes and citizens coexist in terms of rights subject; political nature and governing nature coexist in terms of rights nature; political way and governing way coexist in terms of the way of rights practices. In the dual nature relationship, class status is superior to citizens' status, political nature is superior to governing nature, and politicalized way of implementation is superior to governing way of implementation.[34]

Another view of "dual nature" believes that every fundamental right has the dual nature of positive rights and negative rights.[35] That is to say any fundamental right is featured by comprehensiveness. Accordingly, duties of a state are featured by compositionality. Some scholars referred to German theory of "functional system of fundamental rights" and concluded that the nature of fundamental rights can be layered through defining "the functions of fundamental rights" due to the comprehensive nature of every fundamental right, thus layering duties of the state. The categorization and methodization of duties of the state are conducive to guaranteeing citizens' fundamental rights.[36] Some scholars believed that the fundamental rights are a kind of inverted rights rather than affirmative rights. That means the fundamental rights are negative rights rather than positive rights.[37] Generally speaking, the academic circle has rather rich studies on the functions of fundamental rights and corresponding duties of the state,[38] enabling the conduction of studies on "rights-duties," which is a pair of basic categories of constitutional law, and providing the basic theoretical interpretations for the state's duties of guaranteeing the citizens' fundamental rights from all perspectives.[39]

2.2 *Subjects of Fundamental Rights*

To put it briefly, the subjects of fundamental rights refer to those who are entitled to the fundamental rights. At present, it is generally believed that the subjects of

---

[33]See Footnote 22.

[34]Xiuyi [53].

[35]Piliang [54].

[36]Xiang [55].

[37]Yezhong [56]; "the author has no intention to deny the significance of active freedom in citizens' basic rights but intends to balance the relations between democratic form of government and freedom."

[38]Xiang [57], Di [58], Zheng [59], Chengming [60], Li [61], Xianghe and Yaohui [62], Chun [63], Yinhua [64], Xianghe [65].

[39]Zhiwei [66].

fundamental rights include natural persons (including citizens of the state, foreigners and stateless persons); legal persons; and social organizations. Citizens are the general subjects of fundamental rights. Compared with "individuals," "citizens" as subjects of fundamental rights have richer meanings in many aspects, such as the relations with community, fundamental right system connecting with development and assumption of realistic social obligations.[40] However, with the advent of the era of globalization, citizens of different countries have increasingly frequent contacts and citizens of other countries and stateless citizens are growing in number. If we only take "citizens" as the subject of fundamental rights, then the fundamental rights of all natural persons except for "citizens" would not be effectively guaranteed. Under this circumstance, some scholars pointed out that the inclusion of the concept of human rights in the Constitution indicates that the government has expanded its duties of human rights protections to some fundamental human rights that should be enjoyed by all natural persons living and working within the territory of the People's Republic of China. The scholar also pointed out that these fundamental rights are more functional in fundamental guarantee compared with the fundamental rights of citizens. He added that this kind of common human rights is not contradictory but mutually complementary with the meanings of citizens' fundamental rights as stipulated by the Constitution.[41]

As regards the subject status of foreigners and stateless persons in the fundamental rights, the constitutional circle remains divided, either positively or negatively. The positive theory believes that foreigners as a subject of human rights should be entitled to the fundamental rights as stipulated by the Constitution and should be qualified as a subject of rights other than the rights to participate in political affairs and social basic rights. The negative theory believes that the fundamental rights are the value order combining the social community and foreigners should not be part of this value order. As a matter of fact, according to the stipulations of international human rights documents and constitutions, foreigners' fundamental rights, including right of person, property right and right of action are protected by constitution and laws, and they are simply under strict restrictions as a subject of the fundamental rights, mainly in the right to participate in political affairs, economic freedom and freedom of movement into and out of the country.

With the development of the society, legal person as a subject of the fundamental rights starts to attract the attention of scholars. The research contents are principally concentrated on the reason for legal persons to enjoy fundamental rights and the contents of their fundamental rights.[42] It is generally believed that legal persons should become a subject of fundamental rights and they are simply unable to enjoy the fundamental rights in physicality and spirituality connected with the inherent

[40]Aolei [67].

[41]Jihong [68].

[42]Xiangfei [69], Qiangqiang [70], Qianhong and Daoying [71], Gaoya [72], Yuyin [73], Xiaoxiao [74], Tingting [75].

nature of natural persons, but they are entitled to the right of equality, economic right, property right, right of claim, among other rights.

Besides, some scholars studied the capacities of subjects of fundamental rights, including capacity for rights, capacity for acts and capacity for responsibilities.[43] Normative studies of this kind have provided certain theoretical references for future applicability of constitutional norms. Some scholar studied the changes of subjects of fundamental rights in the texts of the constitution ever since the founding of the PRC in a historical perspective and concluded that the subjects of fundamental rights in China have went through the changes from political subjects to legal subjects, i.e., the changes from people to citizen,[44] which have reflected the progress in the concept of constitutionalism to a certain extent.

To sum up, the Chinese constitutional circle has made some achievements in studying the subjects of the fundamental rights, but still many issues need to be further studied. For instance, could schools and regions be taken as subjects of fundamental rights?[45] Currently, these subjects are faced with many common issues, so studying this subject is highly relevant in theory and practice alike.

2.3 *Categorization, Conflict, Competition and Cooperation of Fundamental Rights*

2.3.1 Categorization of Fundamental Rights

The categorization of fundamental rights belongs to categorized studies. The categorization of fundamental rights could help affirm the value natures of different rights and the relations with state powers and then define the constitutional status and effect of each right.[46] Moreover, categorized studies of fundamental rights could also bridge the pandect of fundamental rights subpandects of fundamental rights, provide knowledge support for improving the fundamental rights system and the texts of constitution, and help guarantee fundamental rights and realize the constitutional values.[47]

The key of categorized studies is to choose the standard for categorization. Most Chinese scholars take content as the standard for categorizing fundamental rights. Besides, some scholars take the subjects, nature and fields of fundamental rights as

---

[43]Yu [76] studies on capacities for the fundamental rights also include: Cheng and Pinpin [77], Jianxue [78].

[44]Xiaomin [79].

[45]Jianxue [80].

[46]Xianjun [31, p. 131].

[47]Lianfan [81].

the standards. Some scholars summarized the categorizations of the fundamental rights[48] and concluded that there are eight types of categorizations with a single standard, which respectively take the subject, object, content, form, field, nature, effect and history of fundamental rights as the standard. There are still some scholars who categorize the fundamental rights based on a variety of standards, such as taking subject and nature as the standards, dividing the fundamental rights into personal rights, political rights, social rights and the rights of vulnerable groups.[49]

Given the functions of fundamental rights, some scholars divided fundamental rights into three parts: individual rights in the sense of self-affirmation and preservation, i.e., classical fundamental rights; political rights reflecting citizens' participation in the sense of self-expression; social rights in the sense of self-fulfillment and development.[50] Some scholars categorized fundamental rights into the fundamental rights at individual level and the fundamental rights at institutional level[51] as believing that the rights at individual level mainly meet the needs of personal lives, while the fundamental rights at institutional level mainly come from the necessity of maintaining a specific system of the state. Some other scholars categorized fundamental rights into the right of freedom, right to benefits and right of equality while taking into consideration the meaning, characteristics and inter-relations of constitutional fundamental rights.[52]

Above academic categorizations of fundamental rights are of great significance in epistemology, but the constitution as a legal norm has clear stipulations on fundamental rights. In this sense, it is quite necessary to categorize fundamental rights in hermeneutics on the basis of norms. For this purpose, many Chinese scholars have categorized fundamental rights pursuant to the stipulations of the Constitution on the fundamental rights, including ten categories,[53] eight categories,[54] five categories[55] and four categories.[56] Regarding these categorizations, scholars have paid attention to absorbing the merits of academic categorizations on the one hand and tried to take into consideration China's constitutional system for the stipulations of citizens' fundamental rights on the other as they strive to establish a logical, integrated and self-accomplishing categorization system.

Categorized studies with constitutional norms as the basis cannot be ignored, but this is not enough. The reason is that many people believe that the rights contained in fundamental rights have not yet been assimilated by the Constitution, such as

48Lianfan [82].

49Haikun [83, p. 122].

50Xianjun [84].

51Qianfan [85, p. 441].

52See Footnote 48.

53Jialin [86, pp. 364–368].

54Laifan [87, p. 93].

55Chongde [88, pp. 400–424].

56Dingren [89, pp. 172–196].

human dignity, personality independence and freedom, right to pursue happiness; freedom of thought and consciousness; freedom of the press; freedom from torture, forced slavery and laboring; freedom of residence, movement, job selection, and leaving and entering the country; freedom of strike; right to peaceful petition; and right to accept a fair trial.[57] Therefore, in the current context, categorized studies on fundamental rights need to combine constitutional norms with academic studies and keep improving the normative system of fundamental rights.

2.3.2 Conflict, Competition and Cooperation Between Fundamental Rights

Conflicts between fundamental rights refer to the case that one subject at the time of exercising the fundamental rights may encroach on the fundamental rights of another subject. Due to the diversified interests and values protected by the Constitution, it is quite common to see the conflicts between the claims for fundamental rights, such as the conflict between freedom of speech and personal dignity.[58] For that reason, some scholars made categorized studies on the conflicts between fundamental rights: conflicts between rights, such as the right to life, the right of freedom, property right and liberty right.[59]

The modes of resolving conflicts between fundamental rights mainly include: rank-ordered principle; specific rules taking precedence over rules summarized; proportionality principle; interest measurement in individual cases[60]; legislative measurement theory.[61] While resolving conflicts between fundamental rights, some scholars supported the idea of taking into account the following several modes. Firstly, it is the prioritized application of common legal norms. Secondly, when common legal norms fail to provide clear-cut principles for resolving conflicts between fundamental rights, justices may individually measure each case, i.e., choosing the interpretations consistent with the constitutional spirit from multiple possibilities of interpretation of legal rules or principles. If common legal provisions for reconciling conflicts between rights are suspected of violating the Constitution, it would be very necessary to carry out review for constitutionality and make constitutional interpretations.[62] Regarding how to make sure that justices do not make subjective assumptions in measuring the interests, some scholars support the application of the basic rights theory with German scholar Alexy's legal

[57]Dayuan et al. [90, pp. 306–308].
[58]Jingbo [91].
[59]Zhihua [92, pp. 390–430].
[60]Laifan and Zhuoming [93].
[61]Xiang [94].
[62]See Footnote 61.

augmentation theory as the supporting point.[63] Besides, some scholars also studied the competition and cooperation between fundamental rights.[64]

This kind of studies has a strong practical significance and could be the guidance for both the settlement of the current conflicts between rights and the application of constitutional norms in the future. One of the legal missions is to guide the settlement of disputes, so are the constitutional norms.

2.4 *Effect of Fundamental Rights*

The effect of fundamental rights refers to a force that can realize the value and specific contents of fundamental rights. Specifically, it is reflected by the binding force of fundamental rights on social life areas, including the effect of fundamental rights on state powers; and the effect of fundamental rights on private activities.

One of the main functions of fundamental rights is to restrict state powers and defend the encroachment of state powers, which can be specifically mirrored in the following aspects. First, it is the binding force on legislators and legislative procedures. Second, it is the direct binding force on activities of administrative powers. Third, it is the binding force on activities of judicial powers. Due to their different natures and expression forms, different fundamental rights showcase different features in binding state powers. As such, there is a need to not only follow general principles but also adopt the individual case analysis method while analyzing the effect of fundamental rights on state powers and interpret the effect value in line with the actual relations in real life. In addition, a controversial issue in the constitutional circle remains to be whether the activities of state in non-power forms are restricted by fundamental rights.

The effect of fundamental rights is mainly applicable to state powers, but with the changes of social life, fundamental rights have started to expand their effect to private areas. Some scholars summarized the causes of this phenomenon as follows. First, it is the change of concept of fundamental rights: Fundamental rights are not just subjective rights, and they start to become the basis of the objective value system. Second, it is the socialization of state powers: The diversification of social relations and socialization of powers have transferred some powers that used to be exercised by the state to organizations beyond public powers, such as political and economic organizations. Third, it is the diversification of basic rights protection: Traditional human rights theories fail to effectively protect private persons from private rights encroachment by private persons. Fourth, it is the amendment of civil law principles in the Constitution: The Constitution may partially amend already established civil law principles to resolve the phenomenon of violating the effect of

[63]Tao [95].

[64]Laifan and Guoqiang [96], Young-sung [23].

fundamental rights in civil laws. Fifth, it is the strengthening of functions of the Constitution as a judgment system.[65] Given these objective requirements, the theory of third-party effect of fundamental rights has taken shape gradually.

The effect of fundamental rights on private activities has attracted much attention of the academic community. Particularly after the occurrence of Qi Yuling Case, the Supreme People's Court made a judicial interpretation of guaranteeing citizens' right to education according to the Constitution in 2001, which triggered continuous studies on such issues as the concept and effect of fundamental rights, constitution and private laws and relations between the Constitution and judicature, etc.[66] In 2008, the Supreme People's Court abolished relevant judicial interpretations, causing another wave of studies. In 2009, the *Law Science* magazine organized conversations by writing for its third and fourth issues on the title of "relations between abolishing the reply for the Qi Yuling Case and constitution applicability." As many as 19 papers were submitted.

At the same time, the academic community has also quoted many foreign research results in this regard, mainly including German theory of the effect of articles about fundamental rights on third person and the theory of "state act" of the constitutional circle of the USA. Furthermore, the Chinese academic circle has also analyzed related theories and practices of Britain, South Africa, Japan and the ROK. These countries with relatively mature constitutional government system are undoubtedly beneficial references for China to study the effect of fundamental rights on third person.

Of course, scholars have different opinions on whether foreign experiences are applicable to China's judicial practices at the current stage. Some scholars observed that the main issues faced by China at the moment are how to effectively restrict state powers, phase in the dualistic structure of "political state-civil society" promoted by contemporary constitutionalism and boost the formation of "autonomy of private law." From the perspective of Western countries, just under the modern concept of constitution and being confined to the slack relations between state and society, the effect of constitutional fundamental rights could go deeper into the private law field. Therefore, when making a choice from these two value orientations, we need to be prudent in line with China's basic political and legal system and social reality.[67] Some scholars observed that the protection of citizens' fundamental rights by Western countries is the expansion process from public law field to private law field, but there are big institutional and conceptual obstacles in China's implementation of the Constitution in the public law field. For that matter, China may explore the constitutional implementation road through privatization of the Constitution and firstly use the Constitution, and then slowly promote the

[65]Dayuan [97, pp. 217–219].

[66]Before this case, there were few studies on the effect of fundamental rights, including Min [26], Yongkun [27]; after the case, there were more studies in this regard, including Zhendong [98], Xiang [99], Dingjian [100], Xianjun [101], Fei [102], Zhiguo [103], Zhenyu [104], Zhigang [42], Hong [105], Zhigang [106], Hong [35], Xiuqun [37].

[67]Xiang [99].

review for constitutionality of public powers in order to take a path that is different from Western countries in the development of constitutionalism.[68]

2.5 *Restriction and Guarantee of Fundamental Rights*

Similar to the systematic studies on the effect of fundamental rights triggered by Qi Yuling Case, abundant studies on the restriction and guarantee of fundamental rights came from Sun Zhigang Case in 2003.[69]

2.5.1 Restriction of Fundamental Rights

Scholars' studies on the restriction of fundamental rights are concentrated on such aspects as the legitimacy of fundamental rights restriction; basic principles of fundamental rights restriction; mode of rules for fundamental rights restriction; standard for fundamental rights restriction, etc.

With regard to the legitimacy of fundamental rights restriction, some scholars believed that the legal philosophical basis of state's restrictions over citizens' fundamental rights is the theory of original evil of human nature and constitutional law basis is the conditionality of fundamental rights, including two aspects. First, it is the mutual constraints between fundamental rights. Second, it is extrinsic constraints allowed by constitutional value goal, which was set for fundamental rights for realizing order, welfare, public order and good custom.[70] Some other scholars observed that the restriction of fundamental rights is an important characteristic of the Constitution in the twentieth century and reflects the relativization and socialization of fundamental rights.[71]

Restricting citizens' fundamental rights is legitimate, but the restriction in itself should be strictly restricted in entity and procedure so as to prevent improper restrictions of citizens' fundamental rights from harming citizens' fundamental rights. In this connection, it is very necessary to clearly define the basic principles that should be followed for restricting citizens' fundamental rights. Some scholars noted that these principles include the principle of harming no fundamental rights, legal reservation principle, crystallization principle and judicial review principle.[72] Some scholars believed that it should include constitutional reservation principle,

[68]Dingjian [100].

[69]Enci and Xianjun [107].

[70]Xiaohua and Jing [108].

[71]Dayuan [109].

[72]Zhongmin and Jichun [110].

constitutional authorization principle, rational restriction principle and procedural restriction principle.[73] Some other scholars discussed the basic principles of basic rights restriction from three levels, namely subject, implementation and relief, including legal reservation principle, legislative balance principle (including equality protection and interest measurement principle (i.e., proportionality principle), constitutionality review principle (constitutionality principle and litigation relief principle).[74]

After comparing the opinions of different scholars, we can see that the basic principles of restricting fundamental rights are rather clear. Given these principles, many scholars especially studied the principle of legal reservation.[75] Through studies on relevant stipulations of *the Legislation Law*, some scholars noted that citizens' fundamental rights should be the original theoretical point of legal reservation.[76] On top of that, some other scholars also especially discussed legislative power restriction and the principle of constitution reserve for guaranteeing fundamental rights.[77]

Regarding the legislative means of constitutional restriction of fundamental rights, some scholars put forward two points, namely generalized legislation models and differentiated legislation models.[78] Some other scholars also added a hybrid-type legislation model,[79] i.e., the combination of generalized legislation models and differentiated legislation models. Taking generalized legislation models as an example, China's Constitution stipulates in Article 51, "The exercise by citizens of the People's Republic of China of their freedoms and rights may not infringe upon the interests of the state, of society and of the collective, or upon the lawful freedoms and rights of other citizens." Differentiated legislation models refer that constitution makes differentiated restrictive stipulations based on different purposes and the different natures of various specific fundamental rights and divides the stipulations into special legal restriction, conditional legal restriction, general legal restriction, implicit legal restriction and reverse legal restriction. Some scholars tended to classify the ways of restriction into specific restriction, lawful restriction and principle restriction.[80] Comparatively speaking, the differentiation between generalized legislation models and differentiated legislation models is rather rational. Specific restrictions and lawful restrictions can be included in differentiated legislation models, but principle restrictions and generalized restrictions have no essential difference. What merits in-depth studies is specific legislative restriction ways in differentiated legislation models.

---

[73]Jinyuan and Pang [111].

[74]See Footnote 70.

[75]Studies on legal reservation and fundamental rights: Jun [112], Rong [113].

[76]Liantai [114].

[77]Lianfan and Qinghua [115], Qinghua [116].

[78]Qianhong [117], Xianjun [118, pp. 208–209].

[79]See Footnote 73.

[80]Shuanghong and Qinghua [119], Huahui [120, p. 204].

How are fundamental rights restricted? In reality, "public interests" are generally taken as the substantial element of basic rights restriction. As for the relations between public interest and fundamental rights, there are two different understandings, which are "internal restriction theory" and "external restriction theory." According to the external restriction theory, public interests are the restrictions on fundamental rights beyond fundamental rights. According to internal restriction theory, the restrictions of public interests are actually generated based on the nature of fundamental rights and are restrictions existing in fundamental rights. External restriction theory clearly distinguishes rights and limit of rights. Given some fundamental right, we firstly define its subjects and contents and then discuss the limit of rights that is to define the rights without support through considering public interests. This kind of theory is clear in logic, but it cannot rule out the risk of "the theory of superior position of public interest" and public interest provisions would probably become empty authorization of state powers and an edge tool for restricting fundamental rights. According to internal restriction theory, rights have natural limits pursuant to their social attribute. When we have defined "what right is," we simultaneously define "what the limit of right is." The composition of rights and restriction of rights are the same issue both exteriorly and interiorly. The problems of the internal restriction theory are as follows. First, there is a need to put fundamental rights in social order for discussions and it is to demonstrate social and super level of law. We are unable to find the basis for a "fixed range" in fundamental rights provisions. Second, a priori and artificial exclusion of some matters from the essential range of fundamental rights may cause a narrow range of fundamental rights. Therefore, some scholars argued that the internal restriction theory has logical problems that cannot be accommodated by rigorous legal theories. As a matter of fact, we can eliminate the risk of external restriction theory through defining certain ideas and rules, such as the denial of the theory of superior position of public interest; denial of the effect of abstract public interest provisions; definition and proportionality principle of laws; and judicial review.[81]

Given the practical issues relating to fundamental rights restriction, some scholars came up with a thinking framework for judging individual cases of fundamental rights restriction: fundamental rights composition—fundamental rights restriction—extra-constitution reason for fundamental rights restriction.[82] Many scholars have studied constitutionality review of the restriction.[83] These studies are beneficial to studies of individual cases of fundamental rights restriction and somewhat beneficial to future specific application of constitutional norms. What's more, many scholars have also paid attention to the restriction and guarantee of citizens' fundamental rights under emergencies, such as major natural disasters, major human accidents, public health emergencies and severe economic crises.[84]

[81]Xiang [121].

[82]Xiang [122].

[83]Jinyuan [123], Xinsheng [124]. Monographs also include Yonghong's [34].

[84]Xuexian and Shu [125], Dayuan [126].

After the amendment to the Constitution in 2004, China has clearly stipulated emergencies in the Constitution, but there is still a need to carry out deep-going studies on the scope, degree and condition of citizens' fundamental rights restriction and fundamental rights guarantee and relief under relevant emergencies.

2.5.2 Guarantee of Fundamental Rights

A perfect system for guaranteeing fundamental rights includes constitutional formulation, constitutional implementation, constitutional monitoring and constitutional relief. After 30 years of implementation, the 1982 Constitution has made great progress in guaranteeing citizens' fundamental rights, but there are still many deficiencies, including incomplete contents of fundamental rights, lacking relevant legal guarantee and the imperfect constitutional supervision system. Given these deficiencies, the constitutional circle has conducted many valuable studies.[85]

The encroachment on citizens' fundamental rights mainly comes from state powers, but scholars start to focus on the encroachment from non-state powers, such as political parties, labor unions, industry organizations, private enterprises, among other social organizations. Controversies exist in the constitutional circle over the relief of encroachment by non-state public powers. One point of view supports the adoption of common legal proceedings without involving constitutional litigation procedure. Another standpoint supports resort to common legal proceedings, and then instituting constitutional proceedings when court judgment fails to eliminate the encroaching behaviors.[86]

Given the relief of fundamental rights, scholars have made a great deal of research on constitutional litigation.[87] Some scholars especially wrote articles to introduce and compare the judicial relief system for fundamental rights of Britain, the USA, Germany, France, and Hong Kong and Taiwan of China.[88] Regarding the model of constitution implementing agency in Chinese mainland, the constitutional circle has the following several standpoints. First, it is constitutional committee review system, by either establishing a constitutional committee paralleling the Standing Committee of the NPC under the NPC or establishing a constitutional committee with the nature of a special committee, and the latter is the mainstream opinion of the Chinese constitutional circle. Second, it is the constitutional court review system, by establishing a special constitution court. Third, it is the Supreme People's Court review system. Fourth, it is the establishment of a compound review system with the parallel of the constitutional committee under the NPC and the review for constitutionality court under the Supreme People's Court. Given the huge influence, the selection of review for constitutionality models needs to be

[85]Yu [127]. Other related works: Yuanxian and Yonghao [128], Weiyan [129], Yan [130].

[86]Zhendong [131].

[87]Shancheng [132], Jianshui and Li [133], Pinghui [134], Xiaoming [135].

[88]Wei [136].

considered thoroughly in line with the specific political ecology and historical and cultural traditions of the state. Some scholars pointed out that, in China against the specific time-and-space background, it is worthy of the wait for applying the thinking of gradual reform from constitutional and human rights committee to government-dominated constitution to the reconstruction of judicial review system.[89] This has reflected the increasing focus of scholars on China's domestic politics to a certain extent as they look forward to establishing an review for constitutionality system that suits China's national conditions.

Constitutional procedures are of great significance to the guarantee of fundamental rights. Some scholars pointed out three essential procedures of the constitutional legislation for guaranteeing citizens' constitutional rights. First, it is launching process. Second, it is the drafting process. Third, it is the process of seeking for relief after the encroachment on citizens' constitutional rights.[90] Some scholars put forward the suggestions for improvement on the basis of introducing Western countries' models of constitutional rights guarantee procedures and in line with China's current situation of fundamental rights guarantee procedures. The suggestions include establishing a just concept of constitutional procedure; adding "due legal process clause" to the Constitution; drawing on Western models of constitutional rights guarantee to improve China's specific constitutional rights guarantee procedures; refer to advanced experiences to perfect the constitutional rights relief procedures.[91]

Besides, some scholars made analyses from the perspective of state finance and tried to provide an institutional guarantee for equal protection of fundamental rights through establishing a mechanism featuring effective financial control, financial power division and financial balance.[92] From this point of view, studies on fundamental rights need to focus on the law and take into consideration the influence of the economic and social system. Only by doing so, the guarantee of fundamental rights could be reliable.

3 Outlook for Theoretical Studies on Fundamental Rights

If we say that the level of fundamental rights protection is the standard for measuring the development level of a country's constitutionalism, then the development of studies on fundamental rights would be the alignment for the country's constitutional law research level. Over the past three decades, China has made remarkable progress in theoretical studies on fundamental rights, but compared with that of developed countries and territories, China still has a long way to go. In particular,

[89]Wanchao [137].

[90]Zhiwei [138].

[91]Wanghong [139].

[92]Zhigang [140].

there is still an obvious gap in meeting the pursuits of the Chinese people for guaranteeing their fundamental rights. Of course, this is not completely the fault of scholars. Theoretical studies on fundamental rights are inevitably restrained by the actuality and advanced by relying on the state system. However, there is still institutional space for caring for every citizen's fundamental rights. Scholars are expected to act upon the actuality of China's basic political system and fully absorb the theoretical results of theoretical studies on fundamental rights of other countries and territories to boost the development of China's theoretical studies on fundamental rights and improve the protection of citizens' fundamental rights. Looking to the future, we just put forward some preliminary opinions for the following three aspects for your references.

1. It is to deepen studies on the theory of fundamental rights from the perspective of respecting and guaranteeing citizens' fundamental rights. Currently, just as some scholars pointed out, the Chinese constitutional circle has reached a basic consensus on the core status of fundamental rights in the constitutional norm system. China' constitutional law studies have gradually turned to centering on fundamental rights.[93] The available academic achievements and themes of annual academic meetings have also demonstrated scholars' academic efforts to make the concept of fundamental rights protection permeate state organs and various public laws and systems so as to establish the constitutional law with fundamental law as the axis. In this sense, disciplinary consciousness of constitutional law with fundamental rights as the core is not reflected by building a standard system with professional language to showcase the differences with other disciplines. Instead, it focuses on caring for citizens' fundamental rights, looking at state and social systems, demonstrating the fundamental right theory for system construction and guaranteeing the basic path for fundamental rights.

From this perspective, theoretical studies on fundamental rights are obviously directed to practices. Scholars' studies on fundamental rights, including individual case studies for fundamental rights and studies in line with branch laws, have all demonstrated this research purpose since 2000. In fact, China's theoretical studies on fundamental rights were also ignited by Qi Yuling Case and Sun Zhigang Case. Just under this context, the method of law hermeneutics has become a research trend although it is not the only advisable method. As a matter of fact, the effectiveness of this method rests with the care and respect for people's dignity and depends on the comprehension of human dignity in the current Chinese society. Just in this context, the so-called studies on the effect of fundamental rights on private laws have become popular and the connection between the Constitution and branch laws has become the necessity. These have, to a large extent, eased the vigorous arguments over whether the effective guarantee of fundamental rights inevitably lies in the absolute constitutional guarantee. However, we can also see from this perspective that China's theoretical studies on fundamental rights have much room for expansion and deepening. It requires reevaluating the legislative

[93] See Footnote 3.

guarantee and restriction of fundamental rights and the fundamental rights relief theory and system. It also requires comprehensively and systematically analyzing the closely related institutional guarantee theory and theory establishment from the perspective of the specific situation of citizens' fundamental rights, such as local autonomy, electoral system, university autonomy and press and publication system, deepening the understanding of the natures and functions of fundamental rights.

2. It is to actively assimilate international achievements in human rights law theories and practices, look at the functional positioning of international human rights protection and constitutional guarantee of citizens' fundamental rights with open mind and deeply reflect on the relations between human rights and fundamental rights to improve theoretical studies on fundamental rights. It is generally believed that fundamental rights are the constitutionalized human rights. In today's globalization of human rights, international human rights documents with *the Universal Declaration of Human Rights*, *the International Covenant on Civil and Political Rights* and *the International Covenant on Economic, Social and Cultural Rights* as the cornerstone have constituted the source of and standard for constitutional protection of fundamental rights in each country. In addition, a series of human rights mechanisms and domestic mechanisms for protecting fundamental rights on the basis of these covenants together have preliminarily formed the rather complete rights protection system. How to look at the interactions between international human rights covenants and domestic constitutions and look at the influence of the resolutions and judgments made by these international human rights organizations on domestic protection of fundamental rights have actually become an important proposition.[94]

Based on this perspective, we can find that it is worthy of reflections on domestic scholars' studies on the relations between human rights and fundamental rights and even on the theory of guaranteeing fundamental rights. Human rights are not self-determined, self-advocated and self-justified moral rights for demonstrating the legitimacy of fundamental rights. At the time of writing the requirement for the state's respect and guarantee of human rights in the Constitution, it is the constitutional commitment to international human rights and the commitment to respecting and guaranteeing a host of rights established by international covenants of human rights. These rights had been clearly defined in meaning and been given the attribute as legal norms from the very beginning. However, in terms of fundamental rights protection, the absolute constitutional guarantee has been taken as an effective means. However, constitutional guarantee of human rights as the fundamental rights is not the only means. Looking from the development of international human rights protection, it may not be the last resort. In fact, effective protection of fundamental rights does not merely rely on the constitutionality review agency. The play of its functions also relies on the effective functional accommodation and operation of various human rights protection institutions in the final analysis.

[94]See Chen [141], Waters [142], Samar [143].

3. It is to keep a foothold on our country's institutional practices in citizens' fundamental rights, comprehensively absorb foreign achievements in theoretical studies on fundamental rights and practical experiences in institutional guarantee and strive to phase in fundamental rights theories with Chinese characteristics. In the face of the citizens' increasingly growing pursuits of fundamental rights after entering the twenty-first century, how to improve the protection of citizens' fundamental rights has become the theme constantly pursued by scholars. The constitutional guarantee system has attracted most attention of scholars. For most scholars, the absolute constitutional guarantee is not only the measurement of a country's guarantee of citizen's fundamental rights but also the criterion for judging a country's development of constitutionalism according to the comparative constitutional history. Correspondingly, the fact is that China has not yet accomplished the mission of constitutionalism and still needs to strengthen the relative guarantee according to the law. So, how to gear to international standards in line with China's actual conditions has become the objective of many scholars. Within this context, scholars have made a great deal of systematic research on the constitutional guarantee systems of Germany, the USA, France and other countries and have therefore written many prescriptions for China to establish a constitutional guarantee system. These academic efforts are undoubtedly worthy to be affirmed and have offered knowledge references for China to ultimately form an effective system for guaranteeing citizens' fundamental rights. Yet, the basic reformation of constitutional system cannot be boosted simply by scholars' rationality of knowledge and passion for ideals. In contrast, a rather steady and realistic choice might be respecting our constitutional system and carefully considering how to effectively leverage on the functions of the current basic system which has long been unpractical.

As guided by the concept of citizens' fundamental rights of the modern constitution, it is necessary for us to rethink the power allocation and function exertion under the dominance of the National People's Congress and its Standing Committee. At the same time, it is also necessary for us to start from fundamental studies on the natures of fundamental rights to absorb foreign achievements and practical experiences in theoretical studies on fundamental rights in an all-round way. We should not be confined to the norms and systems of fundamental rights. For my own part, within the limited reading scope, Raz's studies on the necessity of judicial review from the perspective of the functions of fundamental rights are quite inspiring.[95] Habermas unveiled the homology of the people's sovereignty principle and fundamental rights from the perspective of interactive theory, so applying his discourse theory to interpret the review for constitutionality system is also thought-provoking. Regarding this aspect, some domestic scholars used to make academic attempts to introduce the discourse theory into the implementation of China's Constitution.[96] Likewise, other countries' application of the discourse

[95]See Raz [144, 145].

[96]Xu [146].

theory for understanding and implementing the review for constitutionality system[97]has also provided the basis for our expectations for re-understanding the review for constitutionality model dominated by the Standing Committee of the National People's Congress. We are looking forward to realizing the target of protecting citizens' fundamental rights through the effective functional operations of different power authorities.

References

1. Guan Hua: *Ten Key Words in Constitutional Law Studies within 60 Years – Analysis on the basis of Summaries of Constitutional Law Annual Meetings and Annual Reviews*, *Western Law Review*, 2010, Issue 1.
2. Zhai Guoqiang: *Comment on Theory Development of the Constitutional Rights in the PRC ——From the Methodology Perspective*, *Northern Legal Science*, 2010, Issue 3.
3. Han Dayuan: *The Origin and Transformation of the Concept of Fundamental Rights in China*, *China Legal Science*, 2009, Issue 6.
4. Wang Dexiang: *On the Basic Principles of the Rights and Obligations of Chinese Citizens*, Modern Law Science, 1982, Issue 3.
5. Xiao Fangyang: *On the Unity of the Rights and Obligations of Chinese Citizens*, *Jianghuai Tribune*, 1982, Issue 4.
6. Wu Jialin: *On Fundamental Rights and Obligations of Citizens of Our Country*, *Law Science Magazine*, 1982, Issue 4.
7. Cheng Chunsheng: *Features of the Fundamental Rights and Obligations of Citizens of Our Country*, *Journal of Anhui University*, 1982, Issue 4.
8. Liu Lansheng: *Characteristics of the Fundamental Rights and Obligations in the New Draft Constitution*, *Journal of Social Sciences*, 1982, Issue 6.
9. Li Buyun: *A Brief Account of the Fundamental Rights and Obligations of Citizens – Some Understandings of the Draft Amendment to the Constitution*, *Study and Research*, 1982, Issue 6.
10. Wei Yiwen: *New Constitution and Citizens' Rights and Obligations*, *Social Science Journal of Xiangtan University*, 1983, Issue 3.
11. Gu Naizhong: *Consistency of Rights and Obligations of Citizens of Our Country*, *Weishi*, 1983, Issue 3.
12. Chen Yunsheng: *Legal Characteristics of the Fundamental Rights and Obligations of Citizens*, *Political Science and Law*, 1985, Issue 6.
13. Jiang Bikun: *On the Categories of Chinese Citizens' Fundamental Rights and Obligations and Their Relations*, *Legal Study and Research*, 1988, Issue 2.
14. Wang Xiangming: *Legal Nature of the Fundamental Rights and Obligations of Citizens in Soviet Law Theory*, *Political and Legal Periodicals*, 1982, Issue 3.
15. Chen Huizhen: *Fundamental Rights and Obligations of Soviet Citizens*, *Digest of Modern Foreign Philosophy and Social Sciences*, 1983, Issue 1.
16. E·Poppe, Hermes-Epiteck: *Fundamental Rights and Human Rights in Socialist Countries*, *Social Sciences Abroad*, 1983, Issue 9.
17. Yang Shaotong: *Fundamental Rights of Soviet Citizens in Social and Economic Life*, *Reference Data about Soviet Issues*, 1985, Issue 1.
18. Yang Shuyang: *On the Bill of Rights of the Federal Constitution of the United States of America*, *Journal of Huiyang Normal College* (Social Sciences Edition) 1992, Issue 1.

[97]See Tremlay [147].

19. [U.S.]James Friedman: *Rights Theories in the American Constitutional Tradition*, *Collected Translations of Law Science*, 1986, Issue 1.
20. Kou Yingjie: *Contents and Characteristics of the Fundamental Rights of Citizens of Hong Kong Special Administrative Region*, *Graduate Law Review*, 1998, Issue 1.
21. Wang Shuwen: On the Basic Rights and Obligations of Citizens of Hong Kong Special Administrative Region, Science of Law, 1990, Issue 5.
22. Wang Aihua: *Characteristics of the Fundamental Rights and Duties of Citizens of the Hong Kong Special Administrative Region*, *Journal of Jinan University* (Philosophy and Social Sciences Edition), 1992, Issue 4.
23. [ROK]Kwon Young-sung: *Competition, Cooperation and Conflict of Fundamental Rights*, translated by Han Dayuan, *Foreign Laws Translation and Review*, 1996, Issue 4.
24. Zhou Ke: *Appeal for Protection of the Fundamental Rights of Foreign Countries and Macao*, *The Jurist*, 1997, Issue 4.
25. Zhang Xisheng: *On the Fundamental Rights of Citizens of the European Community*, *The Europe*, 1999, Issue 3, etc.
26. Yu Min: *On the Direct Effect of the Constitutional Principle of Equality between Men and Women in "Civil Field"*, *China Legal Science*, 1995, Issue 6.
27. Zhou Yongkun: *On the Direct Effect of Constitutional Fundamental Rights*, *China Legal Science*, 1997, Issue 1.
28. Xia Yong: *Several Basic Theoretical Issues Concerning the Chinese Constitution Reform*, *Social Sciences in China*, 2003, Issue 2.
29. Zhou Wei: *A Study of Judicial Remedies of Constitutional Fundamental Rights*, People's Public Security University of China Press, 2003 edition.
30. Zhou Wei: *Constitutional Fundamental Rights: Theory, Legislation and its Application*, China Law Press, 2006 edition.
31. Zheng Xianjun: *Principles of Fundamental Rights*, China Law Press, 2008 edition.
32. Ma Ling: *An Interpretation on Constitutional Rights*, People's Public Security University of China Press, 2010 edition.
33. Chief editor Yang Haikun: *A New Research on Fundamental Rights in Constitutional Law*, Peking University Press, 2004 edition.
34. He Yonghong: *Constitutionality review of the Limitation of Constitutional rights: Focusely Research on the Standards of Scrutiny and its Categorization*, China Law Press, 2009 edition.
35. Zhang Hong: *Fundamental Rights and Private Law*, China Law Press, 2010.
36. Qin Aolci: *A Study of Basic Rights System*, Shandong People's Publishing House, 2009.
37. Li Xiuqun: *The Study of the Horizontal Effect of Constitutional Rights*, China University of Political Science and Law Press, 2009.
38. Zhang Xiang: Legal *Construction of Fundamental Rights Norms*, Higher Education Press, 2008 edition.
39. Huan Ji'e: *Study on the Validity of the Norms of Constitutional Fundamental Rights in Penal and Criminal Procedure Law*, Xiamen University Press, 2011 edition, etc.
40. Xu Xianming: *An Analysis of Basic Rights*, *China Legal Science*, 1991, Issue 6.
41. Xia Zhenglin: *From Fundamental Rights to Constitutional Rights*, *Chinese Journal of Law*, 2007, Issue 6.
42. Liu Zhigang: *Limit of Fundamental Rights and Private Legal Rights*, *Law Review*, 2010, Issue 1.
43. Jiang Dehai: *Discussions about the Relations between Fundamental Rights and Legal Rights – Starting from the Nature of Fundamental Rights*, *Tribune of Political Science and Law*, March 2009, Vol. 27, Issue 2.
44. Li Long, Li Xiaoping: On the Communication of People's Sovereignty Principle and Basic Human Rights Principle in Constitution – From the Perspective of Habermas' Theory of Constitution Validity, Science of Law, 2008, Issue 1.
45. Ma Ling: *Differences between Constitutional Rights and Legal Rights*, *Global Law Review*, 2008, Issue 1.

46. Mo Jihong: *On Non-morality of Human Rights*, *Social Sciences in Guangdong*, 2011, Issue 2.
47. Han Dayuan: *Normative Analysis of the Human Rights Clause in the Constitutional Text*, *Human Rights*, 2006, Issue 1.
48. Zhang Yan: *On the Relationship between Human Rights and Fundamental Rights – Taking German Laws and General Law Theory as the Background*, *The Jurist*, 2010, Issue 6.
49. Zhang Xiang: *Double Characters of Basic Rights*, *Chinese Journal of Law, 2005, Issue 3.*
50. Zheng Xianjun: *The Basic Rights as Objective Value Order*, *Science of Law*, 2006, Issue 2.
51. Zhao Hong: *The Subjective Rights and the Objective Value – Two Orientations of Fundamental Rights in German Laws*, *Zhejiang Social Sciences*, 2011, Issue 3.
52. Zhao Hong: *Fundamental Rights as Objective Value and Their Issues*, *Tribune of Political Science and Law*, March 2011, Vol. 29, Issue 2.
53. Han Xiuyi: *Text Structure Practice: A Duality Analysis of Constitutional Rights in China*, *Journal of Liaoning University* (Philosophy and Social Sciences Edition), 2010, Issue 4.
54. Shangguang Piliang: *New Theory on the Nature of Constitutional Basic Rights*, *Journal of Yunnan University Law Edition*, January 2008, Vol. 21, Issue 1.
55. Zhang Xiang: *The Benefiting Function of Basic Rights and the State's Paying Obligation – New Start of the Basic Rights Analysis Framework*, *China Legal Science*, 2006, Issue 1.
56. Zhou Yezhong: *The Nature of Citizens' Basic Rights*, *Journal of Shenzhen University* (Humanities & Social Sciences), January 2004, Vol. 21, Issue 1.
57. Zhang Xiang: *On the Defensive Function of Fundamental Rights*, *The Jurist*, 2005, Issue 2.
58. Wei Di: *State Duty to Protect Basic Rights – to Take Germany and China as the Objects for Examination, Contemporary Law Review*, 2007, Vol. 21, Issue 4.
59. Chen Zheng: *State Protection Obligation and Function of Basic Rights*, *Studies in Law and Business*, 2008, Issue 1.
60. Du Chengming: *On State Duties o.f Basic Rights: Theoretical Basis, Structural Form and China's Practices*, *Law Review*, 2011, Issue 2.
61. Yuan Li*: Limit of State Obligations from the Perspective of the Fundamental Rights of Citizens*, *Modern Law Science*, January 2011, Vol. 33, Issue 1.
62. Gong Xianghe, Liu Yaohui: *State Obligation System of Fundamental Rights*, *Journal of Yunnan Normal University* (Philosophy and Social Sciences Edition), January 2010, Vol. 42, Issue 1.
63. Chen Chun: *On Obligations of the State*, *Law Science*, 2002, Issue 8.
64. Jiang Yinhua: *On State Obligation's Theoretical Origin: Modern Theory of Publicness*, *Law Review*, 2010, Issue 2.
65. Gong Xianghe: *State Obligations are the Guarantee of Civil Rights – New Perspective of the Relations between State and Citizens*, *Science of Law*, 2010, Issue 4, etc.
66. Tong Zhiwei: Constitutional Teaching and Research of China over the Past Three Decades, Science of Law: Journal of Northwest University of Political Science and Law, 2007, Issue 6.
67. Qin Aolei: *On the Meaning of "Citizens" as a Subject of Fundamental Rights – Also on the Comparison between "Citizens" and "Individuals" as Subject of Fundamental Rights*, *Journal of CUPL*, 2010, Issue 5.
68. Mo Jihong: *The Development of the Concept of "Citizen" in the Texts of Chinese Constitution*, *Human Rights*, 2010, Issue 4.
69. Qu Xiangfei: *Studies on the Constitutional Rights of Enterprise Legal Persons in the United States*, *Global Law Review*, 2011, Issue 4.
70. Du Qiangqiang: *On the Subject Status of Legal Person in the Fundamental Rights*, *The Jurist*, 2009, Issue 2.
71. Qin Qianhong, Chen Daoying: *Freedom of Speech of Corporate Legal Person – New Research Subject in the Freedom of Speech of the United States*, *Studies in Law and Business*, 2005, Issue 3.

72. Li Gaoya: *Simple Analysis of the Fundamental Rights of Legal Persons in American Laws – From the Perspective of Empirical Analysis*, *Journal of Southwest Agricultural University (Social Sciences Edition)*, November 2011, Vol. 9, Issue 11.
73. Huang Yuyin: *Preliminary Discussions on the Basic Rights of Legal Persons*, *Journal of Xingtai University*, September 2010, Vol. 25, Issue 3.
74. Liang Xiaoxiao: *On Contents of the Basic Rights of Legal Persons*, *Hunan Agricultural Machinery*, July 2010, Vol. 37, Issue 4.
75. Zhou Tingting: *Fundamental Rights of Legal Persons*, *Journal of Xianning University*, August 2010, Vol. 30, Issue 8.
76. Hou Yu: *Capacities for the Fundamental Rights*, *Chinese Yearbook of Constitutional Law 2008*; *Nature of Capacities for the Fundamental Rights*, *Chinese Yearbook of Constitutional Law 2010*.
77. Chen Cheng, Lin Pinpin: *Implication and Declarations*: *Capacity for Political Rights and Political Acts in Constitution*, *Journal of Guangdong Institute of Public Administration*, October 2010, Vol. 22, Issue 5.
78. Wang Jianxue: *On the Capacity of Legal Persons of Local Organizations for the Fundamental Rights*, *Tribune of Political Science and Law*, September 2011, Vol. 29, Issue 5, etc.
79. Yang Xiaomin: *On Changes of Subjects of Fundamental Rights in the Texts of the Constitution of the PRC*, *Legal Forum*, 2011, Issue 2.
80. Wang Jianxue: *Local Self-government as Fundamental Rights*, *Xiamen University Press*, 2010 edition.
81. Deng Lianfan: *On Reconstruction of the Academic Classification of Constitutional Rights*, *Journal of Xiangtan University* (Philosophy and Social Sciences), November 2008, Vol. 32, Issue 6.
82. Deng Lianfan: *Theoretic Classification of Basic Rights: Significance & Method*, *Wuhan University Journal* (Philosophy & Social Sciences), July 2008, Vol. 61, Issue 4.
83. Yang Haikun: *Constitutional Law*, China Human Resources Publishing House, 2002 edition.
84. Zheng Xianjun: *Constitutional Composition and Demonstration of Fundamental Rights*, *Studies in Law and Business*, 2002, Issue 2.
85. Zhang Qianfan: *Lectures on Constitutional Law*, Peking University Press, 2011 edition.
86. Chief Editor Wu Jialin: *Constitutional Law*, Masses Publishing House, 1983 edition.
87. Lin Laifan: *From Constitutional to Normative Constitution-A Preface of Normative Constitutional Law*, China Law Press, 2001 edition.
88. Xu Chongde: *Constitution of China*, China Renmin University Press, 1989 edition.
89. Wei Dingren: *Constitution*, Peking University Press, 1994 edition.
90. Han Dayuan, Lin Laifan, Zheng Xianjun: *Study on the Subject of Constitutional Law(2nd edition)*, China Renmin University Press, 2008 edition.
91. Xiong Jingbo: *Conflict and Reconciliation between Freedom of Expression and Right of Personality – Observe from the Perspective of the Theory of Fundamental Rights Limit*, *Science of Law*, 2007, Issue 1.
92. Zhang Zhihua: *Conflict between Fundamental Rights and Reconciliation Method*, *Legal Method* (Volume I).
93. Lin Laifan, Zhang Zhuoming: *Rank of Rights in Conflict*, *Journal of Zhejiang University* (Humanities and Social Sciences), 2003, Issue 6.
94. Zhang Xiang: *Standard Structure and Solving Model of the Conflicts in Fundamental Rights*, *Studies in Law and Business*, 2006, Issue 4.
95. Wang Tao: *Fundamental Rights Protection and Measurement: An Initial Review*, *Journal of Nanyang Normal University* (Social Sciences Edition), February 2010, Vol. 9, Issue 2.
96. Lin Laifan, Zhai Guoqiang: *On the Competition and Cooperation between Fundamental Rights*, *The Jurist*, 2006, Issue 5.

97. Han Dayuan: *On the Effect of Fundamental Rights*, published in *Studies on Constitutionalism and Rule of Administrative Law: Collected Works for Celebrating the Fiftieth Anniversary of the Teaching of Professor Xu Chongde*, China Renmin University Press, 2005 edition.
98. Xu Zhendong: *Effect of Constitutional Fundamental Rights in Civil Laws*, *Studies in Law and Business*, 2002, Issue 6.
99. Zhang Xiang: *The Expanding of Fundamental Rights on Private Law – Taking Contemporary China as the Background*, *Peking University Law Journal*, 2003, Issue 5.
100. Cai Dingjian: *Towards a Private Law Approach to the Implementation of the Constitution of China*, *Social Sciences in China*, 2004, Issue 2.
101. Zheng Xianjun: *Re-penetration of Values of Public Laws to Private Law Field – Horizontal Effect of Fundamental Rights and the Principle of Contractual Freedom*, *Zhejiang Academic Journal*, 2007, Issue 1.
102. Yu Fei: *Differentiation of Fundamental Rights and Civil Rights and Influence of the Constitution on Civil Laws*, *Studies in Law and Business*, 2008, Issue 5.
103. Cao Zhiguo: *The Relationship between Constitutional Rights and Civil Rights*, *Hebei Law Science*, 2008, Issue 5.
104. Tu Zhenyu: *Privacy Rights: From Civil Rights to Constitutional Rights – Also on the Relationship between Civil Rights and Constitutional Rights*, *Jin Ling Law Review*, 2009, Issue 1.
105. Zhang Hong: *Method and Target: Two Considerations of the Applicability of Fundamental Rights to Civil Laws*, *Modern Law Science*, 2010, Issue 2.
106. Liu Zhigang: *The Public Order and Moral and the Fundamental Rights*, *Science of Law*, 2009, Issue 3, etc.
107. Li Enci, Zheng Xianjun: *Look at the Limit of Constitutional Fundamental Rights from Sun Zhigang Case*, *The Jurist*, 2004, Issue 2.
108. Hu Xiaohua, Xu Jing: *On the Legitimacy of Citizens' Fundamental Rights Restriction and Restriction Principles*, *Law Review*, 2005, Issue 6.
109. Han Dayuan: *Basic Theories of Constitutional Law*, *China University of Political Science and Law Press*, 2008 edition.
110. Tang Zhongmin, Wang Jichun: *On the Principles of Restricting Citizen's Fundamental Rights*, *Journal of Southwest University (Social Sciences Edition)*, March 2007, Vol. 33, Issue 2.
111. Wang Jinyuan, Chen Pang: *A Comparison of Constitutional-making Models for Rights Restriction*, *Law Review*, 2005, Issue 5.
112. Li Jun: *Legal Reservation Principle for Protecting the Fundamental Rights*, *Journal of Shenzhen University* (Humanities & Social Sciences), 2004, Vol. 21.
113. Hu Rong: *On the Value of Legal Reservation*, *Political Science and Law*, 2010, Issue 9.
114. Liu Liantai: *Review on the "Legal Reservation" System in Article Eight and Article Nine of China's Legislation Law*, *Journal of Henan Administrative Institute of Politics and Law*, 2003, Issue 3.
115. Deng Lianfan, Jiang Qinghua: *On the Constitutional Reservation of Fundamental Rights*, *Journal of Hunan University* (Social Sciences), November 2009, Vol. 23, Issue 6.
116. Jiang Qinghua: *Norms and Values of Constitutional Reservation of Fundamental Rights*, *Political Science and Law*, 2011, Issue 3.
117. Qin Qianhong: *On Stipulations of China's Constitution on Restricting Citizens' Fundamental Rights*, *Journal of Henan Administrative Institute of Politics and Law*, 2005, Issue 2.
118. Zheng Xianjun: *Principles of Fundamental Rights*, China Law Press, 2010 edition.
119. Ao Shuanghong, Jiang Qinghua: *Ways of Stipulating and Restricting Citizens' Fundamental Rights –Comparative Study on Constitution Texts*, *Journal of Hubei University of Police*, September 2005, Issue 5, Issue 86 in total.

120. He Huahui: *Comparative Constitutional Law*, Wuhan University Press, 1988 edition.
121. Zhang Xiang: *Logic of the Limitation of Public Interests on Basic Rights*, *Legal Forum*, 2005, Vol. 20, Issue 1.
122. Zhang Xiang: *Thinking Framework of Limitations of Fundamental Rights*, *The Jurist*, 2008, Issue 1.
123. Wang Jinyuan: *Constitutional Standards of Restricting Fundamental Rights*, *Journal of Political Science and Law*, 2010, Issue 4.
124. Wang Xinsheng: *Constitutional Considerations of Limitations of Fundamental Rights*, *Western Law Review*, 2010, Issue 6.
125. Huang Xuexian, Guo Shu: *On the Guarantee of Citizen's Fundamental Rights under the State of Emergency*, *Contemporary Law Review*, July 2004, Vol. 18, Issue 4.
126. Han Dayuan: *Restriction and Guarantee of Citizen's Fundamental Rights under the State of Emergency*, *Study and Exploration*, 2005, Issue 4, etc.
127. Jin Yu: *Development of Constitutional Guarantee of Fundamental Rights*, *Journal of East China University of Political Science and Law*, 2009, Issue 5.
128. Xu Yuanxian, Cai Yonghao: *On the Improvement of China's System for Guaranteeing Citizens' Fundamental Rights*, *Contemporary Law Review*, 2002, Issue 10.
129. Xie Weiyan: *60 Years of the Republic of China: Changes in Citizens' Fundamental Rights Guarantee*, *Tribune of Political Science and Law*, January 2010, Vol. 28, Issue 1.
130. *Reflection on the Development of China's Guarantee of Fundamental Rights*, *Hebei Law Science*, April 2011, Vol. 29, Issue 4.
131. Xu Zhendong: *Encroachment on and Relief of Fundamental Rights*, *Science of Law*, 2004, Issue 1.
132. Fei Shancheng: *Analysis of the Constitutional Litigation System for Chinese Citizens' Fundamental Rights*, *Journal of Zhejiang University* (Humanities and Social Sciences), July 2001, Vol. 31, Issue 4.
133. Huang Jianshui, Li Li: *On Judicial Guarantee of Constitutional Basic Rights*, *Tribune of Political Science and Law*, August 2002, Vol. 20, Issue 4.
134. Lu Pinghui: *Lawsuits of Basic Rights: A Chinese Way of Realizing Constitutional Government*, *Study and Exploration*, 2004, Issue 4.
135. Li Xiaoming: *Citizens' Fundamental Rights from the Perspective of Constitutional Government*, *Academic Research*, 2006, Issue 2, etc.
136. Zhou Wei: *Comparisons of Judicial Remedy Systems for Constitutional Fundamental Rights of Different Countries*, *Journal of Southwest Nationalities College* (Philosophy and Social Sciences), February 2002, Vol. 23 (total), Issue 2.
137. Bao Wanchao: *Constitutionalism Transformation and China's Judicial Review System*, *Peking University Law Journal*, 2008, Issue 6.
138. Tong Zhiwei: *Initial Research on Several Issues Concerning the Improvement of Constitutional Procedures*, *Tribune of Political Science and Law*, April 2003, Vol. 21, Issue 2.
139. Liu Wanghong: *Brief Review of Constitutional Guarantee Procedures for Citizens' Fundamental Rights*, *Jiangsu Social Sciences*, 2006, Issue 5.
140. Zhou Zhigang: *On Equal Protection of Fundamental Rights*, Journal of Xiamen University: Philosophy and Social Sciences, 2010, Issue 1.
141. Albert H.Y. Chen, "International Human Rights Law and Domestic Constitutional Law: Internationalization of Constitutional Law in Hong Kong", *4 National Taiwan University Law Review* 2009.
142. Melissa A. Waters, "Creeping Monism: The judicial Trend Toward Interpretive Incorporation of Human Rights Treaties", Columbia Law Review, No. 3, 2007.
143. Vincent J. Samar, "Justifying The use of International Human Rights Principles in American Constitutional Law", 37 Columbia Human Rights Review 1 200–2006, etc.

144. Joseph Raz, "Rights and politics", *Indiana Law Journal,* 1995(27).
145. Joseph Raz, *Rights and Individual Well-being*, translated by Song Haibin, published in Tsinghua Journal of Rule of Law (11th series) edited by Gao Hongjun and He Zengke, Tsinghua University Press, 2009 edition.
146. Wang Xu: Discourse Mechanism for the Implementation of the Constitution: Aletheia and Construction, Peking University Law Journal, 2011, Issue 3.
147. luc B. Tremlay, "The Legitimacy of judicial review: The limits of dialogue between courts and legislatures", 3 *Int'l J.Const.L.* 617, 2005, etc.

The 1982 Constitution and Human Rights: Thirty Years of Social Change and Its Constitutional Implications

Zhang Zhen

The relationship between civil rights and state power is not only an essential aspect of constitutional law but also the theoretical foundation for constitutional law. Yet, state power and civil rights are not on an equal footing speaking of their basic contradictory relation in the Constitution. According to contemporary natural law theories, state power is derived and transformed from civil rights and takes civil rights as its foundation, source, and operation purpose. In this sense, civil rights are the core value and ultimate purpose of the Constitution. Human rights are the generalization and abstraction of civil rights, and thus, the core value system for judging the legitimacy of the Constitution. After its foundation, the PRC activated the constituent power and formulated the first constitution in 1954. Then, China activated the amending power and had three times of overall amendments to the 1954 Constitution, meaning the respective formulation of the 1975 Constitution, 1978 Constitution, and 1982 Constitution. At the time of marking the thirtieth anniversary of the promulgation of the 1982 Constitution, which is generally agreed as the best constitution in China's constitutional history, it is necessary to use human rights, the core value of the Constitution, to have a review in order to further improve the 1982 Constitution. The development of rights is inherently connected with social changes, but "right can never be higher than the economic structure of society and its cultural development conditioned thereby."[1] Therefore, it could only be historically truthful and practically significant, when human rights and rights as stipulated in the 1982 Constitution are examined against the background of China's social changes in the past three decades.

[1] Tucker [1, p. 12].

Z. Zhen (✉)
School of Administrative Law, Economic, Social and Cultural Rights Research Office of Human Rights Education and Research Center, Southwest University of Political Science and Law (SWUPL), Chongqing, China
e-mail: 13263169197@163.com

L. Li et al. (eds.), *Constitutional Development in China, 1982–2012*,
Research Series on the Chinese Dream and China's Development Path,
https://doi.org/10.1007/978-981-32-9261-1_8

1 Succession and Sublation: Principal Line of Human Rights Logic

As the first constitution after the foundation of the People's Republic of China (PRC), the 1954 Constitution was formulated in a process filled with the respect for the value of human subjectivity and the care for human rights. The group for drafting this constitution worked for over 2 months and accepted more than 100 of the 5000-plus opinions received nationwide from as many as 8000 people who contributed their views to the draft. After the release of the draft, it is the 4-month-long solicitation of opinions from the whole nation. More than 150 million people from all walks of life took part in the discussions and proposed up to 1.18 million opinions. The entire constitution-making process was featured by a strong democratic atmosphere.[2] Some scholar highly appraised the 1954 Constitution as an important part of the treasury of Marxist theory of the state from the perspective of its historical value.[3] The 1975 Constitution was formulated in the late period of the Cultural Revolution, so the political situation and social background back then determined its neglect and disregard of human rights value. The 1978 Constitution also failed to give enough recognition of the universal values of human rights due to the special historical period and the influence of many factors. The 1982 Constitution was formulated in the context of the termination of the Cultural Revolution, emancipation of the mind and implementation of the reform and opening-up program. Both the ordinary people as subjects of the constituent power and leaders knew the costs and harms of having no democracy and rule of law, so the 1982 Constitution is more realistic than the 1954 Constitution in respecting human dignity and guaranteeing human existence and development.

Looking from the concentrated stipulations of the four constitutions for human rights,[4] the 1975 Constitution contained the fewest provisions on rights, but it is most controversial and problematic. The 1982 Constitution contains the most provisions on rights, but it excludes the freedom to strike and freedom to change residence as provided in the 1954 Constitution. Through comparative analyses, we can conclude the principal line of human rights logic of the 1982 Constitution.

1. Development characteristics of the 1982 Constitution in human rights logic. The 1982 Constitution and the 1954 Constitution have a successive relationship. Except for personal dignity, the right of criticism, right to make suggestions and right to appeal and impeach, all other rights explicitly stipulated in the 1982 Constitution were clearly provided in the 1954 Constitution.[5] The 1982

[2]Chongde [2, pp. 173, 227, and 181].

[3]Chongde [2, p. 277].

[4]For specifics, refer to the 1954 Constitution, 1975 Constitution, 1978 Constitution, and 1982 Constitution.

[5]In the 1982 Constitution, foreigners' rights are stipulated in Article 32, Chapter I "General Principles" rather than Chapter II "The Fundamental Rights and Duties of Citizens," so it is not contained herein.

Constitution is very different from the 1975 Constitution and 1978 Constitution in human rights logic, and its articles about human rights are the sublation of the two constitutions. In the 1975 Constitution, the provisions on rights were put behind that on duties, which was not in conformity with the theoretical relations between rights and duties. The 1975 Constitution took upholding the leadership of the Party as one of the rights and duties of citizens, which confused the constitutional political articles with rights articles. In specific provisions on rights, the 1975 Constitution even had no provision on the right of equality, which is a fundamental right as recognized in constitutional law. The human rights logic of the 1975 Constitution disrespected and even ignored the universal values of human rights. The 1978 Constitution and 1975 Constitution are basically consistent in terms of human rights logic. It is very absurd to take "speaking out freely, airing views fully, writing big-character posters, and holding great debates" as citizens' rights. These two constitutions even emphasized women's right of equality without stipulating the general right of equality, which was self-contradictory in human rights logic.

2. Time features of the 1982 Constitution in human rights logic. Apart from the universal values, human rights also have specific meanings of the times. At the time of its formulation, the 1982 Constitution stipulated the rights based on China's social reality and historical background with the hope of solving existing problems back then. For instance, in the process of formulating the 1982 Constitution, many scholars and ordinary people proposed to restore the freedom to change residence as stipulated in the 1954 Constitution.[6] As a fundamental human right of citizens, the freedom to change residence is clearly stated in the constitutions of other countries and international human rights documents. The freedom to change residence was contained in the 1954 Constitution, but it is virtually in vain due to the constantly changing conditions for the implementation of the 1954 Constitution and the promulgation and enforcement of *the Household Registration Ordinance*. The reform and opening-up policy had been implemented for a few years at the time of the formulation of the 1982 Constitution, but the freedom to change residence, even if being provided in the 1982 Constitution, would have little realistic significance and would be inconsistent with the social reality because of institutional barriers and imperfect social and economic conditions for the freedom to change residence.

3. Chinese characteristics of human rights logic of the 1982 Constitution. The provisions of the 1982 Constitution on rights were established in line with China's actuality and to solve the challenges faced by our country back then. Looking from the world's constitutional history, the stage of modern constitution started from 1919. After the end of the World War II, there were further changes in constitutional concepts and articles about rights. For example, the environmental right and the right to be informed became increasingly popular and were written into constitutions of many countries after 1970s. At the time of making the 1982 Constitution, it seemed that China should make clear these two rights in the Constitution from the perspective of complying with the global development trend

---

[6]Chongde [2, p. 573].

of constitution. However, these two rights seemed to be not particularly significant to China at that time. In this case, the 1982 Constitution did not explicitly write these two rights that reflected the global trend of that moment in the part about rights.

2 Rules and Emphasis: Highlight of Economic Rights

The emergence, realization, and development of human rights, either as a requirement, a political stand, or as statutory rights, must be based on certain economic conditions of the society.[7] In the system of rights, economic rights and economic foundations are most directly and closely connected. Therefore, under the social background centering on economic development, it seems quite natural to lay particular stress on economic rights. After the termination of the Cultural Revolution, China needed to be rebuilt in many aspects and the top priority was to improve economic growth and people's material life. This was the basic historical and social background of the formulation of the 1982 Constitution. The 1982 Constitution is commonly taken by scholars as the constitution for reform and opening up and for development. The focus of reform and development was on the economic field back then, so a major historical and social mission of the Constitution was to facilitate the economic reform and development. This thinking of prioritizing economic development undoubtedly affected the arrangement of articles about rights in the 1982 Constitution. From an overall perspective, the articles about rights of the 1982 Constitution constituted an organic system with development characteristics, time features and Chinese characteristics as the basic logic. However, the articles about economic rights seemed to have a special position in the text of the 1982 Constitution and several amendments to it, which not only most directly met China's economic and social development needs but also most directly reflected China's economic and social development achievements.

The core element of the so-called economic rights is legitimate economic interest. Looking from the 1982 Constitution's Chapter II with concentrated stipulations for rights, the part about rights from Article 33 to Article 50 contains only a few provisions about economic rights, which are respectively the right to work in Article 42, the right to rest in Article 43, the ensured livelihood of retired personnel in Article 44, and the right to material assistance in Article 45. Actually in China, all rights other than the right of equality in Article 33, the right to vote and stand for election in Article 34, the freedom of religious belief in Article 36, and personal dignity in Article 38 have a close relationship with economic rights or legitimate economic interests directly or indirectly. For example, commercial speech, for-profit association, realization of personal freedom, possession of residence, freedom of correspondence, right to education, right to cultural activities, and equal

[7]Han and Lin [3].

pay for equal work irrespective of sex are all closely related to legitimate economic interests. In this connection, the special social and historical background of the formulation, implementation, and revision of the 1982 Constitution is manifested by the prominence given to economic rights in provisions on rights.

With the constantly advanced economic system reform and adjustment, the clauses about the economic system accounted for a large proportion of each previous amendment to the 1982 Constitution. The amendments to the Constitution in 1988 were made for two articles, involving the status of the private sector of the economy and land use right transfer, which both belonged to the economic system in content. The amendments in 1993 were made for nine articles, six of which directly involved the economic system. The amendments in 1999 were made for 6 articles, three of which directly involved the economic system. The amendments in 2004 were made for 14 articles, four of which directly involved the economic system. Due to the inherent relations between civil rights and institutional guarantee, all provisions about the economic system involved economic rights. Article 1 of the 1988 Amendment to the Constitution confirmed the legitimate status of the private sector of the economy and the protection of the lawful rights and interests of the private sector of the economy and confirmed that the great improvement of citizens' material life since the reform and opening up was largely contributed by private economy. Article 2 of the 1988 Amendment to the Constitution stipulated that the land use right could be transferred according to law; under the premise of public land ownership, it is just the existence of this amendment that has enabled Chinese citizens to possess the house property, and "homes for all" has always been taken as a basic economic right of citizens. Relevant amendments to the Constitution in 1993 rather rationally allocated the economic rights and interests of different economic subjects. The amendments to the Constitution in 1999 provided a basic guarantee for the economic rights and interests of different subjects like citizens through further stipulating the structure of ownership and distribution system, etc., covered by the basic economic system. 1999 年的相关宪法修正案通过对所有制结构、 分配制度等基本经济制度的进一步的规定, 对于我国公民等不同主体的经济权利及利益的保障提供了基盘性保障; 通过对农村经济形式的调整, 对农村居民的经济权利及利益的完善提供制度支持; 通过提高非公有制经济的地位, 进一步确认保障非公经济主体的经济权利及利益, 同时为全体公民享有非公经济发展的成果提供了制度前提。 There are a number of points in the 1999 amendments to the Constitution that are noteworthy for this discussion. It contained additional rules and regulations that were meant to provide institutional safeguard for the economic rights and interests of a broad range of economic entities, individual citizens included; it called for structural adjustments to the rural economy that would amount to institutional support for safeguarding rural residents' economic rights and interests; and it further confirmed the guarantee of the economic rights and interests of non-public economic subjects and provided a systematic precondition for all citizens to enjoy non-public economic development results through raising the status of the non-public economic sector. The 2004 Amendment to the Constitution involved the economic rights and interests mainly in further guaranteeing and adjusting the land system and non-public economic forms.

The provisions on private property right improvement and public interests were the most central and significant clauses involving economic rights in the amendments to the Constitution in 2004. The amendments in these two aspects marked the increasing improvement of the 1982 Constitution in revising its provisions on the economic system to some extent. Private property right is one of the three widely accepted fundamental rights. Even among the three major fundamental rights, private property right has its special function as it is the material premise and guarantee for the realization of the right to life and right to freedom.[8] Property right is not only an important legal phenomenon necessarily accompanying the market economy, but also a major legal pillar for the market economic order.[9] The constitutional guarantee of right to private property is conducive to economic prosperity and economic growth; stable protection of right to private property is the requirement for political democracy; constitutional protection of the right to private property is the realistic guarantee for human freedom.[10] The 1982 Constitution stipulated the right of citizens to private property in Article 13, but the concept of the right to private property is not clearly presented and the scope of protection of rights to private property is less accurate and comprehensive. The amendments to the Constitution in 2004 made the stipulations of China's Constitution for private property right conform to the global constitutional development trend and China's actual conditions in concept. In logical structure, these amendments contained guarantee clauses, restriction clauses, and compensation clauses. The values of rights and effects of norms represented the examples of right clauses of the amendments. The amendments of public interests raised the concept that has been commonly contained in constitutions of various countries for the first time in the texts of the Constitution of China.[11] The amendments of public interests also conformed to the theory of restriction of rights and defined the bottom line of restriction of rights.

What needs to be pointed out is that the 2004 Amendment to the Constitution contained fewer clauses directly involving the economic system compared with the previous amendments. The proportion of clauses about the economic system showcased a successively lower level in the amendments, respectively in 1988, 1993, 1999, and 2004. This indicates that the emphasis of the amendments to the 1982 Constitution changed, which was consistent with the trend of transformation from economic development to social development in China in recent years. Therefore, the focus of the rights clauses of the 1982 Constitution on economic rights would also change accordingly. The amendment of private property right comes as the overriding achievement and symbol of the improved economic rights

[8]Zhengbang [4, p. 200].
[9]Laifan [5, p. 182].
[10]Qianfan [6, pp. 282–288].
[11]Xinmin [7, pp. 347–348].

in constitution. In some sense, the amendment also comes as the announcement of the evolution and development changes of the right system with economic rights as the center.

3 Respect and Protection: Confirmation of Human Rights Value

One of the most valuable contents of the 2004 Amendment to the Constitution was the incorporation of respecting and protecting human rights in the Constitution. Incorporating human rights in the Constitution comes as a pioneering contribution to the constitutional history ever since the founding of the People's Republic of China. The concept of human rights experienced a crucial process of law amid twists and turns, from being criticized to being recognized, and to the signing of two covenants on human rights and to the clear definition in the Constitution. Human rights are the standard for judging the legitimacy of politics. If governments protect human rights, then they would be legitimate in themselves and their activities would be legitimate.[12] With human rights written in the Constitution, China's Constitution developed from fundamental rights system to human rights system, reflecting the profound changes of view of the state and the ruling party on human rights and constitution.[13] In the law circle of China, a rather common viewpoint is that "human right" is historically a western term.[14] According to some Chinese scholars, human rights are the rights that are enjoyed and should be enjoyed by humanity according to its natural attributes and social essence.[15] *The Human Rights in China* issued in 1991 began with the writing that "it has been a long-cherished ideal of humanity to enjoy human rights in the full sense of the term."[16] *The Universal Declaration of Human Rights* proclaims human rights "as a common standard of achievements for all peoples and all nations."

From the perspective of governing method, human rights have endowed law-based spirit. The principle of human rights has laid a legitimate foundation for social and political orders. Human rights have offered better approaches to maintain the harmony and stability of social order.[17] "Respect and safeguard human rights" is the specific expression of human rights in China's Constitution. For the first time, the text of China's Constitution included the two concepts, "human rights" and "rights" simultaneously. Many scholars of the academic circle uphold that these two concepts could be equalized or interchanged. As a matter of fact, it is necessary to

[12]Donnelly [8, p. 10].
[13]Dayuan [9].
[14]Xianming [10, p. 3].
[15]Hainian and Jiafu [11, p. 481].
[16]State Council Information Office [12, p. 1].
[17]Yong [13, pp. 177–180].

give a clear response and explanation after the two concepts appeared simultaneously in the text of the Constitution. First, the subject of human rights is humanity while the subject of rights is citizen. Of course, except for natural persons, legal persons may also become a subject of rights to a certain extent and scope.[18] In positive laws, the concepts of humanity and citizen need to be converted rather than being simply equalized. Second, human rights can be either legal rights or moral rights. Human rights are generally believed to be endowed by nature and self-earned, but rights need to be stated in legal texts in the end. Therefore, in our opinion, after incorporating human rights in the Constitution, there is a need to further study the relations between human rights and rights, including the values, functions, and forms of expression of human rights and rights and the conversion between human rights and rights.

Incorporating the provision that "the state respects and safeguards human rights" in the Constitution should not be interpreted simply from the perspective of the law itself. In fact, incorporating human rights in the Constitution is the concentrated manifestation of the change of the state's attitude toward human rights and the citizens' awakening consciousness of human rights against the background of social development and changes. As a major achievement in legal development, incorporating human rights in the Constitution signals the new developments of the human rights logic of the 1982 Constitution. First, it is the combination of the respect for universal values and China's national conditions. As stated above, the rights system established by the 1982 Constitution was to answer and resolve realistic issues related to rights faced by China after the end of the Cultural Revolution. The 2004 Amendment to the Constitution opened the vision of the constitutional text in human rights and improved the cognition of the universal values of human rights. Second, it is the combination of abstract guarantee of rights and specific provisions. The 1982 Constitution stipulates human rights in a listed manner and emphasizes the guarantee of every specific right. The 2014 Amendment to the Constitution has effectively made up for the Constitution in terms of its lacking of enumeration of rights protection and played a role in generalized protection of rights.

4 Being "Conservative" and "Innovative": Extension of the Topic About Rights

The rights system established by the 1982 Constitution has certain defects in itself. All previous amendments to the Constitution contained provisions directly involving rights, but not many. In addition, all the provisions directly involving rights were presented in the form of economic rights or economic interests. The human rights amendments in 2004 provided a more firm stand, more open space

[18]Ashibe [14, pp. 77–78].

and more realistic demand for improving citizens' rights. Apart from the factors within the law, the factors beyond the law, such as our country's economic and social development and citizens' increasingly enhanced awareness of rights could also boost the development of the rights system of the 1982 Constitution. This can be considered from the following perspectives.

4.1 Improvement of Existing Rights

According to the Marxist view of human rights, rights come from the basic economic relations reflecting the position of individuals in some mode of production, so economic and social rights should be taken priority over civil and political rights.[19] Looking from the development trend of constitutional rights in the world, the development of economic, social, and cultural rights has become the focus since the World War II. Since the reform and opening up, China has witnessed 30 years of rapid development and is shifting the focus from economic development to an all-round social development. Taking the above several factors into consideration, the emphasis should be laid on economic, social, and cultural rights when it comes to improving the existing rights system of the 1982 Constitution.

Looking from the text of the 1982 Constitution, all the contents from Article 42 to Article 50 basically belong to the scope of economic, social, and cultural rights. We believe that centering on these rights, the following topics need to be studied. First, as stipulated by Article 43 of the Constitution, "Working people in the People's Republic of China have the right to rest." Rest should be a fundamental right of everyone and every citizen. The subject of the right to rest should not be confined to workers. Article 24 of *the Universal Declaration of Human Rights* stipulates that everyone has the right to rest and leisure. All the four constitutions formulated after the founding of the PRC had stipulations for the right of workers to rest. It is understandable but unscientific to affirm and guarantee the right to rest of citizens of socialist countries after taking part in and loving working and then having the identity of worker. Constitution is made under the preconditions of the existence of political power and ideology of a state, but after the establishment of the political power, a technology-based and scientific constitution-making is the foundation for the improvement of the text of constitution. Second, Article 45 of the Constitution stipulates, "Citizens of the People's Republic of China have the right to material assistance from the state and society when they are old, ill or disabled." Material assistance comes as a fundamental right of citizens after the state went through the state of full socialization and was firstly stated in *Weimarer Verfassung*. The right to material assistance belongs to a typical social right.[20] The realization of this right requires the state's fulfillment of affirmative duties. The stipulation for this

---

[19]Vincent [15, p. 85].

[20]Xinmin [7, p. 691].

right in the 1982 Constitution was related to the characteristics and requirement of the socialist country and was somewhat forward-looking in rights protection. That said, for the time being, the premise for citizens to get material assistance is limited to those who are old, ill or disabled. The protection scope is obviously too narrow and unable to adapt to the new changes of citizens' requirement for material assistance. In addition, the mechanism for protecting the right to material assistance should also become a new research topic. Otherwise, it would become a right of no effect. At present, the law circle has fewer studies on this right. Third, the stipulation of Article 48 of the Constitution for women to enjoy equal rights is worth discussing. According to the Article 33, "All citizens of the People's Republic of China are equal before the law." Logically, this stipulation contains all circumstances including women's equality. Moreover, even considering that women are a specific subject or vulnerable group in China, only emphasizing the protection of the equal rights of a special group is still illogical.

4.2 *Incorporation of New Rights in the Constitution*

Constitutional rights are an open system. With the emergence of constitution in modern sense and the social development and changes, new rights are constantly supplemented to the constitutional rights system. The expansion of civil rights is a common law of development of constitution in different countries and one of the development trends of constitution as supported by multiple versions of law textbooks.[21] Incorporating human rights in China's Constitution has greatly opened the original fundamental rights system of the Constitution and expanded the subject scope and contents of the fundamental rights system.[22] In the law circle of China, scholars have been constantly studying matters related to the incorporation of new rights in the Constitution.[23] For the moment, there is a high expectation for incorporating the freedom to change residence, the right to be informed, right of environment, and other rights in the Constitution.

The logic of incorporating new rights in the Constitution needs to conform to several elements, namely the justification of the attributes of fundamental rights, independent right values, and realistic conditions for the incorporation. This text takes the rights of environment as an example to demonstrate the logic of incorporating new rights in the Constitution. Constitutional rights and fundamental rights are not completely the same, but their concepts are quite similar. Constitutional rights are empirical and constitutionalized fundamental rights and the fundamental

[21]Chongde [16], first section of chapter two; Yezhong [17], first section of chapter two; Zhengbang 4, first section of chapter six.

[22]See Footnote 13.

[23]According to preliminary statistics, articles centering on "incorporating new rights in the Constitution" could be searched via Chinese academic periodical net and numbered around 190 between 1994 and 2011.

rights clearly stipulated in the Constitution. Constitutional rights must be fundamental rights in the first place.[24] In this sense, the incorporation of a right in the Constitution must firstly demonstrate its attribute as a fundamental right. Robert Alexy noted that whether a right could be written in the Constitution is determined by three factors, namely the commonly recognized practical significance, political legitimacy, and the position above legal rights.[25] Given the significance of the environmental rights to China's economic development, to people's living needs, to people's political life, and to the sustainable development of human society, we can conclude the indispensability of environmental rights. The differences between environmental rights for one part and the right to live, the right to health, and the right to residence, etc., for another could justify the independent right value of environmental rights. The inseparable relations between environmental rights and human dignity of the day could justify the higher position of environmental rights. Three aspects could comprehensively demonstrate the attribute of environmental rights as fundamental rights.[26]

Of course, demonstrating the attribute of environmental rights as fundamental rights is only a theoretical premise for incorporating environmental rights in the Constitution. Three points need to be taken into account while discussing the incorporation of environmental rights in the Constitution. First, does the text of China's Constitution contain stipulations or contents about environmental rights? Second, can environmental rights be derived from existing constitutional provisions through constitutional interpretation? Third, it is the unique value of incorporating environmental rights in the Constitution.

As for the first point, the provisions directly related to environment in the 1982 Constitution are Article 9 and Article 26. Article 9 stipulates, "The state ensures the rational use of natural resources and protects rare animals and plants. The appropriation or damage of natural resources by any organization or individual by whatever means is prohibited." Article 26 states, "The State protects and improves the environment in which people live and the ecological environment. It prevents and controls pollution and other public hazards. The state organizes and encourages afforestation and the protection of forests." Article 9 is about the state's protection of natural resources. Article 26 is about the state's protection of the living environment and eco-environment. At the time of formulating the 1982 Constitution, many countries had started to attach importance to environmental issues and come up with the concept of environmental rights. Looking from the actuality after its foundation, China had a special position in the world's political structure, had little connections with other countries and a lower level of openness. We can judge from this actuality that China had not yet formed a conscious reaction to the world's growing trend of environmental protection and rising concept of environmental rights at the time of formulating the 1982 Constitution.

---

[24]Zhen [18, p. 61].

[25]Alexy [19, p. xix].

[26]For specific demonstrations, see Zhen [18, pp. 62–69].

As regards the second point, since the current constitution has no clear stipulations for environmental rights, could environmental rights be derived through constitutional interpretation? In our opinion, there might be the following obstacles to launch a constitutional interpretation of environmental rights from the perspective of the provisions of Article 9 and Article 26 of the Constitution. First, the space for interpretation is not enough. The clauses about environmental protection in the 1982 Constitution contain no explicit meanings of environmental rights and of citizens' environmental obligations. There are such phrases as "state's guarantee, state's protection", but the state's responsibility orientation and power assumption are not clearly defined. It reflects more about the state's principled policy orientation. Second, it lacks constitution-making purpose. Environmental protection should be one of the development trends of constitutions in different countries, but the concept of environmental rights as a kind of new and rather complex rights is somewhat inconsistent with the traditional concept of constitution. If we explain the environmental rights that are not contained in the text of the Constitution, the interpretation results would have certain conflict with the old concept of constitution, which violates the objectivity principle of constitutional interpretation. In fact, taking multiple factors into consideration, we can make the judgment that the formulators of the 1982 Constitution had no consciousness of taking environmental rights as fundamental rights.

Regarding the third point, firstly, the incorporation of environmental rights in the Constitution will lead to an organic interaction of citizens' environmental rights, environmental obligations, and the state's environmental protection responsibility by protecting citizens' environmental interests, enabling humanity, and nature to have a harmonious state. In modern times facing the shortage of resources and crises, the harmony of humanity and nature is the material prerequisite for the harmony between humanity and humanity, and a harmonious state of man-to-man relations pursued. Secondly, constitutionalized environmental rights can help people live a more decent life. Personal dignity is a fundamental right in China's Constitution. Some scholar believed that personal dignity is a fundamental principle in the constitutional value order, and the inviolable personal dignity has become the foundation of the value system.[27] No matter it is to overcome the negative effect brought about by eco-crisis, or to meet the increasingly growing life demands of people, environmental rights are closely related to the factor of "man." Environmental rights were proposed just to resolve difficulties existing in human development toward sustainability, to realize the continuity of human beings with dignity in biological significance and sociological significance. In this sense, environmental rights inherently agree with the core values of the Constitution. As our country's economic and social development reaches a certain level, environmental rights would have some realistic significance for people to live a more decent life.

[27]Zhenshan [20, pp. 3–4].

5 Conclusion or Start of a Problem?

Rights cannot transcend the economic structure of a society and the cultural development of the society restricted by the economic structure.[28] Therefore, historic and social significance is the most essential attribute of rights. The logic of any right generation and protection is based on the realistic social and economic conditions. With the changes and improvements of social and economic conditions, the meaning of rights would also develop in some way. In the last thirty years since the formulation of the 1982 Constitution, China put forward the reform and opening-up policy in the 1980s and the implementation of the market economy in the 1990s, and just recently proposed to build a harmonious society. These keywords in the theme of social developments and changes undoubtedly added obvious meanings of times to constitutional rights. For our part, an equitable access to the development achievements represents the most central proposition in shifting the focus from economic development to social development. In socialist countries, what's most valuable is not individualism and personal rights but the full development of all people in a socialist society.[29]Therefore, the guarantee of the equality of rights should be the most central expression of the topic of human rights. The so-called equality refers that all people, or at least all citizens of a state, or all members of a society should have an equal political status and social status.[30] At the same time, equality should be not only superficial and practical in the realms of state, but also socially and economically practical.[31] Certainly, this is not to deny the natural differences between men. For two persons, they may be unequal sexually.[32] Therefore, the key to safeguarding the equality of rights is the judgment of rational differences and the establishment of different legal conditions. If it is a rational difference, it would not violate the protection of equality of rights. Otherwise, it would go against the protection of equality of rights.

If we say that different evolutions of the focus on rights in the 1982 Constitution belong to an external reflection of the changes within the rights system, then, currently in China, the equal protection of rights would be the most central proposition and ultimate value of human rights logic of the 1982 Constitution. All propositions for right studies need to be discussed by centering on the ultimate value of equal protection.

---

[28]See Footnote 1.

[29]Henkin [21, p. 31].

[30]Tucker [1, p. 143].

[31]Tucker [1, p. 146].

[32]Tucker [1, p. 136].

References

1. Robert C. Tucker: *Anthologies of Marx & Engels*, Volume III, People's Publishing House, 1972 edition.
2. Xu Chongde: *Constitutional History of the People's Republic of China*, Fujian People's Publishing House, 2003 edition.
3. Liu Han, Li Lin: *A Preliminary Study of the Marxist View of Human Rights*, *China Legal Science*, 1991, Issue 4.
4. Chief Editor Wen Zhengbang: *A Course in Constitutional Law*, China Law Press, 2005 edition.
5. Lin Laifan: *From Constitutional to Normative Constitution-A Preface of Normative Constitutional Law*, China Law Press, 2001 edition.
6. Zhang Qianfan: *Constitutionalism, Rule of Law and Economic Development*, Peking University Press, 2004 edition.
7. Chen Xinmin: *Basic Theory of Public Law in Germany* (Volume Two), Shandong People's Publishing House, 2001 edition.
8. Jack Donnelly: *Universal Human Rights in Theory and Practice*, translated by Wang Puqu et al., China Social Sciences Press, 2001 edition.
9. Han Dayuan: *The Origin and Transformation of the Concept of Fundamental Rights in China*, *China Legal Science*, 2009, Issue 6.
10. Chief Editor Xu Xianming: *International Human Rights Law*, China Law Press, 2004 edition.
11. Chief editors Liu Hainian, Wang Jiafu: *The Human Rights Encyclopedia of China*, the Encyclopedia of China Publishing House, 1998 edition.
12. State Council Information Office: *Human Rights in China*, Central Party Literature Press, 1991 edition.
13. Xia Yong: *The Origin of the Concept of Human Rights: A Historical Philosophy of Rights*, China University of Political Science and Law Press, 2001 edition.
14. [Japan] Nobuyoshi Ashibe: *Constitutional Law* (Third Edition), translated by Lin Laifan, Ling Weici and Long Xunli, Peking University Press, 2006 edition.
15. [Britain] R. J. Vincent: *Human Rights and International Relations*, translated by Ling Di, Huang Lie and Zhu Xiaoqing, Knowledge Publishing House, 1998 edition.
16. Chief Editor Xu Chongde: *Constitution*, China Renmin University Press, 2009 edition.
17. Chief Editor Zhou Yezhong: *Constitution*, Higher Education Press, Peking University Press, 2007 edition.
18. Zhang Zhen: *On the Right to Environment as a Fundamental Right*, China Law Press, 2010 edition.
19. Robert Alexy: *A Theory of Constitution Rights*, translated by Julian Rivers, Oxford University Press, 2002, p.xix.
20. Li Zhenshan: *Human Dignity and Human Rights Protection*, ANGLE Publishing Co., Ltd., 2000 edition.
21. [U.S.] Louis Henkin: *The Age of Rights*, translated by Xin Chunying, Wu Yuzhang and Li Lin, Knowledge Publishing House, 1997 edition.

State Organs: Three Decades of Structural Change and Institutional Development

Hongchang Jiao and Qiang Ye

Since the promulgation of the 1982 Constitution 30 years ago, China has undergone tremendous social changes. The values of constitutionalism have taken root deeply in the hearts of the people, and the democracy and the rule of law have been gradually advanced. How to look at the 30-year changes of the Chinese society from the perspective of Constitution is a significant yet tough project.

Since the revision of the Constitution in 1982, Chinese constitutional law studies have also seen considerable progress, from the low-key establishment of Constitutional Research Association to the massive building of the community of constitutional scholars today; from the simple and ideological constitutional research methods to today's multiple research methods and magnificent scene of schools; from lacking constitutional knowledge in early stage to today's competing yet wonderful constitutional studies in various countries. It is time to prudently review and seriously retrospect the Constitution if we take 30 years as a development stage.

1 State Organ Is the Core of China's Constitution Law

Reading various constitutional textbooks being distributed currently, we can see that they are quite different in standpoint but basically the same in style, structure, and basic values. Most constitutionalists have accepted the universal values of constitutionalism, such as people's sovereignty, human rights and rule of law, and power restriction. In the establishment of the constitutional law, the above values have become the logical preconditions for future writing of Constitution and the foundation for analyzing constitutional phenomena. The results will always be the

H. Jiao (✉) · Q. Ye
China University of Political Science and Law, Beijing, China
e-mail: 13263169197@163.com

L. Li et al. (eds.), *Constitutional Development in China, 1982–2012*,
Research Series on the Chinese Dream and Chinaâ s Development Path,
https://doi.org/10.1007/978-981-32-9261-1_9

dilemma between "value and fact" and between "norm and reality." We are not saying that the values of constitutionalism are insignificant. Instead, we mean that if we bind our feet in the mire of values, it would be difficult for us to have a clear picture of real constitutional issues.

What are real constitutional issues? It is difficult to answer the question. If we make a statistical analysis of the works and papers published by constitutionalists in the last 30 years and recap the topics concerned them every year, we may have some clues. But, it requires writing a long article. Among the constitutional issues, what stays at the core of the overall situation? If it is taken as insignificant, studies on constitutional law might always center on peripheral issues.

The core aspect of constitutional law studies has something to do with the life experience of every generation of scholars and the historical background. Up to now, I have not seen any documents on the division of generation of constitutionalists in the past 30 years. Here are some of my humble opinions. If we take 10 years as a stage, the living constitutionalists can be generally divided into three generations: the first generation above 55 years old; the second generation between 45 and 55 years old; and the third generation between 35 and 45 years old. Those under the age of 35 could be included in the third generation, or no generation as they are still growing. Those currently leading the constitutional circle of China are only the first and second generations. There are many promising young constitutionalists in the third generation, but they are less experienced and thus still need to accumulate experiences.

After summarizing the main ideas of the first and second generations of constitutionalists, we can find that the core aspects of constitutional law are constantly examined and discussed in different ways. The first generation of scholars directly raised this question. For example, Professor Xu Chongde pointed out in the article titled *On the Core of Studies on Constitutional Law*, the nature of state and form of state stay at the core of studies on constitutional law in general.[1] Within a same generation, Professor Zhang Guangbo reflected on this question in different ways and explained the categories of "constitution," "nature of state," and "form of government," etc., in the article titled *Recognition of the Basic Categories of Constitutional Law*.[2] By means of extending the categories, the second generation of scholars has laid particular emphasis on this aspect and come up with many different category theories, such as "rights" and "duties," etc.[3]

The way of thinking using categories to replace issues in studies unavoidably leaves an abstract sense of difficulties. As a philosophical term, category used in studies on constitutional law studies has truly enhanced the sense of dignity of constitution, but it is difficult to play a practical role once facing the social reality. After studying the text of the Constitution and in line with the arguments over

[1]Xu [1].

[2]Zhang [2].

[3]Han [3].

studies of constitutional law over the past 30 years, we come up with the proposition that "state organ stays at the core of China's constitutional law."

"People" and "state" are the two terms which occurred most frequently in the text of the Constitution. They are bonded by state organs. Just one year after the promulgation of the 1982 Constitution, Professor Xu Chongde wrote an article, in which he pointed out that the state's missions and functions were mainly realized by state organs. He also pointed out that the constant improvements of state organs of our country had a bearing on the socialist modernization process. Therefore, the stipulations for the principle, organization, and activities of state organs were important contents of the Constitution as the fundamental law of the state.[4] The importance of state organs was clearly stated. If based on later debates over the constitutional law, we can find that state organs were behind every debate.

We take *Records of the Science of Law of the People's Republic of China over the Past Sixty Years* as the object of analysis. This book summarizes the main debates on constitutional law since the founding of the PRC, especially since the formulation of the 1982 Constitution. Let's firstly take a look at the objects of research on constitutional law. No opinion can deny that state organ is an object of research. Secondly, let's have a look at the benign unconstitutional debates called by professor Lin Laifan as "ripples" of China's constitutional law,[5] which is also triggered by various "unconstitutional events" of state organs. Regarding the debates about unconstitutionality of the property law, it is the relationship between the Constitution and civil laws, but it actually has something to do with the legislative power of the National People's Congress, still less the setting of the review for constitutionality institution, and the respect and guarantee of provisions on human rights.

The concept "state organs are the core of China's constitutional law" is most possibly challenged and questioned by "rights-based" theory supporters or liberalists. At the moment, rights have become a universal name card, but scholars holding a negative view of freedom take state organs as fierce floods and savage beasts. Our response to it is that the difference between studying state organs and advocating the standard of right is simply the difference in the angle looking at questions, but the effects of the two may be consistent. For liberalists, state organs due to their various changes have a reciprocal relationship with negative freedom. Studying state organs is not to justify their expansion but to make them well operate and well match their powers and responsibilities.

From the perspective of the text of the Constitution, state organ represents an active subject with rich imageries. Through revealing state organs' four dimensions from inside to outside and from top to down, various constitutional relations can be inter-linked. By using this active subject and based on the vivid examples in the past three decades, we can have an overview of China's social changes in the last three decades and then extract rich constitutional theories.

---

[4]Xu [4].

[5]Lin [5].

2 Horizontal Dimension of State Organs

(1) From centering on administration to centering on legislation

As confirmed by the 1982 Constitution, the people's congress system is the fundamental political system of our country and the National People's Congress and its Standing Committee exercise the legislative power of the state. However, from the very beginning, the National People's Congress and its Standing Committee didn't build the authority of dominating the situation as a whole because of the heavy legislative tasks and rapid social transformation. In this case, the State Council and its departments seized the opportunity. In 1980s, the National People's Congress and its Standing Committee passively played their role in legislation. When the National People's Congress and its Standing Committee started to exercise the legislative power, their working institutions felt difficult to assume the task of drafting laws. In this case, all legal proposals other than relevant criminal and civil laws and laws of state organs were drafted by the State Council and its departments.[6] We can look at this background from two aspects.

By the end of the term of the Eighth National People's Congress in March 1998, the NPC and its Standing Committee had enacted altogether 233 laws and 94 relevant legal decisions apart from the Constitution and two amendments to the Constitution. But by the same time, the State Council had issued and approved 795 administrative laws; departments of the State Council and local governments had made 26,000 rules and regulations within their statutory authority.[7] In number, the rules and regulations were far more than laws. If this is not enough to explain the situation, then the two decisions adopted by the NPC and its Standing Committee in 1980s came as the origin of their authorization in legislation.

The Seventh Session of the Sixth Standing Committee of the National People's Congress on September 18, 1984, adopted *the Decision on Authorizing the State Council to Reform the Industrial and Commercial Tax System and Release Draft Regulations on Taxation for Trial Implementation*. This was to authorize the State Council to draft relevant regulations on taxation and release the draft regulations for trial implementation in the process of reforming taxation for state-owned enterprises and reforming the industrial and commercial tax system. On April 10, 1985, the Third Session of the Sixth National People's Congress adopted *the Decision of the National People's Congress on Authorizing the State Council to Formulate Interim Provisions or Regulations Concerning the Reform of the Economic Structure and the Open Policy*. This was to authorize the State Council to formulate, promulgate, and implement interim provisions or regulations related to the reform of the economic structure and the open policy if necessary in accordance with the Constitution and without contradicting relevant laws and the basic principles of relevant decisions of the NPC and its Standing Committees, and report to the NPC

[6]Cai [6].

[7]*Law Yearbook of China (1987–1997)*, Press of Law Yearbook of China, 1998 edition, page 10.

Standing Committee for record. These two decisions gave a wide range of powers to the State Council in economic legislation. The tax system reform in 1994 especially had a far-reaching influence on the financial system afterward. The dominant role of the State Council in legislation somewhat indicates that the NPC and its Standing Committee were too generous to transfer their powers.

Why did the State Council have such a big power and what's the basis for the authorization of the NPC and its Standing Committee? These two questions are implied in the vague functions and powers of the NPC, NPC Standing Committee, and the State Council in Article 62, Article 67, and Article 89 of the Constitution. The functions and powers of these three organs have generated many controversies over the past three decades. For examples, is the authority of the NPC inherent or authorized by the Constitution? Are all powers and functions of the State Council authorized by the organ of power, or are partially inherent and partially authorized? What are the limit, principle, and procedures of authorization? There are still no final answers to these questions. That said, it is undeniable that the extensive legislative authority of the State Council is abnormal in a law-based country. However, the promulgation of *the Legislation Law* in 2001 came as a symbolic transformation.

The significance of *the Legislation Law* is that it firstly defines matters reserved by laws and restricts authorized legislation through stipulating the authorized content, purpose, and term. At the same time, the legislative ability of the NPC and its Standing Committee has also been strengthened. The legislative space of the State Council and its departments has been restricted through the enactment of backbone branch laws. Following *the Legislation Law, the Supervision Law* adopted in 2006 further consolidated the authority of power organs. The institutional supervisory measures have cleared away obstacles to the enforcement of laws. Regrettably, many laws like *the Constitution*, *the Legislation Law* and *the Supervision Law* have the stipulation for recording and reviewing provisions and regulations by the NPC and its Standing Committee, but this stipulation has failed to be effective in practice. Yet, the regression of power to the NPC and its Standing Committee is an irresistible social fact. The review of administrative laws, provisions, and regulatory documents is expected to come true.

(2) **From centralism to democracy**

The constitutional circle always has different comprehensions of democratic centralism. For example, is it a constitutional principle or an organization principle of state organs? What's the true meaning of it? Does it emphasize centralism or democracy? Looking from its development process in China, it experienced the changes in two meanings in early days. First, democratic centralism was firstly used in the sense of state system. Democracy referred that the election of government and state powers were based on people's support. Centralism referred that administrative powers must be exercised in a concentrated and uniform manner to implement the laws and policies developed by public opinion organs. Second, democratic centralism later became a general norm for the political life of the state and was taken as the norm to handle the relationship between individuals and organizations in case of the occurrence of contradictions among the people and was taken as an approach to strengthen disciplines.[8] In the political life of our country, i.e., during the period before and a long period after the formulation of the 1982 Constitution, there had been the phenomenon of one-sided understanding of democratic centralism and excessive highlight of centralism, but it became constantly divided and began to showcase the trend of turning from centralism to democracy.

On the one hand, the 1982 Constitution stipulates that all state organs implement democratic centralism and administrative organs implement the head responsibility system. How to comprehend the relations between democratic centralism and head responsibility system is prone to disputes.[9] The reason for implementing the head responsibility system by administrative organs was understood from the perspective of administrative efficiency in the past. Administrative organs were thought to deal with all kinds of sudden social events, so it is easy to miss the optimum opportunity if adopting the collective responsibility system. That being said, the practices in the last 30 years indicate that the head responsibility system has resulted in excessive centralization of powers and endless corruptions of all kinds.

Does that mean the head responsibility system is effective while the collective responsibility system is ineffective? This simple mode of thinking usually shields refined theoretical thinking. Taking France as an example, France had been adopting centralization and the administrative authority was powerful in the history. At the time of its establishment in 1958, while being guaranteed, the power of the president was also restricted through various means. As a matter of fact, politically speaking, normal politics went through most part of the history. Normal politics had the law to follow in handling matters, so realizing efficiency through procedure control rather than power concentration could be expected. This is because efficiency is related not only to policy-making but also to all links like execution and supervision. The head responsibility system only sets its target on the decision-making link but overlooks such links as execution and supervision. That means administrative efficiency would not become prominent when the execution and supervision links were not in place even with fast decision-making procedures. This is exactly the administrative situation of China at the moment, which is the situation of poor execution and imperfect supervision.

Out of the reflection on the head responsibility system, the functions of democracy have been recognized. To simply understand, democracy is the majority decision, but democracy has multiple forms of expression. The establishment of the administrative law-enforcing responsibility system is one of its manifestations. Since 1994, the Municipal Government of Shijiazhuang of Hebei, the Municipal Government of Wuhai of Inner Mongolia Autonomous Region, the Government of Fuping County of Shaanxi, and the Municipal Government of Dunhuang of Gansu have tried to establish the administrative law-enforcing responsibility system. As of

[8]Cai [7].

[9]Wu [8].

June 2002, 29 provinces, autonomous regions, and municipalities directly under the central government have developed the systems for various administrative organs to implement the administrative responsibility system through issuing provisions, documents, and other means.[10] The administrative responsibility system has made clear the basis and limit of law enforcement and designed the responsibility examination and assessment system, which have preliminarily resolved the confusion of responsibilities of administrative organs but not yet fundamentally resolved the excessive power of administrative officers.

In 2004, the State Council released *the Notice on Printing and Distributing the Implementation Outlines for Comprehensively Advancing Administration by Law* (Guo.Fa. [2004] No. 10), proposing that, in the 10 years followed, one of the targets of building a law-based government was the basic formation of a scientific, democratic, and normative administrative decision-making mechanism and system. The administrative mechanism for democratic decision making was obviously designed to break the monopoly of the head responsibility system. While stipulating the specific contents of the head responsibility system without denying the head responsibility system, the paradox that "head of an administrative organ assumes the full responsibility for the administrative organ" should be no longer underlined. Regarding major issues that have a bearing on citizens' fundamental rights, collective decision making, or the deployment by other persons in charge should be gradually adopted. At present, auditing bodies and power organs have also worked to intensify the supervision over heads of administrative organs over time, but there is still a long way to go before the formation of an institutionalized form of supervision.

(3) **From cooperation with division of labor to strengthening restriction**

The "tripartite" political system is not the principle for power distribution between state organs in China, but the division of powers between state organs is an unquestioned fact. Taking legal interpretation as an example, in 1981, the 19th Session of the Fifth Standing Committee of the National People' Congress adopted *the Resolution on Strengthening the Work of Interpretation of Laws*, which preliminarily established the system of joint interpretation of laws by the NPC Standing Committee, the State Council and its competent departments, the Supreme People's Court and the Supreme People's Procuratorate. In practice, the interpretation of laws by the Supreme People's Court and the Supreme People's Procuratorate has become the normality. The Supreme People's Court and the Supreme People's Procuratorate have also gone beyond legislation through interpretation of laws, which has been denounced by the academic community and has demonstrated the work style of "cooperation with division of labor" among state organs. In addition, this style of work has also been facilitated by several guiding thoughts followed by China.[11] Over the past 30 years, strengthening the restriction

[10]Zhang [9].

[11]Wang [10].

of powers between state organs has become a consensus. It is also the result of the institutional development step by step.

The Law of Administrative Procedure was successfully adopted in 1989, which is a landmark event in the history of China's contemporary legal system. Just as a famous jurist Luo Haocai said, in China's history, there was no truly effective system under which "people could sue officials." The promulgation and implementation of *the Law of Administrative Procedure* mean the formation of a whole-new judicial system and the availability of a brand-new mechanism for supervising administrative organs to exercise powers and functions and maintaining citizens' lawful rights and interests according to the law. He finally concluded that this had a crucial role in the history of China's legal system. In the 20-odd years from the formulation of *the Law of Administrative Procedure* in 1989 to 2009, people's courts of all levels nationwide accepted 1.52 million administrative cases of trial of first instance of various kinds,[12] which well restricted the supervisions over administrative organs' administration by law. Being subject to the natural deficiency in system, administrative litigation is still faced with twists and turns while moving forward at this point. It is unnecessary for us to be pessimistic about this. Once the institutional gate is opened, the rest would be waiting for the opportunity.

For a long period, people's courts have been in a very awkward position and seemed to be rather exhausted in face of the powerful administrative organs. People's courts are usually squeezed by people's procuratorates and public security organs in practice. The status of these three kinds of organs can be clearly mirrored by the term "public security organs, procuratorates, and courts." Some scholars have vigorously called for changing the order from "public security organs, procuratorates, and courts" to "courts, procuratorates, and public security organs."[13] However, in face of the NPC that is not that powerful, people's courts have attempted to take the place of the NPC through judicial interpretations. As such, strengthening the supervision over judicial interpretations has been gradually included in the work of the NPC and its Standing Committee. *The Legislation Law* and *the Supervision Law* have a concentrated reflection of this. However, if it is poorly operated, it would easily result in excessive supervisions by the NPC and its Standing Committee. "Individual case supervision" used to be taken as an effective mode of supervision for reducing judicial corruptions, but empirical studies show that individual case supervisions have not produced obvious results and could easily cause judicial interference and be utilized by the minority with well-connected relations.[14] Under the current institutional framework, it is difficult for people's courts to restrict the NPC and its Standing Committee. Yet, people's courts are being active in accepting the supervisions of the NPC and its Standing Committee. The sincerity of people's courts to accept supervisions can be reflected

[12]Zhang [11].

[13]Han [12].

[14]Cai [13].

by such documents as *Several Opinions of the Supreme People's Court on the Acceptance by People's Courts of Supervision from People's Congresses and Their Standing Committees* (Fa.Fa. [1998] No. 26), *Decision of the Supreme People's Court on Strengthening the Work for Contacts with Deputies to the National People's Congress* (Fa.Fa. [2000] No. 32), and *the Interim Provisions of the Supreme People's Court for People's Courts to Handle Letters from Deputies to the National People's Congress* (Fa.Fa. [2000] No. 32). The question is that people's courts are at the position of being supervised. Except for certain power of law interpretation, people's courts have no substantive power to restrict the National People's Congress and its Standing Committee. An effective way to change this situation is to give the review for constitutionality power to the Supreme People's Court, but this proposition is difficult to be realized in China. Therefore, the independence status of people's courts could only be realized by pinning the hope on property right protection and independence of justices. At the moment, the review for constitutionality power of people's courts has been confirmed. Going forward, the task of people's courts is how to consolidate the power and strive for development in difficulties.

3 Longitudinal Dimension of State Organs

Over the past three decades, the central–local relationship has witnessed a complex adjustment process. Even today, there are still many arguments over their relations. As a cross section of the central–local relationship, the relationship between central and local state organs has clearly reflected the various changes during the period.

(1) **From central authorization to rational separation of powers**

The third article of the Constitution stipulates that the division of functions and powers between the central and local state organs is guided by the principle of giving full play to the initiative and enthusiasm of the local authorities under the unified leadership of the central authorities. This article has set the master tone for longitudinal state organs: The authorization by central authorities is the principle, so giving play to the initiative of local authorities depends on the powers authorized by the central authorities. The once disordered development of "liaison offices in Beijing" profoundly revealed this principle. The actions of these liaison offices of local governments were vividly called "alleged involvement in corruption." These offices were also called "second administrative centers of local governments."[15] In 2010, the General Office of the State Council issued *the Opinions of the General Office of the State Council on Strengthening and Regulating the Management of Resident Agencies of Various Local Governments in Beijing* (Guo.Ban.Fa. [2010] No. 8) and decided to overhaul and clean up various kinds of "liaison offices in

[15]Li [14].

Beijing." This conduct still showcased the difficulties faced by local state organs in survival.

The first step for local state organs to get substantive powers was the establishment of standing committees of local people's congresses. In June 1979, the Second Meeting of the Fifth National People's Congress adopted *the Resolution of Revising Several Provisions of the Constitution of the People's Republic of China*. According to the resolution, "revolutionary committees" were abandoned and changed into local people's governments of all levels. The resolution stipulated the establishment of standing committees under local people's congresses at and above the county level. The establishment of standing committees of local people's congresses not only fundamentally changed the extremely inappropriate state of the revolutionary committees but also enabled local people's congresses to become more authoritative power organs of the people.[16] In order to comply with the development trend of local state organs, *the Organic Law of the Local People's Congresses and Local People's Governments* was revised for four times respectively in 1982, 1986, 1995, and 2004. Thereby, the functions and powers of local people's congresses and local people's governments were defined in law, but there were still many problems due to the outmoded notions. First, the functions and powers of local people's congresses and local governments were duplicated with that of the National People's Congress and the State Council to a large degree, which easily led to the encroachment on the functions and powers of local state organs by the superior organs. Second, "larger city" is a special phrase in the Constitution because a city would enjoy the legislative power once it has the identity of "larger city." However, the introduction and exit mechanism for "larger city" was still not clearly defined. The control power was firmly mastered by the State Council. Third, since 1990s, with the introduction of the concept of administrative subjects into China's *Administrative Law*, studies on administrative subjects have become a fashion. A prevailing viewpoint is that Chinese administrative organs at all levels should become public legal entities with independent autonomy.[17] Various supporting systems need to be developed for practices of public legal entities, but it is difficult to realize it at this point. Fourth, local people's courts have the responsibility for maintaining the uniformity of the socialist legal system. As the Supreme People's Court monopolizes the formulation of judicial interpretations, higher people's courts and intermediate people's courts also enact some locally applicable law interpretation documents, but the space for law interpretation is narrow. How to ensure the independence of justices of local people's courts remains to be an unsolved problem.

Different from local people's congresses and their standing committees, state organs of ethnic autonomous areas have been given greater powers by *the Regional National Autonomy Law* which was laid down in 1984 and revised in 2001, such as enacting autonomous regulations and separate regulations and implementing these

[16]Xu [15].

[17]Xue [16].

regulations flexibly, etc. In addition, "the right of autonomy" as a formal term also appears in the text of the Constitution, which has greatly enlarged the space for the development of constitutional hermeneutics. The right of autonomy is not the power that is completely free from the control of the central authorities. Instead, there are some restrictions. For example, the enactment of autonomous regulations must be approved by the Standing Committee of the NPC, and flexible regulation implementation must be approved by the superior organs. In general, *the Regional National Autonomy Law* has partially changed the power relationship between central state organs and local state organs, and given prominence to the characteristic of power separation.

A major challenge to the relationship between longitudinal state organs is the adoption and implementation of the two basic laws. Taking *the Basic Law of Hong Kong Special Administrative Region* as an example, the Standing Committee of the NPC has interpreted *the Basic Law* for five times since its entry into force in 1997, which have set off an upsurge of studies on constitutional interpretations and enriched China's practices in constitutionalism. *The Basic Law of Hong Kong Special Administrative Region* was enacted under the principle of "One Country, Two Systems." According to the law, the Hong Kong SAR may maintain the capitalist system and enjoy a high degree of autonomy except in defense and diplomatic affairs; Hong Kong courts have the power of final adjudication. As the democratic process speeds up, the Legislative Council and Executive Council are going to implement "direct elections" after 2017. The political practices of Hong Kong SAR will indirectly promote the political transformation of the Chinese mainland beyond doubt. However, due to the rapid development of organs of Hong Kong, the tensions between the central government and the SAR may be stimulated, which are demonstrated in the following aspects. Firstly, how to maintain the authority of the central government? Secondly, how to make sure that the constitutional order sees no greater changes? Thirdly, how to guarantee the development of special administrative regions without being separated under the precondition of "one country" principle? Power separation might be able to solve the unclear responsibility allocation between the central and local state organs, but excessive separation of powers would harm the stability of the unitary state.

A rational choice is to refer to the practice of *the Basic Law for the Federal Republic of Germany* that is to make clear the contents of power separation between central and local authorities, such as the matters respectively taken charge by central state organs, local state organs, and jointly by central and local state organs. Some scholar proposed the matric power structure: breaking the traditional bureaucracy and establishing the "matrix" train of thought with public affairs as the basis for the division of functions between central and local state organs.[18] It can be said that local vitality should also be realized while maintaining the central authority, which will remain to be an essential principle for measuring the reforms going forward.

---

[18]Dong [17].

(2) **From administrative adjustment to legal regulation and control**

Looking from the experiences of federal states, using judicial means to adjust the relations between longitudinal state organs is a main choice.[19] But, this is backed by strong judicial powers. At the current stage, China is not in the position to go for this method. Besides, under the premise that the central and local powers are not yet refined, administrative adjustment is mostly employed to handle the relationship between longitudinal state organs, but there is a trend of gradual transition to legal adjustment.

We can observe the change of relations between longitudinal state organs from the perspective of administrative division. As an important means for political power building and government management, administrative division is one of the basic forms of the redistribution of state powers and plays a pivotal role in the political life.[20] Article 30 and Article 31 of the Constitution have stipulations for the administrative division structure of our country. Article 62 (12) and (13), Article 89 (15), and clause 3 of Article 107 contain the stipulations for the limit of authority of administrative division. In the last 30 years, except for the establishment of Hainan province and Chongqing city and two special zones, provincial-level organizational construction has been basically stable, but it has been more frequent to see administrative division under the provincial level. This means the power of administrative division has been taken up by administrative organs (the State Council, provinces, and municipalities directly under the central government) in most cases.

The result of administrative organs' control of administrative divisions is that frequent changes of administrative divisions in the name of economic development have triggered many legal issues. A typical case is the emergence and development of development zones. According to Deng Xiaoping's strategic thinking of further expediting the reform and opening up as proposed in 1984, the Central Committee of the Communist Party of China (CPC) and the State Council decided to open 14 coastal cities, including Tianjin, Shanghai, Dalian, Qinhuangdao, and Yantai. During the period between 1992 and 1994, development zones experienced a great upsurge of development. During this period, 18 national economic and technological development zones were established with approval. By late 1990s, development zones had developed unorderly and occupied a large amount of land, so the development zones started to be overhauled vigorously. According to statistics, a land market governance overhaul campaign has been launched since 2003 with the focus on cleaning up development zones. Up to now, the campaign has received fruitful results. Before this nationwide overhaul, there were as many as 6,866 development zones of various kinds with a planning area of 38,600 km^2. After the overhaul, by 2006, the number of development zones was reduced to 1568 with the

[19]Guo [18].

[20]Zhao [19].

planning area being reduced to 9949 km^2, representing a decrease rate of 77.2% and 74.2%, respectively.[21] The first problem of establishing development zones is that the management committees of development zones, as the administrative organs, are not legally defined in terms of the nature, which is also quite controversial in theory. Second, the establishment of state organs in development zones is inconsistent with *the Organic Law of the Local People's Congresses and Local People's Governments*. Most development zones did not establish administrative areas due to their emphasis on heavy industrial and economic development, and their management was mostly taken charge by party working committees and management committees assigned by the superiors. Party committees, people's congresses, governments, and political consultative conferences with complete functions were not in place. Of the 216 state-level development zones (128 state-level economic and technological development zones and 88 state-level high-tech development zones), nearly 80% implemented the mode dominated by management committees and operated by companies. Development zones of this kind had no corresponding people's congresses, still less the building of a perfect people's congress system. In addition, only 10% of the development zones had implemented the people's congress system.[22] Lastly, how to realize a coordinated development between the state organs established by development zones and other state organs also represents a test for the wisdom of the designers.

As with that of development zones, the adjustment of administrative division within cities has also given rise to many legal difficulties. For example, Xiangfang District and Dongli District of Harbin merged; Pudong New District and Nanhui of Shanghai merged, and Dongcheng District and Chongwen District of Beijing merged in an effort to streamline state organs and improve their efficiency. To a certain extent, these mergers have indeed produced the expected effect, but the abolition of administrative divisions has led to the cancel of organs of people's congresses and people's courts along with the cancel of administrative organs. Organs of people's congresses are composed of deputies elected by the people. Without the consent of the people, how could a paper document of the superior administrative organs cancel the subordinate organs of people's congresses? It makes no sense to cancel people's courts which are judicial organs together with the staff due to regional changes even they are not subject to the interference of administrative organs.

Handling the relations between longitudinal state organs through administrative adjustment is no longer adaptable to the needs of building a modern law-based state. It has been separated from democratic decision makings of public opinion organs and lacks the involvement of citizens and thus legitimacy. The current system of law for handling administrative division is imperfect. Apart from the Constitution, the laws, provisions, and regulations relating to administrative division in China mainly include *the Organic Law of the Local People's Congresses*

---

[21]Xia [20].

[22]Hu and Zhang [21].

and Local People's Governments, *Provisions of the State Council Concerning Administrative Division* adopted in 1985, *Administrative Regulations for Geographical Names* adopted in 1986, *Regulations on the Handling of Boundary Disputes between Administrative Areas* adopted in 1989, *Guidelines for Implementing Administrative Regulations for Geographical Names* adopted in 1996, *Regulations on Administration of Administrative Boundaries* adopted in 2002, and *Regulation on the Work of Local Chronicles* issued by the State Council in 2006.[23] Enacting a complete *Administrative Division Law* and incorporating administrative division in the supervision of the National People's Congress turn out to be the direction of administrative division reform down the line. This is also an important measure for guaranteeing local state organs to effectively exercise constitutional and legal functions and powers.[24]

4 State Organs and Citizen Dimension

(1) **From state power to civil rights**

The relationship between state power and civil rights represents a core part of studies on constitutional law and has attracted continuous attentions of the three generations of constitutionalists.[25] Over the past three decades, the civil rights-based values of constitutionalism have been established over time. Right discourse has replaced duty discourse to become the consensus at all levels. From the perspective of state organs, restricting the powers of administrative organs, expanding the contents of civil rights, and improving citizens' rights of appeal and procedure have also been demonstrated in the legislation of the National People's Congress and its Standing Committee.

Compared with the previous three constitutions, the 1982 Constitution has a major change in chapter arrangement, i.e., making the chapter of "the fundamental rights and duties of citizens" ahead of the chapter of "the structure of the state." In *the Report on the Revision of the 1978 Constitution of the People's Republic of China*, Peng Zhen did not give explanations of this revision, but it was cheered by constitutionalists and thought to be a major event that realized the constitutional theory of individuals and state.[26] However, the revision at that moment was more symbolic because the adjustment of these two chapters was mainly based on people's painful memory of the Cultural Revolution, and it is hard to say whether there would be this adjustment or not without the Cultural Revolution. The revision of the Constitution in 1982 might be only minor amendments to the 1954

[23]Pan [22].

[24]Mo [23].

[25]We take three papers of three scholars, respectively, representing each of the three generations as examples, Wu [24], Yin [25], and Zhang [26].

[26]Deng [27].

Constitution. Taking the Constitution of the USA as an example, the Bill of Rights was not yet available at the time of formulating the constitution, but the legislative technology of including prohibitive regulations in the Constitution still left enough space for Americans to add contents about rights. The adjustment of chapter arrangement of the 1982 Constitution simply highlighted the symbol and declaration, but it still satisfied people's expectations for rights and heralded the realization of citizens' rights.

Civil rights were realized on the basis of the understanding of human rights by the Party and the central government. A review of the legislative process of the National People's Congress and its Standing Committee in the past three decades indicates that the legislations in 1980s were to serve the building and improvement of the market-oriented economy but rarely for civil rights. Even if there were legislations about civil rights, they were aimed at restricting civil rights in most cases. The most typical example in this aspect was *the Law on Assemblies, Processions, and Demonstrations*. Assemblies, processions, and demonstrations should be part and parcel of the political rights of citizens, but they were stipulated with extremely strict conditions in *the Law on Assemblies, Processions, and Demonstrations* adopted at the Sixth Session of the Seventh Standing Committee of the National People's Congress on October 31, 1989. Thereby, assemblies, processions, and demonstrations became unrealizable rights.

The State Council released the first white paper on human rights, *Human Rights in China* in 1991. Since then, studies on human rights had become popular, but the gate of ideology had not yet been opened, as it is still unclear about the nature, meaning, and realization of human rights. As a term with rich imagines, human rights had been constantly intertwined with civil rights and had taken root and developed in China. Finally, human rights witnessed revolutionary changes in 2004. In the 2004 Amendment to the Constitution, "the state respects and safeguards human rights" was written into the Constitution. Later, scholars "excessively" explained this stipulation and compared it with the clauses about human dignity of *the Basic Law for the Federal Republic of Germany*. That said, incorporating human rights in the Constitution indeed updated the ruling concept of the Party.

After incorporating human rights in the Constitution, China has gained momentum in protecting human rights. There have also been heated discussions about the structure of human rights institutions. For instance, a full realization of citizens' rights has been taken into consideration at the state level. The implementation and evaluation of *the National Human Rights Action Plan of China* represent the most substantive example under this framework. In April 2009, the State Council Information Office of the People's Republic of China released *the National Human Rights Action Plan of China (2009–2010)*. Its introduction stated, "*The National Human Rights Action Plan of China (2009–2010)* is a document explaining the policy of the Chinese government with regard to the promotion and protection of human rights during the period 2009–2010, covering political, economic, social and cultural and other fields." Governments and government departments at all levels were required to make the action plan part of their responsibilities, and proactively implement it in line with the principle of "each performing its own functions and sharing out the work and responsibilities." All enterprises, public institutions, social and non-governmental organizations, press and media agencies, and the ordinary people were required to give vigorous publicity to this action plan, and expedite its implementation. Initiated by the State Council Information Office and the Ministry of Foreign Affairs, the "joint meeting mechanism for the National Human Rights Action Plan," comprising legislative and judicial organs and departments under the State Council, was responsible for coordinating the implementation, supervision, and assessment of the plan. In July 2011, State Council Information Office issued *the Assessment Report on the National Human Rights Action Plan of China (2009–2010)*, which earnestly summarized and recapped the work of the previous stage. On this basis, in June 2012, the State Council Information Office issued *the National Human Rights Action Plan of China (2012–2015)* as the guideline for future works related to human rights. It can be said that China will advance significantly in human rights through the national plan and regular evaluation mechanism.

While making headway in human rights, administrative organs have felt more and more restricted in power. Well, it is not easy to enact a law restricting public powers. The enactment of every law would involve the game of various interests. Following *the Law of Administrative Procedure* issued in 1989, *the State Compensation Law* gave a full explanation of this question. The first draft of *the State Compensation Law* was accomplished in April 1991. The Administrative Law Research Group submitted the draft to the Legislative Affairs Commission of the Standing Committee of the NPC. After the revision and further solicitation of opinions by the Legislative Affairs Commission, *the State Compensation Law* was drafted. On May 12, 1994, *the State Compensation Law* was adopted at the Seventh Session of the Eighth Standing Committee of the NPC. That said, since the enforcement of *the State Compensation Law* 14 years ago, only 680 million yuan has been delivered for national compensation. The cases compensated only accounted for one third of the total cases applying for state compensation. When it comes to the "Virgin Prostitute Case" involving a rural maiden Ma Dandan in Jingyang County of Shaanxi, the victim only got 74.66 yuan as the compensation for the two-day illegal restriction of personal freedom, altogether 9135 yuan plus the compensation for medical expenses, transportation costs, lodging fees, and 180-day costs for lost labor from the Public Security Bureau of Jingyang County.[27] This law was completely revised 15 years later in 2010. The issuance of *Law of the People's Republic of China on Administrative Penalty, the Administrative Reconsideration Law, the Administrative License Law, the Public Security Administration Punishments Law,* and *the Administrative Compulsion Law* has also intensified the restrictions of administrative authorities, and law-based administration has become the basic principle for building law-based government. Administrative regulations, such as *the Regulations on Disclosure of Government*

---

[27]Wang [28].

Information, the Regulation on the Implementation of the Administrative Reconsideration Law, the Regulation on the Expropriation of Buildings on State-owned Land and Compensation, the Regulation on Detention Facilities, and *the Regulation on the Administration of the Institutional Affairs of Government* released by the State Council also greatly narrowed the space for arbitrary administration of administrative organs. While seeing the accomplishments, there are still many issues pending for solutions, such as issues related to reeducation through labor, prison management, and disclosure of the three public expenditures, which all have a bearing on citizens' fundamental rights. Yet, there are still many difficulties ahead in reforms.

(2) **From emphasizing political function to highlighting public service function**

The stipulation of the Constitution for duties of state organs became a reality through the functions of the state. State is the product of the irreconcilable class contradictions and the tool for class ruling, which is the essential attribute of the state. However, class contradiction, class struggle, and class ruling are not all that need to be faced by the state. As a force overriding the society, apart from handling class contradictions, the state needs to deal with many social affairs to ease social conflicts and maintain the conflicts within the scope of order.[28] That is to say the political and social natures of the state are reflected by political function and public service function of the state. Looking at the state's handling of its relations with citizens over the past three decades from the perspective of the functions of the state, the state went through the transformation from focusing on political function to highlighting public service function. The following part explains this by the comprehensive management of social order.

The comprehensive management of social order is a new national governance plan put forward following the "mobilized governance" during the Cultural Revolution. The comprehensive management of social order refers to a systematic project that all related departments, under the leadership of party committees and governments of all levels, give full play to their functional roles and work together with the involvement and support of the broad masses to prevent and crack down on illegal criminal activities, improve the public security and social order, defuse social conflicts and disputes, maintain social stability, and promote social harmony through multiple means, such as political, economic, administrative, legal, cultural, and educational means.[29] In late 1970s, with the termination of the Cultural Revolution and the recovery of the political power, there was a period of power vacuum with rampant criminal activities and serious juvenile delinquencies. Given this, in August 1979, the Central Committee of the CPC forwarded a notice of eight units including the Propaganda Department of the Central Committee of the CPC, about *the Report on Calling the Entire Party to Pay Attention to Solving Juvenile Delinquency*. The report gave expression to the basic idea of the comprehensive

[28]Liang [29].

[29]Hua [30].

management of social order. Following that, on June 14, 1981, the Central Committee of the CPC approved and forwarded the minutes of the public security symposium held by the Political and Legislative Affairs Committee, CCCPC, with the participation of five large cities, namely Beijing, Tianjin, Shanghai, Guangzhou, and Wuhan. The instructions of the Central Committee of the CPC on strengthening political and legal works on January 13, 1982, the minutes of the national working meeting of politics and law forwarded by the Central Committee of the NPC in 1982, among other documents clearly raised the scientific concept of comprehensive management of social order and preliminarily established the mode of the comprehensive management of social order.

As part of the comprehensive management of social order, the policy of "severe cracking down on criminal activities" was gradually popularized. From November 22 to 26, 1979, Peng Zhen (Secretary of the newly established Political and Legislative Affairs Committee in January 1980), member of the Political Bureau of the CPC Central Committee, chaired a national urban public security meeting. At the meeting, Peng Zhen firstly pointed out to severely crack down on a very few crimes such as murder, robbery, rape, arson, bombing, and other cases seriously disrupting the social order (six kinds of cases) as soon as possible in accordance with the law so as to realize the idea of comprehensive management of social order. On January 23, 1980, after listening to the reports of heads of public security organs, procuratorial organs and people's courts of Shanghai on the public security of Shanghai, Peng Zhen said that, currently, active criminals should be punished seriously as soon as possible rather than leniently and slowly. This was Peng Zhen's first proposal of cracking down on criminal offenses severely as soon as possible. On February 12, 1980, the Thirteenth Session of the Fifth Standing Committee of the National People's Congress approved: the Supreme People's Court may authorize high people's courts of provinces, autonomous regions, and municipalities directly under the central government to examine and approve the cases pertaining to death sentence for serious crimes, such as murder, rape, robbery, and arson, committed in 1980. This decision became the start of the devolution of judicial review power for death penalty cases. *The Decision of the Standing Committee of the National People's Congress Regarding Approval of Cases Involving the Death Sentence* adopted in 1981, *the Organic Law of the People's Courts* revised in 1983, and *the Notice of the Supreme People's Court on Authorizing Higher People's Courts to Approve Some Death Penalty Cases* delegated to higher people's courts the power of examining and approving death sentence in cases seriously disrupting and threatening the public security and social order, such as murder, rape, robbery, and bombing. On August 25, 1983, the Central Committee of the CPC issued *the Decision on Severely Cracking Down on Criminal Activities*, proposing to launch three campaigns lasting 3 years. On September 2, 1983, the Standing Committee of the NPC adopted *the Decision Regarding the Severe Punishment of Criminals Who Seriously Endanger Public Security* and *the Decision of the Standing Committee of the NPC Regarding the Procedure for Prompt Adjudication of Cases Involving Criminals Who Seriously*

Endanger Public Security. As such, the policy of severe crackdown on crimes formally took shape.[30]

The policy of severe crackdown on criminal activities focused on cracking down on crimes but overlooked the rights of criminal defendants, such as their right to defense and procedural right. It could rein in crimes in a short run, but it easily got into a strange cycle, namely occurrence, detection, and arrest; many cases, much detection, and many arrests; more cases, much more detection, and more arrests. In short, there were more cases even after detection.[31] In line with the hands-on experience in severe crackdown on crimes and comprehensive management of social order nationwide, on February 19, 1991, the Central Committee of the CPC and the State Council issued *the Decision Concerning Strengthening Comprehensive Management of Social Order*. On March 2 of the same year, the Eighteenth Session of the Seventh Standing Committee of the NPC adopted *the Decision Concerning Strengthening Comprehensive Management of Social Order*. These two decisions established the basic framework for our country's comprehensive management of social order and represented the programmatic documents in this field. On March 21, the Central Committee of the CPC decided to set up the Central Committee for Comprehensive Management of Public Security (CCCMPS for short) as a permanent body for assisting the Central Committee of the CPC and the State Council of the People's Republic of China to lead the comprehensive management of social order nationwide. Under the CCCMPS, the Office of the Central Committee for Comprehensive Management of Public Security was established as its working body and works in one office with organs of the Political and Legislative Affairs Committee.

During the operation of the mode of comprehensive management of social order, issues became increasingly salient. For example, governance subjects were unclear; responsibilities of institutions were duplicated; there was too much reliance on policies; rights were poorly protected; social conflicts became increasingly protruding; crimes became complex and diversified. With the comprehensive revision of *the Criminal Procedure Law* and *the Criminal Law,* respectively, in 1996 and 1997, this mode had undergone changes in itself. In 2001, the Central Committee of the CPC and the State Council issued *the Decision on Further Strengthening Comprehensive Management of Public Order*, stating that "combining crackdown and prevention and putting prevention first" came as the best guiding principle for comprehensive management of social order. That was to promote crackdown and prevention simultaneously, give consideration to both the symptoms and the root cause, and put the emphasis on prevention and resolving the root cause. In 2004, the Fourth Plenary Session of the 16th Central Committee of the CPC adopted *the Decision of the Central Committee of the CPC on Strengthening the Building of Party's Ruling Capacity*. The decision proposed the new policy of "combining crackdown and prevention, putting prevention first, combining the efforts of both

[30]He [31].

[31]Jiang [32].

professionals and the masses of the people and depending on the masses" and further made clear the importance of relying on the broad masses to do a good job in grassroots security and carry out the comprehensive management of social order in a deep-going way. In 2006, the Sixth Plenary Session of the 16th Central Committee of the CPC added the content of "implementing the criminal justice policy combining punishment with leniency" to the comprehensive management of social order from the height of building a harmonious society in *the Decision of the CPC Central Committee on Major Issues Regarding the Building of a Socialist Harmonious Society*. This indicated major changes in governance policy. From the proposal of the value idea of a harmonious society by the Party, the social building idea has also developed constantly. In 2011, the CPC Central Committee and the State Council released *the Opinions on Strengthening and Innovating Social Management* (Zhong.Fa. [2011] No. 11) and proposed the fundamental policy for strengthening and innovating social management featuring "Party committee leadership, government execution, social coordination, and public participation." Correspondingly, on August 21, 2011, the General Office of the CPC Central Committee and the General Office of the State Council printed and distributed the notice on changing the name of the Central Committee for Comprehensive Management of Public Security into the Central Public Security Comprehensive Management Commission, adjusted the functions of the Central Public Security Comprehensive Management Commission, enriched the leadership, increased the member units, and strengthened the working body. From "public security" to "management," it is not just the change of one term. Professor Wang Yukai noted that the change of the name signified the transformation of functions from simply public security management and cracking down on crimes to today's comprehensive social governance. After the change of the name, the meaning has been enriched and the working scope has been enlarged. In addition, there have been more emphases on social management. This has reflected that the CPC Central Committee has attached more importance to social management.[32]

The changes in the comprehensive governance policy and the setting of CCCMPS have mirrored the shift of focus of functions and powers of the state. This policy was proposed for cracking down on crimes. As the leading organ, the CCCMPS has been targeting at the positioning of cracking down on crimes and maintaining social stability. Along with the update of the ruling idea of the Party, strengthening social construction has become more important and the government function of providing public services has become increasingly prominent. Therefore, the model of government comprehensive management of social order has been transformed from control to service,[33] which has complied with the historical development of the stipulation that "the state respects and safeguards human rights." During this transformation period, *the Criminal Procedure Law* was revised substantially in March 2012, which also complied with this process. Next, greater

[32]Sun [33].

[33]Wang [34].

efforts will be made to relieve criminal victims to enrich the social management innovation and manifest the service functions of state organs.

5 State Organs and Social Organizations Dimension

(1) **From restriction to self-discipline**

Social organizations are also called private organizations. According to the classification system in China, organizations have three types of subjects, namely social groups, private non-public organizations, and foundations. Firstly, the emergence and development of a social organization is closely related to the implementation of citizens' freedom of association as stipulated in the Constitution. Secondly, it is closely linked to the attitude of the state to social issues and how loose social policies are. Over the past 30 years, with the growth of citizens' awareness of civil rights, the vigorous promotion of civil society building, and the state's emphasis on social construction, social organizations have seen a greater development process and these changes happened in their interactions with state organs.

The 1982 Constitution stipulates citizens' freedom of association. But in the entire 1980s, the freedom of association was not exercised. According to the number of papers published on the network of China National Knowledge Infrastructure, few are about the freedom of association, and the focus of the papers was not on the freedom of association but on the restriction of the freedom of association.[34] A paper of Professor Wang Xiangming profoundly revealed this tendency and listed various reasons for the restriction. Even now, they are still cited as reasons for restricting the freedom of association. Moreover, the paper presented a group of data. According to incomplete statistics, by April 1989, the number of lawful social groups registered and confirmed by competent authorities reached nearly 1000; but there were more unregistered but still active ones.[35] Subsequent data indicate that, as of the end of 1989, the number of national social groups had grown to 1600, and the number of local social groups had even reached more than 200,000.[36] Analyzing from the social environment back then, the legally registered social groups were in a small number, and illegal social groups were the objects of crackdown, clearly indicating how vigorous the restriction effort was back then.

Just as laying the legislative stress on the economy by the National People's Congress and its Standing Committee during this period, social legislation was only proposed in late 1980s. Only by 1988, the labor law was prioritized in legislative work. Also during the same period, the State Council formulated two administrative

---

[34]After searching on the network of China National Knowledge Infrastructure, we found that there were only two papers studying the freedom of association in 1980s. These two papers were, respectively, Wu [35] and Wang [36].

[35]Wang [36].

[36]Bi [37].

regulations supporting the legal framework for social organizations. The two regulations were *the Regulations for the Management of Foundations* and *the Regulation on Registration and Administration of Social Organizations* which were, respectively, issued in September 1988 and October 1989. In late 1950s, China's Government Administration Council and Ministry of the Interior enacted *the Tentative Measures on Registration of Social Organizations* and *Rules for the Implementation of the Tentative Measures on Registration of Social Organizations*. But, they were not revised until late 1980s. The revision laid a preliminary foundation for the "dual management system" for Chinese social organizations. That was to firstly get the approval of competent business units and then register with corresponding civil affairs department. In early 1990s, along with the institutional reform of units, some originally state-run public institutions began to become private or social-run. As such, "non-governmental public units" different from "social groups" began to emerge on the horizon beyond the government and the market mechanism. In 1996, the General Office of the CPC Central Committee and the General Office of the State Council released *the Notice Concerning Further Strengthening the Management of Social Groups and People-Run Non-Enterprise Units*, officially calling social organizations as "people-run non-enterprise units" paralleling them with "social groups." In October 1998, the State Council promulgated *the Interim Regulations on Registration and Administration of Private Non-enterprise Unit* and revised *the Regulation on Registration and Administration of Social Organizations*. The registration and management organ and business management unit dually management system were further defined and stressed. Their respective responsibilities were stipulated. The previous reporting system was changed to the registration system for branches and representative organizations. At the same time, the registration conditions and procedures and regulatory punishment measures for social organizations were further improved. At that moment, the dual management system had been reinforced. Besides, the government also irregularly cleaned up and overhauled social organizations nationally. Since the founding of the People's Republic of China, the government carried out three overhauls targeting social organizations respectively started in 1951, 1990, and 1997. These three large-scale overhaul campaigns were closely related to the three important regulations promulgated by the government for the management of social organizations. A case in point is that, from April 1997 to December 2000, Chinese social groups witnessed the third large-scale overhauls. After that, the total number of social groups nationwide was reduced to 136,000 from 200,000, 47,000 of which were canceled, and 12,000 were liquidated. The number of national social groups was decreased from 1849 to above 1500. In 1999, the State Council promulgated *The Interim Provisions on the Formation of Special Fund Management Institutions by Social Groups* and *The Opinions on the Review and Registration of Private Non-enterprise Units*, among other regulations and administrative provisions in order to coordinate the social overhaul work.[37]

---

[37]Qiu [38].

Entering the new century, the Central Committee gradually relaxed the restriction on social organizations with the changes of both international and domestic social environments. In October 2006, the Sixth Plenary Session of the 16th Central Committee of the CPC proposed to give play to the role of various kinds of private organizations in providing services, reflecting appeals, and regulating behaviors and guide private organizations of various kinds to strengthen self-construction and improve self-discipline and integrity. In May 2007, the General Office of the State Council promulgated *Several Opinions on Accelerating the Reform and Development of Industry Associations and Chambers of Commerce*, making directional stipulations for how to actively widen the functions of industry associations. At the same time, the document required industry associations to carry out activities independently in strict accordance with laws, regulations, and rules, and practically address the serious administrative tendency and dependence on the government. The document also clearly required that those presently serving as public servants should not assume a part-time leading position in industry associations and proposed the establishment of the system for governments to purchase the services of industry associations. In addition, the document contained clear stipulations on the supervisory mechanism and self-construction of industry associations and related supporting policy measures. In the meantime, in response to the new development trend of social organizations, the revision of *the Regulation on Registration and Administration of Social Organizations* was also on the agenda. As of the end of 2009, the number of legally registered social organizations nationwide stood at 431,000, of which 238,700 were social groups, 190,400 were private non-enterprise units, and 1843 were foundations. Beyond that, there were more than 40,000 rural professional economic associations and over 200,000 urban community-based social organizations that had records with civil affairs departments at all levels. From 1988 to 2009, the number of Chinese social organizations skyrocketed by nearly 100-fold (China was home to only 4446 social groups in 1988), representing an annual increase rate of around 10% in the decade.[38] According to the spirit of official revision, the most distinct aspects include strengthening the organization and management of social organizations and making social organizations develop toward self-discipline and self-management, highlighting the importance of the bylaw of social organizations and making them conduct activities according to their bylaws. In case of the occurrence of any dispute within a social organization, the direction is to guide the social organizations to develop dispute settlement procedures, such as having discussions through member meetings and council meetings, instead of the compulsory settlement by the government by administrative means. The rights and duties of members meeting, council and secretary general should be distinguished, and the democratic procedures for internal discussions should be developed. In brief, the newly revised *Regulation* was to make clear the legal person governance structure of social

[38]Sun [39].

organizations and make social organizations become self-disciplined and independently managed organizations.[39]

Currently, the three main obstacles to the development of social organizations are as follows. First, it is the dual management system for social organizations. Some local areas, such as Shenzhen and Beijing, have already launched the reform, but it will take some time to realize nationwide abolition of this kind of system. Second, it is the organization structure of social organizations. The organization structure of social organizations has a bearing on the depth of self-discipline and continuous development of their industries. Third, it is how to solve issues related to "grassroots organizations" that are unable to meet the essential conditions for registration. At the moment, these organizations are in large number and play a big role at the grassroots level. In a long run, it is quite necessary to absorb them to become a subject of social management.

(2) **From one-way management to interdependence**

This change in the relationship between state organs and social organizations has something to do with the transformation of government functions. As government functions are gradually transferred from economic management to public service, governments would gradually exit from some fields while some qualified social organizations have the ability to manage work in these fields. Therefore, governments enable social organizations to enjoy certain management power through authorization and entrustment. Comprehending from the subject perspective of administrative legal relationship, social organizations are turning their role from administrative counterpart to administrative subject.[40] Once social organizations have the rights similar to that of administrative organs, the relationship between state organs and social organizations could no longer be classified as that between managing and being managed. Instead, they are interdependent. In order to showcase this change, the practices of Guangdong province in reforming social organizations are taken as the examples for explanations.

As with other provinces, Guangdong province also experienced a development process from slow increment to fast increment for launching the administration of social organizations. The province started to brew the reform in 2003 toward the target of building a perfect society. The overall thinking of reform was steady and step-by-step advancement starting from the economic field. The breakthrough of reform was local legislation for industry associations. In February 2004, the Second Session of the Tenth People's Congress of Guangdong Province was convened. During the session, more than 20 deputies to Guangdong Provincial People's Congress submitted *the Proposal on Developing the Regulations for Industry Associations of Guangdong Province As Soon As Possible*. This proposal was officially listed as a legislation of Guangdong Provincial People's Congress in the first time. Due to the lack of the basis for higher-level law back then, it took another

---

[39]Wu [40].

[40]Jin [41].

three years to finally promulgate the law from being included in the legislative plan.[41] *The Regulations for Industry Associations of Guangdong Province* represents China's first local regulation on adjusting the legal relations of industry associations with innovation highlights in three aspects. First, it has improved the dual management system as provided in *the Regulation on Registration and Administration of Social Organizations*. Second, it clearly stipulates "separation of politics and society" and "separation of enterprises and society," and stipulates private organizations' enjoyment of the right to initiative right, personnel autonomy, and budget control right in order to maintain the independence of non-governmental organizations. Third, it is the first time to make clear in regulations that the specific functions of industry associations are providing services, reflecting appeals, and regulating behaviors, which has provided the legal basis for industry associations to undertake the functions transferred from governments. In 2006, the CPC Guangdong Provincial Committee and the People's Government of Guangdong Province issued *the Decision on Giving Play to the Role of Industry Associations and Chambers of Commerce* (Yue.Fa. [2006] No. 2). In the same year, the Department of Civil Affairs of Guangdong Province issued *the Opinions on the Implementation of the Decision of CPC Guangdong Provincial Committee and the People's Government of Guangdong Province on Giving Play to the Role of Industry Associations and Chambers of Commerce* (Yue.Min.Min. [2006] No. 50). These two documents further refined the mechanism for governments to interact and cooperate with industry associations and chambers of commerce. For instance, *the Decision on Giving Play to the Role of Industry Associations and Chambers of Commerce* mentioned that governments' relations with industry associations and chambers of commerce are guiding and being guided and supervising and being supervised. Governments need to manage the registration of industry associations and chambers of commerce in accordance with the law and actively support and promote their development. The governments also need to gradually transfer the functions to industry associations and chambers of commerce according to laws and regulations and guarantee their independent activities. The governments need to transform their management of industry associations and chambers of commerce into cultivation and service orientation for providing legal basis and conducting legal supervisions. The governments also need to strengthen the post-supervision over industry associations and chambers of commerce rather than directly intervene in their internal operations. At the same time, the governments need to give play to the role of industry associations and chambers of commerce through establishing the entrustment and authorization mechanism, cooperation and interaction mechanism, consultation mechanism, supervision and guiding mechanism, and appraisal and punishment mechanism. In September 2008, the General Office of CPC Guangdong Provincial Committee and the General Office of the People's Government of Guangdong Province issued *the Opinions on Developing and Regulating the Social Organizations of Our Province* (Yue.Ban.Fa. [2008] No. 13), emphasizing that all

[41]Shen [42].

departments of the government should comprehensively review and decompose their functions and come up with specific plans for transferring functions according to *the Opinions* while mentioning “strengthening the transfer of government functions.” *The Opinions* also emphasized that all departments of the government should make clear the matters concerning function transfer in the stipulations for function disposition, internal organization and staffing, separate government departments' functions that are transferrable and no longer exercised to social organizations. Some social organizations with strong representativeness and standard operation could be selected for the experiment. After gaining some experiences, function transfer could be promoted gradually and steadily.

Guangdong province has led the country in this round of reform that started in 2003 and has made great achievements, such as gradually transferring the 17 government functions of 3 categories to social organizations. Among the social organizations, 15% have undertaken the functions transferred from government departments and 9% have accepted government purchase of services. The annual economic aggregate of the social organizations of Guangdong province has surpassed 50 billion yuan. That said, some aspects are still unsatisfactory. 85% of the social organizations have not yet undertaken the functions transferred from government departments and 91% have not received government offer for purchasing services. The existing challenges for the development of the social organizations of Guangdong province are mainly reflected by the slow process of government function transfer and service purchase and the less motivated vigor of social organizations; few supporting measures and more restrictions are also affecting the development of social organizations; unsmooth channels for social organizations to participate in the administration and discussion of state affairs; the imperfect social counseling mechanism; unbalanced development level of social organizations; inadequate strength of registration and management organs, which is unmatched with the development of social organizations, and so on and so forth.[42]

Since the CPC Central Committee and the State Council issued *the Opinions on Strengthening and Innovating Social Management* (Zhong.Fa. [2011] No. 11) in 2011, Guangdong province has speeded up the pace in social organization management. In July 2011, CPC Guangdong Provincial Committee and Guangdong Provincial Government issued *the Decisions on Strengthening Social Construction* (Yue.Fa. [2011] No. 17), representing the prelude to the province's social construction. In September of the same year, the General Office of CPC Guangdong Provincial Committee and the General Office of the People's Government of Guangdong Province printed and distributed another seven supporting documents, namely *the Notice on Printing and Distributing the Seven Documents on Strengthening Social Construction Including the Implementation Opinions for Accelerating the Advancement of Reforming the Social System and Building A Service-oriented Government* (Yue.Ban.Fa. [2011] No. 22). Among which, *the Implementation Opinions for Strengthening the Management of Social Organizations* further defined

[42]Deng [43].

the targets of the next stage of reform.[43] In April 2012, *the Plan on Further Cultivating, Developing, Regulating and Managing Social Organizations* (Yue.Fa. [2012] No. 7) was printed and distributed. *The Interim Measures for Government Purchase of Services from Social Organizations* (Yue.Fu.Ban. [2012] No. 48) was printed and distributed in May. *The Guiding Opinions for Determining the Directory of Social Organizations Qualified for Undertaking the Functions Transferred by Governments and Government Purchase of Services* (Yue.Min.Min. [2012] No. 135) was printed and distributed in June. Thereby, all supporting measures for social organizations to undertake the functions transferred by the government had been accomplished. With the changes of the dual management system, the optimization of the structure of social organizations, and the crystallization of government purchase of social organizations' services, the interdependent relationship between social organizations and state organs will also continue to develop.

6 Conclusion

Back to the text of the Constitution, we found the core element of China's constitutional law— state organs, and demonstrated the significance of state organs as the core of constitutional law. Through presenting the four dimensions of state organs, we had a review of China's social reforms and concluded that none of the reforms was accomplished in an action. Instead, each reform was an incremental change. While analyzing the four dimensions, we discovered that they are not separated but interdependent and mutually affected. That is to say social changes are the result of the synergy of all elements composing the society. If a single element could have a benign interaction with other elements, social changes would be relatively smooth. In social changes, it is easy to have external reform, but it is very difficult to realize internal reform. Internal reform could follow the principle of "step by step." The most typical example in this aspect is the restriction of powers of administrative organs over the past 30 years. Today, the importance of social reform and political reform has become increasingly evident, but blind advancement would not end up beneficially. A feasible train of thought is to make clear the sequencing of reforms, figure out the key elements of each reform, and steadily press ahead with all reforms so as to see the happening of true changes.

References

1. Xu Chongde: *On the Core of Studies on Constitutional Law*, published in *Journal of Political Science and Law*, 1987, Issue 3.

[43]Li [44].

2. Zhang Guangbo: *Recognition of the Basic Categories of Constitutional Law*, published in *Chinese Journal of Law*, 1987, Issue 3.
3. Han Dayuan: *Records of the Science of Law of the People's Republic of China over the Past Sixty Years*, Xiamen University Press, 2009 edition, page 74.
4. Xu Chongde: *Implement the New Constitution and Strengthen the Building of State Organs – Marking the First Anniversary of the Promulgation of the New Constitution*, published in *China Legal Science*, 1984, Issue 1.
5. Lin Laifan: *From Constitutional to Normative Constitution-A Preface of Normative Constitutional Law*, China Law Press, 2001 edition, page 11.
6. Cai Dingjian: *20-year Development and Historical Transition of NPC Legislation*, published in *Journal of Chinese Academy of Governance*, 2000, Issue 5.
7. Cai Dingjian: *The People's Congress System of China (Fourth Edition)*, China Law Press, 2003 edition, page 83–84.
8. Wu Huaiyou: *Analysis of the Relations between Head Responsibility System and Democratic Centralism*, published in *Theoretical Investigation*, 2005, Issue 5.
9. Zhang Jincai: *Building of Legal System in the New Era*, Chinese Communist Party History Publishing House, 2009 edition, page 253.
10. Wang Guisong: *From Coordination to "Coordination + Restriction" – Analysis of the Development Trend of the Relations among State Organs of China*, published in *Social Sciences in Nanjing*, 2005, Issue 9.
11. Zhang Wei: *The 1.5 Million Cases about Suing Officials by Ordinary People Promoted China's Advancement of Building the Rule of Law – Written at the Time Celebrating the 20th Anniversary of the Promulgation of the Law of Administrative Procedure*, published in *Legal Daily*, September 30, 2010, edition 6.
12. Han Dayuan, Yu Wenhao: *Constitutional Relationship between the People's Courts, the People's Procuratorates and the Public Security Organs*, published in *Chinese Journal of Law*, 2011, Issue 3.
13. Cai Dingjian: *Supervision and Judicial Fairness: Research and Case Report*, China Law Press, 2005 edition.
14. Li Song: *Liaison Offices in Beijing: "Second Administrative Centers of Local State Organs"*, published in *Outlook Weekly*, 2005, Issue 30.
15. Xu Chongde: *Establishment and Changes of Standing Committees of Local People's Congresses*, published in *Tribune of Political Science and Law*, 2004, Issue 6.
16. Xue Gangling: *Review of China's Administrative Subject Theory – Also on the Necessity of Comprehensively Studying the Administrative Organic Law*, published in *Tribune of Political Science and Law*, 1998, Issue 6.
17. Dong Keyong: *Rebuild the Central-Local Relationship and Optimize the Public Governance*, published in *Chinese Public Administration*, 2010, Issue 1.
18. Guo Shu: *On the Function of Judicial Adjustment in the Central-Local Relationship – Taking U.S. Federal Judicial Precedents as the Clue*, published in *Studies in Law and Business*, 2008, Issue 5.
19. Zhao Jujun: *Appropriate Application of Administrative Division Devices and Longitudinal Intergovernmental Relations*, published in *Journal of Zhanjiang Normal College*, 2011, Issue 2.
20. Xia Jun: *The Number and Area of Development Zones Nationwide Have Been Reduced by over Seventy Percent*, published in *People's Daily*, September 18, 2007, Section 6.
21. Hu Honghong, Zhang Lei: *Investigation into the General Situation of the Structuring of People's Congresses of National Development Zones*, published in *People's Congress Studying*, 2012, Issue 4.
22. Pan Xiaoqing: *Studies on the Legal System of Administrative Divisions in China: Problems, Defects and Improvement*, 2007 master's thesis of East China University of Political Science and Law, page 16.

23. Mo Jihong: *The Reshuffling of Administration Areas Should be Set on a Legal Track*, published in *Journal of Beijing Union University* (Humanities and Social Sciences), 2010, Issue 3.
24. Wu Jiaqing: *Positioning of Civil Rights and State Power in Constitutional Law*, published in *Studies in Law and Business*, 1999, Issue 3.
25. Yin Xiaohu: *Evolution of Constitutional-making Concept in Modern China – Taking the Relationship between State Power and Civil Rights as the Object*, published in *Oriental Law*, 2010, Issue 5.
26. Zhang Xiaoqin: *Civil Rights and State Power in the Constitution*, published in *Wuhan University Journal (Philosophy & Social Sciences)*, 2006, Issue 3.
27. Deng Lianfan: *A Study of the Setting of "Chapters" of China's Constitution*, published in *Political Science and Law*, 2009, Issue 12.
28. Wang Yanzhao: *It is Not Easy to Enact a Law Restricting Public Powers – from the Rudiment to Legislation of the State Compensation System*, published in *Procuratorate Daily*, September 3, 2009, Section 4.
29. Liang Zhoumin: *On State Functions and Function Changes*, published in *Academic Journal of Zhongzhou*, 2008, Issue 1.
30. Hua Naiqiang: *Investigation into the Source of the Concept of Comprehensive Management of Social Order*, published in *Journal of Zhejiang Police College*, 2009, Issue 3.
31. He Libo: *1983: Whole Story about the Party Central Committee's Decision on Cracking Down on Crimes*, published in *Prosecutorial View*, 2008, Issue 17.
32. Jiang Pusheng: *Review and Thinking of the Strike-hard Campaign*, published in *Policing Studies*, 2003, Issue 7.
33. Sun Yanmin: *From Public Security to Governance: Changes more than Terms*, published in *Procuratorate Daily*, September 27, 2011, Section 5.
34. Wang Yan: *Model Transformation and Element Integration of Comprehensive Management of Social Order*, published in *Journal of Jiangsu Police Institute*, 2009, Issue 2.
35. Wu Daying: *On Freedom of Assembly and Freedom of Association*, published in *Gui Zhou Social Sciences*, 1981, Issue 5.
36. Wang Xiangming: *Look at Issues Concerning China's Social Groups from the Illegal Organization - "Beijing Federation of University Societies" – Also on the Guarantee and Restriction of Freedom of Association*, published in *China Electric Power Education*, 1989, Issue 9.
37. Bi Jianwu: *Revolution of Social Organizations: Economic Analysis of the Development of Social Organizations in China*, Shandong People's Publishing House, 2003 edition, page 85–86.
38. Qiu Li: *The Non-profit Organizations in the Perspective of Social Policy*, published in *Dongyue Tribune*, 2007, Issue 3.
39. Sun Weilin: *Promoting the Healthy Development of Social Organizations*, published in *Outlook Weekly*, 2010, Issue 37.
40. Wu Xiaofeng: *The Revision of the Regulation on Registration and Administration of Social Organizations is Underway – Interview with Director Wu Ming of the Legislative Affairs Office of the Ministry of Civil Affairs*, published in *Legal Daily*, August 3, 2008, Section 3.
41. Jin Guokun: *On Mechanical Innovation for Government Administration of Social Organizations – Thinking of Administrative Law Triggered by Private Non-enterprise Units*, published in *Administrative Law Review*, 2011, Issue 1.
42. Shen Xinwang: *Guangdong: Social Construction First*, published in *China Newsweek*, 2012, Issue 17.
43. Deng Xinjian: *De-administration and Deregulation of Social Organizations of Guangdong Province*, published in *Legal Daily*, November 28, 2011, Section 4.
44. Li Qiang: *Formation of the Policy System of Guangdong for Strengthening Social Construction*, published in *Nanfang Daily*, October 14, 2011, Section A04.

The President as the Head of State: Review and Reflections

Ling Ma

Throughout the history of China's state president system, constitutional provisions on state president have witnessed obvious changes. For example, the state president system was deleted from the 1975 Constitution and 1978 Constitution; the provisions on state president of 1982 Constitution are not identical with those of the 1954 Constitution. Yet, the changes in practice are probably more thought-provoking. While reviewing the history of the state president system, we should make the analysis from two aspects, namely the norms and the facts, but not simply limit ourselves to constitutional norms.

1 1954–1959: The President Was in Fact Head of the State with Real Power

During this period, the president was elected according to the stipulation of the 1954 Constitution. The president had the same power as that of heads of other countries, so the president of China at that time should be considered as head of the state.

According to the stipulation of the 1954 Constitution, the president exercised the power to promulgate laws and decrees in pursuance of decisions of the National People's Congress or its Standing Committee. In this connection, it is widely held in the academic circle that the powers of the president existed in name only. However, these powers were not completely nominal in practice. A case in point is that, on April 7, 1955, president Mao Zedong issued *the Order on Termination of the State of War between the People's Republic of China and Germany* pursuant to the decision of the 9th Session of the First Standing Committee of the National

L. Ma (✉)
Department of Law of China Youth, University of Political Studies, Beijing, China
e-mail: 13263169197@163.com

L. Li et al. (eds.), *Constitutional Development in China, 1982–2012*,
Research Series on the Chinese Dream and China's Development Path,
https://doi.org/10.1007/978-981-32-9261-1_10

People's Congress. Two points of the Order (declaring "The termination of the state of war and establishment of peaceful relations between the PRC and Germany" and "The termination of the state of war between the People's Republic of China and Germany does not change Germany's international obligations. At the same time, it does not affect the rights that the People's Republic of China enjoys and the commitments it undertakes under international agreements involving Germany.") were not contained in the decisions of the NPC Standing Committee. The NPC Standing Committee only determined the spirit of principles. Regarding specific norms, the President made the regulations by order, and such norms must be followed and implemented by the State Council in works.[1] The nomination of the Premier by the President was also both a real and virtual power. In real life, this "real" power could be better manifested by the following practices. On April 13, 1955, Zhou Enlai, Premier of the State Council concurrent Foreign Minister, reported to the President of the People's Republic of China that Vice Premier Chen Yun would act as the Premier and Vice Minister Zhang Wentian would act as the Foreign Minister while he was abroad for attending the Asian-African Conference and visiting Indonesia and requested the approval from the President. On the same day, the President of the People's Republic of China approved this report.[2] These specific examples tell us that the so-called "nominal powers" of the President had become "real powers" in the practice that the NPC Standing Committee determined the spirit of principles while the President made specific regulations by order. Such model of power exercise can also be interpreted as the development of constitution in practice. However, whether this practice was unconstitutional should be judged by the National People's Congress. Since constitutional norms were rather in principle, related constitutional laws were not timely enacted in China back then, the supervision authority of the NPC was not exercised, and special review for constitutionality institution had not yet been established, these acts of the President seemed to be well-reasoned, and became rationalized and legalized with virtually no objections.

A careful analysis of the stipulations of the 1954 Constitution for state president would show us that some provisions are not as simple as we understood them. For instance, Article 43 of the 1954 Constitution stated, "The President of the People's Republic of China, whenever necessary, convenes a Supreme State Conference and acts as its president. The Vice President of the People's Republic of China, the Chairman of the Standing Committee of the National People's Congress, the Premier of the State Council and other persons concerned take part in the Supreme State Conference. The President of the People's Republic of China submits the views of the Supreme State Conference on important affairs of the state to the National People's Congress, its Standing Committee, the State Council, or other bodies concerned for their consideration and decision." For these stipulations, some scholars hold the view that the powers of the President as provided in the 1954

---

[1]Chengmei [1], p. 744.

[2]Chongde [2], p. 207.

Constitution were both real and nominal in characteristics and, among the seven powers exercised by the state president, the military power and power to convene Supreme State Conference were most substantive. The provision of the constitution on convening Supreme State Conference was literally unreal, but it is actually real in essential analysis. Mao Zedong used to explain this provision at the meeting of the Committee for the Draft of the Constitution in 1954. First, he noted that the constitution contained no content and scope of discussions of Supreme State Conference. As he said, what to be discussed was not stated, but it should not go against the National People's Congress. Second, he didn't think this power as frequently exercised. As he noted, "whenever necessary" meant that the conference was less-frequent and only convened in emergency. Third, he thought that the Supreme State Conference was only to offer proposals. He said that the conference could give suggestions, but the suggestions didn't have a decisive role and could be either adopted or not, and nothing could be done about it. It seemed that Mao Zedong said so to demonstrate that convening a Supreme State Conference was a nominal rather than real power of the president. Yet, it is not exactly the case. First and foremost, just as Mao Zedong said, what to be discussed was not stated, which precisely illustrates that the constitution gave the President great discretionary power. The President determined what to be discussed as long as it didn't go against the National People's Congress. All "major state affairs" as defined by the President could be taken as a topic of the conference. The Vice President of the People's Republic of China, the Chairman of the Standing Committee of the National People's Congress, the Premier of the State Council and other persons concerned must take part in the Supreme State Conference once it was convened according to the stipulations of the constitution. Besides, the Supreme State Conference didn't make resolutions or decisions, didn't enact normative documents with legal effect, but only proposed opinions that would be submitted to the National People's Congress, the NPC Standing Committee, the State Council or other departments concerned by the President for discussion and decision. But actually, it is a conference chaired by the President for discussing "major state affairs" with the participation of Vice President of the People's Republic of China, the Chairman of the Standing Committee of the National People's Congress, the Premier of the State Council and other persons concerned, so could general opinions be comparable to the proposals raised after discussions at such a high-level state conference? Was there any reason for anyone not to take them seriously? Thus it can be seen that this power was nominal only in form but real in essence. It is extremely authoritative and actually influential.[3]

The author takes this analysis as pertinent. Notably, the nominal in form and real in essence powers of the President were closely related to the characteristics of China's national conditions and also the demonstration of the big role of latent rules in China's political power. Clauses with the same contents might be nominal in other countries, nominal in both form and essence. Articles on the constitution

[3]Chongde [2]. pp. 206–207.

would have certain development and changes and even transformation in constitutional government practice, but they are generally believed to be normal. The question is what the development direction and changing aspects would be. Should they develop towards constitutionalism or towards the opposite direction? This lies in the competitions between democratic forces within a state. The political wisdom of Mao Zedong was his intentional design of the "nominal" President. On the one hand, there would be no "spanking" and the president would not be held accountable. On the other hand, it could prevent state powers from being concentrated in the hands of individuals legally, which conformed to the democratic principles and the president would certainly not be condemned or attacked for such bad reputations as "individual monopoly of powers" and "dictatorship".[4] This intentionally designed state president indicates that Mao Zedong was shrewd, tactful and sophisticated as a politician. The President's powers were nominal in articles on the constitution, but the designer was very confident that these powers would be nominal in form but real in essence and believed that realistic political power environment would definitely make these powers real, which was exactly expected by the designer. The President could use his intelligence and influence to control the overall situation by virtue of the Constitution and in the form of the Supreme State Conference. We can sense the clear thinking capacity of Mao Zedong and the great originality of China's state president system.[5] The author believes that Article 43 is the core yet the fatal weakness of the 1954 Constitution. Among all articles of the constitution, if one (or a few) article(s) is (are) the key point, then hitting this point would make the whole constitution unworkable. We have to say that this is a profound inspiration of the 1954 Constitution to us. It warns us that, in a country without a perfect democratic legal system, the drafter of the constitution might leave a "fatal weakness" to the constitution, and the activation of this key point could put the entire country into a constitutionalism crisis. For instance, the "anti-rightist" movement in 1957 had a direct connection with the Supreme State Conference. On October 13, 1957, Mao Zedong delivered a speech titled "Have Firm Faith in the Majority of the People" at the Supreme State Conference, "The Rightists are a hostile force because they oppose the Communist Party, the people and socialism." Mao Zedong made the judgment that 10% of the people endorsed or opposed socialism, 2% of whom were diehards who firmly opposed socialism. What's 10% of the 600 million people? It is 60 million. What's 2% of the total population? It is 12 million.[6] What happened proves that these remarks of the President at the Supreme State Conference were effectively followed by state organs. The anti-rightist movement was a nationwide political crisis in essence. The occurrence of this crisis had profound historical, cultural, and social reasons. The power of the President to convene Supreme State Conference provided

---

[4]Chongde [2]. p. 25.

[5]Chongde [2], p. 208.

[6]*Selected Works of Mao Zedong* (Volume V), People's Publishing House, 1977 edition, page 491, 486, 482 and 483.

a legal form of external realization of the crisis and indicated that highly concentrated and unrestricted power would lead to constitutional government crisis sooner or later.[7] In practice, the participants of the Supreme State Conference were not limited to Vice President of the People's Republic of China, the Chairman of the Standing Committee of the National People's Congress, the Premier of the State Council and other persons concerned, but also including dozens of others. The form of "enlarged conference" of the Supreme State Conference was invented, enabling the number of attendees to reach more than one thousand.[8] The clause about the Supreme State Conference was actually at a frozen state with the absence of the President of the state in 1966. The Supreme State Conference was not stipulated in the 1982 Constitution, meaning its formal cancel in the Constitution.

During this period, one person (Mao Zedong) concurrently served as the Chairman of the Party, the President of the state and the Chairman of Central Military Commission. The "trinity" of the Party, the government and the army is generally believed to be and actually is the guarantee and symbol of political stability and social stability and unity. The drawbacks of this system are not exactly the over-concentration of powers but the lack of effective restriction on this concentration of powers. The National People's Congress and its Standing Committee as the supreme organ of power actually have no decision-making power endowed by the Constitution and the right of supervision as stipulated by the Constitution. The supreme organ of power has become virtually symbolic (real in form and

[7]From Mao Zedong's practice of being the President of the People's Republic of China for 5 years, he exercised the constitutional functions and powers and convened 16 sessions of Supreme State Conference, involving major affairs of national life. The most widely known example was the work policy proposed by Mao Zedong for the elimination of counter-revolutionaries at a Supreme State Conference held on May 12, 1955. The policy was to be vigilant and to eliminate all secret agents; prevent deviations and avoid wronging innocent people. This policy played a guiding role in launching a nationwide political campaign to eliminate counter-revolutionaries. Mao Zedong chaired a Supreme State Conference held on January 25, 1956. The conference discussed the *Draft of the National Program of Agriculture Developmentfrom 1956–1959*, which was accepted by the National People's Congress later on and became the charter of our country's agricultural work. At a Supreme State Conference held on May 2, 1956, Mao Zedong raised to "let a hundred flowers bloom; let a hundred schools of thought contend", which became the guiding principle for China's development of scientific technologies and booming of literature and art. Xue Chongde: *Constitutional History of the People's Republic of China* (Volume I), Fujian People's Publishing House, 2005 edition, page 207. Altogether 16 sessions of the Supreme State Conference were held in 5 years, meaning 3 times a year on average, far more than the convocation of the annual NPC. This was not identical with Mao Zedong's explanation that the Supreme State Conference was rarely convened and only convened for discussing major emergencies while formulating the 1954 Constitution. Major emergencies occurred so frequently, making the Supreme State Conference rather than the National People's Congress actually become the supreme organ of state power.

[8]There were 37 participants at a Supreme State Conference held on February 26, 1957. At the enlarged Supreme State Conference held between February 27 and March 1, 1957, the number of attendees reached more than 1800 representing all sectors (at this conference, Mao Zedong made the well-known report titled *On the Correct Handling of Contradictions among the People*). Xianzhi and Chongzhi [3], pp. 620–621.

nominal in essence). We have to say that this is one of the institutional causes for such major constitutional government crises as the Cultural Revolution which occurred later.

2 1959–1966: The "Dual-Head System" Contains Political Crisis

Looking from the constitutional norms during this period, articles on the constitution about President of the state remained unchanged in content. During this period, President of the state still had the real power. For instance, with regard to the power of absolution, the constitution stipulated that the President released a special amnesty based on the decision of the Standing Committee of the National People's Congress. The decision-making power for releasing a special amnesty was in the hand of the NPC Standing Committee while the President of the state just released the amnesty. It seemed that President of the state played a nominal role, but it is not true. On November 19, 1960, the 32nd Session of the Second Standing Committee of the National People's Congress adopted the decision on granting special amnesty to war criminals of the Chiang Kai-shek Clique and the Puppet Manchukoku if they thoroughly reformed themselves. According to this decision, Liu Shaoqi who was the President of the People's Republic of China issued *the Order on Special Amnesty* as follows. First, war criminals of the Chiang Kai-shek Clique and the Puppet Manchukoku could be released if they had been detained for 10 years and indeed turned over a new leaf. Second, for war criminals of the Chiang Kai-shek Clique and the Puppet Manchukoku who were sentenced to death with a two-year reprieve and had turned over a new leaf after one year of the suspension of execution, the death penalty could be changed to life imprisonment or the imprisonment of above 15 years; the life imprisonment… could be changed to more than ten years. This Order was executed by the Supreme People's Court and higher people's courts. This clearly indicates that the President could create new and concrete norms while releasing an order in the principle spirit of the decisions of the NPC Standing Committee. The legal effect of orders of the President was high. For instance, the specific contents of *the Order on Special Amnesty* must be followed and executed by the Supreme People's Court and higher people's courts.[9] Here, it is

[9]Chengmei [1], 743. *The Decision of the Standing Committee of the National People's Congress on Granting Special Amnesty to War Criminals of the Chiang Kai-shek Clique and the Puppet Manchukoku* issued on November 19, 1960, stated that the 32nd Session of the Second Standing Committee of the National People's Congress discussed the suggestions of the State Council for granting special amnesty to truly reformed war criminals of the Chiang Kai-shek Clique and the Puppet Manchukoku and decided to grant special amnesty to war criminals of the Chiang Kai-shek Clique and the Puppet Manchukoku after a certain period of reform.

difficult to explain the President's power to release an order on special amnesty for the Supreme People's Court and higher people's courts to follow by using the term of nominal power.

The changes during this period were mainly manifested in practice—the Party and political system of the state was the "dual-head system", i.e. the President of the state and the Chairman of the Party were served by different persons. This phenomenon could be interpreted as the sign of "separating the functions of the Party from those of the government". In countries with a developed democracy and legal system or with an improving democracy and legal system, the "dual-head system" might facilitate the political system to become more democratic. For example, Mao Zedong as the Chairman of the Party and Liu Shaoqi as the President of the state could take charge of different affairs respectively, which broke the power structure of a high degree of integration of the Party and government. In a society lacking the tradition of democracy and legal system, the "dual-head system" would only aggravate power conflicts, trigger fierce power struggles and cause political instability. The causes for the Cultural Revolution were multiple and complicated. Was the "dual-head system" the political trigger of the Cultural Revolution?[10] In countries like China with the tradition of "creating a job in order to accommodate a person", this is an essential change.[11] In some sense, the position of the President

[10]During the period implementing the "dual-head system", Mao Zedong's status indeed declined. When Mao Zedong appeared at a Party meeting, the audience habitually rewarded his speech with warm applause (according to official records), but most leaders of the Party turned a deaf ear to what he said. He was honored as the revolutionary leader, but he could no longer determine the direction of the new society. He was no longer at the center of the political power, and his position as the Chairman of the Party was nominal. Mao Zedong used to complain that Deng Xiaoping who was the General Secretary in charge of Party affairs management didn't come to him at all from 1959 and 1966. [U.S.] Maurice Meisner: *Mao's China and After*, translated by Du Pu et al., Sichuan People's Publishing House, 1989 edition, page 337–338, 339 and 341. By 1960 s, Mao Zedong had found it difficult to be included in the middle-level leadership that seemed to be in the hand of Liu Shaoqi and the Party. In addition, his words could rarely be heard by the masses of the people. Mao Zedong even admitted that he made "a serious mistake" and this "Great Leap Forward" experiment was "too costly". However, no matter whether the masses of the people knew his self-criticism, the criticisms of him were growing and increasingly bold in the party and state organs. Since 1958, Liu Shaoqi's powers had increased gradually. By 1962, people's impression was that he almost helped the economy get back to normal. ... During this period, Mao Zedong voluntarily accepted the semi-retired life for two years or longer. [Britain] Clare Hollingworth:*Mao and the Men against Him*, Henan People's Publishing House, 1989 edition, page 89, 90. It can be said that the growing power of Liu Shaoqi was directly related to his position as the President of the state (there are other factors). The real power characteristics as the President of the state enabled him to lead the economic work and manage state affairs.

[11]At the time of drafting the Constitution in 1954, it is quite clear that only Mao Zedong could fill the post as the President of the state. Chongde [2], p. 206. No one thought about the case when Mao Zedong was not the President. After 1959, Liu Shaoqi started to serve as the President of the state. If we say that the original design of the Supreme State Conference was tailor made, then will the "dress" still fit when the "figure" is changed? The potential and big role of the power to convene the Supreme State Conference might benefit "others" after personnel changes. This was unexpected. "Man proposes God disposes."

was handed over by Mao Zedong to Liu Shaoqi. As a wise man, Mao Zedong should have thought about the consequence of this kind of "abdication". However, he might be overconfident (overconfident about the realistic political power structure without being constrained by the "doctrines" of constitutional provisions), or too willful (Mao Zedong had been impatient with the specific procedural and ritual works as the President of the state),[12] which usually made those in power pay the price. Even Mao Zedong really wanted to resign from the leading post, it might be an impulse and might not be executed for a long term. Without enough institutional restrictions, only self-consciousness might cause the recovery of power.[13] No one in power could tolerate transferring his power into the hands of others. With his personality, Mao Zedong would not attend to but taking charge of state affairs in the long run. According to the institutional design in 1954, the decisions on major state affairs should be made by the National People's Congress and implemented by the State Council in general.[14] In certain cases, the President of the state called for the Supreme State Conference to propose suggestions in form and decisions in essence. Since Mao Zedong gave up the post as the President of the state, he should no longer take charge of and intervene in state affairs after Liu Shaoqi served as the President of the state. However, what's the division of powers between the President of the state and the Chairman of the Party, and what's the power limitation? It is vague and uncertain in both the Constitution and the Party Constitution. When the two posts are taken by two persons, the President of the state might be subordinate to the Party chairman or the Party chairman consciously maintains a detached attitude, otherwise, it would be difficult to avoid the power collision and easily escalate the conflicts between the two. It can be said that the design of the system made disasters possible, and the realistic political environment and power culture came as the final preparations for disasters. There was no causality between the launch of the Cultural Revolution and Article 43 of the 1954 Constitution. The Cultural Revolution was not launched based on Article 43 of the 1954 Constitution (the launch of the Cultural Revolution had no constitutional basis and didn't even conform with the democratic procedures within the Party), but the really high

[12]When Nixon paid his visit to China and listed a series of specific national, regional and international issues requiring common concerns, Mao Zedong waved his hand and pointed at Zhou Enlai, saying that it is not him but Zhou Enlai who should be talked with. He said that he only talked about philosophical issues. Dunde [4], p. 296.

[13]Some foreign scholar noted that the masses' angry for the Great Leap Forward in 1958 and peer pressure forced Mao Zedong to give up the post of President of the state to Liu Shaoqi in mid-1959 and only maintain the post of the Chairman of the Central Committee of the CPC. [U.S.] Terrill [5], p. 315. Li Rui also agreed that Mao Zedong's resign from the post was to prepare for rallying forces again. Rui [6], p. 123. This might not completely tally with the facts because Mao Zedong said that he would not serve as the President of the state for another term in the leading up to the convocation of the Eighth Congress of the Chinese Communist Party in 1956. He even said that he would resign from the post as the Chairman of the Party in due time. Zheng [7], p. 345.

[14]Article 47 of the 1954 Constitution stipulated that the State Council was the executive organ of the supreme organ of state power.

degree of concentration of powers as confirmed in Article 43 of the 1954 Constitution foreshadowed the later so-called "two commands" and "two lines of struggle".

Taking this for a lesson, when we design the system in the future and when the country's building of democracy and legal system become mature, should we avoid the "dual-head system" and maintain the current structure that the head of the Party concurrently serves as the head of the state, or should we try the "dual-head system" again and take it as the breakthrough of separating the functions of the Party from those of the government? The author believes that the separation of powers is necessary but limited from the perspective of the characteristics of the state power, and the system under which different persons respectively serve as the head of the Party and the head of the government is not necessarily the requirement for power separation as power separation does not refer to the separation of the functions of the Party from those of the government in this sense. On the contrary, the system under which the head of the ruling party and the head of the state with real power are different persons may lead to buck-passing and intensify the conflicts. This malpractice could be avoided and even corrected in countries with the tradition of democracy and rule of law. In countries without the tradition of democracy and rule of law, it would be a bad thing. Even among those countries with a rather perfect democratic system, many have settled for this practice in which the head of the ruling party serves as the head of the state. The design of democratic system has unavoidably resulted in the conflicts between state organs. Within an administrative system with the characteristic of executive power, there is a need to prevent buck-passing and pursue high efficiency. Well, the integration of the head of the Party and the head of the state with real power can help realize this target.

3 1966–1982: The Paralyzed and Finally Canceled State President System

During this period, the state president system was severely undermined and finally canceled. During the period between 1966 and 1975, the constitution was not revised but actually lost its validity. President Liu Shaoqi was brought down in the political movement; the state president system was unable to play its role properly; the legal system was trampled gravely. Yet, Liu Shaoqi's fall from power couldn't illustrate that the state president system was no longer existent. During this period, some functions and powers of the President of the state were exercised by the Vice President. For instance, Song Qingling as the Vice President of the state used to accept the credentials presented by new ambassadors of some countries in China.

Vice President Dong Biwu used to exercise the functions and powers of the President in the name of the Acting President during 1972 and 1975. In this sense, the state president system was still in operation but seriously disrupted.[15]

Between 1975 and 1982, the state president system was clearly canceled in the constitution. The 1975 Constitution contained no stipulations on the original powers of the President of the state, such as the power of diplomacy, power of law promulgation and power of order issuance. Accordingly, part of the functions and powers of the President of the state were transferred to other Party and political departments for exercise. For example, the nomination of the Premier of the State Council and other members of the State Council was transferred to the Central Committee of the Chinese Communist Party.[16] The power to command the armed forces was transferred to Chairman of the Central Committee of the CPC.[17] The right of legation was transferred to the Standing Committee of the NPC.[18] According to the 1978 Constitution, some functions and powers of the President of the state as stipulated in the 1954 Constitution were transferred to the Chairman of the NPC Standing Committee, such as the power to promulgate laws and the power of diplomacy.[19] But the nomination of the Premier of the State Council and other members of the State Council was still controlled by the Central Committee of the Chinese Communist Party.[20] The power to command the armed forces was still controlled by the Chairman of the Central Committee of the CPC.[21]

The Cultural Revolution period was the most disorderly period in the history of the People's Republic of China. It looked very much like the change of the regime. All societies undergoing the change of regime would inevitably see the tendency against the rule of law. The difference is that the person with the highest power remained unchanged during the Cultural Revolution period. The person with the highest power led the revolutionary masses to change persons in power subordinate to the person with the highest power by means of rebellion. This enabled us to see the price of the "empty leader" model. Once the supreme power is constrained, how big the rebounding force would be; how cruel the institutionally unrestricted political struggle would be; how unreliable the self-discipline of power would be; how lawless the willful people would be in self-willed powers. "No rules, no justice!" The "rules" not just refer to moral self-discipline. It should also include

[15]Starting from May 1967, the Central Committee of the CPC issued an instruction on exercising military control or dispatching military representatives to the system affiliated to the State Council. The military control committees have the powers of the Party, the government and the army. In the same year, after the January Storm in Shanghai, revolutionary committees were established across the nation and gradually replaced military control committees. The revolutionary committees had the powers of the Party, the government, the army, legislation and judicature. Lirong [8], pp. 68–69.

[16]Article 17 of 1975 Constitution.

[17]Clause 2 of Article 15 of 1975 Constitution.

[18]Article 18 of 1975 Constitution.

[19]Article 26 of 1978 Constitution.

[20]Article 22(item 4) of 1978 Constitution.

[21]Article 19 of 1978 Constitution.

compulsory norms with legal effects. The "rules" are targeted at rural peasants and paramount and powerful persons, especially at persons with the highest power. Bringing disasters to all the people for indulging only one person was by no means allowed.

4 1982–1993: Recovery of the "Dual-Head System"

The state president system was restored in the Constitution during this period. Compared with the 1954 Constitution, the 1982 Constitution canceled the "power to command the armed forces" and the "power to call for a Supreme State Conference" of the President of the state. In practice, the President of the PRC didn't go beyond the stipulations of the constitution to enact the implementation rules for the decisions of the organ of supreme power. At that time, the functions and powers of the President of the state started to become "nominal".

In the relationship between the Party and the government, the "dual-head system" re-emerged. Under this system, the President of the state and the Chairman of the Party were different persons.[22] Between the two leaders, the power tipped towards the latter. In practice, the President during this period was basically left on the edge of political power and actually only exercised some procedural and ritual powers. In constitution, the only real power of the President, i.e. the power to nominate the Premier failed to be truly exercised in practice. This was the early period of the reform and opening up, so China was witnessing rapid economic development and a new and active climate in politics. However, these had no direct relations with the "dual-head system". In China, the center of political power has always been under the coordination of the Party, the government and the army. The government at that time mainly referred to the State Council while the President had been excluded from the center of power. This was clearly different from the "dual-head system" during the period between 1959 and 1966. During the period between 1959 and 1966, the Chinese President had real powers and took charge of state affairs across the board. This is just the cause for the fierce conflict between the President of the state and the Chairman of the Party in real power. Between 1982 and 1993, the Chinese President's power was only nominal, which had no obvious conflict with the real power of the Chairman of the Party, and their power conflicts were mostly seen in other areas. For instance, between the Chairman of the Party with the real power and the Chairman of the Central Military Commission with real power (or with more real power), the power center had been shifted. The 1982 Constitution canceled the Supreme State Conference and stipulated that the Premier assumed the overall responsibility for the work of the State Council, so the

[22]During the period from 1983 to 1988, the President of the state was Li Xiannian and the Party General Secretary was Hu Yaobang (1982–1987) and Zhao Ziyang (after 1987) successively; during the period from 1988 to 1993, the President of the state was Yang Shangkun and the Party General Secretary was Zhao Ziyang (before 1989) and Jiang Zemin (1989–1993).

President of the state should no longer intervene in administrative affairs. According to the 1982 Constitution, the power of military command was handed over to the Chairman of the Central Military Commission and the Chairman assumed the overall responsibility for the work of the Central Military Commission (but, there were no stipulations for the Chairman of the Central Military Commission to command the national armed forces). It can be said that the 1982 Constitution was indeed to establish a nominal state president (rather than the President of the state with real power even nominal in form as stipulated in the 1954 Constitution). It decomposed the power mode integrating the Party, the government and the army in the 1950s and made the situation featuring parallel troika of the Party, the government and the army.[23] This seemed to be "separation of powers", but this "separation of powers" contained crises. This power mode reflected a certain extent that we had insufficient essential and scientific analyses of the type, structure, function, and nature of powers. Chinese traditional power culture might pay more attention to studies on power tactics while lacking profound comprehension of the power as system.

5 1993-to Date: Return of Head of the State with Real Power

During this period, the constitution was revised for several times, but its articles about the President of the state had few changes.[24] In practice, the powers of the President of the state were even enlarged. As decided by the 27th Session of the Eighth Standing Committee of the National People's Congress on April 29, 1997, Chinese President Jiang Zeming, on behalf of the People's Republic of China, signed *the Agreement on Mutual Reduction of Military Forces along the Border Areas among the People's Republic of China, the Republic of Kazakhstan, the Republic of Kyrgyzstan, the Russian Federation and Republic of Tajikistan* in Moscow on April 24, 1997.[25] In particular, the tradition that Party Chairman

[23]The power structure after the promulgation of the 1982 Constitution was that Hu Yaobang was the Party General Secretary (1982–1987), Zhao Ziyang was the Premier (1982–1987) and Deng Xiaoping was the Chairman of the Central Military Commission (1982–1989). Someone may attribute the defects of the political system in reality to the imbalance among the three. But in fact, this triangle relationship in power was irrational in itself (i.e. the structure under which heads of the Party, government and army were respectively assumed by three different persons easily led to chaos and did no good to stability). But why has it been so difficult to separate the powers of legislation, judicature and administration in China while there had been separation and integration of powers of the Party, government and army. It is thought-provoking.

[24]Only Article 27 of the Amendment to the Constitution in 2004 changed the President's original power from "proclaims martial law" to "proclaims entering of the state of emergency". The stipulation for the state president to "engage in activities involving State affairs" was added to Article 28 of the Amendment.

[25]Bulletin of the NPC Standing Committee, 1997, No. 5, page 617. Quoted in Haikun [9], p. 458.

concurrently served as state president and Chairman of the Central Military Commission during 1954–1959 was restored. After 1996–1997, the power mode featuring the integration of the Party, government and army appeared once again.[26] This power mode repetition 40 years later called for rumination. Does it mean that the powers of the Party, government and army are inseparable unity artificially? If the striking echoes in history indeed contain some rationality, then we should maintain the system appearing repeatedly. Of course, the striking echoes in history may also be irrational, then we need to make persistent improvements. The centralized and unified powers of the Party, government and army are realistic in China, and other countries' practices have also proved its certain rationality. For example, both the U.S. President and Prime Minister of UK control the powers of the Party, government and army, which is incompatible with the democratic decentralization system. China's political power system undoubtedly has its defects, thus requiring political restructuring. But, what are the defects and how to make the improvement? We need to suit the remedy to the case. Power separation and restriction should be implemented between different state organs (such as legislative organs, judicial organs and administrative organs) and between different parties rather than between the Party and the government. The attempts to implement the "dual-head system" from 1958 to 1966 and from 1982 to 1993 might be a dangerous power separation. Separating powers in a wrong place was bound to bring about chaos and even corrupted power order. On the contrary, we refuse power separation in the right place, resulting in less and minor power restriction. Collective leadership is our ideal and personality cult is our habit. Democracy is our objective of struggle over the century and centralized rule is our thousands years of history. Therefore, when we develop a system under a collective leadership, it seems that the system only represents our ideals and probably represents our ideals at the time. When we take the real action, we spontaneously act by habit. In this case, our system would be out of line with our practices from the very beginning and even be more divorced from our practices later on until its alteration beyond recognition. In the past, we used to habitually blame many defects of the national political system for the disruption of the Cultural Revolution, but the happening of the Cultural Revolution has no essential influence on the political system of our country. On the one hand, we especially emphasize collective leadership in system while opposing personal centralization. On the other hand, we usually implement the personal centralization system in practice. This system was not derived from the

[26]China's current constitution has no provision on forbidding the state president to concurrently serve as the Chairman of the Central Military Commission. But in practice, these two posts are assumed by the same person, making the powers of head of the state and the top military power be united in the hand of one person. See Dong Chengmei's *Head of State System*, published in *Comparative Study on Constitution* by Li Buyun, China Law Press, 1998 edition, page 748. The author agrees that the powers of the Party, government and army should be united and controlled by one person, but not the practice that top heads of the two state organs are the same person. The author thinks that the Constitution should have clear stipulations on the state presidents' power of commanding armed forces and serving as Chairman of the Central Military Commission.

Cultural Revolution. Cultural Revolution was only the peak of the system. Before the Cultural Revolution, the system had already taken shape. For instance, the constitution or the law only made the stipulation in principle, a set of latent rules were created in practice to transform the system, and the power center was shifted. It is basically as such for both the actual power system before the Cultural Revolution and the actual power system after the Cultural Revolution. We might have exaggerated the differences between the 1954 Constitution before the Cultural Revolution for one part and the 1975 Constitution during the Cultural Revolution and the 1982 Constitution after the Cultural Revolution. They actually had no essential differences but simply quantitative changes in degree. Blaming the Cultural Revolution for all disastrous effects is the overestimation of the Cultural Revolution and has much simplified the issues. We need to have introspections not only on the Cultural Revolution but also on the power system of the past 50-plus and even 100-plus years and the power culture it contained.

6 Analysis of One Individual Case

The 1982 Constitution restored the election of the state president. The president of the state has played a pivotal role in practice pursuant to the Constitution. For instance, since 2001, the president of China has started to exercise the power to institute state medals and titles of honor and decide on their conferment and has presented awards to scientists who have made outstanding contributions to the country time and again. This has demonstrated that the state attaches great importance to scientific and technological undertakings and encourages and cares for the scientific and technical workers. However, some constitutional issues involved merit the attention of constitutionalists.

1. Looking from the constitutional basis for the state president to present awards, Article 80 of China's Constitution stipulates that the President of the PRC has the power to confer state medals and titles of honor in pursuance of decisions of the National People's Congress and its Standing Committee. But the previous presentation of awards seemed to have nothing to do with the National People's Congress or the Standing Committee of the National People's Congress. For example, on February 28, 2003, academician Jin Yilian received the Highest Science and Technology Awards presented by President Jiang Zemin at the award-giving ceremony organized by the Party Central Committee and the State Council and chaired by Hu Jintao in the name of the General Secretary of the CPC Central Committee. Premier of the State Council Zhu Rongji made a speech at the meeting on behalf of the Party Central Committee and the State Council. Vice Premier Li Lanqing read out *the Decision of the State Council on the State Science and Technology Award for 2002* at the meeting. *The Decision*

stated that this award presentation was approved by the State Council and endorsed by Chinese President Jiang Zemin.[27] However, looking through the Constitution, there was no provision on the state president's endorsement of documents and exercise of power to confer state medals and titles of honor in pursuance of decisions of the State Council.

2. Regarding the functions and powers of the State Council, Article 89 (17) of the Constitution stipulates that the State Council exercises the functions and powers to appoint, remove, and train administrative officers, appraise their work and reward or punish them in accordance with the law. In this connection, there is a constitutional basis for the State Council to give awards, but the objects must be administrative staff. Such scientists as Yuan Longping, Wu Wenjun and Jin Yilian, etc. are working with scientific research units (Yuan Longping was a researcher of Hunan Hybrid Rice Research Center; Wu Wenjun was a researcher of The System Science Institute of Chinese Academy of Sciences; Jin Yilian was a research center director). They are all researchers of scientific research institutions. It may be inappropriate to include them in the list of administrative staff. In addition, if it is the State Council to exercise the power to confer awards, it would be more appropriate for the head of the State Council (such as the premier and vice-premier) to present the award, but the award level would be lowered.
3. According to newspaper reports, in the award-giving activities in 2003, President Jiang Zemin conferred the award in the capacity of President of the state and Chairman of the Central Military Commission.[28] Academician Jin Yilian is an expert in computer. He was awarded because he chaired and accomplished the R&D of many large and supercomputers in China and systematically and innovatively put forward the system structure, design ideas and realization plans for supercomputers, and greatly contributed the leapfrog development of China's computer undertakings, especially supercomputers. It seemed that these achievements had no direct relations with military and army and were obviously different from the honor conferred by President Jiang Zemin in the capacity of Chairman of the Central Military Commission to the PLA commanders and fighters who fought against the flood in 1998. Comrade Jiang Zeming was the President of the state and Chairman of the Central Military Commission back then. Therefore, when he exercised the functions and powers of the state president, he should be in the capacity of the state president. Likewise, when he exercised the functions and powers of the Chairman of the Central Military Commission, he should be in the capacity of the Chairman of the Central Military Commission. The two capacities should not be confused. Otherwise, it would give the people an impression of "unclear functions and powers of state organs".

[27] *Guangming Daily*, March 1, 2003, Front Page.

[28] See footnote 27.

4. When President Jiang Zemin conferred the award to academician Jin Yilian in 2003, some other scientists were also granted with the National Natural Science Award, National Technological Invention Award and National Award for Science and Technology Progress at the award-giving meeting. The presenters included Jiang Zemin, Hu Jintao and other leaders of the Party and the state. Since President Jiang Zemin presented the Highest Science and Technology Awards to academician Jin Yilian (the title conferred by the state president is the highest honor), it is inappropriate for him to present awards to other scientists to demonstrate the differences and levels of honors. For awarding other scientists other than academician Jin Yilian, the presenters could be the Vice President of the state in accordance with the stipulation of Article 82 of the Constitution for the Vice President to assist the works of the President.[29]
5. The State Council's presentation of awards to scientists other than administrative staff is the act beyond its authority. According to Article 67 of the Constitution, the Standing Committee of the National People's Congress should revoke this decision.[30] Then, does the President of the state have the responsibility? If the State Council requires the President of the State to present awards, the President of the state should refuse it because this requirement of the State Council has no constitutional basis (the functions and powers as stipulated by Article 80 of the Constitution are all exercised in pursuance of decisions of the National People's Congress and the NPC Standing Committee). If the President of the state didn't refuse the requirement in such case, the President of the state should bear corresponding responsibilities. It is also the dereliction of duty if the organ of supreme power remained silent about this and failed to exercise the supervisory power endowed by the Constitution.
6. Both decisions of the State Council and decisions of the National People's Congress or the NPC Standing Committee are the acts of the government or the state. The Party is inadvisable to intervene in these specific works (these award-giving meetings were all organized by the Party Central Committee and the State Council, chaired by General Secretary of the CPC Central Committee, and the presenters were Party and state leaders). Otherwise, it would be suspected of replacing government with the Party. The Party can also exercise the power of conferring honors and awards, but it should be targeted at party members, such as conferring the titles of "best communist" and "model party branch" and General Secretary of the Party could be the presenter.

---

[29]As stipulated in Article 82 of the current constitution of China, "The Vice-President of the People's Republic of China assists the President in his work. The Vice-President of the People's Republic of China may exercise such parts of the functions and powers of the President as entrusted by the President." As regards how to assist and in which aspect to assist, a special legislation is needed.

[30]Article 67 of the Constitution stipulates that the Standing Committee of the National People's Congress has the power to annul those administrative regulations, decisions or orders of the State Council that contravene the Constitution or other laws.

References

1. Dong Chengmei: *Head of State System*, published in *Comparative Study on Constitution* by Li Buyun, China Law Press, 1998 edition.
2. Xu Chongde: *Constitutional History of the People's Republic of China* (Volume I), Fujian People's Publishing House, 2005 edition.
3. Pang Xianzhi, Jin Chongzhi: *Biography of Mao Zedong* (Volume I), Central Party Literature Press, 2003 edition.
4. Chen Dunde: *Mao Zedong and Nixon in 1972*, Kunming Publishing House, 1988 edition
5. Ross Terrill: *Mao: A Biography*, translated by Liu Luxin et al., Henan People's Publishing House, 1989 edition.
6. Li Rui: *Mao Zedong's Early Years and Later Years*, Guizhou People's Publishing House, 1982 edition.
7. Huang Zheng: *A Life of Liu Shaoqi*, Central Party Literature Press, 2003 edition.
8. Zhang Lirong: *Comparison of Chinese and Foreign Administrative Systems*, the Commercial Press, 2002 edition.
9. Yang Haikun: Chinese Constitutional Law in the New Century (I), China Human Resources Publishing House, 2001.

Values in the Constitution: Fifteen Years of Exploration

Qian Zhao

In recent years, research on constitutional values has become a spotlight in the academic circle. There are many different viewpoints and impressive works about constitutional values, but few studies directly focus on the concept. The viewing angles are quite different; yet, there has been no consensus on what constitutional values exactly are. The formal logic method might as well be applied for the entry point of studies to identify the logical form and law of the concept of constitutional values. Concept is the thinking form reflecting the special attributes (inherent attribute or essential attribute) of things. While reflecting the special attributes of things, concept also showcases the things with these attributes, thus forming the meaning and extension of concept. The meaning of concept is the special attributes of things as reflected by the concept. The extension of concept is the thing with special attributes as reflected by the concept.[1] Related studies in the academic circle could be recapped from two aspects, namely meaning and extension of the concept of constitutional values.

1 Meaning of the Concept of Constitutional Values

The meaning of the concept of constitutional values is the special attribute of constitutional values as reflected by the concept. The main task of studying the special attributes of constitutional values lies in analyzing the basic elements of

[1]Yuelin [1, p. 18, 22].

Q. Zhao (✉)
Law School of Southwest University, Chongqing, China
e-mail: 13263169197@163.com

Q. Zhao
Constitutional Law and Administrative Law of Law School,
Zhongnan University of Economics and Law, Wuhan, China

L. Li et al. (eds.), *Constitutional Development in China, 1982–2012*,
Research Series on the Chinese Dream and China's Development Path,
https://doi.org/10.1007/978-981-32-9261-1_11

constitutional values and discovering the mutual relations between the basic elements (status and function). The basic elements that constitute constitutional values and their mutual relations can be called the internal structure of constitutional values. The mutual relations between constitutional values and other elements in a larger social system can be called the external structure of constitutional values.

1.1 Internal Structure of Constitutional Values

The studies on the basic elements of constitutional values and their mutual relations can be classified into "single-element theory" and "composite-element theory."

1.1.1 Single-Element Theory

This theory mainly consists of three points of view. First, it is justice element. Equity is the basic value orientation of constitution. The generation of constitution contains the value orientation of equity. The development of constitution enriches and improves this value orientation. Equity as a value orientation of the constitution is the foundation and precondition for improving the overall quality of life of humanity. Equity as a value orientation of the constitution is a necessary requirement for the development of human society.[2] Second, it is democratic element. The value of constitution is to regulate the political order by democratic means and the core is democracy. Constitution is a democratic law. As a basic norm of building a democratic ruling order, constitution reflects the democratic understanding and democratic requirements of the ruling class.[3] Third, it is human rights element. The primary value of constitution is the protection of human rights and the protection of human peace.[4] The ultimate value of constitution is to pursue the protection of human rights.[5]

No matter what elements are applied, all viewpoints of this kind are established under the preconditions of basic value, core value, and primary value or ultimate value and do not deny the existence of other elements while emphasizing a single element. This kind of viewpoints give prominence to the level of value elements but it is inferior in self-sufficiency. What are other non-basic, non-core, non-primary, and non-ultimate value elements? What are the category limits? There are no clear answers to these questions. However, the proposal of these three types of "single element" has pointed out the direction for defining the internal structure of

---

[2]Yi [2].

[3]Heping [3].

[4]Dayuan [4].

[5]Jiaqing and Chengming [5, p. 17].

constitutional values. The status of justice, democracy, and human rights cannot be ignored among the basic elements that constitute constitutional values.

1.1.2 Composite-Element Theory

When defining the basic elements that constitute constitutional values mainly from the perspective of the public's anticipated demand for constitution, the diversity of subject demands has determined the compositionality of the basic elements of constitutional values. People's sovereignty is a substantive value of constitution. The formal values of constitution are for the realization of substantive values. The right—power order is a formal value of constitution. The integration of the dual values of constitution forms the constitutional purpose.[6] Constitutional values are people's anticipated demand for constitution. The value demands reflected in constitution in concentration are justice, freedom, and order. Among which, justice is an inherent value of constitution while freedom and order reflect realistic values of constitution.[7] Constitutional values refer to the effect or benefit of the constitution as the object to people as the subject in the process of interactions. The core of it is democracy, including human rights, freedom, and safety (order).[8] Constitutional value is the public's ideological form of anticipated demand for the ideas of constitution contradictory movement. The compositions of constitutional values are justice, freedom, and order. The value meaning of constitution is social justice, which is the general standard for evaluating constitutional values.[9] Constitutional value refers to the normative target and social significance of constitution as a special branch law for human society. Democracy is the core value of constitution while justice, order, and freedom are the basic values of constitution.[10] Constitutional value is a constituent part of legal value. It is the subject's evaluation of constitutional satisfaction for expectation and constitutional effectiveness on the basis of the attributes of constitution. Specifically, it contains justice, order, and human rights. Justice is the primary value, order is the basic value, and human rights are the core value.[11] Constitutional value signals the special category of relations between humanity and constitution and the significance of constitution to man, covering the relations between the satisfaction of constitution for human demand and people's expectation and evaluation of constitution. It includes three basic values, namely order, freedom, and justice.[12] Constitutional value refers to the value indicator of constitution with the guarantee of democratic system in the

---

[6]Wei [6].

[7]Fuhui [7].

[8]Zhengbang [8, p. 121].

[9]Yi [9].

[10]Yueming [10, p. 64].

[11]Haikun et al. [11, pp. 110–115].

[12]Xikun and Yunya [12, pp. 90, 92–93].

process of human pursuit of constitutional government order, promotion of social justice and social development and realization of fundamental human rights, including people's sovereignty, constitutional government order, social development, and social justice.[13] Constitution is the fundamental law of the state while freedom, equality, democracy, human rights, and corresponding social order are its basic values.[14]

The composite elements of constitutional values as defined by this point of view can be divided into seven groups, namely people's sovereignty and order; justice, freedom, and order; democracy, human rights, freedom, and security (order); democracy, justice, order, and freedom; justice, order, and human rights; people's sovereignty, constitutional government order, social development, and social justice; and freedom, equality, democracy, human rights, and order. It can be seen through comprehensive comparisons that order is included in all the seven groups, so it can be said the primary element of constitutional values, subsequently followed by democracy (people's sovereignty) (included in five groups), justice (equity), freedom (included in four groups), human rights (included in three groups), and equality and development (included in one group). According to the provisions on freedom, equality, and development in Article 1, 2, 3, 7, 22, and 29 of the *Universal Declaration of Human Rights*, and after the comparison among all these categories, we can find that freedom, equality, and development are all included in the category of human rights. In this connection, while defining the elements of constitutional values, it might be appropriate to put human rights before freedom, equality, and development so as to have a better and clearer review of the opinions of the academic circle.

To sum up, the "composite-element theory" could better adapt to the increasingly diversified subject demands being presented currently. Based on the direction pointed out by the single-element theory, comparing the standpoints supporting the "composite-element theory" can make the following conclusions. The basic elements of constitutional values should be democracy, human rights, justice, and order. If we want to figure out the "order of priority" of these four elements (prioritized according to the importance of constitutional values in social and political life),[15] then they should be the same in priority but play different roles in the internal structure of constitutional values. Democracy is the logic starting point, human rights are the ultimate purpose, justice is the means of realization, and order is the basic guarantee.

---

[13] Jiaqing and Chengming [5, p. 40]

[14] Maolin [13].

[15] Jichao [14].

1.2 External Structure of Constitutional Values

To clarify the mutual relations between constitutional values and other elements in a larger social system, we need, first of all, to analyze other elements that may have relevance to constitutional values. The academic circle mainly has the following viewpoints. Constitutional values fall into state values, social values, and legal values of the constitution. The implication is the demand of the state, the society or people, and the law for the constitution and the actual effects of the constitution on the state, the society, and the law.[16] The general meaning of constitutional values typically refers that constitutional values imply instrumental value, target value, formal value, and universality. Individual meaning of constitutional values mainly refers that constitutional values contain special economic, political, and cultural characteristics.[17] The construction and development of China's socialist market economic system have provided a material foundation for the transformation of constitutional values. Under the leadership of the Communist Party of China and on the basis of enabling the people to be masters of the country, governing the country by law and developing the socialist democratic politics with Chinese characteristics have offered a political guarantee for the transformation of constitutional values. Developing a national, scientific, and popular socialist culture with Chinese characteristics oriented toward modernization, toward the world, and toward the future with Marxism as the guidance and with the cultivation of citizens with ideals, moral, culture, and discipline as the target has provided the cultural development direction for the transformation of constitutional values.[18] The instrumental value of constitution is to demonstrate the fundamental economic, political, and cultural system of the state through the constitution and then use the constitution to protect relevant basic systems like the economic, political, and cultural systems as stipulated in the constitution. The target value of constitution is the target of realizing institutionalized and legalized democracy through constitutional functions and functions of relevant legal guarantee systems.[19] Due to the universality of adjustment objects of the constitution, constitutional values have also showcased diversity. Its basic values mainly include the following aspects. First, it is the economic value that is reflected in the function of constitution in guaranteeing the economic system and promoting the economic development. Second, it is the political value, which lies in the realization of people's sovereignty through building the authority of constitution. Third, it is the legal value, which rests with the realization and maintenance of social justice.[20]The value of constitutionalism in a harmonious society refers to the role of building a harmonious society in promoting and facilitating the construction of a country under constitutionalism. Specifically, it

[16]Long [15, pp. 212–223].
[17]Chongying [16].
[18]Chongying [17].
[19]Chongying [18].
[20]Xiaohu [19, pp. 94–96].

includes optimizing power allocation and smoothing the channel for the interactions between the government and the people; eliminating social tensions and building the foundation for social solidarity; rebuilding human-oriented value and giving birth to the spirit of modern citizenship; and improving the authority of the rule of law and nurturing the culture of free constitutionalism.[21]

Other elements defined by above viewpoints can be divided into five groups: state, society, and law; economy, politics, and culture; economy, politics, culture, and law; economy, politics, and law; and harmonious society. Through comprehensive comparisons, we can find that law is contained in all the three groups and has become the consensus of the academic community within a certain extent. The status of constitution as the mother law and higher law and the indirect applicability of the constitution have been well manifested by this point of view. As an ideal form of social development, a harmonious society is the subconcept of society and can be contained in the category of "society." Comparing the group of state and society (harmonious society) for one part and the group of economy, politics, and culture and the group of economy and politics for another in category, different perspectives of category statement make it difficult to have a clear clue. However, we might find out the answer according to the provisions of *the International Covenant on Civil and Political Rights* and *the International Covenant on Economic, Social and Cultural Rights*. The statement of state and society (harmonious society) and the statements of economy, politics, and culture, and economy and politics are rather insular. The statement of appositive concept based on different perspectives of the two groups of state, citizen, and society (harmonious society) and politics, economy, and culture focuses more on the self-sufficiency and universality. It might be appropriate to define the law, the group of state, citizen, and society (harmonious society) and the group of politics, economy, and culture as the three other groups of elements having connections with constitutional values.

To sum up, the mutual relations between constitutional values and other elements in forming a larger social system are more embodied as the philosophical category featuring the dialectical association characteristic of things, namely "general and individual." The basic elements of constitutional values are featured by universality and can be called the general character of various constitutions in the world. Other elements correlated with constitutional values have differences and have demonstrated different forms due to different customs and cultures. Other elements correlated with constitutional values are reflected as the character of various constitutions in the world. Of course, these three groups of elements are also different somewhat in character presentation. The law is the main carrier manifesting constitutional values. State, citizen, and society (harmonious society) are objects of the action of constitutional value. Politics, economy, and culture are the special fields for implementing constitutional values.

[21]Guohua [20].

2 What the Concept of Constitutional Value Refers to

Analyzing what the concept of constitutional values refers to is to analyse the things with the special attributes of constitutional values as reflected by the concept, including three aspects, namely the origin, relations, and realization of constitutional values.

2.1 *Origin of Constitutional Values*

The academic circle mainly studies the origin of constitutional values from the perspective of "humanity." It is believed that humanity is the origin and important basis of constitutional values. Humanity is manifested by the people's needs of interests, freedom, and propositions. Different people have different needs. Public needs are formed in the interaction process of individual needs. Public needs are bound to become common wills. When common wills are confirmed by the state in the form of fundamental law, constitutional value is generated.[22] The formation and development of the constitutional values philosophy would not happen without the fundamental role of humanity in constitution. Natural humanity view has cultivated the sprout of ancient constitution through the rule of law priority theory. The rational view of human nature has promoted the formation of modern constitution with limited government theory. The view of social humanity has stimulated the development of modern constitution by using the communitarianism theory.[23]

This kind of view is just a typical view of the "theory of subjective constitutional values" as the mainstream of the academic community.[24] According to this view, the subject–object relationship is taken as the basis of cognition. In most cases, it is to analyze how constitutional object meets the needs of constitutional subject from the perspective of constitutional subject. Human nature is believed to be the source and basis of constitutional values. Human nature is certainly the source of constitutional values, but is it the only source of constitutional value? Do democracy, human rights, justice, and order as four elements of the internal structure of constitution value all stem from human nature? Our feelings about virtue are not all natural. Some virtues give rise to happiness and appraisal because of the application of measures or designs for coping with human environment and meeting needs. We are certain that justice belongs to this, artificial virtue. Humanity is substantially dominated by images, and man's feelings are mostly proportional to their viewpoints of any object rather than to the real and intrinsic value of this object. This is why people would rather take any realistic yet little profits regardless of maintaining

---

[22]Jiaqing [21].

[23]Chi [22].

[24]Hongxiang [23, p. 305].

social order although social order relies so much on the compliance with justice.[25] With these words, Hume implicitly pointed out that justice was an artificial virtue and people's trample on order was caused by the search for profit, a weakness of human nature, which well confirmed the mainstream idea that justice and order come from human nature.

If we solely take constitution as a pure legal phenomenon from the perspective of object constitution and beyond human nature, could we decompose all or part of the four elements of constitutional values as the internal structure? Kelsen's Pure Theory of Law might provide some clues. Pure theory of law is a theory of positive law and its only purpose is to understand its objects. The pure theory of law tries to answer the question about the actuality of law rather than the idealistic state of law. The latter is a political question while the pure theory of law is a science. It is very difficult to free the concept of law from the concept of justice. The pure theory of law is an effort trying to study law and justice as two different questions.[26] Constitution is also a law. Why not free the concept of constitution from the notion of justice to build a pure constitution? From a scientific perspective beyond political questions, constitution provides an effective guarantee for the development of democratic systems and human rights. Constitutional norms are reflected by fundamental legal norms and specific adjustment of constitutional relations. Different from general legal norms, constitutional norms have their own characteristics, i.e., the political nature, restrictive nature, supremacy, applicability, sanction nature, and historic significance.[27] Specific statement of constitutional norms is usually used to showcase constitutional guarantee of democracy and human rights. Human rights can be said to be the primary goal of constitution. The legalization of democratic facts can be called the spirit of constitution. Different from pure law, pure constitution has the specific nature, systematic nature, authority of democracy, and human rights protection. Human nature has certainly generated human expectation for justice and order. Pure constitution and constitutional norms should become the source of democracy and human rights.

To sum up, the source of constitutional values should be dualistic, meaning that the analysis and studies need to be made from the perspective of both constitutional subject and object constitution.

2.2 *Relations of Constitutional Values*

Studies in the academic circle on the relations of constitutional values can be roughly divided into two categories, namely "theory of subject core" and "theory of subject–object interaction."

---

[25]Hume [24, pp. 517 and 575].

[26]Kelsen [25, p. 275].

[27]Dayuan [26, pp. 69, 82, and 84–88].

2.2.1 Theory of Subject Matter

This theory is the logical starting point of the aforesaid "theory of subjective constitutional value." This theory principally starts from the perspective of constitutional subject to analyze the relations of constitutional values and emphasizes the dominant role of subject demands in the relations of constitutional values. Constitutional values are the effect of the constitution implying subject value needs on the subjects in their interaction process.[28] Constitutional values are the interrelation between the objective attributes of constitution realized through constitutional practical activities of the subjects of constitution for the one part and the subjective requirements of the subjects of constitution for constitution. It includes two aspects, namely incorporating the value requirements of the subjects of constitution in the constitution and the value-based satisfaction of the requirements of subjects of the constitution.[29]

The relation of constitutional values decomposed by this point of view is a dualistic system of relations of constitutional values and gives prominence to the "mirror effect" between constitutional subjects and object constitution based on the demands of subjects. However, is it truly an ideal interaction between the two in the expected state? How is the interaction process? What should be done in case of the occurrence of a paradox between the two laws in the interaction process? The theory of subject–object interaction is born at the right moment and upgrades or improves the theory of subject core.

2.2.2 Theory of Subject–Object Interaction

The studies mainly focus on three aspects, namely the subject, object, and intermediary agent of subject–object interaction (content) and emphasize the core status of subject–object interaction in the relations of constitutional values. The subjects of constitutional value relations are the people and their groups and collectives taking part in constitutional value relations and creating, realizing, and accepting constitutional values. The objects of constitutional value relations are the objects interacting with the subjects and having effects on the subjects, i.e., constitution, the unity of normative constitution, and practical constitution. The intermediary agent of constitutional value relations refers to the means for the interactions between the subjects and objects of constitutional value relations.[30] The evaluation of constitutional values is to judge the values of specific constitution and its function, including the evaluation of constitutional legislation and the evaluation of constitutional functions. The evaluation of constitutional legislation is a static value judgment of constitutional norms, referring to judging the values of the overall

[28]Jiaqing [27].

[29]Dianying and Donghua [28].

[30]Jiaqing [29].

design of constitutional norms, institutional designs, and the legislative performance of constitutional norms with democratic order as the basic value orientation, and then making the conclusion of the goodness or badness, the degree of democracy, and legislation level through static analyses and comparisons. The evaluation of constitutional functions is the dynamic value judgment of the actual utility of constitution, referring to the value judgment of the actual utility of a specific constitution in the practices of constitutional government based on the democratic values of constitutional government. The results of evaluation of constitutional functions fall into positive functions and negative functions.[31] The subjects of constitutional values are citizens, the state (state organs), nationalities, political parties, and various interest groups, among other subjects of constitutional relations. The objects of constitutional values refer to the objects jointly pointed by the subjects of constitutional values in the constitution operational process and include constitutional documents with static significance and constitutional behaviors with dynamic significance. The contents of constitutional values refer to the significance of constitution to the people, including the satisfaction of people's needs and people's expectations, and evaluations of constitution.[32] Constitutional values should at least contain the meaning of three aspects: What values could be protected and promoted by constitution in the implementation process; the value factors of constitution in itself; and standard for evaluating constitutional values.[33]

Compared with the theory of subject core, this theory is more comprehensive. On the one hand, this theory dualistically divides the meaning of subject constitution, namely statically and dynamically. On the other hand, this theory has responded to the possible "paradox" in the aforesaid interaction process through the evaluation of constitutional values. This theory has also designed the composite constitutional value evaluation system covering constitutional legislation evaluation and constitutional function evaluation based on the duality of object constitution. However, the subject–object interaction theory currently seems to be still one sided in studies of the interaction process. Value evaluation is only one side of the interaction process, but how to realize effective demand-based expressions of the subjects of constitution? Only when the subjects' constitutional requirements and value evaluation become the two sides in the interaction process of constitutional value relations, an organic interconnection and interflow could be realized between the subjects and objects of the constitutional value relations.

To sum up, the constitutional value relation system should be established with the subject–object two-way interaction process as the core based on the subject–object interaction theory.

---

[31]See Footnote 3.

[32]Chi [30].

[33]Yezhong [31, p. 156].

2.3 *Realization of Constitutional Values*

The academic circle's studies on the realization of constitutional values mainly center on the relations among constitutional value, constitutional function, and constitutional role.

2.3.1 Constitutional Values and Constitutional Functions

The academic circle's studies on the relations between constitutional values and constitutional functions can be roughly divided into two categories, namely constitutional function inner core theory and constitutional function externalization theory.

According to the constitutional function inner core theory, constitutional value is the external manifestation of constitutional functions. The normative function of constitution is a direct function of constitution. Constitution plays its social and historical functions on the subjects through its normative function to form the constitutional value tradition. The effect of constitution on subjects is directly reflected in the conformity of constitutional functions to the needs of subjects.[34] Constitutional values are formed based on constitutional functions. Constitutional functions are the objective foundation and basis for realizing constitutional values.[35]

According to the constitutional function externalization theory, constitutional functions refer to the effect that should be possessed by constitution as determined by the essence of constitution. In the constitutional value realization system, constitutional functions are the link between constitutional values and constitutional effects, and these three have a level-wise specific relations.[36] Constitutional values are the concentrated manifestation of the relations between constitutional functions and social development direction and the summation of the unique, compliant, and purposive promotion functions of constitution in human social development process. Constitutional function (effect) is the externalization of constitutional values and constitutional values are the internal basis of constitutional function.[37] The values of constitution as the fundamental law of the state are reflected by functions and specific effects and provide a certain target for bringing its functions and effects into play. Constitutional functions refer to the functions and effects of constitution as determined by the essence of constitution. Constitutional functions are the requirement and manifestation of constitutional values.[38] Constitutional function refers to the functions and effects of constitution as determined by the essence of

[34] See Footnote 30.

[35] Zhengbang [8, p. 8].

[36] See Footnote 3.

[37] Lifu [32].

[38] Xiaohu [19, pp. 94 and 97].

constitution and it is the requirement and manifestation of constitutional values and the abstraction of constitutional effects.[39]

In terms of the demarcation of value and function in meaning, the constitutional function inner core theory might arbitrarily expand the value categories. Value should have four basic characteristics. First, value is the attribute of object. Second, the subject of value is humanity in general sense. Third, value is the benefit of object to humanity and the attribute cherished by man. Fourth, the type of value should be individual and shall not change at the requirement of the subject. Function has the following characteristics. First, function is a social consequence. Second, function is not all beneficial to humanity and might be positive, negative, or even have no function. Third, the subjects of function are not fixed and feature individual differences.[40] Through feature comparison, the differences between the two have been quite clear both internally and externally. The value of law in strict sense should refer to the existence of supreme goal and spirit for the purpose of function and effect above the function and effect of law. The value of law takes the relations between law and people as the basis. The value object of law is law. The value of law takes the attribute of law as the basis. The value subject of law is man. The value of law is to meet the needs of humanity and overstep the direction absolutely as established and confirmed in the heart of the subject of law.[41] Constitution is also law. Constitutional value and function as the subordinate concept of the value and function of law should not surpass the basic judgment of the relation between the value and function of the law. Therefore, the constitutional function externalization theory has become the general theory of the academic circle within a certain scope and further studied the relations between constitutional effect and constitutional function and value on this basis.

2.3.2 Constitutional Values and Constitutional Effects

The academic circle's studies on the relations between constitutional values and constitutional effects have been established on the basis of the "constitutional function externalization theory." Constitutional values correlate with constitutional effects through the externalized conduction of constitutional functions. Related studies can be divided into two categories, namely function-effect integration theory and function-effect separation theory.

According to the function-effect integration theory, constitutional effects are also called constitutional functions, referring to the act of constitution to state organs, social groups, and individual citizens, and the active influence of constitution on the social real life and the specific manifestation of the realization of state will.[42] Constitutional

[39]Yueming [10, p. 67].

[40]Yi [33].

[41]Zeyuan [34, pp. 49–52].

[42]Yezhong [35, p. 22].

functions are the intrinsic attribute of constitution that can exert influence on the social life. It is usually manifested as the external effects of constitution.[43] Constitutional effects are the effectiveness of constitution, or the functions and usage of constitution, the result of meeting people's some needs by the constitution, and the influence of constitution on other things. Constitutional effects are the manifestation of constitutional values.[44] Constitutional values are reflected through constitutional effects. Constitutional effects are the external manifestation of the values that the constitution should have. Constitutional effects refer to the actual influence of constitution on human behaviors and social relations through its activities. Constitutional effects and functions can be used as the same concept.[45] Constitutional effects are also called constitutional functions, referring to the beneficial influence that could be exerted by the constitution as expected by the people according to the actual needs of the society.[46] Constitutional effects are also called constitutional functions and refer to the influence of the constitution on other social phenomena under certain conditions.[47]

According to the function-effect separation theory, constitutional effects are the concretization and realization of constitutional functions, but the two have no direct relations. Constitutional functions refer to the effectiveness that the constitution should have as determined by the essence of the constitution, and feature necessity. Constitutional effects are the actual effectiveness of the constitution and feature reality. Constitutional functions refer to active and effective functions from the perspective of effects. Constitutional effects include not only active effects but also passive effects.[48] Constitutional effects refer to the actual effectiveness of constitution on the political power operation and social life. Constitutional functions determine the direction and scope of constitutional effects according to the essence and value of constitution. Constitutional effects are the concrete realization of constitutional functions.[49] Constitutional functions are the abstraction of constitutional effects and have defined the scope and direction of constitutional effects. Constitutional functions feature necessity. Constitutional effects feature actuality. Constitutional effects refer to the actual utility possessed and played by constitutional norms in adjusting constitutional relations.[50] Constitutional functions are the intrinsic and inherent attribute of the constitution. Constitutional effects are determined by constitutional functions and are the external and specific manifestation of constitutional functions. Constitutional functions are rather stable. Constitutional effects change with the changes of the nature and state of other social phenomena. Constitutional effects also have apparent, concrete, and historic characteristics

43 See Footnote 37.

44 Haikun et al. [11, pp. 115–116].

45 Jiaqing and Chengming [5, pp. 40 and 42].

46 Zhiwei [36, p. 35].

47 See Footnote 14.

48 See Footnote 3.

49 Xiuyi and Dayuan [37, p. 223].

50 Xiaohu [19, pp. 97, 100–101].

compared with constitutional functions.[51] Constitutional effects refer to the actual utility possessed and played by constitutional norms in adjusting constitutional relations, referring to the act of constitution to state organs, social groups, and individual citizens, the active influence of constitution on the social real life. Constitutional effects contain normative effects and social effects. Constitutional functions feature necessity, while constitutional effects feature actuality.[52]

These two points of view are equal in strength and both supported. If comparing the categories of constitutional functions and effects, both views have some merits and they are different simply because they are discussed from different perspectives. However, if constitutional values are taken as the footstone to compare the categories of constitutional values, functions, and effects, the function-effect separation theory is clearer in logical reasoning. As the guidance and derivative of the interaction between constitutional subject and object constitution, constitutional values should belong to the category of necessity. The dualistic source of democracy, human rights, justice, and order has determined that its manifestation carrier should coordinate the demand of subjects of constitution and pure constitutional norms and this carrier belongs to the category of necessity but should not have a long distance from the category of necessity and can more specifically provide realistic guidance to give play to the role of actual effects. The functions of law are the intrinsic attribute of law, while the effects of law are endowed and set. The functions of law are stable intrinsic attribute of law, while the effects of law need constant changes. The functions of law are intrinsic necessary attribute of law, while the effects of law have its realistic direction. The realization of the adjustment, guidance, and guarantee functions of law always has an inseparable connection with the realization of such values as legal order, legal interests, and legal justice, and always exists for realizing these legal values to a large extent.[53]Constitution is also a law, so the functions and effects of constitution as the subordinate concept of the functions and effects of law should not surpass the basic judgment on the functions and effects of law. In this connection, the functions of constitution can serve the realization of constitutional values and specifically guide constitution to play its role. So, we can realize the coordination between the diversified demands of subjects of the constitution and the pure constitutional norms through the obvious carriers like constitutional functions. Full play of the role of constitution is subject to the three groups of other elements in the external structure of constitutional law values to a large extent, and so it belongs to the category of necessity. It would demonstrate that constitutional values in the category of necessity have various operational deviations toward different application objects through constitutional functions.

[51]Zhengbang [8, p. 53].

[52]Yueming [10, p. 70]

[53]Wangsheng [38].

In conclusion, the constitutional value realization system featuring level-wise and specific "constitutional value—constitutional function—constitutional effect" shall be established on the basis of the constitutional function externalization theory and the function-effect separation theory.

References

1. Jin Yuelin: *Formal Logic*, People's Publishing House, 2006 edition.
2. Fan Yi: *Equity: Basic Value Orientation of Constitution, Journal of Renmin University of China*, 1999, Issue 1.
3. Dong Heping: *On Constitutional Values and Evaluation*; *Contemporary Law Review*, 1999, Issue 2.
4. Han Dayuan: *Simple Analysis of the Values of Modern Science and Technology and Constitutional Values, The Jurist*, 2000, Issue 3.
5. Wu Jiaqing, Du Chengming: *Constitutional Law, Science Press*, 2008 edition.
6. Hu Wei: *On Constitutional Values, Science of Law*, 1997, Issue 2.
7. Zhu Fuhui: *A Jurisprudential Analysis of Value and Function of the Constitution, Modern Law Science*, 2002, Issue 3.
8. Wen Zhengbang: *A Course in Constitutional Law*, China Law Press, 2005 edition.
9. Fan Yi: *On the Concept, Composition and Meaning of Constitutional Value, Journal of Gansu Political Science and Law Institute*, 2005, Issue 5.
10. Wang Yueming: *Fundamental Issues on Constitution*, China Law Press, 2006 edition.
11. Yang Haikun, Shangguan Piliang, Lu Yongsheng: *Basic Theory of Constitution*, China Democracy and Legal System Publishing House, 2007 edition.
12. Li Xikun, Liu Yunya: *Constitutional Law*, Chongqing University Press, 2007 edition.
13. Liu Maolin: *An Introduction to China's Constitution*, Peking University Press, 2009 edition.
14. Xu Jichao: *A Study of the Order of Priority of Values of China's Modern Socialist Constitution, Theory and Reform*, 2009, Issue 3.
15. Li Long: *Basic Theory of Constitution*, Wuhan University Press, 1999 edition.
16. Wang Chongying: *A Tentative Study on Constitutional Value, Journal of Wuxi University of Light Industry (Social Science Edition)*, 2001, Issue 3.
17. Wang Chongying: *China's Modernization and Change in Constitutional Value, Political Science and Law*, 2002, Issue 3.
18. Wang Chongying: *A Research on Modern Chinese Constitutional Value, Journal of Southern Yangtze University: Humanities & Social Sciences Edition*, 2003, Issue 5.
19. Yin Xiaohu: *Significance of Constitutional Law*, Peking University Press, 2005 edition.
20. Jiang Guohua: *Value of Constitutionalism of a Harmonious Society, Legal Forum*, 2005, Issue 4.
21. Wu Jiaqing: *On Humanistic Basis of Evolution of Constitutional Value, Journal of Guangdong University of Business Studies, 2001*, Issue 1.
22. Chen Chi: *Historical Latitude of the Philosophy of Constitutional Value, Journal of Sichuan Normal University (Social Sciences Edition)*, 2008, Issue 4.
23. Pan Hongxiang: *Social Theory Analysis of Constitution*, People's Publishing House, 2009 edition.
24. [Britain] Hume: *A Treatise of Human Nature (Volume II)*, translated by Guan Wenyun, the Commercial Press, 1980 edition.
25. [Austria] Kelsen: *Pure Theory of Law*, translated by Zhang Shuyou, China Legal Publishing House, 2008 edition.
26. Han Dayuan: *Basic Theories of Constitutional Law*, China University of Political Science and Law Press, 2008 edition.

27. Wu Jiaqing: *On the Nature, Characteristic and Form of Constitutional Value, China Legal Science*, 1999, Issue 2.
28. He Dianying, Shao Donghua: *On the Concept and Characteristic of Constitutional Value, Journal of Henan Administrative Institute of Politics and Law*, 2007, Issue 5.
29. Wu Jiaqing: *Elements of Constitutional Value Relations, Hebei Law Science*, 1999, Issue 3.
30. Chen Chi: *Prescriptive Nature Of the Constitution Value, Journal of Chengdu University of Technology (Social Sciences)*, 2004, Issue 4.
31. Zhou Yezhong: *Constitution*, Higher Education Press, Peking University Press, 2005 edition.
32. Du Lifu: *Further Review of Constitutional Function and Constitutional Value, Contemporary Law Review*, 2001, Issue 9.
33. Chen Yi: *Debate on Value and Function of the law* [J]. *Journal of Southwest University for Nationalities (Philosophy and Social Sciences)*, 2001, Issue 4.
34. Zhuo Zeyuan: *On the Values of Law*, China Law Press, 2006 edition.
35. Zhou Yezhong: *Constitutional Law*, China Law Press, 1999 edition.
36. Tong Zhiwei: *Constitutional Law*, Tsinghua University Press, 2008 edition.
37. Xu Xiuyi, Han Dayuan, *Basic Theory of Modern Constitution*, People's Public Security University of China Press, 2001 edition.
38. Zhou Wangsheng: *Discriminating Between the Function of Law and the Effect of Law, Tribune of Political Science and Law*, 2006, Issue 5.

Implementation of the Constitution: Evaluation Method and Impact Assessment

Jihong Mo

1 Significance of the Concept of Implementation of the Constitution

1.1 Status of Study on the Concept of Implementation of the Constitution

The year of 2012 marked the 30th anniversary of the promulgation of China's current constitution. Over the past three decades, China's constitutional community has carried out comprehensive and extensive studies revolving around the concept, approach, guarantee, and significance of constitutional implementation in accordance with stipulations of implementation of the current constitution and has reached certain results. Specifically speaking, the study results are made in the following aspects. First, some scholars have made special and systematic academic studies and written-related academic works with constitutional implementation as the topic, which have promoted the constitutional circle to conduct profound, systematic, and specialized topic studies of constitutional implementation-related issues. These works include *the Constitutional Text and Realization: Research on Issues Related to Constitutional Implementation* by Hu Zhengchang[1] and *the Enforcement System of the Constitution of China* by Zhai Xiaobo.[2] Besides, there are also some academic works strongly correlated with the special topic of constitutional implementation, such as *Research Reports on Constitutional Development of China (1982–2002)* by Hu Jinguang and Han Dayuan,[3] etc. The

[1]China University of Political Science and Law Press, February 2009.
[2]China Legal Publishing House, April 2009.
[3]China Law Press, April 2004.

J. Mo (✉)
Institute of Law of Chinese Academy of Social Sciences, Beijing, China
e-mail: 13263169197@163.com

L. Li et al. (eds.), *Constitutional Development in China, 1982–2012*,
Research Series on the Chinese Dream and China's Development Path,
https://doi.org/10.1007/978-981-32-9261-1_12

publication of above-mentioned academic works was good theoretic and academic preludes to more profound studies on constitutional implementation in Chinese constitutional circle. Second, nearly 200 papers with constitutional implementation-related issues as the research topic were published on domestically influential academic journals of law. These papers made systematic and comprehensive discussions about issues related to constitutional implementation from different sides and perspectives. Some of these papers have exerted important academic influences in theory and played a positive role in strengthening constitutional implementation in practice. These papers with significant academic influence include *On the Guarantee of the Implementation of the Constitution* by Wang Shuwen,[4] *China's Constitution and Several Issues Related to the Implementation of the Constitution* by Cheng Xiangqing[5] and *the Implementation of the Constitution: An Important Subject of Studies on Constitutional Law* by Zhou Yezhong,[6] etc. Furthermore, comparative studies were conducted in some of the works on the subject of constitutional implementation, such as *On the Guarantee System of the Implementation of Constitution of Different Countries* by Chen Shaoxing and Wu Yufeng[7] and *Condition and Path for the Implementation of Australian Constitution* by Zhu Yingping,[8] etc.

The constitutional circle of China has made positive progress in theoretical studies on the implementation of constitution since the promulgation of the current constitution in 1982, but these research results need to be further studied on their significance as the guiding theories into practices. For instance, certain results are lack of accurate description of the actual situation of the implementation of the Constitution, with weak "problem consciousness and not useful to effectively discover issues and propose effective solutions. Thus, over the past three decades since the promulgation of China's current constitution, there are still absences of authoritative evaluation standard and scientific conclusions of the basic situation of constitutional implementation. When comes to the theoretical research on constitutional implementation, studies were mainly focused on building concept, elaborating significance and paying attention to the assurance of constitutional implementation. However, there were not sufficient accurate definition and classified, leveled, and hierarchical studies of the nature and feature of constitutional implementation. In particular, there have been no comprehensive and systematic normative studies on the evaluation method or evaluation mechanism for the situation of constitutional implementation which should have been the fundamental theory of constitutional implementation. The studies in this aspect are few and were only mentioned in a few works (such as *On Constitutional implementation*

[4]*China Legal Science*, 1992, Issue 6.

[5]Journal of Beijing Union University (Humanities and Social Sciences), 2007, Issue 1.

[6]*Law Science*, 1987, Issue 5.

[7]*Global Law Review*, 1993, Issue 3.

[8]*Academics*, 2006, Issue 2.

Evaluation Principle by Zhang Yan).[9] Obviously, due to the lack of valuable studies on the basic legal features of constitutional implementation, it is difficult to systematically come up with well-targeted policies and advices on enhancing constitutional implementation.

In general, no foreign constitutional theory is specifically about the implementation of constitution. In most law-based countries, the significance of constitutional implementation is not independently and specifically emphasized. Instead, their focus is on how to solve issues related to the applicability of constitution, i.e., to apply constitution as the basis of legal decisions in specific cases. In this sense, while studying issues related to constitutional implementation, foreign constitutional theories lay emphasis on the core issues, namely the applicability of constitution or review for constitutionality, in constitutional implementation. That said, in recent years, some law-based countries have been reviewing their own situation of rule of law and others that have been undergoing the transition toward a democratic system have achieved greater understanding of the issue of constitutional implementation from a general perspective. There is a growing body of publications in this area, include *Constitutional Implementation in South Africa*[10] by J. De Groof, R. Malherbe & A. Sachs and *Constitutional Implementation*[11] by Bezalel Peleg & Eyal Winter, etc. All these monographs directly apply the concept of "constitutional implementation" and comprehensively and systematically elaborate the general theory of constitutional implementation. These works have made up for the deficiency of previous law-based theories in systematic study of constitutional implementation. In some other countries, legislations have been passed to safeguard the implementation of the constitution. For example, the Republic of Serbia enacted *The Constitutional Law on Implementation of the Constitution of the Republic of Serbia* in 2006.[12]

1.2 Changes in the Meaning of Constitutional Implementation

Looking at the studies of China's constitutional circle on the meaning of constitutional implementation, there are a variety of interpretations and the meaning is ever changing. Some scholars pointed out the phenomenon of non-standard usage of the concept of constitutional implementation. The cause for the confusion of

[9]*Theory Horizon*, 2006, Issue 4.

[10]*Constitutional Implementation in South Africa*, edited by: J. De Groof, R. Malherbe & A. Sachs, Mys&Breesch publishers, Belgium, 2003-05-22.

[11]*Constitutional Implementation*, Bezalel Peleg & Eyal Winter, Rev.Econ. Design *7187–204 (2002).*

[12]*Constitutional Law on Implementation of the Constitution of the Republic of Serbia*, *The Official Gazette of the RS No. 98/06.*

concepts relating to constitutional implementation has something to do with the fact that China introduced the constitutional government system from other countries and thus used borrowed words in translating the review for constitutionality systems of different countries. These different words have different meanings in Chinese, resulting in the possibility of establishing different systems. Some work has been done on this topic.[13] In the *Concept of Constitutional Application and the Means thereof* published in *China Legal Science*, professor Cai Dingjian put forward the three aspects for understanding in cognizing and analyzing the meaning of constitutional implementation in detail. According to him, the concept of constitutional implementation is constitutional guarantee and constitutional implementation on the macro-level, constitutional supervision and constitution application in meso-level, and review for constitutionality (judicial review) and constitutional litigation in micro-level or constitutional implementation and the operational level.[14] Professor Cai, especially presented a logically strict definition of constitutional implementation at the macro-level. The definition is that constitutional implementation is the concept relative to the formulation of constitution and refers to a set of theories, notions, systems, and mechanisms of turning the text of constitution into realistic system. Constitutional implementation is the concept with a broad sense, including making the constitution legalized and making administrative organs to enforce the constitution and judicial organs to apply the constitution through legislation. The specific mechanism for constitutional implementation includes constitutional supervision and constitutional interpretation, or review for constitutionality and constitutional litigation. Constitutional implementation goes with the constitutional guarantee system. But, professor Cai also realized that it is difficult to apply this concept on a systematic base as its meaning is too general and broad.[15] Of course, what merits our attention is that the "unified interpretation" methods proposed without defining the nature of constitutional implementation and realizing the conceptual meaning of constitutional implementation still contradicts each other in legal theory. That means constitutional implementation must focus on the objectivity and subjectivity of its objects. It would be imperative to know and study what the constitution is and what is to be implemented, regardless of which sense of constitutional implementation is being used. Academic controversies surrounding the concept of constitutional implementation accurately reflect the objectivity and subjectivity of constitutional phenomena. Without a logically sound set of methods for describing the objectivity and subjectivity of constitutional phenomena, no rigorous theories of constitutional. Implementation would be possible at all.

---

[13]Dingjian [1].

[14]See Footnote 13.

[15]See Footnote 13.

1.3 Significance of the Concept of Constitutional Implementation in Practice

The lack of conceptual and definitional clarity has also made interpretation and evaluation more difficult in practice. Tian Zan is highly critical about this in *On the Present Situation of Constitutional Enforcement, Causes and Measures.* Tian explains why he is not sanguine about the situation, in which two problems stand out. First, the constitution denied relevance in litigation procedures and second, the constitutional supervision system exists in name only. There are mainly three reasons for this: widespread illiteracy about the constitution among the public, political appropriation of the functions of the constitution, and belief in value nihilism with regard to the constitution among many. China's constitutional implementation has fallen into the dilemma in which substance is severed from process.[16] The issue that is more prominent than the one pointed out by Tian Zan is that effective institutionalized definition or institutionalized meaning of constitutional implementation has not yet been formed in practice, therefore, the implementation motivation and implementation effect are seriously dislocated judging from the constitutional implementation phenomenon. A case in point is *the Criminal Procedure Law of the People's Republic of China* which was amended for the second time according to *the Decision on Revising the Criminal Procedure Law of the People's Republic of China* adopted at the Fifth Session of the 11th National People's Congress on March 14, 2012, "respect and safeguard human rights" was written in Article 2 of new provisions. Based on the mutual relations between the Constitution and branch laws, *the Criminal Procedure Law* as the basic law enacted by the National People's Congress has the mission of enacting and specifying constitutional principles and various systems in the Constitution. "The state respects and safeguards human rights" was written in the Constitution at its fourth amendment in 2004, demonstrating the spirit of constitutional respect and protection of human rights. At the time of being revised, *the Criminal Procedure Law* as a branch law reiterates the provision on respecting and protecting human rights in a specific provision. This is highly meaningful in both theory of law and specific legal practice from the perspective of the human rights protection spirit of *the Criminal Procedure Law* and the promotion of constitutional implementation. What needs to be studied is that, after human rights were incorporated in the constitution in 2004, the NPC Standing Committee with constitutional interpretation power according to the Constitution has not yet made clear-cut constitutional interpretation of the specific legal meaning of the term "human rights" as contained in the provision of "the state respects and safeguards human rights". In particular, the NPC Standing Committee has not yet defined the subjects of human rights in the form of constitutional interpretation. Therefore, this might lead to "disunity of legal system",

[16] *Journal of Hunan Public Security College*, 2002, Issue 1.

under which *the Criminal Procedure Law* is divorced from the text of Constitution to independently develop its constitutional principle meaning.

This case illustrates how, when the meaning of constitutional implementation is unclear, good intentions can sometimes lead to bad outcome, causing harm to the authority of the Constitution. The official reply issued on August 13, 2001, by the Supreme People's Court in the Qi Yuling Case drew a great deal of attention. Some even consider it "China's first legal case decided by directly citing the constitution".[17] Instead of helping to raise awareness about the constitution, flaws in the way the case handled led to just the opposite outcome. On December 18, 2008, at the 1457th meeting of the judicial committee of the court, the Supreme People's Court passed *the Decision of the Supreme People's Court on Abolishing the Relevant Judicial Interpretations (the Seventh Batch) Promulgated before the End of 2007*, including taking "already stopped the application" as the excuse to annul *the Official Reply of the Supreme People's Court on Whether the Civil Liabilities Shall Be Borne for the Infringement upon a Citizen's Basic Right of Receiving Education as Protected by the Constitution by Means of Infringing upon the Right of Name* (Fa.Shi. [2001] No. 25), and the Decision started to be enforced on December 24, 2008. The annulment of the "August 13 Reply" by the Supreme People's Court received widespread academic criticisms[18] and exerted adverse and negative social influences. From certain point of view, this has reflected the complexity of constitutional implementation issues, so we should not go off half-cocked, let alone taking it as the bait for attracting public attentions.

In short, constitutional implementation concept not only has the academic value of building constitutional law theories. Constitutional implementation concept is also highly relevant for guiding constitutional practices. Since China has long been lacking scientific and effective theoretical guidance for constitutional implementation, and the practices in implementing the Constitution in practice have been different, some have certain positive influences and triggered arguments over the authority and effect of the Constitution, there is a necessity to build persuasive constitutional implementation concept and its application system in theory.

[17]After the judgment of second instance of the Qi Yuling Case, Huang Songyou, when he was Head of the Civil Law Tribunal No. 1 of the Supreme People's Court, wrote an article titled *Judicialization of Constitution and its Significance:A Discussion Beginning with Today's SPC "Reply"* which was published in *People's Court Daily* on August 13, 2001, believing that this case set a precedent in courts' protection of citizens' fundamental rights as stipulated by the Constitution, and created an example of constitution judicialization.

[18]Professor Hu Jinguang observed that the "August 13 Reply" of the SPC was not constitutional interpretation and thus should not be annulled. Refer to Hu Jinguang: The "Reply" to Qi Yuling Case is not the interpretation of the Constitution and thus shall not be annulled by the SPC, *Law Science*, 2009, Issue 4.

2 Evaluation Method of the Constitutional Implementation Situation and Its Influence on the Evaluation Conclusion

Constitutional implementation is a rather complex constitutional phenomenon mixing theoretical and practical features, so the understanding of constitutional implementation status needs profound analysis in theory and emphasis on studying the purpose of constitutional implementation. Only by combining the theoretic ought with the necessity and feasibility in practices, we could thoroughly comprehend the meaning of constitutional implementation concept and establish a rather comprehensive and systematic analysis system for constitutional implementation.

2.1 Constitutional Implementation Status Lies in a Scientific Evaluation Mechanism

1. Logically, the basic theoretical issues related to constitutional implementation include at least the following aspects. First, it is the definition of subjects of constitutional implementation. Who has the obligation to implement the Constitution and to whom the Constitution has the legal binding power Second, definiteness of objects of constitutional implementation. That is whether the objects of constitutional implementation are limited within the text of the Constitution or include constitutional principles or constitutional values outside of the text. If the objects are only limited to the implementation of the text of the Constitution, the question is what contents in the text of the Constitution should be implemented. The answer to this question differentiated in broad sense and narrow sense. According to the broad sense of constitutional norm theory, all stipulations in the text of the Constitution must be implemented, including the declarative facts contained in the Preamble to the Constitution, the constitutional principles contained in the General Principles of the Constitution and the constitutional norms contained in the text of the Constitution. Of which, constitutional norms are the main object of constitutional implementation. The narrow sense of constitutional norm theory does not include the constitutional provisions which don't have specific relations between rights and duties. Narrow-sensed constitutional norms include fundamental authoritative norms, obligatory norms and prohibitive norms. Narrow-sensed constitutional norms also include function and responsibility-oriented norms, conditioned authoritative norms and mandatory norms, etc., that are formed on the basis of the composition of fundamental constitutional norms. Third, the objectivity of the evaluation objects of constitutional implementation. Constitutional implementation evaluation mechanism is established based on the dualistic relations between the subjectivity of implementation objects and the objectivity of

evaluation objects. The target of constitutional implementation is to turn static constitution into dynamic constitution and its basic institutional function is to keep constitution staying in operation. Therefore, logically, who is operating is objective and what should be kept in operation has a strong subjectivity. The so-called constitutional implementation is inevitably embodied through the combination of the subjectivity and objectivity of the evaluation objects in the evaluation system. Fourth, scientificity of evaluation standard. Constitutional implementation is a subjective evaluation based on objective facts. The direct evaluation object is constitution. No matter it is the constitution in its original sense or it is the constitution surpassing the original meaning of the text, there is a strong subjectivity. Whether it could be implemented in reality, there lies individuality differential. That is to say the implementation of constitutional norms should be based on the evaluation measurements, including "enforceability" and "unenforceability", "complete enforcement", and "partial enforcement" and "no enforcement", "stable and continuous enforcement" and "intermittent enforcement", "effective enforcement", and "ineffective enforcement". Fifth, impartiality of the evaluation procedures. Constitutional implementation is the subjective evaluation of the static constitution in dynamic state, so different evaluation subjects could make different evaluation conclusions of relevant state of constitutional implementation. For a çountry's building of constitutional system, an authoritative evaluation mechanism with legal effects should be established in due time. The evaluation process should follow the principles of justice, openness, and transparency so as to offer reliable reference opinions to properly understanding the institutional significance of constitutional implementation and further improve the constitutional system through summarizing the experience and lessons from constitutional implementation.

2. From the perspective of specific evaluation method for constitutional implementation and along with the purpose of constitutional implementation, evaluation should focus on the following several aspects. First, to analyze, article by article, all provisions of the current constitution, including the Preamble, make accurate analysis and evaluation of the general implementation situation of the current constitution and the implementation situation of every specific article from the angle of chapters and articles, through integration of points and spheres, of generality and key points in evaluation conclusions. Second, to draw related statistical charts in line with certain criteria for classification and based on the article by article analysis of the implementation the current constitution. This is to compare the differences and analyze the implementation status of different types of constitutional norms and highlight the impact factors and differentials in constitutional implementation status rising from the features of constitutional norms. Third, to generalize and summarize the constitutional events beyond the provisions of the text of the Constitution but conforming to

constitutional principles and having the significance of promoting constitutional values, and come up with countermeasures and suggestions for constitutional interpretation and revision. Fourth, to study the constitutional implementation status of a country from historical perspective, analyze the implementation status of constitution in different stages and the continuity and mutual influence of the implementation situations of different texts of constitution and study the continuity and integrity of constitutional implementation. Fifth, to compare the states of constitutional implementation of different countries with the same or similar texts of constitution, analyze the implementation characteristics of domestic constitutional text and raise the suggestions and measures for improving constitutional implementation. Sixth, to analyze the macro influence of the constitutional implementation situation on the social development according to a country's specific political development requirement in certain stage. Pointing out the development direction of the rule of law and clarifying the status and effect of constitution in state political and social life, etc.

2.2 *Methodological Problems and Negative Influences Existing in Constitutional Implementation in China*

Chinese constitutional circle's understanding of constitutional implementation shall be deemed as partial or individual investigations either in theoretic or purposive sense. The Chinese constitutional community has not yet comprehensively and systematically established the concept, composition, and significance of constitutional implementation on the basis of consciously defining the nature of constitutional implementation. This situation will inevitably affect the constitutional implementation practice. Due to the existence of many value contradictions in constitutional implementation in real life, the authoritative status of constitution as the fundamental law has not yet been established. On the contrary, the lack of scientific theoretical guidance has resulted in the formalized and simplified constitutional implementation practice, and constitutional implementation has no obvious and actual influence on the social life. This article cites two examples, respectively, representing the current constitutional implementation at the macro-level and the micro-level, which could fully prove that blind advancement of constitutional implementation without correct theoretical guidance would severely hinder the implementation of constitution, reduce the legal effect of constitution as the fundamental law, especially result in poor practical effects of constitutional implementation.

3 Problems Existing in Constitutional Implementation about "Enacting a Law in Conformity with the Constitution"

At present, China's top legislature lays more emphasis on the legislative principle of "enacting the law in accordance with the Constitution" in making laws. Historically, *the Electoral Law of the National People's Congress and Local People's Congresses* (adopted at the Second Session of the Fifth National People's Congress on July 1, 1979) unprecedentedly and indistinctively stipulated in Article 1 that *the Electoral Law of the National People's Congress and Local People's Congresses* is formulated in accordance with the Constitution of the People's Republic of China. Following that, many basic laws or other laws other than those formulated by the NPC and its Standing Committee all put this principle of "formulating the law in accordance with the Constitution" in the first article to demonstrate the constitutionality in making laws. For examples, "in accordance with the Constitution" has been written in all laws related to the Constitution, such as *the Legislation Law*, *the Electoral Law*, *the Basic Law of Hong Kong Special Administrative Region,* and *the Basic Law of the Macao Special Administrative Region.* The provision of "in accordance with the Constitution" has also been contained in administrative branch laws, such as *the Law of Administrative Procedure*, *the State Compensation Law*, *Law of The People's Republic Of China on Administrative Penalty*, *the Administrative Reconsideration Law*, *Administrative License Law*, but not in *the Public Security Administration Punishments Law*. "In accordance with the Constitution" is also incorporated in such criminal laws as *the Criminal Law* and *the Criminal Procedure Law*; in such civil laws as *the General Principles of the Civil Law*, *the Property Law*, *the Law of Succession* and *the Civil Procedure Law*, but not in *the Contract Law*, *the Marriage Law* and *the Arbitration Law*; in such commercial laws as *the Company Law* and *the Insurance Law*, but not in *the Securities Law*, *the Law of Maritime Commerce* and *the Bankruptcy Law*; in such intellectual property laws as *the Copyright Law*, but not in *the Patent Law* and *the Trademark Law*. The original legislative intention of pointing out that "the law is formulated in accordance with the Constitution" in general terms in the first article is to declare that the legislation follows the stipulations of the Constitution and conduct the constitutional implementation through specifying constitutional principles and constitutional norms. However, this kind of abstract statement of formulating the law in accordance with the Constitution has two fatal deficiencies.

First, it fails to effectively explain the fact that half of the existing 240[19] or so laws have incorporated the statement that "enacting the law in accordance with the Constitution" and the other half has not. Does this mean they were not enacted according to the constitution? Second, those containing "the law is enacted in accordance with the law" fail to logically tell how they followed the Constitution due to the too abstract legislative principle. Therefore, some affaires that are not touched in the text of the Constitution have been formulated "in accordance with the constitution" in specific laws. A typical case is *the Legislation Law* formulated in 2000. Article 1 of the law makes clear, "the law is enacted in accordance with the Constitution with a view to standardizing legislation, establishing a sound legislative system of the State, establishing and improving the socialist legal system with Chinese characteristics, safeguarding and developing socialist democracy, promoting governance by law and building a socialist country under the rule of law." But, the provisions in Article 93 of *the Legislation Law* obviously have no constitutional basis. This article states, "The Central Military Commission, in accordance with the Constitution and laws, formulate military regulations. The General Departments, the various services and arms and the military commands of the Central Military Commission may, in accordance with laws and the military regulations, decisions and orders of the Commission, formulate military rules within the limits of their power. The Central Military Commission has no power to make laws and regulations and its departments, armed services and military regions have no power to develop military rules as granted by the Constitution. Since Article 1 of *the Legislation Law* clearly stipulates that it is enacted in accordance with the Constitution and the current constitution contains no stipulations on enacting military regulations and military rules in the functions and powers of the Central Military Commission, the NPC Standing Committee with the power to interpret the constitution should explain why the Central Military Commission's formulation of military rules and regulations is constitutional in the form of constitutional interpretation. Up to now, there is no explanation and demonstration of this issue. As such, the legal question generated is that "formulating the law in accordance with the law" can be freely applied without having to strictly follow the spirit of the text of the Constitution. The result might be the people's bewilderment and confusion about the meaning of "in accordance with the constitution".

[19]By the end of 2010, the National People's Congress and its Standing Committee had enacted 236 laws. The new laws enacted by the National People's Congress and its Standing Committee as of 2011 include *Vehicle and Vessel Tax Law of the People's Republic of China, the Intangible Cultural Heritage Law of the People's Republic of China, the Administrative Compulsion Law of the People's Republic of China* and *the Military Personnel Insurance Law of the People's Republic of China*. By the end of May 2012, 240 laws had been enacted. However, the National People's Congress didn't release an authoritative number.

4 Look at the Inadequacy of Theories about Constitutional Implementation in the View of Article 100 of the Constitution

Currently, in China's constitutional implementation practices, there is the phenomenon that the laws enacted in accordance with Article 100 of the 1954 Constitution are still valid. According to the white paper titled *China's Efforts and Achievements in Promoting the Rule of Law* issued by the State Council Information Office in February 2008, China's currently effective laws numbered 229 (the actual number should be 240), 79 of which were administrative laws, and the second law was *the Resolution of the Standing Committee of the National People's Congress on Approving the Decision of the State Council on Issues Concerning Reeducation through Labor*. This resolution was adopted at the 78th Session of the Standing Committee of the National People's Congress on August 1, 1957. According to *China's Efforts and Achievements in Promoting the Rule of Law*, this resolution was still an effective law at that moment. The specific content of the "law" was *the Decision of the State Council on Issues Concerning Reeducation through Labor* approved by this resolution. *The Decision of the State Council on Issues Concerning Reeducation through Labor* clearly stipulated that *the Decision* was enacted in accordance with Article 100[20] of the Constitution of the People's Republic of China. From the legal point of view, *the Decision of the State Council on Issues Concerning Reeducation through Labor* was directly enacted in accordance with Article 100 of the Constitution of the People's Republic of China adopted in 1954. From the perspective of the legislative basis, *the Decision* would not be legitimate without this Article 100. Thus it can be reasoned reversely, as *the Decision* is still effective at the moment, the constitutional basis should remain effective. In this case, it would be easy to conclude that Article 100 of the 1954 Constitution, the legislative basis of *the Decision of the State Council on Issues Concerning Reeducation through Labor*, is still effective currently among others confirmed in the white paper titled *China's Efforts and Achievements in Promoting the Rule of Law* issued by the State Council Information Office including *the Resolution of the Standing Committee of the National People's Congress on Approving the Decision of the State Council on Issues Concerning Reeducation through Labor*. Otherwise, the decision would lose its necessary legitimacy. As *the Decision of the State Council on Issues Concerning Reeducation through Labor* supports the direct legal effect of Article 100 of the 1954 Constitution, a question is raised for China's constitutional theories, i.e., how to quote constitutional text in the process of constitutional implementation. The text of constitution generally recognized by the constitutional community is that of the 1982 Constitution. The constitutional circle also calls the 1982 Constitution as the

[20]According to Article 100 of the 1954 Constitution, citizens of the People's Republic of China must abide by the Constitution and the law, observe labor discipline, observe public order and respect public morality.

current constitution. However, the text of the 1982 Constitution does not specify that all previous constitutional texts start to lose their legal effect on the date of the enforcement of the Constitution. This deficiency in provisions of the constitutional text has naturally resulted in the dilemma of difficult selection of currently effective "constitutional text" once the 1954 Constitution is taken as the currently effective law other than the text of the 1982 Constitution as the legal basis for making laws. If we admit this kind of realities, then we can conclude legally that the basic constitutional principles and basic systems of the 1954 Constitution as the first constitution of the People's Republic of China could be taken as the constitutional basis in constitutional implementation. We can also conclude that specific articles of the 1954 Constitution can be quoted as the basis for specific legislations. For instance, the 1954 Constitution had 106 articles, but the 1982 Constitution has 138 articles. 106 entries of the articles of the two constitutions are duplicated. Therefore, if there is a need to take a specific article of the 1954 Constitution as the legislative basis, there is a need to clearly indicate which article of the 1954 Constitution is being quoted so as to differentiate it from the same entry of the 1982. If just broadly referring to a constitution article, it might be difficult to find the corresponding text in constitution. In addition, if specific articles of the 1954 Constitution can be quoted, then there will be a question about whether articles of the 1975 Constitution and 1978 Constitution can be quoted as well. As a whole, the theoretical issue brought about by the still valid Article 100 of the 1954 Constitution is rather severe. Of course, the simplest way to solve this theoretical issue is to annul *the Decision of the State Council on Issues Concerning Reeducation through Labor* enacted in accordance with Article 100 of the 1954 Constitution. If *the Decision of the State Council on Issues Concerning Reeducation through Labor* is annulled on the ground that Article 100 of the 1954 Constitution cannot be taken as a valid article, it would be significant both in theories and practices. Legally, this practice clearly affirms that only the text of the 1982 Constitution could be taken as the applicable constitutional text with specific legal effect and no specific entry of all previous constitutional texts before the 1982 Constitution could be applied anymore. This has affirmed the solely effectiveness of the 1982 Constitution as the current constitution in the field of constitution application, and the so-called "current" would have "currently effective" legal meaning. In practice, the evidence cited to justify annulling *the Decision of the State Council on Issues Concerning Reeducation through Labor* in the past few years was inadequate. *The Decision of the State Council on Issues Concerning Reeducation through Labor* has been invalidated for lack of legislative basis. Thus, the requirement for constitutionality would be raised for laws and regulations, making the Constitution truly become the legal basis for people's behaviors and play its role as the legal standard for judging the right and wrong.

To solve above-said constitutional implementation difficulties generated from quoting specific articles of the constitutional text, one practical and feasible method is to refer to *the Organic Law of the State Council* adopted during the First Session of the First National People's Congress in 1954. Article 1 of *the Organic Law of the State Council* stipulated that *the Organic Law of the State Council of the People's*

Republic of China was enacted in accordance with the second clause of Article 48 of the Constitution of the People's Republic of China.[21] Obviously, "in accordance with the second clause of Article 48 of the Constitution of the People's Republic of China" is accurate. The Fifth Session of the Fifth National People's Congress reformulated *the Organic Law of the State Council of the People's Republic of China* on December 10, 1982. According to Article 1 of this reformulated law, "This *Organic Law* is formulated in accordance with the provisions concerning the State Council in the Constitution of the People's Republic of China." This reformulated *Organic Law of the State Council* just emphasized "in accordance with the provisions concerning the State Council in the Constitution of the People's Republic of China" in general terms. The possible influence of relevant articles of the 1954 Constitution on the reformulated *Organic Law of the State Council* cannot be completely ruled out, but the accuracy and reliability of "in accordance with the Constitution" were rather flexible and clear. *The Regulation on Agriculture Tax* (adopted at the 96th Session of the NPC Standing Committee on June 3, 1958, and annulled at the session of the NPC Standing Committee on December 29, 2005) stated in Article 1 that citizens of the People's Republic of China have the duty to pay taxes by law in accordance with Article 102 of the Constitution.[22] As *the Regulation on Agriculture Tax* was annulled due to the abolishment of agricultural taxes, Article 102 of the Constitution which was the basis for the enactment of *the Regulation on Agriculture Tax* no longer has its influence on constitutional implementation.

5 Several Suggestions for Strengthening the Building of Constitutional Implementation System

Constitutional implementation is an important topic in constitutional theories and constitutional practices. However, for quite a long period of time, systematic studies of China's constitutional circle on constitutional implementation have been inadequate, which have resulted in many misunderstandings of issues related to

---

[21]The second clause of Article 48 of the 1954 Constitution stipulated, "The organization of the State Council is determined by law.".

[22]Article 102 of the 1954 Constitution stipulated, "Citizens of the People's Republic of China have the duty to pay taxes according to law." *The Regulation of the People's Republic of China on Agriculture Tax* was not revised before being annulled on January 1, 2006. As stipulated in its Article 1, in order to ensure the national socialist construction, help consolidate ***the agricultural cooperation system*** and promote agricultural development, this regulation is enacted in accordance with the stipulation of Article 102 of ***the Constitution of the People's Republic of China***, which was "citizens of *the People's Republic of China* have the duty to pay taxes according to law". Obviously, under the circumstance that the 1982 Constitution has come into force, Article 1 of *the Regulation on Agriculture Tax* has a serious referential unclearness, and has the same nature of the legal issues with that of *the Decision of the State Council on Issues Concerning Reeducation through Labor.*

constitutional implementation in the theory of law, and have been applied disorderly in practice. Eventually, theoretical and practical issues related to constitutional implementation will be thoroughly and effectively resolved, but from the perspective of the effectiveness, the research vision on constitutional implementation could be further broadened from the following angles. The currently disordered legal theories about constitutional implementation could be changed through defining the concept and nature of constitutional implementation and effectively applying the analyzing methods of constitutional implementation.

5.1 Further Cognizing the Nature of Constitutional Implementation through Improving the Evaluation Mechanism

"Legislation alone is insufficient." The function of the concept of constitutional implementation as an important concept of constitutional law studies is to turn static constitution into dynamic constitution and turn literal constitution into constitution in action. In recent years, the constitutional community has presented some works about studies on constitutional evaluation,[23] constitutional realization,[24] among other phenomena closely related to the constitutional implementation concept. In terms of the nature of its concept, constitutional implementation is not constitutional activities or constitutional behaviors in purely objective sense. It is similar to the concept and meaning of constitutional practice,[25] but it must rely on a set of scientific evaluation system to confirm its basic meaning. Constitutional implementation is actually aimed at finding a necessary connection in system between the implementation object and implementation result. Therefore, if we talk about the result of constitutional implementation too generally without studies on specific implementation object, it will be hollow, especially in practice. So, it is easy to trigger the deficiencies such as "sidelining the Constitution" and formalizing "the legal effect of the Constitution". Without regard to practical results but simply advocating the significance of constitutional text and using the advocacy effect to replace the implementation result could also make the legal status of the

[23]Master's thesis of Zhong Mingyou: *On Constitutional Evaluation*. This thesis concludes that constitutional evaluation is an important theoretical issue in constitutional law. Better constitutional evaluation has a profound theoretical significance and realistic guiding significance for restricting state powers, protecting citizens' rights, building up constitutional authority and promoting constitutional government building. For historical reasons, China attaches little importance to constitutional studies, and there are few works or papers about constitutional evaluation theories. Guangxi Normal University, 2005, refer to http://dbpub.cnki.net/grid2008/detail.aspx?dbname=CMFD9908&filename=2005142827.nh, lastly visited on April 7, 2014.

[24]Zhengchang [2].

[25]Qiang and Yongzhao [3].

Constitution as the fundamental law a castle in air. Therefore, from the evaluation perspective, constitutional implementation must focus on a high degree of unity of constitutional implementation objects and constitutional implementation effects. Constitutional implementation concept needs to be investigated in a comprehensive and holistic manner in the logical chains mutually connected, such as constitution, constitutional evaluation, and constitution realization. We need to cognize the subjectivity and objectivity of constitutional implementation concept, especially the practicality and social influence of constitutional implementation concept and shall not abuse the constitutional implementation concept to express We shall assess the status of constitutional implementation scientifically based on the constitution, establish the authority of the constitution as the fundamental law, and improve its function in guiding people's actual behaviors as legal norms.

5.2 *Scientifically Classify the Evaluation Objects of Constitutional Implementation*

The conclusion of evaluations of constitutional implementation situation largely depends on the classification of constitutional implementation objects. In regard to constitution law theories, constitutional implementation objects cannot be limited to constitutional text. Actual practice proves that comprehending the constitutional implementation concept within the framework of constitutional text would limit the guiding role of constitutional values. In particular, the guiding role of some important constitutional principles for people's behaviors would be neglected. Theoretically speaking, constitutional text is the reflection of constitutional values, but it is limited to the specific political environment and historical background. It is impossible for the constitutional text of any country to completely demonstrate idealized constitutional value requirement. Therefore, if it is possible to surpass constitutional text and directly apply better constitutional values to guide people's behaviors in constitutional practice, constitutional values should be carried forward without hesitation. For example, from the perspective of the value function and value requirement of democracy, direct democracy should have the value quality better than that of indirect democracy. When direct democracy could effectively adjust people's behaviors, applying the direct democratic measures to resolve constitutional issues should not be deemed as being unconstitutional, even it could be resolved by indirect democratic mechanism as written in the Constitution text.[26]

---

[26]In 2008, the practice of directly electing township head in Buyun Township of Sichuan province had no clear basis from the perspective of the constitutional text. However, looking from the legal theory of constitutional law, under the circumstance that voters could directly elect township head through their behaviors, there would be no need to elect the township head by the representatives elected by the people. Here, it involves the implementation of constitutional principles or constitutional values.

Besides, due to the influence of the evaluation mechanism, both constitutional implementation modality in the macro-sense and specific measures in microsense are the manifestation of the constitutional implementation status. However, these two must be organically united in constitutional practices and the focus should be put on specific measures rather than the political stance in propaganda and macrosense. Regarding the stipulations of constitutional text, there is also a need to make correct classifications. With regard to the constitutional provisions confirming some legal facts, we shall mainly take into consideration whether there are contradictory statements or negative statements against the legal facts confirmed by the Constitution in practice. Regarding the constitutional norms setting the specific rights and duties of state organs, we need to observe the fulfilment of these specific rights and duties. With regard to the citizens' fundamental rights as stipulated by the Constitution and realized through specific legislative measures, there is a need to emphasize the implementation of legislative organs' formulation of laws to protect human rights. When it comes to the events with quantitative relations requirements like the specific time and place as stipulated in constitutional text, there is a need to strictly observe the implementation of constitutional stipulations. On top of that, there is a need to objectively analyze the constitutional stipulations in the constitutional text, especially the normative preciseness of constitutional norms, and sort out constitutional stipulations by classification, such as constitutional provisions with serious problems in constitution-making technology and with too strong political overtones. The stipulations inconsistent with the overall spirit of the Constitution text shall be annulled and prevented from being enforced. In terms of policy-oriented provisions or provisions with strong political overtone, the value appeal of these constitutional provisions shall be realized through other political channels. In short, the conclusion of constitutional implementation evaluation shall be comprehensive and objective rather than being limited to some certain aspects and shall even refrain from taking a part for the whole and maliciously denying the authority of the Constitution

5.3 Grasp the Major Links and Areas of Constitutional Implementation

In view of mainstream values of modern constitutions, the core values of the constitutional system include effectively restricting state organs' state powers, protecting citizens' fundamental rights and the obligation to protect human rights that should be fulfilled by state parties as stipulated by international covenants of human rights through constitution. Therefore, the focus on state organs' correct fulfillment of responsibilities endowed by the Constitution and citizen's fulfillment of fundamental rights enjoyed in accordance with the constitution represents the main links and areas in constitutional implementation all around the world. For this purpose, reviewing whether the laws enacted by the legislative body have substantively encroached the basic human rights and citizens' fundamental rights as stipulated in the Constitution represents the priorities of constitutional implementation and an important institutional guarantee for enhancing constitutional implementation through effective supervision mechanism. For the key areas in constitutional implementation key areas, there should be a corresponding supervision mechanism to guarantee the effective realization of the core values established by the Constitution. The primary issue existing in China's constitutional implementation is the lack of guarantee for the system that protect the supervision of state organs' exercise of state powers and the realization of citizens' fundamental rights. of the deficiencies lie in two parts, one, lack of necessary legal procedures of power exercise in accordance with the Constitution, two, inadequate constitutional implementation supervision mechanism and the lack of institutions to ensure the preservation of constitutional authority and the constitutional implementation.

5.4 Putting in Place a Constitutional Interpretation Mechanism

Constitutional implementation is closely related to constitution evaluation, so the actual situation of constitutional implementation and its influence on people's behaviors have certain subjectivity. The constitutional implementation fields are very extensive, the objects of constitutional implementation subject to scientific evaluation are also complicated, and they basically have the same meanings as the constitution in value form and constitution in textual meaning. In behavioral law, most constitutional implementation phenomena happen automatically and require not much institutional attention. Only in the fields with possible constitutional disputes, there would be the requirement for strengthening constitutional implementation evaluation and establishing a necessary constitutional implementation supervision mechanism. The Preamble to the Constitution of China defines a rather broad and wide concept of constitutional implementation. According to the Preamble, "This Constitution, in legal form, affirms the achievements of the struggles of the Chinese people of all nationalities and defines the basic system and basic tasks of the State; it is the fundamental law of the State and has supreme legal authority. The people of all nationalities, all State organs, the armed forces, all political parties and public organizations and all enterprises and institutions in the country must take the Constitution as the basic standard of conduct, and they have the duty to uphold the dignity of the Constitution and ensure its implementation." According to above statement, all state organs, public organizations, and individual citizens shall shoulder certain duties of constitutional implementation. Therefore, from the perspective of behavioral law, the constitutional implementation effect shall rely on state organs, public organizations and individual citizens to consciously confine their conducts to constitution stipulations rather than relying on external forces such as the constitutional implementation evaluation mechanism or supervisory mechanism for advancement. Priorities of our attention to constitutional implementation and its influences shall lie in constitutionally controversial areas, i.e., there are disputes over how to implement the Constitution in the implementation process and effective settlement of these disputes can greatly promote the effectiveness of constitutional implementation. Therefore, establishing an effective constitutional dispute settlement mechanism is the biggest guarantee of constitutional implementation. According to the stipulations of the current constitution, the National People's Congress and its Standing Committee have the power and duty to supervise constitutional implementation. While the Standing Committee of the National People's Congress has the power to interpret the Constitution pursuant to the provisions of Article 67 of the current constitution. Therefore in China's constitutional implementation, the very core is how to launch the constitutional interpretation mechanism institutionally. If the Standing Committee of the NPC can proactively exercise the power to interpret the Constitution, it could effectively resolve various kinds of constitution disputes in constitutional implementation and facilitate the effective implementation of constitutional text and constitutional principles. From this point of view, addressing the institutional dilemma in constitutional implementation depends on the NPC Standing Committee's timely and effective launch of the constitutional interpretation mechanism. Without the constitutional interpretation mechanism, it is impossible to discuss the situation of constitutional implementation and correctly evaluate the social effects of constitutional implementation in a strict and scientific sense.

References

1. Cai Dingjian: "The Concept of Constitutional Application and the Means thereof", *China Legal Science*, 2004, Issue 1.
2. Hu Zhengchang: *Constitutional Text and Realization*, China University of Political Science and Law Press, June 2009, first edition.
3. Qin Qiang, Xie Yongzhao: Value Unity of Constitutional Text and Constitutional Practice – Thinking based on the Importance of Constitutional Law Methodology, *Theoretical Exploration*, 2011, Issue 5.

Legislative Application of the Constitution: Key Features and Critical Analysis

Jihong Mo

The Constitution as the fundamental law is the legal basis for the generation of other legal forms. In modern law-based society, all legislative actions of legislative organs are illegitimate without constitutional authorization. China's current constitution also clearly stipulates the principle of enacting laws in accordance with the Constitution. Related articles of the Constitution involve the following aspects. According to the third clause of Article 5, "No laws or administrative or local regulations may contravene the Constitution." Article 89 (1) stipulates that the State Council exercises the following functions and powers: to adopt administrative measures, enact administrative regulations and issue decisions and orders in accordance with the Constitution and other laws. As provided in Article 100, "The People's provincial congresses of provinces, and municipalities directly under the Central Government, and their standing committees may adopt local regulations, which must not contravene the Constitution and other laws and administrative regulations, and they shall report such local regulations to the Standing Committee of the National People's Congress for record." Above stipulations of the Constitution clearly indicate this cardinal principle of enacting laws in accordance with the Constitution, especially when it comes to the basic laws and other laws enacted by the National People's Congress and its Standing Committee, administrative regulations enacted by the State Council and local regulations adopted by local People's congresses and their standing committees. This text only takes examples of the laws enacted by the National People's Congress and its Standing Committee to analyze current situations and problems of "enacting laws in accordance with the Constitution" by the top legislative body through studying the manifestation of constitutional concept in legal texts, in order to make some academic recommendations for the top legislative body's strengthening the constitutionality of the law.

J. Mo (✉)
Institute of Law, Chinese Academy of Social Sciences, Beijing, China
e-mail: 13263169197@163.com

L. Li et al. (eds.), *Constitutional Development in China, 1982–2012*,
Research Series on the Chinese Dream and China's Development Path,
https://doi.org/10.1007/978-981-32-9261-1_13

1 Analytical Object and Method

The analytical object of this paper is only limited to the basic laws and other non-basic laws as well as decisions equivalent to laws enacted and promulgated by the National People's Congress and its Standing Committee. To date, the Standing Committee of the National People's Congress as the top legislative body hasn't released accurate data about the enactment of laws in real time. Therefore, this paper could only refer to the statistics about the number of laws contained in the white paper on *the Socialist System of Laws with Chinese Characteristics* (3) (2011),[1] *the Annual Report on Rule of Law Construction in China (2011)*[2] issued by China Law Society and the white paper on *China's Efforts and Achievements in Promoting the Rule of Law*[3](2008). The statistics suggest that the number of current laws totaled 244 (including the Constitution). The analytical method of this paper is mainly the statistical analysis in typological sense. That is to make statistics of the distribution of related data according to the preset statistical target,[4] finally meet the requirement for demonstrating the Constitution in laws enacted by the top legislative body, and grasp the situation of the top legislative body's legislation in accordance with the Constitution and the actual binding force of the Constitution for laws from a macro perspective.

2 Distribution of the Concept of Constitution in Current Laws

Among the 244 samples for analysis, "constitution" appeared for 240 times in total, representing an occurrence rate of 98.36% on average in each law. 149 legal documents contain the concept of constitution, accounting for 59.02% of the 244 sample laws for analysis. The word "constitution" does not appear in 40.98% of the 244 laws. 81 laws clearly contain the stipulation that "the law is enacted in accordance with the Constitution" in the first article, representing 33.196% of all samples. 16 laws stipulate enacting the law in accordance with the Constitution and other laws, making up 6.557% of all samples, and 19.753% of the laws containing that "the law is enacted in accordance with the Constitution". The National People's Congress has enacted 32 basic laws, accounting for 13.114% of the total sample laws, but 5 of these basic laws have no such stipulation in the first article as "the law is enacted in accordance with the Constitution".

[1]Refer to http://politics.people.com.cn/GB/101380/17427549.html, lastly visited on April 7, 2014.

[2]Refer to http://www.legaldaily.com.cn/index_article/content/2012-07/17/content_3716784.htm?node=6148, lastly visited on April 7, 2014.

[3]Refer tohttp://www.iolaw.org.cn/showNews.asp?id=29465, lastly visited on April 7, 2014.

[4]The data about the distribution of "the constitution" in laws are provided by assistant researcher Jin Yuzhen of the Law Branch Library of Chinese Academy of Social Sciences. Heartfelt gratitude is expressed hereby.

Among all laws with the concept of constitution, 26 involve "shall not contravene the Constitution"; 32 contain "exercise functions and powers in accordance with the Constitution"; 14 stipulate constitutional assurance of the rights; 8 provide the guarantee of effective implementation of the Constitution; 35 require abiding by the Constitution (including advocacy and loyal to the Constitution); 7 stipulate that the Constitution shall not be violated; 2 mention supervising the implementation of the Constitution; 10 are interpretations of the Constitution; 4 involve the revision of the Constitution; 10 involve constitutional principles; and 10 involve specific provisions and chapters of the Constitution.

3 Application Characteristic of China's Constitution in Legislation

According to the analyses of the 244 samples, more than half of the laws indicate the attitude of "enacting laws in accordance with the Constitution" with the statement that "the law is enacted in accordance with the Constitution" in their first articles. This indicates that the top legislative body has certain legislative awareness with regard to the constitutional basis for enacting new laws. The Constitution has certain binding force for the legislative activities of legislative organs. The awareness of applying and implementing the Constitution in legislations is relatively ideal. However, if the text provision of enacting laws "in accordance with the Constitution" is further analyzed, the following characteristics can be found.

3.1 Generalized Stipulation of "in accordance with the Constitution" in Most Cases, and Unclear Legal Relations Between the Constitution and Specific Laws

According to sample analyses, altogether 81 laws clearly contain the statement that "the law is enacted in accordance with the Constitution" in their first articles, accounting for 33.196% of all samples, 65 of which just simply state "in accordance with the law", but only one law titled *the Military Service Law of the People's Republic of China* clearly points out in its Article 1 which specific article of the Constitution it followed for the enactment. Article 1 of the law stipulates, "This Law is enacted pursuant to Article 55 of the Constitution of the People's Republic of China which stipulates, 'it is the sacred duty of every citizen of the People's Republic of China to defend the motherland and resist aggression. It is the honorable duty of citizens of the People's Republic of China to perform military service and join the militia in accordance with the law,' and in accordance with other relevant provisions of the Constitution." *The Military Service Law of the People's Republic of China* clearly points out that its legislative basis is Article 55 of the Constitution, so it seems that its constitutional basis is more solid and clearer compared with the legislative attitude of other laws' enaction in the sense of "in accordance with the Constitution".

3.2 Very Few Cases Differentiating Constitutional Norms and Constitutional Principles, and Only a Few Laws with Emphasis on the Status of Constitutional Principles

With regard to whether the provisions of the Constitution contain the code of conduct of two natures, namely constitutional principle and constitutional norm. From the overall situation of these samples, there is no clear-cut legal attitude and only a small number of them emphasize the importance of constitutional principles in legislation. For example, *the Law on Assemblies, Processions and Demonstrations* stipulates in Article 4, "In exercising their right to assembly, procession and demonstration, citizens must abide by the Constitution and the laws, shall not oppose the cardinal principles specified in the Constitution and shall not impair state, public or collective interests or the lawful freedoms and rights of other citizens."

3.3 Only a Small Number of Law Texts Involve Matters Concerning Specific Implementation of Some Specific Article of the Constitution, Indicating Legislative Tendency of Laws as the Embodiment of the Constitution

It has been an authoritative viewpoint recognized in traditional constitutional theories that laws are the embodiment of the Constitution, but few works undertook studies and scientific argumentations in their specific legal texts. At present, the texts of the following laws include the implementation of specific articles of the Constitution: Article 3 of *the Organic Law of the State Council* stipulates that the State Council exercises the functions and powers as provided in Article 89 of the Constitution. Article 4 of *the Regional National Autonomy Law* stipulates, "The organs of self-government of national autonomous areas shall exercise the functions and powers of local organs of the State as specified in Section 5 of Chapter III of the Constitution. At the same time, they shall exercise the power of autonomy within the limits of their authority as prescribed by the Constitution, by this Law and other laws, and implement the laws and policies of the State in light of existing local conditions." Article 11 of *the Basic Law of Hong Kong Special Administrative Region of the People's Republic of China* stipulates, "In accordance with Article 31 of the Constitution of the People's Republic of China, the systems and policies practiced in the Hong Kong Special Administrative Region, including the social and economic systems, the system for safeguarding the fundamental rights and freedoms of its residents, the executive, legislative and judicial systems, and the relevant policies, shall be based on the provisions of this law." Article 11 of *the Basic Law of Macao Special Administrative Region of the People's Republic of China* stipulates, "In accordance with Article 31 of the Constitution of the People's Republic of China, the systems and policies practiced in the Macao Special Administrative Region, including the social and economic systems, the systems for safeguarding the fundamental rights and freedoms of its residents, the executive, legislative and judicial systems, and the relevant policies, shall be based on the provisions of this Law." On the top of that, the second clause(2) of Article 56 of *the Legislation Law of the People's Republic of China* stipulates, "The administrative regulations may be formulated to govern the following matters: matters within the administrative functions and powers of the State Council as provided for in Article 89 of the Constitution." As stipulated in Article 80 (1), "The National People's Congress has the power to alter or annul any inappropriate laws enacted by its Standing Committee, and to annul any autonomous regulations or separate regulations which have been approved by its Standing Committee but which contravene the Constitution or the provision of the second paragraph in Article 66 of this Law." Article 88 (2) also stipulates, "The Standing Committee of the National People's Congress has the power to annul any administrative regulations which contradict the Constitution and laws, to annul any local regulations which contradict the Constitution, laws or administrative regulations, and to annul any autonomous regulations or separate regulations which have been approved by the standing committees of the People's congresses of the relevant provinces, autonomous regions or municipalities but which contravene the Constitution or the provision of the second paragraph in Article 66 of this Law."

3.4 The Lack of Reference Effect of Basic Laws and Other Non-basic Laws Enacted by the National People's Congress and Its Standing Committee

Looking from the samples for analysis, the National People's Congress has enacted 32 basic laws, accounting for 13.114% of the total samples. However, 5 of the basic laws enacted by the National People's Congress have no such stipulation as "the law is enacted in accordance with the Constitution" in the first article. These 5 laws enacted by the National People's Congress have no direct connection with the Constitution in legislative origin, so a question was raised in legal theory: whether the laws enacted by the National People's Congress are allowed not to abide by the Constitution? The most typical example is *the Contract Law of the People's*

Republic of China, but issues still fatally exist,[5]which is what is the constitutional basis for *the Contract Law of the People's Republic of China*? Another example is that the Standing Committee of the National People's Congress has enacted and formulated the laws that are enacted in accordance with the Constitution and the NPC Standing Committee. For instance, Article 1 of *the Regulations on the Military Ranks of Officers of the Chinese People's Liberation Army* stipulates, "These Regulations are formulated in accordance with the relevant provisions of *the Constitution of the People's Republic of China* and *the Military Service Law of the People's Republic of China*." The Second Meeting of the Sixth National People's Congress on May 31, 1984 adopted *Order of the President of the People's Republic of China No. 14. The Military Service Law of the People's Republic of China* was amended for the first time according to *the Decision on Revising the Military Service Law of the People's Republic of China* adopted at the Sixth Session of the Ninth Standing Committee of the National People's Congress on December 29, 1998; for the second time according to *the Decision of the Standing Committee of the National People's Congress on Amending Some Laws* adopted at the Tenth Session of the Eleventh Standing Committee of the National People's Congress **on August 27,** 2009; for the third time according to *the Decision on Revising the Military Service Law of the People's Republic of China* adopted at the 23rd Session of the Standing Committee of the Eleventh National People's Congress on October 29, 2011. One more example, *the Law of the People's Republic of China on Diplomatic Personnel Stationed Abroad* stipulates in its Article 1, "This Law is formulated in accordance with the Constitution and *the Law on Public Servants* for the purposes of building high-quality diplomatic personnel teams stationed abroad, ensuring diplomatic missions stationed abroad perform their duties pursuant to the law, regulating the management of diplomatic personnel stationed abroad, and protecting their legitimate rights and interests." With respect to legislative basis for above sample laws, the Constitution and other laws are taken as the basis, but their slight differences are that *the Regulations on the Military Ranks of Officers of the Chinese People's Liberation Army* takes *the Constitution of the People's Republic of China* and *the Military Service Law of the People's Republic of China* as the legislative basis. *The Law of the People's Republic of China on Diplomatic Personnel Stationed Abroad* takes the Constitution and *the Law on Public Servants*.

Thereby, we can analyze that legislative powers may not be clearly classified even with the additional factor of being in conformity with other laws. *The Regulations on the Military Ranks of Officers of the Chinese People's Liberation Army* is enacted by the Standing Committee of the National People's Congress. The legislative basis of *the Regulations on the Military Ranks of Officers of the Chinese People's Liberation Army* is related provisions of *the Constitution of the People's Republic of China* and *the Military Service Law of the People's Republic of China. The Regulations on the*

[5]Article 1 of *the Rules of Procedure for the Standing Committee of the National People's Congress of the People's Republic of China* stipulates, "These Rules are formulated in accordance with the provisions of the Constitution and *the Organic Law of the National People's Congress* and in the light of the practical experience of the Standing Committee of the National People's Congress."

Military Ranks of Officers of the Chinese People's Liberation Army is enacted by the NPC Standing Committee while *the Constitution of the People's Republic of China* and *the Military Service Law of the People's Republic of China* are enacted by the National People's Congress, so the subordinate NPC Standing Committee shall take the Constitution and the basic laws enacted by the NPC as the basis. However, *the Law of the People's Republic of China on Diplomatic Personnel Stationed Abroad* stipulates, "This Law is formulated in accordance with the Constitution and *the Law on Public Servants*", in which *the Law on Public Servants* is formulated by the NPC Standing Committee. Hereby, a very clear logical question is generated, which is whether the NPC Standing Committee could take the Constitution and its previously formulated laws other than basic laws as the legislative basis. The laws enacted by the NPC Standing Committee can be taken as the basis for enacting another law by itself.

3.5 Failing to Determine the Basis and Source of "in accordance with the Constitution" in Legal Texts Makes the Legislation of the Next Level Less Scientific and Rational

The meaning of formulating a legal form "in accordance with the law" is clearly defined in legal texts, but it is difficult to effectively prove it after careful comparisons with constitutional text. The most typical example is "the Central Military Commission shall, in accordance with the Constitution and laws, formulate military regulations" as stipulated in Article 93 of *the Legislation Law of the People's Republic of China*. Yet, after looking through the constitutional text, it is hard to find such provision as "the Central Military Commission shall formulate military regulations" in the Constitution and difficult to prove it through refined constitutional interpretation. A similar case is the Article 56 of *the Legislation Law of the People's Republic of China*, which stipulates, "The State Council shall, in accordance with the Constitution and laws, formulate administrative regulations." In terms of the State Council's formulation of administrative regulations "in accordance with the Constitution and laws", questions were raised, should it be interpreted as "in accordance with the Constitution" or "in accordance with the laws", or as both "in accordance with the Constitution" and "in accordance with the laws". This question cannot be effectively resolved by referring to the constitutional text.

3.6 Unexplainable Legislative Basis Still Exists

From the perspective of sample analysis, a few effective laws still take related provisions of the 1954 Constitution as the legislative basis. For instance, *the Resolution of the Standing Committee of the National People's Congress on Approving the Decision of the State Council on Issues concerning Reeducation through Labor* stipulates, "The following decision regarding the question of reeducation through labor is made in accordance with the provisions of Article 100 of the Constitution of the People's Republic of China and with a view to reforming those persons who are able to work but insist on leading an idle life, violating law and discipline, or will not engage in honest pursuits, into persons who are able to support themselves through their own labor, and to further maintaining public order, thus facilitating socialist construction." *The Resolution of the Standing Committee of the National People's Congress on Approving the Decision of the State Council on Issues concerning Reeducation through Labor* still takes Article 100 of the 1954 Constitution as the constitutional basis, which has severely affected the mainstream judgment and conclusion of the legal relations between the 1954 Constitution and the 1982 Constitution.

4 Several Comments on the Application Situation of China's Constitution in Legislation

From the simple sample analysis, the following comments are made for the application of the Constitution in legislation.

1. From the 244 samples being analyzed, the National People's Congress and its Standing Committee, as the top legislative body, rather respect the Constitution in legislative concept at the time of enacting basic laws and laws other than basic laws. They unconsciously seek a legitimate basis for "in accordance with the Constitution" for the newly formulated constitution.
2. Currently, "in accordance with the Constitution" is basically still a "declaration" for enacting laws. Most of the laws fail to point out which article of the Constitution is taken as the basis for the enactment. Therefore, the constitutional basis in legislation is too abstract.
3. When it comes to the existing legal texts, the term "constitution", when it does appear, such as in the phrase "in accordance with the Constitution" has little more than symbolic significance, i.e., being taken as a basis for legislation. Under the circumstance of unclear relationship with other legislative bases, paralleling them as the legislative basis is obviously unable to generate real constraining force of the Constitution in legislative activities.
4. The concept and term of constitution appeared in the 244 samples, but basically all of them are for declaration and none is put in a specific social relationship to establish the role of the Constitution in guiding and judging the right or wrong of People's behaviors.
5. The word "constitution" mainly appears in the first article of existing legal documents for stipulating the legislative purpose and legislative basis. Constitution as the legislative basis is basically in the sense of "political attitude". On the one hand, it can build up characteristic that the top legislative body respects the authority of the Constitution. On the other hand, it reflects that the Constitution has not yet had specific binding force to the specific meaning of laws. Currently, the Constitution is only somewhat reflected in legislation, but it still lacks authority and legalpower.

Attached table: "constitution" review

Serial No.	Name of law	Release time, last amendment	Occurrence frequency of "constitution"	Article
1	Organic Law of the Local People's Congresses and Local People's Governments of the People's Republic of China	Adopted in October 2004	12	**Article 3** The organs of self-government of autonomous regions, autonomous prefectures and autonomous counties shall, in addition to exercising the functions and powers specified in this Law, exercise the power of autonomy within the limits of their authority as prescribed by **the Constitution**, the Law on Regional National Autonomy and other laws **Article 7** The People's congresses of provinces, autonomous regions, and municipalities directly under the Central Government may, in the light of the specific conditions and actual needs of their respective administrative areas, formulate and promulgate local regulations, which must not contravene **the Constitution** and other laws, as well as administrative regulations; they shall report such local regulations to the Standing Committee of the National People's Congress and the State Council for the record The People's congresses of cities where provincial and autonomous regional People's governments are located and the People's congresses of relatively large cities with the approval of the State Council may, in the light of the specific conditions and actual needs of their respective cities, formulate local regulations, which must not contravene **the Constitution** and other laws, administrative regulations, and the local regulations of their respective provinces and autonomous regions; they shall report such local regulations to the standing committees of the People's congresses of the respective provinces and autonomous regions for approval before implementation and for submission to the Standing Committee of the National People's Congress and the State Council for the record **Article 8**(1) to ensure the observance and execution, in their respective administrative areas, of **the Constitution** and other laws, administrative regulations and the resolutions of the People's congresses and their standing committees at higher levels, and to ensure the implementation of the State plan and the State budget (15) to safeguard women's rights as endowed by **the Constitution** and other laws, such as equality with men, equal pay for equal work and freedom of marriage **Article 9** (13) to safeguard women's rights as endowed by **the Constitution** and other laws, such as equality with men, equal pay for equal work and freedom of marriage **Article 43** The standing committees of the People's congresses of provinces, autonomous regions, and municipalities directly under the Central Government may, when their respective People's congresses are not in session, formulate and promulgate local regulations in accordance with the specific conditions and actual needs of their respective administrative areas, provided that these regulations do not contravene **the Constitution**, other laws or administrative regulations; they shall report such local regulations to the Standing Committee of the National People's Congress and the State Council for the record The standing committees of the People's congresses of cities where the provincial and autonomous regional People's governments are located and the standing committees of the People's congresses of those relatively large cities with the approval of the State Council may, when their respective People's congresses are not in session, formulate local regulations in accordance with the specific conditions and actual needs of their respective cities, provided that these regulations do not contravene **the Constitution**, other laws, administrative regulations and the local regulations of the respective provinces and autonomous regions; they shall submit such local regulations to the standing committees of the People's congresses of the respective provinces and autonomous regions for approval

(continued)

(continued)

Serial No.	Name of law	Release time, last amendment	Occurrence frequency of "constitution"	Article
				before implementation and for submission to the Standing Committee of the National People's Congress and the State Council for the record **Article 44**(1) to ensure the observance and execution, in its administrative area, of **the Constitution**, other laws, administrative regulations and the resolutions of the People's congresses and their standing committees at higher levels **Article 59** (8) to safeguard the rights of minority nationalities and respect their folkways and customs, assist those areas where minority nationalities live in concentrated communities within its sphere of jurisdiction to exercise regional autonomy in accordance with **the Constitution** and other laws and assist the various minority nationalities in their political economic and cultural development (9) to safeguard women's rights as endowed by **the Constitution** and other laws, such as equality with men, equal pay for equal work and freedom of marriage **Article 61** (6) to safeguard women's rights as endowed by **the Constitution** and other laws, such as equality with men, equal pay for equal work and freedom of marriage
2	Military Personnel Insurance Law of the People's Republic of China	June 30, 2012	No	
3	Extradition Law of the People's Republic of China	Adopted in December 2000	No	
4	Criminal Procedure Law of the People's Republic of China	July 1, 1979	1	**Article 1** This Law is enacted in accordance with **the Constitution** and for the purpose of ensuring correct enforcement of the Criminal Law, punishing crimes, protecting the people, safeguarding State and public security and maintaining socialist public order
5	Organic Law of the Villagers Committees of the People's Republic of China	October 28, 2010	4	**Article 1** This Law is enacted in accordance with **the Constitution** with a view to ensuring self-government by the villagers in the countryside, who will administer their own affairs according to law, developing democracy at the grassroots level in the countryside, protecting villagers' legal rights and interests and promoting the building of a socialist countryside which is materially and ethically advanced
				Article 4 The primary organization of the Communist Party of China in the countryside shall carry out its work in accordance with the Constitution of the Communist Party of China, playing its role as a leading nucleus, supporting and leading villagers committee in exercising official powers; and, in accordance with **the Constitution** and laws, support the villagers and ensure that they carry out self-government activities and exercise their democratic rights directly
				Article 10 The villagers committee and its members shall observe **the Constitution**, laws, regulations and State policies, observe and organize the implementation of villagers charter of self-government, and rules and regulations for the village and villagers pledges, implement decisions of villagers' meetings and villagers' representative conferences, and they shall be impartial in handling affairs, honest in performing their duties and warmhearted in serving the villagers, subject to the supervision of villagers

(continued)

(continued)

Serial No.	Name of law	Release time, last amendment	Occurrence frequency of "constitution"	Article
				Article 27 A villagers assembly may formulate and revise the villagers charter of self-government, rules and regulations for the village and villagers pledges, and submit them to the People's government of the township, ethnic township or town for the record No villagers charter of self-government, rules and regulations for the village, villagers pledges or matters decided through discussion by a villagers assembly or by representatives of villagers may contravene **the Constitution**, laws, regulations, or State policies, or contain such contents as infringing upon villagers' rights of the person, their democratic rights or lawful property rights
6	Administrative Coercion Law of the People's Republic of China	June 30, 2011	1	**Article 1** This Law is formulated in accordance with **the Constitution** of the People's Republic of China in order to regulate prescription and implementation of administrative coercion, guarantee and supervise over lawful exercise and performance of powers and duties by administrative agencies, maintain public interest and social order, and protect the lawful interests of citizens, bodies corporate and other organizations
7	Law of the People's Republic of China on Intangible Cultural Heritage	February 25, 2011	No	
8	Law of the People's Republic of China on Vehicle and Vessel Tax	February 25, 2011	No	
9	Law of the People's Republic of China on Water and Soil Conservation	December 25, 2010	No	
10	Law of the Peoples Republic of China on Deputies to the National People's Congress and to the Local People's Congresses at Various Levels	Revised in October 10, 2010	4	**Article 1** This Law is formulated in accordance with **the Constitution** to ensure that deputies to the National People's Congress and deputies to the local People's congresses at various levels exercise their functions and powers, fulfill their duties and play their roles, according to law and in their capacity as deputies **Article 2 Third Paragraph** Deputies to the National People's Congress and to the local People's congresses at various levels shall, representing the interests and will of the people, participate in the exercise of State power in accordance with the functions and powers vested in the People's congresses at the corresponding levels by **the Constitution** and relevant laws **Article 10** Deputies to the National People's Congress have the right, in accordance with the procedures prescribed by **the Constitution**, to submit to the National People's Congress bills on the amendment to **the Constitution**
11	Law of The People's Republic of China on the Laws Applicable to Foreign-related Civil Relations	October 28, 2010	No	

(continued)

(continued)

Serial No.	Name of law	Release time, last amendment	Occurrence frequency of "constitution"	Article
12	Social Insurance Law of the People's Republic of China	October 28, 2010	1	**Article 1** This law is hereby enacted in accordance with **the Constitution** for the purposes of regulating social insurance relationships, securing citizens' legitimate rights and interests to participate in a social insurance system and receive social insurance benefits, achieving a fair sharing of benefits of development by citizens, and promoting social harmony and stability
13	People's Mediation Law of the People's Republic of China	October 28, 2010	1	**Article 1** To improve the People's mediation system, regulate the People's mediation activities, timely solve disputes among the people and maintain social harmony and stability, this Law is formulated pursuant to **the Constitution**
14	Reserve Officers Law of the People's Republic of China	Revised in August 2010	3	**Article 1** This Law is enacted in accordance with **the Constitution** and the Military Service Law for the purpose of establishing a sound system of reserve officers, improving the mobilization system of the armed forces of the State, and strengthening the reserve forces for national defense **Article 9** Reserve officers shall abide by **the Constitution**, laws and regulations as well as the relevant military rules and regulations, participate in military training and military service activities, receive political education, enhance their organizing and commanding ability and their technical proficiency, and be ready at all times to respond to the call-up for active service **Article 11 (1)** to be loyal to the motherland and to observe **the Constitution**, laws and regulations
15	Law of the People's Republic of China on the Protection of Petroleum and Natural Gas Pipelines	June 25, 2010	No	
16	Law of the People's Republic of China on State Compensation	Revised in April 2010	1	**Article 1** This Law is formulated in accordance with **the Constitution** with a view to safeguarding the right of citizens, legal persons and other organizations entitled to State compensation according to law, and promoting the exercise by State organs of their functions and powers according to law
17	Law of the People's Republic of China on Guarding State Secrets	Revised in April 2010	No	
18	Electoral Law of the National People's Congress and Local People's Congresses of the People's Republic of China	Revised in March 2010	1	**Article 1** The Electoral Law of the National People's Congress and Local People's Congresses is formulated in accordance with **the Constitution** of the People's Republic of China
19	Copyright Law of the People's Republic of China	Revised in February 2010	2	**Article 1** This law is enacted, in accordance with **the Constitution**, for the purpose of protecting the copyright of authors in their literary, artistic and scientific works and the rights and interests related to copyright, encouraging the creation and dissemination of works conducive to the building of a socialist society that is advanced ethically and materially, and promoting the progress and flourishing of socialist culture and sciences **Article 4** in exercising their copyright, no copyright owners may not violate **the Constitution** or laws, nor may they impair public interests. The State supervises and manages the publication and dissemination of works in accordance with the law

(continued)

(continued)

Serial No.	Name of law	Release time, last amendment	Occurrence frequency of "constitution"	Article
20	National Defense Mobilization Law of the People's Republic of China	February 26, 2010	2	**Article 1** To strengthen national defense, improve the national defense mobilization system, guarantee the smooth going of the national defense mobilization work, and maintain the national sovereignty, unification, territorial integrity and security, this Law is formulated pursuant to **the Constitution** **Article 8** Where the sovereignty, unity, territorial integrity or security of the state is threatened, the Standing Committee of the National People's Republic of China shall decide a general or partial mobilization pursuant to **the Constitution** and other relevant laws. The Chairman of the state will issue a mobilization order in accordance with the decision of the Standing Committee of the National People's Congress
21	Tort Liability Law of People's Republic of China	December 26, 2009	No	
22	Renewable Energy Law of the People's Republic of China	December 26, 2009	No	
23	Law of the People's Republic of China on Island Protection	December 26, 2009	No	
24	Law of the People's Republic of China on Diplomatic Personnel Stationed Abroad	October 31, 2009	3	**Article 1** This Law is formulated in accordance with **the Constitution** and the Law on Public Servants for the purposes of building high-quality diplomatic personnel teams stationed abroad, ensuring diplomatic missions stationed abroad perform their duties pursuant to the law, regulating the management of diplomatic personnel stationed abroad, and protecting their legitimate rights and interests **Article 6 (3)** Uphold **the Constitution** of the P.R.C **Article 8 (2)** Be loyal to **the Constitution** and laws of the People's Republic of China and respect the laws and customs of host countries
25	Statistics Law of the People's Republic of China	Revised in June 2009	No	
26	Law of the People's Republic of China on Mediation and Arbitration of Disputes over Rural Land Contract and Management	June 27, 2009	No	
27	Postal Law of the People's Republic of China	April 24, 2009	No	
28	Production Safety Law of the People's Republic of China	Revised in August 2009	No	
29	Military Service Law of the People's Republic of China	Revised in August 2009	2	**Article 1** This Law is formulated pursuant to Article 55 of **the Constitution** of the People's Republic of China, which stipulates, "It is the sacred duty of every citizen of the People's Republic of China to defend the motherland and resist aggression. It is the honorable duty of citizens of the People's Republic of China to perform military

(continued)

(continued)

Serial No.	Name of law	Release time, last amendment	Occurrence frequency of "constitution"	Article
				service and join the militia in accordance with the law," and in accordance with other relevant provisions of the Constitution **Article 6** The active servicemen and reservists must abide by **the Constitution** and the law, and shall perform their duties and at the same time enjoy their rights as citizens; their rights and duties resulting from their joining the military service shall be specified separately in military regulations in addition to the provisions of this Law
30	Grassland Law of the People's Republic of China	Revised in August 2009	No	
31	Product Quality Law of the People's Republic of China	Revised in August 2009	No	
32	Law of the People's Republic of China on the Administration of the Urban Real Estate	Revised in August 2009	No	
33	Electric Power Law of the People's Republic of China	Revised in 2009	No	
34	Trade Union law of the People's Republic of China	Revised in August 2009	5	**Article 1** This Law is enacted in accordance with **the Constitution** of the People's Republic of China with a view to ensuring the status of trade unions in the political, economic and social life of the State, defining their rights and obligations and bringing into play their role in the socialist modernization drive **Article 4** Trade unions shall observe and safeguard **the Constitution**, take it as the fundamental criterion for their activities, take economic development as the central task, uphold the path of socialism, the People's democratic dictatorship, leadership by Communist Party of China, and Marxist-Leninism, Mao Zedong Thought and Deng Xiaoping Theory, persevere in reform and the open policy, and conduct their work independently in accordance with **the Constitution** of trade unions The National Congress of Trade Unions formulates or amends *the Constitution of Trade Unions of the People's Republic of China*, which shall not contravene **the Constitution** of the People's Republic of China or other laws **Article 5** Trade unions shall organize and conduct education among workers and staff members in order that they shall, in accordance with the provisions of **the Constitution** of the People's Republic of China and other laws, give play to their role as masters of the country and participate in various ways and forms in the administration of State affairs, management of economic and cultural undertakings and handling of social affairs; trade unions shall assist the People's governments in their work and safeguard the socialist State power under the People's democratic dictatorship led by the working class and based on the alliance of workers and peasants
35	Highway Law of the People's Republic of China	Revised in August 2009	No	
36	Exit-Entry Administration Law of the People's Republic of China	Adopted on June 30, 2012	No	

(continued)

(continued)

Serial No.	Name of law	Release time, last amendment	Occurrence frequency of "constitution"	Article
37	Law of the People's Republic of China on the Protection of the Rights and Interests of Returned Overseas Chinese and the Family Members of Overseas Chinese	Revised in August 2009	3	**Article 1** This Law is enacted in accordance with **the Constitution** with a view to protecting the lawful rights and interests of returned overseas Chinese and the family members of overseas Chinese **Article 3** Returned overseas Chinese and the family members of overseas Chinese shall be entitled to the citizen's rights prescribed by **the Constitution** and the law and at the same time shall perform the citizen's duties prescribed by **the Constitution** and the law. No organization or individual may discriminate against them
38	Law of the People's Republic of China on National Defence	Revised in August 2009	11	**Article 1** This Law is enacted in accordance with **the Constitution** for the purpose of building up and consolidating national defense and ensuring the smooth progress of the socialist modernization drive **Article 10** The National People's Congress, pursuant to **the Constitution**, decides on issues of war and peace and exercises other functions and powers in respect of national defense as stipulated by **the Constitution** The Standing Committee of the National People's Congress, pursuant to **the Constitution**, decides on the proclamation of a state of war, and on general or partial mobilization of the nation and exercises other functions and powers in respect of national defense as stipulated by **the Constitution** **Article 11** The President of the People's Republic of China, in pursuance of the decisions of the National People's Congress or its Standing Committee, proclaims a state of war, issues mobilization orders and exercises other functions and powers in respect of national defense as stipulated by **the Constitution** **Article 13 (5)** to enact military rules and regulations, and issue decisions and orders in accordance with **the Constitution** and law **Article 18** The armed forces of the People's Republic of China must observe **the Constitution** and law, and they must administer their affairs according to law **Article 44** When the sovereignty, unification, territorial integrity or security of the People's Republic of China is under threat, the State, pursuant to **the Constitution** and law, shall mobilize the entire nation or part of the nation against it **Article 49** The State, pursuant to **the Constitution**, proclaims a state of war, adopts various measures to concentrate human, material and financial resources and leads all citizens in their efforts to defend the motherland and resist aggression **Article 57** Active servicemen must observe **the Constitution** and law in an exemplary way, observe military rules and regulations, execute orders and strictly abide by rules of discipline
39	Law of the People's Republic of China on the National Emblem	Revised in August 2009	1	**Article 1** This Law is enacted, in accordance with **the Constitution**, with a view to upholding the dignity of the National Emblem and ensuring the correct use of the National Emblem
40	National Security Law of the People's Republic of China	Revised in August 2009	1	**Article 1** To maintain national security, safeguard the regime of People's democratic dictatorship and the socialist system, ensure the smooth advancement of reform, opening up, and socialist modernization, this Law is developed in accordance with **the Constitution**
41	Frontier Health and Quarantine Law of the People's Republic of China	Revised in August 2009	No	

(continued)

(continued)

Serial No.	Name of law	Release time, last amendment	Occurrence frequency of "constitution"	Article
42	Law of the People's Republic of China on the National Flag	Revised in August 2009	1	**Article 1** This Law is enacted in accordance with **the Constitution** with a view to defending the dignity of the National Flag, enhancing citizens' consciousness of the State and promoting the spirit of patriotism
43	Law of the People's Republic of China on Red Cross Society	Revised in August 2009	1	**Article 4** The Red Cross Society of China shall abide by **the Constitution** and laws of China, adhere to the Fundamental Principles laid down by the International Red Cross and the Red Crescent Movement, and carry out its work independently in accordance with the Geneva Conventions and their Additional Protocols acceded to by China and the Statutes of the Red Cross Society of China
44	Law of the People's Republic of China on Assemblies, Processions and Demonstrations	Revised in August 2009	4	**Article 1** Pursuant to **the Constitution**, this Law is enacted to safeguard citizens' exercise of their right to assembly, procession and demonstration according to law and to maintain social stability and public order **Article 4** In exercising their right to assembly, procession and demonstration, citizens must abide by **the Constitution** and the laws, shall not oppose the cardinal principles specified in the Constitution and shall not impair state, public or collective interests or the lawful freedoms and rights of other citizens **Article 12 (1)** opposition to the cardinal principles specified in **the Constitution**
45	Metrology Law of the People's Republic of China	Revised in August 2009	No	
46	Teachers Law of the People's Republic of China	Revised in August 2009	3	**Article 8 (1)** to abide by **the Constitution**, laws and professional ethics, and be paragons of virtue and learning **Article 8 (3)** to conduct education among students in the basic principles defined in **the Constitution**, education in patriotism, national unity and the legal system, and education in ideology, morality, culture, science and technology, and to organize and lead students to engage in beneficial social activities **Article 10s Paragraph** All Chinese citizens, who abide by **the Constitution** and laws, take a keen interest in education, have sound ideological and moral character, possess a record of formal schooling as stipulated in this Law or have passed the national teachers' qualification examinations, have educational and teaching ability may, after being evaluated as qualified, obtain qualifications for teachers
47	Organic Law of the Local People's Congresses and Local People's Governments of the People's Republic of China	Revised in 2004	13	**Article 3** The organs of self-government of autonomous regions, autonomous prefectures and autonomous counties shall, in addition to exercising the functions and powers specified in this Law, exercise the power of autonomy within the limits of their authority as prescribed by **the Constitution**, the Law on Regional National Autonomy and other laws **Article 7** The People's congresses of provinces, autonomous regions, and municipalities directly under the Central Government may, in the light of the specific conditions and actual needs of their respective administrative areas, formulate and promulgate local regulations, which must not contravene **the Constitution** and other laws, as well as administrative regulations; they shall report such local regulations to the Standing Committee of the National People's Congress and the State Council for the record The People's congresses of cities where provincial and autonomous regional People's governments are located and the People's congresses of relatively large cities with the approval of the State Council may, in the light of the specific conditions and actual needs of their respective cities, formulate local regulations, which must not contravene **the Constitution** and other laws, administrative regulations, and the local regulations of their respective provinces and autonomous regions; they shall report such local regulations to the standing committees of the

(continued)

(continued)

Serial No.	Name of law	Release time, last amendment	Occurrence frequency of "constitution"	Article
				People's congresses of the respective provinces and autonomous regions for approval before implementation and for submission to the Standing Committee of the National People's Congress and the State Council for the record **Article 8 (1)** to ensure the observance and execution, in their respective administrative areas, of **the Constitution** and other laws, administrative regulations and the resolutions of the People's congresses and their standing committees at higher levels, and to ensure the implementation of the State plan and the State budget (15) to safeguard women's rights as endowed by **the Constitution** and other laws, such as equality with men, equal pay for equal work and freedom of marriage **Article 9 (1)** to ensure the observance and execution, in their respective administrative areas, of **the Constitution**, other law, administrative regulations, and the resolutions of the People's congresses and their standing committees at higher levels (13) to safeguard women's rights as endowed by **the Constitution** and other laws, such as equality with men, equal pay for equal work and freedom of marriage **Article 43** The standing committees of the People's congresses of provinces, autonomous regions, and municipalities directly under the Central Government may, when their respective People's congresses are not in session, formulate and promulgate local regulations in accordance with the specific conditions and actual needs of their respective administrative areas, provided that these regulations do not contravene **the Constitution**, other laws or administrative regulations; they shall report such local regulations to the Standing Committee of the National People's Congress and the State Council for the record The standing committees of the People's congresses of cities where the provincial and autonomous regional People's governments are located and the standing committees of the People's congresses of those relatively large cities with the approval of the State Council may, when their respective People's congresses are not in session, formulate local regulations in accordance with the specific conditions and actual needs of their respective cities, provided that these regulations do not contravene **the Constitution**, other laws, administrative regulations and the local regulations of the respective provinces and autonomous regions; they shall submit such local regulations to the standing committees of the People's congresses of the respective provinces and autonomous regions for approval before implementation and for submission to the Standing Committee of the National People's Congress and the State Council for the record **Article 44 (1)** to ensure the observance and execution, in its administrative area, of **the Constitution**, other laws, administrative regulations and the resolutions of the People's congresses and their standing committees at higher levels **Article 59 (8)** to safeguard the rights of minority nationalities and respect their folkways and customs, assist those areas where minority nationalities live in concentrated communities within its sphere of jurisdiction to exercise regional autonomy in accordance with **the Constitution** and other laws and assist the various minority nationalities in their political-economic and cultural development (9) to safeguard women's rights as endowed by the Constitution and other laws, such as equality with men, equal pay for equal work and freedom of marriage **Article 61 (6)** to safeguard women's rights as endowed by **the Constitution** and other laws, such as equality with men, equal pay for equal work and freedom of marriage

(continued)

(continued)

Serial No.	Name of law	Release time, last amendment	Occurrence frequency of "constitution"	Article
48	Organic Law of The People's Courts of The People's Republic of China	Revised in 2006	1	**Article 3s Paragraph** The people's courts, in all their activities, educate citizens in loyalty to their socialist motherland and voluntary observance of **the Constitution** and laws
49	Organic Law of the People's Procuratorates of the People's Republic of China	Revised in 1986	1	**Article 4s Paragraph** The People's procuratorates, through procuratorial activities, educate the citizens to be loyal to their socialist motherland, to consciously observe **the Constitution** and other laws and to actively fight against illegal activities
50	Nationality Law of the People's Republic of China	Promulgated in 1980	1	**Article 7** Foreign nationals or stateless persons who are willing to abide by China's **Constitution** and laws and who meet one of the following conditions may be naturalized upon approval of their applications
51	Organic Law of the National People's Congress of the People's Republic of China	Promulgated in 1982	8	**Article 1** Sessions of the National People's Congress shall be convened in accordance with the relevant provisions of **the Constitution** of the People's Republic of China **Article 12** Sessions of the National People's Congress shall adopt bills amending **the Constitution**, legislative bills and other bills in accordance with the relevant provisions of **the Constitution** of the People's Republic of China **Article 14** The Premier and other members of the State Council and members of the Central Military Commission other than its Chairman shall be nominated in accordance with the relevant provisions of **the Constitution** **Article 22** The Standing Committee of the National People's Congress shall exercise the functions and powers prescribed in **the Constitution** of the People's Republic of China **Article 37 (3)** to examine and submit reports on items received from the Standing Committee of the National People's Congress which are considered to be in contravention of **the Constitution** or other laws; such items include administrative regulations, decisions and orders issued by the State Council; orders, instructions and regulations issued by the ministries and commissions under the State Council; regulations and resolutions issued locally by the People's congresses of the provinces, autonomous regions, and municipalities directly under the Central Government and their standing committees; and decisions, orders and regulations issued by the People's governments of the provinces, autonomous regions, and municipalities directly under the Central Government **Article 40** Deputies to the National People's Congress must observe **the Constitution** and other laws in an exemplary way, keep State secrets and, in the course of production, other work and the public activities in which they take part, assist in the enforcement of **the Constitution** and other laws
52	Organic Law of the State Council of the People's Republic of China	Promulgated in 1982		This Organic Law is formulated in accordance with the provisions concerning the State Council in **the Constitution** of the People's Republic of China **Article 3** The State Council shall exercise the functions and powers prescribed in Article 89 of **the Constitution**
53	Law of the Peoples Republic of China on Regional National Autonomy	Revised in 2001	8	**Preface** **Last Paragraph** *The Law of the People's Republic of China on Regional National Autonomy* is the basic law for the implementation of the system of regional national autonomy prescribed in **the Constitution** **Article 1** The Law of the People's Republic of China on Regional National Autonomy is formulated in accordance with **the Constitution** of the People's Republic of China **Article 4** The organs of self-government of national autonomous areas shall exercise the functions and powers of local organs of the State as specified in Section 5 of Chapter III of **the Constitution**. At the same time, they shall

(continued)

(continued)

Serial No.	Name of law	Release time, last amendment	Occurrence frequency of "constitution"	Article
				exercise the power of autonomy within the limits of their authority as prescribed by the Constitution, by this Law and other laws, and implement the laws and policies of the State in the light of existing local conditions **Article 5** The organs of self-government of national autonomous areas must uphold the unity of the country and guarantee that **the Constitution** and other laws are observed and implemented in these areas **Article 6s Paragraph** On the principle of not contravening **the Constitution** and the laws, the organs of self-government of national autonomous areas shall have the power to adopt special policies and flexible measures in the light of local conditions to speed up the economic and cultural development of these areas **Article 15 Third Paragraph** The organization and work of the organs of self-government of national autonomous areas shall be specified in these areas' regulations on the exercise of autonomy or separate regulations, in accordance with **the Constitution** and other laws **Article 52** The organ of self-government of a national autonomous area shall guarantee that citizens of the various nationalities in the area enjoy the rights of citizens prescribed in **the Constitution** and shall educate them in the need to perform their duties as citizens
54	Organic Law of the Urban Residents Committees of the People's Republic of China	Adopted in February 1989	4	**Article 1** Pursuant to **the Constitution**, this Law is formulated with a view to improving the urban residents committees as an institution, enabling urban residents to administer their own affairs in accordance with the law, promoting socialist democracy at the grassroots level in the cities, and furthering socialist material development and the building of an advanced socialist culture and ideology in urban areas **Article 2 (1)** publicizing **the Constitution**, the laws, the regulations and the state policies, safeguarding the lawful rights and interests of the residents, educating the residents for the fulfillment of their statutory obligations and for the protection of public property, and conducting various forms of activities for the development of an advanced socialist culture and ideology **Article 12** Members of a residents committee shall observe **the Constitution**, the laws, the regulations and the state policies, be fair in handling matters and serve the residents warmheartedly **Article 15s Paragraph** The joint pledges of the residents shall not contravene **the Constitution**, the laws, the regulations and the state policies
55	Basic Law of the Hong Kong Special Administrative Region of the People's Republic of China	Adopted in April 1990	2	**Preamble** **Second Paragraph**: Upholding national unity and territorial integrity, maintaining the prosperity and stability of Hong Kong, and taking account of its history and realities, the People's Republic of China has decided that upon China's resumption of the exercise of sovereignty over Hong Kong, a Hong Kong Special Administrative Region will be established in accordance with the provisions of Article 31 of **the Constitution** of the People's Republic of China, and that under the principle of "one country, two systems," the socialist system and policies will not be practiced in Hong Kong. The basic policies of the People's Republic of China regarding Hong Kong have been elaborated by the Chinese Government in the Sino-British Joint Declaration **Third Paragraph** In accordance with **the Constitution** of the People's Republic of China, the National People's Congress hereby enacts the Basic Law of the Hong Kong Special Administrative Region of the People's Republic of China, prescribing the systems to be practiced in the Hong Kong Special Administrative Region, in order to ensure the implementation of the basic policies of the People's Republic of China regarding Hong Kong

(continued)

(continued)

Serial No.	Name of law	Release time, last amendment	Occurrence frequency of "constitution"	Article
				Article 11 In accordance with Article 31 of **the Constitution** of the People's Republic of China, the systems and policies practiced in the Hong Kong Special Administrative Region, including the social and economic systems, the system for safeguarding the fundamental rights and freedoms of its residents, the executive, legislative and judicial systems, and the relevant policies, shall be based on the provisions of this Law
56	Law of the People's Republic of China on the Procedure of the Conclusion of Treaties	December 1990	1	**Article 1** The present Law is enacted in accordance with **the Constitution** of the People's Republic of China
57	Law of the People's Republic of China on the Territorial Sea and the Contiguous Zone	Adopted in February 1992	No	
58	Basic Law of the Macao Special Administrative Region of the People's Republic of China	Adopted in 1993	3	**Preamble** **Second Paragraph**: Upholding national unity and territorial integrity, contributing to social stability and economic development, and taking account of its history and realities, the People's Republic of China has decided that upon China's resumption of the exercise of sovereignty over Macao, a Macao Special Administrative Region will be established in accordance with the provisions of Article 31 of **the Constitution** of the People's Republic of China, and that under the principle of "one country, two systems", the socialist system and policies will not be practiced in Macao. The basic policies of the People's Republic of China regarding Macao have been elaborated by the Chinese Government in the Sino-Portuguese Joint Declaration **Third Paragraph** In accordance with **the Constitution** of the People's Republic of China, the National People's Congress hereby enacts the Basic Law of the Macao Special Administrative Region of the People's Republic of China, prescribing the systems to be practiced in the Macao Special Administrative Region, in order to ensure the implementation of the basic policies of the People's Republic of China regarding Macao **Article 11** In accordance with Article 31 of **the Constitution** of the People's Republic of China, the systems and policies practiced in the Macao Special Administrative Region, including the social and economic systems, the system for safeguarding the fundamental rights and freedoms of its residents, the executive, legislative and judicial systems, and the relevant policies, shall be based on the provisions of this Law
59	Judges Law of the People's Republic of China	Revised in 2001	5	**Article 1** This law is enacted in accordance with **the Constitution** to enhance the quality of judges, to strengthen the administration of judges, and to ensure that the people's courts independently exercise judicial authority according to law, that judges perform their functions and duties according to law and that law is administered impartially **Article 3** Judges shall faithfully implement **the Constitution** and laws, and serve the people wholeheartedly **Article 7 (1)** to strictly observe **the Constitution** and laws **Article 9 (3)** to endorse **the Constitution** of the People's Republic of China **Article 11** A judge shall be appointed or removed from the post in accordance with the limit of authority for, and procedures of, appointment or removal as prescribed by **the Constitution** and laws
60	Public Procurators Law of the People's Republic of China	Revised in 2001	5	**Article 1** This Law is enacted in accordance with **the Constitution** to enhance the quality of public procurators, to strengthen the administration of public procurators, and to ensure that the People's Procuratorates exercise legal

(continued)

(continued)

Serial No.	Name of law	Release time, last amendment	Occurrence frequency of "constitution"	Article
				supervision and independently exercise procuratorial authority according to law, that public procurators perform their functions and duties according to law and that law is administered impartially **Article 3** Public procurators must faithfully implement **the Constitution** and laws, and serve the people wholeheartedly **Article 8 (1)** to strictly observe **the Constitution** and laws **Article 10 (3)** to endorse **the Constitution** of the People's Republic of China **Article 12** A public procurator shall be appointed or removed from the post in accordance with the limit of authority for, and procedures of, appointment or removal as prescribed by **the Constitution** and laws
61	Martial Law of the People's Republic of China	Adopted in March 1996	2	**Article 1** This Law is enacted in accordance with **the Constitution** of the People's Republic of China **Article 4** In order to guarantee execution of martial law and preserve public security and public order during the period of martial law, the State may, in accordance with this Law, lay down special rules and regulations regarding the citizens' exercising of their rights and freedom as stipulated by **the Constitution** and laws in the area under martial law
62	Law of the People's Republic of China on Garrisoning the Hong Kong Special Administrative Region	Adopted in December 1996	1	**Article 1** This Law is enacted in accordance with **the Constitution** and the Basic Law of the Hong Kong Special Administrative Region to ensure the lawful performance of functions and responsibilities by the military forces stationed by the Central People's Government in the Hong Kong Special Administrative Region for defense, and to maintain the sovereignty, unity and territorial integrity of the State and the security of Hong Kong
63	Law of the Peoples Republic of China on the Exclusive Economic Zone and the Continental Shelf	Adopted in June 1998	No	
64	Law of the People's Republic of China on Garrisoning the Macao Special Administrative Region	Adopted in June 1999	1	**Article 1** This Law is enacted in accordance with **the Constitution** and the Basic Law of the Macao Special Administrative Region to ensure the lawful performance of functions and responsibilities by the military forces stationed by the Central People's Government in the Macao Special Administrative Region for defense, and to maintain the sovereignty, unity and territorial integrity of the State and the security of Macao
65	Legislation Law of the People's Republic of China	Adopted on March 15, 2000	19	**Article 1** This Law is enacted in accordance with **the Constitution** with a view to standardizing legislation, establishing a sound legislative system of the State, establishing and improving the socialist legal system with Chinese characteristics, safeguarding and developing socialist democracy, promoting the government of the country according to law and building a socialist country under the rule of law **Article 3** Laws shall be made in compliance with the basic principles laid down in **the Constitution**, principles of taking economic development as the central task, adhering to the path of socialism and the People's democratic dictatorship, upholding leadership by the Communist Party of China, upholding Marxism-Leninism, Mao Zetong Thought and Deng Xiaoping theory and persevering in reform and in opening to the outside world **Article 56** The State Council shall, in accordance with **the Constitution** and laws, formulate administrative regulations (2) matters within the administrative functions and powers of the State Council as provided for in Article 89 of **the Constitution**

(continued)

(continued)

Serial No.	Name of law	Release time, last amendment	Occurrence frequency of "constitution"	Article
				Article 63 The People's congresses or their standing committees of the provinces, autonomous regions and municipalities directly under the Central Government may, in light of the specific conditions and actual needs of their respective administrative areas, formulate local regulations, provided that such regulations do not contradict **the Constitution**, the laws and the administrative regulations The People's congresses or their standing committees of the comparatively larger cities may, in light of the specific local conditions and actual needs, formulate local regulations, provided that they do not contradict **the Constitution**, the laws, the administrative regulations and the local regulations of their respective provinces or autonomous regions, and they shall submit the regulations to the standing committees of the People's congresses of the provinces or autonomous regions for approval before implementation. The standing committees of the People's congresses of the provinces or autonomous regions shall examine the legality of such local regulations which are submitted for approval, and shall approve them within four months if they do not contradict **the Constitution**, the laws, the administrative regulations, and the local regulations of their respective provinces or autonomous regions **Article 66s Paragraph** Where certain provisions of the laws and administrative regulations are concerned, adaptation on the basis of the characteristics of the local nationality (nationalities) may be made in autonomous regulations and separate regulations, but such adaptation may not contradict the basic principles of the laws and administrative regulations; where the provisions of **the Constitution** and the Law on Regional National Autonomy as well as the provisions in other laws and administrative regulations specially formulated to govern the national autonomous areas are concerned, no adaptation may be made **Article 78** The legal effect of **the Constitution** is the highest, and no laws, administrative regulations, local regulations, autonomous regulations, separate regulations or rules whatever may contradict it **Article 80 (1)** The National People's Congress has the power to alter or annul any inappropriate laws enacted by its Standing Committee, and to annul any autonomous regulations or separate regulations which have been approved by its Standing Committee but which contravene **the Constitution** or the provision of the second paragraph in Article 66 of this Law **Article 88 (2)** The Standing Committee of the National People's Congress has the power to annul any administrative regulations which contradict **the Constitution** and laws, to annul any local regulations which contradict **the Constitution**, and laws, and to annul any autonomous regulations or separate regulations which have been approved by the standing committees of the People's congresses of the relevant provinces, autonomous regions or municipalities directly under the Central Government but which contravene **the Constitution** or the provision of the second paragraph in Article 66 of this Law **Article 90** When the State Council, the Central Military Commission, the Supreme People's Court, the Supreme People's Procuratorate and the standing committees of the People's congresses of the provinces, autonomous regions and municipalities directly under the Central Government consider that administrative regulations, local regulations, autonomous regulations or separate regulations contradict **the Constitution** or laws, they may submit to the Standing Committee of the National People's Congress written requests for examination, and the working offices of the Standing Committee shall refer the requests to the relevant special committees for examination and suggestions When State organs other than the ones mentioned in the preceding paragraph, public organizations, enterprises and institutions or citizens consider that administrative regulations, local regulations, autonomous regulations or

(continued)

(continued)

Serial No.	Name of law	Release time, last amendment	Occurrence frequency of "constitution"	Article
				separate regulations contradict **the Constitution** or laws, they may submit to the Standing Committee of the National People's Congress written suggestions for examination, and the working offices of the Standing Committee shall study the suggestions and shall, when necessary, refer them to the relevant special committees for examination and suggestions **Article 91** When after examination a special committee of the National People's Congress considers that administrative regulations, local regulations, autonomous regulations or separate regulations contradict **the Constitution** or laws, it may submit written suggestions to the organ that has formulated the regulations for examination; or the Law Committee and other relevant special committees may convene a joint meeting for examination and request the said organ to attend the meeting and give an explanation, and then after examination submit to the organ written comments and suggestions. The organ that has formulated the regulations shall, within two months, study and put forth suggestions as to whether to revise the regulations, and shall give feedback to the Law Committee and other relevant special committees of the National People's Congress If, after examination, the Law Committee and other relevant special committees of the National People's Congress consider that administrative regulations, local regulations, autonomous regulations or separate regulations contradict **the Constitution** or laws and the organ that has formulated such regulations refuses to make revision, they may submit written comments and suggestions on the basis of their examination and propose a motion for annulment of the regulations to the Council of Chairmen, which shall decide whether to submit the motion to a meeting of the Standing Committee for examination and decision **Article 93** The Central Military Commission shall, in accordance with **the Constitution** and laws, formulated military regulations
66	Anti-Secession Law	Adopted in March 2005	1	**Article 1** This Law is formulated, in accordance with **the Constitution**, for the purpose of opposing and checking Taiwan's secession from China by secessionists in the name of "Taiwan independence", promoting peaceful national reunification, maintaining peace and stability in Taiwan Straits, preserving China's sovereignty and territorial integrity, and safeguarding the fundamental interests of the Chinese nation
67	Law of the People's Republic of China on Judicial Immunity from Compulsory Measures Concerning the Property of Foreign Central Banks	October 2005	No	
68	Law of the People's Republic of China on Supervision by the Standing Committees of the People's Congresses at All Levels	Adopted in August 2006	2	**Article 1** This Law is enacted in accordance with **the Constitution** to ensure that the Standing Committee of the National People's Congress and the standing committees of the local People's congresses above the county level exercise their powers of supervision according to law, to develop socialist democracy, and to promote governing the country according to law **Article 2** The standing committees of People's congresses at all levels shall exercise their power of supervision in accordance with **the Constitution** and the provisions of relevant laws

(continued)

(continued)

Serial No.	Name of law	Release time, last amendment	Occurrence frequency of "constitution"	Article
69	Law of the People's Republic of China on Chinese-Foreign Equity Joint Ventures	Revised in 1990	No	
70	Marriage Law of the People's Republic of China	Revised in April 2001	No	
71	Trademark Law of the People's Republic of China	Revised in 2001	No	
72	Patent Law of the People's Republic of China	Revised in 2008	No	
73	Law of Succession of the People's Republic of China	Adopted in April 1985	1	**Article 1** This Law is enacted pursuant to the provisions of ***the Constitution*** *of the People's Republic of China* with a view to protecting the right of citizens to inherit private property
74	General Principles of the Civil Law of the People's Republic of China	Revised in August 2009	1	**Article 1** This Law is formulated in accordance with **the Constitution** and the actual situation in our country, drawing upon our practical experience in civil activities, for the purpose of protecting the lawful civil rights and interests of citizens and legal persons and correctly adjusting civil relations, so as to meet the needs of the developing socialist modernization
75	Law of the People's Republic of China on Wholly Foreign-Owned Enterprises	Revised in 2000	No	
76	Law of the People's Republic of China on Industrial Enterprises Owned by the Whole People	Adopted in April 1988	1	**Article 1** This Law is formulated in accordance with ***the Constitution*** *of the People's Republic of China* with a view to ensuring the consolidation and development of the economic sector under ownership by the whole people, defining the rights and obligations of industrial enterprises owned by the whole people, safeguarding their lawful rights and interests, enhancing their vitality and promoting socialist modernization
77	Law of the People's Republic of China on Chinese-Foreign Contractual Joint Ventures	Adopted in April 1988	No	
78	Adoption Law of the People's Republic of China	Revised in 1998	No	
79	Maritime Code of the People's Republic of China	Adopted in November 1992	No	
80	Law of the People's Republic of China against Unfair Competition	Adopted in September 1993	No	
81	Law of the People's Republic of China on the Protection of Consumer Rights and Interests	Revised in August 2009	No	

(continued)

(continued)

Serial No.	Name of law	Release time, last amendment	Occurrence frequency of "constitution"	Article
82	Company Law of the People's Republic of China	Revised in August 2005	1	**Article 18** Company's staff and workers shall, in accordance with the Trade Union Law of the People's Republic of China, organize a trade union to carry out the trade union activities and protect the lawful rights and interests of the staff and workers. The company shall provide its trade union with conditions necessary for carrying out its activities The trade union of a company represents the staff to sign a collective contract with the company on the staff's labor reward, working time, welfare, insurance and safety hygiene of labor, etc. Companies shall, through staff and workers' congresses or other forms, practice democratic management in accordance with the provisions of **the Constitution** and relevant laws. Companies shall, when making major issues concerning the reorganization and management and making important rules and regulations, listen to the opinions of their trade unions, and listen to the opinions and suggestions of the staff through staff and workers' congresses or other forms
83	Law of the People's Republic of China on Commercial Banks	Revised in 2003	No	
84	Law of the People's Republic of China on Negotiable Instruments	Revised in 2004	No	
85	Guaranty Law of the People's Republic of China	Adopted in June 1995	No	
86	Insurance Law of the People's Republic of China	Revised in February 2009	No	
87	Auction Law of the People's Republic of China	Revised in August 2004		
88	Law of the People's Republic of China on Partnerships	Revised in 2006	No	
89	Law of the People's Republic of China on Securities	Revised in 2005	No	
90	Contract Law of the People's Republic of China	Adopted in March 1999	No	
91	Law of the People's Republic of China on Individual Proprietorship Enterprises	Adopted in August 1999	1	**Article 1** This Law is enacted in accordance with **the Constitution** with a view to regulating activities of individual proprietorship enterprises, protecting the legitimate rights and interests of investors and creditors of individual proprietorship enterprises, maintaining the socio-economic order and promoting the development of the socialist market economy in China
92	Law of the People's Republic of China on Bid Invitation and Bidding	Adopted in August 1999	No	

(continued)

(continued)

Serial No.	Name of law	Release time, last amendment	Occurrence frequency of "constitution"	Article
93	Trust Law of the People's Republic of China	Adopted in April 2001	No	
94	Law of the People's Republic of China on Land Contract in Rural Areas	Adopted in August 2009	1	**Article 1** In accordance with **the Constitution**, this Law is enacted for the purposes of stabilizing and improving the two-tier management system that combines centralized and decentralized management on the basis of household contractual management, granting to the peasants long-term and guaranteed land-use right, safeguarding the legitimate rights and interests of the parties to land contracts in rural areas, and promoting the development of agriculture and rural economy and social stability in the countryside
95	Law of the People's Republic of China on Securities Investment Fund	Adopted in October 2003	No	
96	Electronic Signature Law of the People's Republic of China	Adopted in 2004	No	
97	Enterprise Bankruptcy Law of the People's Republic of China	Adopted in August 2006	No	
98	Property Law of the People's Republic of China	Adopted in March 2007	1	**Article 1** This Law is enacted in accordance with **the Constitution** for the purpose of upholding the basic economic system of the State, maintaining the order of the socialist market economy, defining the attribution of things, giving play to the usefulness of things and protecting the property right of obligees
99	Marine Environment Protection Law of the People's Republic of China	Revised in 1999	No	
100	Cultural Relics Protection Law of the People's Republic of China	Revised in October 2002	1	**Article 1** With a view to strengthening the protection of cultural relics, inheriting the splendid historical and cultural legacy of the Chinese Nation, promoting the scientific research, conducting education in patriotism and revolutionary tradition, and building the socialist spiritual and material civilization, this Law is formulated in accordance with **the Constitution**
101	Water Pollution Prevention and Control Law of the People's Republic of China	Revised in 2008	No	
102	Drug Administration Law of the People's Republic of China	Revised in 2001	No	
103	Compulsory Education Law of the People's Republic of China	Revised in 2006	1	**Article 1** This Law is enacted in accordance with **the Constitution** and the Education Law, for the purpose of ensuring the right of school-age children and adolescents to compulsory education, guaranteeing implementation of compulsory education and improving the qualities of the entire nation
104	Customs Law of the People's Republic of China	Revised in 2000	No	

(continued)

(continued)

Serial No.	Name of law	Release time, last amendment	Occurrence frequency of "constitution"	Article
105	Air Pollution Prevention and Control Law of the People's Republic of China	Revised in 2000	No	
106	Archives Law of the People's Republic of China	Revised in 1996	No	
107	Law of the People's Republic of China on the Protection of Wildlife	Revised in August 2009	No	
108	Law of the People's Republic of China on the Prevention and Treatment of Infectious Diseases	Revised in 2004	No	
109	Environmental Protection Law of the People's Republic of China	Adopted in 1989	No	
110	Law of the People's Republic of China on the Protection of Military Installations	Revised in August 2009	1	**Article 1** This Law is formulated in accordance with **the Constitution** of the People's Republic of China for the purpose of protecting the safety of military installations, ensuring the effective utilization of military installations and normal performance of military activities, promoting modernization of national defense, strengthening national defense and resisting aggression
111	Surveying and Mapping Law of the People's Republic of China	Revised in 2002	No	
112	Law of the People's Republic of China on Progress of Science and Technology	Adopted in July 2008	1	**Article 1** This Law is formulated in accordance with **the Constitution** with a view to promoting progress of science and technology, assigning priority to the development of science and technology and bringing the role of science and technology as the primary productive force into full play in socialist modernization drive, so as to improve the service of science and technology to economic construction
113	Law of the People's Republic of China on Maternal and Infant Health Care	Revised in August 2009	1	**Article 1** This Law is formulated in accordance with **the Constitution** with a view to ensuring the health of mothers and infants and improving the quality of the newborn population
114	Prison Law of the People's Republic of China	Adopted in December 1994	2	**Article 1** This Law is formulated in accordance with **the Constitution** for the purpose of correctly executing criminal punishments, punishing and reforming prisoners, preventing and reducing crimes **Article 13** The People's police of a prison shall strictly abide by the Constitution and the law, be loyal to their duties, enforce the law impartially, strictly observe discipline and be honest and upright
115	People's Police Law of the People's Republic of China	Adopted in February 1995	3	**Article 1** The present Law is enacted in accordance with **the Constitution** for the purpose of safeguarding state security, maintaining public order, protecting the lawful rights and interests of citizens, strengthening the building of the contingent of the People's police, strictly administering the police, enhancing the quality of the People's

(continued)

(continued)

Serial No.	Name of law	Release time, last amendment	Occurrence frequency of "constitution"	Article
				police, ensuring the People's police's exercise of their functions and powers according to law, and ensuring the smooth progress of reform, opening up and the socialist modernization drive **Article 4** People's policemen must take **the Constitution** and laws as the guiding principles for their activities, be devoted to their duties, be honest and upright and highly disciplined, obey orders, and enforce laws strictly **Article 26 (2)** to endorse **the Constitution** of the People's Republic of China
116	Education Law of the People's Republic of China	Adopted in 1995	2	**Article 1** With a view to developing educational undertakings, improving the quality of the whole nationality, accelerating the construction of the socialist material and spiritual civilization and in accordance with **the Constitution** of the People's Republic of China, the present Law is hereby formulated **Article 3** In developing the socialist educational undertakings, the state shall uphold Marxism-Leninism, Mao Zedong Thought and the theories of constructing socialism with Chinese characteristics as directives and comply with the basic principles of **the Constitution**
117	People's Republic of China on Physical Culture and Sports	Adopted in August 1995	2	**Article 1** This Law is formulated in accordance with **the Constitution** for the purpose of developing undertakings of physical culture and sports, building up the People's physique, raising sports performance level and promoting the socialist material, ideological and cultural development
118	Law of the People's Republic of China on Prevention and Control of Environmental Pollution by Solid Waste	Revised in December 2004	No	
119	Food Hygiene Law of the People's Republic of China	Adopted in October 1995	No	
120	Administrative Penalty Law of the People's Republic of China	Revised in August 2009	2	**Article 1** This law is enacted pursuant to **the Constitution**, with a view to standardizing the establishment and administration of administrative punishments, guaranteeing and supervising the effective enforcement of executive commands by administrative organs, safeguarding public interests and social order, and protecting the legitimate rights and interests of citizens, legal persons or other organizations
121	Law of the People's Republic of China on Lawyers	Revised in 2007	2	**Article 3** In his legal practice, a lawyer must abide by **the Constitution** and laws, and strictly observe lawyers' professional ethics as well as discipline governing their legal practice **Article 5 (1)** uphold **the Constitution** of the People's Republic of China
122	Law of the People's Republic of China on Promoting the Transformation of Scientific and Technological Achievements	Adopted in May 1995	No	
123	Vocational Education Law of the People's Republic of China	Adopted in May 1996	No	

(continued)

(continued)

Serial No.	Name of law	Release time, last amendment	Occurrence frequency of "constitution"	Article
124	Gun Control Law of the People's Republic of China	Revised in August 2009	No	
125	Law of The People's Republic of China on The Prevention And Control of Environmental Noise Pollution	Adopted in October 1996	No	
126	Civil Air Defense Law of the People's Republic of China	Revised in August 2009	No	
127	Administrative Supervision Law of the People's Republic of China	Revised in 2010	1	**Article 1** This Law is enacted in accordance with **the Constitution**, in order to strengthen the supervision, guarantee the smooth implementation of government decrees, maintain administrative discipline, facilitate the building of an honest and clean government, improve administration and raise administrative efficiency
128	Construction Law of the People's Republic of China	Adopted in November 1997	No	
129	Law of the People's Republic of China on Blood Donation	Adopted in December 1997	No	
130	Law of the People's Republic of China on Precautions Against Earthquake and Relief of Disaster	Adopted in December 1997	No	
131	Fire Prevention Law of the People's Republic of China	Adopted in October 2008	No	
132	Law of the People's Republic of China on Medical Practitioners	Revised in August 2009	No	
133	Higher Education Law of the People's Republic of China	Adopted in August 1998	3	**Article 1** This Law is enacted in accordance with **the Constitution** and the Education Law for the purposes of developing the cause of higher education, implementing the strategy of reinvigorating the country through science and education and promoting the building of socialist material civilization and spiritual civilization **Article 3** The state adheres to the development of the cause of socialist higher education with Marxism-Leninism, Mao Zedong Thought and Deng Xiaoping's Theory as guidance following the basic principles defined by **the Constitution** **Article 46** Institutions of higher learning practice the teachers' qualification system. Chinese citizens who abide by **the Constitution** and laws, ardently love the educational cause, have good ideology and moral character, have an educational background of graduation of postgraduate course or graduates of regular college course and have corresponding educational and teaching capabilities may, upon confirmation of being qualified, acquire the qualification of teachers of institutions of higher learning. Those citizens without the educational background of

(continued)

(continued)

Serial No.	Name of law	Release time, last amendment	Occurrence frequency of "constitution"	Article
				graduation of postgraduate course or graduates of regular college course who have acquired a specialty from study and passed the state examination for teachers' qualification may also, upon confirmation of being qualified, acquire the qualification of teachers of institutions of higher learning
134	Administrative Reconsideration Law of the People's Republic of China	Revised in August 2009	1	**Article 1** This Law is enacted pursuant to **the Constitution** for the purpose of preventing and correcting any illegal or improper specific administrative acts, protecting the lawful rights and interests of citizens, legal persons and other organizations, safeguarding and supervising the exercise of functions and powers by administrative organs in accordance with law
135	Meteorology Law of the People's Republic of China	Revised in August 2009	No	
136	Law of the People's Republic of China on the Standard Spoken and Written Chinese Language	Adopted in October 2000		**Article 1** This Law is enacted in accordance with **the Constitution** for the purpose of promoting the normalization and standardization of the standard spoken and written Chinese language and its sound development, making it play a better role in public activities, and promoting economic and cultural exchange among all the Chinese nationalities and regions **Article 8s Paragraph** The spoken and written languages of the ethnic peoples shall be used in accordance with the relevant provisions of **the Constitution**, the Law on Regional National Autonomy and other laws
137	Law of the People's Republic of China on Officers in Active Service	Adopted in December 2000	2	**Article 3s Paragraph** Officers shall perform the sacred functions and responsibilities entrusted to them by **the Constitution** and laws, and they shall, in public activities, enjoy the status and honor commensurate with their functions and responsibilities **Article 8 (2)** observing **the Constitution**, laws and regulations, implementing the principles and policies of the State and the rules and regulations of the Army, and obeying orders and commands
138	National Defense Education Law of the People's Republic of China	Adopted in April 2001	No	
139	Law of the People's Republic of China on Prevention and Control of Desertification	Adopted in August 2001	No	
140	Law of the People's Republic of China on Population and Family Planning	Adopted in December 2001	1	**Article 1** In order to achieve the simultaneous development of population with the economy, society, resources and environment, to carry out the family planning, to safeguard the lawful rights and interests of the citizens, and to promote happiness of the families, prosperity of the people and the advancement of society, this Law has been formulated in accordance with **the Constitution**
141	Law of the People's Republic of China on Popularization of Science and Technology	Adopted in June 2002	1	**Article 1** This Law is enacted in accordance with **the Constitution** and other related laws for the purposes of implementing the strategy of invigorating the country through science and education and the strategy of sustainable development, redoubling the efforts to popularize science and technology, raising the citizens' scientific and cultural level and promoting economic and social progress

(continued)

(continued)

Serial No.	Name of law	Release time, last amendment	Occurrence frequency of "constitution"	Article
142	Law of the People's Republic of China on Promotion of Cleaner Production	Adopted in June 2002	No	
143	Law of the People's Republic of China on Evaluation of Environmental Effects	Adopted in October 2002	No	
144	Non-State Education Promotion Law of the People's Republic of China	Adopted in December 2002	1	**Article 1** This Law is enacted in accordance with **the Constitution** and the Education Law with a view to implementing the strategy of invigorating the country through science, technology and education, promoting the sound development of non-state education, and safeguarding the lawful rights and interests of the privately-run schools and the educates
145	Law of the People's Republic of China on Resident Identity Cards	Adopted in June 2003	No	
146	Law of the People's Republic of China on Prevention and Control of Radioactive Pollution	Adopted in June 2003	No	
147	Administrative License Law of the People's Republic of China	Adopted in August 2003	1	**Article 1** In order to regulate the establishment and implementation of administrative licenses, to protect the legitimate rights and interests of citizens, legal persons and other organizations, to safeguard public interests and social order, to ensure and supervise the effective implementation of administrative management by administrative organs, the Law is formulated in accordance with **the Constitution**
148	Law of the People's Republic of China on Road Traffic Safety	Adopted in December 2007	No	
149	Law of the People's Republic of China on Civil Servants	Adopted in April 2005	4	**Article 1** This Law is enacted in accordance with **the Constitution** and for the purpose of regularizing the administration of public servants, safeguarding their lawful rights and interests, improving supervision over them, and building up a contingent of civil servants with high quality, promoting a diligent and clean government and enhancing its efficiency **Article 11 (3)** upholding **the Constitution** of the People's Republic of China **Article 12 (1)** exemplarily observing with **the Constitution** and laws **Article 17** The leading posts under the category of comprehensive administration shall be established in accordance with **the Constitution**, relevant laws, levels of posts and institutions
150	Public Security Administration Punishment Law of the People's Republic of China	Adopted in August 2005	No	

(continued)

(continued)

Serial No.	Name of law	Release time, last amendment	Occurrence frequency of "constitution"	Article
151	Notary Law of the People's Republic of China	Adopted in August 2005	No	
152	Passport Law of the People's Republic of China	Adopted in April 2006	No	
153	Emergency Response Law of the People's Republic of China	Adopted in November 2007	1	**Article 69** Where an especially serious emergency occurs, which posts a major threat to the safety of the lives and property of the people, to national security, public security, environmental safety or social order, and the serious harm which inflicts on the society cannot be eliminated, kept under effective control or mitigated by taking the measures for handling emergency, as provided for in this Law and in other relevant laws, administrative regulations and rules, therefore it is necessary to enter into a state of emergency, the matter shall be subject to decision made by the Standing Committee of the National People's Congress or the State Council within the limits of their power and according to procedure as provided for by **the Constitution** and the relevant laws
154	Urban and Rural Planning Law of the People's Republic of China	Adopted in October 2007	No	
155	Narcotics Control Law of the People's Republic of China	Adopted in December 2007	No	
156	Law of the People's Republic of China on Protecting against and Mitigating Earthquake Disasters	Adopted in December 1997	No	
157	Food Safety Law of the People's Republic of China	Adopted in February 2009	No	
158	Law of the People's Republic of China on the People's Armed Police Force	Adopted in August 2009	1	**Article 4** The People's Armed Police Force shall abide by **the Constitution** and laws, be devoted to its duties and perform its duties in accordance with the provisions of this Law and other relevant laws
159	Law of the People's Republic of China on Individual Income Tax	Revised in 2007	No	
160	Maritime Traffic Safety Law of the People's Republic of China	Adopted in September 1983	No	
161	Forestry Law of the People's Republic of China	Revised in August 2009	No	

(continued)

(continued)

Serial No.	Name of law	Release time, last amendment	Occurrence frequency of "constitution"	Article
162	Accounting Law of the People's Republic of China	Revised in 1999	No	
163	Fisheries Law of the People's Republic of China	Revised in August 2009	No	
164	Mineral Resources Law of the People's Republic of China	Revised in August 2009	1	**Article 1** This Law is enacted in accordance with **the Constitution** of the People's Republic of China, with a view to developing the mining industry, promoting the exploration, development, utilization and protection of mineral resources and ensuring the present and long-term needs of the socialist modernization drive
165	Law of Land Administration of the People's Republic of China	Revised in August 2004	1	**Article 1** This Law is enacted in accordance with **the Constitution** for the purpose of strengthening land administration, maintaining the socialist public ownership of land, protecting and developing land resources, making rational use of land, effectively protecting cultivated land and promoting sustainable development of the society and the economy
166	Water Law of the People's Republic of China	Revised in August 2009	No	
167	Standardization Law of the People's Republic of China	Adopted in April 1989	No	
168	Law of the People's Republic of China on Import and Export Commodity Inspection	Revised in April 2002	No	
169	Railway Law of the People's Republic of China	Revised in August 2009	No	
170	Law of the People's Republic of China on Tobacco Monopoly	Revised in August 2009	No	
171	Law of the People's Republic of China on the Entry and Exit Animal and Plant Quarantine	Revised in August 2009	No	
172	Law of the People's Republic of China on the Administration of Tax Collection	Revised on April 28, 2001	No	
173	Law of the Peoples Republic of China on the Popularization of Agricultural Technology	Adopted in July 1993	No	

(continued)

(continued)

Serial No.	Name of law	Release time, last amendment	Occurrence frequency of "constitution"	Article
174	Agriculture Law of the People's Republic of China	Revised in August 2009	No	
175	Law of the People's Republic of China on Certified Public Accountants	Adopted in October 1993	No	
176	Law of the People's Republic of China on Protection of Investment by Compatriots from Taiwan	Adopted in March 1994	No	
177	Budget Law of the People's Republic of China	Adopted in March 1994	3	**Article 1** This Law is formulated in accordance with **the Constitution** with a view to strengthening the distribution and supervisory function of budget, improving the budget management of the State, intensifying the macroscopic regulation and control of the State, and ensuring the sound development of economy and society **Article 12s Paragraph** The Standing Committee of the National People's Congress supervises the implementation of the central and local budgets, examines and approves the adjustment plan for the central budget, examines and approves the final accounts of the Central Government, annuls administrative rules and regulations, decisions, or orders of the State Council on budget or final accounts, which contravene **the Constitution** or laws, and annuls local regulations or resolutions made by the People's congresses or their standing committees of the provinces, autonomous regions or municipalities directly under the Central Government on budget or final accounts, which contravene **the Constitution**, laws or administrative rules and regulations
178	Foreign Trade Law of the People's Republic of China	Revised in April 2004	No	
179	Audit Law of the People's Republic of China	Revised in February 2006	1	**Article 1** This Law is enacted in accordance with **the Constitution**, with a view to strengthening State supervision through auditing, maintaining the fiscal and economic order of the country, improving the efficiency in the use of fiscal funds, promoting the building of a clean government and ensuring the sound development of the national economy and society
180	Advertising Law of the People's Republic of China	Adopted in October 1994	No	
181	Law of the People's Republic of China on the People's Bank of China	Revised in December 2003	No	
182	Civil Aviation Law of the People's Republic of China	Revised in August 2009	No	
183	Coal Industry Law of the People's Republic of China	Revised in August 2009	No	

(continued)

(continued)

Serial No.	Name of law	Release time, last amendment	Occurrence frequency of "constitution"	Article
184	Law of the People's Republic of China on Township Enterprises	Adopted in October 1996	No	
185	Animal Epidemic Prevention Law of the People's Republic of China	Revised in August 2007	No	
186	Law of the People's Republic of China on Flood Control	Adopted in August 1997	No	
187	Energy Conservation Law of the People's Republic of China	Revised in October 2007	No	
188	Price Law of the People's Republic of China	Adopted in December 1997	No	
189	Seed Law of the People's Republic of China	Revised in August 2004	No	
190	Law of the Peoples Republic of China on the Administration of Sea Areas	Adopted in October 2001	No	
191	Government Procurement Law of the People's Republic of China	Adopted in June 2002	No	
192	Law of the People's Republic of China on Promotion of Small and Medium-sized Enterprises	Adopted in June 2002	No	
193	Law of the People's Republic of China on Ports	Adopted in June 2003	No	
194	Banking Supervision Law of the People's Republic of China	Revised in October 2006		
195	Law of the People's Republic of China on Promotion of Agricultural Mechanization	Adopted in June 2004	No	

(continued)

(continued)

Serial No.	Name of law	Release time, last amendment	Occurrence frequency of "constitution"	Article
196	Animal Husbandry Law of the People's Republic of China	Adopted in December 2005	No	
197	Agricultural Product Quality Safety Law of the People's Republic of China	Adopted in April 2006	No	
198	Law of the People's Republic of China on Anti-money Laundering	Adopted in October 2006	No	
199	Enterprise Income Tax Law of the People's Republic of China	Adopted in March 2007	No	
200	Anti-monopoly Law of the People's Republic of China	Adopted in August 2007	No	
201	Circular Economy Promotion Law of the People's Republic of China	Adopted in August 2008	No	
202	Law of the People's Republic of China on the State-Owned Assets of Enterprises	Adopted in October 2008	No	
203	Law of the People's Republic of China on the Protection of Disabled Persons	Revised in April 2008	1	**Article 1** This Law is formulated in accordance with **the Constitution** for the purposes of protecting the lawful rights and interests of, and developing undertakings for, disabled persons, and ensuring their equal and full participation in social life and their share of the material and cultural wealth of the society
204	Law of the People's Republic of China on the Protection of Minors	Adopted in December 2006	1	**Article 1** This Law is enacted in accordance with **the Constitution** for the purpose of protecting the physical and mental health of the minors, safeguarding their lawful rights and interests, promoting their all-around development morally, intellectually and physically, and training them to be builders of and successors to the socialist cause with lofty ideals, sound morality, better education and a good sense of discipline
205	Law of the People's Republic of China on the Protection of Rights and Interests of Women	Revised in August 2005	1	**Article 1** In accordance with **the Constitution** and the actual conditions of the country, this Law is formulated to protect women's lawful rights and interests, promote the equality between men and women and allow full play to women's role in socialist modernization
206	Law of The People's Republic of China on Safety in Mines	Revised in August 2009	No	

(continued)

(continued)

Serial No.	Name of law	Release time, last amendment	Occurrence frequency of "constitution"	Article
207	Labor Law of the People's Republic of China	Revised in August 2009	1	**Article 1** This Law is hereby formulated in accordance with **the Constitution** in order to protect the legitimate rights and interests of labourers, readjust labour relationship, establish and safeguard the labour system suiting the socialist market economy, and promote economic development and social progress
208	Law of the People's Republic of China on the Protection of the Rights and Interests of the Elderly	Revised in August 2009	1	**Article 1** This Law is enacted in accordance with **the Constitution** to protect the lawful rights and interests of the elderly, develop the undertakings related to the elderly and promote the Chinese People's virtues of respecting and providing for the elderly
209	Law of the People's Republic of China on Prevention of Juvenile Delinquency	Adopted in June 1996	No	
210	Law of the People's Republic of China on Donation for Public Welfare Undertakings	Adopted in June 1999	No	
211	Law of the People's Republic of China on Prevention and Control of Occupational Diseases	Adopted in October 2001	No	**Article 1** This Law is enacted, in accordance with **the Constitution**, for the purpose of preventing, controlling and eliminating occupational disease hazards, preventing and controlling occupational diseases, protecting the health and related rights and interests of workers, and promoting the development of the economy
212	Labor Contract Law of the People's Republic of China	Adopted in June 2007	No	
213	Employment Promotion Law of the People's Republic of China	Adopted in 2007	No	
214	Law of the People's Republic of China on Labour Dispute Mediation and Arbitration	Adopted in 2007	No	
215	Law of the People's Republic of China on the Protection of Disabled Persons	Adopted in April 2008	1	**Article 1** This Law is enacted in accordance with **the Constitution** for the purpose of protecting the lawful rights and interests of disabled persons, developing undertakings for them, and ensuring their equal and full participation in social life and their share of the material and cultural wealth of the society
216	Criminal Law of the People's Republic of China	Revised in August 2009	1	**Article 1** This law is formulated in accordance with **the Constitution** and in light of the concrete experience of China launching a struggle against crime and the realities in the country, with a view to punishing crime and protecting the people
217	Law of the People's Republic of China on Specialized Farmers Cooperatives	Adopted in October 2006	No	

(continued)

(continued)

Serial No.	Name of law	Release time, last amendment	Occurrence frequency of "constitution"	Article
218	Administrative Litigation Law of the People's Republic of China	Adopted in April 1989	1	**Article 1 Pursuant** to **the Constitution**, this Law is enacted for the purpose of ensuring the correct and prompt handling of administrative cases by the people's courts, protecting the lawful rights and interests of citizens, legal persons and other organizations, and safeguarding and supervising the exercise of administrative powers by administrative organs in accordance with the law
219	Civil Procedure Law of the People's Republic of China	Revised in October 2007	2	**Article 1** The Civil Procedure Law of the People's Republic of China is formulated on the basis of **the Constitution** and in the light of the experience and actual conditions of our country in the trial of civil cases **Article 17** The People's congresses of the national autonomous regions may formulate, in accordance with **the Constitution** and the principles of this Law, and in conjunction with the specific circumstances of the local nationalities, adaptive and supplementary provisions. Such provisions made by an autonomous region shall be submitted to the Standing Committee of the National People's Congress for approval; those made by an autonomous prefecture or autonomous county shall be submitted to the standing committee of the People's congress of the relevant province or autonomous region for approval and to the Standing Committee of the National People's Congress for the record
220	Arbitration Law of the People's Republic of China	Adopted in August 1994	No	
221	Special Maritime Procedure Law of the People's Republic of China	Adopted in December 1999	No	
222	Constitution of the People's Republic of China	Revised in March 2004	21	**Last Paragraph of the Preamble** This **Constitution** affirms the achievements of the struggles of the Chinese people of all nationalities and defines the basic system and basic tasks of the state in legal form; it is the fundamental law of the state and has supreme legal authority. The people of all nationalities, all state organs, the armed forces, all political parties and public organizations and all enterprises and undertakings in the country must take **the Constitution** as the basic norm of conduct, and they have the duty to uphold the dignity of **the Constitution** and ensure its implementation **Article 5 Third Paragraph** No laws or administrative or local regulations may contravene **the Constitution** **Article 33 Fourth Paragraph** Every citizen is entitled to the rights and at the same time must perform the duties prescribed by **the Constitution** and other laws **Article 53** Citizens of the People's Republic of China must abide by **the Constitution** and other laws, keep State secrets, protect public property, observe labour discipline and public order and respect social ethics **Article 62 (1)** to amend **the Constitution** (2) to supervise the enforcement of **the Constitution** **Article 64** Amendments to **the Constitution** are to be proposed by the Standing Committee of the National People's Congress or by more than one-fifth of the deputies to the National People's Congress and adopted by a vote of more than two-thirds of all the deputies to the Congress **Article 67 (1)** to interpret **the Constitution** and supervise its enforcement

(continued)

(continued)

Serial No.	Name of law	Release time, last amendment	Occurrence frequency of "constitution"	Article
				(7) to annul those administrative regulations, decisions or orders of the State Council that contravene **the Constitution** or other laws **Article 76** Deputies to the National People's Congress must play an exemplary role in abiding by the Constitution and other laws and keeping State secrets and, in public activities, production and other work, assist in the enforcement of **the Constitution** and other laws **Article 95 Third Paragraph** Organs of self-government are established in autonomous regions, autonomous prefectures and autonomous counties. The organization and working procedures of organs of self-government are prescribed by law in accordance with the basic principles laid down in Sections 5 and 6 of Chapter III of **the Constitution** **Article 99** Local People's congresses at various levels ensure the observance and implementation of **the Constitution** and other laws and the administrative regulations in their respective administrative areas. Within the limits of their authority as prescribed by law, they adopt and issue resolutions and examine and decide on plans for local economic and cultural development and for the development of public services **Article 100** The People's congresses of provinces and municipalities directly under the Central Government, and their standing committees may adopt local regulations, which must not contravene **the Constitution** and other laws and administrative regulations, and they shall report such local regulations to the Standing Committee of the National People's Congress for the record **Article 115** The organs of self-government of autonomous regions, autonomous prefectures and autonomous counties exercise the functions and powers of local organs of State as specified in Section 5 of Chapter III of the Constitution. At the same time, they exercise the power of autonomy within the limits of their authority as prescribed by the Constitution, the Law of the People's Republic of China on Regional National Autonomy and other laws and implement the laws and policies of the State in the light of the existing local situation
223	Provisions of The Standing Committee of the National People's Congress for the Direct Election of Deputies to People's Congress at Or below the County Level	Adopted in March 1983	No	
224	Decision of the Standing Committee of the National People's Congress on the Establishment of Maritime Courts in Coastal Port Cities	Adopted in November 1984	No	
225	Regulations of the People's Republic of China Concerning Diplomatic Privileges and Immunities	Adopted in September 1986	No	

(continued)

(continued)

Serial No.	Name of law	Release time, last amendment	Occurrence frequency of "constitution"	Article
226	Rules of Procedure for the Standing Committee of the National People's Congress of the People's Republic of China	Revised in April 2009	1	**Article 1** These Rules are formulated in accordance with the provisions of **the Constitution** and the Organic Law of the National People's Congress and in the light of the practical experience of the Standing Committee of the National People's Congress
227	Decision of the Standing Committee of the National People's Congress Approving the Central Military Commission's Regulations for Conferring on Retired Officers Honorary Medals of Meritorious Service in the Chinese People's Liberation Army	Adopted in July 1988		
228	Rules of Procedure for the National People's Congress of the People's Republic of China	Adopted in 1989	4	**Article 1** These Rules are formulated in accordance with **the Constitution**, the Organic Law of the National People's Congress and the practical experience of the National People's Congress **Article 34s Paragraph** The Premier and other members of the State Council and members of the Central Military Commission other than its Chairman shall be nominated in accordance with the relevant provisions of **the Constitution** **Article 52s Paragraph** An amendment to **the Constitution** shall be adopted by two thirds or more of the votes of all the deputies **Article 53s Paragraph** An amendment to **the Constitution** shall be passed by ballot
229	Regulations of the People's Republic of China Concerning Consular Privileges and Immunities	Adopted in October 1990	No	
230	Measures for Election of Deputies from the Chinese People's Liberation Army to the National People's Congress and Local People's Congresses at or Above the County Level	Revised in 2012	1	**Article 1** These Measures are enacted in accordance with the relevant provisions of ***the Constitution*** *of the People's Republic of China* and *the Electoral Law of the National People's Congress and Local People's Congresses of the People's Republic of China*

(continued)

(continued)

Serial No.	Name of law	Release time, last amendment	Occurrence frequency of "constitution"	Article
231	Resolution of the Standing Committee of the National People's Congress on Approving the Decision of the State Council on Issues concerning Reeducation through Labor	Adopted in 1957	1	**Begin with**: The following decision regarding the question of rehabilitation through labour is made in accordance with the provisions of Article 100 of **the Constitution** of the People's Republic of China and with a view to reforming those persons who are able to work but insist on leading an idle life, violating law and discipline, or will not engage in honest pursuits, into persons who are able to support themselves through their own labour, and to further maintaining public order, thus facilitating socialist construction
232	Regulations on Household Registration of the People's Republic of China	Adopted in January 1958		
233	Resolution of the Standing Committee of the National People's Congress on Approving the Temporary Measures of the State Council on Providing for Old, Weak, Sick, and Handicapped Cadres	Adopted in May 1978	No	
234	Resolution of the Standing Committee of the National People's Congress Approving the Supplementary Provisions of the State Council for Rehabilitation Through Labour	Adopted in November 1979	No	
235	Regulations of the People's Republic of China on Academic Degrees	Revised in 2004	No	
236	Resolution of the Standing Committee of the National People's Congress on Approving the Interim Provisions of the State Council for Veteran Cadres to Leave Their Posts in Order to Rest	Adopted in 1980	No	

(continued)

(continued)

Serial No.	Name of law	Release time, last amendment	Occurrence frequency of "constitution"	Article
237	Regulations on the Military Ranks of Officers of the Chinese People's Liberation Army	Revised in 1994	1	**Article 1** These Regulations are formulated in accordance with the relevant provisions of ***the Constitution*** *of the People's Republic of China* and *the Military Service Law of the People's Republic of China*
238	Regulations of the People's Republic of China on the Police Ranks of the People's Police	Adopted in July 1992	1	**Article 1** These Regulations are formulated in accordance with **the Constitution**, with a view to strengthening the revolution, modernization and standardization of the contingent of the People's police, enhancing their sense of responsibility, sense of honor and sense of discipline and facilitating their command and management as well as the performance of their duty
239	Regulations of the People's Republic of China on the Customs Titles	Adopted in February 2003	1	**Article 1** These Regulations are enacted in accordance with **the Constitution**, with a view to strengthening the contingent of the Customs personnel, enhancing their sense of responsibility, their sense of honor, and their sense of organization and discipline, and facilitating their performance of duties according to law
240	Resolution of the Standing Committee of the National People's Congress on Approving the Regulations on Special Economic Zones in Guangdong Province	Adopted in 1980	No	
241	Decision of the Standing Committee of the National People's Congress Concerning the Application of Interim Regulations on Such Taxes as Value-added Tax, Consumption Tax and Business Tax to Enterprises with Foreign Investment and Foreign Enterprises	Adopted in 1993	No	
242	Resolution of the Standing Committee of the National People's Congress Approving the "Interim Measures of the State Council on the Workers' Retirement and Leaving of Posts"	Adopted in 1978	No	

(continued)

(continued)

Serial No.	Name of law	Release time, last amendment	Occurrence frequency of "constitution"	Article
243	Resolution of the Standing Committee of the National People's Congress Approving the Provisions of the State Council for Home Leave for Workers and Staff	Adopted in March 1981	No	
244	Decision of SCNPC Regarding Exercising Criminal Jurisdiction over the Crimes Prescribed in the International Treaties to Which the People's Republic of China is a Party or has Acceded	Adopted in June 1987	No	

Study of the Applicability of the Constitution in Judicial Proceedings

Mo Jihong

Ever since the Supreme People's Court made clear in the "August 13" Official Reply in 2001 for protecting citizens' right to education as endowed by the Constitution, the applicability of the Constitution in judicial judgment has received wide attention from the constitutional community and judicial practice departments. However, China's constitutional community has long been lacking in-depth and systematic studies in this aspect and, in practice, the Standing Committee of the National People's Congress and the Supreme People's Court lack clear-cut legal attitude toward the way of applying the Constitution in judicial judgment. Therefore, there have been no strong theoretical demonstrations about whether the Constitution should be taken as the legal basis for people's courts to make judicial judgments and about how to apply the Constitution in judicial judgment. There has also been short of effective practices in judicial judgment. The applicability of the Constitution in judicial judgment has not been well studied, so there have been no effective discussions about relevant theoretical and practical questions, including whether people's courts could carry out review for constitutionality s in judicial adjustment in accordance with the Constitution, or make corresponding interpretations of the Constitution, etc. For that matter, it is necessary to conduct comprehensive and systematic studies on the applicability of the Constitution in judicial judgment so as to promote China's studies of review for constitutionality theories and building of a review for constitutionality mechanism.

M. Jihong (✉)
Institute of Law of Chinese Academy of Social Sciences, Beijing, China
e-mail: 13263169197@163.com

L. Li et al. (eds.), *Constitutional Development in China, 1982–2012*,
Research Series on the Chinese Dream and China's Development Path,
https://doi.org/10.1007/978-981-32-9261-1_14

1 Basic Standpoint of the Supreme People's Court on Applying the Constitution in Judicial Judgment Since the Foundation of PRC

After the founding of the People's Republic of China, the 1954 Constitution stipulated that the National People's Congress had the function and power to supervise the enforcement of the Constitution. In addition, the 1954 Constitution stipulated in Article 31 (5) that the Standing Committee of the National People's Congress had the function and power to supervise the work of the State Council, the Supreme People's Court, and the Supreme People's Procuratorate. That said, the 1954 Constitution did not make clear whether the work of the Standing Committee of the National People's Congress to supervise the State Council, the Supreme People's Court, and the Supreme People's Procuratorate contains the constitutional supervision over the aforesaid three organs. Neither did the 1954 Constitution stipulate that the Supreme People's Courts have the responsibility for guaranteeing the implementation of the Constitution, especially whether people's courts could directly quote the Constitution as the legal basis for judicial judgment.

The Constitution has no clear stipulations for whether people's courts at various levels including the Supreme People's Court have the duty to guarantee the implementation of the Constitution and whether the Constitution can be taken as the legal basis for judicial judgment, so the Supreme People's Court is also conservative and cautious about whether people's courts could take the Constitution as the legal basis for judging cases. The Supreme People's Court issued *the Reply on Not Citing the Constitution as the Basis for Determining Guilt or Sentences in Criminal Judgments* on July 30, 1955. In the reply, the Supreme People's Court made the statement, "Higher People's Court of Xinjiang, your court's (55) Xing.Er.Zi. No. 336 Report has been received. The Constitution of the People's Republic of China is the fundamental law of our country and the 'mother law' of all laws. In the report on the draft constitution of the People's Republic of China, NPC Chairman Liu Shaoqi pointed out that constitution stipulates what's legitimate and illegitimate, or what must be statutorily executed, and what is illegal and must be prohibited concerning the most important matters in national life. In criminal aspect, the Constitution has no stipulation of the way of punishment and sentence. Given this, we agree with your court's opinion that it is inappropriate to cite the Constitution as the basis for determining the punishment and sentence in criminal judgment.

Viewing from legal principle, we cannot definitely judge that the Supreme People's Court clearly denied the citing of the Constitution in criminal judgment for punishment and sentence in above-said reply, but we can at least see from the wording of "inappropriate to cite" that the Supreme People's Court held a passive and unsupportive attitude toward citing the Constitution in criminal judgment for punishment and sentence. The Supreme People's Court has an ambiguous attitude toward the application of the Constitution in judicial judgment, so people's courts at the grass-roots level have basically never cited the Constitution as the basis for criminal punishment and sentence in judicial practice. The Constitution has been excluded by people's courts from the group of laws being taken as the basis for criminal judgment.

The 1975 Constitution and 1978 Constitution even failed to resolve the question about whether people's courts could take the Constitution as the legal basis for judging cases in judicial judgment.

In another judicial interpretation in 1986, the Supreme People's Court interpreted the legal basis for judging civil cases by people's courts without affirming that the Constitution could be taken as the legal basis by people's courts for civil trials. Yet, the Supreme People's Court did not deny people's courts' reference to the Constitution as the legal basis in civil trials. On October 28, 1986, the Supreme People's Court issued *the Reply Concerning How People's Courts Are to Cite Legally Normative Documents When Producing Legal Document*. Given the request of Jiangsu Provincial Higher People's Court for instructions, the Reply wrote, "The receipt of your court's Su.Fa.Min. [1986] No. 11 Request for Instructions has been received. Regarding the question about how people's courts are to cite legally normative documents to prepare legal documents, after studies, the reply is as follows. According to relevant stipulations of the Constitution and the organic law of local people's congresses and local people's governments at various levels, the legislative power of the state is exercised by the National People's Congress and its Standing Committee; the State Council has the power to formulate administrative regulations in accordance with the Constitution and laws; people's congresses of provinces and municipalities directly under the central government, and their standing committees may adopt local regulations, which must not contravene the Constitution, laws and the administrative regulations; people's congresses of national autonomous areas have the power to adopt special autonomous regulations and separate regulations in light of local political, economic and cultural characteristics. Therefore, when people's courts prepare legal documents for trying civil cases and cases related to economic disputes, they could cite the laws enacted by the National People's Congress and its Standing Committee and administrative regulations formulated by the State Council. When a people's court prepares the legal document for trying a civil case and case related to civil and economic disputes, in which both litigants are within the administrative region, the court may cite local regulations, which are formulated by people's congresses of provinces and municipalities directly under the central government and their standing committees and must not contravene the Constitution, laws and administrative regulations, and cite autonomous regulations and separate regulations formulated by people's congresses of national autonomous areas in light of local political, economic and cultural characteristics. In handling cases, people's courts may refer to but not cite orders, instructions, rules, and regulations issued by ministries and commissions under the State Council, decisions and resolutions adopted and issued by people's congresses of counties and municipalities, decisions, orders, rules, and regulations issued by local people's governments at various levels, but all must not contravene the Constitution, laws and administrative regulations. The opinions and replies of the Supreme People's Court on implementing laws should be carried out, but inappropriate to be directly cited.

Looking from the above-mentioned reply of the Supreme People's Court, although the Supreme People's Court did not affirm that people's courts could take the Constitution as the legal basis for civil trials, it put forward a clear judicial requirement that the legal basis taken by people's courts for trying civil cases and cases related to economic disputes shall not contravene the Constitution. That is to say, the Supreme People's Court still has a passive and evasive attitude toward applying the Constitution in civil trials. That said, this reply shows that the Supreme People's Court's attitude toward applying the Constitution in judicial trials seems rather moderate and flexible when compared with its judicial reply issued in 1955 on not citing the Constitution as the basis for determining punishment or sentence in criminal judgments.

At the same time, in judicial practice, the Supreme People's Courts inclined to support grass-roots people's courts to cite the Constitution as the legal basis for judicial judgments. In the judicial reply on Qi Yuling Case, the Supreme People's Court clearly defined the protection of citizens' right to education as stipulated in the Constitution by means of civil remedy.

Given the paper of civil mediation (87) Jin.Tang.Fa.Min.Tiao.Zi. No. 517. issued by the People's Court of Tanggu District of Tianjin Municipality in the lawsuit brought by the plaintiffs, Zhang Lianqi and Zhang Guoli, against the defendant, Zhang Xuezhen, for disputes over compensation for damages, the Supreme People's Court gave *the Reply Regarding Whether the "No Liability for Work-related Injury" Clause in Labor Contract Is Effective* on October 14, 1988. The Supreme People's Court pointed out in the reply, "Tianjin Municipal Higher People's Court, the receipt of your (1987) No. 60 Request for Instruction is acknowledged hereby. According to the request, Zhang Xuezhen and XuGuangqiu of your city's Tanggu District opened a new village youth service station and hired Zhang Guosheng (male, aged 21) in June 1985 as a temporary worker, and the "no liability for work-related injury" was clearly indicated in the employment registration form. On November 17 of the next year when the station was demolishing the old buildings in Tianjin Soda Plant, Zhang Guosheng was injured on the left ankle by the fallen beam and died of toxic sepsis caused by infected and necrotic local tissues. Before death, Zhang Guosheng spent 14,151.15 yuan for medical treatment of the injury. For that matter, Zhang Guosheng's parents Zhang Lianqi and Jiao Ronglan claimed for compensation against Zhang Xuezhen, who refused to bear the civil liability on the ground of the "no liability for work-related injury" clause. Zhang Lianqi and Jiao Ronglanthen filed a lawsuit to the court. After studying the case, the Supreme People's Court believes that China's Constitution has clear stipulations for labor protection which is the right enjoyed by workers. Zhang Xuezhen and XuGuangqiu, as the employers, should provide labor protection to their employees by law. Instead, they added the "no liability for work-related injury" clause to the recruitment registration form, which goes against the provisions of the Constitution and related laws and severely violates socialist ethics and thus shall be regarded as an invalid civil act. With regard to the legal consequence, compensation, among other aspects after confirming the invalidity of this act, your court should properly handle the case in accordance with related stipulations of such laws as the *General Principles of the Civil Law* and in line with this particular case. It is obvious that, in this judicial reply, the Supreme People's Court cited the Constitution to support the grass-roots people's court to make the judgment for "no liability for work-related injury" in line with the spirit of the Constitution.

In the Qi Yuling Case, the Supreme People's Court even more directly showed its judicial attitude in the "August 13" Reply toward how to protect citizens' right to education as stipulated in the Constitution.

The Judicial Committee of the Supreme People's Court adopted *the Reply on Whether the Accused Shall Bear Civil Liability for the Infringement of the Citizen's Fundamental Rights of Receiving Education under the Protection of Constitution by Means of Infringing the Right of Name* (Fa.Shi [2001] No. 5) at the 1183rd meeting held on June 28, 2001. The Supreme People's Court pointed out in the reply: Shandong Provincial Higher People's Court, the receipt of your court's *Request for Instructions on the Cases related to the Disputes over Infringing the Right of Name between Qi Yuling and Chen Xiaoqi, Chen Kezheng, Jining Business School of Shandong Province, the Eight Middle School of Tengzhou City, Shandong Province and the Education Committee of Tengzhou City, Shandong Province* ([1999] Lu.Min.Zhong.Zi. No. 258) is acknowledged hereby. After studies, we conclude that, in accordance with the facts of the case, Chen Xiaoqi et al. have violated Qi Yuling's fundamental right to receive education as stipulated by the Constitution by means of infringing the right of name and caused specific damages and consequences, so they shall bear corresponding civil liabilities.

In above-said judicial reply, the Supreme People's Court made clear that civil remedy could be given to citizens whose right to receive education as stipulated in the Constitution is infringed. This judicial attitude clearly indicates that the Supreme People's Court as the highest judicial organ in China has put forward its own judicial proposition about how to realize citizens' fundamental rights as stipulated in the Constitution. In fact, this means that the Supreme People's Court has assumed the responsibility for guaranteeing the implementation of the Constitution, which is realized by directly taking the Constitution as the legal basis for judicial judgment.

Nevertheless, different from the judicial attitude of actively advancing the application of the Constitution in civil trials, the judicial stance of the Supreme People's Court in criminal judgment remains to be at the same level with the judicial replies made in 1955. In administrative judgment, the Supreme People's Court even clearly evades the application of the Constitution.

The Supreme People's Court printed and distributed *the Summary of the Symposium on Issues Concerning Applicable Legal Norms for the Trial of Administrative Cases* (Fa. [2004] No. 96) on May 18, 2004. The Supreme People's Court kept silent about whether the Constitution could be directly cited as the legal basis for administrative judgment, completely avoiding the application of the Constitution in this regard. This evidently showcased the passive and evasive tendency of the Supreme People's Court. This kind of equivocal judicial attitude actually goes against the spirit of the Constitution and *the Legislation Law* that laws, regulations, and rules shall not contravene the Constitution. In addition, this judicial standpoint is far less clear than the judicial reply given in 1986 on whether the Constitution could be cited in civil judgment. *The Summary of the Symposium* clearly stipulates the following aspects.

Administrative judgment involves many levels and categories of legal norms. After the enforcement of *the Legislation Law*, great changes have happened to the rules for the application of laws. In law application, there are always difficulties of all kinds, such as how to identify legal basis and resolve conflicts between legal norms. Whether these issues could be properly resolved has a direct influence on the justice and efficiency of administrative judgment. Furthermore, as China improves its rule of law and adapts to the needs of its entry into the World Trade Organization, administrative judgment has played an increasingly prominent role in resolving conflicts between legal norms and maintaining the uniformity of the legal system. For the purpose of accurately applying legal norms, ensuring impartial administrative trials, safeguarding the uniformity and dignity of the legal system and promoting law-based administration, the Administrative Tribunal of the Supreme People's Court used to conduct special investigations into the protruding issues related to the application of legal norms in administrative cases and solicited the opinions of related departments. In October 2003, the Supreme People's Court convened a symposium in Shanghai on administrative judgment of nationwide courts. During the proceedings of the symposium, a special discussion was held on issues related to the application of legal norms in hearing administrative cases. The participants reached the consensus on some universal issues on the basis of summarizing trial experiences and in accordance with stipulations of *the Legislation Law, the Administrative Procedure Law,* and other relevant laws. The summary is as follows.

1.1 Basis for Trying Administrative Cases

According to related provisions of *the Administrative Procedure Law* and *the Legislation Law*, people's courts take laws, administrative regulations, local regulations, autonomous regulations, and separate regulations as the basis and take rules as the reference in hearing administrative cases. While referring to rules, the legitimacy and efficacy of provisions of the rules shall be judged and legitimate and effective rules shall be applied. According to the stipulations of *the Legislation Law, the Regulation Regarding Procedures for the Formulation of Administrative Regulations* and *the Regulation on the Procedures for the Formulation of Rules* for the interpretation of laws, administrative regulations and rules, the legal interpretations by the Standing Committee of the National People's Congress, and the interpretations of administrative laws and regulations by the State Council or the departments authorized by the State Council are taken by people's courts as the legal basis for trying administrative cases. In trying administrative cases, people's courts may refer to and apply the interpretations of rules that are made by the enacting bodies of the rules and have the same effect with the rules.

Considering the evolution of China's legislative procedures after the funding of the People's Republic of China, the currently valid administrative regulations can be classified into three types. First, it is the type of administrative regulations formulated and promulgated by the State Council. Second, it is the type of administrative regulations promulgated by departments of the State Council with the approval of the State Council and pursuant to the effective procedures of formulating administrative regulations before the enforcement of *the Legislation Law*. After the enforcement of *the Legislation Law*, the normative documents promulgated by departments of the State Council with the approval of the State Council no longer belong to administrative regulations. Third, it is the type of other administrative regulations confirmed by the State Council while sorting out administrative regulations.

In practice, administrative judgment usually involves the specific application interpretations and other normative documents made and formulated by relevant departments for guiding law enforcement or implementing administrative measures. These specific application interpretations and normative documents mainly include the interpretations made by the State Council and people's governments of provinces, municipalities, autonomous regions and larger cities or their competent departments for specific application of laws, regulations or rules; generally binding decisions, orders or other normative documents issued by people's governments above the county-level and their competent departments. Administrative organs frequently take these specific application interpretations and other normative documents as the direct basis for specific administrative acts. These specific application interpretations and other normative documents aren't formal legal source and could not restrain people's courts in sense of legal norms. However, when people's courts believe after investigations that the specific application interpretations and other normative documents taken as the basis for specific administrative acts being sued are legitimate, effective, rational and appropriate, then the effectiveness shall be admitted while affirming that the specific acts being sued are legitimate. People's courts may make comments on whether the specific application interpretations and other normative documents are legitimate, effective, rational, or appropriate in judicial reasons.

1.2 Rules for the Application of Conflicting Legal Norms

When there is a conflict between two or more legal norms adjusting the same object for their different stipulations of legal consequences, the rules for judging and selecting the legal norms for application are generally that higher-level laws are superior to lower-level ones; later laws prevail over those which precede them; and special laws are superior to general laws. When conflicting legal norms involve major matters, related organs have different viewpoints on whether there are conflicts, there are still questions about the legitimacy and validity of the legal norms being applied, or it is unable to determine how to apply the legal norms according to the law application rules, the judgment shall be determined by competent authorities level by level according to the procedures as stipulated by the Legislation Law.

1.2.1 Judgment and Application When the Lower-Level Law Is not in Conformity with the Higher-Level Law

In case that the provisions of the lower-level law are not in conformity with that of the higher-level law, the people's court handling the case shall apply the higher-level law in principle. At present, many specific administrative acts are performed by taking lower-level laws as the basis but not citing and applying higher-level laws. Under this circumstance, people's courts should also judge whether the lower-level law is in conformity with the higher-level law while examining the legitimacy of specific administrative acts to maintain the uniformity of the legal system. If the judgment is that the lower-level law contravenes the higher-level law, the higher-level law shall be taken as the basis for judging the legitimacy of specific administrative acts being sued. Looking from judicial practice, the lower-level law is not in conformity with the higher-level law in the following common aspects: The lower-level law narrows the scope of subjects of rights as stipulated by the higher-level law or violates the legislative purpose of the higher-level law by expanding the scope of subjects of rights as stipulated by the higher-level law. The lower-level law restricts or expropriates the rights as stipulated by the higher-level law or violates the legislative purpose of the higher-level law by expanding the scope of rights as stipulated by the higher-level law. The lower-level law expands the scope of subjects of administration or their functions and powers. The lower-level law extends the terms of performing statutory duties as stipulated by the higher-level law. The lower-level law expands or narrows the scope, nature or conditions of duties or subjects of duties as stipulated by the higher-level law by means of reference and application approval. The lower-level law adds, or narrows, or violates the application conditions as stipulated by the higher-level law. The lower-level law expands or narrows the scope of behaviors, types, and degrees for administrative punishment as stipulated by the higher-level law. The lower-level law changes the nature of unlawful acts as stipulated by the higher-level law. The lower-level law exceeds the application scope, types and ways of coercive measures as stipulated by the higher-level law and adds or narrows its application conditions. Regulations, rules or other normative documents provide administrative permits violating stipulations of the administrative permission law or add administrative permission conditions violating higher-level law. There are also other inconsistent circumstances.

When the enforcement rules for laws, administrative regulations or local regulations after being revised are not abolished in writing, people's courts should differentiate the following circumstances in application. When the enforcement rules contravene the revised laws, administrative regulations or local regulations, they shall not be applied. When corresponding enforcement rules have lost the basis and cannot be separately enforced due to the revision of laws, administrative regulations or local regulations, the enforcement roles shall not be applied. When the enforcement rules do not contravene the revised laws, administrative regulations or local regulations, they can be applied.

1.2.2 Application Relations Between Special Regulations and General Regulations

When different provisions of the same law, administrative regulation, local regulation, autonomous regulation and separate regulation and rule have general and special stipulations for the same matter, the special ones shall prevail.

When the new general stipulations are inconsistent with the old special stipulations for the same matter between laws, between administrative regulations and between local regulations, people's courts shall determine the application in light of the following situations in principle. When new regulations permit the continuous application of old special regulations, the old special regulations shall be applied. When new general regulations annul old special stipulations, the new general stipulations shall prevail. When it is unable to confirm whether new general stipulations permit the continuous application of old stipulations, the people's court shall suspend the hearing of the administrative case, and if it is a legal stipulation, the court shall report the case to the corresponding higher people's court for being submitted to the Standing Committee of the NPC for judgment; if it is an administrative regulation, it shall be reported to the Supreme People's Court for being submitted to the State Council for judgment; if it is a local stipulation, the higher people's court shall submit it to the formulating organ for judgment.

1.2.3 Application Selection When a Local Regulation Contravenesy Departmental Rule

When the stipulations of a local regulation are consistent with that of a departmental rule for the same matter, people's court may follow the following point in application selection. (1) When a legal or administrative regulation authorizes a departmental rule to make enforcement rules, the rules should prevail. (2) When laws and administrative regulations are not yet available, the stipulations of departmental rules shall prevail for matters authorized by decisions and orders of the State Council, or for matters requiring the macro-control of the central government, or matters requiring national unified market activity rules and matters like foreign trade and foreign investment that require national unified stipulations. (3) When local regulations contain specific stipulations made in line with the actual situation of the administrative region as authorized by laws or administrative regulations, the specific stipulations shall prevail. (4) The stipulations of local regulations for matters belonging to local affairs shall prevail. (5) When laws and administrative regulations are not yet available, the stipulations made by local regulations for matters beyond that require national unified provisions in line with the local administrative regions shall prevail. (6) Other circumstances under which local regulations can be directly applied. When it is unable to determine the way of application, the hearing of administrative cases shall be suspended and submitted to the Supreme People's Court for power organs' handling in accordance with the stipulations of the first clause (2) of Article 86 of *the Legislation Law*.

1.2.4 Application Selection of Conflicting Rules

When the provisions of departmental rules are inconsistent with that of local government rules for the same matter, people's courts may determine the application as follows. (1) If laws or administrative regulations authorize departmental rules to make enforcement rules, the enforcement rules shall prevail. (2) When laws and administrative regulations are not yet available, the provisions prescribed in departmental rules for matters as authorized by decisions and orders of the State Council, for matters belonging to the macro-control of the central government, and for matters requiring national unified market activity rules and matters related to foreign trade and foreign investment shall be prioritized in application. (3) Specific provisions prescribed in local government rules in line with the actual situation of local administrative regions as authorized by laws or administrative regulations shall be prioritized in application. (4) The provisions prescribed in local government rules for specific administrative management matters of the local administrative regions shall be prioritized in application. (5) Other circumstances under which rules can be directly applied. When it is unable to determine the way of application, the hearing of administrative cases shall be suspended and reported level by level to the Supreme People's Court and then to the State Council for adjudication.

When the rules developed by different departments of the State Council are inconsistent for the same matter, people's courts may determine the application pursuant to the following situations. (1) Departmental rules, and regulations that do not contravene the higher-level law shall be applied. (2) If both provisions do not contravene that of the higher-level law, the provisions prescribed in the rules as required by exclusive authority shall be prioritized in application. (3) The rules, and regulations jointly formulated by two or more departments of the State Council for matters involving their functions and powers shall take precedence over provisions made by one department. (4) Other circumstance under which the application can be selected. When it is unable to determine the way of application, the hearing of the administrative cases shall be suspended and reported level by level to the Supreme People's Court and then submitted to the State Council for judgment.

When the provisions of other normative documents formulated by departments of the State Council, or people's governments of provinces, municipalities and autonomous regions are inconsistent for the same matter, above spirit shall be taken as the reference for the application.

1.3 Rules for Application of New and Old Legal Norms

According to the universal recognition and practices in administrative judgment, if the acts of an administrative counterpart are performed before the enforcement of a new law and specific administrative acts are performed after the enforcement of the new law, then people's courts, at the time of examining the legitimacy of specific administrative behaviors, shall apply provisions of the old law for practical issues but apply that of the new law for procedural issues, provided that: 1. There are stipulations otherwise specified by laws, regulations or rules; 2. applying the new law is more conducive to protecting the lawful rights and interests of the administrative counterpart; 3. the practical provisions of the new law should be applied pursuant to the nature of the specific administrative acts.

1.4 About the Interpretation of Specific Legal Norm Application

Interpreting legal norms in judging cases is an important part of people's courts' application of laws. People's courts usually interpret the applied legal norms in general semantics. When there is a special professional meaning, this meaning shall be prioritized in application. When it is semantically unclear or ambiguous, the meaning could be confirmed with reference to the context and the legislative purpose, objective, and principle.

When legal norms use such words as "etc." and "other" in the statement after listing applicable typical matters, they belong to exemplary provisions of an incomplete list. All matters using "etc.," "other," among other general terms shall be taken as matters beyond clearly listed matters in writing and the generalized circumstances should be matters similar to the listed matters.

People's courts should properly handle the relations between legal effect and social effect while interpreting and applying laws. That is to strictly apply legal provisions and uphold the seriousness of legal provisions to ensure determined, unified, and continuous application of laws. That is also to keep abreast with the times, lay emphasis on social effects in handling cases, avoid rigid and inflexible understanding and application of legal provisions, and safeguard national interests and public interests in law application.

Through summarizing the judicial position of the Supreme People's Court on the applicability of the Constitution in judicial judgment after the founding of the PRC, we can conclude that the Supreme People's Court as the highest adjudicative organ has not made any clear statement to deny the applicability of the Constitution in judicial judgment. That said, in specific judicial practice, the Supreme People's Court prefers to take the Constitution as the legal basis for civil judgment. In criminal judgment and administrative judgment, the Supreme People's Court has basically taken an evasive judicial attitude toward whether the Constitution can be used as the basis for judging criminal cases and administrative cases. The main reason behind this is that civil judgment involves the legal relations between equal subjects, and applying the Constitution in civil judgment would neither involve state organs exercising state powers nor antagonize state organs and hinder state organs' exercising state powers. In criminal judgment and administrative judgment, citing the Constitution as the legal basis for judging cases, it is bound to involve whether state organs' acts of exercising state powers are constitutional, which would easily trigger the rejection of state organs and form adverse political pressures, and consequently affect the application result of the Constitution in criminal judgment and administrative judgment.

2 Current Situation and Existing Problems in Applying the Constitution in Judicial Judgment

The Supreme People's Court has an ambiguous attitude toward whether the Constitution can be clearly applied in judicial judgment. In judicial practice, many local people's courts have actively and boldly cited the Constitution as the legal basis, which have demonstrated a diversified and complex trend. Summarizing various cases of applying the Constitution in judicial judgment by people's courts at various levels concludes the following classifications.

2.1 The Constitution Has Been Commonly Cited in Criminal, Civil, and Administrative Cases

The Supreme People's Court has not made clear statement to affirm that the Constitution can be directly cited as the legal basis for judging criminal, civil, and administrative cases. However, the Supreme People's Court has neither denied in any judicial interpretation the application of the Constitution as the legal basis for judicial judgments. Therefore, in judicial practice, local people's courts used to directly cite provisions of the Constitution in criminal, civil, and administrative cases. Looking from criminal cases, in the defamation case involving Shen Yafu and Mou Chunlin, Intermediate People's Court of Shanghai Municipality proposed in the ruling paper on the civil suit collateral to criminal proceedings (87) Hu. Zhong.Xing.Shang.Zi. No. 531[625]: There is a need to point out the state's protection of citizens' freedom and rights of speech, freedom of press and rights. However, just like all citizens, journalists also must fulfill their duties prescribed by the law while exercising their rights, i.e. "shall not impair state, public or collective interests or the lawful freedoms and rights of other citizens," and "insult, libel, false charge or frame-up directed against citizens by any means is prohibited." From the perspective of civil cases, a large number of civil cases cited related stipulations of the Constitution. Such as in the "case filed by Wu Fennv after being released upon completion of her sentence against the Municipal Engineering Management Office of Changning District for the restoration of pension benefits," the Civil Judgment of the People's Court of Changning District of Shanghai (1997) Chang.Min.Chu.Zi. No. 1248626 pointed out, "Our court concludes that, Article 44 of *the Constitution of the People's Republic of China* clearly stipulates that 'The State applies the system of retirement for workers and staff members of enterprises and institutions and for State functionaries according to law. The livelihood of retired persons is guaranteed by the State and society.' Pension benefit is one of the important social and economic rights enjoyed by citizens and the critical guarantee for retirees to live a settled life." Looking from administrative cases, many administrative judgments citied related provisions of the Constitution. For example, in the case of "Wang Hongjun refusing to accept the decision of Langzhong Public Security Bureau on the public security punishment," the Administrative Judgment of the Intermediate People's Court of Nanchong City of Sichuan Province (1999) Nan.Zhong.Fa.Xing. Zhong.Zi. No. 136[1] pointed out, "Our court concludes that, the right to vote and the right to be elected are the rights of citizens endowed by the Constitution. Ma Xinyun was not given the right to elect deputies to the township people's congress on behalf of his families, but it is legitimate for Ma Xinyun's to request the personnel chairing the electoral meeting to give him his vote in order to safeguard his lawful rights and interests."

Thus, it can be seen that, in current judicial practice, local people's courts haven't given up the application of the Constitution, though the Supreme People's Court has not clearly affirmed that the Constitution can be cited as the legal basis for judicial judgment. Local people's courts at various levels used to cite the Constitution as the legal basis for judging criminal, civil and administrative cases pursuant to the specific requirements of the cases. The Constitution has been widely applied in judicial practice, which has demonstrated diversified application characteristics.

2.2 The Constitution Is Both Independently and Dependently Applied in Judicial Judgment

In practice, local people's courts cite the Constitution as the legal basis for handling specific cases in judicial judgment in different ways. In some judgments, the

[1]Yu [1, pp. 61–63].

Constitution was simply cited as the legal basis for supporting other legal forms, and it is still the specific laws and regulations cited by people's court that truly have a decisive role in specific cases. In some judgments, the specific disputes over rights and duties were settled completely by taking related provisions of the Constitution as the basis, making the Constitution become the only and most important legal basis for settling legal disputes. Therefore, from the perspective of its role in being cited in judicial judgment, the Constitution was applied both dependently and independently. In most cases, the Constitution was cited with other legal forms by courts as the basis for interpreting the legality and legitimacy of other legal forms. In the lawsuit filed by WuFengdi against Andong Township Environmental Sanitary Management Station of Cixi City for the disputes over retirement treatment, the Civil Judgment of People's Court of Cixi City in Zhejiang Province (2001) Ci.Min.Chu.Zi. No.1862[2] pointed out, "Hereby, in accordance with Article 44 and the first paragraph of Article 45 of *the Constitution of the People's Republic of China* and the first paragraph (1) of Article 73 of *the Labor Contract Law of the People's Republic of China*, and by referring to *the Interim Measures of the State Council on the Retirement and Resignation of Workers*, the judgment is made as follows." It is obvious that the Constitution was applied as the legal basis for the labor contract law and other legal forms in judgment. The purpose of applying the Constitution was to further strengthen the legitimacy and rationality of the application of specific laws and regulations by people's courts. There are not many cases in which the Constitution is independently applied in judicial judgment. But in this kind of cases, judgment of legal disputes involved totally relied on the practical stipulations of the Constitution. It can be said that legal disputes involved in such cases would not be settled effectively in law without related stipulations of the Constitution. For instance, in the case filed by Fan Xuezhen, Fan Changqi, Fan Guidi, Fan Changbo, and Fan Xiaorong against Shanghai Municipal Housing and Land Administration Bureau for Issuing the Property Ownership Certificate, the Administrative Judgment of the No. 2 Intermediate People's Court of Shanghai Municipality (1998) Hu.Er.Zhong.Xing.Zhong.Zi. No. 102[3] pointed out, "According to the stipulations of the 1982 Constitution on making urban land become state-owned land, the land used for No. 5 residence in 234 Nong, Zhoushan Road is sate-owned land. There is a legal basis for confirming the ownership of the building and the state-owned land use right as stated on the property ownership certificate issued by the appellee Shanghai Municipal Housing and Land Administration Bureau. The five appealers' claim for the right of inheritance of the land after it became state-owned goes against the law." Evidently, in this case, the stipulations of the Constitution were the main basis for the people's court to make the judgment. Without citing related stipulations of the Constitution, the legal disputes involved in this case would not be effectively settled.

[2]Yu [1, pp. 155–159].

[3]Yu [1, pp. 28–31].

2.3 *The Constitution Is Used for Both Protecting and Restricting Citizens' Rights*

When being applied in judicial practice, the Constitution is taken by some people's courts as the legal basis for protecting citizens' rights while by others to restrict citizens' rights. However, on citing the Constitution as the basis for protecting and restricting citizens' rights, it is taken as the legal basis for protecting citizens' rights in most cases. On taking it as the legal basis for protecting citizens' rights, a case in point is the "case filed by Wu Fennv after being released upon completion of her sentence against the Municipal Engineering Management Office of Changning District for the restoration of pension benefits." The Civil Judgment of the People's Court of Changning District of Shanghai (1997) Chang.Min.Chu.Zi. No. 1248[4] pointed out, "Our court concludes that, Article 44 of *the Constitution of the People's Republic of China* clearly stipulates, 'The State applies the system of retirement for workers and staff members of enterprises and institutions and for State functionaries according to law. The livelihood of retired persons is ensured by the State and society.' Pension benefit is one of the important social and economic rights enjoyed by citizens and the critical guarantee for retirees to live a settled life." However, when some local people's courts make judgment, they also cite-related stipulations of the Constitution to restrict citizens' rights or give relevant duties to citizens. In the lawsuit filed by Xu Yuechao against Fan Xiuqun for child-rearing dispute, the Civil Judgment of the People's Court of Xinye County of Henan Province (1999) Xin.Shang.Min.Chu.Zi. No. 079[630] pointed out, "Our court concludes that, according to the stipulation of China's Constitution and Marriage Law, parents have the duty to rear and educate their minor children, which is a compulsory provision." In the case lodged by Wang Sulan against Tu Men and Zhu Dongli for infringing the right of reputation, Beijing Xicheng District People's Court issued the Civil Judgment (1998) Xi.Min.Chu.Zi. No. 547[631] stated, "In accordance with the stipulations of China's Constitution, Citizens of the People's Republic of China enjoy the freedom of speech, of the press, of assembly, of association, of procession and of demonstration. Therefore, the freedom of speech, of expression, of publication and of the press belongs to the fundamental freedom of citizens as confirmed and protected by the Constitution. However, there is no absolute freedom. While endowing the right of freedom to subjects of rights, the law also formulates necessary restrictions of the right of freedom. It is the same for the freedom of speech, of expression, of publication and of the press, which is not an absolute right. The maximum restriction on exercising the freedom of speech, of expression, of publication and of the press is that infringing others' private rights on the excuse of the freedom of speech, of expression, of publication and of the press is prohibited." Besides, some local people's courts also cite the principles consistent with the rights and duties as defined by the Constitution in judgment to require the

---

[4]Yu [1, pp. 21–22].

parties involved to also bear the duties prescribed by the law while enjoying the rights endowed by the law. For example, in the case filed by Liu Shao against Li Zhi, Li Jintian and Beijing Electroplate Coordinating Center Hongxing Branch, the Civil Judgment of People's Court of Jinghai County in Tianjin(1997) Jing.Min. Chu.Zi. No. 349[632] for compensation disputes pointed out, "This wrongful act means Hongxing Branch enjoyed the right to benefits of overloading, which has a certain causal relationship with the traffic accident. According to the constitutional principle that rights and obligations are consistent and the principle of liability for fault in civil tort debt, Hongxing Branch shall bear civil joint responsibilities within the object scope of the contract for fulfillment."

2.4 The Constitution Is Applied Sometimes by Directly Citing the Articles and Sometimes by Making Substantive Interpretations of Articles on the Constitution

The way to cite the Constitution in judicial judgment has a direct bearing on whether courts have the function and power to supervise and guarantee the implementation of the Constitution. In particular, whether courts can make substantive interpretations of articles on the constitution involved in the process of citing the Constitution has a bearing on the system for constitutional implementation. According to provisions of China's current constitution, people's courts have no power to interpret the Constitution no matter this kind of interpretations is for the public in abstract sense or for specific cases to come into force. However, in judicial practice, many local people's courts have gone beyond the limit of substantively interpreting the meanings of the Constitution and played the role as interpreters of the Constitution while citing the Constitution as the legal basis for judging cases. For instance, in the cases brought to the court by the People's Government of Hezhe Ethnic Township against Guo Song, CCTV and Beijing North Star Shopping Center about the disputes over the infringement upon the copyright of folk literary and artistic works, the Civil Judgment of Second Intermediate People's Court in Beijing (2001) Er.Zhong.Zhi.Chu.Zi. No. 223[633] noted, "The plaintiff as the government of an ethnic township is not an autonomous organ of a national autonomous area, but this ethnic township government is a county-level state power established within a concentrated area of nationalities according to the stipulations of China's Constitution and special laws. This has demonstrated the characteristic of the legal system of regional ethnic autonomy. This ethnic township government is the political representative of some groups of Hezhe nationality and the representative of the public interests of some Hezhe groups. When the folk literature and arts of Hezhe nationality are likely to be compromised, given the specificity of the status of right subjects, the plaintiff as the township government may take legal action in its own name in order to protect the public rights and interests of local

Hezhe nationality under the preconditions of demonstrating the principle of the regional ethnic autonomous legal system as stipulated by the Constitution and laws of China and violating no prohibitive stipulation of laws. It is easy to see that the Civil Judgment of Beijing Second Intermediate People's Court made substantive legal reasoning for relevant stipulations of the Constitution while citing stipulations of the Constitution and establishing the qualification of the plaintiff as a subject of a lawsuit, which typically belonged to a substantive judicial interpretation of constitutional provisions through judicial actions. It can be said that this was a bolder judicial action.

2.5 Some Cases Accurately Cited Constitutional Provisions While Some Other Cases Generally Applied Constitutional Principles and Spirit in Judicial Judgment

Courts' citation of the Constitution as the legal basis for judicial judgment involves a question that is how to comprehensively and accurately apply the Constitution. Generally speaking, the way of citing articles on the constitution without any change and making judicial judgment according to the clear and errorless meaning of articles on the constitution relatively accords with the requirement for applying the Constitution in judicial judgment. Under this circumstance, even if the Constitution is cited in judicial judgment, the meaning of the Constitution would not change, making it not easily or less likely to see wrong applications of the Constitution. However, if a court digresses from articles on the constitution in judicial judgment by only abstractly citing related spirit of the Constitution, it would easily cause subjective judgment of the meaning of the Constitution by the judge. This would also prompt judges to make substantive interpretations while citing the Constitution as the legal basis for judicial judgment. At the moment, local people's courts are mostly capable of citing the original text of the Constitution while citing the Constitution as the legal basis for judicial judgment. They basically apply the Constitution literally. In the case filed by Quan Taiyuan against Liaoyuan Mining Bureau Meihe Coal Mine for occupational disability compensation, the Civil Judgment of People's Court of Meihekou City in Jilin (1999) Mei.Min.Chu. Zi. No. 319–2[634] noted, "Article 42 of *the Constitution of the People's Republic of China* promulgated on December 4, 1982, stipulates, 'Citizens of the People's Republic of China have the right as well as the duty to work.' The plaintiff has the right to work and the defendant has the duty to strengthen labor protection, improve labor condition and increase labor remuneration and welfare on the basis of developing production." However, some other courts did not strictly point out which articles they cited when they applied the Constitution as the legal basis for judgment. They just pointed out that the Constitution had some related principles and spirit in general terms. A case in point is the lawsuit instituted by Ningxiang

County Meitanba Town Cement Plant against Huang Chunxiang about the disputes over their purchase and sales contract. The Civil Judgment of People's Court of Ningxiang County (2000) Ning.Jing.Zai.Chu.Zi. No. 1[635] noted, "This kind of contract signed between unequal parties would obviously not result in the so-called consideration of the sales contract between equal subjects and violates the Constitution and relevant labor laws and regulations. In addition, the contents of this contract are obviously unfair and inconsistent with the nature of sales contract. The true debtor is placed outside of the disputes, making it unable to recover the debt. Therefore, this contract shall be regarded as invalid according to the law and shall not be protected by the law." Another example, in the case filed by Liu Ming against No. 8 Engineering Company of Division No. 2 of the No. 20 Engineering Bureau of the Ministry of Railways for occupational injury compensation, the Civil Judgment of People's Court of Meishan County in Sichuan (1999) Mei.Min.Chu. Zi. No. 9–10[636] noted, "The No. 8 Engineering Company and its employee LuoYoumin signed the contract and agreed that LuoYoumin shall be responsible for any work-related injury if happened, which has shirked the risk responsibility that should be assumed by the enterprise to the natural person with limited risk-taking ability. This goes against the protection of workers and violates China's Constitution and socialist ethics, thus belonging to invalid civil act. When LuoYoumin is unable to bear the protection responsibility, the No. 8 Engineering Company shall undertake the joint liability in accordance with the law."

2.6 Some Cases Cited the Constitution in a Simple Way While Some Others Conducted Review for Constitutionality of Case-Related Acts

An important characteristic of the modern review for constitutionality system is that the review for constitutionality body, at the time of citing the Constitution as the basis for making relevant decisions, shall primarily make a legal judgment of whether the reviewed matters are unconstitutional. For both ordinary courts and special review for constitutionality body, such as constitutional court, all undertake the responsibility for making substantive legal judgment of the constitutionality of the objects being reviewed at the time of applying the Constitution. Applying the Constitution to handle specific cases is closely connected with review for constitutionality s of specific cases. At present, when China's local people's courts cite the Constitution as the legal basis for judging cases, they fail to make unconstitutional judgment in most cases. However, in a few judgments, substantive judicial conclusions have been made on the constitutionality of matters involved. Applying the Constitution in judicial judgment as such has produced the legal result that is close to review for constitutionality. That being said, due to the shortage of theoretical guidance for review for constitutionality s, the objects of some review for constitutionality s do not have the legal nature as they should have. Some cases directly conduct review for constitutionality s on the legal norms formulated by legislative organs. For instance, in the lawsuit brought by Baoshan Labor Reeducation Management Committee against Yang Chaofu about the reeducation through labor, the Administrative Judgment of Intermediate People's Court of Baoshan in Yunnan (1999) Bao.Zhong.Fa.Xing.Zhong.Zi. No. 2[637] noted, "Rules must not contravene the Constitution, laws and administrative regulations, which is the basic principle of China's legal system. To this, *the Provisions of the People's Government of Yunnan Province on Regulation and Rule Making Procedures* clearly stipulate in its Article 5 that the enactment of regulations and rules must follow the principles of not contravening the Constitution, laws, and administrative regulations and coordinating other laws, regulations, and rules. The provisions of the Third Paragraph (1) and (2) of Article 3 of *the Temporary Provisions of Yunnan Province on Approving and Reconsideration Works for Reeducation through Labor* as a rule obviously contravene the provisions of *the Tentative Measures for Reeducation through Labor* on "all persons who need to be reeducated through labor shall be confirmed by the management commission of reeducation through labor after reviews." *The Administrative Procedure Law of the People's Republic of China* provides in Article 53, "In handling administrative cases, the people's courts shall take, as references, administrative rules and regulations—formulated and issued, in accordance with the law and administrative rules and regulations of the State Council, by the people's governments of provinces, autonomous regions and municipalities directly under the Central Government." "As reference" means the rules have no absolute binding force to people's courts in general. When people's courts judge the specific administrative acts performed by administrative organs according to the rules, they have the right to make judgment in accordance with the provisions of laws and regulations if the rules are inconsistent with the laws and regulations. In the aforesaid Administrative Judgment of Yunnan Baoshan District Intermediate People's Court, the court cited the Constitution to judge that the rules violated the constitutional principle of "must not contravene the Constitution, the statutes and the administrative rules and regulations," which belong to review for constitutionality in typical sense.

In the case about Lin Shuchao's refusal to obey the decision of Hainan Reeducation-through-labor Management Committee on reeducation through labor, the Constitution was cited as the legal basis for protecting citizens' fundamental rights. With regard to the decision on the case, the Administrative Judgment of People's Court of Haikou City in Hainan (1999) Hai.Zhong.Fa.Xing.Zhong.Zi. No. 1[638] noted, "The decision of the appealer for reeducating the appellee through labor for one year was aimed at quieting down the appellee from petition without considering that the personal freedom is the most fundamental right of citizens protected by the Constitution. Reeducation through labor as the highest administrative penalty for restricting personal freedom should be prudently and impartially applied. The appellee is the victim in the case, so being reeducated through labor is indiscreet and unjust."

Of course, when some courts make the review for constitutionality s of some acts by citing constitutional provisions, these acts under review for constitutionality s do not conform to the characteristics of the objects of review for constitutionality. This is clearly beyond the scope of review for constitutionality. For instance, in the case filed by Long Jiankang against Zhongzhou Building Engineering Company, Jiang Jianguo and the Road Transport Bureau of Yongsheng County about the disputes over compensation, the Civil Judgment of People's Court of Yongsheng County in Yunnan (2000) Yong.Fa.Min.Chu.Zi. No. 03[639] held, "Zhongzhou Building Engineering Company, after becoming the contractor, agreed with Jiang Jianguo in the *Construction Contract* that all work-related injuries shall be borne by Jiang Jianguo, which shifted the safety risk that should be assumed by the enterprise to the natural person with limited ability. This agreement has harmed the lawful rights and interests of the worker, violated related provisions of the Constitution and *Labor Law of the People's Republic of China*, so it shall be regarded as invalid and shall not be protected by the law." In above-said judgment, the review for constitutionality of the "Construction Contract" involved in this case is actually similar to the "Third Party Effect Theory" admitting constitutional rights and takes the Constitution as the legal basis for handling private legal disputes. Another example is the case filed by Luo Daixi and Ling Zhifen against Liu Min about the dispute over compensation for water caused injury and loss of life. The Civil Judgment of Beihai Maritime Court (2000) Hai.Shi.Chu.Zi. No. 003[640] held, "Our investigations conclude that this agreement has seriously harmed the lawful rights and interests of LuoJiajin and his relatives, violated related provisions of China's Constitution, Labor Law and Contract Law, so the agreement belongs to the obviously unfair act as provided in the second paragraph of Article 59 of the *General Principles of the Civil Law* and shall be modified and void in accordance with the law.

2.7 In Judicial Practice, Some Courts Cited Constitutional Stipulations in Judgment with the Purpose of Resolving "Conflicts of Rights," Demonstrating the Nature of Authority Conflicts Between Review and Formulation Power and Legislative Power

Some local people's courts, in judicial judgment, have doubts about the legitimacy of the legal basis for judging cases, so they cite constitutional provisions in an attempt to resolve the value conflict between constitutional provisions and other legal provisions. For instance, in the case filed by Zhao Zhongxiang against Zhang Lin and Xinhua Daily for defamation, the Civil Judgment of People's Court of Haidian District in Beijing(2000) Hai.Min.Chu.Zi. No. 7230[641] held, "In this case, the focus of disputes between both litigants is the conflict between citizen's right of reputation and journalist's press coverage right. The legitimacy and suitability of both litigants' exercise of civil rights are confirmed pursuant to the facts of the case and the evidence to balance this right conflict. China's Constitution stipulates that citizens have the freedom of speech. *The General Principles of the Civil Law* stipulates that citizens shall enjoy the right of reputation; the personality of citizens shall be protected by law, and the use of false reports, insults, libel or other means to damage the reputation of citizens shall be prohibited." Regarding this judgment, what needed to be resolved was the value conflict between two rights, but the Civil Judgment of the People's Court of Haidian District in Beijing equalized the rights stipulated by the Constitution and the rights stipulated by *the General Principles of the Civil Law* for settling this kind of conflicts, which further affirmed the priority of the rights as provided in *the General Principles of the Civil Law*. It is clear to see that the court failed to properly understand the value relations between constitutional rights and general legal rights in making the standpoint with regard to rights protection.

In brief, the application of the Constitution is non-standard and multifarious in judicial judgment. On more occasions, the Constitution are applied by courts as the legal norm just the same with other general legal forms without thinking more about the value relations behind constitutional norms. Some forms of applications are similar to the direct validity of the Constitution between privates, some involve substantive interpretations of constitutional provisions, some make review for constitutionality s in accordance with the Constitution, and some others make application selections between the Constitution and general laws, and so on and so forth. All these circumstances have something to do with the long-term lack of theories and guidance in China's constitution application in judicial judgment and with the ambiguous attitude and unclear stance of the Supreme People's Court in the applicability of the Constitution in judicial judgment.

Contrasted with inappropriate or random application of the Constitution by courts in judicial judgment, in judicial practice, people's courts did not give clear-cut support for the appeal of some litigants for citing the Constitution as the basis for making judgment or protecting their rights in many cases. For instance, in the case filed by Jiang Tao against the People's Bank of China Chengdu Branch for the height requirement in recruiting civil servants, the plaintiff who was a student admitted by Sichuan University in 1998 argued that the height requirement of the People's Bank of China Chengdu Branch for employing civil servants as announced on *the Notice of the People's Bank of China Chengdu Branch on Staff Enrollment* on December 23, 2001, was discrimination against the applicants including himself who failed to meet the height requirement. Therefore, the plaintiff's right of equality as endowed by the Constitution to serve as a public servant was encroached. But the Administrative Judgment of People's Court of Wuhou District in Chengdu (2002) Wu.Hou.Xing.Chu.Zi. No. 3[642] dismissed the plaintiff on the ground that the case didn't belong to the scope of cases for acceptance as stipulated by *the Administrative Procedure Law* of our country. This caused the loss of an opportunity for citing the Constitution in judicial judgment to protect citizens' fundamental rights. Besides, even many contents of the Supreme People's Court's judicial interpretations obviously violate the Constitution, but no review mechanism is available for solving these issues. For example, the Supreme People's Court enforced *the Interpretation on Some Issues concerning the Application of Law for the Trial of Cases on Compensation for Personal Injury* on May 1, 2004. The Interpretation stipulates in Article 29 that the death compensation shall be calculated according to the per capita disposal income of urban residents or per capita net income of farmers in the previous year in the hearing court's locality by twenty years. This stipulation is called "the same destiny with different compensations" in the law community. There is no doubt that, from the perspective of the constitutional theory that the value and dignity of life are equivalent, the above judicial interpretation of the Supreme People's Court was clearly unconstitutional. However, this kind of judicial interpretations has been explained as meeting China's national conditions by some scholars or judicial officials. This point of view is an evident misunderstanding of the constitutional principle that human dignity is inviolable and individuals are equal in personality, and having no idea how to understand the basic spirit of protecting the right of equality as stipulated by Constitution [643].

3 Institutional Countermeasures for Strengthening the Applicability of the Constitution in Judicial Judgment

China's constitutional circle had already elaborated the applicability of the Constitution in judicial judgment a decade ago [644]. Especially after the Supreme People's Court promulgated the "August 13 Reply" in 2001, whether the Constitution can be taken as the legal basis for people's courts in judicial judgment has attracted the attention of the theoretical community and the comments from all walks of life and has formed a social upsurge of constitution judicialization.[5]

Actually, looking at the "constitution judicialization" from the perspective of review for constitutionality, we can find that review for constitutionality only involves part of the contents of constitution judicialization or involves the core of constitution judicialization. Constitution judicialization is a broad concept in constitutional theory and is basically the same with or equivalent to the applicability of the Constitution in judicial judgment in terms of the meaning. The Constitution has been applied in judicial judgment in various forms in China, but how to scientifically and rationally interpret the applicability of the Constitution in legal theory turns out to be a theoretical issue that must be highly valued and highlighted for a long period of time to come.

Looking at China's current situation of constitution application in judicial adjustment, it can be said that most applications are questionable in the theory of law. According to the stipulations of the current constitution of China, the

[5]Lei [2].

Constitution must be interpreted by the Standing Committee of the National People's Congress. As judicial organs, people's courts are unable to interpret meanings of constitutional provisions with substantive influence on judicial judgment. Therefore, the practice of interpreting the meaning of the Constitution while citing the Constitution as the legal basis for judicial judgment has actually gone beyond the powers prescribed by the Constitution and should be taken as unconstitutional acts under the current constitutional system. There is even a lack of constitutional basis for citing the Constitution in judicial judgment by people's courts for review for constitutionality of matters involved in cases. That is to say, people's courts' review for constitutionality of the acts or matters involved in ordinary cases in accordance with the Constitution has no legal basis and is questionable in the theory of law. Particularly when some local people's courts conduct review for constitutionality of some cases, the objects of review for constitutionality are actually general civil agreements or contracts and these objects under review are actually not true in the theory of law. Even according to the "Third Party Effect Theory," civil agreements or contracts cannot be freely included in the scope of review for constitutionality. For the time being, there are inadequate constitutional and legal basis for applying the Constitution in judicial judgment by taking the Constitution as an independent legal basis, or making substantive judgment in accordance with the Constitution, which has legal effects on the litigants in real sense. Of course, the review for constitutionality mechanism as provided in Article 90 of *the Legislation Law* only involves the review of administrative regulations, local regulations, autonomous regulations and separate regulations but not all objects that conforms to the nature of review for constitutionality. Therefore, there is still a large institutional space for people's courts to carry out, in accordance with the Constitution, review for constitutionality s of matters beyond that as stipulated by Article 90 of *the Legislation Law*. However, this requires a definite authorization in law because the current constitution only stipulates that the National People's Congress and its Standing Committee have the power to supervise the implementation of the Constitution and other state organs have no such constitutional power. Therefore, constitutionality review is actually excluded from the judicial actions of people's courts in general. In this connection, in legal system, the scope of objects for constitutionality review can be expanded in two directions. First, all review for constitutionality matters can be included in the scope of review for constitutionality by the Standing Committee of the National People's Congress. That means only the Standing Committee of the National People's Congress has the power to conduct review for constitutionality. Second, the power of review for constitutionality of some objects can be given to people's courts at various levels through the form of legislation. In particular, the constitutional appeals involving the protection of citizens' fundamental rights could be reviewed by people's courts at various levels.

Of course, beyond review for constitutionality, whether the Constitution could be applied in judicial judgment merits exploration and discussions. At the moment, some cases of applying the Constitution in judicial practices did not involve the monitoring of constitutional implementation as stipulated by the Constitution but only took the Constitution as the supplementary or auxiliary legal basis in judicial judgment. This practice of applying the Constitution not as an independent basis for determining the result of cases but simply as the supplementary instruction of the legitimacy of the laws and regulations being taken as the basis for people's courts' judicial judgment is very helpful for making the application of laws by people's courts in judicial judgments more scientific and rational. Therefore, this can be reserved conditionally, but this is only limited to the accurate citation of constitutional provisions. General citation of the Constitution may not be adopted because it makes little sense to supporting the legitimacy of the legal basis for judicial judgment. However, the practice of using constitutional provisions to further emphasizes the rationality of the legal basis for judicial judgment is worth keeping. For instance, in the case filed by Song Xiulin against Wang Ke for disputes over the compensation for mariculture damages, the Civil Judgment of Maritime Court of Qingdao (2001) Qing.Hai.Fa.Hai.Shi.Chu.Zi. No. 23 stated, "Article 51 of *the Constitution of the People's Republic of China* stipulates, 'Citizens of the People's Republic of China, in exercising their freedoms and rights, may not infringe upon the interests of the State, of society or of the collective, or upon the lawful freedoms and rights of other citizens.' Article 7 of *the General Principles of the Civil Law* also stipulates, 'Civil activities shall have respect for social ethics and shall not harm the public interest, undermine State economic plans or disrupt social economic order.' Extensively interpreted, the content of this article includes one of the basic principles of the civil law, namely the principle to prohibit the abuse of rights." In above-said judgment, Article 51 of the Constitution was applied to support the rationality of the provisions of Article 7 of *the General Principles of the Civil Law*. This way of applying the Constitution is helpful for enhancing the rationality of the legal basis for judicial judgment and thus making the application of laws by people's courts in judicial judgment more scientific.

In conclusion, under the current circumstance that no law or regulation affirms whether the Constitution can be taken as the legal basis for judicial judgment, especially when the Supreme People's Court has no clear attitude toward whether the Constitution can be applied in judging criminal, civil and administrative cases, local people's courts at all levels must be prudent in citing the Constitution as the legal basis for judicial judgment. With regard to matters involving constitutional interpretation or review for constitutionality, they should try to avoid the application. When it comes to applying the Constitution to further strengthen the rationality and legal effect of the legal basis for judging cases, the application could be reserved prudently. This is because this way of constitution application does not involve the power of constitutional interpretation and the power of review for constitutionality. On the contrary, the citation of the Constitution in judicial judgment could further consolidate the legal relations between the Constitution and other branch laws and help improve the legal theories and principles of branch laws.

References

1. Wang Yu: *Judicialization of the Constitution in China: Case Analysis*, Peking University Press, August 2005, 1st edition.
2. Wang Lei: *Judicialization of the Constitution*, China University of Political Science and Law Press, February 2000, 1st edition.

Postscript I

A great many major political events made 2012 a year of historic significance. The year marked 30 years since the 1982 Constitution was passed and adopted. Having begun at ground zero with practically nothing, China's constitutional law and constitutional system have over these three decades seen rapid growth and admirable achievements. As we look forward to the 18th National Congress of the Communist Party of China, the Chinese people's collective belief in the prospect of realizing moderate prosperity for all in the not-too-distant future is stronger than ever. For constitutional scholars, this promises to be a particularly busy year, with many articles to write, and conferences and ceremonies to attend. A bit tired, perhaps, but certainly excited, too.

We were contacted by Ms. Liu Xiaojun from Social Sciences Academic Press (SSAP) at the end of 2010 about the possibility of a book series on China's constitutional developments and achievements over the past three decades. Soon afterward, shortly after 2011 Spring Festival, a number of renowned scholars from the Chinese Academy of Social Sciences (CASS) Institute of Law attended a gathering at the invitation of SSAP president Xie Shouguang, who urged us to spare no effort in putting together such a series. The weight of the high expectations was a bit overwhelming. We wasted little time before getting started, putting together a team made up of the right people, and preparing the materials needed for the project. Our hope was to formulate advice and suggestions for constitutional, legislative and legal practices on the basis of what can be learned from past experiences in these and other related areas. As it happened, the CASS Institute of Law is home to the office of The Secretariat of the Committee for Revision of the Constitution in 1982, so it made perfect sense for scholars from this institute, noted for their academic caliber, to undertake such a monumental task. It took us more than six months, many discussions among participating scholars and consultation sessions with pertinent departments of the National People's Congress to draw up a blueprint, that included the basic what and how for the series. A detailed writing plan was agreed upon by September 2011. A mere one year later, the manuscript

L. Li et al. (eds.), *Constitutional Development in China, 1982–2012*,
Research Series on the Chinese Dream and China's Development Path,
https://doi.org/10.1007/978-981-32-9261-1

was completed, a feat that would not have been possible had it not been for the commitment and perseverance of everyone involved.

We gratefully acknowledge funding support for this project from the State Administration of Press and Publication (SAPP, now State Administration of Press, Publication, Radio, Film and Television, SAPPRFT). Of course, just as important, we draw on the collective strength of constitutional scholars in the country. All these propitious conditions boosted our confidence in our ability to accomplish the task. We were also ably assisted throughout the process by a strong team of editors at SSAP, whose hard work ensured the timely publications of the series. The original plan called for five volumes: (1) a collections of outstanding works from the Proceeding of the 2011 Xi'an Annual Meeting of China Constitutional Research Association (*Constitutional Study* Vol. 13); (2) an edited volume featuring articles first presented at the 2012 Beijing Annual Meeting of China Constitutional Research Association and marking the 30th anniversary of adoption of the current constitution (*Constitutional Study* Vol. 14); (3) a collection of works by researchers affiliated with the CASS Institute of Law commemorating the 30th anniversary of the adoption of the current constitution; and (4) and (5) collections of articles written by researchers working under the leadership of Mo Jihong on "uniformity of the legal system" and "construction of the national people's congress system." After further discussions with Ms. Liu Xiaojun from SSAP and factoring in input from SAPP, we decided on presenting the series as a three-volume set, in which the three volumes are organically connected with one another, instead of each being a self-standing book. In addition to articles based on presentations at the Annual Meetings over the years of China Constitutional Research Association, we also included works by CASS Institute of Law researchers on major topics of constitutional law studies. The work is both broad in scope and vast in depth, providing not only a panoramic view but also fine analyses of constitutional development in China over the course of three decades. We believe that the series will still be relevant and valuable to future researchers when they mark the 40th or 50th anniversary of the Constitution.

Volume I gives an overview of the major achievements in the country's constitutional development, as well as development of the academic studies of the constitution. Volume II covers two major topics, namely "rule of law" and "governing the country in accordance with the Constitution." Volume III focuses on the "technical issues" related to the constitutions, i.e., the "how" question. Articles in this volume are strongly informed by practice on the frontline and are meant to provide guidance for improving the way things are done in the future.

Ideally, we would like to list all the individuals to whom we owe a debt of gratitude for helping us finish this work. But the sheer number of them makes that infeasible. Suffice it to say that CASS Institute of Law, CASS Institute of

International Law and China Constitutional Research Association were instrumental to our effort to put together the series, and we thank from the bottom of our hearts all constitutional scholars in China, the works of many of who are featured in these pages, for making this an intrinsically rewarding experience.

Editor

Shatan, Beijing, September 2012

Postscript II

The Chinese language edition of *Constitutional Development in China, 1982–2012*, published by Social Sciences Academic Press (SSAP) was well received by scholars in the field and the general public. Thanks to the approval of more funding from the government for the project, we decided to produce an abridged edition. It was Ms. Liu Xiaojun from SSAP who broke the news about the funding to us, and who shepherded the production of the concise edition to completion. It was no easy task to decide on the articles that would be included in the abridged edition, which we were told must be kept under one-tenth the aggregate size of the multi-volume set. We had to let go, albeit painfully, many articles with scholarly merit. Still, we are happy to say that the result is a collection of articles that together do justice to the process by which China's experience with the constitution went from nascency to maturity.

It is, of course, our hope that readers who find the concise edition useful would be interested in engaging with the topic more deeply, say, by reading the multi-volume set. They will not be disappointed.

Here, I wish to express my heartfelt thanks again to Ms. Liu and her colleagues at SSAP, for their commitment to the project, their professional skills and their encouragement. In them, we saw the stuff of which excellence in academic publishing is made. It gives us hope and propels us forward, reaching for greater heights.

Mo Jihong

No. 15, Shatan North Street, Beijing, April 5, 2014

L. Li et al. (eds.), *Constitutional Development in China, 1982–2012*,
Research Series on the Chinese Dream and China's Development Path,
https://doi.org/10.1007/978-981-32-9261-1

References

Chinese-Language References

1. *Collected Works of Karl Marx and Friedrich Engels*, volume 1, People's Publishing House, 1995 edition;
2. *Collected Works of Karl Marx and Friedrich Engels*, volume 17, People's Publishing House, 1958, edition 1;
3. *Collected Works of Karl Marx and Friedrich Engels*, volume 3, People's Publishing House, 1972 edition;
4. *Collected Works of Lenin*, edition 3, volume 1, People's Publishing House, 1995 edition;
5. *Selected Works of Mao Zedong*, volume 3, volume 4, People's Publishing House, 1991 edition;
6. *Selected Works of Mao Zedong*, volume 5, People's Publishing House, 1977 edition;
7. *Selected Works of Deng Xiaoping*, volume 2, People's Publishing House, 1994 edition;
8. Jiang Zemin: *On "The Three Represents"*, Central Party Literature Press, 2001 edition;
9. CCCPC Party Literature Research Office: *Since the Third Plenary Session* (I, II), People's Publishing House, 1982 edition;
10. *Compilation of the Documents of the 17th National Congress of the Communist Party of China*, People's Publishing House, 2007 edition;
11. Wang Hanbin: *Collected Works on the Socialist Democracy and Legal System(I)*, China Democracy and Legal System Publishing House, 2012 edition;
12. Zhang Youyu: *Collections of Academic Works of Zhang Youyu*, Beijing Normal University Publishing House, 1988 edition;
13. Wang Shuwen: *Introduction to the Basic Law of Hong Kong Special Administrative Region*, Press of Party School of the Central Committee of CPC, 1997 edition;
14. Wang Shuwen, Zheng Chengsi: *Introduction to the Basic Law of Macao Special Administrative Region*, Press of Party School of the Central Committee of CPC, 2001 edition;
15. *Complete Works of Xu Chongde*, volume 7, China Democracy and Legal System Publishing House, 2009 edition;
16. Xu Chongde: *Constitutional Law*: China Renmin University Press, 1999 edition.
17. Wu Jialin: *Constitutional Law*, Masses Publishing House: 1983 edition;
18. He Huahui: *Comparative Constitutional Law*, Wuhan University Press, 1988 edition;
19. Zhang Qingfu: *A Brief Introduction to Constitutional Law Research*, Tianjin Education Press, 1989 edition;

L. Li et al. (eds.), *Constitutional Development in China, 1982–2012*,
Research Series on the Chinese Dream and China's Development Path,
https://doi.org/10.1007/978-981-32-9261-1

20. Zhang Qingfu: *Basic Theory of Constitutional Law* (I), Social Sciences Academic Press, 1999 edition;
21. Zhang Qingfu, Han Dayuan: *Chinese Yearbook of Constitutional Law 2005*, Law Press China, 2006 edition;
22. Xu Xiuyi and Han Dayuan: *Basic Theory of Constitutional Law*, Chinese People's Public Security University Press, 2001 edition;
23. Han Dayuan: *Research on Asian Constitutionalism*, Chinese People's Public Security University Press, 1996, edition 1;
24. Han Dayuan: *Basic Theories of Constitutional Law*, China University of Political Science and Law Press, 2008 edition;
25. Han Dayuan and Mo Jihong: *Cases of Foreign Constitution*, China Renmin University Press, 2005 edition;
26. Mo Jihong: *Logical Foundation of Modern Constitution*, Law Press China, December 2001 edition;
27. Mo Jihong: *Constitutional Law*, Social Sciences Academic Press, 2004 edition;
28. Dong Heping, Han Dayuan, Li Shuzhong: *Constitutional Law*, Law Press China, 2000 edition;
29. Hu Jinguang and Han Dayuan: *Constitution of China*, Law Press China, 2004 edition;
30. Zhou Yezhong: *Constitution*, Higher Education Press, Peking University Press, 2000 edition;
31. Jiao Hongchang: *Constitutional Law* (Fourth Edition), Peking University Press, 2004 edition;
32. Jiao Hongchang: *Legal Guarantee of the Right to Vote*, Peking University Press, 2005 edition;
33. Liu Maolin: *An Introduction to China's Constitution*, Peking University Press, 2005 edition;
34. Tong Zhiwei: *Legal Rights and Constitutionalism*, Shandong People's Publishing House, 2001 edition;
35. Hu Jinguang: *Analysis of China's Top 10 Administrative Law Cases*, Law Press China, 2005 edition;
36. Zhang Qianfan: *Introduction to Constitutional Law*, Law Press China, 2004, edition 1;
37. Lin Laifan: *From Constitutional Norms to Normative Constitution-A Preface of Normative Constitutional Law*, Law Press China, May 2001, edition 1,
38. Zhu Fuhui: *Constitutional Law*, Xiamen University Press, 2007 edition;
39. Cai Dingjiang: *The People's Congress System of China*, Law Press China, 2003 edition;
40. Cai Dingjian: *On Constitutional Issues*, Phoenix Publishing & Media Group, Yilin Press, 2011 edition;
41. Wang Lei: *Judicatory Actualization of Constitution*, China University of Political Science and Law Press, 2000;
42. Zheng Xianjun: *Principles of Fundamental Rights*, Law Press China, 2008 edition;
43. Zhang Xiang: Legal Construction of Fundamental Rights Norms, Higher Education Press, April 2008 edition;
44. Jiang Guohua, *Introduction to Constitutional Philosophy*, The Commercial Press, 2007 edition;
45. Wang Yu: *Judicialization of the Constitution in China: Case Analysis*, Peking University Press, 2005 edition;
46. Jiang Jingsong: *The Mother of Parliaments*, China Democracy and Legal System Publishing House, July 1998, edition 1;
47. Jiang Shilin et al.: *World Constitutions*, Qingdao Publishing House, 1997 edition;
48. Gong Xiangrui: *Comparative Constitution and Comparative Administrative Law*, Law Press China, 1985 edition;
49. Lin Feng: *One Century of Constitutional Development and the Future of Constitutionalism in China*, City University of Hong Kong Press, 2011 edition;

50. Wu Geng: *The Interpretation and Application of the Constitution*; San Min Book Co., Ltd., June 2004, edition 3;
51. Xu Zhi-xiong: Changes in Constitutional Order, Angle Publishing Company, 2000 edition;
52. Fa Jyh-Pin and Dong Bao-cheng: *The Constitution of the Republic of China*, National Open University Press, 1997 edition;
53. Jiunn-Rong Yeh: *Democratic Transitions and Constitutional Changes*, Angle Publishing Company, 2003 edition;
54. Yue-Dian Hsu: *Freedom of Religion and Religious Law*, Angle Publishing Company, 2005 edition;
55. Wang Shijie and Qian Duansheng: *Comparative Constitution*, The Commercial Press, 1999 edition;
56. Zhang Wenxian: *Jurisprudence*, Law Press China, October 1997, edition 1;
57. Zhang Jinfan, Zeng Xianyi: *Brief History of Chinese Constitution*, Beijing Publishing House, 1979 edition;
58. Xu Chongde: *A Constitutional History of the People's Republic of China*, Fujian People's Publishing House, 2003 edition;
59. He Qinhua and Zhang Haibin: *The History of Western Constitution*, Peking University Press, 2006 edition;
60. Bian Xiuquan: *Historical Interpretation of the Constitution Text of Modern China*, Intellectual Property Publishing House, 2006 edition,
61. Li Buyun: *Comparative Research on Constitution*, Law Press China, 1998 edition;
62. Shen Zongling: *Modern Western Jurisprudence*, Peking University Press, 1992 edition;
63. Wang Tieya: *International Law*, Law Press China, 1995 edition;
64. Chen Shin-Min: *On Public Law*, San Min Book Co., Ltd., 1996 edition;
65. Ma Qibing and Chen Wenbin et al.: *Forty Years in Power of the Chinese Communist Party*, CPC History Publishing House, 1989 edition;
66. [Britain]Blackstone: *Commentaries on the Laws of England* (volum 1), translated by You Yunting and Miao Miao, Shanghai People's Publishing House, 2006 edition;
67. [Britain] Jennings: *The Law and the Constitution*, translated by Gong Xiangrui et al., Beijing, SDX Joint Publishing Company, 1997 edition;
68. [Britain] Locke: *Two Treatise of Government*, translated by Ye Qifang and Zhai Junong, the Commerial Press, 1964 edition;
69. [Britain]Karl Popper: *The Poverty of Historicism*, translated by Du Ruji and Qiu Renzong, Shanghai People's Publishing House, 2009 edition;
70. [Britain] John Mill: *Freedom*, translated by Cheng Chonghua, The Commercial Press, 1959 edition;
71. [Britain] A.V. Dicey: *Introduction to the Study of the Law of the Constitution*, translated by Lei Binnan, China Legal Publishing House, 2001 edition;
72. [U.S.] Huntington: *The Clash of Civilizations and The Remaking of World Order*, translated by Zhou Qi et al., Xinhua Publishing House, 2002 edition;
73. [U.S.] Hamilton, Jay and Madison: *The Federalist Papers*, translated by Cheng Fengru, Zai Han and Shu Xun, The Commercial Press,1980 edition;
74. [France] Sieyes: *On Privilege: What is the Third Estate?*, translated by Feng Tang, The Commercial Press, 1990 edition;
75. [U.S.] Edward S. Corwin: *The "Higher Law" Background of American Constitutional Law*, translated by Qiang Shigong, Joint Publishing Company, 1996 edition;
76. [U.S.] Merryman: *Civil Law Tradition*, translated by Gu Peidong and Lu Zhengping, Law Press China, 1984 edition;
77. [U.S.] Jack Donnelly: *Universal Human Rights in Theory and Practice*, translated by Wang Puqu, Beijing: China Social Sciences Publishing House, 2001 edition;
78. [U.S.] Scott Gordon: *Controlling the State: Constitutionalism from Ancient Athens to Today*, translated by Yingqi et al., Jiangsu People's Publishing LTD, 2001 edition;

79. [U.S.]Bruce Ackerman: *We the People: Foundations*, translated by Sun Li and Zhang Chaoxia, Law Press China, 2004 edition;
80. [U.S.] Louis Henkin and Albert J. Rosenthal: *Constitutionalism and Rights*, translated by Zheng Ge et al., SDX Joint Publishing Company, 1996, edition 1;
81. [U.S.]Jon Elster and [Norway] Rune Slagstad: *Constitutionalism and Democracy: Studies in Rationality and Social Change*, translated by Pan Qin and Xie Pengcheng, Joint Publishing Company, 1997 edition;
82. [U.S.] Hendrik Willem van Loon: *Tolerance*, translated by Lian Wei and Jin Cuiwei, SDX Joint Publishing Company, 1985 edition;
83. [Germany]Dieter Grimm: *Birth, Operation and Prospect of Modern Constitution*, translated by Liu Gang, Law Press China, 2010 edition;
84. [Germany] Schmitt: *Constitutional Theory*, translated by Liu Feng, Shanghai People's Publishing House, 2005 edition;
85. [Germany] Carl Schmitt: *The Concept of the Political*, translated by Liu Zongkun et al., Shanghai People's Publishing House, 2004 edition;
86. [Germany] Karl Schmidt: *Karl Schmidt the Guardians of the Constitution*, translated by Li Juntao and Su Huijie, The Commercial Press, 2008 edition;
87. [Germany] Kaufman: *Postmodern Jurisprudence*, translated by Mijian, Law Press China, 2003 edition;
88. [Germany] Gustav Radbruch: *Introduction to Legal Science*, translated by Mi Jian et al., The Encyclopedia of China Publishing House, 1997 edition;
89. [Austria] Hans Kelsen: *General Theory of Law and State*, translated by Shen Zongling, Encyclopedia of China Publishing House, 1996 edition;
90. [France] Rousseau: *The Social Contract*, translated by He Zhaowu, Hongqi Press,1997 edition;
91. [Japan] Nobuyoshi Ashibe: *Constitutional Law*, translated by Wang Guisong, China University of Political Science and Law Press, 2012 edition;
92. [Japan] Minobe Tatsukichi: *Constitutional Theory*, translated by Ou Zongyou and He Zuolin, proofread by Tang Wei, China University of Political Science and Law Press, 2003, edition 1;
93. [Japan] Takashi Miura: *Constitutional Law in Practice*, translated by Li Li and Bai Yunhai, Chinese People's Public Security University Press, 2002, edition 1;
94. [The Netherlands] Henk van Marcy and Ger van der Tang: *Written Constitution: Comparative Studies via Computer*, translated by Chen Yunsheng, Peking University Press, 2007 edition;

Foreign-Language References

95. Gustavsson Sverker, Thick and Thin Constitutionalism, Statsvetenskaplig tidskrift, 112 (1), 2010.
96. Hayek, The Constitution of Liberty, Chicago: University of Chicago Press, 1960.
97. J. Rawls, Two Concepts of Rules(1995), in J. Rawls: Collected Papers, edited by S. Freeman, Harvard University Press, 2001.
98. Carol Harlow, The Political Constitution Reworked, in Public Interest Litigation: New Zealand Experience in International Perspective, edited by Rick Bigwood, Wellington: LexisNexis, 2006.
99. C. Gearty, Principles of Human Rights Adjudication, Oxford University Press, 2003.
100. Richard Bellamy, Political Constitutionalism: A Republican Defence of the Constitutionality of Democracy, Cambridge University Press, 2007.
101. Adam Tomkins, Our Republican Constitution, Hart Publishing, 2005.
102. Martin Loughlin, Sword and Scales: An Examination of the Relationship between Law and Politics, Hart Publishing, 2000.

103. A.V. Dicey, An Introduction to the Study of the Law of the Constitution, MacMillan, 1959.
104. Jeffrey Goldsworthy, The Sovereignty of Parliament: Contemporary Debates, CambridgeUniversity Press, 2010.
105. M. Elliot, Parliamentary Sovereignty and the New Constitutional Order: Legislative Freedom, Political Reality, and Convention, 22 Legal Studies, 2004.
106. Alison L Young, Parliamentary Sovereignty and the Human Rights Act, Hart Publishing, 2009.
107. Richard Bellamy, Political Constitutionalism: A Republican Defence of the Constitutionality of Democracy, CambridgeUniversity Press, 2007.
108. Yash Ghai.Hong Kong's New Constitutional Order. Hong Kong University Press, 1999.
109. V. Jean Carbonnier, La codification dans les états de droit: le cas français, Année Canonique 1996.
110. Jean Carbonnier, Le Code Civil, Les Lieux de Mémoire, tone 2, La Nation, Pierre Nora (dir.), Paris: Gallimard, 1986.
111. Jacques Bouineau et Jérôme Roux, 200 ans de Code Civil, Paris: Association pour la diffusion de la pensée française, 2004.
112. Louis Favoreu, « La constitutionnalisation du droit », in Mélanges en l'honneur de Roland Drago, L'unité du droit, Paris, Economica,1996.
113. Wienholtz, Normative Verfassung und Gesetzgebung.Die Verwirklichung von Gesetzgebungsauftraegen des Bonner Grundgesetzes, Freiburg i. Br. 1968.
114. H. Kelsen, Über Grenzen zwischen Juristischer und Soziologischer Methode, Tübingen 1970, S. 7ff.; ders., Hauptprobleme der Staatsrechtslehre, 2. Aufl. 1923, Nachdruck 1984.
115. H. Dreier, Rechtslehre, Staatssoziologie und Demokratienlehre bei Hans Kelsen.
116. N. Luhmann, Evolution des Rechts, in: ders., Ausdifferenzierung des Rechts. Beiträge zur Rechtssoziologie und Rechtstheorie, Suhrkamp 1. Aufl. 1999.
117. J. Habermas, Faktizität und Geltung. Beiträge zur Diskurstheorie des Rechts und des demokratischen Rechtsstaats, Surkamp1994.
118. E. –W. Böckenförde, Geschichtliche Entwicklung und Bedeutungswandel der Verfassungs, in: ders., Staat, Verfassung, Demokratie, 2. Aufl. 1992.
119. Bassam Tibi, Europa ohne Identität?: Leitkultur oder Wertebeliebigkeit: Die Krise der multikulturellen Gesellschaft,btb Verlag 2000.
120. Wolfgang Kahl, Sprache als Kultur- und Rechtsgut, VVDStRL 65, Berlin 2006.
121. Edouard Campiche, Die verfassungskonforme Auslegung: Stellung in der Auslegungslehre und Abgrenzung zur Normenkontrolle, Zürich: Schulthess Polygraphischer Verlag (1978).
122. Jörn Lüdemann: Die verfassungskonforme Auslegung von Gesetzen, in: JuS 2004.
123. Jörg P. Müller, Der Verfassungsgerichtbarkeit im Gefüge der Staatsfunktionen, im Martin Bullinger, Veröffentlichung der Vereinigung der Deutschen Staatslehrer, Bd.39, Berlin, New York: de Gruyter 1981.
124. Georg Hermes, Verfassungsrecht und einfaches Recht-Verfassungsgerichtbarkeit und Fachgerichtbarkeit, im Jörn Ipsen, Veröffentlichung der Vereinigung der Deutschen Staatslehrer, Bd.61, Berlin, New York. de Gruyter 2002.
125. Закон Российской Федерации 《О гражданстве Российской Федерации》 // Ведомости Съезда народных депутатов Российской Федерации и Верховного Совета Российской Федерации, 1992, N 6.
126. Федеральный закон 《О политических партиях》 // Рос. газ. 2001. 11 июля.
127. Конституция Российской Федерации (комментарий).Под общей редакции Б·Н·Тпорнина,Ю·М·Батурина,Р·Г·Орехова. М.Юридическая литература,1994.
128. Статьи 11—12 Федеральный конституционный закон 《О референдуме Российской Федерации》 // Конституционное право России (Сборник конституционно-правовых актов).Том 1 . Под редакции О·Е·Кутафина.М.:Юристь.1999.
129. HiguchiYouchiandOsugaAkira: *NationalConstitutionofJapan*, edition 4, Sanseido, 2000, edition 4.

The manufacturer's authorised representative in the EU is Springer Nature Customer Service Centre GmbH, Europaplatz 3, 69115 Heidelberg, Germany. If you have any concerns regarding our products, please contact ProductSafety@springernature.com

Printed and bound by CPI Group (UK) Ltd, Croydon, CR0 4YY
30/09/2026
02225510-0016